INNOVATIONS IN EVIDENCE AND PROOF

Innovations in Evidence and Proof brings together 15 leading scholars and experienced law teachers based in Australia, Canada, Northern Ireland, Scotland, South Africa, the United States and England and Wales to explore and debate the latest developments in evidence and proof scholarship. The essays comprising this volume range expansively over questions of disciplinary taxonomy, pedagogical method and computer-assisted learning, doctrinal analysis, fact-finding, techniques of adjudication, the ethics of cross-examination, the implications of behavioural science research for legal procedure, human rights, comparative law and international criminal trials. Communicating the breadth, dynamism and intensity of contemporary theoretical innovation in their diversity of subject matter and approach, the authors nonetheless remain united by a common purpose: to indicate how the best interdisciplinary theorising and research might be integrated directly into degree-level Evidence teaching.

Innovations in Evidence and Proof is published at an exciting time of theoretical renewal and increasing empirical sophistication in legal evidence, proof and procedure scholarship. This ground-breaking collection will be essential reading for Evidence teachers, and will also engage the interest and imagination of scholars, researchers and students investigating issues of evidence and proof in any legal system, municipal, transnational or global.

D1394436

Innovations in Evidence and Proof

Integrating Theory, Research and Teaching

Edited by

Paul Roberts
and
Mike Redmayne

·HART·
PUBLISHING

OXFORD AND PORTLAND, OREGON
2009

Published in North America (US and Canada) by
Hart Publishing
c/o International Specialized Book Services
920 NE 58th Avenue, Suite 300
Portland, OR 97213–3786
USA
Tel: +1 503 287 3093 or toll-free: (1) 800 944 6190
Fax: +1 503 280 8832
E-mail: orders@isbs.com
Website: www.isbs.com

First published in 2007. Reprinted in paperback in 2009

Hart Publishing, 16C Worcester Place, OX1 2JW
Telephone: +44 (0)1865 517530 Fax: +44 (0)1865 510710
E-mail: mail@hartpub.co.uk
Website: http://www.hartpub.co.uk

British Library Cataloguing in Publication Data
Data Available

ISBN: 978-1-84113-706-3
978-1-84113-978-4 (paperback)

Typeset by Columns Design Ltd, Reading
Printed and bound in Great Britain by
CPI Antony Rowe, Chippenham

Acknowledgements

The colloquium on *Teaching Evidence Scholarship* at which the papers published in this volume were first presented was generously sponsored by the *Modern Law Review*'s Annual Seminar Competition. Supplementary funding was provided by Vathek Publishing (publisher of E & P, the *International Journal of Evidence & Proof*) and the University of Nottingham School of Law.

Although each chapter of this book (with the exception of Chapter 1) was written for the *Teaching Evidence Scholarship* colloquium and has been specially revised and edited for publication in this volume, several of them draw substantially on previously published material. We are grateful to Oxford University Press for permission to reprint Paul Roberts, 'Rethinking the Law of Evidence: A Twenty-first Century Agenda for Teaching and Research' (2002) 55 *Current Legal Problems* 297–345 as Chapter 1 of the present volume; and to Cambridge University Press for permission to reprint William Twining, 'Taking Facts Seriously – Again' from Twining, *Rethinking Evidence: Exploratory Essays* 2/e (2006) as Chapter 2 of the present volume. In accordance with the terms of the MLR's Annual Seminar Competition, an earlier version of Chapter 11 appeared as John D Jackson, 'The Effect of Human Rights on Criminal Evidentiary Processes: Towards Convergence, Divergence or Realignment?' (2005) 68 *MLR* 737–764, and is reprinted here, in substantially revised form, by kind permission of the MLR and Blackwell Publishing.

We would like to thank, again, everybody who presented and participated in the original Nottingham colloquium in September 2004 for making that meeting such a stimulating and collegial event. Particular thanks are owed to Anne Crump and Jane Costa for their administrative assistance in preparing for the conference, and to Olga Pleshkova for organisational help during the event itself. Over and above their contributions at the colloquium, we want to pay tribute to those who agreed to write polished papers for this volume for their expertise, patience and good humour in keeping faith with the project over its several years of gestation whilst responding, always promptly and obligingly, to successive waves of editorial questions, suggestions, requests and revisions. We are also grateful to Richard Hart for taking a chance on a book that aspires to take the pedagogy and theory of Evidence seriously, because these are serious subjects rather than the stuff of bestsellers. Everybody at Hart Publishing worked with their customary professionalism and efficiency to ensure that this book was published before 31 December 2007.

Paul especially thanks Jill Hunter and her colleagues in the University of New South Wales School of Law for their kind hospitality during Paul's tenure of a professorial visiting fellowship during March – May 2007. This refreshing break from normal duties, spent in fine and friendly surroundings, came just at the right time to supply the opportunity and 'head-space' (adopting the Australian vernacular) to bring this long-running project finally to fruition.

PR   MR
Sydney,   London
ANZAC Day 2007

Contents

List of Contributors

Roderick Bagshaw, Tutor and Fellow in Law, Magdalen College, Oxford

Christine Boyle, Professor of Law, University of British Columbia

Craig Callen, Professor of Law, Michigan State University College of Law

Robert Cryer, Professor of International and Criminal Law, University of Birmingham

Jill Hunter, Professor of Law, University of New South Wales

John Jackson, Professor of Law, Queen's University Belfast

Jeroen Keppens, Lecturer in Computer Science, King's College London

Andrew Ligertwood, Reader in Law, University of Adelaide

Jenny McEwan, Professor of Law, University of Exeter

Mike Redmayne, Professor of Law, London School of Economics and Political Science

Paul Roberts, Professor of Criminal Jurisprudence, University of Nottingham; Professorial Visiting Fellow, University of New South Wales Faculty of Law, 2007

Burkhard Schafer, Senior Lecturer in Computational Legal Theory, University of Edinburgh

PJ Schwikkard, Professor of Law, University of Cape Town

Qiang Shen, Professor in Computer Science, University of Wales, Aberystwyth

William Twining, Quain Professor of Jurisprudence Emeritus, University College London; Visiting Professor, University of Miami School of Law

Abbreviations

AI	artificial intelligence
ATMS	assumption-based truth maintenance system
CJA	Criminal Justice Act
CJPOA 1994	Criminal Justice and Public Order Act 1994
DSS	decision support system
ECHR	European Convention on Human Rights
ECtHR	European Court of Human Rights
EIE	evidence interpretation and evaluation
EPF	evidence, proof and fact-finding
ICC	International Criminal Court
ICCPR	International Covenant on Civil and Political Rights
ICrimL	international criminal law
ICrimJ	international criminal justice
ICTR	International Criminal Tribunal for Rwanda
ICTY	International Criminal Tribunal for the former Yugoslavia
IHL	international humanitarian law
IR	international relations
PACE	Police and Criminal Evidence Act 1984
PIL	public international law
RPE	Rules of Procedure and Evidence
YJCE Act 1999	Youth Justice and Criminal Evidence Act 1999

Introduction: Teaching Evidence Scholarship

PAUL ROBERTS AND MIKE REDMAYNE

WITH THE EXCEPTION of Chapter 1, the essays comprising this volume are based on presentations made at a *Modern Law Review*-sponsored colloquium on 'Teaching Evidence Scholarship', hosted by the University of Nottingham on 10–11 September 2004. The inspiration for the colloquium derived from the speculation that Evidence teaching in university law schools, in Britain and elsewhere, currently fails to make the best use of an increasingly dynamic and diverse corpus of scholarship on evidence, proof and fact-finding in legal proceedings. Indeed, at some slight risk of unfairness and over-generalisation, the point can be expressed much more vividly: when scholarship on evidence and proof has never been more exciting in its range, methodologies and ambition,[1] how is it that textbooks and courses on the Law of Evidence are generally so predictable and even—dare one say it—a little bit dull? The primary purpose of the colloquium, and subsequently of the essays collected in this volume, is to bridge the apparent gap between teaching and scholarship in the Law of Evidence, not least by providing inspiration and practical advice to fellow Evidence teachers who might share our desire to re-energise our subject.

The notion of 'Teaching Evidence Scholarship' was intentionally conceived to be ambiguous. Contributors to the colloquium were left to decide for themselves whether they wanted to talk about teaching *Evidence scholarship* or to place the emphasis of their presentation on the more overtly pedagogical dimensions of *teaching Evidence* scholarship. In either event, the following indicative list of topics and questions was proposed:

(1) What can be learnt from comparing curricula, teaching practises, and teachers' experiences in different jurisdictions?

---

[1] For a review of recent scholarship, see RC Park and MJ Saks, 'Evidence Scholarship Reconsidered: Results of the Interdisciplinary Turn' (2006) 47 *Boston College Law Review* 949.

(2) What are the relationships between evolving legal practice, Evidence teaching and scholarly research and publication in the fields of evidence and proof?

(3) How do, and how should, Evidence teaching and scholarship inform legislative reform, judicial reasoning and other pertinent legal developments? Are the answers to these questions jurisdiction-bound and/or culturally specific?

(4) To what extent is curriculum design and delivery influenced by distinctive traditions of legal education in particular jurisdictions (including the type and level of students being taught)?

(5) How, if at all, is Evidence teaching influenced by the teaching materials traditionally employed, or currently available, in particular jurisdictions?

(6) To what extent is Evidence teaching multidisciplinary in different jurisdictions? What are the benefits, and costs, of a multidisciplinary approach? (To what extent are these costs and benefits specific to particular jurisdictions, or generalisable to all?)

(7) Which other (extra-legal) perspectives do Evidence teachers bring into their teaching? Epistemology (eg theories of truth and fact-finding)? Moral and political philosophy (eg questions of procedural justice or due process)? Social psychology (eg behavioural science data on the accuracy of eye-witness testimony, or juror assessments of credibility)? Economics (eg theories of efficient evidence production and adjudication)? Probability theory (eg Bayesian analysis of fact-finding)? Anything else? How far is each of these perspectives pursued? With what advantages, and at what cost?

(8) To what extent are the challenges, and opportunities, created by globalisation impacting on traditional practices of teaching and research? To what extent *should* they impact?

(9) How, if at all, has information technology impacted on Evidence teaching? Does it have untapped potential that Evidence teachers ought to exploit (and/or hidden dangers that Evidence teachers need to guard against)?

(10)To what extent does Evidence teaching incorporate international and/or comparative dimensions? Why (not)?

(11)How should the Law of Evidence be conceived and taxonomised, as a discrete curriculum within law school curricula, and as an object of scholarly investigation?

(12)What is the Law of Evidence?

This list had no pretensions to comprehensiveness, but it was hoped that it might at least indicate the range of issues that could profitably be discussed at the colloquium, and that it might stimulate further interest and reflection. In the event, we were richly rewarded by our contributors' generous and imaginative responses. All of these questions, and more, are addressed in one way or another in the following pages, sometimes as part of the author's central theme, at other times more implicitly or as asides to the main narrative.

Chapter 1 reproduces a previously published essay that was circulated to contributors in advance of the colloquium.[2] In a paper originally prepared as a *Current Legal Problems* lecture, Paul Roberts sketches out an agenda for 'rethinking the law of evidence' in the twenty-first century. Broadly allying himself with William Twining's project of 'taking facts seriously', Roberts identifies and elaborates on four key methodological dimensions of rethinking Evidence: taxonomy, epistemology, political morality and cosmopolitanism. This chapter fleshes out some of the issues and questions previously listed, and indicates a promising direction of travel; but the general mood is indicative rather than rigidly prescriptive, and the essay concludes by inviting further discussion and debate, at the colloquium and beyond.

William Twining is 'taking facts seriously ... again' in chapter 2, revisiting and up-dating a thesis first presented in print in 1980. This essay is part restatement, part reply to Roberts, and part tantalising glimpse of ongoing and future work. The basic thesis remains that the subject of evidence, proof and fact-finding (EPF) deserves a more central place in legal scholarship and law teaching. For Twining, this is not only a question about the design and delivery of courses on the Law of Evidence: legal scholarship in general, and jurisprudence and legal theory in particular, are seriously impoverished by their lamentable neglect of factual and evidentiary issues. So far as the theory and pedagogy of Evidence teaching are concerned, Twining (correctly) perceives a large measure of agreement with Roberts on the core issues. However, Twining is concerned to underline the important distinction between actually *taking* facts seriously, and merely talking about doing so. And when it comes to inculcating skills of fact management, interpretation and analysis in the classroom, there is still no substitute, in Twining's experience, for a modified version of Wigmore's chart method. The merits of Wigmore's much-maligned system are reiterated and promoted as an efficient way of dealing with complex factual arguments and 'mixed masses' of data, and some common misapprehensions are dispelled. This prompts reflection on the implications for legal scholarship and law teaching of the emergence of Evidence as an interdisciplinary field of inquiry, which might be regarded as a belated revival, and vindication, of Wigmore's early twentieth century adventures in the science

---

[2] See Roberts (2002) 55 *CLP* 297. The version reprinted in this volume has undergone a modicum of up-dating and redrafting.

of proof. The chapter concludes with some snapshots and 'tasters' indicating the remarkable range, diversity and innovation of the interdisciplinary research currently being undertaken on evidence, proof and fact-finding, which also serve to corroborate another one of Twining's nostrums, that 'the study of evidence in law is fundamentally and inescapably related to the study of evidence generally'.[3]

Twining's writings on evidence and proof supply part of the inspiration for Christine Boyle's contribution to this volume. Twining once likened Anglo-American law of evidence to the Cheshire Cat in *Alice in Wonderland* 'who keeps appearing and disappearing and fading away' so that one can never be confident what the law of evidence truly looks like, or even whether it exists at all. In Chapter 3, Boyle puts this trope to work in her quest for 'a principled approach to relevance', which takes her on a voyage of discovery through some well-known landmarks and lesser explored regions of Canadian jurisprudence bearing on evidence and fact-finding. The orthodox positions are easy to restate: relevance is determined by the logical relation of one fact to another, which, for the more mathematically-minded, can be expressed in terms of comparative probabilities. But after undertaking a wide-ranging examination of Canadian judges' approaches to factual inferences in different legal contexts, Boyle is driven to doubt whether 'logic' is truly determinative. A large dose of 'policy' seems to be in play when the courts meditate on the factual inferences that legitimately may be drawn from the accused's failure to report a murder, or a complainant's failure to record incidents of abuse in her diary, or an asylum-seeker's ignorance of Toronto's 'gay pride' day. It is tempting to conclude that the legal concept of relevance is just as obscure and intangible as the enigmatic Cheshire Cat. Fortunately, however, Boyle has more constructive advice to offer to fact-finders, judges and commentators. The process of drawing factual inferences is clearly governed by law in certain circumstances, as where the equality norm established by the Canadian Charter of Rights and Freedoms is engaged. For the rest, critical self-reflection on the defensibility of one's assumptions—structured by a series of helpful guidelines which Boyle elucidates—points the way to a principled approach to relevance (and a less elusive Cheshire Cat).

The significance of relevance as the conceptual and practical bridge between fact-finding and legal doctrine is something on which Roberts, Twining and Boyle are all agreed. In Chapter 4, Mike Redmayne develops this insight more systematically by re-examining the nature and durability of the factual inferences that were made in several cases which will be very familiar to teachers of English Evidence law. *Blastland*[4] and *Kearley*[5] are

---

[3]   William Twining, Chapter 2, 86. For a sense of the possibilities of a 'general science of evidence', see the material for the UCL evidence project at www.evidencescience.org/
[4]   *R v Blastland* [1986] 1 AC 41, HL.

(or have been[6]) staples of classroom explorations of the relationship between relevance and hearsay in English law. Redmayne shows, however, that buried under the more obvious jurisprudential contortions of these authorities are complexities of factual reasoning that legal commentators (let alone judges) rarely perceive. The theme of complexity finds more obvious resonance when Redmayne turns his attention to the notorious jurisprudential quagmire of inferences from silence, but here again Redmayne is able to demonstrate that careful attention to the logic of inference brings fresh illumination to recurring doctrinal puzzles. Redmayne is offering insight rather than simplification: indeed, in many respects the type of analysis that he advocates tends to complicate rather than simplify matters, but this only goes to show that law and legal adjudication can be a messy business. Here, we see facts being taken seriously, in just the way that Twining recommends, but in the comparatively unusual context of case law that would be encountered in any Evidence textbook or course on English law. Redmayne's essay thus supplies material assistance to Evidence teachers, both in substance and by way of example.

The next two chapters are equally concerned with the practicalities of Evidence teaching, but interpret this brief in ways which are at once striking and instructive in their contrasting styles and subject matter. In Chapter 5 Burkhard Schafer, Jeroen Keppens and Qiang Shen describe a computerised 'decision support system' (DSS) which they have developed as a practical aid to teaching their course on 'evidence interpretation and evaluation' (EIE) at the University of Edinburgh. Whilst computer-aided learning is not an entirely novel proposition for law students and teachers, the distinctive quality of the authors' system is its ability to simulate creative thinking about the relationships between pieces of evidence and alternative causal hypotheses that might account for the presence of that evidence, and for the absence of other evidence more consistent with competing hypotheses. Moreover, the system's user-interface can accommodate both 'backward-chaining' case theory-building from evidence to causal hypothesis (eg, Does the presence of a head wound indicate that the deceased was more likely to have been murdered than does the absence of such evidence? Do blood-shot eyes in a corpse differentiate between homicide and suicide?); and also 'forward-chaining' hypothesis construction followed by further inquiries for evidence which would be expected to confirm, or undermine, the hypothesis (the kind of intellectual process

---

[5]　*R v Kearley* [1992] 2 AC 228, HL.

[6]　*Kearley* has (at least temporarily) been stripped of its precedent status by the Criminal Justice Act 2003, though the pedagogical value of reading contrasting judicial analyses of the scope and application of the hearsay rule is barely diminished.

dubbed 'abductive reasoning' by the American philosopher Charles Sanders Peirce).[7] Inspired by computing models first imagined in science fiction, the Edinburgh DSS is a practical – albeit, at this stage, still evolving – solution for teaching law students transferable skills of creative thinking about facts through their active engagement with virtual crime scenes and criminal investigations. The authors have made their prototype available on the website of Edinburgh's Joseph Bell Centre for Forensic Statistics and Legal Reasoning[8] and encourage law teachers and students to try it out for themselves.

Craig Callen also presents a model for reasoning about factual inferences in Chapter 6, but he focuses rather more narrowly on terrain very familiar to common law Evidence teachers, the scope of the hearsay prohibition and the problem of 'implied assertions'. Implied (or *imputed*) assertions present notorious theoretical puzzles for legal analysis, whilst the House of Lords' decision in *Kearley*, the US Supreme Court's ruling in *Crawford v Washington*[9] and the UK Parliament's major reform of the law of hearsay in the Criminal Justice Act (CJA) 2003 have turned classroom hypotheticals into pressing problems for practising lawyers and judges (by extension, reinforcing their significance for law teachers and students as well). Callen's method for getting some traction on these seemingly timeless issues is both interdisciplinary and comparative.

Research on the theory and practice of communication, Callen argues, illuminates the 'cognitive strategies' employed by speakers to convey information to their intended audience in the most economical fashion. This is directly relevant to legal practice, not only in modelling the strategies probably relied on by jurors to draw factual inferences from the evidence presented to them in court, but also in analysing the significance of equivocal utterances (eg, 'I didn't tell them anything about you') and non-verbal communication and other ambiguous conduct which have traditionally posed problems for the application of hearsay doctrine. Insights derived from communications theory are built into Callen's graphical representation of hearsay analysis, which also encompasses the fruits of his comparative legal survey of the range of contrasting approaches to implied assertions to be found in different US state jurisdictions, under the Federal Rules of Evidence, in England and Wales pre- and post-CJA 2003, and under the Supreme Court's Confrontation Clause analysis. Although the shortcomings of various approaches are pointed out along the way, it is not Callen's purpose in this essay to promote any particular conception of the scope of the hearsay prohibition. Rather, the

---

[7] For a brief introduction, see eg, the entry on Peirce in the *Stanford Encyclopedia of Philosophy*: www. plato.stanford.edu/entries/peirce/#dia/

[8] www.cfslr.ed.ac.uk/ (site undergoing reconstruction at the time of writing).

[9] *Crawford v Washington* 541 U.S. 36, 124 S.Ct. 1354 (2004).

essay aims to explain how different approaches to hearsay apparently rest on different assumptions, both about the nature of communication in natural settings and about the conduct of fact-finding in legal adjudication. Students (and lawyers and judges) might better understand knotty problems of hearsay doctrine if they examined more carefully the types of argument that need to be constructed to support any particular conception of the scope of the hearsay rule, and reflected more systematically on the implications for fact-finding of choosing one conception over another. Callen's essay maps and summarises eligible strategies of argumentation about hearsay and implied assertions. Moreover, '[c]omparative analysis (whether across national or doctrinal borders) affords an additional perspective from which we can assess the degree to which evidence law seems to respond to jurors' cognitive needs'.[10]

The next pair of chapters underscores the significance of interdisciplinarity in Evidence teaching and scholarship. In Chapter 7, Jenny McEwan undertakes a wide-ranging survey of the implications of psychological and other 'behavioural science' literature for legal practice, adjudication and law reform. Behavioural scientists have studied various aspects of legal proceedings and generated masses of empirical data with a direct bearing on law and legal process. The reliability of eyewitness identification has been a particularly popular topic of investigation over the years, but psychologists and socio-legal researchers have also undertaken interesting studies on interviewing and false confessions, the durability of witnesses' memories, the significance of demeanour in assessing witness credibility, the comprehensibility of judicial instructions to juries, and the impact of hearing 'prejudicial' character evidence on mock jurors' verdicts, amongst other experimental designs with evident salience for the law of evidence. Reconsidered within the context of this discussion, it is hard to see how a legislature contemplating procedural reform, a judge formulating an advisory instruction to the jury, or a university teacher aspiring to inculcate techniques of critical evaluation in law students, could properly proceed without at least taking account of these extensive research findings.

In advocating greater resort to behavioural science literature as an empirical basis for legislation, adjudication, law reform and law teaching, McEwan is careful to emphasise limitations as well as untapped potential. Common-sense assumptions—dubbed 'fireside inductions' by Paul Meehl—should not necessarily be abandoned at the first sign of conflicting research findings, especially if they are 'gold-star fireside inductions' which appear to have withstood the tests of time and judicial experience. Nor can empirical data settle normative arguments about 'fairness' and other moralised legal standards. However, McEwan does insist that the law's

---

[10] Craig Callen, Chapter 6, 161.

approach to behavioural science evidence should be consistent and reasonably comprehensive, and here the track-record of legislators, courts and commentators leaves much to be desired. Rather than consistency and comprehensiveness, McEwan's survey finds cherry-picking and irrational distinctions. Behavioural scientists' criticisms of eyewitness testimony have been substantially taken on board by the legal establishment,[11] but similar caution has not been extended to the analogous context of voice identification, in which the dangers of wrongful conviction are, if anything, greater. More generally, the argument for 'free' (or at least, *freer*) proof, which would appear to be supported by a very substantial corpus of mutually reinforcing research studies, has not recommended itself to a critical mass of legal practitioners and commentators in relation to traditional exclusionary doctrines of hearsay or character evidence, notwithstanding the advocacy of Lord Justice Auld's *Review of Criminal Courts in England and Wales*. McEwan not surprisingly finds this piecemeal approach indefensible: 'if psychological theory is to be invoked in order to challenge lay competence, psychology must also be allowed a voice on the question of the accuracy of the assumptions underpinning the rules of exclusion'.[12] In short, 'the law of evidence, in particular, cannot afford to treat the findings of behavioural scientists as merely an interesting sideshow'.[13]

In the course of her discussion, which takes in an impressive array of legal issues and empirical studies, McEwan still finds time to acknowledge certain methodological limitations of behavioural science research, including its reliance on more-or-less artificial simulations as approximations to real-world events and frequent use of college students as experimental subjects. Roderick Bagshaw takes up these methodological issues in a much more systematic fashion in Chapter 8. Granted that it might be useful to know about behavioural science data in evaluating legal norms and institutions, how should law teachers equip their students (and themselves) to become competent consumers and users of such information? What steps should we take to make empirical data, and the predictably reformist arguments based upon them, safe(r) for legal education? These are the preoccupations of Chapter 8, and Bagshaw is a cultured sceptic. Like any accomplished presenter, he begins with a joke: the one about the engineer, the physicist, the mathematician and the Scottish black sheep. There is a serious point, of course: the meaning and significance of any empirical information is sensitive to the perspectives and motivations of its consumers. The mathematician might come across

---

[11] Which does not necessarily rule out scope for improvement. McEwan, Chapter 7 in this volume, advocates adapting the classic *Turnbull* warning in certain scenarios.

[12] *Ibid* 196.

[13] *Ibid* 216.

as a boring pedant at dinner parties,[14] but his insistence on meticulously limiting the inferences that can safely be drawn from empirical observations might, suggests Bagshaw, provide a valuable object-lesson for lawyers trying to assess the implications of behavioural science data for law, legal adjudication and procedural reform.

As McEwan also recognises, behavioural science experiments employ various 'substitutions' in modelling real-world legal phenomena like identification parades, police interviews and criminal trials. Practical necessity, ethical considerations and resource limitations understandably dictate the nature of these substitutions, but their undeniable implications, Bagshaw notes, are not only confined to limiting the generalisability of research findings, but also serve to restrict the type and range of issues that are investigated in the first place. Thus, 'often lawyers have to decide how to deal with evidential issues of a type or within a timescale which precludes primary reliance on the experimental method'.[15] In any case, as McEwan has already stated, legal decision-making is often normative in a way that empirical information may potentially inform, but can never—ultimately— dictate. Bagshaw adds the further complexity that existing legal norms, as much as proposals for their reform, may impact unevenly on different sections of society and require the law to mediate between competing interests. In other words, legal adjudication is an object of political contestation and compromise, and consequently an inevitably 'risky' undertaking. Indeed, for Bagshaw, 'it is irresponsible to treat reasoning from experimental data as a process which is free from risk ... [A]nxiety will never be *entirely eliminated* by a strategy of further experimentation. This strategy must consequently be supplemented by an approach to making decisions *despite* lingering anxiety'.[16] It may well be educational, Bagshaw suggests, for students of the law of evidence to appreciate that they are not the only ones who may experience anxiety when confronted with the demands of adjudication. Since uncertainties inevitably persist after all pertinent information has been taken into account, legal adjudication might be conceptualised, and experienced by its participants, as an occasion of inescapable social and personal anxiety.

Yet, one might still ask: is there anything more constructive to teach a student who has experienced the edifying anxiety of uncertainty, but still remains baffled about the place of behavioural science data in legal adjudication and law reform? Careful to keep his inferential conclusions securely anchored in their empirical moorings, Bagshaw sensibly eschews sweeping generalisations in favour of endorsing two modest principles.

---

[14] We should add, in the interests of balance, that the woolly thinking of engineers is the butt of the mathematicians' version of the joke.
[15] Roderick Bagshaw, Chapter 8, 229.
[16] *Ibid* 233.

First, the risks—what is at stake in any 'wager' on legal doctrine or its proposed reform—must be carefully specified, always recognising that there are risks of inaction as well as of wrong action, for example the risk of failing to heed the warnings of reliable behavioural science, mirroring the risk of relying on ill-conceived or methodologically inept studies. Secondly, the distributional dimension of legal adjudication implies the desirability of a legislative procedure in which the full range of societal perspectives, preferences and interests can be ventilated and afforded due weight in decision-making. With these guiding principles established, more detailed questions of institutional design can be left to another day (though Bagshaw cautions against chasing chimerical standards of perfection).

For the next two chapters, coincidentally[17] both written by Australian scholars, the focus of attention shifts to the institutional contexts of legal adjudication and their significance for Evidence teaching. Andrew Ligert-wood, in Chapter 9, is keen to emphasise the practical nature of the law of evidence and its subservience to the instrumental goals of adjudication in terms of effective dispute resolution. Whilst truth-finding is obviously central to litigation, and illuminating parallels can be drawn between factual inquiries in law and fact-finding in other social contexts, it does not follow that epistemology, probability theory or other relatively arcane theoretical inquiries will provide much insight into the complexities of legal adjudication. Rather, Ligertwood insists, 'within the discipline of law, evidential issues are most effectively analysed and understood in the context of the practical legal process within which they arise ... and the parameters of the discipline are defined by what those appealing to legal norms are trying to achieve'.[18] Legal practice, then, should be the starting point, both for evidentiary scholarship and for Evidence teaching.

Ligertwood acknowledges that the objectives of civil and criminal litigation diverge, but insists that legal approaches to fact-finding are essentially similar in both institutional contexts such that 'it is preferable not to hive off evidential issues into separate criminal and civil compart-ments'.[19] He proceeds to give a detailed outline and summary of an innovative approach to Evidence teaching pioneered at the University of Adelaide, which is organised around mock trials, advocacy exercises and student role-plays as well as incorporating more traditional-style lectures on legal procedure and the exclusionary rules. Though admittedly some-what resource-intensive, this practically-focused, participation-based cur-riculum design has proved popular and effective in 'bring[ing] Evidence

[17] Or possibly not: the structure of Australian legal education, which does not incorporate the British split between the 'academic' and 'vocational' stages, might conceivably encourage a more practically-orientated approach to Evidence teaching.
[18] Andrew Ligertwood, Chapter 9, 239, 241.
[19] *Ibid* 250. Cf P Roberts and A Zuckerman, *Criminal Evidence* (Oxford, OUP, 2004) § 1.1.

doctrine to life'.[20] Whilst there may be some passing resemblances to practitioner-orientated 'how-to' courses on litigation procedure and advocacy, Ligertwood stresses the more elevated pedagogical ambitions of his model, the point of which is not teaching advocacy skills per se, but rather to inculcate in students a deeper, critical understanding of the laws of evidence through the experience of trying to apply procedural norms in hypothetical litigation scenarios. In this way, students learn by doing, not simply by talking about evidence and fact-finding, in accordance with the principle of active learning advocated by Twining, and implemented with the assistance of computing technology by Schafer, Keppens and Shen. Ligertwood also echoes Twining in insisting on the largely unacknowledged significance of evidence and fact-finding for legal theory more generally: 'Every judgment studied in a substantive law subject is a consequence of the contingencies of legal process. This is an important insight for anyone seriously interested in studying and understanding law'.[21]

In Chapter 10, Jill Hunter takes the intimate connection between rules of evidence and adjudicative processes in a rather different direction. Her 'cross-examination' of 'the failure of the law of evidence' is in large part an indictment of the failure of judges, and of legal rules and processes, to protect vulnerable witnesses from excessive cross-examination in criminal trials. A large body of empirical information has by now accumulated, from behavioural science research (including studies cited in Jenny McEwan's chapter), socio-legal trial observations and official inquiries, demonstrating that adversarial trial process in general, and cross-examination in particular, imposes often severe burdens on witnesses without any compensating gains in forensic truth-finding. Indeed, many researchers argue that adversarial trial process is peculiarly ill-suited to the task of securing reliable testimony. How has this situation arisen and been perpetuated? An important part of the answer, Hunter indicates, is to be found in the combination of the historical development of common law criminal trials and modern professional legal culture.

Langbein has shown how the 'lawyerisation' of the eighteenth century criminal trial resulted in the evolution of the adversarial, party-dominated forensic contest that later came to symbolise common law adjudication.[22] This was also the opportunity for lawyers to make a name for themselves as talented advocates, the epitome of their art being the skilfully devised, rhetorically pyrotechnic demolition of an opponent's witnesses in cross-examination; or failing that, straightforward character assassination. Today, whilst some of the antics of Garrow and his ilk would no longer be

---

[20] Andrew Ligertwood, Chapter 9, 259.
[21] *Ibid* 258.
[22] JH Langbein, *The Origins of Adversary Criminal Trial* (Oxford, OUP, 2003).

tolerated in most courtrooms,[23] advocates still employ essentially the same techniques of case construction and story-telling to run rings round vulnerable (or just relatively unsophisticated) witnesses and to engage the sympathies and prejudices of lay jurors. Hunter is in no doubt about the law's complicity in perpetuating this lamentable situation: the legal rules governing witness examination are 'tired, sad and inadequate'. Part of the problem is that ethical constraints on overbearing cross-examination, which appear in advocates' professional codes of conduct, are far too flimsy to encourage real restraint, especially within a professional culture which values aggressive cross-examination styles and an institutional context which erects legal and pragmatic barriers to effective judicial intervention on behalf of harried witnesses. The situation is exacerbated by pointless legal technicalities which serve only to distract attention from more substantive issues of justice and humane treatment, and further frustrate the search for truth.

For Hunter, then, the true significance of rules of evidence and procedure can only emerge when they are placed in their institutional and professional-cultural context, where their true effects become apparent. For example, the baroque technicalities of the collateral-finality rule, which might seem only harmlessly eccentric when contemplated in abstraction, appear more sinister by these lights, since (Hunter argues) they are directly implicated in the institutional structures which continue to expose witnesses to distressing, demeaning and—perhaps worst of all, in view of the centrality of truth-finding to legal adjudication—*counterproductive* cross-examinations. Adopting an institutional perspective, which is also sensitive to the history and professional culture of adversarial trial, should encourage law students and their teachers (as well as practising lawyers, judges and legislators) to construct different, and better, 'stories' about the law of evidence and its practical implementation. This is not so much a question of abandoning our adversarial heritage—Hunter is a realist on this score, cautioning that '[c]ulturally-embedded practice does not vanish overnight'[24]—but, rather, of refining existing norms and adapting current practice so that criminal adjudication can better serve the ends of justice and maintain public confidence in a modern constitutional democracy.

Comparative perspectives feature prominently at various points in the essays already mentioned, for example in Craig Callen's comparative

---

[23] On Garrow's style of cross-examination, see JM Beattie, 'Scales of Justice: Defense Counsel and the English Criminal Trial in the Eighteenth and Nineteenth Centuries' (1991) 9 *Law and History Review* 221 at 236ff. For later concerns provoked by the adversarial tactics of Lord Henry Brougham, and their modern-day extensions, see AW Alschuler, 'How to Win the Trial of the Century: the Ethics of Lord Brougham and the OJ Simpson Defense Team' (1998) 29 *McGeorge Law Review* 291; L Ellison, 'The Mosaic Art? Cross-Examination and the Vulnerable Witness' (2001) 21 *Legal Studies* 353.

[24] Jill Hunter, Chapter 10, 287.

analyses of hearsay doctrine in US and English law, in Jill Hunter's reflections on the cultural foundations of adversarialism (citing Italy's rather mixed experience of adversary trial as a cultural-institutional 'transplant')[25] and in Paul Roberts' advocacy of 'cosmopolitanism' in Evidence teaching and scholarship. For this volume's final four essays, however, the comparative and international dimensions of our discipline move centre-stage.

John Jackson begins, in Chapter 11, with some conceptual reflections on the meaning and methods of 'comparative' scholarship and its place within the Evidence curriculum. As Jackson insists, there is much more to comparative legal studies than a narrow focus on 'comparing and contrasting' domestic and foreign laws. Illuminating comparisons can also be drawn between truth-seeking inquiries in legal and non-legal contexts (Twining would readily concur), between fact-finding in different institutional settings (as Ligertwood also contends), and between evidence gathering and evaluation at different stages of the same proceedings, comparing, for example, the pre-trial, trial and post-verdict phases of criminal adjudication (reprising the argument advanced by both Hunter and Roberts for greater attention to pre-trial process). Indeed, 'comparison might be regarded as the quintessential mode of legal scholarship',[26] as well as affording the perfect vehicle for teaching skills of critical thinking and analysis to Evidence students. There is, moreover, a burgeoning comparative legal literature on which to draw, albeit that little of this material has thus far found its way into the standard Evidence texts. But the neophyte, Jackson cautions, should be made aware of certain biases and blindspots which threaten to 'skew our understanding of the manner in which processes of proof are changing and to impede attempts to conceptualise desirable reforms'.[27] In this respect, Jackson's project echoes Roderick Bagshaw's approach to behavioural science data, in seeking to make somewhat less familiar areas of pertinent research and scholarship safe for consumption by Evidence students and their teachers.

Comparative studies of criminal procedure routinely invoke stylised contrasts between 'adversarial' and 'inquisitorial' legal systems as a cornerstone of their analytical frameworks. Jackson does not deny that the 'adversarial-inquisitorial dichotomy' can be an illuminating heuristic, but he does question its theoretical coherence and continuing durability. The danger perceived by Jackson is that 'if we use the terms inappropriately, as though they were comprehensive, all-inclusive categories, we my lose sight

---

[25] See WT Pizzi and M Montagna, 'The Battle to Establish an Adversarial Trial System in Italy' (2004) 25 *Michigan Journal of International Law* 429; E Grande, 'Italian Criminal Justice: Borrowing and Resistance' (2000) 48 *American Journal of Comparative Law* 227.

[26] John Jackson, Chapter 11, 329.

[27] *Ibid* 304.

of important aspects of legal process which cannot be categorised as either "adversarial" or "inquisitorial" at all'.[28] Close analysis of Article 6 ECHR jurisprudence on the right to a fair trial seems to bear out this contention. The Strasbourg institutions have not so much engineered a 'convergence' between adversarial and inquisitorial traditions in criminal adjudication, as many commentators understand it, but have rather improvised a sui generis model of fair trial rights implicitly designed to combine the *theorie de la procédure contradictoire* of continental jurisprudence with common law conceptions of adversarialism. This is, on Jackson's account, a distinctive 'vision of participatory proof'[29] which eludes the staid dichotomy between 'adversarial' and 'inquisitorial' procedural systems. Whether or not Jackson's theoretical analysis is accepted in its entirety, the argument for 'taking comparative evidence seriously' seems both telling and timely when rapid normative and institutional innovation appear to demand 'a new vocabulary for describing and explaining what is taking place'.[30] For as Jackson concludes, 'Evidence teachers, too, will need to learn this new jurisprudential language if they are serious about participating in the comparative study of evidence and proof'.[31]

The notion of 'convergence' is revisited by PJ Schwikkard in Chapter 12, in a way which departs from, and to a certain extent qualifies, Jackson's analysis. Schwikkard squarely confronts the question of the appropriate criterion by which 'convergence' might be assessed. For her, moral and political 'values' are the decisive arbiters (partly answering Roberts' plea in Chapter 1 for more systematic reflection on the political morality of evidence and proof). On this account, 'identifying the values shaping evidence rules has the potential to inform assessments of the extent of convergence in national and international Evidence law, as well as providing a basis for evaluating the merits of importing or exporting rules between jurisdictions'.[32] By examining the broader political environment beyond the 'internal' procedural values of truth-seeking and due process, we can, suggests Schwikkard, gain some purchase on a more substantive notion of convergence capable of looking past relatively superficial differences, or indeed apparent similarities, in procedural forms. If one is concerned with the political legitimacy of criminal adjudication, convergence on substantive conceptions of equality and human rights may be more significant than idiosyncratic local variations in institutional design

---

[28] *Ibid* 311.
[29] *Ibid* 329.
[30] *Ibid* 330.
[31] *Ibid.*
[32] PJ Schwikkard, Chapter 12, 332.

or criminal legislation.[33] Conversely, from the point of view of social justice, the political realities dictating whether a particular polity has the capacity to recruit and train defence lawyers and to fund expert legal advice and representation for the accused may provide a far better indication of the quality of justice dispensed in the world's courtrooms than near-universal agreement on aspirational 'fair trial' standards in international human rights treaties. In short: '[c]onvergence, on this view, is therefore not a measure of superficial similarities between legal doctrine or process in different jurisdictions, but a search for a deeper underlying unity of moral and political values'.[34]

Schwikkard is effectively calling for the elucidation of comparative moral and political philosophies of government, legislation and adjudication. Some might regard that as a daunting and rather ethereal project, at some distance removed from conventional debates about the extent of convergence in comparative procedural systems (let alone the more parochial contents of the standard Evidence curriculum). However, moral and political values are never far from the surface of evidentiary discourse, and frequently force themselves into the discussions and analyses of our contributors, for example, in Christine Boyle's appeals to the Canadian Charter's equality norm and in Jill Hunter's critique of the excesses of adversarial cross-examination from the normative perspective of dignity and humane treatment. If rules of criminal evidence and procedure are conceptualised as a pivotal point of contact between adjudication in individual cases and broader landscapes of political legitimacy, constitutionalism, human rights and social justice, this opens up new possibilities for collaborative interdisciplinary research in which studies of criminal evidence might inform conceptions of liberal democracy at the same time as procedural law and practice are contextualised in terms of theories of legitimate government. This suggestion is a methodological analogue of Schwikkard's insistence that '[t]he impact of broader political, social and cultural forces on rules of evidence and procedure is often particularly pronounced. Evidentiary rules and doctrines may consequently serve as a tangible index, both of social progress within a particular legal jurisdiction and of international convergence upon a shared set of values'.[35] Another way of encapsulating the essential connection is to say that, if you want to find out about a society's cherished values and political culture, its criminal courts would be one good place to look.[36]

---

[33] Also see P Roberts, 'Theorising Procedural Tradition: Subjects, Objects and Values in Criminal Adjudication' in A Duff, L Farmer, S Marshall and V Tadros (eds), *The Trial on Trial*, vol 2, *Judgment and Calling to Account* (Oxford, Hart, 2006).

[34] PJ Schwikkard, Chapter 12, 345.

[35] *Ibid* 344.

[36] This is, of course, an adaptation of Churchill's celebrated aphorism that 'the mood and temper of the public in regard to the treatment of crime and criminals is one of the most

In Chapter 13, Paul Roberts makes his second contribution to this volume, with some ruminations on the question 'Why international criminal evidence?'. As it was for Jackson in contemplating the merits of comparative study, Roberts' starting point is conceptual analysis of basic terminology. Having clarified the meanings of 'Evidence' and 'International Criminal Justice' (ICrimJ), it becomes evident that their interrelationships can be characterised in different ways. On a broad view, the march of cosmopolitanism implies that Evidence teaching and scholarship *are already* engaging with international criminal justice. However, the argument can be developed and refined to emphasise some relatively under-developed applications. Roberts illuminates the untapped potential of ICrimJ for Evidence scholarship and teaching with some concrete examples focusing on the political morality, institutional architecture and cultural contexts of international criminal adjudication. As well as being immensely important in their own right (who does not care about global justice after 9/11 and war in Iraq?), Roberts urges Evidence scholars and teachers to seek out, and learn from, traces of the familiar in the international community's juridical responses to extreme events in world history. This connection between humanity's blackest deeds and the routine demands of criminal adjudication was prefigured in Robert H Jackson's opening speech to the Nuremberg International Military Tribunal in 1945 in which Jackson promised to provide the eight-member multinational tribunal with 'undeniable proofs of incredible events'.[37] Roberts commends ICrimJ to Evidence specialists, firstly as the disciplinary locus for a distinctive brand of comparativism which 'helps to make explicit what is often relatively opaque at the domestic level';[38] and secondly, as a unique source of primary materials (including full trial transcripts) potentially generating 'valuable insights which are generally absent from English criminal juris-prudence'.[39]

The theme of international criminal justice is ably taken up again by Robert Cryer in Chapter 14. Cryer's specific focus is witness evidence and the problems to which it gives rise in international criminal proceedings. An immediate challenge is presented by the need for translation in multicultural trials in which witnesses, advocates and each member of a collegiate tribunal may all speak different mother-tongues. These issues have been addressed by international criminal courts, and with increasing

---

unfailing tests of the civilisation of any country', quoted in Sir L Radzinowicz and R Hood, 'Judicial Discretion and Sentencing Standards: Victorian Attempts to Solve a Perennial Problem' (1979) 127 *University of Pennsylvania Law Review* 1288 at 1348.

[37] *Nuremberg Trial Proceedings*, vol 2, Second Day, 21 November 1945, Mr Justice Jackson's Opening Speech to the Tribunal, 98: see the Avalon Project Transcript at www.yale.edu/lawweb/avalon/imt/imt.htm#proc/

[38] Paul Roberts, Chapter 13, 372.

[39] *Ibid* 373.

cultural sensitivity, since the post-war Nuremberg and Tokyo trials, culminating in the Codes of Practice on translation adopted by the United Nations' international criminal tribunals for the former Yugoslavia (ICTY) and Rwanda (ICTR). However, as Cryer shows, problems of translation penetrate far below the surface appearances of linguistic difference, burrowing deep into the culture, mores and psyche of particular language-communities and helping to define membership in them. International criminal tribunals must grapple with the 'thick' cultural-conditioning of language in order to interpret and evaluate witness evidence successfully. This task is exacerbated by various factors, some of which characterise the unusual circumstances of war crimes trials (eg, the difficulty of finding reliable interpreters who are not already themselves implicated in the conflict in some way) whilst other considerations will be perfectly familiar to Evidence scholars and teachers from their studies of domestic legal process: problems in interpreting witnesses' demeanour in the courtroom, devising appropriate measures to accommodate the seriously traumatised witness within the parameters of a fair trial, controlling for factors liable to 'contaminate' a witness's testimony, and so on. Here, Cryer draws on some of the psychological research surveyed in Jenny McEwan's chapter, and also touches on issues discussed more systematically, in the domestic context, by Jill Hunter. Indeed, Elizabeth Loftus, known to most Evidence specialists as a pioneering researcher on the reliability of eyewitness identification, has appeared before the ICTY as an expert witness on the psychology of memory and the potentially confounding impact of trauma. In demonstrating, once again, the link between the extreme and the mundane in criminal adjudication, Cryer concludes almost exactly where Roberts' essay began:

> Particularly in the light of international judges' apparent willingness to discuss problems of evidence and fact-finding quite openly, all Evidence scholars, and not only those with a developed interest in international criminal law, might readily be encouraged to learn from and contribute towards studies of the practice and procedures of the international criminal tribunals.[40]

We have said enough by way of introduction; it is high time to allow our contributors to speak for themselves. This brief foretaste of what readers can expect to find in the following pages will hopefully suffice to indicate both the rich variety and diversity of the essays in this volume, and the significant measure of commonality in their underlying themes and preoccupations. At one level, this collection of essays is intended to contribute, in the conventional manner, to the 'jewelled mosaic'[41] of scholarly writings

---

[40] Robert Cryer, Chapter 14, 400.
[41] EW Marsh, 'Teachers of Evidence and their Jeweled Mosaic' (2003) 21 *Quinnipiac Law Reivew* i.

on evidence and proof. However, in its explicit focus on relatively neglected aspects of pedagogical theory and practice, we hope that this volume also contributes something particularly distinctive to the existing literature. In these pages Evidence teachers will find practical tips and suggestions, as well as grand theorising, committed advocacy, and even a little bit of gentle provocation, to encourage and facilitate their participation in teaching Evidence scholarship.

1

Rethinking the Law of Evidence: a Twenty-First Century Agenda for Teaching and Research*

PAUL ROBERTS

TIME FOR RETHINKING

THIS ESSAY PROCEEDS from the simple conviction that rethinking the Law of Evidence[1] is a permanent, indispensable and even *routine* dimension of teaching and writing about the Law of Evidence, or at least of the best teaching and writing in this field. If, after all, university scholars and teachers decline to keep their subject in good theoretical, pedagogical and practical shape, who else will be motivated or qualified to take up the challenge? In this threshold sense, it is always time for rethinking Evidence, and the only question is whether Evidence teachers can find the time for it.

Though university teachers never need an excuse for rethinking their subject, there are, moreover, strong positive reasons for rethinking the Law of Evidence at the start of the twenty-first century. The discipline-specific factors on which this chapter will mainly concentrate are framed by the backdrop of contemporary trends in British higher education. These trends prominently include unprecedented expansion in student numbers, turning

* The substance of this chapter was first presented in my *Current Legal Problems* lecture delivered at UCL's Faculty of Laws on 29 November 2001, and subsequently published in revised form at (2002) 55 *CLP* 297. I am indebted to Roderick Bagshaw, Andrew Choo, Sean Doran, Steve Gilmore, Mike Redmayne, Alex Stein, Peter Tillers and William Twining for their generous comments on previous drafts, as well as to the scores of other Evidence teachers and successive generations of students who have constantly kept me rethinking what I should teach and research.
[1] Herein, the 'Law of Evidence' (capitalised) means the legal subject, course or topic of that name. The shortened-form 'Evidence' is employed synonymously. This usage is not intended to imply that the specifically juridical aspects of the *law* of Evidence take precedence over the more generic components (fact analysis, moral reasoning etc) of an agenda for rethinking the Law of Evidence.

an elite into a mass system of university tuition,[2] relatively inflexible and intrusive mechanisms of 'quality audit' (Research Assessment Exercise (RAE); Teaching Quality Assessment (TQA)), and an insidiously pervasive instrumental philosophy of education, which characterises learning as the handmaiden of employment and promotes 'consumer choice' and 'customer satisfaction' in priority to intellectual growth and pedagogical expertise.[3] For those of us who judge instrumental conceptions of legal education to be seriously inadequate and lamentably misguided, now is the time to say so, and loudly. Though traditional liberal values are currently on the defensive, debate has not (yet) been foreclosed. For example, the voluminous documentation demanded by quality audit, which is time-consuming and tedious to generate, nonetheless provides genuine opportunities to reiterate alternative conceptions, values and rationalisations of higher education.

Such pressures and opportunities are reinforced by the contemporary demands of law teaching in general, and of Evidence teaching in particular. The interwoven, mutually reinforcing consequences of globalisation and new information technologies have inaugurated continual revolution in legal education and scholarship. One very tangible impact is an explosion in the volume of pertinent legal information, downloadable via the Internet to every law teacher's desktop within minutes of its parliamentary or judicial production.[4] Access to transcripts of unreported cases, now archived on commercial and educational Internet sites, is a significant innovation.[5] Vast, searchable databases of primary and secondary legal

---

[2] In the last 30 years, Britain has moved from a highly selective, elitist model of higher education, in which perhaps 5 per cent of school leavers went on to university, to a system of mass higher education catering for one-third of all school-leavers, with a target of 50 per cent participation by the end of the decade: D MacLeod, 'Ministers Aim High with HE Recruitment Campaign', *The Guardian*, 15 November 2001.

[3] These developments have been satirised by Tony Bradney in a series of SPTL *Reporter* editorials, which would be comedy pieces, but for the fact that they only lightly embellish reality: see T Bradney, 'The Future of Law Schools' (1998) 16 *SPTL Reporter* 1; 'Quality or Cant?' (1998) 17 *SPTL Reporter*, 1; 'This Brave New World' (2000) 20 *SPTL Reporter* 1; 'Making Students Suffer' (2000) 21 *SPTL Reporter* 1; 'Law Schools and the Egg Marketing Board' (2001) 22 *SPTL Reporter* 1; 'Rejoice, Rejoice' (2001) 23 *SPTL Reporter* 1.

[4] No English judge has yet to my knowledge followed the example of Judge Hiller Zobel, who presided at the 'British nanny' trial of Louise Woodward, by actually rendering judgment on the Internet: see WR Leibowitz, 'Growing Pains of Major Web Sites Broadcast Problems and Potential' (1998) 20 *National Law Journal* B9 (2 March 1998); *Commonwealth v Woodward* 7 Mass L Rptr 449 (10 November 1997) (Mass Superior Court), affirmed 694 N E 2d 1277 (1998) (Mass Supreme Judicial Court). But when the decisions of English courts are accessible to Evidence teachers worldwide to download onto their desktop pc within an hour, it seems to me that the information revolution has already happened in advance of any local judge resorting to this gimmick.

[5] See in particular the British and Irish Legal Information Institute (BAILII) website at www.bailii.org/. The Court of Appeal has already taken steps to control its own information-saturated environment, admonishing counsel to stick to reported cases if at all possible:

information, of which LEXIS and WESTLAW are perhaps the best known and most useful, are another revolutionary deliverance of modern information technology.

These new technologies are still in their infancy, yet it is already barely possible to keep abreast of every judicial decision or dictum bearing on the Law of Evidence. Nor is it necessarily a wise use of a teacher's finite time, effort and motivation to attempt to do so. The aspiration to comprehensiveness becomes obsessive and chimerical if taken to extremes. Time spent agonising over the potential implications of the Court of Appeal's latest pronouncement, though undeniably gainful employment,[6] nonetheless entails that material of greater juridical or pedagogic value is probably escaping one's attention. This is most evident with regard to comparative and international materials, as English lawyers in the post-Human Rights Act era are beginning to realise (themes addressed below, under the rubric of 'cosmopolitanism'). The point to stress by way of introduction is that there are positive as well as negative reasons for rethinking Evidence teaching in the twenty-first century. On the positive side, current technologies and modern law's cosmopolitan tendencies have opened up new vistas of possibility for Evidence teaching and scholarship; whilst, on the negative side, these same developments render the ongoing task of up-dating traditional texts and syllabi both inordinately demanding and excessively narrow.

It is essential periodically to take stock of the unremarked incremental changes that build up over time to shift the ground beneath our feet. In times of rapid change more than ever, there should surely be periodic checks to ensure that our discipline has not ossified or been left behind. Nor is this only a question of pre-empting anachronism and irrelevance. We should constantly be on the look out for new opportunities to enrich Evidence teaching and scholarship. My agenda for rethinking the Law of Evidence is intended to encourage fellow teachers to consider taking advantage of

---

Practice Direction (Citation of Authority) [2001] 1 WLR 1001, CA; *Practice Direction (Judgments: Form and Citation)* [2001] 1 WLR 194.

[6] This remark hints at a (hypo)thesis, which cannot be developed or tested here, about the precedential value of Evidence decisions. Briefly, my sense is that, taken in the round, Evidence cases lie somewhere on the continuum between the relatively strict precedential significance of decisions on points of substantive criminal law (underpinned by the principle *nullum crimen, nulla poena sine lege*) and the relatively loose judicial guidelines established by sentencing decisions. Evidence has always generated more than its fair share of case law. Part of the explanation is that advocates frequently take a shopping list of evidentiary points to a single appeal, provoking more or less extemporary judicial rulings and observations that, in their turn, are ripe for revision in later appeals. A more profound explanation is that since Evidence is so intimately bound up with facts, and facts are infinitely variable, the scope for appeals on points of Evidence is also infinite. The 'latest case' must therefore always be tested against evidentiary principle *as a matter of precedent* (Bentham's 'expository jurisprudence'), in addition to being checked for conformity with (moral) standards of justice ('censorial jurisprudence').

important and exciting new pedagogical opportunities. Less aspirationally, it might function as a palliative for current anxieties or contribute towards a survival guide for the modern university Evidence lecturer.

TAKING TWINING SERIOUSLY

My starting point for rethinking the Law of Evidence as a law school option is a particular conception of the value of higher education in general. Teaching and learning in a university setting should ideally be a collegial enterprise of intellectual discovery and personal development, which properly embraces instrumental goals, but is not reducible to them. Thus, law schools are in the business of training lawyers, but that is far from all they can or should do. A law degree is first and foremost, for the majority of British undergraduates,[7] the final formal stage of a liberal education, a basis for life-long learning and a finishing school for responsible citizenship. This conception of university education supplies a foundational principle for Evidence teaching:

> *Foundational Principle*: The Law of Evidence should make its contribution to the overarching goals and values of university education, by inculcating relevant, robust and adaptable (more or less) transferable skills, helping students to become life-long learners (self-teachers), and promoting responsible citizenship. Evidence courses will naturally develop skills and provide information that will be useful to the minority of students who after graduation forge careers in related spheres of legal practice, such as criminal advocacy. But this instrumental objective is only a subsidiary, component part of the broader remit of Evidence teaching.

As an intensely practical subject, concerned with such patently transferable skills as managing, analysing, presenting and evaluating facts and arguments, the Law of Evidence is pre-eminently well-placed to deliver these pedagogic objectives. But after more than a decade of teaching, learning and writing about Evidence I have come to think that its potential remains largely unrealised. A report card stamped 'Promising, but could do much better' seems a fair assessment, of both the subject and its teachers.[8] And this is as much a confession of my own sins as a criticism of academic colleagues.

---

[7] In the United Kingdom the 'academic stage' of legal training comprises a three (sometimes extended to four) year undergraduate programme. This aspect of the argument obviously applies with less force to jurisdictions where a law degree is a postgraduate qualification (as in the United States), or effectively so (eg, the five-year combined degrees offered in Australia and South Africa).

[8] Cf W Twining, *Theories of Evidence: Bentham and Wigmore* (London, Weidenfeld & Nicolson, 1985) 178: 'Evidence scholarship has a lot to offer and a lot to learn'.

In England, at least,[9] Evidence teachers have rather complacently accepted and perpetuated a standardised, and increasingly deficient, model of the Law of Evidence. Indeed, when one considers that the standard model replicated in the vast majority of textbooks is basically the nineteenth-century conception distilled by Thayer and perfected and popularised by Wigmore and Cross, it should hardly occasion surprise that, as we orientate ourselves in the twenty-first century, its cracks are beginning to show. In late modernity change is not only constant but also increasingly rapid, a kaleidoscope of social, political, economic and cultural relations in perpetually increasing motion. There is no earthly reason why Evidence teaching should somehow be immune to these tectonic reconfigurations. But whilst the world has turned, the Law of Evidence—as we read and write it in our textbooks, and teach it to our students—has remained more or less static, barely shifting its ground.

This diagnosis of our current predicament is influenced (as my title should have hinted) by William Twining's ground-breaking work on theorising and teaching Evidence.[10] Twining has identified and criticised two defining features of Anglo-American Evidence scholarship: its rationalist assumptions, and its almost exclusive concentration on exclusionary rules to the detriment of any serious or sustained examination of the processes of fact-finding and adjudication. Rationalist assumptions, Twining concedes, can be invested with different shades of significance, and can be held with varying degrees of confidence and critical reflection. For the most part, however, Twining discerns that the modern Law of Evidence has been built upon largely unexamined and basically crude positivistic assumptions about the existence of objective facts in the world and the ability of legal process to recover, establish and make them manifest in adjudication:

> [T]here is a truly remarkable homogeneity about the basic assumptions of almost all specialist writings on evidence from Gilbert through Bentham, Thayer and Wigmore to Cross and McCormick. Almost without exception, Anglo-American writers about evidence show very similar assumptions, either explicitly or implicitly, about the nature and ends of adjudication, about knowledge or belief about past events and about what is involved in reasoning about disputed questions of fact in forensic contexts . . . In brief: almost all the leading writers in the mainstream of Anglo-American evidence scholarship were aspirational rationalists, most were optimistic rationalists most of the time and many, but by

---

[9]   Though phrases like 'Anglo-American Evidence scholarship' and 'common law systems of Evidence' trip off the tongue rather (too?) easily, my limited familiarity with US and Commonwealth Evidence texts and teaching makes it prudent to limit specific claims to England and Wales.

[10]   W Twining, *Rethinking Evidence: Exploratory Essays* (Oxford, Blackwell, 1990; 2nd edn, Cambridge, CUP, 2006). My title also respectfully references IH Dennis, 'Reconstructing the Law of Criminal Evidence' (1989) *CLP* 21.

no means all, were fairly complacent about the general operation of the adversary system in their own jurisdiction in their day.[11]

This mild critique is subsequently sharpened:

> The general tendency of Anglo-American evidence scholarship is not only optimistic, it is also remarkably unsceptical in respect of its basic assumptions. Hardly a whisper of doubt abut the possibility of knowledge, about the validity of induction, or about human capacity to reason darkens the pages of Gilbert, Best or Thayer, Wigmore or Cross or other, lesser writers . . .[C]onfident assertion, pragmatic question-begging, and straightforward ignoring are the characteristic responses to perennial questions raised by philosophical sceptics.[12]

Evidence scholarship's skewed focus on exclusionary rules, for which Twining has suggested memorable similes, is a logical outgrowth of rationalist assumptions: for if one assumes that forensic fact-finding is pretty much self-evident, there is nothing more to be said about the handling of facts in adjudication and the Law of Evidence is free to devote its undivided attention to formulating and refining normative standards for excluding protected, unreliable, or morally objectionable evidential material from the trial:

> The Thayerite metaphor is of a great silence punctuated by spasmodic noises of varying duration and intensity or a piece of Gruyère that consists of more holes than cheese ... In one of our classics of literature, *Alice in Wonderland*, one of the characters is the Cheshire Cat who keeps appearing and disappearing and fading away, so that sometimes one could see the whole body, sometimes only a head, sometimes only a vague outline and sometimes nothing at all, so that Alice was never sure whether or not he was there or, indeed, whether he existed at all. In practice, our rules of evidence appear to be rather like that.[13]

Or, more prosaically:

> [T]he subject of evidence is typically treated as being coextensive with the law of evidence; topics such as probabilities, which are not governed by legal rules, are either totally ignored or uneasily slotted into discussions of the law; books and courses on evidence are either very narrowly conceived, incoherently organized, or both . . . [E]vidence doctrine has yet to be put in its proper place as just one part of the science of proof; instead, in so far as the science has not been entirely ignored, it has typically been treated as a satellite of the law of evidence. That is rather like treating England as a suburb of London.[14]

---

[11]   Twining, above n 8, 13, 17.
[12]   *Ibid* 177.
[13]   Twining, above n 10, 197.
[14]   Twining, above n 8, 164.

Twining's well-rehearsed argument[15] for 'taking facts seriously' is, I would suppose, reasonably familiar to Evidence teachers. Yet (and the irony is inescapable), the argument has never been taken very seriously in these circles, if the structure and content of most Evidence texts is anything to go by. One inference from the absence of any noticeable impact on mainstream Evidence teaching, two decades after Twining first made the argument in print, is that, like betamax video, the Sinclair C5, and wap phones, 'taking facts seriously' is a dud. For those impressed by the predictive power of history, this suspicion may be strengthened by the sorry fate that befell Wigmore's attempts to have fact-finding taken seriously in the first decades of the twentieth century. Wigmore's *The Principles of Judicial Proof*,[16] setting out his 'chart method' for organising and analysing facts in adjudication, was first published in 1913 and went through two further editions in the 1930s. Though Wigmore himself used these materials in his teaching at Northwestern University Law School, where he served as Dean between 1901 and 1929, his book and its method were almost entirely ignored by other Evidence teachers, until a fairly recent mini-revival sparked renewed interest. Twining records that '[d]uring his lifetime and for many years after his death, the reception of Wigmore's chart method ranged from polite scepticism to complete indifference'.[17] And the final verdict: 'the *Principles* seems to have sunk like the proverbial lead balloon'.[18] So Twining's argument for taking facts seriously, which has made little headway, draws inspiration from a book that few read, and still fewer seriously credited, and which had sunk almost without trace, until Twining and others set about reclaiming it from oblivion. Put this way, an impertinent question will not be suppressed: has Twining been flogging a dead horse?

It is my contention that, far from being lifeless, 'taking facts seriously' should be a vital, animating force infusing the agenda for rethinking

[15] First published in N Gold (ed), *Essays on Legal Education* (Toronto, Butterworths, 1982) and at (1984) 34 *Journal of Legal Education* 22, and reprinted as Twining, *Rethinking Evidence*, ch 2 (above n 10).

[16] JH Wigmore, *The Principles of Judicial Proof, as Given by Logic, Psychology, and General Experience and Illustrated in Judicial Trials* (Boston, Little, Brown & Co, 1913). The third edition published in 1937 was retitled *The Science of Judicial Proof*, a revision which Twining attributes to marketing strategy and doubtless reflects the scientist conceits of the day: Twining, above n 8, 119.

[17] Twining, above n 8, 134.

[18] *Ibid* 165. Twining later reprised this simile, accented with gallows humour, in a preface thanking his publisher for agreeing 'to risk floating the "lead balloon" once more': T Anderson and W Twining, *Analysis of Evidence* (London, Weidenfeld & Nicolson, 1991) xxix. Having recruited another publisher and a third co-author, this remarkably buoyant lead balloon has recently been treated to a second re-launch: T Anderson, D Schum and W Twining, *Analysis of Evidence* (2nd edn, Cambridge, CUP, 2005).

Evidence teaching and research in the twenty-first century.[19] In sketching out my own version of that agenda I will try to indicate where and how 'taking facts seriously' should figure. A preliminary task is to neutralise some of the apparent hostility and indifference to Twining's thesis amongst Evidence teachers, by clarifying the terms of the argument, as I understand it, and by offering an alternative explanation for its neglect.

The first thing to establish is that one does not have to be a Wigmorean chart methodist to take facts seriously. Twining and his longstanding co-author Terry Anderson have proclaimed that 'Wigmore's presentation of the principles applicable in judicial trials . . . remains the most useful account [of the principles of proof] available'.[20] Their book on *Analysis of Evidence*, subtitled 'how to do things with facts,' affords Wigmore and a modified version of his chart method pride of place.[21] However, Anderson and Twining also discuss alternative styles of fact analysis, including narrative and story-telling,[22] which Twining further develops elsewhere,[23] and the most recent edition recruits David Schum as a third co-author to give the exposition a stronger foundation in probabilistic reasoning.[24] The forensic applications of narrative have been explored by the social psychologists Pennington and Hastie,[25] and by the American Evidence scholar Ron Allen,[26] with no mention of either Wigmore or charts. And for a final example of non-Wigmorean taking facts seriously, one need look no further than the lively debates in, predominantly American, Evidence scholarship concerned with probability (especially Bayesian) theory.[27] It is

---

[19] Also see D Nicolson, 'Facing Facts: the Teaching of Fact Construction in University Law Schools' (1997) 1 *E & P* 132.

[20] Anderson and Twining, above n 18, 48.

[21] *Ibid* 142–53 where suggested modifications are summarised, the reader having been informed (calling to mind Marx's estrangement from Marxism) that 'Wigmore was not a very good Wigmorean'.

[22] *Ibid* 155–72, 278–89.

[23] 'Lawyers' Stories' and 'Thompson and Wigmore: Fresh Evidence and New Perspectives' in *Rethinking Evidence*, chs 7 and 9 (above n 10). And see D Hirsch, 'The Trial of Andrei Sawoniuk: Holocaust Testimony under Cross-Examination' (2001) 10 *Social & Legal Studies* 529; T Jefferson, 'The Tyson Rape Trial: the Law, Feminism and Emotional "Truth"' (1997) 6 *Social & Legal Studies* 281; C Bell and M Fox, 'Telling Stories of Women who Kill' (1996) 5 *Social & Legal Studies* 471.

[24] Anderson, Schum and Twining, above n 18.

[25] N Pennington and R Hastie, 'The Story Model for Juror Decision Making' in R Hastie (ed), *Inside the Juror: the Psychology of Juror Decision-Making* (Cambridge, CUP, 1993).

[26] RJ Allen, 'Factual Ambiguity and a Theory of Evidence' (1994) 88 *Northwestern University Law Review* 604; RJ Allen and A Carriquiry, 'Factual Ambiguity and a Theory of Evidence Reconsidered: a Dialogue between a Statistician and a Law Professor' (1997) 31 *Israel Law Review* 464; RJ Allen, 'The Nature of Juridical Proof' (1991) 13 *Cardozo Law Review* 373.

[27] M Redmayne, 'Bayesianism and Proof' in M Freeman and H Reece (eds), *Science in Court* (Aldershot, Ashgate, 1998); R Allen and M Redmayne (eds), *Bayesianism and Juridical Proof*, Special Issue 1(6) *E & P* (London, Blackstone, 1997); RD Friedman, 'Assessing Evidence' (1996) 94 *Michigan Law Review* 1810; B Robertson and GA Vignaux, 'Probability:

not my purpose here to investigate the relative merits of these different approaches to reasoning about facts (my suspicion is that they are partial and complementary techniques rather than mutually incompatible, comprehensive analytical frameworks). The point for present purposes is that, although (modified) Wigmorean analysis may be a prominent method of taking facts seriously, the success and value of the whole enterprise most emphatically does *not* begin and end with Wigmore.

A second important clarification is that taking facts seriously is not conceived as being coterminous with Evidence teaching and scholarship. On the one hand, the transferable skills imparted through fact analysis are relevant across the legal curriculum, and could be taught in a range of alternative formats and modules concerned with 'legal skills and method'; and on the other, Evidence scholarship obviously has a range of objectives in addition to developing teaching materials. It is not my argument that Evidence teachers should relieve their colleagues of the responsibility for teaching essential skills as a magnanimous gesture of self-sacrifice. But if the Law of Evidence has special potential for realising the objectives and values of university education, as I am suggesting, then Evidence teachers are presented with enhanced opportunities (and additional responsibilities?) to contribute more than their collegial fair share. Moreover, Evidence teachers should have the motivation as well as the opportunity to shoulder a significant portion of this labour, because our subject makes fact management and analysis practically inescapable.

In the standard textbook curriculum, the bridge between fact analysis and legal doctrine is supplied by the topic of relevance. Yet relevance is one of the least explored and most frequently abused concepts in the Law of Evidence. The neglect of factual analysis in Evidence teaching and the poor conceptual health of relevance seem to me to be intimately related, if they are not two sides of the same coin. Pertinent decisions squarely confronting issues of relevance are few, and whilst the best known cases, *Blastland*[28] and *Kearley*,[29] are in their way excellent vehicles for critical analysis, they manifestly fail to provide either authoritative guidance for trial courts or helpful conceptual elucidation for students of Evidence. Every September I

---

the Logic of the Law' (1993) 13 *Oxford Journal of Legal Studies* 457; W Twining, 'Debating Probabilities' (1980) 2 *Liverpool Law Review* 51; D Kaye, 'The Laws of Probability and the Law of the Land' (1979) 47 *University of Chicago Law Review* 34. Cf LH Tribe, 'Trial by Mathematics: Precision and Ritual in the Legal Process' (1971) 84 *Harvard Law Review* 1329.

[28] [1986] 1 AC 41, HL. See DJ Birch, 'Hearsay-Logic and Hearsay-Fiddles: *Blastland* Revisited' in P Smith (ed), *Criminal Law: Essays in Honour of JC Smith* (London, Butterworths, 1987); AL-T Choo, 'The Notion of Relevance and Defence Evidence' [1993] *Crim LR* 114; and see Mike Redmayne, Chapter 4.

[29] [1992] 2 AC 228, HL. See R Pattenden, 'Conceptual versus Pragmatic Approaches to Hearsay' (1993) 56 *Modern Law Review* 138; M Hirst, 'Conduct, Relevance and the Hearsay Rule' (1993) 13 *Legal Studies* 54.

renew the campaign to persuade fresh cohorts of undergraduates that relevance is a concept underpinning and pervasive throughout the Law of Evidence, and not just something 'we did in tutorial one' which can subsequently be put aside until revision time. 'Relevance' might be included in the first chapter, or tutorial, on 'Basic Concepts,' but how often do Evidence scholars and teachers follow through in their treatments of previous misconduct evidence, character evidence going to credit, hearsay or silence? Could it be that our feeble collective grasp on relevance is traceable to the neglect of the processes of fact management, assessment and inference-making in teaching and learning Evidence, and that this omission leads directly to an impoverished understanding of other familiar evidentiary topics? If these rhetorical speculations bear serious reflection, conscientious Evidence teachers will need no further prompting to re-examine the scope for greater attention to factual analysis in their own teaching and research.

My third, and final, preliminary clarification of the argument for taking facts seriously concerns the nature of Twining's advocacy. It is not difficult to read into, or extrapolate from, Twining's reiterated thesis messages that might alienate Evidence teachers. However, just as fact analysis is not inevitably Wigmorean, Twining has no monopoly on the argument for taking facts seriously. My suspicion is that Evidence teachers may have taken exception to incidental, and severable, idiosyncrasies of Twining's presentation, which have no bearing on the merits of the argument per se. Though somewhat speculative, this rationalisation may partly account for Twining's patent lack of success in recruiting Evidence teachers to the cause.

Twining himself observes that Bentham's Evidence writings would have suffered in the eyes of lawyers on account of Bentham's disregard for practical legal wisdom and his penchant for launching virulent broadsides against legal professionals, denouncing them as pedants and blood-suckers.[30] Twining's criticisms of Evidence teachers are nowhere near as sustained or intemperate, but there are barbs that might sting nonetheless. In contemplating what he takes to be an unfortunate lack of enthusiasm for Wigmore's chart method, for example, Twining asks:

> What explains the continuing scepticism of both teachers and practitioners . . .? In the education context, any advocate of the method has first to overcome the inertia and conservatism of most academic lawyers. Many teachers of evidence

---

[30] Twining, above n 8, 168. Bentham's calumnies are summarised *ibid* 75ff. Revisionist histories converge on the conclusion that Bentham's influence on nineteenth century law reform was probably less, and certainly less direct, than an earlier generation of historians had assumed: C Allen, *The Law of Evidence in Victorian England* (Cambridge, CUP, 1997); KJM Smith, *Lawyers, Legislators and Theorists: Developments in English Criminal Jurisprudence 1800–1957* (Oxford, OUP, 1998) ch 2.

continue to cling to the absurd fallacy that the subject of evidence is co-extensive with the rules of evidence. Others, more understandably, assert that they are not competent to teach the method. This is often [note, only *often*!] due more to lack of confidence than to incompetence; both are quite easily remediable.[31]

The history of the *Principles* and the author's experiences of attempting to introduce Wigmore's approach to the analysis of evidence make it clear that it is wise to anticipate resistance from readers . . . This can be due to a combination of one or more factors, such as distrust of novelty (conservatism); dislike of symbols (literalism); aversion to hard work (indolence) and scepticism about careful analysis (irrationalism). I have pandered to these weaknesses by trying to keep the exposition simple.[32]

At other times lawyers are portrayed as verging on innumeracy ('Most lawyers confronted with symbols or mathematical formulae just switch off'),[33] and—possibly cruellest of all—it is said to be 'an ironic comment on both practising and academic lawyers that the fate of the *Principles* was to be treated as an entertaining anthology rather than as a path-breaking educational work'.[34] What a bunch of literal-minded drones these lawyer-folk must be!

Anyone familiar with Twining's *oeuvre*, characterised as it is by honesty, open-mindedness, generosity and wit,[35] could not read these passages as deliberately malicious. Momentary insensitivity in wielding a sharp pen, or

---

[31] Twining, above n 8, 174.

[32] *Ibid* 126.

[33] *Ibid* 130. The charge of mathematical ineptitude comes round from time to time: see eg, P Hawkins and A Hawkins, 'Lawyers' Probability Misconceptions and the Implications for Legal Education' (1998) 18 *Legal Studies* 316. In fact, a close reading of this article reveals that statisticians can be at least as confused about judicial evidence and fact-finding as lawyers are supposed to be about statistics. But the importance of the issue cannot be denied after the 'Adams family' trilogy: *R v Adams* [1996] 2 Cr App R 467, CA; *R v Doheny and Adams* [1997] 1 Cr App R 369, CA; and *R v Adams (No 2)* [1998] 1 Cr App R 377, CA. For discussion, see M Redmayne, *Expert Evidence and Criminal Justice* (Oxford, OUP, 2001) chs 3–4; M Redmayne, 'Presenting Probabilities in Court: the DNA Experience' (1997) 1 *E & P* 187; B Steventon, 'Statistical Evidence and the Courts: Recent Developments' (1998) 62 *Journal of Criminal Law* 176; D Hodgson, 'Probability: the Logic of the Law: a Response' (1995) 15 *Oxford Journal of Legal Studies* 51.

[34] Twining, above n 8, 175. It could be said that Wigmore himself rather encouraged a trivialisation of his formal system for modelling proof by instructing his readers that '[t]he ensuing Problems may be used for thorough analysis and study, by the method expounded . . . or merely for mental entertainment and stimulus as curious problems of fact': *The Principles of Judicial Proof* (Boston, Little, Brown & Co, 1913) 744. Contemporary commentators judge Wigmore's analysis of fact-finding and inference deficient in various respects. However, whilst the inherent weaknesses of Wigmorean analysis are reasons for it now to be refined or superseded, they do not explain why the *Principles* have languished, rather than being celebrated as a trail-blazing, if flawed, pioneer of taking facts seriously.

[35] See in particular, W Twining, 'Hot Air in the Redwoods, a Sequel to the Wind in the Willows' (1988) 86 *Michigan Law Review* 1523, in response to KW Graham Jr, '"There'll Always be an England": the Instrumental Ideology of Evidence' (1987) 85 *Michigan Law Review* 1204. In this piece Twining deftly interweaves a merciless parody of his reviewer with a serious and compelling argument about the shortcomings of Evidence scholarship.

the *hauteur* of an impatient prophet frustrated by the recalcitrant masses, are more plausible charges, if any indictment could be made to stick. In any case, though such remarks are hardly calculated to win friends and favourably influence people, I am not suggesting that Evidence teachers are so thin-skinned, flaky or humourless as to discount Twining's ideas just because he occasionally goes in for a little gentle goading and baiting. But there is something else here, of deeper significance, in the way in which Twining's commentary betrays him as an outsider to the Law of Evidence. Twining is not, of course, a legal practitioner, but nor, I venture to suggest, is he really an Evidence scholar, either. He is, rather, a jurist, who has applied himself to the problems of Evidence, and with no little success. Yet whilst Twining has made significant theoretical, historical and pedagogic contributions to the discipline, this has always been from the position of an outsider commentating on the Law of Evidence, rather than a fully-fledged participant in the enterprise developing it from within. This, at least, is how it may appear to those of us who are insiders to the Law of Evidence (and one can presumably infer from Twining's argument that he does not consider himself to be part of the mainstream Evidence tradition).

What follows if I am right in thinking that most Evidence scholars do not see Twining as 'one of us'? More fundamentally, and irrespective of the validity of my impertinent attempt to pigeonhole him, why should Twining's disciplinary affiliations have any bearing on the value, or otherwise, of what he has to teach us? First, there is the suspicion that Twining, as a jurist, is intent on turning the Law of Evidence into a branch of jurisprudence. That is not a project to which Evidence teachers could be expected to subscribe. Like the doctrinal lawyers first confronted with the challenge of socio-legal perspectives in the late 1970s and 1980s, they might cheerfully concede that sociology or philosophy or history are worthwhile forms of inquiry, but still insist that law teaching should be about the rules of law that are applied, argued over and developed in law courts, which in the present context means teaching the Law of Evidence as Thayer and Cross intended it.

In reality, it is preposterous to portray Twining as a kind of academic infiltrator intent on betraying the Law of Evidence to the expansionist ambitions of Jurisprudence. To the contrary, Twining's concentration on fact-finding and proof makes his approach to Evidence far more 'practical' than the traditional focus on exclusionary rules, since fact management is a feature of every case, for every participant and at every stage of forensic process, whereas points of law are comparatively localised and infrequent. Yet suspicions about Twining's motives and objectives may persist amongst the relatively uninitiated. For after all, he does not publish articles in the doctrinal *Reviews*, and there is little to suggest that he is particularly well-versed in the case law.[36]

Which brings me to a second point, regarding the methodology and presentation of Twining's arguments. The lamentable neglect of Wigmore's ground-breaking work on fact-finding and proof is partly explicable, Twining suggests, by a mundane misjudgement of marketing strategy. *Principles of Judicial Proof* was published as a self-contained volume, splitting off Wigmore's theory of forensic fact-management from his *Treatise*'s magisterial commentary on the exclusionary rules of evidence. Wigmore himself described the *Principles* and the *Treatise* as encompassing separate, but closely related, fields of inquiry, whilst Twining makes the case for viewing them as two complementary halves of a unified theory of Evidence.[37] However, as we have seen, Wigmore's legal readers just didn't catch on: whilst the *Treatise* became one of the most influential law books ever written, the *Principles* enjoyed a brief career as a coffee table curiosity before sliding into obscurity. The problem, it seems, is that although Wigmore himself perceived a significant connection, he never developed it systematically or spelt it out clearly enough for others to follow his lead. His readers, failing to grasp the logic of the connection or to appreciate its significance, lacked the intellectual resources to join the dots or solve further pieces of the puzzle for themselves.

My suspicion is that modern Evidence teachers, repeating the historical pattern, may have encountered similar difficulties in engaging with Twining's work on Evidence. Twining's arguments for taking facts seriously are clear and persuasive enough in their own terms, but the retort may still come: 'What has this got to do with the Evidence course I teach?' 'Too little, judging by your syllabus!' a once-more frustrated Twining might reply. 'Ah, but you want to turn my Evidence course into an outgrowth of Jurisprudence', counters Evidence Teacher emphatically and, as it seems to her, vindicated. We may conclude that the argument for taking facts seriously is unlikely to make much headway until it can be shown, in some detail, how a concern with facts is relevant to, and can be integrated with, the traditional subject matter of Evidence courses.

Since I began teaching Evidence 14 years ago my own position in this debate has shifted from sharing the reflex response of Evidence Teacher to siding with Twining. The reasons for this change of heart have already

---

[36] Cf Twining's self-description of the jurist as 'a licensed dilettante as well as a hired subversive': *Globalisation and Legal Theory* (London, Butterworths, 2000) 90. This is hardly a startling admission, if one thinks about it, since it is impossible that jurists should know everyone else's subject as well as—indeed, as part of—their own. But no less candid for that.

[37] '[T]he *Principles* and the *Treatise* were based on a shared conceptual framework and even overlapped to some extent, so that it is more accurate to treat Wigmore's principles of proof as part of an integrated theory of evidence and proof': Twining, above n 8, 156.

been intimated in general terms, and will now be further developed and substantiated. The argument for taking facts seriously resonates through the agenda for rethinking Evidence sketched out in the remaining sections of this chapter. Guided by the previously stated 'foundational principle' of Evidence teaching, and in light of my diagnosis of the challenges and opportunities currently confronting university Evidence teachers, I will argue that the desiderata for a twenty-first century Law of Evidence prominently include the following four, interrelated themes:

(a) taxonomy;
(b) epistemology;
(c) political morality; and
(d) cosmopolitanism.

The next four sections seek to elaborate and defend each item on the agenda with specific illustrations, mindful of the moral I have just drawn against Twining: proposals for rethinking Evidence are unlikely to be taken up by Evidence teachers unless explicit links can be made with the detailed subject matter of standard Evidence textbooks and curricula. The task of individuating my four agenda items must contend with the fact that they are overlapping and mutually reinforcing. Though an element of repetition is unavoidable in approaching a limited set of legal and pedagogical issues from multiple perspectives, I will endeavour to show that all four items independently merit inclusion on the agenda for rethinking Evidence. Of course, neither comprehensive elucidation nor complete defence is achievable in a single essay. The more modest objective is to inform and engage the interest of fellow Evidence teachers, and possibly even to drum up a measure of enthusiasm for radical rethinking. To this end, the final section responds pre-emptively to the most obvious questions and challenges that this proposal is likely to provoke, on the hopeful assumption that readers take any interest in it.

TAXONOMY

Evidence teachers need to concern themselves with questions of taxonomy in two dimensions. First, there is the basic set of questions: what is the territory or subject matter of the Law of Evidence? How is the province of Evidence to be determined? Or, simply and most fundamentally, as Thayer in fact framed the question: what is our Law of Evidence?[38] Linked to this

---

[38] JB Thayer, *A Preliminary Treatise on Evidence at the Common Law* (Boston, Little, Brown & Co, 1898) 263. It is salutary to recall that the fathers of the subject took basic questions of taxonomy seriously, even if their answers are now being called into question. And see Twining, above n 10, ch 6.

first set of questions, but at a somewhat more practical 'hands-on' level, is a collection of issues about the categorisation, organisation and presentation of the subject matter of the Law of Evidence. How is one topic to be differentiated from another? How are the topics to be arranged into a coherent, or at least an illuminating, package? If it is useful to have labels for these primary tasks of conceptualisation, the first might be called *external taxonomy*, being the task of differentiating Evidence from related legal, quasi-legal or non-legal disciplines, and the second, lower order task of organising the subject matter of Evidence, *internal taxonomy*.

Let me affirm right away that, having argued for traditional assumptions and disciplinary boundaries to be rethought and possibly recast, I am not in the business of proposing their replacement with an alternative vision no less prescriptive, unitary and rigid than the tradition it confronts. A key challenge of taking taxonomy seriously is to keep the boundaries and organisation of one's subject sufficiently fluid and flexible in order to satisfy the demands of a rapidly changing world, whilst at the same time ensuring that fluidity and flexibility do not dissolve one's subject into an incoherent mush, either in the design of syllabi, in classroom presentations, or in the imperfectly articulated conceptual frameworks that Evidence teachers carry with them in their heads. So what is to be done? I will give two concrete proposals in relation to external taxonomy, and then share some dissatisfactions at the level of internal taxonomy, by way of elaboration and illustration.

The territory of the Law of Evidence, it seems to me, needs both to expand and to contract; or, rather, it needs to expand and differentiate, because we probably now need at least two disciplines to do the jobs that a unified Law of Evidence has been struggling, with declining plausibility, to undertake single-handedly. Expansion is required along the temporal dimension, in order to accommodate the reality of adjudication as a dynamic process with an evolving institutional history, as opposed to a discrete event that can meaningfully be compressed into a narrow temporal frame. In practical terms this means that the Law of Evidence must develop away from its traditional near-exclusive focus on the trial stage of legal process and take a much greater interest in pre-trial proceedings. The pressure to do so emanates from a number of sources which, in combination, represent an irresistible force for change.

First, the judges have already made this intellectual journey, in tandem with procedural reforms that reflect and reinforce a new appreciation of the significance of pre-trial proceedings. A pronounced illustration is the way in which evidentiary standards regulating the admissibility of confessions and the general judicial discretion to exclude improperly obtained evidence (now Police and Criminal Evidence Act 1984 (PACE) 1984, s 78) have been developed to require judges to take a far keener interest in the details of police investigations, and to assess their propriety. As is well known, the old Judges Rules spelt out worthy standards, but in the absence of effective scrutiny and enforcement it was possible for the police and the judges to inhabit different, almost mutually exclusive, normative worlds.[39] The judges upheld rules and procedures that would not embarrass a modern liberal democracy, whilst the police drew practical authority from the Ways and Means Act to do whatever occupational routines and private conscience deemed necessary to keep the peace and put known criminals behind bars.[40] However, once PACE had furnished a firmer juridical basis for intervention, judges were encouraged to pierce the veil of secrecy surrounding police detention and interrogation. Some senior members of the judiciary seemed genuinely shocked at what subsequently came to light.[41] It is not my concern here to evaluate such reactions. The point for present purposes is that Evidence teachers need to follow judicial practice in, for example, getting to grips with the realities of police detention and interrogation. How else can one apply PACE, s 76(2)'s 'oppression' and 'unreliability' tests for excluding confessions in concrete situations? Lord Lane CJ determined early on, as I suppose he was bound to say, that 'the word "oppression" means something above and beyond that which is inherently oppressive in police custody'.[42] But what *are* the standard, inherently oppressive conditions of detention? A reasonably detailed knowledge of PACE Code C seems essential, and we should also be looking to socio-legal accounts of police investigations and social-psychological analyses of detention and interrogation for further clues as to the reality of the conditions under which admissions are 'volunteered', and the legal implications that should follow.[43] Similar considerations apply to s 78, which places such matters as undercover operations, covert surveillance, stings, honey-traps and investigative tactics generally, squarely within the

---

[39] AAS Zuckerman, *The Principles of Criminal Evidence* (Oxford, OUP, 1989) 311–14; A Sanders and R Young, *Criminal Justice* (3rd edn, Oxford, OUP, 2007) chs 4–5.

[40] It is interesting to compare the experiences of common law jurisdictions that have thus far escaped any comparable procedural revolution, and in which traditional policing prerogatives consequently appear to endure. On New South Wales, see D Dixon, *Law in Policing: Legal Regulation and Police Practices* (Oxford, OUP, 1997) ch 5. And see JB Hunter, C Cameron and T Henning, *Litigation II: Evidence and Criminal Process* (7th edn, Chatswood, NSW, LexisNexis, 2005).

[41] See eg, *R v Mason* [1988] 1 WLR 139, CA (Watkins LJ); *R v Paris, Abdullahi and Miller* (1993) 97 Cr App R 99, CA (Lord Taylor CJ); *R v Fell* [2001] EWCA Crim 696.

[42] *R v Fulling* [1987] QB 426, CA.

[43] Dixon, above n 40, chs 4–6; M McConville, J Hodgson, L Bridges and A Pavlovic, *Standing Accused* (Oxford, OUP, 1994) chs 4–5; RA Leo, 'Police Interrogation and Social Control' (1994) 3 *Social and Legal Studies* 93; J Baldwin, 'Police Interview Techniques: Establishing Truth or Proof?' (1993) 33 *British Journal of Criminology* 325; M McConville, 'Videotaping Interrogations: Police Behaviour On and Off Camera' [1992] *Crim LR* 532; GH Gudjonsson, *The Psychology of Interrogations and Confessions: a Handbook* (Chichester, Wiley, 2003); *Wolchover and Heaton-Armstrong on Confession Evidence* (London, Sweet & Maxwell, 1996) §1–084– §1–147.

province of Evidence.[44] To the extent that these practices are governed by soft law regulations and codes of practice, internal force orders and informal occupational routines and working rules, as well as by an increasing volume of primary and secondary legislation, it seems inevitable that the theoretical complexity, range of sources and practical challenges of teaching the Law of Evidence must accordingly expand, if Evidence is to move with the times.

European law is a second force operating in the same direction. Deferring for the moment some more general observations, the European Court of Human Rights has already told us that the concept of 'fair trial' under Article 6 of the ECHR extends to such matters as the conduct of police officers in encouraging or inciting criminality,[45] suspects' access to custodial legal advice in the police station (with implications for the admissibility of confessions at trial),[46] the right to silence,[47] pre-trial disclosure[48] and the propriety of pre-trial mechanisms for evaluating witness testimony.[49] Police surveillance operations, meanwhile, fall within the purview of Article 8.[50] The European Court's temporally expansive understanding of the 'fair trial' norm and other pertinent Convention standards, mediated via the Human Rights Act, can only serve to reinforce

---

[44] A Ashworth, 'Should the Police be Allowed to Use Deceptive Practices?' (1998) 114 *LQR* 108; D Birch, 'Excluding Evidence from Entrapment: What is a "Fair Cop"?' (1994) 47 *CLP* 73; G Robertson, 'Entrapment Evidence: Manna from Heaven, or Fruit of the Poisoned Tree?' [1994] *Crim LR* 805; James Chalmers, 'Test Purchasing, Entrapment and Human Rights' (2000) 150 *New Law Journal* 1444 (6 October).

[45] *Teixeira de Castro v Portugal* (1999) 28 EHRR 101. See A Ashworth, 'Re-drawing the Boundaries of Entrapment' [2002] *Crim LR* 161; D Ormerod and A Roberts, 'The Trouble with *Teixeira*: Developing a Principled Approach to Entrapment' (2002) 6 *E & P* 38.

[46] *Magee v United Kingdom* (2001) 31 EHRR 35; *Averill v United Kingdom* (2001) 31 EHRR 36; *Murray v United Kingdom* (1996) 22 EHRR 29. See R Munday, 'Inferences from Silence and European Human Rights Law' [1996] *Crim LR* 370.

[47] *Condron v United Kingdom* (2001) 31 EHRR 1; *Saunders v United Kingdom* (1997) 23 EHRR 313. See A Jennings, A Ashworth and B Emmerson, 'Silence and Safety: the Impact of Human Rights Law' [2000] *Crim LR* 879, 879–87; AS Butler, '*Funke v France* and the Right against Self-Incrimination: a Critical Analysis' (2000) 11 *Criminal Law Forum* 461.

[48] *Edwards v United Kingdom* (1993) 15 EHRR 417; *Edwards and Lewis v United Kingdom* (2005) 40 EHRR 24, ECtHR (Grand Chamber); *Rowe and Davis v United Kingdom* (2000) 30 EHRR 1. See RJ Toney, 'Disclosure of Evidence and Legal Assistance at Custodial Interrogation: What Does the European Convention on Human Rights Require?' (2001) 5 *E & P* 39; SD Sharpe, 'Article 6 and the Disclosure of Evidence in Criminal Trials' [1999] *Crim LR* 273; S Field and J Young, 'Disclosure, Appeals and Procedural Traditions: *Edwards v UK*' [1994] *Crim LR* 264.

[49] *SN v Sweden* (2004) 39 EHRR 13; *Doorson v Netherlands* (1996) 22 EHRR 330; *Van Mechelen v Netherlands* (1998) 25 EHRR 647. See A Benjer, C Cobley and A Klip, 'Witness Evidence, Article 6 of the European Convention on Human Rights and the Principle of Open Justice' in P Fennell *et al* (eds), *Criminal Justice in Europe: a Comparative Study* (Oxford, OUP, 1995).

[50] *Khan v United Kingdom* (2001) 31 EHRR 45; *Halford v United Kingdom* (1997) 24 EHRR 523; *Schenk v Switzerland* (1991) 13 EHRR 242. See S Nash, 'Secretly Recorded Conversations and the European Convention on Human Rights: *Khan v UK*' (2000) 4 *E & P* 268.

the established trend towards an expanded and intensified focus on pre-trial proceedings in England and Wales, exemplified by the judicial development of PACE, ss 76 and 78.[51]

A third force for temporal expansion is the pedagogical case for taking facts seriously, for which Twining argues directly, but which can also be presented as an auxiliary buttress to accommodating the legal developments just mentioned. The strengths of the pedagogical argument are hard to deny in this context: (1) the identification, selection, management, categorisation, presentation and analysis of facts are pervasive aspects of modern human existence, the more so in an information-rich age: in these respects, the demands of employment in the major divisions of legal practice are only a specific institutional inflexion of a general condition; (2) a focus on the early stages of legal process allows one to explore the generation of facts in the raw, and to trace their progress as they are added to and subtracted from, manipulated and refined through successive procedural stages, rather than encountering facts for the first time as they appear at trial, a relatively polished evidential product more or less concealing the institutional history of its production; *ergo* (3), expanding the temporal focus of Evidence would greatly facilitate the teaching of key transferable skills to law students. Of course, there are no guarantees that such opportunities will properly be exploited, even in a curriculum attuned to the significance of pre-trial proceedings. But it should be understood that this potential pedagogic windfall comes directly from what Evidence teachers and scholars should already be doing, in the established way of responding to contemporary legal developments. Taking facts seriously should not be thought to require heroic efforts of curriculum realignment or self-education.

My second exemplar of external taxonomy involves rethinking the peculiarly Anglophone conception of a unified Law of Evidence, and moving in a more continental direction[52] by splitting the subject into two: Criminal Evidence and Procedure, and Civil Procedure. Pragmatically, a contraction of subject matter can be viewed as offsetting the first proposal for an expanded temporal frame; but the primary motivation has nothing to do with keeping Evidence syllabi within manageable proportions (important though this is, from a practical point of view). It is a commonplace of Evidence teaching, reflected in the leading texts, that as the law of criminal evidence has expanded over the last 20 years or so, the

---

[51] The temporal expansion of criminal proceedings has also been noted by JD Jackson, 'Silence and Proof: Extending the Boundaries of Criminal Proceedings in the United Kingdom' (2001) 5 *E & P* 145.

[52] See JF Nijboer, 'Common Law Tradition in Evidence Scholarship Observed from a Continental Perspective' (1993) 41 *American Journal of Comparative Law* 299; MR Damaška, *Evidence Law Adrift* (New Haven, Yale UP, 1997) ch 1.

civil law of evidence has withered on the vine. Most Evidence texts, and therefore (one must assume) most Evidence courses, have become notably lopsided. Whilst orthodoxy still insists on the fiction of a single Law of Evidence in principle applicable equally to civil and criminal proceedings,[53] in reality the modern subject is at least four-fifths criminal evidence, with a rump presence on the civil side centred on legal professional privilege and 'public policy'. But the product of unplanned organic development is no more defensible in principle as a basis for taxonomising the Law of Evidence than the traditional preoccupation with exclusionary rules. Both fail to register modern evidentiary realities.

Whilst it is undeniable that Parliament has gradually exempted civil litigation from the ambit of traditional evidentiary doctrines,[54] it is unlikely that the underlying issues addressed by rules of evidence have suddenly disappeared or been conclusively resolved. Rather, it seems, the legislature and the courts have been engaged in a process of realigning the balance in civil litigation between formal and informal regulation, passive and active judicial case-management, consensual and mandatory timetables, minimalist and maximalist pre-trial disclosure and so forth, culminating in Lord Woolf's reforms. Underpinning these changes is an evolving new conception of the appropriate balance between fairness, justice and economy in civil proceedings,[55] which cries out for careful description and searching critical appraisal.[56] Procedural developments need to be set in the context of wider issues of civil justice, including problems of access and unmet legal need, the organisation and delivery of legal services, negotiation, conciliation, arbitration and settlement, themes and practices which have been marginalised in traditional legal curricula, at least as serious topics for sustained analysis. Unfortunately, I am sceptical whether the existing cadre of local Evidence scholars will fully grasp this nettle, for two reasons. First, with a handful of notable exceptions, most of us are Crime specialists with relatively little professional interest in civil justice issues (which, of course, is a self-fulfilling prophesy, inasmuch as a predominantly

[53] An extension of this anachronistic misconception is the dubious notion that rules of evidence must apply equally to 'both parties' to criminal litigation. Cf *R v Harry* (1988) 86 Cr App R 105, CA, *R v Beckford and Daley* [1991] Crim LR 833, CA, and *Sparks v R* [1964] AC 964, PC, for prime illustrations of how undiscriminating 'party-blind' application of the rules of evidence risks injustice to the accused.

[54] Eg the progressive erosion of the hearsay rule culminating in the Civil Evidence Act 1995.

[55] AAS Zuckerman, 'Quality and Economy in Civil Procedure: the Case for Commuting Correct Judgments for Timely Judgments' (1994) 14 *Oxford Journal of Legal Studies* 353.

[56] See AAS Zuckerman, *Zuckerman on Civil Procedure: Principles of Practice* (2nd edn, London, Sweet & Maxwell, 2006); J Shapland, A Sorsby and J Hibbert, *A Civil Justice Audit*, LCD Research Series No.2/02 (London, LCD, 2002); AAS Zuckerman (ed), *Civil Justice in Crisis: Comparative Perspectives of Civil Procedure* (Oxford, OUP, 1999); AA Paterson and T Goriely (eds), *A Reader on Resourcing Civil Justice* (Oxford, OUP, 1996); Lord Mackay of Clashfern, *The Administration of Justice* (London, Stevens and Sons, 1994).

criminal Law of Evidence attracts exponents with predominantly criminal law interests). Secondly, the pace with which major new legislation and case law accumulates on the criminal law side is simply too great to allow a significant bifurcation of scholarly focus and effort. Thus, it seems that the disaggregation of the civil and criminal components of a unified Law of Evidence is necessary, not only to facilitate a more rounded study of criminal evidence and procedure, but also in order that justice might be done to Civil Justice, as a theoretically challenging, socially significant, juridically differentiated, empirically grounded and pedagogically coherent discipline in its own right. In the absence of any notable tradition of civil procedure teaching in English universities, this is going to be a tall order even in the event of disciplinary specialisation.

This is not to say that criminal and civil evidence lack common features, or that there is nothing to be gained by studying them in tandem. On the contrary, it is clear that fact-finding and dispute resolution share significant features in common, and this is very much to my purpose, since it implies that the pedagogic benefits of taking facts seriously might be available to teachers of dedicated Civil Procedure/Civil Justice courses, as much as to teachers of Criminal Evidence and Procedure. But general family resemblance becomes less salient as one's focus gains particularity and the analysis becomes correspondingly fine-grained and context-specific. Case construction by the police, for example, has rather more unique aspects than features in common with case preparation by the average civil litigant, and one's understanding of the former would be seriously deficient if limited to generalised aspects of fact-management applicable to both. True, this still leaves open the possibility of fruitful comparison. One might, for example, contrast the predominantly cards-on-the-table style of post-Woolf civil adjudication with the still significantly cards-to-chest orientation of criminal litigation.[57]

It is not my intention to downplay, much less to deny, the value of such comparisons. What should be challenged, however, is the normative assumption implicit in the traditional conception of a unified Law of Evidence that comparison begins and ends with the juxtaposition of civil and criminal trial rules of evidence. Why not compare, instead, the trial rules of criminal adjudication with the rules (such as they are) regulating plea bargaining? Or trial rules operative in trials on indictment, with

---

[57] The Criminal Procedure and Investigations Act 1996 notwithstanding. Comparison with the very limited extent of pre-trial 'discovery' in most US criminal proceedings in fact places English criminal litigation somewhere towards the mid-point of the chest/table continuum. See R Hochman, '*Brady* v *Maryland* and the Search for Truth in Criminal Trials' (1996) 63 *University of Chicago Law Review* 1673; C Yablon, 'Stupid Lawyer Tricks: an Essay on Discovery Abuse' (1996) 96 *Columbia Law Review* 1618; WT Pizzi, *Trials Without Truth* (New York, NYU Press, 1999) 121–4.

criminal evidence and procedure in the magistrates' courts?[58] Criminal trials in other jurisdictions are an obvious source of comparative material (this is, after all, the narrow meaning usually ascribed to Comparative Law), as is—perhaps less obviously—criminal adjudication in supranational and sub-national fora. And if the past is 'another country', why not look for comparative material there, too?[59] This all really comes down to a question of focus and emphasis in choosing the most illuminating subject matter, given the inescapable limitations of curriculum, time and effort available for teaching Evidence. These precious resources would be better employed, in my submission, if the external taxonomy of Evidence were rethought and, in particular, if my two specific proposals for temporal expansion and procedural specialisation were taken up.[60] The orthodox model of a unified Law of Evidence appears, on reflection, to rest on two, not entirely reconcilable assumptions: first, that criminal and civil proceedings are sufficiently similar to fall under a single procedural regime; and secondly, that the differences between criminal and civil litigation make for the most illuminating comparisons. Neither assumption will bear serious scrutiny, at least from a British perspective.[61]

Turning now to internal taxonomy, further scope for rethinking Evidence can be demonstrated by relating topical evidentiary issues to the organising principles of curriculum design. We may begin by observing that developments in positive law are more intimately related to issues of internal taxonomy than to the overall shape and superstructure of the Law of Evidence. We should therefore expect Evidence teaching to be more reactive at this level than at the level of external taxonomy, and experience confirms that prediction.

---

[58] Cf P Darbyshire, 'An Essay on the Importance and Neglect of the Magistracy' [1997] *Crim LR* 627; P Darbyshire 'For the New Lord Chancellor: Some Causes for Concern about Magistrates' [1997] *Crim LR* 861; and P Darbyshire 'Previous Misconduct and Magistrates' Courts: Some Tales from the Real World' [1997] *Crim LR* 105.

[59] Historical context, albeit fleeting, is an admirable feature of Christopher Allen's *Practical Guide to Evidence* (3rd edn, London, Cavendish, 2004). For more extended treatments, see JH Langbein, *The Origins of Adversary Criminal Trial* (Oxford, OUP, 2003); C Allen, *The Law of Evidence in Victorian England* (Cambridge, 1997); BJ Shapiro, *Beyond Reasonable Doubt and Probable Cause: Historical Perspectives on the Anglo-American Law of Evidence* (Berkeley, University of California Press, 1991). On legal historiography and pedagogy generally, see KJM Smith and JPS McLaren, 'History's Living Legacy: an Outline of "Modern" Historiography of the Common Law' (2001) 21 *Legal Studies* 251; W Twining, 'RG Collingwood's Autobiography: One Reader's Response' (1998) 25 *Journal of Law and Society* 603.

[60] These recommendations were put into practice in P Roberts and A Zuckerman, *Criminal Evidence* (Oxford, OUP, 2004).

[61] The argument strikes me as particularly compelling in its application to England and Wales. It is possible, however, that features of US law and practice, including the retention of juries in civil litigation, constitute an appreciable counterweight in favour of a unified Law of Evidence.

The abolition of corroboration warnings over a decade ago left a gap in Evidence books and courses that had to filled, either by substituting an entirely new topic, or by reconstituting corroboration as a topic with continuing significance. This might have been achieved, for example, by bringing corroboration under the more general rubrics of 'quantitative evidentiary standards' or 'forensic reasoning rules'.[62] The Evidence teachers at Nottingham constructed a new tutorial topic on 'Children's Evidence', drawing on post-Pigot debates and legislation,[63] which has subsequently evolved into a 'Vulnerable Witnesses' tutorial, to take account of policy-makers' more recent attention to the needs of adult witnesses.[64] Collecting together *Turnbull* directions on eyewitness identification testimony, *Beck* 'suspect witness' warnings,[65] *Lucas* lies directions,[66] and a raft of highly particularistic jury instructions on eligible factual inferences[67] under the capacious umbrella of 'forensic reasoning rules' would, I think, have been a no less imaginative and equally profitable way of exploiting the opportunity for curriculum development presented to Evidence teachers as a side-effect of legislative reform. This would also have secured the incidental advantage of facilitating cross-jurisdictional comparisons, since 'corroboration' is a traditional requirement of proof in continental criminal justice systems[68] (and, of course, in Scotland)[69]; which

---

[62] Now see Roberts and Zuckerman, above n 60, ch 10 on going 'Beyond Quantitative Standards'.

[63] See JR Spencer and R Flin, *The Evidence of Children: the Law and the Psychology* (2nd edn, London, Blackstone, 1993).

[64] Youth Justice and Criminal Evidence Act 1999, Pts II and III. See Roberts and Zuckerman, above n 60, 280–6; D Cooper and P Roberts, *Special Measures for Vulnerable and Intimidated Witnesses: an Analysis of Crown Prosecution Service Monitoring Data* (London, CPS, 2005); D Birch and R Leng, *Blackstone's Guide to the Youth Justice and Criminal Evidence Act 1999* (London, Blackstone, 2000).

[65] *R v Beck* [1982] 1 WLR 461, CA; *R v Spencer* [1987] AC 128, HL.

[66] *R v Lucas* [1981] QB 720, CA; *R v Goodway* (1994) 98 Cr App R 11, CA.

[67] On the inference of 'intention to supply' illegal drugs from the accused's possession of drug-dealing 'paraphernalia' (plastic bags, weighing scales, guns and ammunition, etc) or large amounts of ready cash, see M Redmayne, 'Drugs, Money and Relevance: *R v Yalman and R v Guney*' (1999) 3 *E & P* 128. For comparative analysis of judicial warnings in cases of 'historic' child abuse, see P Lewis, 'Delayed Complaints in Childhood Sexual Abuse Prosecutions: a Comparative Evaluation of Admissibility Determinations and Judicial Warnings' (2006) 10 *E & P* 104. Further types of evidence and inferences that have been singled out for tailor-made jury directions include 'good character' (*R v Vye* [1993] 1 WLR 471, CA), previous convictions (*R v Edwards; R v Fysh; R v Duggan; R v Chohan* [2006] 1 Cr App R 3, CA), voice identifications (*R v Chenia* [2003] 2 Cr App R 6, CA), prisoners' confessions allegedly volunteered to a cellmate (*Benedetto v R* [2003] 1 WLR 1545, [2003] UKPC 27 PC (BVI): cf *R v Kinsella (Christopher)* [2006] EWCA Crim 1288), lip-reading evidence (*R v Luttrell* [2004] 2 Cr App R 31, CA), cut-throat defences (*R v Petkar and Farquhar* [2004] 1 Cr App R 22, CA), and legally-advised silence during police questioning (*R v Howell* [2005] 1 Cr App R 1, CA).

[68] In accordance with the maxim '*unus testis, nullus testis*'. The 'two-witness rule' was, infamously, part of the rationale for the development of judicial torture in the Roman-canon system of proof: JH Langbein, 'Torture and Plea Bargaining' (1978) 46 *University of Chicago*

is not to say that the topic of vulnerable witnesses is devoid of comparative potential. Indeed, there are striking points of comparison in the literature – the Israeli children's 'inquisitor' is surely amongst the most surprising to English eyes,[70] and therefore an excellent foil for classroom debate – as well as pertinent Strasbourg jurisprudence to draw upon.[71]

Whilst there is scope for fine-tuning internal taxonomy at many points in the modern curriculum,[72] the right to silence is perhaps the best example of a topic of great contemporary significance, indubitably within the fold of standard texts and syllabi, which the Law of Evidence has struggled to accommodate over the years, and with which it still remains somewhat uncomfortable. In historical perspective, silence is categorised as part of the law on 'informal admissions' or 'admissions by conduct'.[73] Today this is doubly[74] problematic, first because we now think of 'admissions' in terms of confessions governed by PACE, s 76, but silence is not obviously an 'admission' or even any kind of meaningful communication;[75] secondly, because the significance of silence turns crucially on its contextual meaning, that is to say, on that most abused and neglected of evidentiary concepts, *relevance*. Marginalisation of the right to silence goes hand-in-hand with neglect of the complexities to which factual inferences from silence may give rise. Both can be viewed, in terms of the argument developed here, as more foul crops from the rotten harvest of failing to take facts seriously.

Law Review 3. But note the historical corrective entered by M Damaška, 'Rational and Irrational Proof Revisited' (1997) 5 *Cardozo Journal of International and Comparative Law* 25 and 'The Death of Legal Torture' (1978) 87 *Yale Law Journal* 860; and the possibility that modern continental systems have evolved beyond the maxim.

[69] F Raitt, *Evidence* (3rd edn, Edinburgh, W Green, 2001) ch 7; D Sheldon, *Evidence: Cases and Materials* (Edinburgh, W Green, 1996; 2nd edn, 2002) ch 5; M Redmayne, 'Corroboration and Sexual Offences' [2006] *Juridical Review* 309.

[70] Spencer and Flin, above n 63, 397–8.

[71] WE O'Brian Jr, 'The Right of Confrontation: US and European Perspectives' (2005) 121 *LQR* 481; LCH Hoyano, 'Striking a Balance between the Rights of Defendants and Vulnerable Witnesses: Will Special Measures Directions Contravene Guarantees of a Fair Trial?' [2001] *Crim LR* 948; RD Friedman, 'Thoughts from Across the Water on Hearsay and Confrontation' [1998] *Crim LR* 697; L Ellison, 'The Protection of Vulnerable Witnesses in Court: an Anglo-Dutch Comparison' (1999) 3 *E & P* 29; NW Perry, 'When Children Take the Stand: Permissible Innovations in the US Courts' (1992) 1 *Expert Evidence* 54.

[72] Another important example, expert evidence, is discussed below.

[73] *Phipson on Evidence* (15th edn, London, Sweet & Maxwell, 2000) § 28–16; PB Carter, *Cases and Statutes on Evidence* (2nd edn, London, Sweet & Maxwell, 1990) 336ff.

[74] Confusion is tripled by the traditional habit of describing confessions as exceptions to the hearsay rule. Post-PACE, this is another evidentiary anachronism whose only apparent merits are circumlocution and avoidable taxonomic complexity.

[75] The meaning of silence is thoroughly contextual. Silence is often enigmatic or inscrutable, when it is not radically indeterminate. See PJ Schwikkard, 'Is It Constitutionally Permissible to Infringe the Right to Remain Silent?' (2001) 5 *E & P* 32; Rosemary Pattenden, 'Inferences from Silence' [1995] *Crim LR* 602.

Under the influence of European human rights law and the post-Human Rights Act judicial development of Criminal Justice and Public Order (CJPO) Act 1994, ss 34–38,[76] the way forward is to reconceptualise the right to silence in the police station as one component of a conception of the privilege against self-incrimination and an auxiliary (insofar as it still is, after Parliament's legislative intervention) of the presumption of innocence. The broader ramifications of such normative reconstruction are taken up below.[77] Here I want to stress, as a matter of internal taxonomy, that some topics which have traditionally been marginalised or, as a consequence of unplanned organic growth, inserted only awkwardly into the Evidence syllabus merit greater prominence within a more coherent and contemporary disciplinary structure. The status of silence should certainly be rethought. Socio-legal empirical research has established beyond contention the crucial significance of the police station as *the* primary site of 'case construction' in criminal proceedings. What is said—or not said—in police interview heavily influences (some say *determines*) the conduct and outcome of subsequent procedural stages (including whether there are going to be any further stages, and if so which, in any given case). Custodial confession and its *alter ego*, silence, should therefore be topics of pre-eminent concern for Evidence scholars and teachers trying to understand criminal procedure, and to propagate their insights. The claims of silence, from the perspective of internal taxonomy, thus converge with and reinforce the argument supplied by external taxonomy for an expanded temporal frame in the Law of Evidence.

EPISTEMOLOGY

Words like 'epistemology' have a propensity to fall on deaf ears: the science of knowledge and belief is a topic conspicuous only by its absence from the standard Evidence texts and practitioner works.[78] Still, I want to insist that epistemology must be on the agenda for rethinking Evidence in the

---

[76] *R v Webber* [2004] 1 WLR 404, HL; *R v Hoare and Pierce* [2005] 1 Cr App R 22, CA; *Brown (Margaret) v Stott* [2003] 1 AC 681, PC; *R v Hertfordshire CC, ex p Green Environmental Industries* [2000] 2 AC 412, HL.

[77] On the (rather shaky) theoretical foundations of the privilege against self-incrimination, see Roberts and Zuckerman, above n 60, § 9.3; M Redmayne, 'Rethinking the Privilege against Self-Incrimination' (2007) 27 *Oxford Journal of Legal Studies* 209.

[78] Cf RJ Allen and B Leiter, 'Naturalized Epistemology and the Law of Evidence' (2001) 87 *Virginia Law Review* 1491, who comment at 1493 that '[i]n the field of evidence, while there is some interest in post-modern epistemology, more typical is either the search for the appropriate algorithm ... or simply the complete neglect of epistemological matters'. This US perspective chimes with my reading of the British situation, although now see L Laudan, *Truth, Error and Criminal Law: an Essay in Legal Epistemology* (Cambridge, CUP, 2006); MS Pardo, 'The Field of Evidence and the Field of Knowledge' (2005) 24 *Law and Philosophy* 321.

twenty-first century. For one thing, engagement with epistemology is necessitated by the expanded temporal frame of a rejuvenated external taxonomy. Evidence teachers who commit themselves to taking facts seriously in the investigative and pre-trial phases of criminal proceedings soon run up against a profound and initially very disturbing empirical reality, namely, that legal evidence is the product of more or less active and conscious, institutionally co-ordinated processes of construction.

What does it mean to say that criminal evidence, or criminal cases, are 'constructed'? This question has received some attention from criminal justice scholars,[79] but very little from Evidence specialists.[80] For the most part, those few[81] Evidence teachers who have responded to Twining's challenge to concern themselves with epistemological questions have tended to adopt avowedly 'critical' or post-modern perspectives. Though praiseworthy in seeking to engage with important neglected themes, this style of work tends to be heavily and self-consciously theoretical, jargon-laden and – for my money – too fond of rhetoric, paradox, irony and scepticism. The effect is likely to be decidedly discouraging for any potential reader not already predisposed towards a particular genre of theorising. The uninitiated must find this branch of epistemology incomprehensible, indigestible, irrelevant, and possibly all three at once.

My own, far from exhaustive, epistemological researches[82] lead me to the provisional assessment that 'post-modern' perspectives typically draw or invite unwarranted inferences from what are, nonetheless, often challenging and illuminating analyses. A recurrent, and fundamental, mistake

---

[79] M McConville, A Sanders and R Leng, *The Case for the Prosecution* (London, Routledge, 1991); A Sanders, 'Constructing the Case for the Prosecution' (1987) 14 *Journal of Law and Society* 229. And see P Roberts, 'Science in the Criminal Process' (1994) 14 *Oxford Journal of Legal Studies* 469.

[80] But cf M Redmayne, *Expert Evidence and Criminal Justice* (Oxford, OUP, 2001) ch 2; G Edmond, 'Azaria's Accessories: the Social (Legal-Scientific) Construction of the Chamberlains' *Guilt* and *Innocence*' (1998) 22 *Melbourne University Law Review* 396; AAS Zuckerman, 'Miscarriage of Justice: a Root Treatment' [1992] *Crim LR* 323.

[81] Notably, D Nicolson, 'Truth, Reason and Justice: Epistemology and Politics in Evidence Discourse' (1994) 57 *Modern Law Review* 726; D Nicolson, 'Gender, Epistemology and Ethics: Feminist Perspectives on Evidence Theory' in M Childs and L Ellison (eds), *Feminist Perspectives on Evidence* (London, Cavendish, 2000). Cf the more cautious analyses developed by JD Jackson, 'Theories of Truth Finding in Criminal Procedure: an Evolutionary Approach' (1988) 10 *Cardozo Law Review* 475; and M Damaška, 'Truth in Adjudication' (1998) 49 *Hastings Law Journal* 289.

[82] Useful sources include A Musgrave, *Common Sense, Science and Scepticism: a Historical Introduction to the Theory of Knowledge* (Cambridge, CUP, 1993); J Ziman, *Reliable Knowledge: an Exploration of the Grounds for Belief in Science* (Cambridge, CUP, 1978); S Haack, *Defending Science—Within Reason: Between Scientism and Cynicism* (Amherst, NY, Prometheus Books, 2003); M Moore, 'Moral Reality Revisited' (1992) 90 *Michigan Law Review* 2424; M Williams, *Unnatural Doubts: Epistemological Realism and the Basis of Scepticism* (Princeton, Princeton UP, 1996); J Raz, 'Liberalism, Scepticism, and Democracy' reprinted in his *Ethics in the Public Domain* (Oxford, OUP, 1995); and J Raz, *Engaging Reason* (Oxford, OUP, 1999).

is to imply or assume that strong forms of scepticism or cultural relativism are in any sense default positions that follow by necessary implication from critiques of more traditional, rationalist epistemologies.[83] Far from being commonsensical truths, strong forms of scepticism and relativism can plausibly be defended only through sophisticated theoretical arguments, that are seldom forthcoming in Evidence scholarship (or, for that matter, in legal scholarship generally). In their sophisticated forms, moreover, such arguments eschew the kinds of sceptical or relativistic conclusions that naïve accounts embrace.[84] Evidence teachers should therefore take heart. We can, and must, work with apparently dangerous ideas like case 'construction' without fear of surrendering to a fatal self-deconstruction, or sawing off the branch of the tree of knowledge on which Evidence is perched. The pedagogy of fact-finding demands nothing less.

There are also substantial positive benefits to be garnered from taking epistemology seriously in Evidence teaching. Indeed, this is part and parcel of getting more intimately acquainted with our old friend, relevance. Recalling that 'relevance' is a matter of 'logic and common sense', forensic proof must at least overlap with epistemological inquiries into the adequacy of grounds for belief. This thought suggests that Twining's apparently theoretical critique of the Rationalist Tradition of Evidence Scholarship[85] may have very tangible, practical implications for the operation of forensic techniques for presenting, challenging and evaluating evidence in court. A key intellectual and practical task, I suggest, is to develop and apply principles for distinguishing between two categories of uncertainty in litigation. The first is an intractable feature of the fallible human condition, an 'inert' component of the epistemological context with no practical bearing on adjudication. For example, judges and juries should not be deflected from discharging their respective forensic duties by the philosophically ineliminable possibility that the world is an illusion or that the life forms we recognise as people are really brains in vats. The second type of uncertainty is attributable to factors which are in principle remediable, and is 'actively' at play in criminal trials. The active/passive metaphor can be commended as an illuminating heuristic for clarifying the epistemological foundations of forensic proof.

Epistemology combines with internal taxonomy in hypothesising the eminently plausible link between the neglect of epistemological questions

---

[83] A Green, 'How the Criminal Justice System Knows' (1997) 6 *Social and Legal Studies* 5 exemplifies the sort of thing I have in mind. Cf the more illuminating approach of AE Taslitz, 'An African-American Sense of Fact: the OJ Trial and Black Judges on Justice' (1998) 7 *Boston University Public Interest Law Journal* 219; and for an uncompromising general rebuttal, see SG Gey, 'Why Rubbish Matters: the Neoconservative Underpinnings of Social Constructionist Theory' (1999) 83 *Minnesota Law Review* 1707.

[84] See, especially, Williams, above n 82.

[85] Twining, above n 10, ch 3; Twining, above n 18, 94–104.

and the relatively under-developed state of the law and learning of expert evidence in England and Wales. English law is perhaps the last of the common law family yet to devise modern rules for the admissibility of expert evidence. English judges have made-do-and-mended in typically pragmatic fashion, whilst courts in North America and Australasia have grappled with the task of up-dating old legal ideas to meet the new challenges of scientific evidence.[86] The parlous state of this aspect of English law is fully reflected in standard Evidence texts, in which expert evidence is typically marginalised to the position of a bolt-on afterword to the core chapters. Here it will be found harnessed together with another largely unrelated topic—rules regulating the extent to which ordinary witnesses of fact are permitted to draw inferences from their observations—under the stifling yoke of 'Opinion Evidence'.[87] This out-moded piece of internal taxonomy simultaneously obscures the centrality of scientific evidence in modern criminal investigations, and gratuitously under-utilises one of the most illuminating topics for exploring and evaluating the underlying (epistemological) assumptions of fact-finding and adjudication in criminal proceedings.[88] Science has its own routines for generating, testing and validating knowledge claims.[89] Do these rou-tines reinforce or conflict with legal methodologies for arriving at the

---

[86]   On North America, see P Roberts, 'Tyres with a "Y": an English Perspective on *Kumho Tire* and its Implications for the Admissibility of Expert Evidence' 1(2) *International Commentary on Evidence* Article 5, www.bepress.com/ice/ (posted 2 July 1999); P Roberts, 'Expert Evidence in Criminal Proceedings: More Lessons from North America' in H Reece (ed), *Current Legal Issues*, vol 1, *Law and Science* (Oxford, OUP, 1998); B Black, FJ Ayala and C Saffran-Brinks, 'Science and the Law in the Wake of *Daubert*: a New Search for Scientific Knowledge' (1994) 72 *Texas Law Review* 715; E Cunliffe, 'Without Fear or Favour? Trends and Possibilities in the Canadian Approach to Expert Human Behaviour Evidence' (2006) 10 *E & P* 280. For contrasting interpretations of Commonwealth jurispru-dence, see DE Bernstein, 'Junk Science in the United States and the Commonwealth' (1996) 21 *Yale Journal of International Law* 123; I Freckelton, 'Contemporary Comment: When Plight Makes Right—the Forensic Abuse Syndrome' (1994) 18 *Criminal Law Journal* 29; SJ Odgers and JT Richardson, 'Keeping Bad Science Out of the Courtroom: Changes in American and Australian Expert Evidence Law' (1995) 18 *University of New South Wales Law Journal* 108; G Edmond and D Mercer, 'Keeping "Junk" History, Philosophy and Sociology of Science Out of the Courtroom: Problems with the Reception of *Daubert v Merrell Dow Pharmaceuticals Inc*' (1997) 20 *University of New South Wales Law Journal* 48.

[87]   With a little effort and ingenuity it is even possible to shoehorn the admissibility of previous judgments into this obliging residuum, on the theory that *res judicata* are merely the opinions of other courts. Cf IH Dennis, *The Law of Evidence* (2nd edn, London, Sweet & Maxwell, 2002) 719ff.

[88]   Now see Roberts and Zuckerman, above n 60, ch 7; P Roberts, 'Science, Experts and Criminal Justice' in M McConville and G Wilson (eds), *The Handbook of the Criminal Justice Process* (Oxford, OUP, 2002).

[89]   D Nelken, 'A Just Measure of Science' in M Freeman and H Reece (eds), *Science in Court* (Aldershot, Ashgate, 1998); G Edmond, above n 80; PH Schuck, 'Multi-Culturalism Redux: Science, Law and Politics' (1993) 11 *Yale Law and Policy Review* 1; B Wynne, 'Establishing the Rules of Laws: Constructing Expert Authority' in R Smith and B Wynne (eds), *Expert Evidence: Interpreting Science in the Law* (London, Routledge, 1989).

truth? What should happen when science presents law with alternative proofs, rooted in different procedures for investigating the material and social world? Should expert witnesses attempt to educate the fact-finder in specialist knowledge, or ask the fact-finder to defer to their expertise?[90] Questions like these are theoretically fundamental and yet intensely practical. Judges and juries are effectively required to answer them whenever scientific or other expert evidence is proffered at trial (though, of course, the prominence of such issues in particular cases depends on the status of individual experts, the nature of their evidence, its relation to the facts in issue, whether they are contradicted or corroborated by other expert testimony, and so forth).

A firm grounding in the Law of Evidence should not skimp on such an elemental and practically significant topic as expert evidence. This should include at least a basic grasp of the epistemological foundations of scientific expertise and their implications for legal adjudication. Another, rather different way in which epistemological questions are going to intrude into Evidence teaching is opened up by the Human Rights Act 1998. Once Evidence teachers have assimilated the discourse of human rights into their lectures and textbooks, it will not be long before the more perceptive students start to articulate the gnawing doubts of scepticism and cultural relativism that unvarnished references to extra-legal 'human rights' inevitably provoke amongst a thoughtful audience. If we are not to be wrong-footed by legitimate challenges to our underlying assumptions, if not by our own potentially debilitating self-doubt, there had better be a secure niche for (moral) epistemology on the agenda for rethinking Evidence.[91]

POLITICAL MORALITY

It is only a short intellectual step from moral epistemology to the political morality of government, yet, from a worm's eye view of the case law, it is easy to forget that criminal evidence and procedure is a (very) applied

---

[90] See Roberts and Zuckerman, above n 60, § 7.2; EJ Imwinkelreid, 'The Next Step in Conceptualizing the Presentation of Expert Evidence as Education: the Case for Didactic Trial Procedures' (1997) 1 *E & P* 128; G Edmond, 'The Next Step or Moonwalking? Expert Evidence, the Public Understanding of Science and the Case against Imwinkelreid's Didactic Trial Procedures' (1998) 2 *E & P* 13; EJ Imwinkelreid, 'Correspondence: Didactic Trial Procedures' (1998) 2 *E & P* 205; RJ Allen, 'Expertise and the *Daubert* Decision' (1994) 84 *Journal of Criminal Law and Criminology* 1157.

[91] Further exploration might profitably begin with HJ Steiner and P Alston, *International Human Rights in Context: Law, Politics, Morals* (2nd edn, Oxford, OUP, 2000) chs 5–6; M Freeman, *Human Rights* (Cambridge, Polity, 2002); MJ Perry, *The Idea of Human Rights: Four Inquiries* (New York, OUP, 1998); DL Coleman, 'Individualizing Justice through Multiculturalism: the Liberals' Dilemma' (1996) 96 *Columbia Law Review* 1093.

branch of moral and political philosophy. Criminal law is amongst the principal public institutions in which the rights and responsibilities of citizenship are articulated, contested, elaborated and enforced. Criminal procedure, as the adjectival counterpart of substantive criminal law, is directly concerned with basic rights and liberties in the performance of essential public functions: censure and sanction of criminal wrongs, maintenance of law and order and vindication of political authority. On reflection, it should occasion no surprise that key procedural rights, including variegated bundles of fair trial rights, are standard components of modern national constitutions and international human rights treaties.

Normative moral and political reconstruction merits its own independent entry on a twenty-first century agenda for Evidence scholarship and teaching, as well as being an implicit requirement of rethinking disciplinary taxonomies. Both from the point of view of knowing which values animate rules of evidence, and from the complementary perspective of appreciating criminal procedure's contribution to the broader enjoyment of liberty, democracy and justice, it is essential for students and teachers (and policy-makers, judges and legislators) to be able to trace evidentiary doctrines into their philosophical foundations. How are we to evaluate whether rules are good or bad if we cannot say what they stand for in terms of deeper human interests? How are rules to be applied and extended to new situations, as part of the process of identifying and resolving (or at least managing) normative conflict, without an appreciation of the values they instantiate?

Common lawyers have tended to think in terms of narrowly functional technical rules rather than thickly-textured procedural standards with transparent normative underpinnings. Thus, we have traditionally spoken of a localised and relatively bloodless 'right to silence' rather than a more rounded conception of the privilege against self-incrimination, and of the burden and standard of proof in preference to the more grandiloquent presumption of innocence.[92] After decades of neglect, the project of normative reconstruction in the Law of Evidence has been boosted by the ground-breaking work of Ian Dennis,[93] Peter Mirfield,[94] Adrian Zuckerman[95] and, latterly, Andrew Ashworth,[96] amongst others.[97] Antony Duff

---

[92] See, further, P Roberts, 'Criminal Procedure, the Presumption of Innocence and Judicial Reasoning under the Human Rights Act' in H Fenwick, R Masterman and G Phillipson (eds), *Judicial Reasoning under the UK Human Rights Act* (Cambridge, CUP, 2007).

[93] IH Dennis, 'Rectitude, Rights and Legitimacy: Reassessing and Reforming the Privilege against Self-Incrimination in English Law' (1997) 31 *Israel Law Review* 24; 'Reconstructing the Law of Criminal Evidence' [1989] *CLP* 21.

[94] P Mirfield, *Silence, Confessions and Improperly Obtained Evidence* (Oxford, OUP, 1997); *Confessions* (London, Sweet & Maxwell, 1985).

[95] AAS Zuckerman, 'Miscarriage of Justice and Judicial Responsibility' [1991] *Crim LR* 492; 'Illegally-Obtained Evidence: Discretion as a Guardian of Legitimacy' [1987] *Current Legal Problems* 55.

remarks that 'recent years have seen a striking growth in theoretically sophisticated and philosophically informed work on, for instance, the law of evidence, the criminal trial, and the criminal process as a whole, as well as on broader issues of criminal justice'.[98] These are assuredly encouraging signs: yet there is still far to go in clarifying the concepts and elucidating the moral content of basic evidentiary rules, doctrines and other standards.

Two aspects of the contemporary procedural landscape make normative reconstruction in the Law of Evidence especially pressing and timely. First, the Human Rights Act 1998 has imported into English law unfamiliar concepts like 'respect for private life', 'equality of arms', '(substantive) proportionality' and even 'fair trial'. Yet the European Court of Human Rights itself has made little firm progress towards conceptual clarification or normative elaboration of Convention rights.[99] Evidence teachers, no less than English judges, must face up to the challenge of interpreting and applying Conventional language with only patchy, uneven and sometimes apparently contradictory guidance from Strasbourg.

A second development tending to place greater emphasis on the moral and political foundations of Evidence is the well-documented trend,

---

[96] A Ashworth, *The Criminal Process* (1st edn, Oxford, OUP, 1994; 3rd edn with M Redmayne, 2005) chs 2–3; 'Testing Fidelity to Legal Values: Official Involvement and Criminal Justice' (2000) 63 *Modern Law Review* 633; 'Should the Police be Allowed to Use Deceptive Practices?' (1998) 114 *Law Quarterly Review* 108. These more recent publications pick up the thread of earlier work, especially his still-influential 'Excluding Evidence as Protecting Rights' [1977] *Crim LR* 723.

[97] Exemplars of a 'second generation' of, broadly speaking, 'philosophical foundations' English law Evidence scholarship include Roberts and Zuckerman, above n 60; Redmayne, above n 77; A Duff, L Farmer, S Marshall and V Tadros (eds), *The Trial on Trial*, vol 1, *Truth and Due Process* (Oxford, Hart Publishing, 2005) and *The Trial on Trial*, vol 2, *Judgment and Calling to Account* (Oxford, Hart Publishing, 2006); D Hamer, 'The Presumption of Innocence and Reverse Burdens: a Balancing Act' (2007) 66 *Cambridge Law Journal* 143; V Tadros and S Tierney, 'The Presumption of Innocence and the Human Rights Act' (2004) 67 *MLR* 402; P Roberts, 'The Presumption of Innocence Brought Home? *Kebilene* Deconstructed' (2002) 118 *LQR* 41; P Roberts, 'Double Jeopardy Law Reform: a Criminal Justice Commentary' (2002) 65 *MLR* 39; AL-T Choo, *Abuse of Process and Judicial Stays of Criminal Proceedings* (Oxford, OUP, 1993); P Roberts, 'Taking the Burden of Proof Seriously' [1995] *Crim LR* 783.

[98] RA Duff, 'Theorizing Criminal Law: a 25th Anniversary Essay' (2005) 25 *Oxford Journal of Legal Studies* 353, 365 (footnotes omitted).

[99] Cf the remarks of Judge Martens, dissenting in *Borgers v Belgium* (1993) 15 EHRR 92: 'the concept of "fair trial"... calls for careful handling. To begin with the concept is vague and "open-ended". It needs "filling in". This gradually occurs as case-law develops more specific rules. The Court, however, has a tendency always to rule *in concreto*, taking into account the specific features of the case at hand. Thus elaborating the notion of "fair trial" is not without risks: the rules that emerge from such a case-law develop a momentum of their own and a tendency to engender specific new rules. These new rules may overstrain a concept which, after all, refers to very basic principles of procedure. As long as it has not elaborated a more comprehensive analytical view of the notion of "fair trial" the Court should be aware of these risks ... It may be that those who are completely unfamiliar with a particular procedural institution will be more readily inclined to find it incompatible with the requirements of "fair trial" than those who form part of the same tradition' (dissenting opinion of Judge Martens, paras 4.4 and 4.5).

characteristic of all modern common law systems, for determinate particular rules to be superseded by more general, open-ended principles and standards.[100] Where 20 or 30 years ago there might have been an applicable rule providing trial judges with reasonably specific guidance as to the admissibility of a piece of evidence or the appropriate terminology of a jury direction, today one is quite likely to find generalised standards of 'reasonableness' or 'fairness' entrusting judges with the responsibility of judgement in the exercise of their 'discretion'. This is not the place to re-run the perennial jurisprudential contest between rules and principles, or to hazard predictions about the future shape and style of evidentiary standards. The recently-revived prospect of codification,[101] and the less trumpeted but more immediate impact of the Judicial Studies Board's specimen jury directions (partial codification by stealth?),[102] are complicating factors meriting closer scrutiny, sustained reflection and careful appraisal at all levels. Suffice it here to observe that open-ended general principles are more prevalent than they used to be; and to flag up the genuine possibility, particularly in the light of Commonwealth experience,[103] that English law may yet have further to travel along this axis.

To the extent that rules of Evidence are being remade as 'guides, not chains', the project of normative reconstruction in terms of underlying moral and political values becomes more urgent. For the application of

[100] In England this trend can be discerned in legislation, including PACE ss 76 and 78, and at common law, for example in the progressive reduction in technicality of the hearsay exceptions: *R v Andrews* [1987] AC 281, HL; *Mills v R* [1995] 3 All ER 865, PC. One should add, however, that there are also discernible contradictory trends towards greater rigidity and technicality, eg in CJPO Act 1994, ss 34–38, Youth Justice and Criminal Evidence (YJCE)Act 1999, s 41 and Criminal Justice Act (CJA) 2003, Pt 11. For comparative context, see W Twining, 'Freedom of Proof and the Reform of Criminal Evidence' (1997) 31 *Israel Law Review* 439; CM Bradley, 'The Emerging International Consensus as to Criminal Procedure Rules' (1993) 14 *Michigan Journal of International Law* 171.

[101] Codification, 'comprising, for example, substantive criminal law, rules of evidence, procedure and sentencing', featured on the reform agenda set out in Home Office, *Criminal Justice: the Way Ahead* (Cm 5074, London, Home Office, 2001) paras 3.57–3.59, and was strongly endorsed by Lord Justice Auld's *Review of the Criminal Courts of England and Wales* (London, TSO, 2001) 20–21. See, further, JR Spencer, 'The Case for a Code of Criminal Procedure' [2000] *Crim LR* 519 (arguing that 'the case for codifying both criminal law and criminal procedure is unanswerable').

[102] The JSB directions have been published at www.jsboard.co.uk/. For illuminating commentary, see R Munday, 'Judicial Studies Board Specimen Directions and the Enforcement of Orthodoxy: a Modest Case Study' (2002) 66 *Journal of Criminal Law* 158; R Munday, 'The Bench Books: Can the Judiciary Keep a Secret?' [1996] *Crim LR* 296.

[103] Eg, the innovation of a 'safety-valve' inclusionary discretion covering otherwise inadmissible hearsay, introduced into English law by CJA 2003, s 114(1)(d), was anticipated by common law developments in Canada: see C Boyle, MT MacCrimmon and D Martin, *The Law of Evidence: Fact Finding, Fairness, and Advocacy* (Toronto, Emond Montgomery Publications, 1999) 567ff; AL-T Choo, *Hearsay and Confrontation in Criminal Trials* (Oxford, OUP, 1996) ch 7; PB Carter, 'Hearsay: Whether and Whither?' (1993) 109 *LQR* 573.

general principles in concrete situations requires policy-makers, adjudicators and administrators to be well-informed, skilful interpreters of the values, objectives and rationales underpinning evidentiary norms and doctrines, faithful executives of their practical implementation, and intelligent sponsors of sympathetic legal reforms.

COSMOPOLITANISM

A cosmopolitan sensibility pervades the first three items I have proposed for inclusion on a twenty-first century agenda for rethinking the Law of Evidence. This ubiquitous yet elusive characteristic of modern legality nonetheless merits independent emphasis, as the fourth and final item on my programmatic agenda. In recent work Twining has helpfully mapped a complex, multilayered normative and legal pluralism,[104] which is ill-served by an all-too-neat tripartite division into concentric global, international and domestic legal orders. It is more accurate, and therefore more helpful, to conceptualise legal phenomena at a range of levels from the truly global to the immediately local and all points in between, suspended in a complex web of 'interlegality'.[105] The grain of one's analysis must run from coarse to fine, according to context, subject matter and objective. 'Cosmopolitanism' is a flexible idea, well-suited to contemporary juridical realities. With newly stipulated terminology one may at least start afresh and without too many theoretical pre-commitments.

Contemporary legal orders are characterised by simultaneous pressures towards consolidation *and* fragmentation, centralisation *and* subsidiarity, sameness *and* difference. Nowhere are such pressures currently felt more keenly than in Europe. For all practical purposes, the Law of the European Union is now as much a source of English law as the statutes of the United Kingdom Parliament and the decisions of English appellate tribunals. Whilst the media spotlight has settled on macro-constitutional issues of opt-outs, enlargement and the *bête noir* of a European Superstate, EU and national policy-makers, judges and administrators have quietly gone about the business of expanding the remit of EU laws, European institutions, formalised working agreements and informal practical routines. The old idea that European Law is essentially the economic law of the 'common market' has run its course. Most significantly for present purposes, EU competence now extends to rules of criminal evidence and procedure, as

[104]   Twining, above n 36, chs 3, 6–8.
[105]   B de Sousa Santos, 'Law: a Map of Misreading: Toward a Postmodern Conception of Law' (1987) 14 *Journal of Law and Society* 279, 288.

one aspect of EU criminal justice policy within the 'Third Pillar' (Justice and Home Affairs) of the Treaty of Amsterdam.[106]

The phrase 'European Law' has hitherto been a serviceable synonym for EC or EU Law, but the Human Rights Act 1998 has put paid to that usage.[107] 'European Law' should now also refer to the law of the European Convention on Human Rights (ECHR), which s 2 of the 1998 Act translates into an additional formal source of English law. Strasbourg jurisprudence made an immediate impact on English evidence law, principally (but not exclusively) through the application of Article 6 fair trial rights.[108]

The pressure on law, and therefore on law teaching, towards cosmopolitanism does not stop at the norms of European institutions. Analysis may extend further 'upwards' and 'outwards' towards more international and global perspectives, or 'downwards' and 'inwards' in the direction of greater localism—to the extent that such a contrast can sensibly be drawn, since the local is always simultaneously present in the global.[109] Supra-national legal orders typically incorporate or adapt ideas, concepts, norms, procedures and institutions borrowed from domestic national legal systems. The concept of 'private life' in Article 8 ECHR,[110] the principle of 'equality of arms' in Article 6,[111] and the proportionality norm employed both in ECHR and EC jurisprudence[112] are prominent examples of supra-national doctrines with municipal origins. Supra-national legality is better taught and understood by unearthing its roots in the foreign law sources, implying a commitment to comparative legal scholarship. More ambitiously, if supra-national law is based on foreign law, and supra-national European norms are sources of English law, then can it not be said that (certain) foreign laws are also sources of English law? International

---

[106] Generally, see E Baker, 'Taking European Criminal Law Seriously' [1998] *Crim LR* 361; S Peers, *EU Justice and Home Affairs Law* (2nd edn, Oxford, OUP, 2006).

[107] For conceptual elaboration, see C Harding, 'The Identity of European Law: Mapping out the European Legal Space' (2000) 6 *European Law Journal* 128; Twining, above n 36, ch 6.

[108] B Emmerson and A Ashworth, *Human Rights and Criminal Justice* (London, Sweet & Maxwell, 2001) esp chs 9, 14 and 15; AL-T Choo and S Nash, 'Evidence Law in England and Wales: the Impact of the Human Rights Act 1998' (2003) 7 *E & P* 31; Roberts, above n 92; Redmayne, above n 77; A Ashworth, 'Criminal Proceedings after the Human Rights Act: the First Year' [2001] *Crim LR* 855; T Murphy and N Whitty, 'What is a Fair Trial? Rape Prosecutions, Disclosure and the Human Rights Act' (2000) 8 *Feminist Legal Studies* 143; A Ashworth, 'Article 6 and the Fairness of Trials' [1999] Crim LR 261; JR Spencer, 'English Criminal Procedure and the Human Rights Act 1998' (1999) 33 *Israel Law Review* 664.

[109] An insight spawning such fearsome neologisms as 'glocalisation'.

[110] B Markesinis, 'Privacy, Freedom of Expression, and the Horizontal Effect of the Human Rights Bill: Lessons from Germany' (1999) 115 *LQR* 47.

[111] *Borgers v Belgium* (1993) 15 EHRR 92; *Rowe and Davis v United Kingdom* (2000) 30 EHRR 1, para 60.

[112] E Ellis (ed), *The Principle of Proportionality in the Laws of Europe* (Oxford, Hart Publishing, 1999).

human rights law, in the eyes of some, is developing precisely along these lines, so that one may speak of a nascent 'common law of human rights',[113] a universally applicable body of human rights norms to which international tribunals and municipal constitutional courts around the world make their distinctive contributions and take their lead in adjudication. The right to a fair trial, incorporating such paradigmatically evidentiary topics as the presumption of innocence, the privilege against self-incrimination, the right to compulsory process to acquire testimony and the right to an impartial, rational and reasoned adjudication, is a central component of this now flourishing human rights tradition.[114]

European human rights law exemplifies contemporary legal pluralism. Many of the ECHR's key concepts are borrowed from national legal systems, and their subsequent development has drawn inspiration from international treaties, regional legal orders (especially the EU with which it overlaps), the emergent common law of international human rights, national constitutions and municipal domestic law. An imaginative and modestly expansionist jurisprudence might easily regard a diverse range of international, comparative and foreign law materials as having been incorporated by reference into sources of English law under the Human Rights Act. European law (in the broad sense) immediately became a contentious object of English criminal litigation after 2 October 2000.[115] It is fair to point out that English Evidence lawyers have always been mild comparativists, inasmuch as Australian, Canadian and other Commonwealth judgments are a longstanding and oft-cited reservoir of persuasive authority (*sed quaere* the extent to which this reflects a romantic conception of a unified common law of Evidence rather than anything properly equated with comparative methodology or an interest in foreign law as such). But, in our modern cosmopolitan era, the days of confining one's comparative gaze to a handful of Anglophone municipal jurisdictions are numbered.

Even the briefest survey of legal cosmopolitanism and its implications for Evidence would be inexcusably deficient if the remarkable phenomenon

---

[113] C McCrudden, 'A Common Law of Human Rights?: Transnational Judicial Conversations on Constitutional Rights' (2000) 20 *Oxford Journal of Legal Studies* 499.

[114] S Trechsel and S Summers, *Human Rights in Criminal Proceedings* (Oxford, OUP, 2006); A Ashworth and M Redmayne. *The Criminal Process* (3rd edn, Oxford, OUP, 2005) ch 2; MC Bassiouni, 'Human Rights in the Context of Criminal Justice: Identifying International Procedural Protections and Equivalent Protections in National Constitutions' (1993) 3 *Duke Journal of Comparative and International Law* 235; S Trechsel, 'Why Must Trials be Fair?' (1997) 31 *Israel Law Review* 94. Also see S Zappalà, *Human Rights in International Criminal Proceedings* (Oxford, OUP, 2003).

[115] Indeed, the first salvos were fired *before* 2 October when the Human Rights Act entered fully into force: see in particular, *R v DPP, ex p Kebilene* [2000] AC 326, HL, discussed by P Roberts, 'The Presumption of Innocence Brought Home? *Kebilene* Deconstructed' (2002) 118 *LQR* 41.

of international criminal justice was passed over without mention. Until quite recently, *realpolitik* dominated international relations, with the implication that most perpetrators of international crimes and gross human rights violations could be confident in their expectations of impunity. Following a fleeting moment of post-1945 enthusiasm for international criminal justice, encapsulated and subsequently symbolised by the Nuremberg trials of Nazi war criminals,[116] Cold War machinations swiftly put paid to serious attempts to implement accountability for the next four decades. Despicable client regimes were propped up by Superpowers concerned only with calculations of strategic geo-political advantage. State sovereignty became a convenient legal fig-leaf for tyrants and military *juntas* to terrorise their own civilian populations, eliminate political opposition and prosecute 'local' wars of aggression against their neighbours. Yet with the fall of the Berlin Wall in 1989 and the subsequent dissolution of the Soviet Union, unprecedented developments in international criminal justice occurred with astonishing rapidity.

The UN Security Council, no longer deadlocked by Superpower veto, was able to create, in quick succession, two ad hoc Criminal Tribunals for former Yugoslavia (ICTY) and Rwanda (ICTR) as an innovative application of its Chapter VII powers to maintain international peace and security.[117] The ICTY and ICTR have now been hearing cases and handing down judgments for over a decade.[118] The initial momentum was subsequently carried forward to an international conference held in Rome in 1998, where, contrary to the expectations of many seasoned observers, and

---

[116] For useful introductions to a massive literature, see M Lippman, 'Nuremberg: Forty-Five Years Later' (1991) 7 *Connecticut Journal of International Law* 1; M Lippman 'The Other Nuremberg: American Prosecutions of Nazi War Criminals in Occupied Germany' (1992) 3 *Indiana International and Comparative Law Review* 1; JE Persico, *Nuremberg: Infamy on Trial* (Harmondsworth, Penguin, 1994).

[117] Article 39 (within Chapter VII) of the UN Charter provides that 'The Security Council shall determine the existence of any threat to the peace, breach of the peace, or act of aggression and shall make recommendations, or decide what measures shall be taken in accordance with Articles 41 and 42, to maintain or restore international peace and security'. There is no explicit reference to creating judicial tribunals in Chapter VII, but Art 41 is drafted in sufficiently broad terms to accommodate such measures on a literal reading, even though it is unlikely that Arts 41–42 were originally contemplated in this light: 'The Security Council may decide what measures not involving the use of armed force are to be employed to give effect to its decisions, and it may call upon the Members of the United Nations to apply such measures'.

[118] See eg, JRWD Jones and S Powles, *International Criminal Practice* (3rd edn, Oxford, OUP, 2003); PM Wald, 'Rules of Evidence in the Yugoslav War Tribunal' (2003) 21 *Quinnipiac Law Review* 761; MP Scharf, 'Trial and Error: an Assessment of the First Judgment of the Yugoslavia War Crimes Tribunal' (1997–98) 30 *New York University Journal of International Law and Politics* 167; PL Robinson, 'Ensuring Fair and Expeditious Trials at the International Criminal Tribunal for the Former Yugoslavia' (2000) 11 *European Journal of International Law* 569; KL Fabian, 'Proof and Consequences: an Analysis of the *Tadic* and *Akayesu* Trials' (2000) 49 *DePaul Law Review* 981.

after more than a century of false starts,[119] 120 states were able to agree a text for the Statute of the International Criminal Court (ICC).[120] The ICC become fully operational on 1 July 2002, having secured the requisite 60 treaty ratifications.[121] By January 2007 there were 104 fully-ratified States Parties, though significant absentees still include China, Russia, India and the United States. According to one of the Court's most energetic and longstanding proponents, 'The world will never be the same after the establishment of the International Criminal Court'.[122] Whether or not this optimistic prediction will in time be fully vindicated, it is indisputable that when the dam of accountability broke, it did so with precipitous speed and tremendous creative force.[123] The United Nations' pioneering interventions have been emulated by a slew of improvised quasi-international penal tribunals created in the aftermath of recent conflict or historical oppression in such troubled regions of the world as Sierra Leone, Cambodia, East Timor, Kosovo and Iraq.[124] This unprecedented level of activity means that we can now sensibly speak of 'international criminal justice' as a functioning (albeit emergent and complex) reality, rather than merely an idealist's pipe-dream.

Procedural law is an essential component of any functioning system of adjudication, whether the forum is municipal or international or a blended hybrid. Supra-national tribunals are to a considerable extent institutionally and normatively sui generis, fashioning their law and practice from unique blends and combinations of municipal and international norms.[125] Nonetheless, it is evident that the United Nations' ad hoc tribunals base themselves on a recognisably Anglo-American model of Evidence law,[126]

---

[119] See R Cryer, *Prosecuting International Crimes: Selectivity and the International Criminal Law Regime* (Cambridge, CUP, 2005) 25ff.

[120] In the final vote, 120 states voted in favour of the final Draft Statute, seven voted against and 21 abstained: see MC Bassiouni, 'Negotiating the Treaty of Rome on the Establishment of an International Criminal Court' (1999) 32 *Cornell International Law Journal* 443.

[121] ICC Statute, Art 126.

[122] Bassiouni, above n 120, 468.

[123] It is perhaps worth noting that this assessment is entirely compatible with the consequent deluge having caused a great deal of collateral damage, and also with the possibility of its being securely dammed up again in relatively short order.

[124] See eg, CPR Romano, A Nollkaemper and JK Kleffner (eds), *Internationalized Criminal Courts: Sierra Leone, East Timor, Kosovo, and Cambodia* (Oxford, OUP, 2004); Human Rights Watch, *Judging Dujail: the First Trial before the Iraqi High Tribunal* (November 2006) available at www.hrw.org/reports/2006/iraq1106/; R Cryer, 'A "Special Court" for Sierra Leone?' (2001) 20 *International and Comparative Law Quarterly* 435.

[125] See P Roberts, 'Comparative Law for International Criminal Justice' in E Örücü and D Nelken (eds), *Comparative Law: a Hart Handbook* (Oxford, Hart, 2007); M Delmas-Marty, 'The Contribution of Comparative Law to a Pluralist Conception of International Criminal Law' (2003) 1 *Journal of International Criminal Justice* 13.

[126] R May *et al* (eds), *Essays on ICTY Procedure and Evidence in Honour of Gabrielle Kirk McDonald* (The Hague, Kluwer, 2001); Wald, above n 118; R May and M Wierda, 'Trends in International Criminal Evidence: Nuremberg, Tokyo, the Hague and Arusha'

from which the ICC has also taken its lead (albeit in modified and tempered form). A Romanist influence is somewhat more prominent within the EU system, but the ECHR ensures that detailed procedural codes like the *Corpus Juris*[127] bear strong family resemblance to common law norms and concepts; and, in any event, practices, processes and problems of case construction, information management, inference, evidence, proof and adjudication are in some measure common to all systems of criminal justice, irrespective of their historical origins or prevailing procedural ideology.

Should international criminal proceedings be the exclusive preserve of public international lawyers? That question answers itself. Of course the judges, lawyers and scholars of international penality must be familiar with relevant public international law (PIL) norms, but they no less urgently need to appreciate the objectives, values, institutions and operational realties of criminal process. The potential scope for Evidence scholars to make major contributions to the theory and practice of this emergent discipline is immense. Amongst the most urgent tasks is to provide assistance to the ad hoc tribunals to clarify, systematise and consolidate their quickly evolving jurisprudence of criminal procedure. But this should by no means be all one-way traffic. As I will endeavour to demonstrate in Chapter 13, Evidence teachers have much to learn, and to pass on to their students, from observing the attempts of the international community to get to grips with traditional problems of evidence and proof in novel supra-national contexts.

PLEASE DISCUSS

My motivation in writing this essay was, first, to articulate and develop more systematically some recurring thoughts about Evidence teaching, distilled from various sources and inchoate thoughts which had occurred to me over more than a decade of learning and teaching the subject; and, secondly, to share these ideas with other Evidence teachers in the hope of generating lively debate about the current health and future directions of our discipline. I am well aware that the essay draws heavily on my own experiences as student and teacher, which could conceivably be atypical. But I hope the intermittently confessional tone can be forgiven, since my experiences are relevant to the issues and they are my best source of information. In the meantime we might ask why, collectively, Evidence

(1999) 37 *Columbia Journal of Transnational Law* 725; R Dixon, 'Developing International Rules of Evidence for the Yugoslav and Rwanda Tribunals' (1997) 7 *Transnational Law and Contemporary Problems* 81.

[127] See *Corpus Juris 2000* at www.law.uu.nl/wiarda/corpus/index1.htm; E Bell, 'A European DPP to Prosecute Euro-Fraud?' [2000] *Crim LR* 154.

teachers know so little about each other's methods and approaches. In the absence of any better indication, this chapter made the plausible assumption that the structure and content of university Evidence courses broadly reflect the leading textbook treatments, as did the courses I have studied and taught at Oxford, Nottingham and Leicester.[128]

Legal academics being accomplished exponents of the art of talking past one another, I conclude by trying to anticipate what I imagine to be some of the most obvious potential objections to my arguments and agenda for rethinking Evidence. I hope this will further clarify my thesis, pre-empt avoidable misunderstanding, and generally facilitate a worthwhile debate about issues close to the hearts of all Evidence teachers.

Objection 1: Twining's Fifth Column?

First, I will confess a nagging worry that, despite all I have said, some Evidence teachers will read my arguments for rethinking Evidence as a project of Jurisprudence, external to the Law of Evidence, rather than, as I insisted, an indispensable, but neglected, task internal to the enterprise itself. Those who view Twining as a campaigner for the expansionist ambitions of legal theory might by extension see me as a kind of fifth columnist or Quisling ready to betray the evidentiary citadel to the enemy at the gate. Naturally, I emphatically deny all charges (though Twining, of course, can defend himself).

The best evidence I can offer of my commitment to the Law of Evidence is a previous record of publications, a substantial proportion of which would qualify as doctrinal scholarship on any reckoning. It is certainly not necessary to become an accomplished philosopher or theorist in order to acquire enough of a working knowledge of epistemology, moral and political philosophy, and social and cultural theory to inform one's Evidence teaching. The key is to remember that, for our purposes, epistemology, political philosophy and social theory must serve Evidence teaching, not the other way round.[129] Pragmatically, it will sometimes be necessary to adopt and adapt the products of other disciplines wholesale, and more or less on trust. Off-the-peg garments are invariably inferior to bespoke tailoring, but they are better than going completely naked.

There remains, for all that, a sense in which practically-minded readers might understandably be frustrated. For this chapter has first and foremost

---

[128] The Evidence course taught at Nottingham was substantially revised following the publication of Roberts and Zuckerman's *Criminal Evidence* in 2004.

[129] For an analogous, and more developed, argument about the significance of epistemology and other forms of theorising for the disciplines of Criminology, Criminal Justice and Criminal Law Theory, see P Roberts, 'On the Preconditions and Possibilities of Criminal Law Theory' (1998) 11 *South African Journal of Criminal Justice* 285, 290–301.

been about *the project of* rethinking Evidence, and has only actually engaged in rethinking by way of example and illustration. In this sense what has gone before is fairly characterised as abstract and theoretical. Yet abstraction is an unavoidable feature of any set of generalisations. My hope is that this essay will inspire, or provoke, readers to reconsider the structure, content and disciplinary parameters of the Law of Evidence as an ongoing project of reconstruction and refinement, inseparable from the general business of teaching or learning Evidence. And precisely because the project of rethinking Evidence is conceived as a dynamic, collective, ongoing activity, it follows that—of course—this essay has not completed the job, rethought Evidence, period. An agenda can be no more than a menu or recipe. The proof of the pudding remains in the teaching.

Objection 2: A New Credo?

Readers are bound to take issue with some or all of the particular proposals and examples on my agenda. Although, as I have said, specific examples are intended primarily as illustrations of the rethinking methodology, I have naturally chosen what I take to be good examples calculated to command broader appeal. Further contributions to the shared pool of ideas and experiences are fulsomely invited and eagerly anticipated.

A further, related point merits emphasis. It is no part of my thesis that Evidence teachers should collectively reconstruct a single normative conception of the Law of Evidence (much less that they should defer to my idiosyncratic version of it). To the contrary, I want to promote theoretical, methodological and topical pluralism. There could be many diverse, and equally valid, versions of the Law of Evidence, each with its own particular focus and objectives, strengths and limitations. In a vibrant, stimulating, developing discipline, individual teachers will—and must—work through the details for themselves. When I advocate 'rethinking the Law of Evidence', this project is intended to embrace, or to stimulate, a broader range of ideas and interpretations than those currently at my disposal. The foil for this essay has been the one-dimensional, anachronistic, prescriptive conception of the Law of Evidence which is Thayer & Co's historical bequest.[130] I have absolutely no desire to see one conceptual straitjacket exchanged for another.

---

[130] It has been suggested to me by William Twining that, far from being part of the problem, Thayer points the way to the solution, inasmuch as he conceptualised the Law of Evidence (merely) as a set of disparate exceptions to a general principle of common-sense proof (recall the gruyère cheese and London suburb metaphors quoted from Twining, above). I have no difficulty in reading Thayer as a radical, visionary thinker whose ideas have shaped Evidence scholarship for the last century, but I am yet to be convinced that his inclusion in the orthodox tradition criticised in this chapter is unfair. Not for nothing is Thayer's best-known

Objection 3: A Bonfire of Strawmen?

To the charge that I have been assuming an unrealistically homogenous, simplistic model—or caricature—of (predominantly English) Evidence textbooks and teaching, and in the process have unjustly discounted a substantial corpus of innovative Evidence scholarship, I am obliged to confess and avoid. Discussing general conceptualisations and trends over time requires one to generalise, and generalisation is always in some measure reductive and potentially misleading. Even at the time when I first publicly addressed these themes in my CLP lecture in 2001 there were several well-respected texts which already exemplified core features of my agenda for rethinking Evidence.[131] These works have subsequently been joined on the bookshelves by like-minded treatments which, notwithstanding their many significant differences, share a foundational commitment to pedagogic innovation and theoretical renewal in the Law of Evidence.[132]

Numerically, however, textbooks of this nature are in the minority, and, I would guess, their influence is probably restricted to a minority of students. There is currently a proliferation of Evidence texts, most of which follow the standard format pioneered in England by Sir Rupert

work entitled *A Preliminary Treatise on Evidence at the Common Law*, since it reads as a ground-clearing exercise preliminary to the main business of restating the *law* of Evidence. Thus, Thayer tells us that 'the main errand of the law of evidence is to determine not so much what is admissible in proof, as what is inadmissible ... Admissibility is determined, first by relevancy—an affair of logic and experience, and not at all of law; second, but only indirectly, by *the law of evidence*, which declares whether any given matter which is logically probative is excluded' (268, 269, my emphasis). Meditating on the 'present and future of the law of evidence', Thayer proceeds to instruct his readers that fact-finding is no part of the Law of Evidence, which 'does not re-enact, nor does it displace, the main rules which govern human thought. *These are all taken for granted.* But it does exclude, by rules, much which is logically probative. It also regulates the production of witnesses, documents, and visible objects offered for inspection as the basis of inference' (527, my emphasis). Whilst it is undeniable that Thayer himself took a keen interest in the processes of proof, and their historical evolution, remarks such as these make it difficult to credit Thayer as a pioneer of taking facts seriously in Evidence teaching. According to Twining, above n 8, 6: 'Wigmore was his disciple and, in a sense, completed Thayer's work by producing a systematic treatise based on a coherent theory of judicial proof. In this view, Thayer paved the way and Wigmore completed the task'. But if Twining is right about the significance of Thayer's *Preliminary Treatise*, Wigmore's self-promotion of *Principles of Judicial Proof* (1st edn, 1913) 2, as 'the first attempt in English, since Bentham, to call attention to the principles of judicial Proof (distinguished from Admissibility) as a whole and as a system' must be considered rather ungenerous to his teacher. Also cf E Swift, 'One Hundred Years of Evidence Law Reform: Thayer's Triumph' (2000) 88 *California LR* 2437, 2440: '[Thayer] narrowed the field of evidence law to the study of rules pertaining only to the trial court's decision to admit or exclude evidence'.

[131] IH Dennis, *The Law of Evidence* (London, Sweet & Maxwell, 1999; 2nd edn, 2002); AAS Zuckerman, *The Principles of Criminal Evidence* (Oxford, OUP, 1989).

[132] See J Hunter, '*Criminal Evidence* and *Analysis of Evidence*: Laws unto Themselves?' (2006) 10 *E & P* 327; C Callen and J Jackson (eds), *Special Issue: Commentaries on Roberts and Zuckerman's* Criminal Evidence (2005) 2(2) *International Commentary on Evidence*; T Anderson, D Schum and W Twining, *Analysis of Evidence* (2nd edn, Cambridge, CUP, 2005).

Cross, though seldom with the same range, depth or authority as the master or his pupil and posthumous collaborator.[133] Further down the publishing food chain from the *Cross*-lite clones are various crib books, 'study aids', outlines, digests and the like which promise to put it all in a nutshell for the 'strategic learner' and the work-shy.[134] Much as we might wish it otherwise, those students whose primary objective is to pass their course with a good grade may prefer perceived shortcuts to the road less travelled.[135] Even supposing, optimistically, that innovative texts are widely read, it will be necessary to keep making the argument for rethinking Evidence for as long as the less challenging materials continue to flood the market.

Objection 4: Where are the Materials to Teach from? (What's Research Got to Do with It?)

It is reasonable to suppose that Evidence teachers are obliged to work with the teaching materials to hand. Even teachers who are dissatisfied with their existing texts and curricula may feel constrained to persevere in the absence of readily available alternatives. In the mutually-reinforcing, narrow, orthodoxy of Evidence texts and syllabi one may discern, as though in bas-relief, the intimate connection between teaching and research. Ultimately, if 'the market' is not supplying Evidence teachers with the materials they want and need to teach a reconstructed Evidence course, Evidence teachers will have to supply the market. My agenda for a twenty-first century Law of Evidence invites teachers and scholars to venture beyond conventional disciplinary boundaries in order to recover the full evidentiary potential of work in allied fields such as Criminal

---

[133] The fifth edition (1979) was Cross' last *Evidence*, and the sixth (1985) Colin Tapper's first *Cross on Evidence*. In the eighth (1995) and subsequent editions Colin Tapper is credited as sole author, and the book was retitled *Cross and Tapper on Evidence*.

[134] Such study aids may have their proper (i.e. marginal) place in a rounded evidentiary education. But they contribute nothing to the health or development of the discipline of Evidence, and students are ill-served by over-reliance on them. Cf my review of M Barrett, *Blackstone's Law of Evidence Index: Case Precedents 1900–1997* (London, Blackstone, 1998) at (1999) 3 *E & P* 138.

[135] The only negative review of Roberts and Zuckerman, *Criminal Evidence*, I have read was posted on Amazon by one disgruntled undergraduate, who wrote: 'This is a terrible textbook for students . . . If you want pages and pages of abstract analysis, theoretical waffle and social policy, then by all means go for this book. However, most students want more hard law in their textbooks to actually get them through exams. There is very little emphasis on cases and I don't find the structure to be very helpful or even logical in some places. I think that while this would be a good book to dip into for essay writing, it is terrible for week to week learning and I dread picking it up'.

Procedure, Criminal Justice, Criminology, Sociology, Politics, Economics, Philosophy and History, as well as material located in other sections of the law library.

Without prejudice to the broader ambitions of Evidence scholarship, it is worth drawing attention to the unrealised pedagogical potential of the fruits of academic legal research. Successful Evidence teaching is crucially dependent on a healthy and well-developed research base, certainly including up-to-the-minute doctrinal scholarship, but extending to much more besides. Unless teachers are able to inform themselves about current court practice, and gain insights into the development of cases before they go to court, the content and structure of Evidence courses will lose touch with the contemporary realities of legal process and adjudication, to the detriment of university education and students' legitimate expectations. A theoretical 'Law of Evidence' bearing little or no resemblance to what actually happens in litigation would ill-serve intending practitioners (rather like learning classical Greek in preparation for two weeks' holiday on Rhodes) and misinform all students about the performance of important public institutions.[136]

The 'gap problem' identified by socio-legal scholars since the 1970s[137]— that the 'law in the books' is often far removed from 'the law in action'—has particular resonance for adjectival law, whose *raison d'etre* is precisely the regulation of real-world disputes and their practical resolution. Still, the harmonious integration of Evidence teaching and research is a two-way street. Whilst reliance is placed on researchers to produce information needed for teaching, teachers must be active in identifying, mediating and disseminating new materials for classroom consumption. Scholars who are both teachers and researchers should have no difficulty in recognising this symbiosis, yet the contribution of research to Evidence teaching remains deficient in both directions. There are extensive gaps and blind-spots in our knowledge of the practical operation of particular evidentiary rules and doctrines,[138] and our teaching of the processes of fact management, case construction, inference and proof leaves much to be desired.

---

[136] This is not to discount the intellectual value, rigour or discipline of abstract learning. But if the Law of Evidence were nothing more than mind-training, the rules of chess might provide an equally valuable and vigorous intellectual work-out, and there would be no particular reason for law schools to provide the venue.

[137] A classic theoretical treatment remains D Nelken, 'The "Gap Problem" in the Sociology of Law: a Theoretical Review' (1981) 1 *Windsor Yearbook of Access to Justice* 35; recently revived, for example, by K Daly, 'Mind the Gap: Restorative Justice in Theory and Practice' in A von Hirsch, J Roberts, AE Bottoms, K Roach and M Schiff (eds), *Restorative Justice and Criminal Justice* (Oxford, Hart Publishing, 2002).

[138] English law's restrictions on jury research, though a significant constraint, cannot completely explain this dearth.

This situation is far from beyond amelioration. Valuable empirical data have recently been accumulating,[139] and take their place in a steadily expanding corpus of innovative interdisciplinary research with great potential for classroom application. A healthy crop of books, articles, and research reports,[140] on which this essay has liberally drawn, as well as substantial Internet resources,[141] already supplies the raw material for rethinking Evidence. John Jackson and Sean Doran's socio-legal study of Diplock courts,[142] and the comparative collaboration between Chrisje Brants and Stewart Field,[143] exemplify innovative methodologies for deepening our knowledge and understanding of Evidence in sympathy with the

[139] See eg, HMCPSI/HMIC, *Without Consent: a Report on the Joint Review of the Investigation and Prosecution of Rape Offences* (London, HMIC, 2007); L Kelly, J Temkin and S Griffiths, *Section 41: an Evaluation of New Legislation Limiting Sexual History Evidence in Rape Trials* (HO-OLR 20/06, London, Home Office, 2006); D Cooper and P Roberts, *Special Measures for Vulnerable and Intimidated Witnesses: an Analysis of Crown Prosecution Service Monitoring Data* (London, CPS, 2005); B Hamlyn, A Phelps, J Turtle and G Sattar, *Are Special Measures Working? Evidence from Surveys of Vulnerable and Intimidated Witnesses* (HORS 283, London, Home Office, 2004); S Lloyd-Bostock, *The Effects on Magistrates of Learning that the Defendant has a Previous Conviction*, LCD Research Series No 3/00 (London, Lord Chancellor's Department, 2000); T Bucke, R Street and D Brown, *The Right of Silence: the Impact of the Criminal Justice and Public Order Act 1994* (HORS 199, London, Home Office, 2000); G Davis *et al*, *An Assessment of the Admissibility and Sufficiency of Evidence in Child Abuse Prosecutions* (London, Home Office, 1999); J Harris and S Grace, *A Question of Evidence? Investigating and Prosecuting Rape in the 1990s* (HORS 196, London, Home Office, 1999).

[140] The following contributions, though in other respects extremely varied (and in various ways problematic), share the aspiration to rethink Evidence: Roberts and Zuckerman, above n 60; Anderson, Schum and Twining, above n 18; RJ Allen, 'Factual Ambiguity and a Theory of Evidence' (1994) 88 *Northwestern University Law Review* 604; J Hunter and K Cronin, *Evidence, Advocacy and Ethical Practice: a Criminal Trial Commentary* (Sydney, Butterworths, 1995); J McEwan, *Evidence and the Adversarial Process: the Modern Law* (2nd edn, Oxford, Hart Publishing, 1998); M Childs and L Ellison (eds), *Feminist Perspectives on Evidence* (London, Cavendish, 2000); A Stein, *Foundations of Evidence Law* (Oxford, OUP, 2005); RA Posner, 'An Economic Approach to the Law of Evidence' (1999) 51 *Stanford Law Review* 1477.

[141] Valuable sites devoted specifically to Evidence include the homepages of the *International Journal of Evidence and Proof* (*E & P*) www.vathek.com/ijep/submission.shtml and *International Commentary on Evidence* (*ICE*) www.bepress.com/ice/; and Peter Tillers' 'Dynamic Evidence Page' at http://tillers.net/home.html. The Association of American Law Schools' Evidence Section webpages are still well worth a visit, though they do not appear to have been updated for some time, www.law.umich.edu/thayer/. For gateways to comparative materials, try the United Nations Crime and Justice Information Network www.uncjin.org/; Cornell Law School Legal Information Institute www.law.cornell.edu/world/; Australasian Legal Information Institute http://austlii.law.uts.edu.au/; Florida State University School of Criminology and Criminal Justice www.criminology.fsu.edu/cjlinks/; Washburn University School of Law www.washlaw.edu/; Findlaw www.findlaw.com/.

[142] J Jackson and S Doran, *Judge Without Jury: Diplock Trials in the Adversary System* (Oxford, OUP, 1995), reviewed at (1996) 112 *LQR* 513.

[143] C Brants and S Field, 'Legal Cultures, Political Cultures and Procedural Traditions: Towards a Comparative Interpretation of Covert and Proactive Policing in England and Wales and the Netherlands' in D Nelken (ed), *Contrasting Criminal Justice* (Aldershot, Ashgate, 2000). Now also see J Hodgson, *French Criminal Justice: a Comparative Account of the*

agenda sketched in this chapter. Until such material is fully reflected in the content and structure of standard Evidence texts, however, its impact on teaching is likely to remain muted. Quite apart from the pragmatic consideration of ease of access for teachers and students, whilst a topic, idea, concept, illustration or research finding remains excluded from the received pedagogical canon, it can all too easily be overlooked or marginalised.

Objection 5: Where is the Time?

I never encountered an Evidence teacher, or any law teacher, with too little material to fill their allotted contact hours. There is always more to be said than lecture hours to say it in, and the time-guillotine only falls harder and faster in the rationalising higher education world of modularisation and semesterisation. Even without the extra effort involved, proposals for rethinking Evidence are likely to run into the objection that syllabi have already been pared down to the absolute minimum required for respectable coverage of the essential subject matter. There is simply no room to accommodate the fruits of rethinking, however tempting or tasty they might look on the menu of notional possibilities.

Having wrestled with my conscience to accept that there was no tutorial time to spare for *Jones v DPP*[144] and the absorbing technicalities of Criminal Evidence Act 1898, s 1(f)(i),[145] I am compelled to confess a genuine sympathy for this objection. But perhaps there is a tendency to look at the problem from the wrong end of the telescope. Rather than asking 'What in my current teaching is of negligible value and could be cut out without loss?' (to which the answer is inevitably 'Nothing!'), the challenge should be to make the *most effective* use of the limited time available. Slavish, unreflective adherence to traditional practices cannot be relied upon to deliver maximum effectiveness by serendipitous coincidence.

Investigation and Prosecution of Crime in France (Oxford, Hart Publishing, 2005); S Field, 'State, Citizen, and Character in French Criminal Process' (2006) 33 *Journal of Law and Society* 522.

[144] [1962] AC 635, HL. And see Sir John Smith's commentary [1962] *Crim LR* 244.

[145] See CFH Tapper, 'The Meaning of Section 1(f)(i) of the Criminal Evidence Act 1898' in Tapper (ed), *Crime, Proof and Punishment: Essays in Memory of Sir Rupert Cross* (London, Butterworths, 1981). Parliament subsequently delivered the *coup de grâce* when the CJA 2003 substantially repealed the 1898 Act and dispensed entirely with English law's time-honoured 'character shield'. As if by way of compensation, however, Parliament thoughtfully supplied a new set of exquisitely intricate linguistic contortions which will probably keep Evidence scholars occupied for another 100 years. For a critical overview of the legislation, see Roberts and Zuckerman, above n 60, ch 11.

One final thought. Of all the choices that might be made, the struthious strategy[146] of refusing to think about the issues addressed in this chapter is the least attractive option of all. Critical (re)thinking is an indispensable ingredient of scholarship and teaching, and a rightly treasured inheritance of liberal academic traditions and professional culture. In order to be successful in communicating this most essential of transferable skills to our students we need first to apply some of it to the design and content of our courses (and in the production of texts and supporting materials). Added to which, as a simple matter of enlightened self-interest, the world is changing and we must adapt to survive, or expect—and perhaps deserve— natural deselection.

---

[146] Cf T Bradney, 'The Future of Law Schools' (1998) 16 *SPTL Reporter* 1, 3: 'Today, to ignore discussion of educational theory, practice and policy, in the belief that it will have no impact on one's professional life, is to adopt the same strategy as the ostrich with approximately the same likelihood of finding oneself for sale, pre-packaged, on higher education's equivalent of Sainsbury's exotic meats counter. Those in law schools must contribute to educational debate or they will be controlled by it'.

2

Taking Facts Seriously—Again

WILLIAM TWINING*

INTRODUCTION

IN 1980 I DELIVERED a paper entitled 'Taking Facts Seriously' which is quite well known but has made almost no impact.[1] I think that the argument is both correct and important for our ideas and practice in academic law in respect of legal method, legal theory, the Law of Evidence and legal education generally. Its fate reminds me of a dictum of Karl Llewellyn: 'When Cicero made a speech, you said: "No mortal man is so eloquent"; when Demosthenes made a speech, you yelled: "WAR!!"'. It seems to have been a failure of advocacy.

My thesis was that the subject of evidence, proof and fact-finding (EPF) deserves a more salient place in the discipline of law. The paper argued that fact investigation, fact management and argumentation about disputed questions of fact in legal contexts (not just in court) are as worthy of attention and as intellectually demanding as issues of interpretation and reasoning about questions of law. It was an argument about the importance of the study of facts in legal education and it was addressed to a general legal audience

When the paper was published it was received politely, but failed to persuade, perhaps because it fell between audiences: Practitioners quite liked it, but it was about legal education; many academic lawyers perceived it as addressed to specialists in Evidence and so no concern of theirs; some Evidence teachers perceived it as a radical and undiplomatic critique of

* Different versions of this paper have previously been published in (2005) 55 *Journal of Legal Education* 360 and W Twining, *Rethinking Evidence: Exploratory Essays* (Cambridge, CUP, 2006) (hereafter *RE*). I am grateful to Terry Anderson, Mike Redmayne, Paul Roberts, David Schum and participants in seminars in London, Nottingham and Champaign, Illinois for comments and suggestions.

[1] Originally published in N Gold (ed), *Essays on Legal Education* (Toronto, Butterworths, 1982) and reprinted in (1984) 34 *J Legal Education* 22 and in W Twining, *Rethinking Evidence: Exploratory Essays* (Cambridge, CUP, 2006) (hereafter *RE*) ch 2.

traditional courses on the Law of Evidence; while others saw it as poor salesmanship for improbable Wigmore charts.

Here, the intended audience is both specialists in Evidence and academic lawyers generally. My aim is threefold: first, to restate the original thesis and to argue that it deserves support, not mainly or solely to mitigate curricular pressures, but rather because many of the issues are important to understanding and practising law; secondly, to consider how a coherent single law school course on Evidence can be constructed in conditions of curriculum overload and neglect of evidentiary issues in other parts of the curriculum;[2] thirdly, to suggest some ways in which the recent emergence of Evidence as a multidisciplinary field in its own right might affect the study and teaching of Evidence in law.

THE SUBJECT OF EVIDENCE DESERVES A MORE CENTRAL PLACE IN THE DISCIPLINE OF LAW

Rather than go over the ground covered by the earlier paper, I will briefly restate the reasons why our subject is important. The argument in outline falls under five main heads:

Understanding Evidence is an Important Part of Understanding Law

(a) *Evidence is important for legal theory* because it raises a range of theoretical issues that generally are not included in the agenda of most legal theorists. The practice of treating 'legal reasoning' as being solely concerned with, typically hard, questions of law is merely symptomatic of more fundamental distortions in the agendas of jurisprudence, as I have argued at length elsewhere.[3]

It is odd that issues of fact determination rarely play a significant part in theories of adjudication.[4] How can one have a coherent and comprehensive theory of judging that ignores decisions on questions of fact, procedure and disposition? How can the separation of two bodies of literature

---

[2]   This chapter is concerned with the subject of Evidence in first degrees in law in common law countries. The general argument applies to undergraduate degrees (as in England) and to postgraduate first degrees in law (as in the United States and some other common law countries). However, account is taken of the fact that pressures on curriculum, whether from professional examinations, shortage of time or other factors, vary between jurisdictions.

[3]   W Twining, *Law in Context: Enlarging a Discipline* (Oxford, OUP, 1997) ch 6 (hereafter *LIC*); *RE*, above n 1, ch 8.

[4]   For example, the most prominent modern theory of adjudication, as developed by Ronald Dworkin in *Taking Rights Seriously* (London, Duckworth, 1977) and *Law's Empire* (London, Fontana, 1986), almost completely ignores such matters as fact determination and sanctioning.

be justified on the fragile basis of the notoriously problematic distinction between questions of fact and questions of law?[5]

It is strange that basic concepts in the subject of Evidence, such as relevance, materiality, probative force, probability, credibility and presumptions have received little sustained attention from analytical jurisprudence.[6]

It is odd that nearly all discussions of legal reasoning and interpretation concentrate on questions of law, with little or no reference not only to questions of fact, but more generally to reasoning and rationality in other legal contexts such as investigation, negotiation and sanctioning.[7] The relations between these various kinds of lawyers' reasonings are not adequately explored.

It is odd that issues about the relationship between narrative and argument, between 'holism' and 'atomism', and questions of coherence should not be perceived to be central to theories of legal reasoning and rationality.[8] The role of narrative in legal discourse and questions about the relations between narrative, reasoning, argumentation and persuasion are distorted if narrative and stories are only considered in relation to disputed questions of fact in adjudication.[9] Stories and story-telling are also important in investigation, mediation, negotiation, appellate advocacy, sentencing and predictions of dangerousness,[10] for example. A general theory of narrative in law and legal argumentation needs to encompass all

---

[5] Cf R Allen and MJ Pardo, 'Facts in Law and Facts of Law' (2003) 7 *E & P* 153 and P F Kirgis, 'Questions of Fact in the Practice of Law: a Response to Allen and Pardo's "Facts in Law and Facts of Law"' (2004) 8 *E & P* 47.

[6] A classic exception is JL Montrose, 'Basic Concepts of the Law of Evidence' (1984) 70 *LQR* 527. The case for a broadened conception and agenda for analytical jurisprudence is developed in W Twining, 'Have Concepts: Will Travel' (2005) 1 *Inernational J Law in Context* 5.

[7] If one adopts a 'total process model' of litigation, issues of inferential reasoning arise at all stages of the process. T Anderson, D Schum and W Twining, *Analysis of Evidence* (2nd edn, Cambridge, CUP, 2005) (hereafter *Analysis*) now devotes a whole chapter to reasoning in investigation and considers evidentiary issues from the standpoints of all major participants in legal processes.

[8] Neil MacCormick, 'Coherence in Legal Justification' in W Krawietz *et al* (ed), *Theorie der Normen* (Berlin, Dunker & Humblot, 1984) has stimulated an extensive literature, but still mainly in relation to interpretation and application of legal rules. See now, N MacCormick, *Rhetoric and the Rule of Law* (Oxford, OUP, 2005).

[9] These themes are explored in W Twining, *The Great Juristic Bazaar: Jurists' Texts and Lawyers' Stories* (Aldershot, Ashgate, 2002) (hereafter *GJB*) chs 12–16.

[10] See generally, *RE*, above n 1, 286–306; D Schum, *Evidential Foundations of Probabilistic Reasoning* (New York, Wylie, 1994) 195–9; D Binder and P Bergman, *Fact Investigation* (St Paul, MN, West, 1984); K Llewellyn, *The Common Law Tradition: Deciding Appeals* (Boston, MA, Little, Brown, 1960); J Shapland, *Between Conviction and Sentence: the Process of Mitigation* (London, Routledge, 1981); Erica Beecher-Monas, 'The Epistemology of Prediction: Future Dangerousness Testimony and Intellectual Due Process' (2003) 60 *Washington and Lee LR* 353.

such questions. Some of these topics have been canvassed rather eclectically under the heading of 'law and literature',[11] but a comprehensive framework has yet to be developed within which all these lines of enquiry can be considered in relation to each other.

Jurisprudence needs to take issues relating to evidence more seriously within a balanced conception of what is involved in understanding law.[12] Neglect of those issues results in a distorted picture of adjudication, litigation, legal reasoning and legal practice.

(b) *Evidence in other specialisms*: Questions of fact and other evidentiary issues arise in every field of law: discrimination, land disputes and rape are standard examples. This point is widely recognised, but unevenly acted on. There are also familiar problems of overlap between courses on Evidence and procedure, legal institutions (for example, the jury, police interrogation) and legal processes; there is a developing literature on problems of proof in international criminal tribunals (not only about rules of evidence, but whether crimes against humanity raise any special issues about proof).[13] Some of these matters relate to general questions about the extent to which principles of proof are context-independent and substance-blind.[14] Such issues arise not only in legal contexts, but more generally and acutely in considering evidence from multidisciplinary perspectives.[15]

Evidence is Important in Legal Practice

When Jerome Frank argued that over 90 per cent of adjudication and pre-trial work is more concerned with doubts and uncertainties about facts than with disputed questions of law he partly understated the case, because he was only concerned with litigation and his main focus was on the contested jury trial.[16] But the general message is basically correct: that inferential reasoning and other aspects of information processing are

[11] For example, L Ledwon, 'The Poetics of Evidence: Some Applications from Law and Literature' (2003) 21 *Quinnipiac LR* 1145.

[12] Eg Paul Roberts reports that 'there is the suspicion that Twining, as a jurist, is intent on turning the Law of Evidence into a branch of Jurisprudence': P Roberts, 'Rethinking the Law of Evidence' (2002) 55 *Current Legal Problems* 297, 310 (now see, with slight modifications, Chapter 1). I might be an evidentiary imperialist, but my main point is that neglect of such issues within Jurisprudence tends to promote a distorted understanding of law and legal phenomena. As relatively faithful disciples of Karl Llewellyn, both my co-author, Terry Anderson, and I reject sharp distinctions between 'theory' and 'practice', but as Roberts, *ibid*, points out, our teaching of 'Analysis of Evidence' claims to be far more directly practical than study of the formal law of evidence.

[13] See below n 26.

[14] See D Schum in W Twining and I Hampsher-Monk (ed), *Evidence and Inference in History and Law* (Evanston, Northwestern University Press, 2003) (hereafter *Evidence and Inference*) ch 1.

[15] See below.

[16] On Frank see *RE*, above n 1, 116–19.

important in most contexts of legal practice and have been relatively neglected in legal education and training. The emphasis on the Federal Rules in American bar examinations and on the rules of evidence in police training to the neglect of inferential reasoning are prime examples.[17]

EPF is a Good Vehicle for Developing Some Basic Transferable Intellectual Skills

Skill in inferential reasoning is as much a part of 'legal method' as questions of law and as demanding.[18] Within EPF, the main ingredients are (i) managing complex data and constructing and criticising complex arguments, including such techniques for marshalling evidence as chronological tables, classifying evidence by source, Wigmore charts and stories;[19] (ii) skills of inferential reasoning and microscopic analysis; (iii) some basic numeracy skills; (iv) constructing, communicating and countering persuasive stories;[20] (v) ethical questions relating to all of these. Some seek to develop such skills within courses on Evidence. This can work quite well, but involves two costs. First, some of these topics are important in other contexts. Isolating them in contexts where the focus is on fact management artificially separates them both theoretically and practically from other relevant contexts. For example, numeracy skills apply to more than

---

[17] R Leary, *Evidential Reasoning and Analytical Techniques in Criminal Pre-Trial Fact Investigation* (PhD thesis, University College London, 2004) ch 1.

[18] On the response to objections that intellectual 'skills' are illiberal, see *LIC*, above n 3, ch 9.

[19] Different methods of marshalling evidence and structuring arguments are discussed at length in *Analysis*, above n 7, chs 4–6. For those who are not familiar with it, Wigmore's 'chart method' is a specific technique for analysing a complex body of evidence. In respect of a given case or disputed issue of fact, all of the data that are relevant and potentially usable in an argument for or against a particular conclusion ('the ultimate probandum') are analysed into simple propositions that are incorporated in a 'key-list' of propositions. The relations between all the propositions on the key-list are then represented in charted form using a prescribed set of symbols, so that the end product is a chart of a (typically complex) argument. The method is like chronological tables, indexes, stories and other devices in that it is useful for 'marshalling' or 'managing' complex bodies of data so that they can be considered as a whole; it differs from these in that the organising principle is the logical relationships between propositions in an argument rather than time sequence, narrative coherence, source, alphabetical order or taxonomy. The method is also useful for identifying strong or weak points in an argument and subjecting these key points to rigorous, detailed, 'microscopic' analysis. On the original method see JH Wigmore, *Science of Judicial Proof* (3rd edn, Boston, MA, Little, Brown,1937) ch XXI. For a description of the method modified for contemporary use, see *Analysis*, above n 7, chs 4 and 5.

[20] If one believes that stories play an important role in fact determination, but are also prime vehicles for 'cheating', then teaching skills of persuasive story-telling raises some difficult ethical issues, analogous to classic problems of teaching rhetoric as an art.

probabilities and proof.[21] Secondly, if some of these matters are not dealt with elsewhere it puts a very heavy pressure on Evidence courses.

As the Discipline of Law Becomes More Cosmopolitan Interesting New Issues of Comparison, Generalisation and Hybridisation are Raised in respect of EPF

Recently, increasing attention has been given to comparative procedure and evidence and to the implications of globalisation for the study of law. For example, Mirjan Damaška's pioneering work has provided a framework for comparing not only procedural systems, but also how evidentiary issues are treated within such systems.[22] Hans Crombag, Peter von Koppen and Willem Wagenaar applied ideas and hypotheses developed by psychologists and others in the United States to cases in the Netherlands.[23] This work raises questions about the extent to which logical principles, evidentiary concepts, empirical findings and particular doctrines 'travel well' across legal traditions and cultures.[24] I am told by civil lawyers that the ideal types of 'The Rationalist Tradition' seem to fit civilian systems better than common law ones.[25] Truth and Reconciliation Commissions, international criminal tribunals and international commercial arbitration raise interesting issues about evidence and proof in these special contexts.[26] And, of course, the European Convention on Human Rights has had both a direct and an indirect influence on the Law of Evidence in the United Kingdom.[27]

---

[21] See eg, the range of topics covered in MO Finkelstein, *Quantitative Methods in Law* (New York, Free Press, 1978), JL Gastwirth (ed), *Statistical Science in the Courtroom* (New York, Springer, 2000); P Dawid in *Analysis*, above n 7, Appendix I.

[22] MR Damaška, *The Faces of Justice and State Authority* (New Haven, Yale University Press, 1986); *Evidence Law Adrift* (New Haven, Yale University Press, 1997).

[23] WA Wagenaar, P Von Koppen and H Crombag, *Anchored Narratives* (London, Harvester Wheatsheaf, 1993); cf M Malsch and H Nijboer (ed), *Complex Cases* (Amsterdam, Thela Thesis, 1999); P van Kampen, *Expert Evidence Compared* (Antwerp, Intersentia, 1998). See now, W Wagenaar and H Crombag, *The Popular Policeman and Other Cases: Psychological Perspectives on Legal Evidence* (Amsterdam, Amsterdam University Press, 2005).

[24] On 'travelling well' see Twining, above n 6.

[25] RE, above n 1, 85–6.

[26] Consider eg, the very different issues raised by A Krog, *Country of my Skull* (London, Vintage, 1999) (on South Africa's Truth and Reconciliation Commission); JK Cogan, 'The Problem of Obtaining Evidence for International Criminal Courts' (2000) 22 *Human Rights Quarterly* 404; R May *et al* (ed), *Essays on ICTY Procedures and Evidence* (The Hague, Kluwer Law International, 2001); P Wald, 'Rules of Evidence in the Yugoslav War Tribunal' (2003) 21 *Quinnipiac L Rev* 761 (ICTY); Y Dezalay and B Garth, *Dealing in Virtue* (Chicago, University of Chicago Press, 1996) (international commercial arbitration); D Roebuck, *Ancient Greek Arbitration* (Oxford, Holo Press, 2001).

[27] See eg, the Table of International Instruments and Comparative Legislation in P Roberts and A Zuckerman, *Criminal Evidence* (Oxford, OUP, 2004) (hereafter *Criminal Evidence*) xxvi. The UK Human Rights Act 1998, which enacted the substance of the European

The Subject of Evidence is Coming into its Own as a Distinct Multidisciplinary Field

This is perhaps the most interesting development in recent years and will be discussed in the last section.

TEACHING EVIDENCE AT FIRST-DEGREE LEVEL: A SUGGESTED FRAMEWORK

The thesis that EPF deserves a more central place within the discipline of law implies that the subject deserves more space within undergraduate and postgraduate degree programmes. Either more attention should be given to evidentiary issues under the rubrics of legal method, jurisprudence, legal system, comparative law or the like, or there should be room for at least two courses in the general area. However, until that thesis gains acceptance, we have to confront the problems of designing coherent single courses on Evidence in a context of curriculum overload.

In an interesting paper entitled 'Rethinking the Law of Evidence',[28] Paul Roberts supported my argument, but criticised my advocacy. He focused on teaching courses on Evidence at undergraduate level, which is the most problematic in terms of overload. While careful to reassert his commitment to pluralism in undergraduate legal education, Roberts has constructed a model for an undergraduate course on Evidence that can be contrasted with more narrowly focused courses on the Law of Evidence.[29] Roberts sets out a foundational principle for Evidence teaching based on an orthodox view of the first law degree as the final formal stage of a liberal education. It can contribute to this enterprise by 'inculcating relevant, robust, and adaptable (more or less) transferable skills, helping students to become life-long learners, and promoting responsible citizenship'.[30]

Let us accept this as a recognisable starting-point for constructing a course on Evidence as part of a basic law degree.[31] The building blocks for

Convention, has significant potential implications for evidence and procedure, but it is too early to judge the full extent of its impact. See A Choo and S Nash, 'Evidence Law in England and Wales: the Impact of the Human Rights Act 1998' (2003) 7 *E & P* 31.

[28] Roberts, above n 12, 297.

[29] This is now implemented and made concrete by Roberts and Zuckerman's stimulating book *Criminal Evidence*, above n 27.

[30] Roberts, above n 12, 301.

[31] Roberts' lecture was confined to England and Wales, where law is studied as a first (undergraduate degree). But our main arguments also apply in situations where law is a second rather than a first degree. See above n 2. It is worth noting the paradox that one would expect American law schools to be more vocationally oriented, but the biggest obstacle to developing intellectual skills of analysis and argumentation about questions of fact are the Bar examinations, which place heavy emphasis on detailed knowledge of and ability to apply the Federal Rules of Evidence rather than on skills of analysing, managing and constructing

Roberts' conception of an Evidence course (assuming a degree programme that does not deal with evidentiary issues in a sustained way elsewhere) are as follows:[32]

(1) The study of the Law of Evidence should be situated in its procedural, institutional and theoretical contexts.[33]
(2) The study of Evidence should encompass all stages of legal process and should not be confined to contested trials, let alone jury trials. In particular, there is a greater need than in the past for focus on pre-trial process, including fact investigation. In short, the procedural context involves a total process model of litigation.
(3) The theoretical context includes questions about epistemology, inferential reasoning and principles of political morality (including feminism, economic analysis, critical theory and post-modernism).[34]
(4) The connections between fact analysis and the rules of evidence need to be made clear and treated as part of a coherent whole.
(5) The main bridge between fact analysis and legal doctrine is supplied by the topic of relevance:
(a) relevance is the most important mechanism of exclusion;
(b) to understand relevance involves understanding the principles and characteristics of inferential reasoning;
(c) The principles of proof are anterior to the other exclusionary rules because they deal with the exclusion of relevant evidence.
(d) The Law of Evidence can be treated as a coherent whole by Thayer's inclusionary and exclusionary principles, which are both expressed in terms of relevance within a basic framework of argumentation.[35]
(6) The logic of proof is an important element in studying, for example,

---

arguments based on mixed masses of evidence. Thus, as so often happens, a liberal educational philosophy may be better placed to contribute to the development of useful transferable practical skills.

[32] I here restate the underlying assumptions of this model in my own words and then make some comments that may carry the ideas a bit further, but in ways that I understand are acceptable to Roberts.

[33] Preface, *Criminal Evidence*, above n 27. Nearly all of these ideas are canvassed in *RE*, above n 1.

[34] EG, M Childs and L Ellison (eds), *Feminist Perspectives on Evidence* (London, Cavendish, 2000); R Posner, 'An Economic Approach to the Law of Evidence' (1999) 51 *Stanford LR* 1477; R Lempert, 'The Economic Analysis of Evidence Law: Common Sense on Stilts' (2001) 87 *Virginia LR* 1619; M Siegel, 'A Pragmatic Critique of Modern Evidence Scholarship' (1994) 88 *Northwestern University LR* 995; Donald Nicolson, 'Truth, Reason and Justice: Epistemology and Politics in Evidence Discourse' (1994) 57 *MLR* 726. For my views on post-modernist epistemology, see *GJB*, above n 9, 289–309 (steering a course between Susan Haack and Italo Calvino).

[35] JB Thayer, *A Preliminary Treatise on Evidence at Common Law* (Boston, MA, Little, Brown, 1898), discussed in *RE*, above n 1, ch 6.

scientific evidence, judicial notice, similar facts, prejudicial effect/probative value, burdens and standards of proof (and for other decisions) and presumptions.[36]

(7) The increasingly important subject of scientific and expert evidence is a good peg on which to hang some of the central epistemological questions concerning evidence.[37]

(8) Evidentiary issues arise in all types of proceeding, in all types of legal processes, and at every stage. However, the subject becomes more manageable and coherent if one focuses on one type of proceeding, ie criminal process, which has in practice become the main focus of attention in Evidence courses in England.[38]

(9) Despite (8), basic principles of reasoning and analysis about questions of fact and basic concepts, such as relevance, credibility and probative force, are both substance-blind (Schum) and context-blind, in that they transcend not only the criminal/civil divide, but also travel well across Western legal traditions and even disciplinary boundaries.[39]

(10) As the discipline of law becomes more cosmopolitan, more attention will inevitably have to be paid to the European, international, transnational and comparative aspects of evidence.

(11) Given time, a course on Evidence can be one vehicle for the development of law-related numeracy skills.

(12) Evidence-based narrative plays a central role in constructing and presenting arguments about questions of fact.[40]

---

[36] On the broader concept of 'standards for decision', see *Analysis*, above n 7, ch 8. In arguing for more attention to be paid to relevance, Roberts suggests that after a preliminary consideration at the start of a course, the lessons can be reinforced by explicit consideration of it in relation to other topics such as previous misconduct evidence, hearsay and silence (306–7). I agree. See further *Criminal Evidence*, above n 27, *passim*.

[37] Roberts, above n 12, 324–8. The links between epistemology and scientific evidence have been brilliantly explored by the philosopher, Susan Haack: See especially, *Defending Science: Within Reason* (New York, Prometheus Books, 2003) ch 9 and 'Truth and Justice, Inquiry and Advocacy, Science and Law' (2004) 17 *Ratio Juris* 15.

[38] While agreeing with the idea that it is desirable to integrate the law of civil and criminal evidence quite closely with their specific procedural contexts, it is worth reiterating that the logic of proof is highly transferable, as are basic concepts such as relevance, credibility and probative force (cf Roberts, above n 12, 317). The new edition of *Analysis* (2005), above n 7, includes exercises on criminal cases, civil cases, intelligence scenarios and historical events in order to emphasise this transferability.

[39] On crossing disciplinary boundaries, see Schum, above n 10, and 'Twining's hypothesis' in *Evidence and Inference*, above n 14. On transcending legal cultures, see above n 24. For an attempt to apply modified Wigmorean analysis to a historical problem (the date of the demise of cuneiform), see T Anderson and M Geller, 'The Last Wedge' in *Evidence and Inference*, chs 3–5.

[40] 'Evidence-based narrative' is similar to the notion of 'anchored narratives' developed by Wagenaar, Von Koppen and Crombag, above n 23, except that they place too much emphasis on generalisations rather than on particular evidence as 'anchors' for stories (*GJB*, above n 9, 428–31).

Roberts and I seem to be in broad agreement about these 12 propositions. However, I wish to develop some general points that may bring out some differences, at least of emphasis and priorities.

Evidence Theory is Important in Providing a Coherent Framework for the Study of Evidence in Law (EPF)

Wigmore divided the subject of Evidence in legal contexts into two complementary parts: the 'Principles of Proof' ('as given by logic, psychology, and general experience') and 'the Trial Rules'. He argued that the Principles of Proof are anterior to the Trial Rules, are more important in practice and had been neglected by scholars and teachers of Evidence.[41] This neglect continued until the rise of the 'New Evidence Scholarship' in the 1970s and 1980s, which to date seems not to have been matched by a comparable development of 'New Evidence Teaching'. One reason for this is the lack of a coherent framework.

If we accept that Evidence is best studied in the context of a total process model of litigation (civil, criminal and other), then Wigmore's focus on contested jury trials and his concept of 'Trial Rules' are too narrow. However, his conception of the subject of Evidence in law as consisting of two closely related parts has much to commend it. I refer to these parts as the principles of proof (or the logic of proof) and the Law of Evidence, rather than subsuming both under an expanded conception of the Law of Evidence. But that is mainly a matter of labelling.[42]

To construct a coherent framework for the study of Evidence in law requires two further steps: a coherent picture of each of the two component parts and a coherent conception of the relationship between the two parts.

I suggest that the model of 'the Rationalist Tradition of Evidence Scholarship' provides the most coherent view of the principles of proof.[43] This can be encapsulated in the Benthamite proposition that the direct end of legal procedure is the pursuit of justice under the law through achieving rectitude of decision by rational means. One does not have to subscribe to

---

[41] Wigmore, above n 19, 3–6. Wigmore first expressed this view in 'The Problem of Proof' (1913) 8 *Illinois LR* 77.

[42] However, there are good reasons for the preference: the term 'the law of evidence' has too strong an association with the exclusionary rules and often leads to the fallacious assumption that the subject of Evidence in law is co-extensive with the rules of evidence. See eg, a successful American casebook entitled *Evidence*, which defines the subject of the book as follows: 'Evidence law is about the limits we place on the information juries hear' (G Fisher, *Evidence* (New York, Foundation Press, 2002) Preface). This in turn leads to exaggerating the importance of the rules (*RE*, above n 1, 210–18) and paying insufficient attention to aspects that are not governed by formal rules, such as relevance, weight and argumentation.

[43] *RE*, above n 1, chs 3 and 4.

all of the elements in this ideal type to use it as an organising device; indeed, my particular formulation of 'the Rationalist model' was specifically designed to signal potential significant points at which it might be challenged by various kinds of sceptics and others. Rather the model is robust for two reasons. First, because it represents a stable set of assumptions that have generally been shared by leading writers on the Law of Evidence in the common law tradition for over two centuries. These assumptions also underpin important attempts to rationalise the Law of Evidence, including the American Federal Rules. Secondly, the ideal type sets the study of Evidence at the outset in its ideological context, that is to say the underlying values involved in the design and operation of legal procedures. Since the main values involved—truth, reason, justice and the public interest—are regularly, perhaps essentially, contested, far from being a naïve, dogmatic, functionalist model, it provides a context for considering controversial issues.

Historically, most of the controversies in Anglo-American evidence scholarship can be accommodated *within* the Rationalist model, because they relate to priorities between truth and other values or represent different views of rationality (for example, Baconians versus Pascalians) or different epistemological theories (for example, correspondence versus coherence theories of truth) or contested political priorities (for example, process values/due process versus social control). These can be seen as debates within the Rationalist Tradition. However, the model identifies a range of potential points of departure from one or more of the assumptions of that tradition, for example, challenges from strong philosophical sceptics, cultural relativists, post-modernists, or those who doubt the desirability, or the feasibility, or the sense in expecting litigation to be centrally concerned with truth, justice or reason.[44]

The Rationalist model provides a starting-point for considering the subject of Evidence in law (EPF) as a coherent whole, including giving a context to the logic of proof. In our culture this has its roots in the empiricist tradition of Sir Francis Bacon, Jeremy Bentham, John Stuart Mill, Stanley Jevons and Henry Sidgwick, a tradition since carried on by figures such as Jonathan Cohen, Stephen Toulmin, Douglas Walton and David Schum.

Can the Law of Evidence be given a coherent framework so that it is not just seen as a rather fragmented and confusing collection of loosely related topics? Some advance has been made by the admirable efforts of Ian Dennis, Adrian Zuckerman, Andrew Ashworth and others to expound the

---

[44] *Ibid* ch 4. On post-modernism, see above n 35. Cf the interesting article by DM Risinger, 'Unsafe Verdicts: the Need for Reformed Standards for Trial and Review of Factual Innocence Claims' (2004) 41 *Houston LR* 1281 (arguing for the special moral position of 'innocence in fact' to be recognised within the Rationalist Tradition).

law on the basis of underlying principles,[45] but I still come across students in both London and the United States whose impression is that the subject consists of a rather arbitrary collection of technical rules. This happens even with those who have studied the Federal Rules, which has a discernible framework; still more so with students who have been exposed to the seeming jumble of piecemeal legislation and case law that we have in England. The problem is that students have not been presented with a coherent overview and generally they have been short-changed on the topic of relevance.[46] Maybe this is because relevance is not a matter of law and to understand relevance one has to understand the logic involved. As Thayer put it, 'the law has no mandamus on the logical faculty'.[47]

There are, no doubt, several ways to present the rules of evidence within a coherent framework. My view, which is quite orthodox, is that our Law of Evidence is based on the Thayerite theory that the rules of evidence are a series of disparate exceptions to a principle of free proof, where free proof means ordinary principles of practical inferential reasoning.[48] One needs to understand the principle before studying the exceptions. That means understanding the logic of proof. Thayer may have exaggerated the importance of the jury in the historical development of the Law of Evidence; he may have taken an unnecessarily narrow view of the Law of Evidence by equating it with exclusionary rules in disputed trials (but he did write about presumptions, burdens of proof and judicial notice); but he was surely right in maintaining that the rules of evidence need to be conceived within a framework of *argumentation*.

From the point of view of pedagogy, the topic of relevance is the obvious bridge between the logic of proof and the rules of evidence.[49] Understanding relevance involves understanding the logic of proof within a framework that treats both the principles of proof and the rules of evidence as belonging to a single, coherent subject. I completely agree with Paul Roberts that the topic of relevance should not be seen as something merely to be introduced in the first week and then ticked off.[50] Rather it should be a constant theme in studying all other topics in the Law of Evidence. In the next section I go further and argue that understanding the logic of proof involves skills as well as knowledge. Studying that topic directly for a substantial period at the start of a course and reinforcing the concepts and

---

[45]   A Zuckerman, *The Principles of Criminal Evidence* (Oxford, OUP, 1989); A Ashworth, *The Criminal Process* (2nd edn, Oxford, OUP, 1998); I Dennis, *The Law of Evidence* (2nd edn, London, Sweet & Maxwell, 2002).

[46]   cf Roberts, above n 12, 306: 'relevance is one of the least explored and most frequently abused concepts in the Law of Evidence'.

[47]   Thayer, above n 35, 314n.

[48]   *RE*, above n 1, ch 6.

[49]   Roberts, above n 12, 306–7.

[50]   *Ibid.*

skills throughout is a more economical and effective way of understanding evidence. Further, it develops some valuable general intellectual skills.

Studying about and Learning How

A clear distinction needs to be drawn between learning about reasoning and learning how to reason. Basic skills of inferential reasoning about questions of fact need to be as much a part of 'legal method' or 'thinking like a lawyer' as basic skills of constructing and criticising arguments about questions of law.

It is one thing to describe, interpret, and analyse the reasoning of judges or counsel; it is quite another to master the skills involved in constructing valid, cogent and appropriate arguments on questions of law. It is one thing to describe Hercules; it is another to emulate him. Most teaching and literature on 'legal reasoning' talks *about* it. Some books and courses on 'legal method' blur the distinction.[51] Similar considerations apply to reasoning about questions of fact. Roberts and Zuckerman's *Criminal Evidence* is the latest in a succession of evidence texts that have moved in the direction of explicitly recognising that the logic of proof (or fact analysis) is an integral part of understanding the subject of evidence in law. But few of these books move beyond giving an account of the kinds of reasoning involved. For example, Roberts and Zuckerman under the heading of 'taking facts seriously', devote over 20 pages to introducing basic concepts of inferential reasoning, probabilities and debates about Bayes' Theorem in legal contexts. It is one thing to consider such debates, it is another to learn how to manipulate the theorem.[52] This section of the book clearly falls within the category of studying about rather than learning how. Given the textbook format, this is understandable and some Evidence teachers may consider it to be a sufficient advance. But the question arises: is it desirable and feasible to go beyond this, to try to help students to master the basic reasoning skills involved?

Paul Roberts explicitly acknowledges that a course on Evidence is a good vehicle for 'inculcating relevant, robust and adaptable (more or less transferable) skills'.[53] I would be more emphatic than Roberts for two reasons: first, mastery of basic skills of inferential reasoning (and, only

---

[51] An exception is S Hanson, *Legal Method and Reasoning* (2nd edn, London, Cavendish, 2003), which deals in detail with reasoning about both law and fact.

[52] On Bayesians and 'Bayesio-skeptics' see *Criminal Evidence*, above n 27, 123–32. The main disagreements are about the conditions for the applicability of Bayes' Theorem rather than its validity. For a less sceptical view, see P Dawid, 'Bayes's Theorem and the Weighing of Evidence by Juries' (2002) *Proceedings of the British Academy* 71 and *Analysis*, above n 7, Appendix I.

[53] Roberts, above n 12, 301.

slightly less so, some basic numeracy skills) is one of the most valuable things that a good liberal education in law can offer. Such mastery is best achieved by direct study rather than osmosis.[54] Secondly, if the principles of proof, ie ordinary practical inferential reasoning, underpin the law of evidence, experience suggests that this is an area where learning how is the quickest and fastest route to understanding.

If inculcating basic skills of inferential reasoning is desirable, how is this best done and how much time is needed? What Wigmore called 'the logic of proof' involves applying general principles of inferential logic in legal contexts. One possibility might be to require students to take a course on logic either as part of their degree or in a pre-law programme (which is a more likely option in the United States). Another possibility might be to use a standard book on logic or critical thinking, supplemented by a few legal examples. Unfortunately, this does not work very well for two reasons: first, most courses and texts on logic deal with formal logic, with an emphasis on deduction, whereas inferential reasoning in law is generally recognised to be inductive, and is thought by some to be better modelled by informal logic.[55] Secondly, there is the point that one of the most important skills in law relates to structuring complex arguments—what is variously referred to as 'fact management' or 'evidence marshalling'. Almost all general books and courses on logic focus on quite limited examples involving only a few propositions. When non-lawyers discuss legal examples they tend to present an over-simple picture of what is involved in an argument about a case as a whole, even in quite straightforward cases.[56]

---

[54]   *LIC*, above n 3, 181–3.

[55]   There are good books *about* informal logic, eg D Walton, *Informal Logic: a Handbook for Critical Argumentation* (New York, CUP, 1989), and *Legal Argumentation and Evidence* (University Park, State University of Pennsylvania Press, 2002); S Toulmin, *The Uses of Argument* (Cambridge, CUP, 1964); but there are few that claim to teach the relevant skills and techniques. Perhaps the best is still M Black, *Critical Thinking: an Introduction to Logic and Scientific Method* (2nd edn, Englewood Cliffs, NJ, Prentice-Hall, 1952). On 'fuzzy logic' see R Yager, S Ovchinnikov, R M Tong and H T Nguyen (eds), *Fuzzy Sets and Applications: Selected Papers by L A Zadeh* (New York, Wiley, 1987) and the criticisms by S Haack, *Deviant Logic, Fuzzy Logic* (Chicago, University of Chicago Press, 1996).

[56]   In England there has been a spate of high profile cases concerning cot deaths. The most prominent case, involving a solicitor (Sally Clark), is a striking example of how even distinguished medical experts can grossly over-simplify what is involved in proving a charge of murder: *R v Clark* [2003] EWCA Crim 1020, discussed in symposium on 'Statistics and Law' in (2005) *Significance* 2(1), J Batt, *Stolen Innocence: the Story of Sally Clark* (London, Ebury Press, 2004), and D Dwyer, 'The Duties of Expert Witnesses of Fact and Opinion: *R v Clark* (Sally)' (2003) 7 *E & P* 264.

The Chart Method and Alternatives

Roberts states: 'one does not have to be a Wigmorean chart methodist to take facts seriously'.[57] That is, no doubt, true, but if 'taking facts seriously' in teaching includes inculcating skills of fact analysis, as Roberts claims, then one needs to be clear about the options. Roberts mentions, as alternative approaches to fact analysis, narrative and story-telling and Bayesian theory. He considers these to be complementary rather than rival approaches.[58] But the literature he cites consists of discussions *about* these methods, rather than vehicles for developing the particular skills involved in constructing arguments about questions of fact. Other alternatives can be found, for example, in the work of the Amsterdam School of Argumentation[59] or some developments of computer applications, for example by Henry Prakken.[60] However, in my view, these approaches tend to over-simplify the nature of argumentation in legal contexts. In any case, they are quite similar in conception to Wigmore's approach. I argue that teaching analysis of evidence as a set of basic skills is a more efficient and economical way into studying the Law of Evidence than most traditional treatments of relevance.[61]

---

[57] Roberts, above n 12, 305.

[58] This is in accord with the views of Schum, above n 10, and *Analysis*, above n 7.

[59] On the Amsterdam School, see E Feteris, *Fundamentals of Legal Argumentation* (Dordrecht, Kluwer Academic, 1999). For contrasting applications of the Amsterdam approach and the chart method to the bizarre 'Ballpoint case' (Netherlands), see the contributions of E Feteris and AM Dingley in M Malsch and J Nijboer (eds), *Complex Cases* (Amsterdam, Thela Thesis, 1999) chs 8 and 9.

[60] H Prakken, 'A Dialectical Model of Assessing Conflicting Arguments in Legal Reasoning (1996) 4 *Artificial Intelligence and Law* 331; 'Analysing Reasoning about Evidence with Formal Models of Argumentation' (2004) 3 *Law, Probability and Risk* 33.

[61] See T Anderson and W Twining, *Analysis of Evidence* (1st edn, Boston, MA, Little, Brown, 1991) Preface and 117–31; W Twining, *Theories of Evidence: Bentham and Wigmore* (Stanford, Stanford University Press, 1986) 179–86. Perhaps the best argument in favour of teaching the chart method is: 'It works'. The authors of *Analysis*, above n 7, Anderson, Schum and Twining, estimate that between them they have accumulated more than 50 years of experience of teaching this approach in several institutions, mostly to law students, but also in Schum's case to intelligence analysts and engineers. This experience tells us that the standard objections do not apply. Almost all our students have found the process of learning the method challenging and hard work (the motto of our courses has been 'tough, but fun'); nevertheless, the vast majority have succeeded in mastering the basic techniques and many have produced work of outstanding quality. Interestingly, the subject has worked best with first year law students in Miami, where it is a popular elective in the second semester. Of those who have gone on to practise law, many have reported that they have found the approach very helpful in practice, some claiming that it was the most useful course that they had in law school. Of course, they do not spend time drawing elaborate charts in straightforward cases, but the basic techniques of evidence marshalling and argument construction can be become part of habits of mind that are invaluable and efficient in handling both simple and complex cases. This is hardly surprising because Wigmore's method is essentially a systematisation of the 'best practice' of good lawyers.

As Roberts recognises, the chart method is only one of several ways of organising data for the purposes of constructing an argument. Chronologies, stories, and the outline method (organising evidence by source as is done in some American trial books) are other standard methods.[62] However, none of these organises the material in the form of a structured argument; typically each is a useful preliminary to constructing an argument, whereas the chart method represents the argument itself. And, if one follows Thayer, argumentation is the context in which the rules of evidence are best understood and used.

The most common complaint about the chart method is that it is too time-consuming and too laborious to be fitted into a standard course on evidence or to be of practical value. This argument has some force, but it needs to be considered in the light of two distinctions.

First is the distinction between mastering a skill and applying it in practice. Learning to master the chart method thoroughly is difficult and time-consuming. But that is true of any other important intellectual skills that may be developed in formal legal education. One can introduce the basics quite quickly, but real skill can only be developed if it is reinforced by repeated exercises and experience. Mastery of a skill includes an understanding of its uses and limitations. Once a skill is mastered, one is in a position to make sensitive judgements as to when to use it informally and when to apply it in its full rigour. Once one has mastered the basic skills, the method inculcates disciplined habits of mind that can be exercised routinely in an informal way.

A second distinction is between macroscopic analysis of the case as a whole and microscopic analysis of selected phases of the argument in the case. First, the method is an extremely useful technique for managing facts, marshalling evidence and structuring arguments in complex cases. Structure is achieved by working backwards from the ultimate conclusion ('the top of the chart') and organising different phases of the argument into discrete, manageable sectors. The key lies in anchoring the arguments about the case as a whole in a defined standpoint, clear questions and precisely formulated hypotheses or conclusions. Plotting the basic structure of an argument is a simplifying device. Even in very complex cases, it is typically not time-consuming, but rather the reverse: it saves time.[63]

---

[62] All four approaches are dealt with explicitly in *Analysis*, above n 7, where they are treated as complementary.

[63] Constructing the top of the chart is problematic if the applicable law is uncertain or there are multiple charges or claims. But such problems arise independently of which method is adopted. The Louise Woodward (Boston Nanny) case, which involved several possible gradations of homicide, is a good vehicle for exploring these difficulties: see *Commonwealth v Woodward* 7 Mass. L. Reptr 449, WL 694119 (Mass. Super); (www.courttv.com/trials/woodward/).

The second aspect involves precise and detailed analysis of important phases of the argument. This 'microscopic analysis' is often perceived as extremely arduous and time-consuming. However, the skilful analyst learns some basic principles of economy, by identifying crucial or important phases within an argument and focusing mainly on these. In advocacy 'going for the jugular' means concentrating one's attack on the weakest point in an opponent's argument or, more positively, building up support for a proposition, which, if established, will ensure success. The chart method of analysis is particularly useful in identifying key propositions in an argument or, in investigation, in guiding enquiry by identifying potentially important propositions that are needed. The standard objection of practitioners is that the pure Wigmorean method is too cumbersome and too time-consuming to be a practical tool for trial preparation.[64] But that refers to attempts to do a complete chart of a whole case. Nearly always, microscopic analysis can be confined to a few key phases in an argument.

Structuring an argument need not be time-consuming—precise microscopic analysis can be selective—but mastering the skills takes time. The problem of how to combine fact analysis and the Law of Evidence in a single coherent whole remains. Clearly there are questions of priorities, but the problem is soluble. The solution that has worked best in my view has been that adopted at the University of Miami Law School: to make Analysis of Evidence a free-standing first year option (two credits). A second possibility is to integrate fact analysis with legal analysis in a skills-oriented legal method course. That integration can lay a foundation that can be reinforced later. If neither of these are viable options, then the principles of proof and the rules of evidence have to be fitted into a single course, with proof/fact analysis taking the place of relevance as the first topic, but with a bit more time allotted to it. Terry Anderson has done this in the first three to four weeks of a four credit standard Evidence course at Miami, and I have done this in a quite different way in the first five to six weeks of the year-long course on Evidence and Proof in the London LLM programme.[65] While some topics in the Law of Evidence may be squeezed,

---

[64] Eg Peter Murphy: 'Despite efforts to portray Wigmore's method as a viable practical tool ... the pure Wigmorean method involves an unnecessary and impracticable expenditure of time from the point of view of the practitioner': *Murphy on Evidence* (7th edn, London, Blackstone Press, 2000) 1n. Compare the more sympathetic treatment in P Murphy, *Evidence, Proof and Facts: a Book of Sources* (Oxford, OUP, 2003) 3. Since we teach *selective* use of the chart method rather than 'the pure Wigmorean method', there is no disagreement. An Australian book, A Palmer, *Proof and Preparation for Trials* (Pyrmont, New South Wales, Law Book Co, 2003) provides an excellent introduction to simplified Wigmorean analysis for practitioners.

[65] Solely by way of illustration (for there are many ways of doing this), let me describe what I do in the first six to seven weeks of my part of the London LLM course (involving one two-hour seminar weekly): the first step is to give the students a list of 20 or so concepts and work through most of these using simple examples from a hypothetical police investigation

the approach is economical because (i) the basic concepts of the logic of proof and the rules of evidence are largely shared; (ii) thinking about evidence in terms of inferential reasoning and argumentation lays a foundation for the Thayerite view of the Law of Evidence as a coherent whole; (iii) after the basic skills have been introduced they can be reinforced throughout the course, if relevance and fact analysis are treated as part of other topics in the Law of Evidence; and (iv) once over an initial hump, most students find this approach both interesting and realistic.

This approach is efficient because, as the students learn the basics of the chart method, they begin to grasp a lot else besides. In about six weeks I aim to have introduced (i) the basic concepts of both the Law of Evidence and the logic of proof; (ii) the underlying theory of the chart method (including comparison with chronological tables, stories and the outline method); (iii) a detailed application of each element of the seven step protocol to a complex *cause célèbre*; and (iv) the Thayerite conception and overview of the rules of evidence[66] and the relationship between the principles of proof and the rules of admissibility.[67]

(see *Analysis*, above n 7, 40–5 and 'Two Murders', 10), illustrating them with very simple pictures using only squares and circles as symbols. It takes about three classroom hours to elucidate, illustrate and discuss the most important concepts. Relevance, of course, is central. It is first elucidated by distinguishing it from materiality, admissibility, weight and credibility. It is further elucidated in relation to background generalisations, chains of inferences, convergence, corroboration and—a bit more sophisticated—Jonathan Cohen's problem of conjunction in relation to the case as a whole. Meanwhile the students have read the engaging story, 'The Nine Mile Walk' (*Analysis*, above n 7, 11–18), which illustrates a number of points, including the significance of abduction and imaginative reasoning. We then move directly on to the chart method, presented in outline, systematised in a seven-step protocol, and illustrated by the same murder investigation. The best way to learn the method is by doing, so during the first six weeks the students are set three written exercises of ascending difficulty, one or two of which are done in law firms. We usually spend up to three weeks in class working through the seven step procedure systematically in relation to *R v Bywaters and Thompson* (Schum uses *Sacco and Vanzetti*, Anderson the hypothetical cases of Abel and Archer and one or two US Supreme Court cases). Later the introductory lessons are reinforced by feedback discussions of the exercises, mini-trials and one or two sessions on the relationship between the principles of proof and the law of evidence. The time-consuming part for the students is a major exercise: a full-scale analysis of a complex case (but involving selective microscopic analysis) done out of class. This counts for 35 per cent of the assessment for the full course. It does not have to be handed in until the end of the year, after a day-long workshop in June ('Wigmore Day'). In my eight week section I usually find time to deal with stories, generalisations and standards for decision. A further three to four weeks are devoted to probabilities and proof (taught by Prof Philip Dawid). In an undergraduate course one would not expect students to reach such a high standard in respect of the chart method and something (perhaps the statistics part) might have to be sacrificed. In an intensive one-week mini-course at the University of Puerto Rico in 2004, the students grasped the basics but needed more time for doing exercises and for other reinforcement.

[66]   *RE*, above n 1, ch 6.

[67]   In the new edition of *Analysis*, above n 7, much more emphasis is placed on this last point throughout the book, and ch 11 is devoted to 'Principles of Proof and the Law of Evidence'.

To sum up: understanding the logic of proof is a precondition to understanding the subject of Evidence in law; understanding logic is best developed by a combination of theory and practice; *mastering* the methods of analysis involved in the chart method is laborious and time-consuming, learning the basics is less so. Despite its image, the chart method used intelligently and selectively is an efficient way of dealing with complex arguments about questions of fact and provides a foundation and a context for understanding and using the rules of evidence.

EVIDENCE AS AN EMERGING INTERDISCIPLINARY FIELD: SOME IMPLICATIONS FOR LAW

Perhaps the most important development regarding Evidence in the past 10 years or so has been the emergence of Evidence as a distinct multidisciplinary field with a high public profile.[68] A number of largely unrelated occurrences have contributed to this: DNA analysis and advances in forensic science were followed by the heightened profile of forensic scientists in fiction and on television. Dope testing of athletes, authentication of art works and problems of proving genocide regularly feature in the news. Among historians, Simon Schama and others stirred up controversy about the relationship between narrative and evidence.[69] Tragic events in Eastern Europe, Rwanda, South Africa and Latin America have stimulated an enormous interest in 'memory', not only because of Truth and Reconciliation Commissions and international criminal tribunals, but also in a range of academic disciplines.[70] The 'narrative turn' has extended beyond obvious disciplines, such as history, anthropology and theology, to less obvious ones such as philosophy of science, geography and economics.[71] In the 1980s, 'evidence-based medicine' and 'evidence-based policy' became fashionable in certain quarters, not without controversy. My colleague at UCL, Trisha Greenhalgh, having published a best-selling student text on evidence-based medicine, followed it up with a book entitled *Narrative Based Medicine*.[72] There are even signs of a Medicine-and-Literature

---

[68] For a longer discussion see *RE*, above n 1, ch 15.

[69] Eg, S Schama, *Dead Certainties* (New York, Knopf, 1991).

[70] Eg, C Nino, *Radical Evil on Trial* (New Haven, Yale University Press, 1996); A Krog, above n 26; I Amadiume and A An Na'im (eds), *The Politics of Memory, Truth, Healing, and Social Justice* (London, Zed Books, 2000).

[71] C Nash (ed), *Narrative and Culture* (London, Routledge, 1986).

[72] T Greenhalgh, *How to Read a Paper: the Basics of Evidence Based Medicine* (2nd edn, London, BMJ Books, 2001); T Greenhalgh and B Hurwitz (eds), *Narrative Based Medicine* (London, BMJ Books, 1998). See also T Greenhalgh, *What Seems to be the Trouble? Stories in Illness and Healthcare* (London, Radcliffe Publishing, 2006).

Movement analogous to that in law and literature.[73] Of course, evidence has been headline news in relation to Iraq: the weapons inspections, Colin Powell's presentation to the Security Council, the question of links with Al Qaeda, the search for 'weapons of mass destruction', the 'dodgy dossiers' and, in Britain, the Hutton and Butler enquiries were all centrally concerned with evidentiary issues.[74] There are many other examples.

Undoubtedly the most influential development has been the fall-out from September 11, 2001. A common judgement has been that the intelligence services had enough information to anticipate the event, but lacked the capability to analyse it and 'to connect the dots'. As a consequence, the US intelligence services are being reorganised, billions are being invested in new computer systems and programmes (much of it wasted in my view), and modest efforts have been made to increase the analytical component in the training of intelligence analysts.[75] An article in the *New Yorker* in February 2003 reported Donald Rumsfeld, George Tenet and others concerned with making intelligence analysis more analytical using terms and spouting aphorisms that can be traced back directly or indirectly to Wigmore and Schum.[76]

During the same period there have been developments in academic disciplines that have paralleled or responded to these stimuli. Not surprisingly, there is now a movement to draw all of these disparate elements together into a single, coherent multidisciplinary field. Pre-eminent among these efforts has been the work of David Schum, whose *Evidential Foundations of Probabilistic Reasoning* is still the best place to begin.[77] In Britain, the Joseph Bell Institute in Edinburgh, the Darwin lectures in

---

[73] Greenhalgh and Hurwitz (1998), above n 72, 273–8; cf KM Hunter, *Doctors' Stories* (Princeton, Princeton University Press, 1991).

[74] See WG Runciman (ed), *Hutton and Butler: Lifting the Lid on the Workings of Power* (Oxford, OUP, 2004) (discussing the two main British Reports).

[75] There is a massive literature. A good starting-point is the very readable *The 9/11 Commission Report* (New York, Norton, 2004).

[76] Jeffrey Goldberg, 'The Unknown: the CIA and the Pentagon take on Al Qaeda and Iraq', *The New Yorker*, 10 February 2003, 40–7. The starting-point was a judgment that 'American intelligence agencies did not possess the analytic depth or the right methods of analysis accurately to assess [possible threats]'. My reaction was: 'The diagnosis and the prescriptions were expressed largely in terms that are familiar to students of evidence and inference: the dangers of hypothesis-driven enquiries; the need to distinguish between constructing a hypothesis and testing it against the available data; the different problems that arise from a surfeit of information and absence of evidence; the difference between ambiguity and incompleteness; the value of alternative interpretations of ambiguous evidence; the dangers of 'mirror imaging', that is 'projecting of American values and beliefs onto America's adversaries and rivals'; a tendency to confuse the unfamiliar with the improbable; the relationship between calculus of risk and thresholds of credibility; the likelihood of political bias entering into judgements where the situation is uncertain' (*RE*, above n 1, 437).

[77] Schum, above n 10; *Evidence and Inference*, above n 14, was a modest attempt to advance Schum's agenda.

Cambridge in 2004[78] and the major programmes on Evidence funded by the Leverhulme Foundation and ESRC at the London School of Economics and University College London are indicative of the vitality of the efforts to develop a genuinely multidisciplinary field.[79]

Clearly, law has something to contribute to and a lot to learn from these developments.[80] In the present context, the question arises: what might be their significance for courses on Evidence in law schools? During the twentieth century Evidence scholarship was open to a variety of influences from other disciplines—forensic science, forensic psychology, statistics, logic, narrative theory, artificial intelligence, complexity theory and computer applications are familiar examples.[81] This well-established tradition of interdisciplinary work has fed into teaching. The development of a distinct *multidisciplinary* field promises at the very least to raise some profound questions about the transferability of ideas about evidence across disciplines, cultures and different practical contexts. It will also greatly broaden the range of cases, concrete examples and issues that may be worthy of attention by lawyers.

Perhaps the central theoretical question should be: how far can we generalise about evidence and inferential reasoning across disciplines, contexts and types of enquiry? If so, more specific issues that need to be addressed include:

(1) Are there universal principles of reasoning from evidence?
(2) What counts as 'evidence' has varied across time, language, cultures, practical contexts and academic disciplines. Is it possible to construct an analytic concept or framework of concepts that transcends these various contexts?
(3) Can a substance-blind approach to evidence (Schum) also be context-blind?
(4) What is the relationship between narrative and reasoning in the context of argumentation? To what extent does that relationship vary according to disciplinary and practical contexts? What exactly is meant by the claim that stories help us 'to make sense of the world'? What can narrative legitimately achieve that reasoning cannot?
(5) To what extent and in what respects can concepts and methods developed in one discipline or practical environment be applied, with or without modification, to other disciplines and contexts?

---

[78] K Tybjerg, KJ Swenson-Wright and A Bell (eds), *Evidence* (Cambridge, CUP, 2007).

[79] See www.casa.ucl.ac.uk/; http://www.lse.ac.uk/collections/economicHistory/Research/How%20Well%20do%20facts%20travel.htm

[80] On the limitations of law in this context, see 'Evidence as a Multi-Disciplinary Subject' in *RE*, above n 1, 446–8.

[81] Cf the classic formulation by J Michael, *Elements of Legal Controversy* (Brooklyn, Foundation Press, 1948), cited in *RE*, above n 1, 14–15.

(6) What are the uses, limitations and dangers of formal representations of inferential arguments (Bayes' nets, Wigmore charts, etc)?

(7) What are the uses and limitations of evidence-based approaches to medicine, policy or other activities?

(8) What can reasonably be expected of computers and artificial intelligence as aids to inferential reasoning?

(9) What general lessons can be learned from recent developments in handling evidence in police investigation, intelligence analysis, forensic science and other practical operations?

(10) To what extent should study of evidence be driven by questions about how people actually deal with evidence rather than how they should think and act in relation to it?

Much of the work that is going on is of an applied nature. These are exciting but relatively recent developments. A rich range of seemingly disparate activities is burgeoning. In University College London, for example, individuals from over 20 departments are involved in the Leverhulme-ESRC programme, which began in January 2004. In addition to specific projects on formal tools for handling evidence, enquiry and detection, historical evidence, human attitudes to evidence (psychology), geography, economics, the history and philosophy of science and primary healthcare, there are three active multidisciplinary groups on causality, narrative and prediction, and a case study of interdisciplinarity.[82] Other multidisciplinary projects are proliferating elsewhere in several countries.

It may be some time before their implications for teaching Evidence in law schools become apparent. But Evidence teachers would do well to watch this space. By establishing links with other disciplines, the range of accessible ideas and concrete examples is becoming much richer. Of course, non-legal and quasi-legal examples have been used in Evidence teaching in the past: the judgment of Solomon, the Rosetta Stone, famous historical puzzles and mysteries and Sherlock Holmes have featured in Evidence courses and texts. This stock of examples that might be used in teaching is rapidly increasing. For example, in the aftermath of 9/11 David Schum has designed a series of scenarios for training intelligence analysts—some frighteningly realistic—that can be used in teaching law students about inferential reasoning and fact management. Such non-legal examples, in addition to being interesting in themselves, reinforce the message that the study of evidence in law is fundamentally and inescapably related to the study of evidence generally.

---

[82] For details, see above n 79.

3

A Principled Approach to Relevance: the Cheshire Cat in Canada

INTRODUCTION

RELEVANCE IS A basic yet relatively neglected concept in Canadian case law and evidence scholarship. It seems to be an obvious requirement of fairness—even of rationality—that fact determination be based only on information which has some legitimate connection to a material issue. Inferences should not be drawn from irrelevant information. Thus it is possible to say that, generally, while a witness' prior inconsistent statements are relevant to her credibility, her race is not. However, it would be a challenge to provide fact-finders, such as judges, administrative decision-makers or students of the law of evidence more generally, with an authoritative analytical structure including a legal test of how to distinguish relevant from irrelevant information. This raises a question of whether basic decisions about relevance are governed by the law of evidence and thus by the rule of law at all.

This chapter is an attempt to answer that question. Using examples drawn from English-speaking Canada, it considers the possibility of developing a principled approach to relevance, one in tune with Canadian constitutional values of equality and fairness.[1] As a preliminary, the chapter provides a brief survey of the current state of Canadian evidence

* The author wishes to thank Jesse Nyman and Sam de Groot for their assistance as well as Sydney Lederman J, and Professors Shi-Ling Hsu, Marilyn MacCrimmon, Ken MacCrimmon, Paul Roberts and Moin Yahya for their helpful comments on drafts. Errors and opinions are of course my own.

[1] My focus is on consideration of irrelevant evidence by fact-finders rather than on whether judges should exclude irrelevant evidence. Though see *Re Application under s 83.28 of the Criminal Code* (2004) 21 CR (6th) 82, at 106, for the view that '[r]elevance is a common law rule'. Further, '[r]elevance is a matter to be decided by the judge as a question of law': *R v Dimitrov* (2003) 18 CR (6th) 36 (Ont CA), at 52. Most legal fact-finding does not

law. Attention to the concept of relevance and inferential reasoning is to some extent influenced by perspectives on the law of evidence in general. The question 'What is the Law of Evidence?' was asked by William Twining, in his collection of exploratory essays, *Rethinking Evidence*.[2] As part of his argument that the exceptions to the principle of free proof had been given an exaggerated importance, Twining suggested that the law of evidence resembles the Cheshire Cat in *Alice in Wonderland*:[3]

> who keeps appearing and disappearing and fading away, so that sometimes one could see the whole body, sometimes only a head, sometimes only a vague outline and sometimes nothing at all, so that Alice was never sure whether or not he was there or, indeed, whether he existed at all.[4]

The challenges confronting any attempt to analyse this legal Cheshire Cat are obvious. In what ways, if any, does Anglo-Canadian law actually discipline determinations of relevance and the inferential process in its many different legal contexts?[5] The concept of relevance is found where the Cat (or law of evidence) is least visible.

'Sometimes Nothing at All'

The most familiar part of the subject of Evidence is the extensive legal doctrine relating to rules of procedure (such as competence and the examination of witnesses) and rules of exclusion (such as hearsay).[6] The other part of the subject concerns the inferential process, including determinations of relevance and weight. It is trite to say that the process of fact determination is a human one, governed by fact-finders' sense of logic, common sense and human experience. There is some legal guidance of this

---

involve juries, and even where juries are involved it is not self-evident that they should not be trusted to filter out irrelevant information not caught by any other rule. However, cases can arise where there are costs to the admission of irrelevant evidence, in terms of efficiency and the interests of witnesses, including accused persons. I draw on my own experience of one case where a witness was asked whether she was a lesbian, a question she was not required to answer. For some notes on inadmissibility and non-consideration of irrelevant evidence, see P Tillers, 'Rethinking Relevance' http://tillers.net/home.html, accessed 16 August 2007.

[2] W Twining, *Rethinking Evidence* (Cambridge, MA, Blackwell, 1990) 178.

[3] L Carroll, *Alice in Wonderland* (Vancouver, Douglas & McIntyre, 1993). Canadian admiration of the Cheshire Cat metaphor is not, of course, original to this chapter. See eg, DA Rollie Thompson, 'The Cheshire Cat, or Just his Smile? Evidence Law in Child Protection' (2003) 21 *Child and Family Law Quarterly* 319.

[4] *Ibid* 197.

[5] See C Boyle and M MacCrimmon, 'To Serve the Cause of Justice: Disciplining Fact Determination' (2001) 20 *Windsor Yearbook of Access to Justice* 55.

[6] Wigmore divided the subject of Judicial Evidence into two parts: the Principles (or Science) of Proof, involving 'Logic, Psychology and General Experience' and the Trial Rules of Evidence. Now see generally JH Wigmore, *Evidence in Trials at Common Law*, Chadbourn rev (Boston and Toronto, Little Brown & Co, 1979) and *The Science of Judicial Proof* (3rd edn, Boston, Little, Brown & Co, 1937).

process: the doctrines of judicial impartiality, judicial notice, constitutional norms such as those relating to privacy and equality, legislation governing inferences and precedent about particular inferences, either forbidding them altogether or structuring their application. However, in much fact determination, there is very little Cat at all.

One example, of particular interest in the Canadian context, should be sufficient for this introduction. The test for Aboriginal title requires proof of pre-sovereignty occupation and the continuation of that occupation to present times. In two leading cases, *R v Van der Peet*[7] and *Delgamuukw v British Columbia*[8], the Supreme Court of Canada recognised the difficulties inherent in demonstrating continuity between current Aboriginal activities and pre-contact practices, customs and traditions of Aboriginal societies. Is evidence of present practices, customs and traditions relevant to show pre-contact occupation of land? The trial judge in *Delgamuukw* thought not. He held that the oral history evidence of current practices and even of the practices of immediate ancestors going back 100 years could not demonstrate the requisite continuity between present occupation and past occupation in order to ground a claim for Aboriginal title. Effectively, he held that there was no inferential link between post-contact and pre-contact practices. On appeal, the Supreme Court held that evidence of post-contact practices, customs and traditions is relevant to prove pre-contact practices, customs and traditions. In commenting on the trial judge's failure to find a link between post- and pre-contact practices based on oral history, the court stated that even 'if oral history cannot conclusively establish pre-sovereignty ... occupation of land, it may still be *relevant* to demonstrate that current occupation has its origins prior to sovereignty'.[9] In this particular instance, the ultimate decision-maker had the last word, but is there a way in which that last word can be seen as flowing from law governing how we find facts? This will be discussed below.

---

[7] [1996] 2 SCR 507.

[8] [1997] 3 SCR 1010.

[9] *Ibid* [101]. The court's summary of the trial court's decision ((1991), 79 DLR (4th) 185) can be found at [15]–[30]. Difficulty in mapping the field of Evidence is especially acute with respect to Aboriginal issues. Courts must 'approach the rules of evidence, and interpret the evidence that exists, with a consciousness of the special nature of aboriginal claims' (*Van der Peet*, above n 7, [68]). This approach was reaffirmed in *Delgamuukw*, above n 8. The majority stated, at [81]–[82]: 'The justification for this special approach can be found in the nature of aboriginal rights themselves ... Those rights are aimed at the reconciliation of the prior occupation of North America by distinctive aboriginal societies with the assertion of Crown sovereignty over Canadian territory ... In other words aboriginal rights are truly *sui generis*, and demand a unique approach to the treatment of evidence, which accords due weight to the perspective of aboriginal peoples'.

'A Vague Outline'

The reasoning of adjudicative fact-finders is governed by the constitutional norms, including equality, guaranteed by the Canadian Charter of Rights and Freedoms.[10] Equality rights can be found in s 15:

> (1) Every individual is equal before and under the law and has the right to the equal protection and equal benefit of the law without discrimination and, in particular, without discrimination based on race, national or ethnic origin, colour, religion, sex, age or mental or physical disability.

> (2)Subsection (1) does not preclude any law, program or activity that has as its object the amelioration of conditions of disadvantaged individuals or groups including those that are disadvantaged because of race, national or ethnic origin, colour, religion, sex, age or mental or physical disability.

The jurisprudence on ensuring that evidential practices are egalitarian has now developed to the point where it can be seen in vague outline, if one looks hard enough.

In terms of the Charter itself, its extensive constitutional protections for suspects and accused persons can be seen as an effort to achieve some balance between them and the state.[11] Parliament has explicitly grounded statutory provisions relating to the admissibility of sexual history evidence and the production of the private records of sexual assault complainants in Charter-based equality and fair trial rights. For instance, the Preamble to Bill C-49[12] states:

> Whereas the Parliament of Canada is gravely concerned about the incidence of sexual violence and abuse in Canadian society and, in particular, the prevalence of sexual assault against women and children;

> Whereas the Parliament of Canada intends to promote and help to ensure the full protection of the rights guaranteed under section 7 [fundamental justice] and section 15 [equality] of the Canadian Charter of Rights and Freedoms...[13]

More recently, the Preamble to Bill C-46[14] states:

---

[10]   Constitution Act, 1982, Canada Act 1982 (UK), RSC 1985, c C-11, App 11, No 44, as amended (the Charter).

[11]   Charter, ss 7–14.

[12]   An Act to amend the Criminal Code (Sexual Assault), SC 1992, c 38, adding ss 276–277 to the Criminal Code, RSC 1985, c C-46 (the Criminal Code).

[13]   For discussion of this legislation, see C Boyle and M MacCrimmon, 'The Constitutionality of Bill C-49: Analysing Sexual Assault as if Equality Really Mattered' (1998) 4 *Criminal Law Quarterly* 198.

[14]   An Act to amend the Criminal Code (Production of Records in Sexual Offence Proceedings), SC 2002, c 13, adding ss 278.2–278.9 to the Criminal Code. These sections were enacted by Parliament in reaction to the decision in *R v O'Connor* [1995] 4 SCR 411. *O'Connor* involved a defendant's request for disclosure of sexual assault complainants' school and therapeutic records. The issue required the court to fashion a test and procedure for compelling disclosure of records in the hands of third parties; particularly in the context of

Whereas the Parliament of Canada recognizes that violence has a particularly disadvantageous impact on the equal participation of women and children in society and on the rights of women and children to security of the person, privacy and equal benefit of the law as guaranteed by sections 7, 8, 15 and 28 of the Canadian Charter of Rights and Freedoms.

Controls on the production of private records to the defence were upheld as constitutional in *R v Mills*,[15] in part because of their role in promoting equality. Thus, 'an appreciation of the equality dimensions of records production in cases concerning sexual violence highlights the need to balance privacy and full answer and defence in a manner that fully respects the privacy interests of complainants'.[16]

Other legislative initiatives aimed at the protection of vulnerable witnesses can be seen as grounded in equality. Thus, in *R v DOL*,[17] the Supreme Court upheld a provision permitting the use of videotaped accounts of child complainants in sexual assault cases, as a response to 'the power and dominance which adults ... have over children. Accordingly, s 715.1 [of the Criminal Code] is designed to accommodate the needs and to safeguard the interests of young victims of ... sexual abuse'.[18]

The common law of evidence, too, is evolving with equality explicitly in mind. For instance, *R v Salituro*[19] developed an exception to the common law rule of spousal incompetence. Irreconcilably-separated spouses were made competent witnesses for the prosecution, the court taking the view that the old rule reflected 'a view of the role of women which is no longer

---

a sexual assault complaint. The majority fashioned a test whereby a judge had only to be convinced of a low threshold of 'likely relevance' before examining the records in order to determine what, if anything, should be disclosed. The majority also held that the effect of disclosure on the trial process was not a factor in ordering disclosure and that there were other avenues available to a judge to ensure that disclosure did not frustrate society's interest in the reporting of sexual assaults. The justices dissenting on this issue were of the view that a more onerous burden of showing relevance rested upon the accused before a judge would be required to examine a third party record. It would be insufficient to make bare assertions that were unsupported. They were also of the opinion that in ordering disclosure, the trial judge had to balance the accused's right to full answer and defence with the complainant's rights of privacy and equality. Further, the probative value of the record had to outweigh the prejudicial effect of disclosure on the proper administration of justice and the harm to the privacy rights of the witness. Finally, they set out a list of seven factors, including society's interest in the reporting of sexual assaults. Sections 278.2–278.9 of the Criminal Code essentially codified the dissenting opinion in *O'Connor*, except that the language appeared to create an even higher standard of 'likely relevance' in that a defendant was unable to meet the burden solely on the basis of 11 enumerated assertions. However, in *R v Mills* [1999] 3 SCR 668, the Supreme Court of Canada upheld the constitutionality of the sections.

[15] *Ibid.*
[16] *Ibid* [91].
[17] [1993] 4 SCR 419.
[18] *Ibid* [1]. See also, with respect to screens, *R v Levogiannis* [1993] 4 SCR 475.
[19] [1991] 3 SCR 654.

compatible with the importance now given to sexual equality ... [P]reserving the rule would be contrary to this Court's duty to see that the common law develops in accordance with the values of the Charter'.[20]

Similar attention to egalitarian reasoning can be seen occasionally in the application as well as the development of doctrine. For instance, in *R v Diu*,[21] the trial judge had said of the accused in a criminal case that the Vietnamese 'are notoriously hostile to giving statements to the police' and 'I'm sure in Vietnam there's no oath, so it's foreign to them'. A unanimous Court of Appeal stated:

> To the extent that these comments are indicative of the adoption of a racial stereotype as to the attitudes of persons of Vietnamese origin to the police or to telling the truth, they are plainly unacceptable.[22]

As mentioned above, when it comes to Aboriginal people, the evidence case law shows some awareness of their distinctive social location. However, it would be optimistic to say that attention to equality provides us with anything other than a vague outline. We are at an early stage in testing our fact-finding methods, the policies underlying legal doctrine and our inferences against a standard of equality. Nevertheless, it may be possible to draw on this vague outline to develop a more substantial legal basis for drawing factual inferences.

'Sometimes One Could See the Whole Body, Sometimes Only a Head'

Established legal doctrine relating to exclusionary rules, such as hearsay and privilege, seems to be the obvious place to look for the body of the Cat. Much of a traditional course on the Canadian law of evidence is devoted to such rules, in spite of Twining's argument that they are given 'exaggerated importance'.[23] Recent developments in Canada suggest, however, that even here we cannot expect to see the whole Cat. The Supreme Court has emphasised that the traditional exclusionary rules should be interpreted, not as sharp rules, but as broad principles to be interpreted in the light of the underlying policy. As the leading Canadian textbook puts it:

> The [Supreme] Court [of Canada] has abandoned the formerly fossilized structure which Estey J. once described in *Graat v R* [24] as a 'large number of cumbersome rules, with exclusions, and exceptions to the exclusions and

---

[20]   *Ibid* [38].
[21]   (2000) 144 CCC(3d) 481 (Ont CA).
[22]   *Ibid* [78].
[23]   Above n 2, 179.
[24]   [1982] 2 SCR 819, 835.

exceptions to the exceptions', and has adopted a flexible, principled case by case approach in which the competing policy interests at stake are closely weighed in the context of the circumstances of a particular case.[25]

The most striking example is what is termed the principled approach to hearsay: striking in part because of the contrast between recent legal history in Canada and in England and Wales. In 1965, the House of Lords in *Myers v DPP*[26] held that it would no longer create exceptions to the hearsay rule: creating exceptions was a legislative task, one Parliament promptly undertook.[27] In Canada, the same period has seen major judicial reform. In 1970, in *Ares v Venner*[28] the Supreme Court of Canada started down the road of analysis based on the principles of reliability and fairness, a road still being travelled today.[29]

Similar developments have taken place with respect to other doctrines, for instance replacing privilege,[30] corroboration,[31] and possibly expert opinion,[32] rules with a more flexible approach. A principled approach may be anticipated with respect to other doctrines, such as those relating to prior consistent statements or collateral facts. Detailed analysis of such developments is beyond the scope of this chapter. However, if one considers such reforms, taken in the aggregate, as a move in the direction of indeterminacy, then it is only the head of the Cheshire Cat (namely the principles) that is visible. Indeterminacy leaves room for uneven effects. Thus, there is some concern that enthusiasm for the principled approach generates more appeals and may result in the admission of more prosecution than defence evidence.[33] Nevertheless, even if there is a cost in terms of reduced visibility of the law in such developments, a principled approach may be of some assistance when one turns to the largely uncharted area of determining relevance.

---

[25]   J Sopinka, SN Lederman and AW Bryant, *The Law of Evidence in Canada* (2nd edn, Toronto and Vancouver, Butterworths, 1999) 6.

[26]   [1965] AC 1001 (HL).

[27]   For the subsequent history in the United Kingdom, see P Roberts and A Zuckerman, *Criminal Evidence* (Oxford, OUP, 2004) ch 12, particularly paras 12.5 and 12.6.

[28]   [1970] SCR 608.

[29]   For example, hearsay exceptions are now subject to challenge as being inconsistent with the principled approach: see *R v Starr* [2000] 2 SCR 144.

[30]   See *Slavutych v Baker* [1976] 1 SCR 254.

[31]   See *R v Vetrovic* [1982] 1 SCR 811, though interestingly there may be a move back to categories with the concern about jailhouse informers. See eg, F Kaufman, *Report of the Kaufman Commission on Proceedings Involving Guy Paul Morin* (Ontario, Ministry of the Attorney General, 1998).

[32]   See *R v Mohan* [1994] 2 SCR 9.

[33]   For discussion of the development of the principled approach to hearsay in Canada and of systemic concerns, see DA Rollie Thompson, 'The Supreme Court Goes Hunting and Nearly Catches a Hearsay Woozle' (1995) 37 CR (4th) 282.

RELEVANCE AND DRAWING FACTUAL INFERENCES

We have seen that the modern law of evidence in Canada leaves much of the fact-finding process regulated by broad principles rather than strict rules. This disappearing Cheshire Cat leaves a broad space where the process of drawing inferences, and hence underlying principles of relevance, are important. My argument here is that fact-finders may be assisted by consideration of relevance in three stages, involving the following questions:

(1) Is there any law governing the particular information in question?
(2) If there is no law on the particular issue, is there a general, legal test of relevance?
(3) What assumptions am I making with respect to relevance and are they defensible?

While (1) is a separate question, efficiently asked first, I will suggest below that (2) and (3) are interconnected.

Is There Any Law Governing the Particular Information in Question?

At times there are legal rules which govern the drawing of particular inferences. These are not only important in their own right, but may supply helpful analogies. One familiar example, which takes legislative form in Canada, is that of sexual history evidence in sexual assault trials. Section 276 of the Criminal Code states:

> [E]vidence that the complainant has engaged in sexual activity, whether with the accused or any other person, is not admissible to support an inference that, by reason of the sexual nature of that activity, the complainant
>
> (a) is more likely to have consented to the sexual activity that forms the subject-matter of the charge; or
>
> (b) is less worthy of belief.

Another example is that it is permissible, under the Canada Evidence Act, to take the criminal record of a witness into account in assessing credibility.[34]

---

[34] Canada Evidence Act, RSC 1985, c C-5, s 12. With respect to an accused witness, the judge has a discretion to exclude all or part of the criminal record: *Corbett v The Queen* [1988] 1 SCR 670.

Legislation governing the drawing of inferences is relatively uncommon, but further examples can be found in case law. There is, of course, the well-worn example of an inference of intention from conduct. Here are others.[35]

(1) '[T]he simple fact is that knowledge [of the privilege against self-incrimination] does not yield an inference in relation to truthfulness one way or the other' and is therefore irrelevant.[36]
(2) Evidence that a person accused of drug importing and possessing cocaine associated with drug importers has been held to be irrelevant.[37]
(3) The failure of an accused to testify may weaken his alibi.[38]
(4) The inability of children to recount precise details 'does not mean that they have misconceived what happened to them and who did it'.[39]
(5) The accused's opinion as to why a Crown witness would lie is irrelevant.[40]

Sometimes the issue of whether an appropriate inference can be drawn is seen as depending on context. Questions that have arisen in Canada include:

(a) is evidence of poverty relevant to motive to commit profit-oriented crime?[41]
(b) is the fact that a person did not go to the police with a story of extortion he now invokes as a defence relevant to his credibility?[42]
(c) is the fact that a complainant in a sexual assault trial has not written about the alleged assault in her diary relevant to her credibility?[43]

Sometimes, of course, cases may appear to be wrongly decided, and thus of weak precedential value (though that begs the question of how error is legally assessed). An example may be *Trembliuk v Canada (Minister of*

---

[35] It appears that there may be more developed precedents in the United Kingdom. See generally the discussion of 'The New Forensic Reasoning Rules' in Roberts and Zuckerman, above n 27, 482–90. For instance, they discuss '*Lucas*' directions, relating to when negative inferences can be drawn from exculpatory lies, the 'probative boot-strapping' involved in concluding that an accused's testimony was false and using that conclusion as evidence of guilt, and variations on the theme of jumping to premature conclusions.

[36] *R v Noël* [2002] 3 SCR 433, [60].

[37] *R v Ejiofor* (2002) 5 CR (6th) 197 (Ont CA).

[38] *Vézeau v R* [1977] 2 SCR 277. But this is exceptional. On the general issue of drawing an inference from, and judicial comment on, the exercise of the accused's right not to testify, see *R v Noble* [1997] 1 SCR 874.

[39] *R v B(G)* [1990] 2 SCR 30, 55.

[40] See eg, *R v Ellard* (2003) 10 CR (6th) 189 (BCCA), [21].

[41] *R v Mensah* (2003) 9 CR (6th) 339, leave to appeal denied, [2003] SCCA No 207.

[42] See *R v W(MC)* (2002) 3 CR (6th) 64 (BCCA) and *R v Turcotte* [2005] 2 SCR 519. This issue is discussed below.

[43] *R v Shearing* [2002] 3 SCR 33. This issue is discussed below.

Citizenship and Immigration).[44] This case involved an application for judicial review of a decision of the Immigration and Refugee Board rejecting the applicant's claim for refugee status. The applicant was a young man from Ukraine who claimed to be fleeing persecution based on the fact that he was homosexual. The Board found his evidence about his sexual orientation implausible, pointing to his failure to seek out the gay community in Toronto, ignorance about gay pride day and attendance at a Roman Catholic school. The application for judicial review was successful because the Board had applied a 'stereotypical view of the life-style and preoccupations of homosexual persons'.[45] The inferences 'simply cannot be assumed to be appropriate to all persons of homosexual orientation'.[46]

It could be argued that the Federal Court was simply wrong in terms of legal doctrine, since the test of relevance, discussed below, should not require an invariable connection in order for information to form the basis of an inference. But, that point aside, we lack legal doctrine governing inferences about sexual orientation. How does one draw the line between permissible and impermissible inferences? This is a significant issue. Gay people can hardly be expected to carry some sort of stamp on their foreheads, or to pass a standard test of authenticity. By what standard, then, can we assess the validity of inferences such as the one at issue in *Trembliuk?* This brings us to whether there is a test, recognised by law, for the relevance of information in areas not governed by established rules.

Is There a General Legal Test of Relevance?

While there are different perspectives on the appropriate approach to relevance, an extensive body of evidence literature discusses the role of logic in structuring permissible inferential links between pieces of information and facts in issue. One possibility is that the law turns to logic for the test of relevance. Indeed, it is not uncommon for courts to invoke the language of logic and probability. For instance, the Supreme Court of Canada has said:

> To be logically relevant, an item of evidence does not have to firmly establish, on any standard, the truth or falsity of a fact in issue. The evidence must simply

---

[44] [2003] FCJ No 1590 (Fed Ct). Compare *Laszlo v Canada (Minister of Citizenship and Immigration)* [2005] FCJ No 561 (Fed Ct), where the court, at [10], characterised a somewhat similar inference as a 'logical plausibility finding that a person belonging to a persecuted minority would be interested in how members of that persecuted minority is treated in his country of refuge'.
[45] *Ibid* [5].
[46] *Ibid* [8].

tend to 'increase or diminish the probability of the existence of a fact in issue'...
As a consequence, there is no minimum probative value required for evidence to
be relevant.[47]

This is consistent with what Tillers has termed the 'orthodox view in
America'. '[T]he modern scholarly consensus favored an extremely narrow
notion of relevancy known as "logical relevancy"... [T]hat evidence is
relevant if it has the *slightest* probative value'.[48]

However, there is a large body of literature, and continuing debate,
about how fact-finders do and should find facts. The quotation from *Arp*
suggests some reliance on probability theory,[49] and indeed analysis of
possible inferences (relating to weight as well as relevance) may be assisted
by attention to probabilistic maxims, such as the following observation by
Friedman: 'The general insight is that evidence may tend to prove a given
hypothesis, even though it is unlikely to arise given that hypothesis, if it is
even less likely to arise given the negation of that hypothesis'.[50]

An ideal piece of information about credibility, for instance, would be
something that always occurs when the witness is telling the truth and
never occurs otherwise.[51] Of course, such ideal pieces of information are
very unusual, or, as with credibility, non-existent. We know that truthful
and reliable witnesses can be argumentative and that witnesses with an
interest in the matter can still tell the truth. We know that people with
criminal records can tell the truth and that people with impeccable
reputations for veracity can lie. Thus, the best we can do is ask whether the
piece of information in question is more likely to occur in relation to
truthful, rather than false, testimony.

Although, unfortunately, we lack the massive amounts of information
about the world that would allow us to be confident about making
probability calculations (a point addressed further below), the general
approach can be helpful in providing a check on what otherwise might
pass for common sense. For example, suppose that a child complaining of
sexual abuse bites her nails:

> [A] doctor might observe that a high proportion of abused children display signs
> of stress such as nail-biting. This will be evidence of abuse if and only if abused

---

[47]   *R v Arp* [1998] 3 SCR 339, at [38], per Cory J writing for the court. For a sense of the
debate in which the SCC here appears to be taking a position, see IH Dennis, *The Law of
Evidence* (2nd edn, London, Sweet & Maxwell, 2002) ch 3.
[48]   Above n 1, 3.
[49]   See IH Dennis, above n 47, 103–22, for a discussion of 'Theories of Factfinding'
including Wigmorean analysis, mathematical models of reasoning, including Bayes' theorem,
and narrative and story-telling.
[50]   See RD Friedman 'Assessing Evidence' (1996) 94 *Michigan L Rev* 1810, 1824. See also
Roberts and Zuckerman, above n 27, 111–32.
[51]   See B Robertson and GA Vignaux, *Interpreting Evidence: Evaluating Forensic Science
in the Courtroom* (Toronto, Wiley, 1995) 12.

children are more likely to bite their nails than other children. If it turned out that abused and non-abused children are equally likely to bite their nails then this observation is useless as evidence of abuse.[52]

Sir Richard Eggleston discussed another example in *Evidence, Proof and Probability*:[53]

James ['Relevancy, Probability and the Law'[54]] came to the conclusion that most people would be unwilling to accept the proposition that men's fixed designs (to kill) are probably carried out, but if the major premiss is expressed in the form 'Men having such a fixed design are more likely to kill than men not having such a fixed design', then most people will accept it.

Before turning to the question of whether this approach does indeed provide us with a legal test of relevance, I want to explore the implications of its use through two examples. The first example suggests that a probabilistic approach is reflected in Canadian law relating to sexual history evidence in sexual assault trials. The second example demonstrates, however, that this focus on probabilities is not consistently applied.

Could an Inference of Consent Logically be Drawn from a Sexual Assault Complainant's History of Sexual Activity?

Section 276(1) of the Criminal Code, quoted above, reflects the common law as expressed by the Supreme Court of Canada in *R v Seaboyer*.[55] In *Seaboyer* the court grounded its approach in 'the basic tenet of relevance which underlies all our rules of evidence',[56] stating that 'nothing is to be received which is not logically probative of some matter requiring to be proved, and everything which is probative should be received, unless its exclusion can be justified on some other ground'.[57] The court then linked its view of sexual history evidence to relevance:

As all counsel on these appeals accepted, the reality in 1991 is that evidence of sexual conduct ... in itself cannot be regarded as logically probative of either the

[52] *Ibid* 13. This is a simple version of the debate over Child Abuse Accommodation Syndrome: see eg, *R v Edwards* (1996) 28 OR (3d) 54 (CA), leave to appeal refused 29 August 1996.
[53] R Eggleston, *Evidence, Proof and Probability* (2nd edn, London, Weidenfeld & Nicolson, 1983) 80.
[54] (1941) 29 *California LR* 689.
[55] Prior to 1991, s 276 barred the use of sexual history evidence with three exceptions. In *R v Seaboyer* [1991] 2 SCR 577, the court struck down this provision as infringing ss 7 and 11(d) of the Charter. In the course of that decision the majority set out an approach to the admissibility of sexual history evidence. In *R v Darrach* [2000] 2 SCR 443, the court upheld the current version of s 276, noting, *ibid* [20], that the current version is in essence a codification of the guidelines in *Seaboyer*.
[56] *Ibid* [36].
[57] *Ibid*.

complainant's credibility or consent [an aspect of the actus reus of offences such as sexual assault or rape]. Although they still may inform the thinking of many, the twin myths which [the former] s 276 sought to eradicate are just that—myths—and have no place in a rational and just system of law. It follows that the old rules which permitted evidence of sexual conduct and condoned invalid inferences from it solely for these purposes have no place in our law.[58]

The issue of whether there is any logical connection between sexual activity and consent continues to be the subject of debate.[59] It is a complex issue. To some extent one's view of the probabilities depends on how one frames the issue. In my view, there has been a tendency to frame the issue in terms of the behaviour of the complainant, thus inviting arguments that there is a logical inference that sexually-active persons are more likely to consent to sexual activity than non-sexually-active persons.[60] However, framing the issue in terms of the behaviour of the accused casts the probabilities in a different light. For example, in arguing against the relevance (in general) of sexual history with the accused himself, I have criticised the inference that 'people who have had consensual sex in the past would not rape their partners'.[61] Far from it being the case that consensual sex with the accused makes rape less likely to have happened, it may in fact make it more probable. There is no obvious common sense in thinking that sexual relations with men decrease the danger of sexual assault.[62] Indeed the view that such sexual relations increase the danger has some statistical support.[63]

---

[58] *Ibid* [90]. Both the current legislation and the common law allow sexual history evidence to be admitted for some purposes.

[59] For a sense of that debate in Canada, see Boyle and MacCrimmon, above n 13. For a contribution to it in the United Kingdom see M Redmayne, 'Myths, Relationships and Coincidences: the New Problems of Sexual History' (2003) 7 *E & P* 75.

[60] See eg, Roberts and Zuckerman, *Criminal Evidence*, above n 27, 275, for the view that previous sexual contact between the complainant and the accused almost invariably has a significant bearing on the factual aspect of consent. The legal framing of a material concept, in this case, consent, can also, of course, have an important influence on the drawing of inferences. In Canada, since *Seaboyer*, consent has been held to be subjective and determined by reference to the complainant's state of mind toward the touching, at the time it occurred. If the complainant's testimony that she did not consent is believed, then the absence of consent has been proved. See *R v Ewanchuk* [1999] 1 SCR 330, [26]–[30].

[61] C Boyle, 'Sexual Assault in Abusive Relationships: Common Sense About Sexual History' (1996) 19 *Dalhousie L J* 223, 245.

[62] There is also no obvious common sense in thinking that women's decisions to avoid sexual relations altogether, as reflected in a vow of chastity, for example, would decrease the probability of sexual assault.

[63] The *Full Report of the Prevalence, Incidence, and Consequences of Violence Against Women* found that 'nearly two-thirds (61.9 percent) of the women who reported being raped since age 18 were raped by a current or former spouse, cohabiting partner, boyfriend, or date. In comparison 21.3 percent were raped by an acquaintance, 16.7 were raped by a stranger, and 6.5 percent were raped by a relative': P Tjaden and N Thoennes, *Full Report of the Prevalence, Incidence, and Consequences of Violence Against Women: Findings from the National Violence Against Women Survey* (Washington, DC, National Institute of Justice,

Given that the Supreme Court in *Seaboyer* held that sexual history is logically irrelevant to consent[64] or credibility, the court's perspective, albeit one presented as focusing on the complainant, finds support in the latter focus on the probability of sexual assault, rather than on the probability of consent. In my view, the outcome of the case is consistent with a common-sense view that sexually-active women are not less likely to be raped than non-sexually-active women, and thus sexual history does not help us to decide whether sexual assault occurred or not.[65] In my view, if a Canadian judge were to say something to the effect that the complainant was a sexually-active woman and not a nun, from which it followed that she was less likely to have been subjected to non-consensual sexual contact, this would not only be overturned on appeal on the basis of legal error, it would rightly be criticised as illogical.

If one takes this approach, *Seaboyer* can be viewed as a case which both adopts a logical assessment of the probabilities as the test of relevance *and* rejects sexual history evidence as logically relevant to the actus reus of sexual assault or the credibility of the complainant. Nevertheless, some might see *Seaboyer* as a case in which the court appears to endorse the test of logical relevance while actually doing something more akin to weighing probative value against potential prejudice. I now turn to case law which more openly raises the issue of an approach to relevance which does not purport merely to assess probabilities. *Trembliuk*, introduced above, provides an example.

Could a Negative Inference about Trembliuk's Credibility Logically be Drawn from his Lack of Knowledge of the Gay Community and its Activities?

If we think in terms of relative probabilities, the question in *Trembliuk* is whether knowledge about the gay community is more consistent with being homosexual than with being heterosexual or vice versa. However unlikely it is that a homosexual refugee claiming asylum in Toronto would know about the local gay community, a negative inference about credibility

---

CDC, 2000) (NCJ publication no 183781) ch 7. One difficulty in compiling accurate statistics is that many, if not most, rapes are unreported. One study found a significantly lower reporting rate for victims of sexual assault committed by a known assailant as opposed to assaults by a stranger: KM Feldhaus, D Houry, and R Kaminsky, 'Lifetime Sexual Assault Prevalence Rates and Reporting Practices in an Emergency Department Population' (2000) 36 *Annals of Emergency Medicine* 23. It is thus likely that the majority of unreported rapes are rapes committed by a known assailant.

[64] *Seaboyer* and the current statutory provisions leave the door open to sexual history being relevant to mistaken belief in consent in some cases.

[65] An alternative view is that when the Supreme Court refers to logical relevance it means something other than an assessment of probabilities. Or it may illustrate that where there are different ways of framing the issue, logic cannot dictate the choice.

might still be drawn from lack of knowledge if a heterosexual refugee claimant is even less likely to have such knowledge.[66] Nevertheless, the court flatly rejects the drawing of an inference from lack of knowledge to lack of credibility. Moreover, the illegitimacy of the inference is seen as self-evident, needing no analysis in terms of a test of relevance. The decision suggests an approach based on intuition, rather than on a rigorous assessment of relative probabilities.

It is, of course, vital to examine critically whatever subjective assumptions are being slotted into an assessment of relevance, a point that *Trembliuk* well illustrates. It may not at all be a matter of common sense that a person claiming asylum because of persecution on the basis of his homosexuality is more likely to know about the gay community than a heterosexual claimant. Perhaps we should not be comparing individuals on the basis of sexual orientation at all, but rather residents of Toronto and relative new-comers (or new-comers fleeing particular forms of persecution). I will revisit the question of assumptions below. First, I explore the issue, implicitly raised by *Trembliuk*, whether courts apply an approach to relevance based in the logical assessment of probabilities. For it turns out that there is no simple answer to the question of how to distinguish, legally, between relevant and irrelevant information.

A Legal Test?

First, the way judges talk about relevance is often inconsistent with an assessment of relative probabilities.[67] While the Supreme Court of Canada has sometimes used the language of logical relevance, as in *Seaboyer*, its usage is not consistent. The case which is usually cited as the leading Canadian authority on relevance is *R v Morris*,[68] which involved a charge of conspiracy to import heroin from Hong Kong. One issue was the relevance of a newspaper clipping, found in Morris' home, dealing with the heroin trade in Pakistan. The court unanimously agreed that the clipping was relevant. On this point at least, the majority was in agreement with the dissenting judges.[69] McIntyre J, speaking for the majority, stated:

---

[66] Friedman, above n 50, uses the helpful example of drawing an inference that a car is heading towards the airport because it takes the exit from the highway which leads most directly to the airport. He states, *ibid* 1823, that 'the fact that the car takes the exit may tend strongly to prove that the car is on the way to the airport, even though only a minority of the cars that take the exit are heading toward the airport, because a far higher proportion of the cars that are heading to the airport than of those that are not take the exit'.

[67] Judges may be subject to criticism when this happens, on the ground of illogicality. My basic argument, however, is that it is not evident that legal reasoning should follow some particular form of logic, no matter how imperfect our information about the world or dubious our common sense.

[68] [1983] 2 SCR 190.

[69] The dissenting judges would have excluded the clipping as going to disposition.

In my view, an inference could be drawn from the unexplained presence of the newspaper clipping among the possessions of the appellant, that he had an interest in and had informed himself on the question of sources of supply of heroin, necessarily a subject of vital interest to one concerned with the importing of the narcotic ... [A]n inference could possibly have been drawn or could have been supported to the effect that preparatory steps in respect of importing narcotics had been taken or were contemplated.[70]

The dissenting judges, however, went further. They quoted extensively from Thayer, beginning with his familiar view on the admission of any logically probative evidence, but adding the following passages:

> To this general statement should be added the discretionary power judges exercise to exclude logically relevant evidence:
>
>> as being of too slight a significance, or as having too conjectural and remote a connection; others, as being dangerous, in their effect on the jury, and likely to be misused or overestimated by that body; others, as being impolitic, or unsafe on public grounds; others, on the bare ground of precedent. It is this sort of thing, as I said before—the rejection on one or another practical ground, of what is really probative—which is the characteristic thing in the law of evidence; stamping it as the child of the jury system. [Thayer, 266]

It was through the exercise of this discretionary power that judges developed rules of exclusion. As said Thayer, at 265, when speaking of the rule of general admissibility of what is logically probative:

> [I]n an historical sense it has not been the fundamental thing, to which the different exclusions were exceptions. What has taken place, in fact, is the shutting out by the judges of one and another thing from time to time; and so, gradually, the recognition of this exclusion under a rule. These rules of exclusion have had their exceptions; and so the law has come into the shape of a set of primary rules of exclusion; and then a set of exceptions to these rules.[71]

Morris is generally understood to stand for the proposition that relevance has a low threshold. However, while it starts with the concept of logical relevance, it is clear that evidence can be excluded on various grounds, such as having too slight a significance, or as being too conjectural, or unsafe on policy grounds, and of course on the basis of precedent, even when such grounds have not gelled into an established rule of exclusion. This suggests a rather indeterminate dividing line between relevance and the exclusion of relevant yet prejudicial evidence. While excluding evidence on the basis that it may be misused by the jury seems to fall on the latter

---

[70]   Above n 68, 191–2.
[71]   *Ibid* at 201 (quoting Thayer, *A Preliminary Treatise on Evidence at the Common Law* (Boston, Little Brown & Co, 1896)). The dissenters then applied the rules about disposition evidence.

(prejudice) side of the line, excluding information as inviting too specula-tive an inference could be seen as an aspect of the former (relevance) side. Put another way: fact-finders' sense of a lack of information, or the danger of making assumptions in a particular context, may prompt resistance to framing a relevance issue strictly along probability lines. It is hard to express this contrast without making the distinction appear too linear. I am not suggesting that fact-finders may consider certain information logically relevant on the basis of their assessment of the probabilities but then go on to treat it as legally irrelevant because of some concern extraneous to logic. Rather, fact-finders might consider an assessment of the probabilities too speculative, given their lack of pertinent information about the world and the dangers of discriminatory speculation.

R v Portillo[72] illustrates concern about avoiding conjecture. A logical structure combined with imperfect information can be dangerous, even where there are no countervailing considerations (such as the need to be attentive to the vulnerability and dignity of witnesses) in play. During a murder investigation, shoes which may have left prints at the scene of the crime were found near the accused's apartment. The Court of Appeal rejected the relevance of the shoes, holding that there would have been a logical connection[73] only if two inferences were 'reasonably available':[74] that the shoes made the prints and that the shoes belonged to the accused. But it could be argued that, as a matter of logic, the probability of the accused being guilty would be higher if similar shoes were found near his apartment than if they were not. (Indeed this resembles a scenario where a witness says the murderer was wearing a white coat and a white coat was found near the accused's home.) In *Portillo* the concern seems to be with over-speculation, both about the undetermined number of shoes which could have made the prints and about whether the shoes fit or had been worn by the accused:

> The 'footwear' evidence could not, absent assumption of facts not proved, or speculation, support either the inference that the shoes made the prints found at the scene or that the shoes belonged to [the accused]. The evidence was not relevant.[75]

A concern, obviously heightened in the case of Crown evidence, may be that there must be limits, grounded in fairness, to the assessment of probabilities. In other words, evidence may be irrelevant because there is

---

[72] (2003) 17 CR (6th) 362 (Ont CA).

[73] *Ibid* [32].

[74] *Ibid* [31]. This suggests quite a high threshold for relevance, an impression heightened by other wording suggesting that there had to be evidence establishing that the shoes belonged to the accused: see *ibid* [34].

[75] *Ibid* [35]. Note that the issue is framed in terms of relevance, and not discretion to exclude relevant but prejudicial information.

too much guesswork involved.[76] The evidence is simply not helpful either way because any inference would be too speculative.[77] The difficult thing, however, will be to distinguish speculation from permissible inference.

While *Morris* suggests a low relevance threshold, more recent cases, including *Portillo*, have used language suggesting a higher threshold. The court in *Trembliuk* rejected the invited inference from the applicant's lack of knowledge of the gay community because it could not be assumed that *all* homosexual persons would have such knowledge.

A higher threshold is also suggested in *R v Shearing*.[78] Shearing, the leader of a cult called the Kabalarians in Vancouver, was charged with 20 counts of sexual offences against seven young women between 1965 and 1989. One of the complainants kept a diary, which did not mention the alleged abuse. One issue raised on appeal concerned the appropriate limits on her cross-examination about the diary, which had come into the hands of the defence. Defence counsel wished to invite a negative inference about the credibility of the complainant from the diary's omissions. Counsel for the complainant, who was independently represented on this issue, argued that there was no probative value in a lack of complaint in the diary (in other words, the silence in the diary was not relevant to credibility) and any linkage was discriminatory.[79] The trial judge permitted questions on actual entries but prohibited questions on the absence of entries.

In the Supreme Court of Canada, the majority decision, delivered by Binnie J, found the trial judge to have been in error. The judgment contains a number of contrasting elements. On the one hand, there is a focus on the need for a rational basis for the inference:

> What was objectionable about the defence approach here was that it overlooked (or perhaps resolutely resisted) the need to lay before the jury a rational basis for

---

[76] This may be similar to the exclusion of hearsay where a jury would not be able to assess its ultimate reliability.

[77] It might be countered that normative standards such as fairness should not apply to the concept of relevance. Inferences are either correctly drawn from information or not. My argument here is that *Portillo* supports the proposition that basing an inference on too much guesswork, an inference incapable of being tested for correctness, is unfair, in this case to the accused. Along these lines, the Federal Court of Canada has held that basing inferences upon speculation is a patently unreasonable error: *Mohammadi v Canada (Minister of Citizenship and Immigration)* [2003] FCJ No 1302 (QL), [29]: 'The jurisprudence of this Court establishes that where the [Immigration and Refugee] Board finds a lack of credibility based on inferences, including inferences concerning the plausibility of the testimony, there must be a basis in the evidence to support the inferences. In my opinion, the Board in the case at bar fails to articulate a sufficient basis on the evidence for this key point. Behind the Board's conclusions in this regard lie a host of assumptions and speculations for which there is no real evidentiary basis. For the Board to have proceeded in this way was a [patently unreasonable] reviewable error'.

[78] (2002) 2 CR (6th) 213 (SCC).

[79] *Ibid* [79].

the inference it ultimately wished to draw, namely that the non-recording of a certain type of information was circumstantial evidence that the alleged abuse never happened.[80]

Further: 'On what logical basis would such a non-record give rise to an inference of testimonial deficiency or fabrication?'[81]

On the other hand, the court exhibits a failure of rationality, in two senses. First, the majority allowed the appeal on this issue without actually articulating any possible rational basis for the cross-examination:

> The defence was rightly precluded from *assuming* the truth of that premise [that abuse would have been recorded], but it did not follow that the defence should also be precluded from attempting to *demonstrate* it with this particular diary on the particular facts of a case.[82]

This point was challenged by L'Heureux-Dubé J in dissent: 'I think the bottom line is that the defence simply *did not have* a rational basis for its proposed line of questioning'.[83] But the majority ruled otherwise. In essence, the result was that the defence should have been allowed to cross-examine the complainant on the silence in her diary, with attendant consequences for her privacy and equality[84] rights, without having to suggest any potential legitimate inference.

Secondly, while the court says that cross-examination should have been permitted on some (unexpressed) rational basis, the threshold for establishing a foundation for such cross-examination appears to be remarkably demanding:

> In the absence of some evidentiary basis for the premise that abuse ought to have been recorded, the result of allowing the cross-examination to proceed as proposed by the defence ('the entire contents are fair game') would be to allow the defence to go to the jury at the end of the trial and to point to the absence of entries in an effort to suggest —nod nod wink wink—that women and children who are sexually and physically abused do not suffer in silence, but *must and do* confide their inner hurt even if only to their private diaries.[85]

And even more strongly: 'Why assume that a diary devoted to "mundane" entries would *necessarily* report on episodes of ... abuse'?[86]

---

[80]   *Ibid* [119].
[81]   *Ibid* [120].
[82]   *Ibid* [146].
[83]   *Ibid* [181].
[84]   Attention to equality rights is more explicit in the dissenting than majority judgments, but the majority stated in para 121 that: '[While] in most cases the adversarial process allows wide latitude to cross-examiners ..., sexual assault cases pose particular dangers. [Several SCC decisions] make the point that these cases should be decided without resort to folk tales about how abuse victims are expected by people who have never suffered abuse to react to the trauma: *Mills* [[1999] 3 SCR 668] at paras 72, 117–19'.
[85]   *Ibid* [120], emphasis added.
[86]   *Ibid* [120], emphasis added.

Shearing casts doubt on the assessment of relative probabilities as the legal test of relevance in two ways: by using language suggesting a higher threshold, but also by permitting cross-examination unsupported by any express rationale. Is an alternative analysis available? It could be argued that silence about an alleged incident (abuse) tends to show that it did not occur, because no matter what the likelihood of silence given the hypothesis of abuse (and it might well seem quite likely, in general terms, that a victim of sexual abuse would not write about it in a diary), silence is even more likely given the hypothesis of non-abuse. Using this approach, the silence in the diary would therefore tend to support the defence case.[87]

One problem with this, with respect to silence as a piece of information, is that it implies that a great deal would be relevant. If silence in a diary is relevant, then silence at large is relevant. Complainants could always be cross-examined on when and why they did not tell their mothers, their friends and the police. But the approach adopted by the court in *Shearing* suggests that silence at a particular time is a neutral factor, unless it is given meaning by comparison to a default assumption about how genuine victims of abuse, including rape victims, behave. The absence of particular conduct is rendered meaningful by comparison with what we think we, or other people, or reasonable people, would do in the same situation. It is trite law that silence is an admission where denial would be reasonably expected in the circumstances. Indeed, that is what the court said: 'The omission to record some piece of information is only probative if there is a reasonable expectation that such a record would be made'.[88] This test departs from a comparison of probabilities, since it compares silence to the expected behaviour of a victim rather than considering the hypotheses of abuse and non-abuse. It is an approach which requires a foundation in the particular case for an inference to be drawn from silence, thus providing some protection from general fishing expeditions.[89] A fact-finder may, on the basis of common sense, think that silence is so ambiguous and that so little is known about the behaviour of rape victims generally, that silence is simply not helpful. Such a fact-finder then looks for something more particular which would make that information helpful, a foundation on which to take the relevance assessment beyond pure guesswork in a

[87] I am indebted to Burkhard Schafer for this example. The strength of the inference depends on what we assume about human behaviour. Certainly defence counsel could invite a jury to give some weight to the silence in the diary without suggesting that rape victims 'must and do' record their experience.

[88] *Ibid* [119].

[89] The judicial tendency to discourage 'fishing expeditions' can be seen as reflecting concern about over-speculation. In *O'Connor*, above n 14, [24], the majority noted that the reason for requiring the defence to establish that a third party record is 'likely-relevant' before ordering its disclosure 'is simply a requirement to prevent the defence from engaging in "speculative, fanciful, disruptive, unmeritorious, obstructive and time-consuming" requests for production'.

particular case. *Shearing* takes us to the possibility of a foundation (albeit one envisaged as emerging after the very cross-examination objected to) but the absence of even a hypothetical example leaves doubt that such a foundation could exist in that case.

The rejection of certain information at large as irrelevant, while remaining open to it in particular contexts, is not uncommon in fact determination. To continue with the topic of drawing inferences from silence, Canadian courts have been struggling with the issue of permissible inferences from pre-detention silence. In *R v W (MC)*,[90] the accused, W, was charged with aggravated assault and assault with a weapon. He argued at trial that the police had not adequately investigated the offence and that the principal attacker was another person, B. The Crown asked the investigating officer about his efforts to contact the accused. After W testified that B committed the assaults, the Crown was permitted to cross-examine him about why he had not told the police about B prior to his arrest or gone to the police to report his fear of B. On appeal, a new trial was ordered on the basis of inadequate instruction to the jury.

The court addressed the question of whether an inference could be drawn from W's silence during the investigation. The judges expressed divergent views of the interaction between relevance and the right to silence, but the majority held that the evidence was relevant on the particular facts of the case. Huddart JA held that inferences are allowed to be drawn from silence where there is 'real relevance'.[91] On the facts of this particular case, the accused had, for instance, alleged flaws in the police investigation, which made the evidence relevant. Levine JA held that the evidence was 'relevant to rebut defence allegations that the police investigation was biased and to test the probative value of the defence, which was akin to an alibi'.[92] Ryan JA stated more generally:

> [W]here a witness testifies at trial that he or she has important information about a crime, the fact that the person did not go to the police with the information is something that the jury may wish to take into account in assessing whether the witness's story is true or not.[93]

Ryan JA emphasised that she was addressing evidence of failure to report something to the police, rather than silence in the face of police questioning.

While it could be argued in terms of logic that going to the police with information about a crime is more consistent with the truth of evidence reflecting that information at trial than its falsity, we may be concerned

---

[90] Above n 42. For information about the right to silence in Canada, see Sopinka, Lederman and Bryant, above n 25, 835ff.
[91] *Ibid* [47], quoting Cory J in *R v Chambers* [1990] 2 SCR 1293, 1318.
[92] *Ibid* [94].
[93] *Ibid* [79].

about the degree of speculation involved in drawing inferences from a failure to report, given the inherent ambiguity of silence. *R v W (MC)* suggests, in general terms, that the fact that a witness did not go to or assist the police is relevant to credibility where a foundation can be laid in a particular case, an approach very similar to that in *Shearing* (although here the foundation is stated). In *R v W(MC)*, as in relation to our knowledge of what raped women might or might not write in their diaries, a common-sense concern about drawing on assumptions relating to contact with the police may make silence in general so unhelpful as to be irrelevant,[94] unless there is some expectation of speech in the particular circumstances.

The Supreme Court of Canada has addressed the relevance of silence in another British Columbia case, *R v Turcotte*.[95] The accused was charged with a triple murder on a ranch. He had gone to the police and told them to send a car to the ranch (where three bodies were later discovered) but would not explain why. Evidence of his silence was admitted at trial as post-offence conduct, the Crown inviting the jury to draw an inference of guilt from the accused's failure to respond to questions by the police prior to his detention as a suspect. The Court of Appeal found this to be in error, in part on the basis that the 'refusal to respond to questions was irrelevant to any material issue'.[96] The Supreme Court unanimously dismissed the appeal. Abella J's judgment seems grounded in two different, albeit intermingled, lines of analysis: evidence of Turcotte's silence should be inadmissible because it was irrelevant, or alternatively because, though relevant, it was excluded under the right to silence.

Turning first to relevance, the court stated that 'post-offence conduct' only includes conduct that is probative of guilt.[97] This seems to be a straightforward statement of the principle that only relevant evidence should be considered. However, in this instance the 'traditional common law' that 'everyone has the right to be silent in the face of police

---

[94] What might some underlying 'common-sense' assumptions be? If people are aware of a crime, they would tell the police? People who are telling the truth would not avoid an interview with the police? Innocent people volunteer to help the police? *or* People often avoid contact with the police, even when they are the victims of crime? Even innocent people may try to avoid getting involved in investigations? There are various reasons, other than guilt, why people may avoid contact with the police? These may involve contact with people, such as domestic assaulters, terrorists or other criminals, who may be dangerous if aware of contact with the police? Such reasons may be difficult or unsafe to explain? People may tell the truth while under oath, even though they would not have volunteered the information to the police?

[95] [2005] 2 SCR 519.
[96] (2004) 184 CCC (3d) 242 (BCCA), [69].
[97] Above n 95, [37].

questioning'[98] determined the parameters of relevance. Since individuals are not under a duty to assist the police, silence 'says nothing'.[99] And again:

> Since there was no duty on Mr Turcotte's part to speak to the police, his failure to do so was irrelevant, no rational conclusion can be drawn from it.[100]

Silence is, however, admissible in limited circumstances, including when 'the defence raises an issue that renders the accused's silence relevant', as occurred in *R v W (MC)*, discussed above, or in cases involving an alibi. Silence could also be admissible as narrative, with appropriate instructions to the jury.[101]

With respect to the right to silence, the court noted its common law and constitutional dimensions, that its temporal limits have not been fully defined, and that drawing a negative inference from silence would be a 'snare and a delusion'. There is an unanalysed shift in reasoning from the 'snare and delusion' of drawing negative inferences from the constitutionally-protected right to silence enjoyed by those in the power of the state, to a conclusion that the exercise of the common law right not to speak to the police cannot generally be used as evidence of guilt. However, the court is clearly saying that the common law right to silence exists at all times against the state, including periods before arrest or detention. Since the court was addressing the issue of silence in the face of police questioning and not engaging in any comprehensive doctrinal exposition of the right to silence, it remains uncertain how its reasoning applies to evidence, for example, of a decision not to go to the police, as in *R v W (MC)*. However, reference to this case in *Turcotte* as an example of relevance in a particular context suggests that the court was assuming a very broad scope for the right to silence.

The focus of this chapter is on relevance rather than rules excluding relevant evidence, but the intermingling of relevance and the right to silence in *Turcotte* causes difficulty. It is notable that the court does not base its relevance determination on a comparison of probabilities, or on any kind of principled approach to relevance, but specifically on the existence of a liberty not to speak to the police. The fact that the court does this in terms of relevance, rather than exclusively in terms of the right to silence, suggests, however, that the court was not clarifying a protective exclusionary rule but addressing inference-drawing more generally. The decision seems to be authority for the proposition that a negative inference

---

[98] *Ibid* [41].
[99] *Ibid* [46], quoting, with approval, *R v B(SC)* (1997) 36 OR (3d) 516 (CA), 529. See also *ibid* [55].
[100] *Ibid* [56].
[101] *Ibid* [47]–[59].

cannot be drawn from the exercise of a legally-protected liberty. Failure to act can only be relevant where there is a duty to act.

A duty-based test of relevance, in place of an assessment of probabilities in a particular context, seems troublesome, no less for the defence than the prosecution. After all, women have no duty to report sexual abuse to their diaries, any more than people in general have a duty to answer police questions. People whose spouses go on to die in suspicious circumstances are at liberty to have taken out insurance on their lives, or not, as they please. Absent a legal duty, people are free to remove themselves from the presence of the police, at whatever speed they see fit. It may have been preferable for the court to have expressed its conclusions differently in *Turcotte*. Irrespective of the relevance of Turcotte's behaviour, a negative inference should not be drawn, for policy reasons, from his exercise of the common law right not to answer police questions.

If the issues of relevance and the right to silence were disentangled, should Turcotte's silence have been treated as relevant? In terms of probabilities it is at least arguable that an innocent person is more likely than a guilty one to alert the police to a murder scene and the possibility of ongoing danger. Failure to warn 'there may still be a murderer out at the ranch—be careful' seems more likely to arise given the hypothesis of guilt than on the assumption that the speaker is innocent.

What picture can be painted from these sample cases? Canadian courts sometimes refer to logical relevance involving the assessment of probabilities, but also sometimes use language requiring a higher threshold. These alternative formulations range from the rejection of trivial asides, to the notion (possibly reflecting a desire to avoid discriminatory stereotypes and to promote fairness to the accused) that if information is not conclusive it is not relevant at all. In addition, there is evidence of a reluctance to speculate, linked to an inclination to look for a foundation in the context of a particular case. *Turcotte*, and arguably *Seaboyer*, may illustrate a willingness to merge policy concerns with relevance determinations. At the very least it can be said that there is uncertainty about the legal test of relevance, and a rather blurred line between relevance, exclusion on policy grounds and weight. The Cat, indeed, is not very visible.

Triers of fact do not have the luxury of postponing fact-finding until they have a clear legal test of relevance and sufficient empirical data to resolve doubtful issues. Within the legal framework of burden and standard of proof, fact-finders must combine what quantifiable data they have with other evidence in a case and with the common sense they are permitted to use. I want to conclude by turning to examine that common sense, the realm of fact determination left over by the legal doctrines of impartiality, judicial notice, equality, fairness, the rules of admissibility and the operation of legislation and precedent relating to inferences.

What Assumptions am I Making and are they Defensible?

Fuzziness about the distinctions between relevance, weight and the exclusion of evidence on the basis, for instance, that it might be prejudicial, may not matter in many situations. For example, if a judge in a jury trial excludes certain evidence or does not permit a certain line of questioning, it might not really matter whether her decision was grounded in a test of relevance permitting the exclusion of logically probative but trivial or speculative evidence or whether her decision was grounded in her discretion to exclude relevant but prejudicial evidence. It may not be important for an administrative tribunal to struggle with the line between evidence which is relevant and evidence which is relevant but insignificant. However, there are instances where more clarity would certainly be helpful. Appeals can turn on whether irrelevant evidence was taken into account, thus distorting the search for truth, as the court found in *Trembliuk*. Defence counsel may complain of the exclusion of relevant evidence, as in *Shearing*. Erring on the side of admitting irrelevant but pro-defence evidence may also have costs, in terms of witnesses' interests in privacy and equality. Sexual history evidence encapsulates this conflict. A strong case can be made for a more visible Cat, to clarify the concepts governing factual inferences, relevance and weight.

Whatever the legal test of relevance, however, given incomplete and imperfect information it is often necessary to draw on 'common-sense' assumptions or pre-existing beliefs in order to decide whether to draw an inference and, if so, what weight to attach to it.[102] Indeed juries are routinely urged to do so.[103] The existence of multiple common senses in a jury provides some response to a concern that fact-finding is at best a lottery and at worst the exercise of prejudice. However, most facts, in the legal context, are determined by judges and administrative decision-makers, often sitting alone.

There are obvious dangers in judicial fact-finding. The cases discussed in this chapter give cause for concern. No matter how logical the structure of

---

[102] Linkages between factual findings and pre-existing beliefs have been the subject of some academic analysis. See eg, information about a conference on 'Inference, Culture, and Ordinary Thinking in Dispute Resolution', http://tillers.net/inferencebelief.html, accessed 16 August 2007.

[103] See eg, one model jury instruction on witness credibility: 'Generally, I would suggest that you use your common sense and experience as men and women of the community to assess the credibility of each witness. In doing so, you should keep the following points in mind...': Ferguson and Bouck, *Canadian Criminal Jury Instructions (Crimji)*, vol 1 (3rd edn, Looseleaf, Vancouver, Continuing Legal Education Society of British Colombia, 2002) 4.12(3); and see the model instruction on proof beyond a reasonable doubt: 'A reasonable doubt is not an imaginary or frivolous doubt. It must not be based on sympathy or prejudice. Rather, it is based on reason and common sense. It must logically come from the evidence or the lack of evidence': *Crimji*, 4.04(2).

analysis, assumptions about raped women, homosexual men and criminal suspects may distort analysis of both relevance and weight, and thus call particular inferences (or their absence) into question. Consider other possible examples. A witness' inability to remember details may range from irrelevant to highly probative. Judges who have practised as lawyers, and usually possess good memories, may be overly sceptical about a claim of lack of memory.[104] Avoiding the police may also be equivocal. Persons without cause to fear the police may be quick to judge others' disinclination to co-operate. Is there any way in which this inevitable common-sense component, which feeds into assessments of relevance whatever the legal test, can be disciplined by law or even by good habits of advocacy and judging?[105] In other words, is it possible to develop any criteria for assessing the legitimacy of hypothetical probabilities? Might such criteria have implications for our approach to relevance?

I want to suggest some possible criteria, which I hope might structure a principled approach to relevance, starting with the relatively obvious.

Evidence May be Too Equivocal to be Helpful

I believe this point to be uncontroversial but illustrations may be useful. Evidence is irrelevant where it is equally consistent with different hypotheses. For instance, in *R v White*[106] the court found evidence of flight and concealment irrelevant where 'it can be said that [such] conduct … is "equally explained by" or "equally consistent with" two or more offences'.[107] Further, in *R v Noël*[108] the majority said that 'the simple fact is that [knowledge of the privilege against self-incrimination] does not yield an inference in relation to truthfulness one way or the other'.[109]

Common-sense Assumptions should Reflect Insights Drawn from the Law of Evidence as a Whole

The law of evidence is a rich source of assumptions about human behaviour crystallised into doctrine. An example is the familiar idea that people are more likely to be telling the truth when making statements

---

[104] See Eggleston, above n 53, 197. In a Canadian example, a judge suggested a negative inference could be drawn from the fact that the accused had been able to remember what he had for breakfast on the day the murder took place but not what he was wearing. But my common sense tells me that people are far more likely to be creatures of habit with respect to their breakfasts than their clothing, so this seems very plausible to me.

[105] It should be clear that I am not here talking about cases where expert evidence can supply the information needed. DNA evidence is a possible example.

[106] [1998] 2 SCR 72.

[107] *Ibid* [28].

[108] [2002] 3 SCR 433. See also *R v Jabarianha* [2001] 3 SCR 430, [18].

[109] *Ibid* [60].

against their own interests.[110] Again, *Shearing* provides a useful illustration. Whether one frames the issue as the comparison of probabilities or in terms of a reasonable expectation that a rape victim would refer to her experience in her diary, reflection on common-sense assumptions about the behaviour of rape victims is required. The relevance of silence must, however, be addressed in the context of the legal rule against narrative. A prosecutor's attempt to use a reference to the alleged assault in the diary, as a basis for a positive inference, would run afoul of the prior consistent statement rule. It is generally thought that repetition does not make an allegation more credible:

> The complainant's entry in her diary in no way made it more likely that the allegations of sexual assault she made in court were true. The credibility of a statement is not enhanced by the fact that it was made more than once.[111]

Silence at one point and speech at another are consistent with each other, of course. We are all silent unless we are speaking, so treating silence as a prior inconsistent statement links silence in general with a lack of credibility. The point here is that there should be reasonable consistency in the overall common sense of the law of evidence. Thus, if recording an incident, without more, cannot make an allegation more credible, then failure to record, without more, should not make it less credible.[112]

Still on the theme of common sense influenced by insights from other parts of the law of evidence, there are many reasons for rape victims (especially those who have complained to the police or who plan to do so) not to discuss or record their experience. Canada does not have a privilege for communications with rape crisis workers or therapists in general.[113] A commonly-expressed concern about rules of evidence relating to sexual assault is that victims may be discouraged, by the absence of privilege and other legal rules, from reporting to the police or testifying. This implies a common-sense assumption that the behaviour of rape victims can be influenced by legal developments.[114]

---

[110]   Although this can be seen as contrasting with the view in *Noël*, above n 108.

[111]   *R v SRC* [2004] PEIR No 50 (App Div), [38]. Sopinka, Lederman, and Bryant, above n 25, [7.3], point out that superfluity is one possible rationale for the rule, given the view that a 'story is not made more probable or trustworthy by any number of repetitions of it'.

[112]   I am not suggesting here that there should be symmetry between rules relating to witnesses and accused persons. Rather, common sense cannot be seen in isolation from the assumptions underlying the rules of evidence in general.

[113]   Case by case privilege arguments may be made, including for partial privilege. See *AM v Ryan* [1997] 1 SCR 157. As well there are provisions in the Criminal Code, mentioned above, which set some controls, grounded in relevance and necessity, on pre-trial production of private records to the defence.

[114]   For instance, the Preamble to An Act to amend the Criminal Code (Production of Records in Sexual Offence Proceedings), above n 14, states that 'the Parliament of Canada wishes to encourage the reporting of incidents of sexual violence'. Further, s 278.5(2) of the

*Some Human Behaviour may be of Such Broad, General Significance as
to be Incapable of Supporting any Inference without a Foundation in a
Particular Case*

Again we can turn to the silent diary for an illustration. Silence about the
subject of sexual assault (including the silence of those who have not been
victimised, since it seems unlikely that people would announce to others,
or to their diaries, that they have *not* been sexually assaulted), may be so
pervasive as to have very little meaning. While it is debatable whether
defence counsel would be permitted to cross-examine a complainant about
silence at large (in a diary or letters, to a therapist, friend, or police
officers, etc), adverse inferences may not be drawn from delay. In *R v D
(D)*,[115] the Supreme Court of Canada held that a judge should instruct the
jury that there is no inviolable rule dictating how victims behave: 'A delay
in disclosure, standing alone, will never give rise to an adverse inference
against the credibility of the complainant'.[116] It appears that the court in
Shearing did not, at least in theory, regard the existence of a diary as taking
the case beyond the 'standing alone' threshold.

Overly Speculative Assumptions should be Avoided

Portillo required more than an abstract assessment of the probabilities
suggested by the common sense of the fact-finder. Further examples may be
obscured by a tendency to fudge the line between relevance and weighing
probative value against prejudicial effect, reflected in phrases such as 'little
or no probative value'. In *R v Savoy*,[117] for instance, a murder case in
which cause of death was difficult to establish because the deceased's
corpse had been eaten by a bear, the British Columbia Court of Appeal
held that there was little or no probative value in 'highly prejudicial'
evidence that the accused was a nurse with access to drugs:

> The jury were left to speculate whether the appellant had administered a drug to
> [the deceased], rendering him unconscious or causing his death.[118]

Criminal Code states that encouraging reporting and access to treatment are factors to be
taken into account by the judge in deciding whether (s)he will even examine private records at
all.
    [115] [2000] 2 SCR 275.
    [116] *Ibid* [65]. This appears to make clear that an adverse inference is not the default
position in the absence of an explanation for delay, but it does not make clear that
cross-examination on the issue of delayed disclosure, in the absence of a suggested permissible
inference, will not be permitted. This case is a further example of the approach of being open
to possible inferences in the context of particular cases.
    [117] (1997) 6 CR (5th) 61 (BCCA).
    [118] *Ibid* [43]. I am indebted to Gregory Fitch for drawing my attention to this example.

The Charter Proscribes Discriminatory 'Common Sense'

The requirement for state fact-finders to be impartial and to conform to s 15 of the Charter means that inferences must be fair[119] and egalitarian. For example, it would normally be neither fair nor egalitarian to draw an inference from the colour of a witness' skin to their lack of credibility.[120] This would be utterly speculative as well as discriminatory.[121] Both legal doctrine and influential legal commentary have a long history of conjuring the distinctive figure of the disturbed, fantasising or mendacious woman as a default assumption.[122] In a sense, defence counsel's invitation to draw a negative inference from a silent diary is an attempt to extend that story-schema to the complainant, whilst simultaneously drawing on a common-sense assumption that women would never, or would rarely, make false claims in their diaries. Care needs to be taken, in the drawing of inferences, not to create default assumptions which portray women as distinctively likely to bring false charges. Indeed, modern efforts to reject such discriminatory default assumptions through rules relating to delayed complaints, production of private records to the defence and sexual history evidence, provide positive role models for drawing inferences not directly governed by legal rules.

Fact-finders should be Self-consciously Critical of the Assumptions they are Using

It seems obvious that the assessment of relevance and the process of drawing inferences generally could be improved by more self-conscious attention to both their legal regulation and the inferential process. Fact-finders and appellate bodies should go beyond the kinds of bare assertions of stereotyping found in *Trembliuk*, or worse, the 'nod nod wink wink' approach rightly criticised in *Shearing*. While a fact-finder will not necessarily be able to bring her whole reasoning process to a conscious

---

[119] Alan Mewett suggested that fairness is the standard on which logical relevance is based. A fair trial, 'to be meaningful, must include not only substantive fairness and due process, but also a "fair" inference-drawing process': AW Mewett, 'Secondary Facts, Prejudice and Stereotyping' (1999) 42 *Criminal Law Quarterly* 319, 323.

[120] An example of where this could be permissible is the case of concern about cross-racial bias in identification. See *R v McIntosh* (1997) 35 OR (3d) 97, leave to appeal dismissed 19 March 1998.

[121] In a leading Canadian case on judicial impartiality, *R v RDS* [1997] 3 SCR 484, the court was divided on whether a judicial comment that police officers sometimes over-react against non-white persons was too speculative and in any event discriminatory. However, the majority found that the comment did not raise a reasonable apprehension of bias.

[122] See eg, G Williams, 'Corroboration: Sexual Cases' [1962] *Crim LR* 662, suggesting lie detector tests, since sex cases are prone to false charges.

level of articulation, some explicit attention to possible counter-assumptions[123] and recognition of the steps involved in a chain of inferences[124] would increase the legitimacy of fact-finding as a process governed by law.

CONCLUSION

The linear structure of this chapter's analysis might unintentionally convey the impression that a superior analysis of relevance proceeds in two stages. The first step is to establish clear legal authority for a logical assessment of relative probabilities. The second step demands a critical approach to the common-sense assumptions underpinning the initial assessment of probabilities. However, I doubt that such a clear separation between the two stages is possible in reality.

It should be evident that I do not regard reasoning about relevance as somehow extra-legal, beyond the control of the law of evidence. Such reasoning is properly encompassed within the scope of that body of law[125] and governed by legal standards. Conceptualising relevance as a matter of pure rationality or science beyond the discipline of law ironically (to the extent that egalitarianism is rational) leaves too much room for inegalitarian intuitions. In the legal context, attention to logic needs to interact with legal standards for confining common sense within legitimate boundaries, in an attempt to serve law's overarching rationalist aspirations.[126]

One response (which I experience as a fairly dominant view) is that relevance is a matter of pure logic, and that any deviations from probability assessments are a matter of 'policy', policy having a distinctly second-class ring when contrasted with rationality or logic. Who wants to argue for an irrational approach to fact determination? Or to deny rectitude of decision when the fate of an innocent man or a genuine asylum-seeker or a future rape victim is at stake?[127] Debate designed to shift the focus from

---

[123] For a case which can be seen as encouraging the consideration of counter-hypotheses, see *R v ZL* (2000) 144 CCC (3d) 444 (BCCA), affirmed [2001] 1 SCR 528.

[124] See *R v White*, above n 106, for discussion of when a trial judge should give a 'no probative value' instruction to a jury with respect to post-offence conduct such as flight, the concern being about when a jury might mistakenly leap from ambiguous post-offence conduct to a finding of guilt.

[125] For a summary of different views, see JL Montrose, 'Basic Concepts of the Law of Evidence' (1954) 70 *LQR* 527, 532.

[126] See W Twining, 'The Rationalist Tradition of Evidence Scholarship' in *Rethinking Evidence*, above n 2, 32, including his discussion of aspirational, complacent and optimistic rationalism. Another way of making my point might be that attention to legal norms for common sense addresses the danger of complacent rationalism.

[127] Donald Nicolson has argued that 'fact positivism creates a form of closure that helps isolate the study and practice of fact-finding from feminist challenge': 'Gender, Epistemology

logic to content, as I have attempted above, may be resisted by those undisturbed by the content of common-sense assumptions.[128]

While constitutional norms and the principled approach to doctrinal rules may be criticised as indeterminate and inadequate protections against inappropriate intuition, I have tried to indicate what a principled approach to inferences might entail. In summary, while the basic test of relevance is logical relevance, it should be tempered by precedent, by the fact-finder's critical self-consciousness and the rejection of discriminatory or overly speculative common sense. In essence, this approach merges a comparison of probabilities with a critical attitude towards their common-sense reappraisal. The concept of prejudice would then be restricted to concerns about misuse of relevant evidence by the fact-finder.

So what can we tell Alice, the student (or practitioner, or even the judge) of law, who asks the Cheshire Cat to tell her, please, which way to go from here? We could reply that she is sure to get somewhere if she only walks, or considers evidence doctrine, or argues both sides of an issue, or considers fact-finding in its procedural and social context, long enough. But with the costs of both legal education and dispute resolution rising in Canada, Alice may well think that she should be going somewhere in particular, and not just wherever she ends up. I think the problem boils down to this. She is not going to a place called Logical Relevance, using a compass such as Bayes' Theorem, nor to a place called Legal Relevance, using a map of principles from the Law of Evidence. She is going to a place we might characterise as Self-Consciously Critical Open-Mindedness about Fact-Finding in Context, and she may consequently have trouble knowing whether she is there or not, or, indeed, whether such a place exists at all.

and Ethics: Feminist Perspectives on Evidence Theory' in M Childs and L Ellison (eds), *Feminist Perspectives on Evidence* (London, Cavendish , 2000) 16.

[128] 'Formal logic tends to be adopted by those content with the premises involved in a reasoning process': *ibid* 18.

4

Analysing Evidence Case Law

MIKE REDMAYNE

INTRODUCTION

C AREFUL ANALYSIS OF evidential inference is one of the key
skills in understanding evidence law. Inference is involved at several
different levels of evidence law. Most fundamentally, perhaps, it is
the staple work of judges and juries: in every case, the fact-finder must
draw inferences from evidence in order to work out what happened. In
criminal litigation, this level of inference is often hidden from us, which
leaves us little material to work with when teaching and researching
evidence law.[1] At a higher level, inferential assumptions sometimes form
the background to major rules of evidence. The rules on character evidence
(including sexual history evidence), for example, depend on assumptions
about the sorts of inference that can be drawn from a person's past
conduct.[2] This chapter scrutinises a 'middle level' of inference in evidence
law. The reasoning in particular cases, which sometimes comes to inform
rules of evidence at the higher level, is often inferentially rich. Thinking
carefully about the inferences involved in reported cases provides a deeper
understanding of the cases and rules associated with them.

A guiding assumption behind this essay is that the analysis of evidence is
a skill that can be learned: it is not just a matter of common sense. The
cases I shall discuss, which have been controversial in the sense that people
disagree about the inferences to be drawn from their facts, supply ample

---

[1] Though some trials leave a rich documentary base from which to work: see eg, J Kadane
and D Schum, *A Probabilistic Analysis of the Sacco and Vanzetti Evidence* (Chichester, Wiley,
1996).

[2] I have discussed these examples in detail elsewhere: see M Redmayne, 'The Relevance of
Bad Character' (2002) 61 *CLJ* 684; 'Myths, Relationships and Coincidences: the New
Problems of Sexual History' (2003) 7 *E & P* 75. For another example of the utility of close
analysis of inferential structure in this area, see D Hamer, 'The Structure and Strength of the
Propensity Inference: Singularity, Linkage and the Other Evidence' (2003) 29 *Monash U L
Rev* 137.

demonstration.[3] Analysis of evidence is also a skill which is too often overlooked in Evidence teaching. Although a number of evidence text-books now include some discussion of Bayesianism or Wigmorean analysis—typically in an introductory chapter—this is rarely incorporated in the analysis of rules and cases which forms the major part of the text.[4] In fact, textbooks sometimes contain claims about the implications of evidence which are difficult to justify, claims which might not have been made had the authors been more fully committed to the close analysis of evidential argument.

A second guiding assumption is that there are right and wrong ways to analyse evidence.[5] This does not imply that analysing evidence is easy; as already noted, common sense alone will sometimes lead us astray. Teaching the careful analysis of evidence can be difficult and time-consuming, but there exist excellent materials for getting the essentials of evidential reasoning across to novices.[6] The cases discussed in this chapter are an excellent vehicle for demonstrating the principles involved. Thus, when teaching inference, rather than starting from the bottom up, with an abstract description of ways of reasoning about evidence, one may proceed more or less directly to the examples in order to illustrate the sorts of analysis which can elucidate them. While this chapter's principal aim is to illustrate the detailed analysis of evidential problems, a subsidiary theme will emerge: inference is often distorted by policy concerns. Such distortion occurs in different ways, and the effects are sometimes subtle.

BLASTLAND: HYPOTHESIS CHOICE

My first example, *R v Blastland*,[7] is a notorious decision about relevance and hearsay. Although the focus here is on the relevance issue, the hearsay

---

[3] For exemplary analysis of various other examples, see Christine Boyle, Chapter 3.

[4] I have made this point before. See M Redmayne, 'Evidence Rethought? A Commentary on Ian Dennis's *The Law of Evidence*' (2001) 1(2) *International Commentary on Evidence* (at www.bepress.com/ice/vol1/iss2/).

[5] See D Nicolson, 'Truth, Reason and Justice: Epistemology and Politics in Evidence Discourse' (1994) 57 *MLR* 726; 'Gender, Epistemology and Ethics: Feminist Perspectives on Evidence Theory' in M Childs and L Ellison, *Feminist Perspectives on Evidence* (London, Cavendish, 2000). Nicolson launches an attack on 'foundationalism' and the 'rationalist tradition' in Evidence scholarship. Although aspects of the argument are opaque, Nicolson implies deep scepticism about the ability to justify evidential argument. But at 36 of the latter paper he calls for empirical research as a means of evaluating law reform, which surely implies some faith in our ability to draw justified conclusions from evidence.

[6] Kadane and Schum, n 1 above, have very useful sections with good illustrations of Wigmorean analysis. On Bayesianism, *Adams* [1996] 2 Cr App R 467 is a wonderful, and provocative, illustration. G Gigerenzer's *Reckoning with Risk* (London, Penguin, 2002) is a very useful source which shows how the basics of Bayesian inference can be explained simply and intuitively.

[7] [1986] AC 41.

context is important. Blastland was trying to avoid the exclusionary effects of the hearsay rule by introducing evidence through an exception to the rule. In this situation, judges are perhaps particularly sceptical of relevance arguments. It is also significant that Blastland's trial strategy was to suggest that another person may have committed the crime. This is a strategy which courts are generally keen to curtail.[8] The decision in *Blastland* is often explained in terms of 'legal relevance' or 'insufficient relevance';[9] the analysis that follows sheds a slightly different light on the decision.

Blastland was charged with the buggery and murder of a 12 year-old boy.[10] He admitted having sexual contact with the boy near the place where the body was found, but denied both buggery and murder. His story was that he had had a sexual encounter with the boy, but had then seen another man nearby; worried that the man had observed him committing sexual offences, he ran away, leaving the boy alive. He gave a description of the man which bore some similarity to a man referred to in the proceedings as 'Mark'. Blastland's defence at trial involved suggesting that Mark may have committed the murder. Mark had in fact been suspected by the police, and had even confessed. He later retracted the confession and after further investigation the police ruled him out as a suspect. At the trial, the prosecution agreed to reveal certain information about Mark: that he had been fully investigated by the police, and what his movements were on the night of the murder. The defence had wanted to call Mark to testify at trial, but the judge refused leave to do so.[11] With that avenue closed, the defence sought to build a case against Mark using reports of statements he had made to others. First, there was his confession. However, because the defence would have been relying on the confession to prove the truth of assertions contained in it, it was hearsay and inadmissible; the confession need not concern us further here.[12] Secondly, the defence sought to call evidence from people whom Mark had spoken to on the night of, and the morning after, the murder. On these occasions, which were before the body

---

[8] See D McCord, "'But Perry Mason Made it Look so Easy!'": the Admissibility of Evidence Offered by a Criminal Defendant to Suggest that Someone Else is Guilty' (1996) 63 *Tennessee L Rev* 917; KA Findley and MS Scott, 'The Multiple Dimensions of Tunnel Vision in Criminal Cases' [2006] *Wisconsin L Rev* 291, 342–9.

[9] R Munday, *Evidence* (London, Butterworths, 2001) para 10.31; P Roberts and A Zuckerman, *Criminal Evidence* (Oxford, OUP, 2004) 105; C Allen, *Practical Guide to Evidence* (2nd edn, London, Cavendish, 2001) 14–15; A Choo 'The Notion of Relevance and Defence Evidence' [1993] Crim LR 114.

[10] See [1986] AC 41. The facts are set out in more detail in the unreported judgment of the Court of Appeal, available on LEXIS.

[11] This may seem strange, but, if called, Mark would have been treated as a hostile witness. He may well also have refused to testify, relying on his privilege against self-incrimination, in which case his appearance would have had a dramatic, rather than testimonial, impact on the jury.

[12] This is a straightforward application of the hearsay rule, even if the outcome is controversial. See *R v Turner* (1975) 60 Cr App R 80.

had been discovered by the police, Mark had reported that a boy had been murdered. The trial judge and the Court of Appeal held that this evidence was rightly excluded as hearsay. The argument before the House of Lords concerned whether such evidence might nevertheless be admitted for a non-hearsay purpose.

The argument for admissibility is quite simple. Mark's statement 'a boy has been murdered' was not being used to prove the truth of the assertion that a boy had been murdered—the boy's death was not a contested issue at trial. What, it was argued, the statement showed beyond this was that Mark knew that a boy had been murdered; and this was significant because Mark knew it at a time when it could be presumed that very few people (among them, the boy's killer) knew of the murder. In the House of Lords Lord Bridge seemed to admit that this chain of inference escaped the hearsay rule.[13] He nevertheless objected to the evidence on the grounds that it was irrelevant, explaining:

> The issue at the trial ... was whether it was proved that the appellant had buggered and murdered Karl Fletcher. Mark's knowledge that Karl had been murdered was neither itself in issue, nor was it, per se, of any relevance to the issue. What was relevant was not the fact of Mark's knowledge but how he had come by that knowledge. He might have done so in a number of ways, but the two most obvious possibilities were either that he had witnessed the commission of the murder by the appellant or that he had committed it himself. The statements which it was sought to prove that Mark made, indicating his knowledge of the murder, provided no rational basis whatever on which the jury could be invited to draw an inference as to the source of the knowledge. To do so would have been mere speculation.[14]

Other cases where 'state of mind' evidence had been admitted were distinguished by Lord Bridge on the grounds that the evidence had been 'directly relevant' on those occasions.[15]

---

[13]   He allows that use of a statement to prove state of mind is not hearsay, but still objects to the evidence 'in the light of the principles on which the exclusion of hearsay depends' (above n 7, 54). The better view is probably that the evidence was not hearsay. For a useful discussion, see D Birch, 'Hearsay Logic and Hearsay Fiddles: *Blastland* Revisited' in P Smith (ed), *Criminal Law: Essays in Honour of JC Smith* (London, Butterworths, 1987).

[14]   Above n 7, 54. Note the JSB direction on circumstantial evidence: 'you should be careful to distinguish between arriving at conclusions based on reliable circumstantial evidence, and mere speculation. Speculating in a case amounts to no more than guessing, or making up theories without good evidence to support them, and neither the prosecution, the defence nor you should do that' (www.jsboard.co.uk/criminal_law/cbb/mf_04.htm#19). It will obviously be difficult to draw a clear distinction between speculation and evidence-based reasoning.

[15]   Above n 7, 54 (distinguishing *Thomas v Connell* (1838) 4 M & W 267); and 59 (distinguishing *R v Ratten* [1972] AC 378). The notion of 'direct relevance' is unhelpful. No evidence is directly relevant, in that it can only be linked to a probandum through a process of inference.

People often seem to have conflicting intuitions about *Blastland*. On first considering the facts of the case, they will take the view that evidence of Mark's knowledge is relevant to the proposition 'Blastland killed Karl'. But on reading the passage just quoted, they may become persuaded that Mark's knowledge is irrelevant. This wavering reaction is actually quite instructive: Lord Bridge's argument is sound, but it is based on questionable premises.

There is one easy way to make Lord Bridge's argument look specious. Ask: what if the prosecution had evidence that Blastland had been telling people that a boy had been killed before the body had been discovered; would it have been prevented from presenting this evidence on grounds of irrelevance? It surely would not have been. Drawing on the Bayesian framework, we can say that evidence is relevant if it allows us to distinguish between the hypotheses we are considering.[16] In our example, Blastland's knowledge would be relevant because it can distinguish between the hypotheses 'Blastland killed Karl' and 'someone other than Blastland killed Karl'. Blastland would be far more likely to know about the killing shortly after it had been committed if he had committed the murder than if someone else had. On the actual facts of the case, the same goes for Mark. But Lord Bridge's argument is more subtle than this analysis suggests. Whether or not evidence is relevant can depend on the precise hypotheses being considered:[17] an obvious example is that DNA evidence linking the defendant to the scene of crime is relevant if the hypotheses are 'D killed V' / 'someone else killed V', but not if the hypotheses are 'D killed V in self-defence' / 'D killed V not in self-defence'. Because choice of hypotheses can have significant effects on the relevance and probative value of evidence, it is important to note that Lord Bridge appears to set up his argument with different hypotheses to the ones just considered. He is thinking, not in terms of 'Mark Killed Karl' / 'Someone else killed Karl', but in terms of 'Mark killed Karl' / 'Mark saw Blastland kill Karl'. If these are the right hypotheses to consider, it follows that evidence of Mark's knowledge is irrelevant. On either hypothesis he is bound to know about the murder before it is public knowledge. Evidence about his statements cannot distinguish between the hypotheses, so it is irrelevant.[18]

---

[16] See eg, R Friedman, *The Elements of Evidence* (2nd edn, St Paul, MN, West Publishing, 1998) 45–57.

[17] See B Robertson and GA Vignaux, *Interpreting Evidence: Evaluating Forensic Science in the Courtroom* (Chichester, Wiley, 1995) ch 3.

[18] Actually, it is a bit more complicated than this. The evidence is not that Mark knew that a boy had been murdered, but that he made statements reporting this. Arguably, he would be less likely to make such statements if he had committed the murder than if he had just come across the body or seen the murder. If so, Mark's statements may be evidence for the prosecution.

This analysis does not quite let Lord Bridge off the hook. It simply reveals that the crucial question is whether these were indeed the only two hypotheses in play. It is not difficult to think of other possibilities: Mark may have killed Karl; he may have seen Blastland kill Karl; he may have come across the body after the murder; he may have heard about the murder from someone else; he may never have seen or heard about the body at all. The evidence of Mark's knowledge cannot distinguish between the first four of these hypotheses; but it can distinguish between the first four and the fifth. In effect, the evidence knocks the fifth hypothesis out of the running. Looking at the passage quoted above, Lord Bridge seems to count the fifth hypothesis out from the start: the examples he gives are both hypotheses on which Mark's knowledge of the murder is bound to occur, and he says that what is important is how Mark came by that knowledge. Consider an analogy: a detective finds the offender's blood at the scene of the crime; the blood is of a type shared by 30 per cent of the population, and the suspect has that blood type. No one would respond to this scenario by saying: 'the blood may have been left there by the offender or it may have been left there by someone else with that blood type; therefore evidence about the blood is irrelevant unless we know how the blood came to be there'. Yet that is essentially how Lord Bridge is analysing the knowledge evidence in *Blastland*. In the blood example, the evidence eliminates 70 per cent of the population from suspicion: the probability of guilt that was spread among this part of the population must therefore be redistributed over the remaining 30 per cent (including the defendant), thus the evidence is relevant. In the same way, in *Blastland* the elimination of the fifth hypothesis affects the probability of the remaining four: each becomes more probable than it was before, including the hypothesis that Mark killed Karl. That the evidence cannot distinguish between the remaining hypotheses is of no consequence: what matters is that the evidence lends support to a hypothesis incompatible with Blastland's guilt, possibly creating reasonable doubt. This is not to say that Lord Bridge's analysis is wrong. What really matters is whether his selection of hypotheses is fair. If the defence were running their case on the theory that Blastland had left the boy who had then been killed by Mark, and the prosecution's case was that Mark had either seen the murder or discovered the body because he was in the area, then Lord Bridge is probably right to hold the evidence irrelevant. The case reports provide scant factual detail, but it seems that this was not quite the state of play. We know that the prosecution produced evidence about Mark's movements on the night of the murder, which presumably put him close to the spot where the killing took place. But this is not the same as the prosecution admitting that Mark actually knew about the killing; thus evidence of Mark's knowledge could have done some useful work for the defence by establishing that he did.

It was previously mentioned that the courts may be unsympathetic to defences that involve suggesting that another named person may have committed the crime with which the defendant is charged. This is puzzling: one might expect courts to be cautious about limiting defence strategies. Pondering the reasons why courts are sceptical towards 'someone else did it' defences may provide us with further insight into *Blastland*. In a paper which has generated some controversy, Davis and Follette argue that evidence that a defendant was having an extra-marital affair is not relevant to the question whether he murdered his wife, at least when there is little other evidence to incriminate him.[19] The reason for this claim seems to be that, even if unfaithful men are three times more likely to murder their wives than faithful men, evidence of infidelity will have relatively minor impact on the probability of guilt when there is not much other evidence to incriminate D. It will have rather more impact where there is other evidence throwing a fair amount of suspicion on him. For example, if the initial probability of guilt (P(G)) is 0.01, then the infidelity evidence will only increase P(G) to 0.03. Compare this with the situation where P(G) is initially 0.5; the same evidence now increases P(G) to 0.75.[20] Now there is something of a cognitive illusion here: the strength of the infidelity evidence does not change; in each case it makes guilt three times as likely as it was initially. It is just that when we express the likelihood of guilt in terms of the finite scale between 0 and 1, the impact of the evidence appears to be unimpressive when we have a very small (or, indeed, very large) starting point.[21] The illusion involved here, however, is a significant one. It explains why evidence may look more significant when adduced against someone whom we already have independent reasons to think guilty. Thus, in *Blastland*, because it is Blastland who is on trial, we tend to assume that there is a reasonable amount of evidence against him. If the prosecution were to produce evidence that Blastland had been telling people that a boy had been murdered before this fact was generally known, then this evidence would seem significant. The same does not necessarily

---

[19] D Davis and W Follette, 'Rethinking the Probative Value of Evidence: Base Rates, Intuitive Profiling, and the "Postdiction" of Behavior' (2002) 26 *Law and Human Behavior* 133 and 'Towards an Empirical Approach to Evidentiary Ruling' (2003) 27 *Law and Human Behavior* 661. Cf R Friedman and R Park, 'Sometimes what Everybody Thinks They Know is True' (2003) 27 *Law and Human Behavior* 629; D Kaye and J Koehler, 'The Misquantification of Probative Value' (2003) 27 *Law and Human Behavior* 645.

[20] The calculations are as follows: in the first example, odds on guilt are 1:99, rising to 3:99 with the evidence of infidelity; thus there is a posterior probability of 3/102 = 0.29 of guilt. In the second example, odds on guilt are 1:1, rising to 3:1, thus there is a posterior probability of 3/4 = 0.75 of guilt.

[21] A useful analysis, with clear illustrations of these effects, is G Wells, 'Murder, Extramarital Affairs, and the Issue of Probative Value' (2003) 27 *Law and Human Behavior* 623.

follow for Mark: because the spotlight is not directed at him, evidence making his guilt appear somewhat more likely does not seem so significant.

Blastland shows that judgements of relevance are sometimes quite difficult. Thinking about the evidence in simple terms—by asking 'what if the prosecution had similar evidence against Blastland?'—suggests that it is relevant. But focusing more carefully on the relevant hypotheses, which are moulded by the various admissions made by prosecution and defence, complicates things. All the same, Lord Bridge appears to have dismissed the argument for relevance rather too quickly. And this may well have been because he was worried that the defence was attempting to subvert the hearsay rule. As he comments: the argument for admissibility 'does appear to lead to the very odd result that the inference that Mark may have himself committed the murder may be supported indirectly by what Mark said, though if he had directly acknowledged guilt this would have been excluded'.[22] Policy concerns are moulding Lord Bridge's approach to the relevance issue.

KEARLEY: DETECTING BELIEF

In *Kearley*,[23] as in *Blastland*, an attempt to avoid the hearsay rule raised a difficult question about relevance. The police had searched Kearley's house, looking for drugs. They found a small amount of amphetamines, enough to charge Kearley with possession, but not with the more serious crime of supplying drugs. However, while on the premises, the police answered the door to a number of people asking for Kearley by his nickname, Chippie, and requesting to be supplied with drugs. This looks to be strong evidence against Kearley on the charge of supplying, but the hearsay rule caused problems. The prosecution did not attempt to get the callers to testify at trial (they presumably would not have co-operated), so it was necessary to rely on the police officers' testimony about the callers and what they had said. Suppose the callers had said 'Can I buy some drugs from Chippie?' This looks to be a question, rather than an assertion, so it may avoid the hearsay rule. The House of Lords, however, looked carefully at the way the question was being used. The majority held that it was only relevant via a chain of inference which involved relying on an assertion hidden in the statement. Such 'implied assertions' were held to be caught by the hearsay rule.[24]

---

[22]   Above n 7, 53.

[23]   [1992] 2 WLR 656.

[24]   The definition of hearsay in the Criminal Justice Act 2003 probably overrules *Kearley* on this point: the exclusionary factors in the Act apply to matters stated in a statement not made in oral evidence in the relevant proceedings (s 114). A statement is defined as a

To spot the assertion supposedly hidden in the statement, we need to break down the chain of inference involved here, as if we were constructing a Wigmore chart. This will identify 'the caller believed that Chippie would sell him drugs' as a crucial link in the chain between the statement and the conclusion 'Chippie has supplied drugs in the past'. The decision of the House of Lords in *Kearley* seems to have been that the hearsay rule is activated by reliance on the caller's belief, because the belief involves an implied assertion that Chippie has supplied drugs.[25] Lord Browne-Wilkinson, however, argued in dissent that there is a route from the question 'Can I buy some drugs from Chippie?' to the conclusion that Chippie has sold drugs in the past which avoids relying on this belief. His argument, in essence, is that 'the fact that there were a number of people seeking to buy drugs was legally relevant and admissible as showing that there was a market to which the appellant could sell'.[26] The market gave Kearley the opportunity to sell drugs which, in turn, increased the probability that he was selling drugs. To shore up his point, Lord Browne-Wilkinson deploys an analogy. He imagines a shop which sells only coffee. If, on a certain day, there was a queue of customers outside the shop, it can be inferred that there are potential buyers of coffee from the shop. And from this it can be inferred that the proprietor has an intent to sell coffee.

This analysis seems vaguely plausible, but does it really avoid relying on the beliefs of the customers? Although the existence of potential buyers may be evidence of drug (or coffee) selling, in some cases it will be extraordinarily weak evidence. Anyone who visits a rock music festival doubtless has a large market of potential drug buyers, but it is going a little far to argue that presence at the festival is evidence of intent to supply drugs.[27] Kearley and the coffee shop proprietor are in a slightly different position. Rather than just a market, they have queues at their doors. But

---

'representation of fact or opinion', and a matter stated is only caught by the exclusionary factors if one of the purposes of the person making the statement was to cause a person to believe the matter stated, or to act on the basis of its being true (s 115). It is just arguable, however, that the question 'can I buy some drugs from Chippie' represents, among other things, the speaker's opinion that Chippie is a drug supplier, and thus is a statement; that a matter stated in the statement is that the speaker believes that Chippie can supply drugs; and that one of the speaker's purposes is to cause the person spoken to, to act on the basis that the speaker believes Chippie to be a drug supplier. For fuller discussion, see Craig Callen, Chapter 6. See also *R v Singh* [2006] Crim LR 646 (and commentary).

[25] Though other reasons are given for distrusting beliefs: they are seen as being irrelevant because merely opinion (an unhelpful conflation of the opinion rule and the relevance rule); and because they may be founded on a second layer of hearsay—the callers may be visiting Kearley because they have heard rumours that he is a drug dealer.

[26] Above n 23, 699.

[27] And of course the police officers in *Kearley* had a market for drugs—they could easily have sold amphetamines to the people knocking on Kearley's door. Would Lord Browne-Wilkinson take this to be evidence of the police officers' intent to supply drugs?

our whole understanding of what a queue is seems to involve an assumption that the people in it have a particular belief. When we see a line of cars coming off a factory assembly line, we do not refer to it as a queue (cars, of course, do not have beliefs). And only in a loose metaphorical sense would we talk of the cars waiting to leave the factory. But when we see a line of cars outside a supermarket car park we think of it as a queue; that seems to be because we attribute beliefs to the drivers of the cars. These beliefs will refer to such things as there being something worth getting (a parking space, food) by waiting in the queue. Some people, perhaps, will join a queue for no good reason: they just fall in with the crowd. But if we thought the queue outside the coffee shop was formed entirely of such compulsive queuers we would no longer take it to be evidence of the proprietor's intent to supply coffee. Or, to approach the problem from a slightly different angle, suppose we chopped the heads off the people standing outside the coffee shop and discovered them to be merely very realistic waxwork dummies. We would then surely question whether their presence outside the shop implied anything at all about the proprietor's intentions. Subtracting beliefs from the picture,[28] then, seems to stymie Lord Browne-Wilkinson's argument for the relevance of the callers to Kearley's intentions. This implies that beliefs play a crucial role in his argument.

Hirst has suggested a slightly different hearsay-avoiding argument for the relevance of the callers in *Kearley*.[29] If Kearley was dealing drugs from his house, Hirst argues, one would expect him to have a large number of callers. Thus, the callers are evidence of drug dealing. This would be fairly weak evidence, for there are many reasons, apart from drug dealing, why Kearley may have had several visitors during the short period when the police were in his house. But Hirst has a way to bolster the argument:

> If the mere fact that [Kearley] had so many callers would be of some limited significance, then the added fact that the callers were clearly drug users must surely have enhanced that relevance. It might be compared to a case in which a suspected spy is seen to receive frequent visits from persons known to be agents or military attachés of foreign powers.[30]

---

[28] A riposte is that if a group of cats gathered outside Kearley's door every morning, this would be evidence that Kearley intended to feed them. Supposing that cats do not have beliefs (something which philosophers dispute), we seem to be able to reason from the presence of cats to Kearley's intentions without relying on beliefs. Nevertheless, cats have something in their heads (let us say a Pavlovian stimulus-response mechanism) which stands in the same relationship to Kearley's intentions to feed them as do the callers' beliefs to his intentions to sell them drugs. If we discovered that the cats had nothing inside their heads (they turn out to be stuffed), surely we would no longer take their presence to be an indication of Kearley's intentions.

[29] M Hirst, 'Conduct, Relevance and the Hearsay Rule' (1993) 13 *Legal Studies* 54, 65.

[30] *Ibid* 65.

This is certainly a clever argument, but it is not clear that it avoids reliance on the beliefs of the callers. As before, it seems that the very notion of being a caller is bound up with beliefs about the occupant of the house where one calls. Someone is a caller, as opposed to, say, an electrician who is just ringing a door bell to see whether it works, because she believes that there is a possibility that the person on whom she is calling can help her out in some way. If this is right, then even Hirst's argument for the relevance of the evidence in *Kearley* is vulnerable to hearsay objections—at least, on the understanding of hearsay developed in *Kearley*.

The evidence in *Kearley* poses rather different relevance problems to those encountered in *Blastland*. Anyone can see that the visitors asking for drugs is evidence that Kearley is a drug dealer. The issue is not one of probability, but of trying to isolate the precise route through which the relevance argument runs in order to see whether it involves beliefs which are vulnerable to hearsay objections. Here, a useful technique is to conduct thought experiments. This is what Lord Browne-Wilkinson does with his coffee shop example. This example, however, is opaque: the hypothetical needs further testing to establish whether the inferential chain involved actually does depend on beliefs. And this process reveals that what is important is not just a market, but queues or calls, concepts which do seem to involve beliefs. Admittedly, this is a difficult area. Our understanding of human action is so intimately bound up with our attribution of beliefs to actors that it is not easy to separate the two, to ask 'what role is belief playing in our interpretation of these actions?' Nevertheless, the basic technique to be utilised is not too mysterious. The technique should be familiar to any common lawyer: the construction of hypotheticals to test how far a rule can be extended, and the careful variation of the hypotheticals to isolate the crucial factors. The only difference here is that, rather than testing the scope of a rule, we are trying to isolate the essential steps in an inferential process.

INFERENCES FROM SILENCE

My third example is rather more complex than the two analysed so far. It is also of more immediate practical importance. Since the changes to the right to silence in the police station and at trial introduced by ss 34 and 35 of the Criminal Justice and Public Order Act (CJPOA) 1994, the Court of Appeal has developed a complex case law regulating the drawing of inferences from a defendant's pre-trial silence.[31] An impression of this complexity can be gained by glancing at the Judicial Studies Board specimen direction on s 34 which, together with its explanatory notes, is over 2,000 words long.[32] Section 34, in particular, has given rise to some interesting inferential puzzles and once more illustrates the difficulty courts sometimes experience when drawing inferences.

The appropriate starting point is the wording of s 34 itself. To condense slightly, the section provides that, 'Where in any proceedings against a person for an offence, evidence is given that the accused at any time before he was charged with the offence, on being questioned under caution by a constable trying to discover whether or by whom the offence had been committed, failed to mention any fact relied on in his defence in those proceedings, the court or jury may draw such inferences from the failure as appear proper'. Here, I shall concentrate on three aspects of the s 34 case law.

The first is the requirement, laid down by the Court of Appeal[33] and seemingly adopted by the European Court of Human Rights,[34] that the jury should not draw an inference from the defendant's failure to mention during police interview a fact later relied on at trial, unless it is satisfied that the only explanation for the defendant's silence is that he fabricated the fact after the interview or did not want it exposed to police questioning and investigation. Put another way, the jury must be 'sure'[35] that no 'innocent' explanation exists, or be able to eliminate innocent explanations for the failure. Although some commentators see this as a logical require-ment for the drawing of an inference from silence,[36] it is not. As a matter of logic, an inference can be drawn from the defendant's failure so long as the 'suspicious' explanation for the silence is more plausible than the 'innocent' explanation.[37] To be sure, the strength of the inference will vary

---

[31] Significantly, away from the front line of criminal litigation, the House of Lords in *R v Webber* [2004] UKHL 1 shows a more relaxed attitude, with several references to common sense as opposed to detailed judicial directions as the appropriate basis for inferences from silence.

[32] See www.jsboard.co.uk/criminal_law/cbb/mf_05.htm#40.

[33] *R v Cowan* [1996] QB 373; *R v Condron* [1997] 1 WLR 827.

[34] *Condron v United Kingdom* (2001) 31 EHRR 1; *Beckles v United Kingdom* [2002] 36 EHRR 162.

[35] *R v Chenia* [2003] 2 Cr App R 6.

[36] *Blackstone's Criminal Practice 2003* (Oxford, OUP, 2003) para 19.7 (cf the slightly weaker statement in the 2005 edition, para 19.8); Roberts and Zuckerman, above n 9, 443; D Birch, 'Suffering in Silence: a Cost-Benefit Analysis of Section 34 of the Criminal Justice and Public Order Act 1994' [1999] *Crim LR* 769, 776; J Jackson, 'Interpreting the Silence Provisions: the Northern Ireland Cases' [1995] *Crim LR* 587, 600. Cf C Tapper, *Cross and Tapper on Evidence* (10th edn, London, Butterworths, 2004) 686.

[37] This simplifies things a little. For example, reliance on legal advice is an 'innocent' explanation for silence, but if lawyers are more likely to advise silence where the case against the defendant is strong and D offers no explanation for it, then an inference to guilt may still be possible.

depending on the relative plausibility of suspicious and innocent explanations, and will be at its strongest when the innocent explanation can be discounted. But it is a mistake to think that an inference is not worth drawing because it is weak; even an inference of modest power can have a significant impact on the overall strength of the prosecution's case.[38]

The requirement to eliminate innocent explanations may, of course, be defensible even if it is not logically mandated on purely inferential grounds. I have discussed the issues involved here at greater length elsewhere, so only touch on them here.[39] It is possible that there are policy reasons for limiting the inference in the way described above, though I doubt that any such reasons stand up to scrutiny. Another possibility is that the rule requiring the elimination of innocent explanations is sensitive to the way people actually reason about evidence. That possibility certainly makes the issues more complex,[40] but for the moment, the main point is that a little understanding of the conditions in which inferences can be drawn exposes apparent misconceptions on the part of courts and commentators as to how to draw inferences from evidence.

A second issue related to inferences from silence involves the Court of Appeal's judgment in *Mountford*.[41] M and W were both present in a flat raided by police; there was considerable evidence to suggest that heroin was being supplied from the flat. M said nothing during police interview. At trial, M and W each accused the other of being the dealer. The question for the Court of Appeal was whether an adverse inference could be drawn from the fact that M had not mentioned during interview that W was the dealer, when M's explanation for this failure was that he did not want to get W into trouble. The Court of Appeal held that no inference could be drawn in this situation, owing to a problem of circularity:

'The fact' not revealed in interview constituted the defence to the charge. In other words whether 'the fact' not revealed was or may have been true was the issue in the case the resolution of which would determine the verdict. It is difficult to see how the jury could have rejected the appellant's reason for not mentioning 'the fact' without also rejecting the truth of 'the fact' – the truth of each depended on the truth of the other. In our judgment, this element of circularity could only be resolved by a verdict founded not in any way upon the Section 34 point but upon the other evidence in the case. A verdict of 'guilty' would obviously establish that 'the fact' not mentioned was untrue and accordingly that the explanation for not mentioning it was equally untrue. In

---

[38] Kadane and Schum, above n 1, 45, comment that 'one of the most interesting, but often counterintuitive, characteristics of Bayes's rule is how quickly it can allow weak evidence items to add up to a strong case'.

[39] 'Rationality, Naturalism and Evidence Law' (2003) 4 *Michigan State L Rev* 849, 868–76.

[40] See *ibid.*

[41] [1999] Crim LR 575.

this case, as it seems to us, the evidence which resolved the Section 34 issue was the very evidence which resolved the issue in the case and therefore determined the verdict.

The judgment in *Mountford* has provoked a number of reactions. It was followed by the Court of Appeal in *Gill*,[42] but doubted in later cases and, spectacularly, 'consigned to oblivion' in a judgment given by the then Lord Chief Justice, Lord Woolf, in *Gowland-Wynn*.[43] But *Gowland-Wynn* eschews the sort of close analysis advocated in this chapter; Lord Woolf makes no attempt to assess the reasoning in *Mountford*. His reason for rejecting the *Mountford* approach seems to be partly policy driven: he suggests that the judgment would have the effect of 'emasculating and defeating the very purpose of section 34'.[44] Beyond this, the only observation is that 'where a defendant does not comment about something which goes right to the heart of his defence, it seems to us that section 34 has the largest and most significant part to play'.[45] *Mountford* has also met with the disapproval of the House of Lords in *Webber*, this time with a little more analysis:

> The jury had to decide whether the appellant was in possession of the drug with intent to supply. Had they concluded that only one of the two men was or might be a supplier and that that one was or might have been Williams, that would have defeated the prosecution. But if Williams was the supplier, and the jury were not impressed by the appellant's explanation for not naming him, it was open to the jury to regard the appellant's failure to mention this fact as a pointer towards the untruth of that explanation, thus strengthening the prosecution case and weakening his own.[46]

Academic commentary on *Mountford* has been somewhat more positive. Birch[47] and Grevling[48] give qualified support to the decision. In a more sustained analysis, Munday concludes that there is no circularity involved in drawing an adverse inference in the *Mountford* situation.[49] Ultimately, however, none of these commentaries is completely satisfying.

The *Mountford* problem is rather intractable, and it may be helpful to approach it indirectly. The central claim in *Mountford* is that there is a circularity problem if an adverse inference is drawn. A similar, and much simpler, example of circularity can be found in the jurisprudence on lies

---

[42] [2000] 1 Cr App R 160.
[43] [2002] 1 Cr App R 569.
[44] *Ibid* [9].
[45] *Ibid*.
[46] Above n 31, [26].
[47] In her case commentary [1999] Crim LR 576.
[48] K Grevling, 'Silence, Lies and Vicious Circularity' in P Mirfield and R Smith (eds), *Essays for Colin Tapper* (London, Butterworths, 2003).
[49] R Munday, 'Inferences and Explanations' (2000) 2 *Archbold News* 6.

directions.[50] In some circumstances, an adverse inference can be drawn against a defendant who is thought to have told lies relating to the offence for which he is on trial.[51] An obvious example is where a false alibi is given. But it is recognised that there is no mileage in drawing an adverse inference from a lie on a 'central issue'. If the defendant in an assault case testifies that 'I didn't hit V', while several eyewitnesses testify that D did in fact do so, the fact-finder may well infer that D is lying. But the fact-finder cannot then proceed to draw a guilty lie inference against D on the issue of whether or not he hit V. It is important to understand that in such situations the guilty lie inference is circular, not superfluous: the problem is not that, having already concluded that D hit V, there is no point in drawing a further inference. Rather, the problem is one of bootstrapping, or double-counting. Thus, the circularity is present even if the fact-finder is not quite sure whom to believe. If it is thought that there is, say, a 0.6 probability that the eyewitnesses are correct, then, although D is probably lying, no adverse inference can be drawn, because the fact-finder has already deduced that D probably hit V. The probability that he did cannot be increased beyond 0.6 by taking the suspiciousness of the lie into account. To do so would involve reasoning in a circle, as follows: 'D is probably lying. It is suspicious that he should lie, therefore I think it is even more likely that he is lying than I thought it was a few seconds ago'. To put the point more abstractly: the lie cannot be used to support its negation but only, as in the false alibi example, to support a separate inference. All this is reasonably straightforward. The contention in *Mountford* is that the same reasoning applies to inferences from silence, whenever the explanation for the silence is the same as D's defence to the charge.

To understand the issues in *Mountford*, one needs to appreciate that M makes two claims: (1) 'W was the dealer' and (2) 'I didn't want to get him into trouble'. In this respect it differs from most cases involving inferences from silence. If we concentrate on (1), and presume that only M or W (but not both) was dealing, then we have an exact parallel to the guilty lie inference where the lie is on the central issue: it is just like D saying 'I didn't hit V'. The fact-finder may reject (1), but in doing so she concludes that D is guilty. She will also conclude that D was lying about (1), but with guilt already ascertained, there is no room for a guilty lie inference. Even if the fact-finder thinks it 0.6 probable that W was not the dealer, she cannot use the inference from the probable lie to boost her belief in M's guilt beyond 0.6. To that extent, the reasoning in *Mountford* is impeccable. So far, however, the analysis has concentrated on lies, not silence. Obviously,

---

[50]   This parallel is recognised by Grevling, above n 48.
[51]   *R v Lucas* [1981] QB 720. See the valuable discussion in D Hamer, '"Hoist with his Own Petard"? Guilty Lies and Ironic Inferences in Criminal Proof' (2001) 54 *Current Legal Problems* 377.

if (1) is rejected, an inference from silence will be superfluous. But what if (1) is merely thought improbable? Can the fact-finder then use an inference from silence to conclude that M's defence was a later fabrication? The reasoning here involves the inference 'if W was the dealer, M would have said so earlier'. This inference does not depend at all on the probability that either M or W was the dealer (except to the extent that the inference would be superfluous if one were sure that M was the dealer). However, the soundness of the inference depends on (2)—M's claim that he did not want to get W into trouble. If the fact-finder is sceptical about (2) (along with any other possible reasons for the silence), she can draw an adverse inference without having already concluded that M was the dealer. This seems to be the point intended by the House of Lords in *Webber*, though the way the argument is expressed is confusing (the second reference to 'explanation' is unclear: it would make more sense to substitute 'the claim that it was W who was the dealer').

There is, however, a further layer of complexity to consider. It was noted above that the courts require the rejection of innocent explanations for silence before an adverse inference is drawn. Though this requirement was questioned, let us take it seriously. On this approach, it will be very difficult for the fact-finder to reject the claim that M's silence was protective of W. The claim is perfectly plausible as a matter of human psychology; indeed, what empirical evidence we have suggests that the desire to protect others was a common reason for 'no comment' responses at police interview before the CJPOA reforms,[52] and – though data are scant – that it is the most common reason for the (far more damaging) decision to confess falsely.[53] It would not be impossible for the fact-finder to reject M's explanation for silence, but there are further logical problems in doing so. M's explanation might be rejected if, for example, the fact-finder decides that M is a ruthless individual who would not think twice about implicating W.[54] But M cannot be all that ruthless: one of the few things we know for sure is that M did not implicate W at the police interview, which would have been the obvious strategy for a ruthless individual, whether guilty or not. Further, the fact-finder cannot reason as follows: 'I believe W, therefore M is a drug dealer, drug dealers are ruthless, ruthless people would have no qualms about implicating a co-defendant', for that would raise the very circularity problems described above. Thus, while it is not logically impossible to draw an inference against M, or other

---

[52] M McConville and J Hodgson, *Custodial Legal Advice and the Right to Silence* (London, HMSO, 1993).

[53] G Gudjonsson, *The Psychology of Interrogations and Confessions: a Handbook* (Chichester, John Wiley, 2003) 176–7.

[54] An inference similar to one employed by Judge Weinstein in *United States v Shonubi* 895 F. Supp. 460 (EDNY), on the basis of Shonubi's behaviour at trial.

defendants in similar positions, it does appear to be difficult to do so. To that extent, the Court of Appeal was right in *Mountford* and *Gill*.

Mountford does not exhaust the inferential intricacies of the s 34 case law. My third example has attracted more attention; it arises where D's explanation for silence is that he was relying on legal advice. Here, policy issues loom especially large: the courts are worried that, if they allow reliance on legal advice to block adverse inferences, all lawyers will advise silence in the police station and the legislation will be defeated.[55] Thus, in the first cases to address the issue, it was said that only if there were good reasons for advising silence would reliance on that advice operate as a bar to adverse inferences.[56] This is one area of the s 34 case law where there has been some astute analysis. As Dennis has explained, so long as reliance on legal advice is genuinely D's reason for silence, one cannot infer that he later fabricated the defence or did not want it investigated.[57] As usual, however, there are complications: D may well have mixed motives for silence; the reasonableness of the advice may be relevant to the question of whether D's reason for silence really was that he was following his lawyer's advice; and if legal advisers are more likely to counsel silence where D admits his guilt to them, or offers them no explanation for the incriminating evidence against him, then an adverse inference might be drawn from legally advised silence.

The basic point—that silence based on legal advice blocks adverse inferences—was recognised by the Court of Appeal in *Betts and Hall*.[58] This, however, was a short-lived victory for the logic of inference. Notoriously, in *Howell* policy took the lead again:

> The public interest that inheres in reasonable disclosure by a suspected person of what he has to say when faced with a set of facts which accuse him, is thwarted if currency is given to the belief that if a suspect remains silent on legal advice he may systematically avoid adverse comment at his trial. And it may encourage solicitors to advise silence for other than good objective reasons. We do not consider, *pace* the reasoning in *Betts and Hall*, that once it is shown that the advice (of whatever quality) has genuinely been relied on as the reason for the suspect's remaining silent, adverse comment is thereby disallowed. The premise of such a position is that in such circumstances it is in principle not reasonable to expect the suspect to mention the facts in question. We do not believe that is so … There must always be soundly based objective reasons for silence, sufficiently cogent and telling to weigh in the balance against the clear public interest in an account being given by the suspect to the police.[59]

---

[55] See *Condron*, above n 33, 191.
[56] *Ibid*.
[57] I Dennis, *The Law of Evidence* (2nd edn, London, Sweet & Maxwell, 2002) 156–9.
[58] [2001] 2 Cr App R 257.
[59] [2005] 1 Cr App R 1, [24].

The mistake here is a direct result of mixing policy factors with inferential considerations. Even if one takes the view that it is unreasonable to fail to mention important facts to the police contrary to legal advice not to do so, it does not follow that an inference can be drawn from such silence. That something is unreasonable does not make it evidence of fabrication. Fabrication can only be inferred from silence if silence is more likely on the hypothesis of fabrication than on the hypothesis of non-fabrication, and this is a different issue to the question of reasonableness (one might, for example, conclude that D is simply an unreasonable individual). Even if it is in the public interest that suspects give an account to the police, it does not follow that not giving an account is evidence of fabrication. Unfortunately, it seems that at present the reasoning in *Howell* has considerable influence on the Court of Appeal.[60]

An analogous illustration of careful reasoning being swamped by policy factors can be found in the case law under s 35 of the CJPOA 1994. This section allows a court or jury to draw an inference from a defendant's failure to testify in court.[61] Some defendants may be reluctant to testify because doing so can result in the jury being informed that they have previous convictions (this, at least, was the situation under the Criminal Evidence Act 1898;[62] by broadening the admissibility of previous convictions, the Criminal Justice Act 2003 makes the decision to testify less momentous for defendants who are concerned about disclosing their criminal record, though it is possible that not testifying will continue to make a difference in some cases)[63]. The basic logic of the s 35 inference is that failure to testify implies that the defendant has no answer to the prosecution's case, or none that would stand up to cross-examination. As with s 34, the jury should be told to consider possible innocent explanations for silence.[64] However, it will not be suggested to the jury that a desire to hide previous convictions may be a reason for not testifying, because such a direction is likely to do more harm than good to the defendant's prospects. One of the first questions to be raised about the

---

[60]   *R v Turner* [2004] 1 Cr App R 24, [26]; *R v Knight* [2004] 1 Cr App R 9; *R v Robinson* 2003 WL 21990392. Cf the JSB directions, above n 14, which follow the 'more favourable' line in *Betts and Hall*, above n 58.

[61]   For a detailed analysis of the inferences that can be drawn, see D Hamer, 'The Privilege of Silence and the Persistent Risk of Self-Incrimination: Part I' (2004) 28 *Criminal Law Journal* 160, and 'Part II' at 200.

[62]   See, in particular, the decision on this point in *R v Butterwasser* [1948] 1 KB 4.

[63]   Sections 101(1)(g) and 106(1) are drafted so as to undo *Butterwasser* with respect to attacks on a witness' character. But ss 101(1)(d) and 103(1)(b) allow bad character evidence on the question whether D has a propensity to be untruthful, and it is likely that D's decision to testify will be a factor here, because D's lack of truthfulness is more likely to be thought to be in issue if he testifies (but, for the insight that D's propensity to lie is never relevant to the question of whether he is lying in court, see RD Friedman, 'Character Impeachment: Psycho-Bayesian [!?] Analysis and a Proposed Overhaul' (1991) 38 *UCLA L Rev* 637).

[64]   JSB, above n 32, [4].

operation of s 35 was whether the jury should be told not to draw an inference in a case where a defendant might have been worried that testifying would reveal his previous convictions. The Court of Appeal held that this possibility should not be a barrier to the operation of the section; to accept such an argument would be to 'drive a coach and horses through the statutory provisions'.[65] The question was reconsidered by the House of Lords in *Becouarn*.[66] The defendant's case included the claim that prosecution witnesses had deliberately identified him falsely, a claim that would have led to his being cross-examined on his previous convictions had he testified. He chose not to testify, and the jury were invited to draw an adverse inference.

The House of Lords rejected the claim that the combined effect of s 35 and the character evidence rules placed Becouarn in an unfair position. To protect a defendant in his position would be 'misleading to a jury' and it would be 'wrong if he could stay out of the witness box and avoid having legitimate comment made about his failure to give evidence. It would also create [a] quite unjustifiable distinction between defendants'.[67] There may be some truth in the first and third of these propositions, but they do not confront the real question: is drawing an inference against Becouarn rational? The closest the judgment comes to addressing this point is the claim that 'fear of allowing in his previous convictions may be one element in his decision not to give evidence, but reluctance to face cross-examination may be another and much more predominant element'.[68] The question, of course, is: how is the jury to decide which factor predominates in the decision not to testify when it cannot be alerted to one of them? The problem is especially pressing given that the jury should be directed not to draw an inference under s 35 unless satisfied 'that the only sensible explanation for his silence is that he has no answer, or none that would bear examination'.[69] At the very least, the jury is being kept in the dark about a factor which might persuade it to moderate the inference drawn, an arrangement that hardly seems conducive to fairness. The parallels with the problem of legal advice under s 34 are strong. The courts are keen to make the law workable, but this is achieved only at the price of ignoring the rationality of the inferences in play. The better conclusion may be that Parliament simply created an unworkable law.

---

[65] *R v Cowan and others* [1996] QB 373, 380.
[66] [2005] UKHL 55.
[67] *Ibid* [23].
[68] *Ibid* [24].
[69] See www.jsboard.co.uk/criminal_law/cbb/mf_05.htm#39.

CONCLUSION

The examples presented in this chapter are designed to show that there is considerable value in thinking carefully about inference. Inferential analysis can help to unravel the mysteries of well known cases, such as *Blastland* and *Kearley*, and can also have considerable practical importance, as seen in the discussion of the s 34 and s 35 jurisprudence, where questions about the proper limits of adverse inferences recur from case to case.

In stressing the importance of taking facts, and factual reasoning, seriously, I am to a considerable extent repeating a message widely broadcast by Twining.[70] That message is always worth repeating, if only for the fact that many evidence scholars have not taken it to heart (taking it to heart is very different from nodding to Wigmorean and Bayesian analysis in an introductory chapter of a textbook).[71] That close analysis of inference is so often ignored is surprising. Engagement with factual inference is the main feature that marks our subject, evidence law, out from others taught in the law curriculum. But perhaps therein lies part of the explanation for the existing state of affairs: academics are far more comfortable with the sort of rule and policy analysis which is familiar to them from other doctrinal subjects, and are not prepared to make the effort to get to grips with the markedly different discipline of factual analysis. Perhaps, too, the close analysis of individual cases can seem rather uninspiring to academics more used to making broad arguments about the shape of the law.

While I am more than happy to repeat the message that we should take facts seriously, it is probably also worth observing that Twining has pursued his agenda in the main by using examples that evidence lawyers do not encounter within their day to day work.[72] With important exceptions – such as a careful analysis of *United States v Huddleston*[73] by Anderson[74] – evidence lawyers seem to lack, as a resource, close analyses of the cases or rules which they usually teach. I hope that the examples used in this chapter will do something to fill that gap.

---

[70]   See W Twining, *Rethinking Evidence: Exploratory Essays* (Evanston, IL, Northwestern University Press, 1994); for more recent comments, see W Twining, 'Evidence as a Multidisciplinary Subject' (2003) 2 *Law, Probability and Risk* 91; 'Taking Facts Seriously – Again', ch 2 in this volume.
[71]   As textbooks increasingly do: see Dennis, above n 57, ch 4; Roberts and Zuckerman, above n 9, ch 3. Cf the more integrated approach in Friedman, above n 16.
[72]   See sources cited above n 70.
[73]   485 U.S. 681 (1988). The case is usually discussed on the question of standard of proof of prior wrongdoing; Anderson's analysis focuses on the more basic question of relevance.
[74]   TJ Anderson, 'On Generalizations I: A Preliminary Exploration' (1999) 40 *S Texas L Rev* 455. See also the discussion of exclusionary rules in T Anderson, D Schum and W Twining, *Analysis of Evidence* (2nd edn, Cambridge, CUP, 2005) ch 11.

5

Thinking With and Outside the Box: Developing Computer Support for Evidence Teaching

BURKHARD SCHAFER, JEROEN KEPPENS, AND QIANG SHEN*

INTRODUCTION

THAT EVIDENCE EVALUATION and interpretation should be taught as part of the law curriculum is a point all contributors to this volume agree on, and several of them set out the case better than we possibly could. *How* these skills should be taught, however, remains a matter of some controversy. A starting point for thinking about these issues is the debate between Twining and Roberts.[1] From their contributions, we tentatively draw a number of requirements and desiderata for courses on evidence interpretation and evaluation (EIE), which inform our own thinking:

(1) A course in EIE should be informed by sound theoretical, epistemological and philosophical principles, but it should not simply be a way of sneaking Jurisprudence onto an Evidence course.
(2) A course in EIE should not confine itself to an analysis of the trial process, but also cover the investigative stage and pre-trial proceedings.
(3) A course in EIE should be multidisciplinary. Also, it should not just be an introduction to the various branches of forensic science, but link the 'logic of proof' with the 'trial rules'.
(4) A course in EIE should not just teach students *about* fact interpretation, but also *how* to do it.

* Work on this chapter was supported by EPSRC grant GR/S63267/02 and ESRC grant RES-000–23–0729.
[1] See Paul Roberts, Chapter 1 and William Twining, Chapter 2.

(5) A course in EIE should make clear that issues of fact evaluation arise in all branches of law and are not confined to contested criminal cases. Witness reliability is as important in determining what the parties to a contract really said during their negotiations as it is in criminal law; psychological expert evidence plays a role not just in the glamorous world of criminal profiling, but also in family law, etc.

(6) By the same token, students must not compartmentalise. The skills they learn should be transferable, and they should ideally take what they have learned and apply it in their courses on substantive law.

(7) A course in EIE must not overburden an already cramped curriculum.

Unfortunately, some of these requirements, while perfectly sensible in isolation, are in tension with each other. As a consequence, *any* course in EIE will be a compromise between conflicting demands. In this chapter, we present an approach to computer-assisted teaching of evidence evaluation that is designed to make the compromise as workable as possible.

Let us for a moment forget the seventh requirement, and assume that we could construct the ideal Evidence course without any consideration of resources, time constraints and willingness or ability of the students we teach. It would probably look something like this: in the first year, students would receive a rigorous grounding in scientific method, including epistemology, argumentation theory and statistics. In addition, they would also learn enough to be able later to study the often highly formalised subdisciplines of science that may come up in court, including, for instance, sufficient biology to fully understand DNA evidence, sufficient chemistry to understand modern toxicology and sufficient medicine to understand pathologists' reports. In subsequent years, they would study different disciplines in which science interacts with law, and, since it is not possible to foresee which disciplines will be encountered in later life, students would need to study a wide range: forensic linguistics and psychology, forensic medicine and forensic engineering, and so on. Students would study not just 'about' these disciplines, they would need to be taught to the level where they could carry out the necessary analysis themselves. To ensure that this knowledge becomes 'active', all substantive law courses would incorporate evidentiary issues. In Contract Law, students would discuss cases where the authenticity of a signature under a contract document is contested, in Environmental Law, they would discuss epidemiological data and the correlation between certain medical conditions and the level of chemicals found in drinking water, and in Torts, they would discuss whether it can be established that a car accident was caused negligently by examining skid-marks on the road.

Back in reality, this idealised vision is obviously impossible. Nor is it strictly necessary: lawyers do not need to be forensic scientists, they only need to work with them, to translate their results into legal arguments and to ask the right questions in court. Both Roberts and Twining, in varying degrees, consequently emphasise abstract method over substantive content. There is, of course, a price to be paid for this. It puts Twining's ideal close to courses in Jurisprudence, and makes Roberts' into a course in 'criminal procedure plus'. Their proposals may also fail to tap into student enthusiasm for the more substantive issues in forensic science. Feedback from the Edinburgh version of an advanced course in EIE consistently demanded more in-depth studies of aspects of forensic science. And there is good reason for this: episdoes such as the *McKie*[2] fingerprinting case in Scotland indicate that misuse of forensic science is frequently difficult to reduce to questions of method: to understand what went wrong in this case requires at least some understanding of the 'science' underlying fingerprint identification.

Bearing these issues in mind, we suggest that computer technology is a good candidate for supplementing courses such as those sketched by Roberts and Twining. There are two main reasons: first, computers are adept at knowledge-intensive tasks, and one of the obstacles faced by EIE courses is that there is so much knowledge about evidence interpretation available. Considerable amounts of information about the relevant disciplines can be stored on a single DVD, and made available to students on an 'if needed' basis. This leads to the second advantage: as experience with distance learning courses teaches us, computer-supported learning is not tied to the time scheduling of traditional classes. Digital formats allow students to explore the material in their own time, in parallel with the substantive law courses they take throughout their degree. Experience from distance learning shows how tasks can be set, and the results automatically evaluated, in a digital medium. In our 'business model', after having studied a course along the lines Twining proposes, students would then be able to use predefined examples, or indeed develop their own, that take up themes from say Contract or Environmental Law, and would then carry out their analysis and receive automatic feedback from the software. In this way, no additional demands are made on teaching time or other resources in the substantive law subjects.

In the examples we have mentioned, we follow Twining's arguments in another important respect by focusing on the investigative stage. At present, our system is less capable of dealing with the trial setting itself, but we indicate how it could easily be extended to cover more of the

---

[2] *The Scotsman* maintains a very comprehensive archive of press reports on this case at http://news.scotsman.com/topics.cfm?tid=1385. The BBC also ran a programme on fingerprint evidence that focused on the *McKie* case: transcripts can be found on the BBC website at http://news.bbc.co.uk/1/hi/programmes/panorama/4986570.stm. James Mackay, retired Deputy Chief Constable of Tayside Police, was asked by the Crown Office to investigate the case. His report can be found at http://news.bbc.co.uk/1/shared/bsp/hi/pdfs/04_05_06_mckiereport.pdf.

procedural legal issues that become relevant in adjudication; here, we take Twining's (and Roberts') emphasis on 'relevance' as our starting point. In one important aspect though, we deviate from Twining's lead (though we emphasise that we see our method as complementary to a course like his, not as a replacement). Twining focuses on the correct construction of arguments establishing facts as the main transferable skill taught in an EIE course. By contrast, we focus on spotting wrong or weak arguments. The transferable skill this approach emphasises is 'creativity': students learn to develop alternative explanations of the established facts. We will suggest more reasons for the desirability of this approach as the argument proceeds. At this point, we only want to emphasise that this corresponds to the typical professional perspective of a legal practitioner. Few of our students will become judges, but substantial numbers will represent clients in litigation. The usual division of labour means that experts establish the basic facts, while lawyers need to ask 'critical questions' about these facts and offer alternative narratives that can account for them.

ARGUING THE CASE FOR CREATIVITY IN LAW AND COMPUTING

Papers on artificial intelligence frequently start with a reference to HAL, Stanley Kubrick's famous computer in *2001: A Space Odyssey*. While HAL's ability to understand and communicate in natural language is unmatched by any existing system, and its ability to learn, formulate its own plans and execute them are undoubtedly impressive, HAL lacks a crucial aspect of creativity—the ability to question its own reasoning and conclusions. HAL learns, but its learning is purely cumulative. It invents new methods of getting rid of the spaceship's crew, but only because it follows unrelentingly and unquestioningly its initial assessment of the situation. In this respect, HAL compares unfavourably with another much less well-known SF computer, Peter Griese's ContraComputer or CoCo.[3] In Griese's story, CoCo is employed in tandem with a conventional computer. CoCo's only task is to develop alternative explanations of the available data, and to defend them vigorously. In doing so, it allows its human operators to 'think outside the box', to see alternative courses of action and to remain healthily sceptical regarding the solutions proposed by the main computer (or any other authority, for that matter). The ability to challenge received wisdom, to come up with the least plausible as well as the most plausible explanation consistent with the evidence, is all part of what we commonly understand as 'creativity'. CoCo, though, has its own problems. To use it, the operator must have the right level of security clearance. By its very nature, however, CoCo can always come up with

---

[3] P Griese, *Angriff der Brutzellen* (Perry Rhodan, Issue 1011).

reasons not to give you security clearance, regardless of the evidence you provide, because it is always possible to offer alternative explanations as to how you came into possession of the evidence. You might have stolen the security code, cut off the finger of the authorised person (fingerprints) or cloned him entirely (DNA match). You could even be an evil doppelganger from a parallel universe. Getting CoCo to work with you might therefore be an uphill struggle. Creativity unrestrained (or restricted only by a very weak concept of consistency) can be as unproductive as unreflective rule-following.

This chapter describes our attempts to build a computing system just like CoCo, suitably modified for legal environments, at the Joseph Bell Centre for Forensic Statistics and Legal Reasoning in the University of Edinburgh. We will first give a real life scenario demonstrating how desirable a suitably modified CoCo would be in a legal context. This new approach to using ICT in courses on the interpretation and evaluation of evidence is based on ideas developed for teaching science in schools, emphasising in particular the importance of modelling and qualitative reasoning skills.

Premature Case Theories and Miscarriages of Justice

In the late 1980s, a string of high profile miscarriages of justice shook the foundations of the British legal system.[4] In 1991, the Runciman Royal Commission on Criminal Justice was established with the following terms of reference:

> to examine the effectiveness of the criminal justice system in England and Wales in securing the convictions of those guilty of criminal offences and the acquittal of those who are innocent having regard to the efficient use of resources, and in particular to consider whether changes are needed in:
>
> (i) the conduct of police investigations ...
>
> (ii) the role of the prosecutor ...
>
> (iii) the role of experts ...
>
> (iv) the arrangements for the defence of accused persons ...
>
> (v) the opportunities available for an accused person to state his position on the matters charged ...
>
> (vi) the powers of the courts in directing proceedings ...
>
> (vii) the role of the Court of Appeal in considering new evidence ...

---

[4] For a comprehensive overview, see C Walker and K Starmer (eds), *Justice in Error* (London, Blackstone Press, 1993).

(viii) the arrangements for considering and investigating allegations of miscarriages of justice.[5]

The system proposed here is addressed in particular to points (i) and (iii). In the wake of the Runciman Commission, a significant body of knowledge has been produced analysing the potential for errors in criminal investigations and prosecutions. The establishment of the Criminal Cases Review Commissions in England and Scotland subsequently provided extensive material for case studies, in addition to published ad hoc inquiries into high profile cases of wrongful convictions like the Birmingham Six and the Guildford Four.[6]

One recurrent theme in these studies is the problem of premature case theories. Instead of establishing in a neutral fashion what has happened, police officers tend to decide on the most likely suspects at a very early stage of an investigation, and from then on investigate *against* them.[7] In the words of David Dixon:

> If any factor in investigative practice had to be nominated as most responsible for leading to miscarriages of justice, it would have to be the tendency for investigators to commit themselves to belief in a suspect's guilt in a way that blinds them to other possibilities.[8]

The use of such 'case theories' is probably inevitable.[9] The problem is therefore not that case theories are used at all, but rather the restricted scope of alternatives actively considered. As Greer argues:

> no criminal justice system could work without them. The dangers stem instead from the highly charged atmosphere surrounding an investigation, the haste with which the theory has been formed and the tenacity with which the police have clung to their original view in spite of strong countervailing evidence.[10]

Irving and Dunningham address possible solutions to this problem.[11] They argue for the need to improve officers' reasoning and decision-making by challenging institutionalised presumptions about criminals and crimes. Officers develop 'working rules' that identify certain patterns of behaviour as relevant or worth investigating, and link them through common-sense

---

[5]   Royal Commission on Criminal Justice, *Report* (London, HMSO, 1993) i–ii.
[6]   The reports of the Criminal Cases Review Commission can be found at www.ccrc.gov.uk/publications/publications_get.asp.
[7]   S Sedley, 'Whose Justice?', *London Review of Books*, 23 September 1993, 60.
[8]   D Dixon, 'Police Investigative procedures' in C Walker (ed), *Miscarriages of Justice* (London, Blackstone Press, 1999). See also M McConville, 'Weaknesses in the British Judicial System', *Times Higher Education Supplement*, 3 November 1989.
[9]   M McConville, A Sanders and R Leng, *The Case for the Prosecution* (London, Routledge, 1991).
[10]   S Greer, 'Miscarriages of Criminal Justice Reconsidered' (1994) 58 MLR 71.
[11]   B Irving and C Dunningham, *Human Factors in the Quality Control of CID Investigations and a Brief Review of Relevant Police Training* (London, HMSO, 1993).

assumptions about their causal connectedness. Challenging these assumptions then becomes the main challenge for reform of police training. From our perspective, the problem might be reformulated in the following way: police officers and lawyers behave like HAL when they should behave a bit more like CoCo.

Legal education has to shoulder some of the blame for this. Not only do we fail to teach students evidence interpretation and evaluation, but the way substantive law is taught reinforces an uncritical attitude towards facts.[12] In exams, students are typically given a problem that they have to evaluate from a legal perspective. Questioning whether or not the facts as given in the exam problem really exist or can be proven by the parties is actively discouraged. In the reminder of this chapter, we introduce and discuss some of the more technical features of the system that we have developed. We will focus on those features of the system most directly motivated by our pedagogical aims, confining discussion of the overall system architecture to a bare outline.[13]

DEAD BODIES IN LOCKED ROOMS

Consider the following scenario: a dead body has been found in a room. The police have collected a certain amount of evidence and submitted a report. The student, taking the role of a prosecutor, has to decide if, on the basis of the available evidence: a case against a suspect can be constructed; whether the evidence is conclusive; if additional evidence for or against the suspect should be collected; and how he or she would use the accumulated evidence to convince others that the prosecution theory is correct. Pictures of the crime scene, forensic reports and witness statements are supplied. The computer should provide ongoing guidance and feedback; for instance, if the student overlooks possible explanations of the evidence, appropriate prompts should be given. If 'the prosecutor' decides to carry out additional investigative actions, such as requesting a toxicology report, the computer should supply this information, and keep track of which possible theories have now been eliminated. To achieve all this, the computer has to operate in a similar fashion to a decision support system for crime investigation, utilising an appropriate knowledge-base.

Robust decision support systems (DSSs) for crime investigation are difficult to construct because of the almost infinite variation of plausible crime scenarios. Generally speaking, systems are said to be robust if they

---

[12] See D Nicolson, 'Facing Facts: the Teaching of Fact Construction in University Law Schools' (1997) 1 *E & P* 132.

[13] For full technical details, see J Keppens and B Schafer, 'Knowledge Based Crime Scenario Modelling' (2006) 30 *Expert Systems with Applications* 203.

remain operational in circumstances for which they were not designed. In the context of crime investigation systems, robustness requires considerable adaptability to unforeseen crime scenarios. We propose a novel model-based reasoning technique which places reasoning about crime scenarios at the very heart of the system, by enabling the DSS to construct representations of crime scenarios automatically. It achieves this by exploiting the assumption that unique scenarios consist of regularly recurring component events that are combined in a unique way. Generic formal descriptions of such component events, called scenario fragments, are selected from a knowledge-base incorporating a given set of available evidence, and combined into plausible scenarios. This approach addresses the robustness issue because it does not require a formal representation of all, or even a subset, of the possible scenarios that the system might encounter. Instead, only a formal representation of the possible component events is required. Because such events can be concatenated into an exponentially large number of combinations to form myriad scenarios, it should be much easier to construct a knowledge-base of relevant component events rather than trying to imagine all possible relevant scenarios in advance. In teaching terms, this technique resembles the way in which law teachers devise problem questions for examinations, re-using and re-configuring tried-and-tested 'stock' examples.

We can illustrate this point by returning to the dead body in the room. Imagine a police officer arriving at a potential scene of crime. He notices a person, identified to him as the home owner, lying prone on the floor of a second-storey flat, an electric cable around his neck and blood seeping from his head. The window of the room is broken, and there are signs of a struggle such as overturned furniture. Outside the broken window, lying on the ground, a ladder is found. The officer now has to make a series of decisions: Is this a crime scene? Are further (costly) investigations necessary? Should all known burglars in the area be rounded up for interrogation?

Conventional DSS models are not particularly suitable for solving such problems owing to their lack of robustness, ie their limited flexibility in dealing with unforeseen contingencies. This objective is difficult to achieve because 'low volume', serious crimes tend to be virtually unique, and conventional artificial intelligence (AI) techniques have difficulties in handling previously unseen problem settings. A traditional rule-based approach, for instance, would require the officer to consult explicit generalisations about ladders and windows to apply to the current situation. Quite apart from the fact that this reasoning process is psychologically implausible, the desired reasoning rules would be difficult to identify in the absence of any organised discipline of 'ladderology' or the like.

The underlying cognitive theory underpinning our approach is taken from gestalt psychology, a psychological approach that shares historical roots with the naïve physicist or qualitative world perspective.[14] Our investigator would (probably pre-linguistically) arrange the features of the scene into a coherent whole or gestalt mental picture of what has occurred. This is a process of 'sense making', an interpretative activity. Just as one cannot but see a forest when confronted by many trees, the investigator will at a very early stage 'see' a scenario in which a burglar used the ladder to gain entry through a window of the second floor flat, but was disturbed by the home owner leading to a struggle in which the home owner was first restrained with the cable and then injured on the head, with the precise cause of death yet to be determined. This whole 'picture' or 'story' is influenced by typical associations, eg 'burglar' is associated with 'ladder'. Our system is designed not so much to emulate or improve on the process by which individual aspects of a scenario are combined, but rather to assist the user to perform a 'gestalt-switch', that is, to see the same individual scenario fragments re-arranged to produce a completely different narrative. In our example, the key scenario fragments are the broken window, the dead body, the wounds on the body and the ladder. Whilst the obvious hypothesis is that of a burglary gone wrong, the system should be able to rearrange the scenario fragments into alternative stories. On the basis of this evidence, it is also (though not necessarily equally) possible that the dead person did some DIY in his flat, trying to fix an electric cable, the ladder collapsed under him, he got entangled in the cable, hit the ground and the ladder fell through the window. This creative reconstruction involves several 'switches': the ability to see the ground as a 'blunt instrument', the window as an opening permitting egress as well as entry, and the entire scenario as a domestic accident rather than murder. These 'switches' in turn are the basis for formulating the 'critical questions' which are a primary learning outcome of our system.

In our mini-case, the two alternative hypotheses both explain the evidence collected so far. But, of course, this evidence is still incomplete. If the student gets stuck, the system should indicate which pieces of additional evidence might discriminate between the two theories, and give advice about where to look for further information. If the student suggests an investigative action, the system should perform it virtually and then eliminate scenarios inconsistent with the new evidence. This is the critical and analytic aspect of the simulation, which complements the creative and synthetic approach of the first interpretative step.

The generation of possible scenarios from collected evidence is a process of 'back-chaining', working back from the available evidence to plausible causal hypotheses. This may be complemented by a 'forward-chaining'

---

[14] B Smith and R Casati, 'Naive Physics: an Essay in Ontology' (1994) 7 *Philosophical Psychology* 225.

process, which re-examines the deductive closure effected under a hypothetical scenario. Assuming that the accident scenario is correct, we would
expect to find the dead person's fingerprints on the ladder. Assuming that
the murder hypothesis is correct, we would possibly expect to find
fingerprints of a third party on the ladder, and almost certainly not the
fingerprints of the deceased. Instead of looking for evidence that supports
an initial hypothesis, the system identifies further information that would
permit the investigator to discard one explanation in favour of another.

In argumentation-theoretical terms, the 'new' evidence functions as an
'undercutter' for the arguments that support alternative explanations.[15]
However, undercutting propositions are in turn based on hypothetical,
defeasible reasoning. Thus, for example, the murder hypothesis is not
conclusively refuted even if new evidence appears to contradict it. The
absence of a third party's fingerprints can be explained by the use of
gloves, the presence of the victim's fingerprints by an extended story in
which the burglar stole the ladder from the victim's garden shed and then
used it to gain entry to the flat, and so on.

Model-based Diagnosis

To implement this system with its two complementary modes of reasoning,
synthetic and analytic, we employ a novel model-based reasoning technique, derived from compositional modelling technology,[16] to generate
crime scenarios from the available evidence automatically. Consistent with
existing work on reasoning about evidence, our method is an application
of abductive reasoning.[17] That is, the scenarios are modelled as the causes
of evidence, and their detailed specifications are inferred from the evidence
they would have been expected to produce. This protocol corresponds to
the typical situation lawyers encounter in litigation: the evidence has
already been collected by someone else; the lawyer's task is to decide if the
evidence was caused by events that correspond to a relevant legal category
such as 'murder', 'consent' or 'negotiation'. The goal of our system, as a
novel form of DSS, is to identify the set of hypotheses corresponding to
scenarios capable of accommodating all of the available evidence.

---

[15] B Verheij, 'Arguments and Defeat in Argument-Based Nonmonotonic Reasoning' in C
Pinto-Ferreira and NJ Mamede (eds), *Progress in Artificial Intelligence: 7th Portuguese
Conference on Artificial Intelligence*, Lecture Notes in Artificial Intelligence 990 (Berlin,
Springer, 1995).

[16] B Falkenhainer and K Forbus, 'Compositional Modelling: Finding the Right Model for
the Job' (1991) 51 *Artificial Intelligence* 95.

[17] H Prakken, 'Analysing Reasoning about Evidence with Formal Models of Argumentation' (2004) 3 *Law, Probability and Risk* 33.

The central component of our system's architecture is an assumption-based truth maintenance system (ATMS). An ATMS is an inference engine that enables a problem-solver to reason about multiple possible worlds or situations. Each possible world describes a specific set of circumstances—here, a crime scenario—under which certain events and states are true and others are false. What is true in one possible world may be false in another. The task of the ATMS is to maintain the coherence of what is true in each possible world.

The ATMS uses two separate problem-solvers. First, the *scenario instantiator* constructs the space of possible worlds. Given a knowledge-base that contains a set of generic re-usable components of crime scenarios (the dead body, the locked door, the jealous partner, etc) and a set of pieces of evidence (Peter's fingerprints, John's DNA etc), the scenario instantiator builds a space of all the possible crime scenarios, called the *scenario space*. This scenario space contains all the alternative explanations for the currently preferred investigative theory, consistent with the complete set of evidence.

Once the scenario space is constructed, it can be analysed by the *query handler*. The query handler provides answers to the following questions:

(1) Which hypotheses are supported by the available evidence?
(2) What additional pieces of evidence would be found if a certain scenario or hypothesis is true?
(3) Which individual pieces or sets of additional evidence are capable of differentiating between two rival hypotheses?

We will return to the ATMS mechanism below, but first we clarify some basic concepts that are necessary for understanding our illustrations.

Scenarios

Scenarios describe events and situations that may have occurred in the real world. They form possible explanations for the evidence that is available to the user and support certain hypotheses under consideration.

Within our DSS, scenarios are represented by means of predicates denoting events and states, and causal relations between these events and states. The causal relations, which enable the scenarios to explain evidence and support hypotheses are represented by the connecting 'branches' between the nodes containing the predicates. The causal graph shown in Figure 5.1 represents a sample scenario of a suicide by hanging.

The scenario in Figure 5.1 contains five pieces of evidence:

(a) n1: a hanging corpse of a person identified as johndoe has been found;

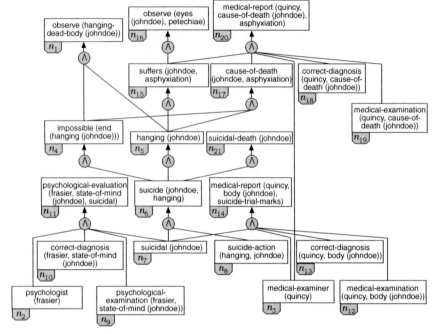

Figure 5.1: Sample scenario: suicide by hanging

(b) n11: a report by a psychologist identified as frasier (n2) stating that johndoe may have been suicidal prior to his death;

(c) n14: the observation of suicide trial marks on the body of johndoe;

(d) n16: the body of johndoe exhibits signs of petechiae;

(e) n20: a report by a medical examiner identified as quincy (n7) stating that the cause of death of johndoe was asphyxiation.

There are many possible combinations of events and states that may lead to this set of evidence, and the scenario of Figure 5.1 shows but one of them. It demonstrates how the first three pieces of evidence may be explained by suicide by hanging. The hanging corpse (n1) and the assumed cause of death (n20) are the consequents of johndoe's hanging (n5), which he was unable (unwilling) to end (n4). The petechiae are caused by asphyxiation (n15) resulting from the hanging. Suicide by hanging requires that johndoe is suicidal (n7) and the remaining two pieces of evidence are a consequence of his suicidal state.

Different types of information feature in abductive reasoning. Some information is certain, ie known to be true, whereas other information is uncertain, ie merely presumed to be true. Some information is explicable, ie causes for its truth can be inferred, whereas other information is inexplicable, ie causes for its truth cannot be inferred or their explanations are irrelevant.

Three different types of information can be identified on the basis of these two distinctions: First, *facts* are pieces of inexplicable, certain information. Typical examples include nodes n2 and n3 in Figure 5.1, which denote that frasier is a psychologist and quincy is a medical examiner. These pieces of information are deemed basic truths that need not be explained further. From a technical perspective, this prevents infinite regress in the analysis. From a teaching perspective, it corresponds to the type of problem-question typically given in an exam. One of the skills a student has to develop is the ability to decide which issues are worth discussing, and which features of the description can be taken at face value. In a problem question that starts: 'Mary complains that the delivered goods did not match the description she gave to the supplier', we might well want the student to consider whether Mary can prove this asserted fact, but the student should not get sidetracked into speculating whether Mary is a human being, of the right age and mental capacity, if there is no indication that such matters are in point.

Investigative actions performed by investigators are a special type of fact, whereby investigators seek to obtain additional evidence. In this respect, our scenario differs from the typical problem-questions used to teach substantive law. There, a student may point out that crucial facts are missing, and even develop answers that hypothetically assume that additional information is present. But they do not ordinarily have the chance of actually procuring the missing information. A great strength of ICT is that we can replicate the more realistic situation in which a lawyer would seek to acquire missing information. Cultivating legally permissible and pragmatically efficient strategies for generating new evidential material is an integral part of legal practice.

Secondly, *evidence* is information that is certain and explicable. Typical examples include nodes n1 and n16 in the scenario of Figure 5.1, which denote that johndoe's hanging corpse has been found and that it exhibits petechiae. Evidence is deemed certain (it truly exists) because it can be observed by the human user and it is explicable because its possible causes are of interest to the user.

Assumptions are a third type of information. Assumptions are uncertain and (at the given point in time) unexplained information. Typical examples include nodes n19 (quincy determines the cause of death of johndoe), n18 (quincy makes the correct diagnosis of the cause of death of johndoe) and n1 (johndoe was suicidal). Generally speaking, it is not possible to rely solely on facts when speculating about the plausible causes of the available evidence. Ultimately, the investigator has to presume that certain information at the end of the causal path is true. Such pieces of information are designated assumptions in our system.

As we have said, the distinctive objective of our approach is automatically to generate scenarios that could have caused the available evidence in an investigation. We proceed from the observation that the constituent parts of particular scenarios are not normally unique. Figure 5.1, for instance, includes the information that asphyxiation causes petechiae on the body of johndoe. This causal relation applies to most humans, irrespective of whether the asphyxiation occurs in the context of a hanging or a suicide. Thus, the causal rule, asphyxiation →petechiae is generally applicable and can be instantiated in all scenarios involving evidence of petechiae or possible asphyxiation.

The knowledge-base of our system consists of a set of such causal rules, designated scenario fragments. For example, the rule

if {suffers(P,C), cause-of-death (C,P), medical-examiner (E)} assuming {determine (E,cause-of-death(P)), correct-diagnosis (E,cause-of-death(P))} then {cod-report(E,P,C)}

states that if a person P suffers from ailment or injury C, C is the cause of death of P, and there is a medical examiner, E, and assuming that E determines the cause of death of P and makes the correct diagnosis, then there will be a piece of evidence in the form of a cause-of-death report indicating that, according to E, the cause of death of P is C. The causal relations between assumptions, states and events are thereby formalised in scenario fragments.

The resulting knowledge-base in the system's architecture for Figure 5.1 consists, at a minimum, of the following constructs:

(a) property definitions describing which types of predicate correspond to a symptom, fact, hypothesis or investigative action;
(b) a set of scenario fragments describing re-usable component causal relations from which completed scenarios are composed;
(c) a set of inconsistencies describing which combinations of states and events are logically impossible.

From these basic constructs, a universe of competing hypotheses may be generated and tested.

The Inference Mechanism

Another way to characterise the ATMS is as a mechanism that maintains how each piece of inferred information depends on presumed information and facts, which also demonstrates how inconsistencies arise.[18] The scenario space generation algorithm can be illustrated by showing how it can be employed to reconstruct the scenario introduced in Figure 5.1.

---

[18] J de Kleer, 'An Assumption-based TMS' (1986) 28 *Artificial Intelligence* 127.

Assume that the system is given one observation (hanging-dead-body(johndoe)), and two facts (psychologist(frasier) and medical-examiner(quincy)). The initialisation phase of the algorithm will simply create an ATMS with nodes corresponding to that piece of evidence and those two facts. As the facts are justified by the empty set, they are deemed true in all possible worlds. The backward-chaining phase then expands this initial scenario space by generating plausible causes of the available evidence by instantiating the antecedents and assumptions of scenario fragments whose consequences match nodes already in the scenario space. For example, the consequent of scenario fragment:

if {hanging(P),

impossible(end(hanging(P)))}

then {observe(hanging-dead-body(P))}

matches a piece of evidence already in the scenario space, and this allows the creation of new nodes corresponding to hanging(johndoe) and impossible(end(hanging(johndoe))) and justifies connecting the latter two nodes with the former. The forward-chaining phase expands the scenarios created during the backward-chaining phase by supplying additional evidence and associated new hypotheses.

The scenario space as a whole is too large to display here. Instead, Figure 5.2 presents an informal overview of the information contained in the scenario space. The blocks on the left-hand side of the figure represent sets of nodes and justifications between them that correspond to a sufficient explanation for a death by hanging. Note that, although these blocks appear to be separated, they do have a number of nodes and lines of justification in common. Therefore, the scenario space does not only contain the six primitive scenarios described in Figure 5.1, but also their various combinations. The middle and right-hand columns for Figure 5.2 show the possible pieces of evidence that might be expected in each scenario, and the hypotheses that logically follow in each case.

Query Handler

The query handler operates in two distinct modes. In the 'marking mode', the student formulates a theory and the system then checks her answer against its own solution, pointing out, for instance, that the evidence might also support alternative theories. In its 'guidance mode', the student directly queries the system, asking questions such as: what additional evidence would distinguish between the two explanations that I have formulated?

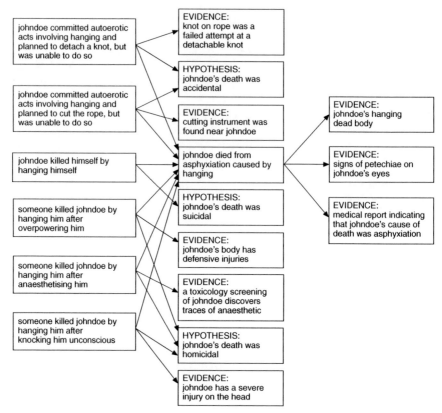

Figure 5.2: Scenario space

USER INTERFACE

The theoretical ideas presented in the previous two sections have been developed into a prototype decision support software. This section briefly discusses how this prototype is employed.

User Input

After the initial set-up of the application, which involves choosing a knowledge-base and starting a new session, the user/investigator must specify which facts and evidence are available in a given case. From a teaching perspective, this operation corresponds to determining what information is pertinent to the case, what facts can be assumed at face value for the time being, and what information requires further analysis

The same set of facts or evidence can be reorganised in different ways, according to contrasting classificatory schemas. This allows the student to take on the perspective of a defence lawyer, a prosecutor or a judge. Within each taxonomy, evidence is organised according to various distinctive attributes, such as the type of object that constitutes the evidence or the evaluation method that generated it. Once the user has found a classification that corresponds to the appropriate piece of evidence, further details must be entered to give the people and objects involved in each scenario their unique identity.

System Output

Once all the available evidence and facts have been entered into the system, the user can generate the scenario space. Once entered, three types of analysis become available. First, the system can display the hypotheses consistent with the available evidence, and the plausible scenarios that support them. Currently, scenarios can be visualised in two different ways. The default approach summarises each scenario by listing the assumptions on which they are based and the hypotheses they support. This representational format facilitates prompt identification of the distinctive features of each scenario, uncluttered by underlying causal reasoning. An alternative view represents each scenario in the form of a causal hypergraph. Causal hypergraphs are particularly suitable for describing causal reasoning, and as such, they are a useful tool for explaining a scenario to the user.

Secondly, the user can query the system for scenarios that produce certain evidence and support particular hypotheses. This is a useful facility for 'what-if' analysis. For example, the investigator might note that a 'cutting instrument', say a knife, has been recovered from the crime scene and consider whether this rules out accidental death. The system can answer this type of question by requesting it to search for a scenario that supports the available evidence—the discovery of a knife near the body—with a hypothesis of accidental death. In response, the system generates such a scenario by suggesting, for example, that the victim may have engaged in autoerotic strangulation and tried to use the knife to cut the rope.

Finally, the decision support system can suggest additional pieces of evidence that might foreseeably be collected if a given scenario were true. Whenever the user has selected a scenario generated by the system (using one of the aforementioned two facilities), there is the option to request additional evidence that could be discovered if the selected scenario were true.

FUTURE WORK

We have made a prototype of our system available on our website.[19] One of the main goals is to enrich this prototype with a large database that can handle real-life scenarios. The great advantage of our approach over more conventional AI tutoring systems is its almost unlimited flexibility. In the past, 'intelligent' tutoring software was case specific: students were given one hypothetical case which only allowed for slight modifications, and then answered questions specific to that case. Depending on their answer, follow-up questions would be generated. But once students had worked through a case, they were unlikely to use the system again. By contrast, the present system allows the teacher to vary the scenarios. The same fragments can be reconfigured to construct civil, criminal or environmental cases. In one variation of a problem, a witness may corroborate crucial evidence, but the next time the student 'plays' the game this witness may be absent or unreliable. Variations in difficulty are also easy to incorporate, by restricting the pieces of evidence the computer offers when queried, or by including cross-domain evidence (such as eyewitness reports, medical and psychological evidence).

Taking up a theme from the introduction, we can now see how our system could move the teaching of evidence a little bit closer to the ideal we briefly described. It can be used in parallel with every substantive law course, its database and models being reusable at will. This way, students develop an understanding of how evidentiary issues permeate all fields of legal studies, and also learn a more careful, 'creative-critical' approach to the interpretation of evidence

A qualitative approach seems suitable for most legal contexts. It means that students can reason, in a scientifically correct way, about substantive issues in the relevant sciences, without having to puzzle over their mathematical underpinnings.[20] Unproblematic mathematical operations are hidden from the user, in the background of the system. Of course, as indicated above, some mathematical issues are relevant for lawyers, including probabilistic assessments of evidence. The present system operates in a binary fashion: a piece of evidence is either caused, or is not caused, by a specific evident. The next step would be to incorporate those parts of the mathematical structure of forensic theories that are relevant for lawyers, in particular the concept of probability. We have shown elsewhere how this might be done in principle;[21] whether the technologically possible

---

[19]   See www.cfslr.ed.ac.uk.

[20]   See D Weld and J de Kleer, *Readings in Qualitative Reasoning about Physical Systems* (Los Altos, Morgan Kaufmann,1989).

[21]   J Keppens, Q Shen, and B Schafer, 'Probabilistic Abductive Computation of Evidence Collection Strategies in Crime Investigations' in *Proceedings of the Tenth International Conference on AI and Law* (Amsterdam, ACM, 2005).

is also pedagogically desirable is a different question requiring further empirical investigation. The present 'mathematics free' approach, rooted in qualitative reasoning, has been highly successful in teaching basic scientific concepts to school children and undergraduate science students,[22] and ought to appeal to law students who typically have little background in the formal sciences.

At present, our DSS is confined to verbal narrative descriptions of the crime scene and the evidence found in it. Ideally, future systems will combine this text-based application with visual representations. The student would see a 3D model of a crime scene, together with evidence already collected (eg an expert witness report in the appropriate format). She might then carry out actions in this three-dimensional space, checking, for instance, if the victim was actually visible from the point where the shot was allegedly fired. Students would next input their findings and reasoning, as previously described, which the system would check against its database, making corrections where appropriate. The system would also make new evidence available, if this option has been authorised by the teacher-programmer. Other parameters can then be added to make the scenario more realistic. One possible extension would be to make further investigative actions subject to budgetary constraints. A time dimension might also be added, to account for the fact that certain investigative actions need to be carried out promptly, owing to deteriorating physical traces or the possibility that a potential witness will die or disappear, etc.

An explicitly legal dimension is so far missing. This reflects the intended use of the system as a supplement to substantive law courses. On the other hand, integrating an explicitly legal dimension ought not to be difficult. Twining, in his contribution to this book, emphasises the central role of the concept of 'relevance'. Major aspects of this concept are implicit in the approach described here, especially through the notion of 'investigative action'. A justified investigative action, according to our system, is one that discovers facts that help to distinguish between two alternative accounts of what has happened. Conversely, an investigative action that uncovers facts that are not able to differentiate between two alternative stories would yield evidence that is irrelevant. Once probabilities are added, a more nuanced view is possible. As a first and very tentative definition, we would expect relevant evidence to increase the probability of one explanation over the other, assuming that the inference(s) supported by that evidence

---

[22] See, in particular, K Forbus, 'Articulate Software for Science and Engineering Education' in K Forbus, P Feltovich, and A Canas (eds), *Smart Machines in Education: the Coming Revolution in Educational Technology* (Boston, AAAI Press, 2001); K Forbus, K Carney, B Sherin and L Ureel, 'Qualitative Modeling for Middle-school Students' in G Biswas (ed), *Proceedings of the Fifteenth International Workshop on Qualitative Reasoning* (San Antonio, St Mary's University, 2001).

remain undefeated by any other evidence already in-hand. (This last qualifier ensures, for example, that fingerprints on a knife are only included if it has not already been proved that the knife is not the murder weapon.) While our system arguably does not exhaustively model the legal concept of relevance, it can nonetheless be used to explain its core aspects, in the form of feedback to students when proposing investigative actions.

Only marginally more difficult would be to incorporate Roberts' more traditional focus on exclusionary rules. Again, the impact of exclusionary rules would be represented as properties of investigative actions. The database associated with a specific case might contain, for example, three items of additional evidence, each of which is capable of differentiating between rival case theories. These items of evidence can be uncovered through appropriate investigative actions. The student would be invited to choose between alternative investigative actions in order to procure additional evidence, say, ordering a toxicology test, wire-tapping the suspect's phone or asking a psychic. An appropriate knowledge-base would ensure that only the first two actions uncover any facts at all. If the student chose action 2, he would be asked about the correct procedure, or warned of possible inadmissibility. 'Being inadmissible' in this sense is not a 'sticky' property of facts, but a property of the investigative actions that lead to particular evidence being obtained. Each dimension of decision-making gives rise to a cascade of further possibilities and variations on stock scenarios. As a result, the number of possible commutations increases with very little work on the part of the teacher. In one setting, crucial evidence may be recoverable only through 'problematic' investigative actions. At the click of a button, this can be changed to a scenario where the evidence is easily recoverable by lawful means, or in a third variation, categorically unavailable.

6

Interdisciplinary and Comparative Perspectives on Hearsay and Confrontation

CRAIG R CALLEN*

INTRODUCTION

LANGUAGE OFTEN CONVEYS a great deal more than its narrowest possible meaning. That rather obvious point is at the heart of a continuing problem in the law of evidence. When the prosecution or the defence offers evidence of out-of-court communications to prove propositions that the communications do not literally or directly convey, courts in both England and the United States must determine whether to apply the hearsay rule. Moreover, under a recent decision in *Crawford v Washington*,[1] American courts must also decide whether the Confrontation Clause of the US Constitution limits the admissibility of that evidence.

Many decisions and much commentary have suggested that the definition of hearsay is settled in one way or another. That seems to be an exaggeration, at least in the United States, though recent legislation in England may prove to clarify things in that jurisdiction. In particular, the extent to which the Confrontation Clause may require exclusion of evidence of implied assertions is clearly unsettled in the United States. In the light of this uncertainty, this chapter addresses the difficult question of hearsay definition by providing an analytical aid to model interdisciplinary and comparative analysis. This simple graphic technique can help teachers, students, courts and advocates to analyse the special evidentiary issues that out-of-court statements present.

---

* I owe particular thanks to Rosemary Pattenden, Michael Pardo and Mike Redmayne for stimulating comments about this topic, to Emma Haas and Adam Keith for excellent research assistance, and to Michigan State University College of Law for a research grant that supported the preparation of this chapter.
[1] 541 U.S. 36, 124 S. Ct. 1354 (2004).

American evidence law unquestionably has roots in English law. For example, American courts still frequently mention *Wright v Tatham*[2] when applying the definition of hearsay.[3] Even so, there are marked contrasts between the two systems. One notable cause of that divergence is the persistence of jury trials in American civil litigation, protected by the Seventh Amendment to the national Constitution[4] and various provisions in state constitutions. By the same token, English legal culture has had effects on evidence law that seem decidedly 'foreign' to Americans.[5] Once *Myers v DPP*[6] renounced judicial creation of further hearsay exceptions in English case law, it was clear that the definition of hearsay would play a more important role in English evidence law than in its American counterpart.[7]

Whatever the source and degree of divergence between the two systems may be, American and English evidentiary doctrine share at least one difficult problem, to which no approach on either side of the Atlantic has been wholly successful: deciding whether to treat out-of-court statements as hearsay when offered to prove matters that they suggest, but do not explicitly communicate (the problem of 'implied assertions'). The framers of the Federal Rules of Evidence tried to resolve that issue in hearsay doctrine, with mixed success.[8] *R v Kearley*[9] sought to resolve the question in English law, and met with a very hostile reception. Eventually that critical reception led to the provisions on hearsay in the Criminal Justice Act 2003, but those provisions are not completely clear.[10] In the United

---

[2]   (1837) 7 Ad and E 313, 112 ER 488.

[3]   See eg, *State v Dullard*, 668 N.W. 2d 585, 591 (Iowa S. Ct. 2003); *Stoddard v State*, 850 A. 2d 406, 407 (Md. Ct. Spec. App. 2004).

[4]   US Const amend VII.

[5]   Eg, RC Park, 'The Definition of Hearsay: To Each Its Own' (1995) 16 *Mississippi College LR* 125, 150.

[6]   [1965] AC 1001 (HL).

[7]   In the United States, the Federal Rules and state Evidence law recognise numerous exceptions to the rule excluding hearsay; classifying evidence as hearsay is well short of holding that it is inadmissible in a US court. See eg, Fed R Evid 803(1)–(23), 804 (b)(1)–(4), 804(b)(6), 807; Cal Evid Code ss 1220–1380 (West 1995).

[8]   The current reporter for the Federal Rules of Evidence has noted that the committee that originally drafted the Federal Rules endeavoured to define hearsay so that 'a statement would be hearsay only if it were offered to prove the truth of the express assertion in the statement; offering it to prove the truth of any implied assertion would escape hearsay proscription'. Yet, he concluded, the courts have generally rejected that 'highly constricted definition of hearsay' in favour of an interpretation of the hearsay rule that would reach implied assertions that speakers '*intended* to communicate'. DJ Capra, 'Case Law Divergence from the Federal Rules of Evidence' (2000) 197 *Federal Rules Decisions* 531, 538. Some other authorities conclude that the federal circuits are evenly split on the point. See eg JB Weinstein and MA Berger, *Weinstein's Federal Evidence* (2nd edn, JM McLaughlin (ed), New York, Matthew Bender, 2003) s 801.10[2][c], pp 801–10 to 801–12.

[9]   [1992] 2 AC 228.

[10]   See *R v Singh* [2006] EWCA Crim 660, [2006] 170 JP 222, [14]: 'The interrelationship between ss 114 and 115 is deeply obscure'.

States, *Crawford v Washington*[11] recently held that the Confrontation Clause of the Sixth Amendment restricts the admissibility of some out-of-court statements against criminal defendants. In other words, out-of-court statements may be inadmissible under that Clause, even though the hearsay rules in the Federal Rules would not exclude them.[12]

Whether courts apply English hearsay doctrine, American hearsay doctrine or American Confrontation Clause doctrine to out-of-court statements, they will still ask jurors to rely on their everyday experience to evaluate evidence. Successful problem solvers, particularly those who deal with problems that are not formalised, rely on cognitive strategies to identify critical information and make decisions based on that information. Given the limitations on our cognitive capacity and time, and competing demands on resources, we learn to use strategies from our own experience, training or education. Grice developed a relatively complicated theory to explain how we can communicate a great deal of information in relatively few words, with comparatively little effort on the part of the speaker or hearer. Wilson and Sperber recently simplified Grice's theory in a way that makes the significance of implicit aspects of communication quite clear.

Their research can help us to analyse the cognitive task that confronts jurors when they assess the probative value of out-of-court statements offered for their truth. Comparative analysis (whether across national or doctrinal borders) affords an additional perspective from which we can assess the degree to which Evidence law seems to respond to jurors' cognitive needs. That is not to say that structuring the fact-finder's task is Evidence law's only concern. Among other things, as Posner's recent economic analysis of Evidence law points out,[13] Evidence law may affect out-of-court behaviour or establish (i) incentives for parties to gather and submit data that are useful for fact-finders and (ii) disincentives for waste of resources. Yet the common human practice of communication does provide one fairly consistent perspective from which to analyse alternative approaches. Students who compare legal systems' delineation of the hearsay rule in light of research on communication may better understand the practical significance and relative strengths and weaknesses of various approaches, and would be better able to formulate and assess arguments drawn from alternative approaches.

---

[11] See *Crawford*, above n 1, 50–1.

[12] Cf *People v Morgan*, 23 Cal. Rptr. 3d 224, 232–3 (Cal. Ct. App. 2005) (classification of statement under California Evidence Code provisions governing hearsay does not determine whether statement is testimonial for Confrontation Clause purposes).

[13] RA Posner, *Frontiers of Legal Theory* (Cambridge, MA, Harvard UP, 2002) 340–1, 347–51. For earlier commentators arguing similar points, see eg, JS Johnston, 'Bayesian Fact-finding and Efficiency: Toward an Economic Theory of Liability under Uncertainty' (1987) 61 *Southern California LR* 137, 145–7, 157 (effect on behaviour); DA Nance, 'The Best Evidence Principle' (1988) 73 *Iowa LR* 222, 240.

The chapter proceeds in four steps. First, a hypothetical illustrates the practical significance of disparate understandings of the definition of hearsay, or of testimonial evidence under the Confrontation Clause. The chapter then turns to research on communication that helps us to delineate the processes jurors would use to assess evidence of out-of-court statements, particularly those offered to show propositions that they do not directly convey, sometimes called 'implied assertions'.[14] That research suggests that legal folk psychology may conceive of the intended content of a communication too narrowly. Third, the US Supreme Court's recent Confrontation Clause decision in *Crawford v Washington* provides a perspective from a different doctrine: *Crawford* stresses the importance of cross-examination for fact-finding, but relies relatively little on traditional hearsay theory. Research on communication can help to delineate the reach of new Confrontation Clause doctrine. Finally, a relatively simple graphic device, based on both scholarship on communication and comparative analysis of the hearsay rule, demonstrates how the ideas developed here can help us to understand the complexities of hearsay definition and to appraise alternative interpretations of it.

AN ILLUSTRATION

Suppose that the police arrested W, believing that he committed a bank robbery. After his arrest, the police took W to the station house for booking and other processing. While he was there, aware that he was in the presence of police officers, W saw D walking past him to an interview room. W said to D, 'I didn't tell them anything about you'.[15] During D's trial for the bank robbery, the prosecution offered W's statement as evidence of D's guilt. The question would be whether the statement, which did not explicitly assert that D had engaged in the bank robbery, would be hearsay if offered to show that he did so.

---

[14]   This terminology is somewhat misleading. When one of a communicator's purposes was to convey an idea, we would normally say that the communication asserted the idea without regard to whether it articulated the idea. The term 'implied assertion' refers not only to assertions that the communicator consciously sought to convey, but also propositions that (i) the communicator intended to convey, in the sense that conveying the propositions would be a natural consequence of the communication, and (ii) non-communicative conduct, offered as evidence of the actor's opinion about a relevant fact, as proof of the relevant fact. Law Commission, *Evidence in Criminal Proceedings: Hearsay and Related Topics* (Law Com 245, London, TSO, 1997) [7.7]–[7.9] (hereinafter 'Law Commission Report'). This chapter uses the term despite its imprecision, because courts and commentators have traditionally done so, and for reasons of brevity.

[15]   This hypothetical is loosely based on *United States v Reynolds* 715 F. 2d 99 (3d Cir. 1983).

The Federal Rules of Evidence say that hearsay is an out-of-court statement 'offered in evidence to prove the truth of the matter asserted'.[16] The Criminal Justice Act 2003 says that a statement is hearsay evidence if offered to prove a matter and 'the purpose, or one of the purposes, of the person making the statement appears to the court to have been (a) to cause another person to believe the matter, or (b) to cause another person to act or a machine to operate on the basis that the matter is as stated'.[17] The Law Commission Report which formed the basis for the provisions in the 2003 Act takes the view that a declarant's purpose is something she consciously desires to achieve, rather than something that is 'an inevitable side-effect' of achieving that end.[18] It also notes that a declarant may have more than one purpose in communicating, and concludes that a statement is hearsay if one of the declarant's purposes was to produce a belief, or to cause an action based on the belief, in the matter for which the proponent offers it.

In regard to the bank robbery hypothetical, case law in at least one US circuit holds that 'Don't worry, I didn't tell them anything about you', would be hearsay if offered against D, on the theory that W intended to assert D's involvement in the crime.[19] The probative value of the statement for the prosecution's case depends on whether the trier could rely on it to conclude that W did not tell the prosecutor that D was involved, even though D was involved in the crime.[20] It would not be evidence of guilt if the trier concluded only that W said nothing about D. In contrast, a significant portion of American cases and commentators take the position that a statement can only be hearsay if offered to show the truth of a matter that it directly or explicitly asserts.[21] The utterance 'I didn't tell them anything about you', would not expressly or directly convey that W had any information that could incriminate D. Rather, taken alone and in its narrowest sense, it would only say that W did not give any information about D to the police. As the Law Commission sees its 'purpose' requirement, causing D 'to believe' in his own guilt would not have been one of W's purposes.[22]

---

[16] Fed R Evid 801(c).
[17] Criminal Justice Act 2003, s 115(3).
[18] Law Commission Report, above n 14, [7.36].
[19] *Reynolds*, above n 15, 104.
[20] *Ibid* 103.
[21] Eg, *United States v Zenni*, 492 F. Supp. 464, 466 n 7 (ED Ky. 1980); *United States v Lewis*, 902 F. 2d 1176, 1179 (5th Cir. 1990); *United States v Long*, 905 F. 2d 1572, 1579–80 (D.C. Cir. 1990) (then-Judge Clarence Thomas); *United States v Oguns* 921 F. 2d 442, 448–49 (2d Cir. 1990); JH Wigmore, *A Treatise on the System of Evidence in Trials at Common Law* (Boston, Little, Brown and Co, 1904) vol 3, ss 1715, 1788, 1790; KS Broun *et al* (eds), *McCormick on Evidence* (6th practitioners' edn, St Paul, MN, West, 2006) vol 2, s 250, pp 144–46.
[22] Law Commission Report, above n 14, [7.27].

COGNITIVE STRATEGY

Recent Research

The narrow American interpretations of the hearsay rule that I just described, and the 'purpose' requirement in the Criminal Justice Act 2003, each rest on assumptions that conflict with scholarship about the communicative process. As a result, they fail to account for some of the difficulties that evaluation of out-of-court statements like W's can present for fact-finders.

In the absence of further information about the context in which W spoke, fact-finders who relied on their experience to assess the value of W's out-of-court statement would understand it to communicate W's belief that W could have said something that would affect D adversely in the eyes of the police. That is, they would assume that W would not have spoken to D as he did unless W thought that his utterance would be of significant benefit to D (for example, by providing information D might want in deciding how to respond to interrogation) and would convey the information efficiently. To explain this, I must briefly touch on some findings in cognitive psychology.

Successful problem solvers, particularly those who deal with common inferential problems that are not formalised, rely on cognitive strategies to identify critical information and make decisions based on that information. Given the limitations on our cognitive capacity and time and the competing demands on resources, we learn to use strategies from our own experience, training or education. Researchers have devoted considerable attention to the cognitive strategies that we exploit in order to convey a significant amount of information in relatively few words, symbols or actions, or to understand messages communicated to us.

W's statement to D that 'I didn't tell them anything about you', would convey little useful information if one took it literally. If W only communicated what he articulated in words, D would not care whether the police overheard it, since the message would be that W had said nothing. Intuitively, however, we know that the police would tend to interpret it more broadly, as suggesting D's involvement in the robbery. Their doing so would be rational, in accord with the natural cognitive effects of the statement, which would reach beyond the words in which W made it. Utterances have effect beyond communicating the propositions they articulate, because hearers rationally and intuitively take account of the cognitive strategies that we use to convey information in order to gather a great deal of information from communications that are, in form, only a limited number of words, symbols or actions.

Wilson and Sperber recently simplified Grice's explanation of the strategies on which we rely in interpreting and evaluating conversations. Essentially, they concluded that when a speaker communicates, she employs not only words, symbols or actions, but also two implicit claims. First, she claims that the information she conveys is worth the hearer's attention, that is, worth the effort to process the information.[23] Information benefits the hearer to the extent that it contributes to his knowledge or helps him to make decisions with less effort. As Posner points out, the costs of information are the resources needed to process it and the extent to which the information may adversely affect the quality of decisions.[24] That new information can benefit the hearer is obvious. The benefits from lowering cognitive effort may be less clear. To illustrate those benefits, consider a statement that ostensibly repeats something that the hearer would be likely to know, such as 'Remember our game next week'. At a minimum, reminding the hearer of a matter lowers the hearer's cognitive effort: the hearer can more easily obtain the information from the reminder than from her own memory.[25] Folk psychology might assume that the cognitive effort needed to recall information is negligible or insignificant. Yet the process of recall may be heavily dependent on reconstruction rather than simple retrieval. One explanation of the process through which we recall information argues that we retain relatively little specific information about past events in our memory. Instead, our recollections are reconstructions that employ the specific information, but cannot be accomplished without heavy reliance on our attitudes to all of our past reactions and experiences.[26] An ostensible reminder or assumption may convey information that is, for most practical purposes, new to the hearer—and that the speaker reconstructed for the purpose. At the very least, the hearer may rely on it rather than attempting a difficult reconstruction in her memory with uncertain results. That reliance would be based on the assumption that the speaker would not articulate the reminder unless the benefits of the information were worth the hearer's trouble.

The second implicit claim that a speaker makes is that the form in which the speaker conveys the information will produce the greatest possible surplus of benefits over costs consistent with the speaker's interest. In other words, the speaker may express herself ironically, loosely, indirectly or through figures of speech—she need not articulate all the messages that she wishes to convey, so long as what she does say, taken with the implicit

---

[23]   See D Wilson and D Sperber, 'Truthfulness and Relevance' (2002) 111 *Mind* 583, 604.

[24]   RA Posner, *Frontiers of Legal Theory* (Cambridge, MA, Harvard UP, 2002) 340–1.

[25]   D Sperber and D Wilson, *Relevance: Communication and Cognition* (2nd edn, Oxford, Blackwell, 1995) 149–50.

[26]   See I Rosenfeld, *The Invention of Memory: a New View of the Brain* (New York, Basic Books, 1988) 192–3.

claims, would lead the hearers to infer the content of her message. Take W's statement, with the limited additional information that the hypothetical provides. Given that limited information, reliance on the second implicit claim would lead us to infer that W could have provided the police with information that incriminated D. Our inferences might proceed as follows: first, the statement that W had told 'them' nothing would be of greatest interest to D if 'them' referred to the police, and if the information affected D's immediate interests. Secondly, given that D might well be concerned that the police suspected him of the crime, W's statement would be likely to refer to withholding of information that might otherwise adversely affect D. Thirdly, the form of W's statement would have reinforced that inference: W might have omitted explicit references to the information that he sought to convey out of fear that someone would overhear him. Hearers, including fact-finders, will rely on the information they have and the speaker's implicit claims to interpret and evaluate any of her communications.[27]

If the analysis only went this far, one might say that W's statement seems only to be designed to assure D that W did not reveal information that D knew that W had. If so, then W would not have made the statement to cause D to believe in his own guilt.[28] Yet such a superficial interpretation of W's utterance could be extremely misleading. Information about knowledge that W and D shared, their perceptions of each other, and their relevant interests, could drastically influence jurors' assessment of the probative value of W's statement. W might have made the statement as a veiled threat that W could provide false information to the police implicating D in the bank robbery, or information implicating D in some other crime. W might have intended his statement to reassure D that W knew nothing that would be harmful to D. W's reconstruction of the relevant facts from his memory could be inaccurate. Finally, W's statement could be an effort to be ironic, intended to indicate that suspecting D would be absurd, and to express a lack of respect for police investigatory efforts. Even if W meant to convey only the message that a narrow interpretation would suggest, the utterance might be misleading: W's perception of the effect of the information he had, or his recollection of events, could be inaccurate.

In each case, D's failure to respond or deny might have little or no probative value (and could well be inadmissible, at least in the United States) given general knowledge of the inadvisability of speaking to the

---

[27] See Wilson and Sperber, above n 23, 604. Wilson and Sperber encapsulated their conclusions in terms to which they gave their own technical definition, which could be very confusing in a discussion of Evidence law: 'Every utterance conveys a presumption of its own optimal relevance' (*ibid*).

[28] See eg, Park, above n 5, 137.

police in the absence of counsel.[29] Without further information about the interests of W and D and their relationship, fact-finders could rationally, but erroneously, rely on the cognitive strategies they learned from experience and credit the evidence in the belief that the court considered it probative of D's guilt.

From a broader perspective, the two conventions that Wilson and Sperber identified bear on hearsay and confrontation on two levels. Initially, they bear on exclusionary rules in general, suggesting that admission of evidence without regard to whether it is worthwhile would be inadvisable. Based on research on communication in general, and the effect of admission of evidence in particular, jurors may interpret admission of evidence as an implicit judicial communication that the evidence warrants the resources needed to process it.[30] To that extent, admission of evidence that does not warrant the effort to evaluate it may lead jurors to misinterpret the evidence or the legal criteria.[31]

More specifically, the conventions have implications for hearsay and confrontation. Communications have cognitive effects on their hearers.[32] They produce or strengthen hearers' beliefs in propositions that speakers could reasonably expect their hearers to infer from the words, symbols or acts that the speaker employed and the implicit claims in the speaker's communication. When the probative value of a communication depends on its implicit claims, special evidentiary rules may be warranted to tailor the fact-finding process to the cognitive processes that fact-finders will use in evaluating the communications.

---

[29] See eg, *United States v Flecha* 539 F. 2d 874, 877 (2d Cir. 1976): '[I]t is clear that many arrested persons know, without benefit of warnings, that silence is usually golden'.

[30] See eg, J Sanders, 'From Science to Evidence: the Testimony on Causation in the Bendectin Cases' (1993) 46 *Stanford LR* 1, 39–41 and n 199; E Beecher-Monas, 'Heuristics, Biases and the Importance of Gatekeeping' [2003] *Michigan State LR* 987, 1005–6.

[31] Eg, SA Saltzburg, 'A Special Aspect of Relevance: Countering Negative Inferences Associated with the Absence of Evidence' (1978) 66 *Caifornia LR* 1011, 1014 f 7; CR Callen, 'Hearsay and Informal Reasoning' (1994) 47 *Vanderbilt LR* 43, 65. A number of commentators argue that special exclusionary rules for hearsay evidence stem from legislative or judicial lack of respect for the cognitive capacities of jurors. Eg, Law Commission Report, above n 14, [3.19]–[3.28]; JB Weinstein, 'Alternative to the Present Hearsay Rules' (1967) 44 *Federal Rules Decisions* 375, 377; G Tullock, *The Logic of the Law* (New York, Basic Books, 1971) 93–4. The argument in the text is not that jurors are cognitively inferior, merely that they are human and subject to errors when using cognitive strategies that we use in everyday life to allocate cognitive resources efficiently: see Callen, above, 66–8. There is no doubt that advocates of excluding hearsay did sometimes distrust jurors, but to conclude on that basis that lack of respect for jurors would be the only reason for a rule against hearsay would be to commit the genetic fallacy, making the assumption 'that explaining the causal origins of a view is sufficient to show that the view is false': JR Searle, *Mind, Language and Society: Philosophy in the Real World* (New York, Basic Books, 1998) 33. See also 'Informal fallacy' in R Audi (ed), *The Cambridge Dictionary of Philosophy* (New York, CUP, 1995) 373.

[32] For the sake of brevity, this chapter will often refer to a communicator as a speaker, and the audience of a communication as a hearer.

Non-Communicative Conduct and Morgan's Theory

Non-Communicative Conduct

Given that we ask jurors to rely on their everyday experience to evaluate evidence, we should anticipate that they would rely on the cognitive strategies they have learned to help them to evaluate evidence, including evidence of out-of-court statements. Evaluating evidence of out-of-court behaviour is much less challenging when the evidence is not hearsay for the purpose for which it is offered. Assessing such evidence does not require appraisal of implicit claims in communication.

Courts, commentators and jurisdictions differ on the precise definition of hearsay. Nevertheless, one useful place to start is Morgan's hearsay risks. Morgan argued that hearsay is suspect evidence because it presents four inferential dangers that cross-examination could mitigate, if not control.[33] He concluded that the distinctive characteristic of hearsay is that its value depends on whether the actor[34] was honest or sincere, whether the conduct was ambiguous, and whether the actor's beliefs were based on accurate perceptions and recollections. Evidence of an out-of-court communication offered for a non-hearsay purpose, such as to show that the statement established a legally operative fact, has probative value without regard to the declarant's sincerity, narrative ability (or clarity), perceptiveness and memory. For example, if the statement 'I'll kill you if you don't open that safe', were offered to show that the person who opened the safe did so as a result of a threat, the evidence would have probative value even if the speaker was lying, spoke imprecisely, had a bad memory or misperceived the situation. The words themselves could constitute the threat.[35]

---

[33]   EM Morgan, 'Hearsay Dangers and the Application of the Hearsay Concept' (1948) 62 *Harvard LR* 177, 178–9. In the United Kingdom, see eg, P Roberts and A Zuckerman, *Criminal Evidence* (Oxford, OUP, 2004) 598.

[34]   Or declarant.

[35]   See eg, *Subramaniam v Public Prosecutor* [1956] 1 WLR 965 (PC). Morgan's theory seems to simplify the hearsay issue in the recent decision of *R v Singh*, above n 10. There, one question was whether the contents of the memories of cell phones, which showed a number of calls between them and to other alleged co-conspirators, would be inadmissible hearsay as unintentional implied assertions. Morgan would argue that the memory contents are not hearsay, since they raise none of the four dangers, certainly not in any sense that might suggest a need to cross-examine. Accuracy of the phone's memory and its display would be authentication questions. Once they were resolved, there would be no issues of sincerity, narrative ability, perception or memory if the Crown offered the cell phone's memory to show calls made on it. See *State v Armstead*, 432 So. 2d 837, 839 (La. S. Ct. 1983) (computerised record of incoming calls not hearsay); *People v Holowko*, 486 N.E. 2d 877, 878–79 (Ill. S. Ct. 1985) (printouts of computerised telephone tracing not hearsay); *Tatum v Commonwealth*, 440 S.E. 2d 133, 135–36 (Va. Ct. App. 1994) (caller ID display not hearsay).

Even so, modern evidence doctrine holds that Morgan's approach extended the reach of the hearsay rule a little too far. Out-of-court conduct, whether communicative or not, often suggests that the actor held beliefs about facts in issue. Morgan relied on the common law to argue that when parties offer out-of-court conduct as evidence of facts that the actor ostensibly believed, that evidence should be hearsay because it presents the distinctive hearsay risks. In other words, Morgan would have argued that non-communicative conduct can be hearsay. That position went back to *Wright v Tatham*.[36] The letters at issue in *Wright* were offered to show the mental condition of their addressee, the testator, and were communicative by definition. In classifying them as hearsay, however, the court offered illustrations of hearsay that included non-communicative conduct, such as 'the conduct of a deceased captain on a question of seaworthiness, who, after examining every part of a vessel, embarked in it with his family'.[37] At best, that portion of *Wright* was confusing. At worst, it dramatically over-extended the reach of the hearsay rule.

The Federal Rules and the Criminal Justice Act 2003 exclude non-communicative conduct from the hearsay rule. Under the Federal Rules, non-verbal conduct of a person can only be hearsay if 'intended by the person as an assertion'. The hearsay rule in the Criminal Justice Act applies to 'statements' offered as evidence of any 'matter stated'.[38] Section 115(3) provides that the Act's hearsay rule only applies to matters stated if one of the declarant's purposes 'appears to the court to have been . . . to cause another person to believe the matter, or . . . to cause another person to act or a machine to operate on the basis that the matter is as stated'.[39] That approach would exclude non-communicative actions from the hearsay rule; that is, if the declarant did not intend to convey information through his action, no purpose of his action would have been to cause a belief or an action based on a belief.[40]

In excluding non-communicative conduct from the hearsay rule, the Federal Rules and the Criminal Justice Act are consistent with Wilson and Sperber's work and the empirical research that supports it. Because non-communicative acts are not intended to convey any information, let alone implicit messages, evaluating them involves a much simpler, less risky process than evaluation of communications offered for hearsay purposes.

---

[36] *Wright*, above n 2.
[37] *Ibid* 516.
[38] Criminal Justice Act 2003, s 114.
[39] *Ibid* s 115(3)(a) and (b).
[40] *Ibid* s 115(2) also suggests that non-communicative conduct cannot be hearsay. It provides that a 'statement is any representation of fact or opinion made by a person by whatever means; and it includes a representation made in a sketch, photofit or other pictorial form'. A representation of fact or opinion would necessarily be intended to convey a message, if only to make a record for the future.

Consider again *Wright*'s ship captain example.[41] An observer who saw the captain examine the vessel would have one fairly firm bit of evidence about the captain's state of mind: clear physical behaviour. If, on the other hand, all we knew was that the captain referred to the vessel in question as 'a classic bucket of bolts', jurors might have a much more difficult problem. Without information about the context in which the captain spoke, including information about his relationship with the hearer, jurors would be unable to decide whether the reference to the 'classic bucket of bolts' pertained to seaworthiness of the vessel, and, if so, whether the captain's judgement was favourable. The phrase might be ironic praise, or have some favourable meaning from the captain's prior relationship with his hearer. On the other hand, it might be critical of the vessel or idle chatter of no significance.

Hearsay Exceptions and Communication

Clarifying ambiguities in communications (or even noticing them) could be very difficult for jurors who lacked necessary information to support conclusions bearing on the context and the degree to which the speaker complied with the norms of communication. Of course, jurors might not be certain about the weight to give a physical inspection of the vessel and subsequent action suggesting seaworthiness. Even so, assessment of evidence of communications differs from evaluation of the probative value of non-communicative physical actions. Jurors may have difficulty determining the content of the communication itself without evidence of the speaker's state of mind and perspective, that is, without considering whether and to what extent the speaker's implicit claims were true. Determining whether the captain inspected the vessel and embarked with his family is more straightforward, and does not require jurors to consider any claims that would be implicit in a communication.

Hearsay exceptions help to adapt the fact-finding process to fact-finders' use of cognitive strategies in assessing out-of-court statements. The exceptions generally require that the proponent of evidence produce information about the context or the declarant's motive in making a statement. Information that fulfils the exceptions' requirements tends to show that the statement is worth the jurors' effort to evaluate it, to make the jurors' task easier, or both. For example, if the company that owned the vessel required all of its captains to fill out a form on the condition of the vessel before departing, and the captain wrote 'classic bucket of bolts' on the form, it would suggest doubts about seaworthiness. If, on the other hand, he had completed a form to request command of the 'classic bucket of bolts', that

---

[41] *Wright*, above n 2, 516.

would suggest that his opinion of the vessel was more favourable. So, the facts needed to trigger the hearsay exception for records of regularly conducted activities under the Federal Rules, including keeping of the record in the course of a regularly conducted business activity, would tend to suggest the probative value of the captain's statement. In the process, such facts would reduce the cognitive effort required for the jurors to appraise the evidence. Satisfaction of the analogous exception in s 117 of the Criminal Justice Act would have the same effect.

I have argued elsewhere that research on communication should inform our judgements about the definition of hearsay and our applications of that definition.[42] My goal in this chapter is more modest. It is to show that research on communication can help us to explain the definition of hearsay, assess different approaches to it, and teach students how to make and evaluate alternative arguments when the definition of hearsay (or of 'testimonial' evidence in the context of the US Confrontation Clause) is uncertain. Application of the hearsay definition has never been completely predictable. With the disagreements about the effect of the Federal Rules in the United States, and novel theories in both Confrontation Clause doctrine and s 115 of the Criminal Justice Act 2003, it seems likely that the law will be less than clear for some time to come. Students who have been exposed to interdisciplinary and comparative approaches are better able to understand the reasons for that lack of clarity, deal with it and, in some cases, resolve it.

COGNITION AND CONFRONTATION

The most troublesome new topic in Evidence is confrontation—a particularly timely topic in the United States. Research on communication can help us analyse whether evidence of a statement should be considered testimonial and subject to the requirements of the Confrontation Clause as the Supreme Court recently reinterpreted it in *Crawford v Washington*.[43] Among the issues *Crawford* raises is a very tricky one about the status of implied assertions under the Confrontation Clause.

The Confrontation Clause of the Sixth Amendment to the US Constitution provides that the accused in a criminal case 'shall enjoy the right . . . to be confronted with the Witnesses against him'.[44] While that might be interpreted to refer only to those testifying at trial, case law prior to *Crawford* interpreted the Confrontation Clause to limit the admissibility of hearsay against criminal defendants, unless the hearsay fell within a 'firmly

---

[42] Callen, above n 31, 86–112
[43] *Crawford*, above n 1.
[44] US Const amend VI.

rooted' exception to the hearsay rule, or bore 'particularised guarantees of trustworthiness'.[45] The *Crawford* Court, per Justice Scalia, took the view that the Clause was principally aimed to avoid 'the civil law mode of criminal procedure' and especially 'its use of ex parte examinations as evidence'.[46] It rejected not only the view that the Clause should only reach in-court testimony, but also the argument that the Clause's effect should depend on the law of evidence. Justice Scalia wrote that dependency on the law of evidence could render the Clause itself 'powerless to prevent even the most flagrant inquisitorial practices'.[47] Relying on the Court's reading of English and American legal history,[48] *Crawford* held that only out-of-court statements that are 'testimonial' implicate the Clause's core concerns, based on an interpretation of the word 'witnesses' in the Clause as persons who 'bear testimony'.[49] Further, it concluded that the Confrontation Clause prohibits the admission of out-of-court testimonial statements against defendants in criminal cases unless the declarant is unavailable and the defendant had a prior opportunity for cross-examination.[50]

The court admitted that it did not 'spell out' the meaning of 'testimonial'. Instead, it offered three possible interpretations of the term, of increasing degrees of breadth, which might well co-exist.[51] The broadest is that testimonial statements are those 'made under circumstances that would lead an objective witness reasonably to believe that the statement would be available for use at a later trial'.[52] Under this interpretation, post-arrest statements in the presence of police officers at the station house that might seem to concern a related crime would qualify. The other two interpretations classify statements as testimonial if they are either (i) the functional equivalent of in-court testimony or (ii) 'formalized admissions', such as affidavits and confessions. They might apply to W's statement in the bank robbery hypothetical (which might be the equivalent of a confession, or an unsworn statement in a custodial examination). W's statement would not be hearsay under some circuits' interpretation of the Federal Rules if offered to show D's guilt, and, to that extent, would not be barred from admission. Yet the Federal Rules, as creatures of statute, do

---

[45] *Ohio v Roberts*, 448 U.S. 56, 66, 100 S. Ct. 2531, 2539 (1980).

[46] *Crawford*, above n 1, 50.

[47] *Ibid* 51.

[48] But see JH Langbein, *The Origins of Adversary Criminal Trial* (Oxford, OUP, 2003) 233–4 (n 241) ('I have been puzzled at the failure of the English common law to identify and develop the confrontation policy as a matter of doctrine').

[49] *Crawford*, above n 1, 51.

[50] *Ibid* 68.

[51] RD Friedman, The Confrontation Blog, 'The Formality Bugaboo' http://confrontationright.blogspot.com/search?q=formality+bugaboo accessed 8 August 2007.

[52] *Ibid.*

not trump constitutional doctrine,[53] and *Crawford* emphasises that the law of evidence does not determine the reach of the Confrontation Clause.

Looking at the issue more closely, the question of whether a statement is testimonial under *Crawford* seems to have two related dimensions. The first concerns the extent to which the declarant would have intended or expected the statement to play a part in an arrest or prosecution of the defendant, which the court's interpretations of its term 'testimonial' seem to address.[54] The second dimension concerns the extent to which the statement, and the purpose for which it is offered, suggest that the statement should be cross-examined. *Crawford* foresaw the issue in part, but gave it little attention because the prosecution offered the statements at issue in that case to prove facts that the statements explicitly asserted in circumstances in which cross-examination would clearly have benefited the trier of fact. In a footnote, *Crawford* did say that a statement is not

---

[53] Eg, *People v Morgan*, 23 Cal. Rptr. 3d 224, 232–3 (Cal. Ct. App. 2005) (classification of statement as non-hearsay does not determine whether statement is testimonial for Confrontation Clause purposes). In his recent opinion for the US Supreme Court in *Davis v Washington*, 126 S.Ct. 2266, 2274 (2006) Justice Scalia wrote, 'We must decide, therefore, whether the Confrontation Clause applies only to testimonial hearsay', but one should not read too much into that. First, the statement at issue in *Davis* was clearly hearsay, so the court faced no issue about the status of non-hearsay under the Confrontation Clause. Secondly, as Michael Pardo pointed out in a private communication, if the Confrontation Clause only applied to evidence that state law treated as hearsay, the state could simply abolish the hearsay rules in criminal cases (or in all cases) and negate defendants' constitutional confrontation rights.

If we were to look at the issue in terms of what 'hearsay' usually means, the text of Federal Rule 801 is relatively unclear on whether statements offered to show matters they do not expressly articulate are, for purposes of the rule, offered to prove what they assert. See eg, OG Wellborn III, 'The Definition of Hearsay in the Federal Rules of Evidence' (1982) 61 *Texas LR* 49, 79–81; DE Seidelson, 'Implied Assertions and Federal Rule of Evidence 801: a Quandary for Federal Courts' (1986) 24 *Duquesne LR* 741, 759. In light of the court's earlier, albeit isolated, cases interpreting the scope of the hearsay rule broadly, one may doubt whether the court intended a narrow interpretation when it promulgated Rule 801. *Krulewitch v United States*, 336 U.S. 440, 441, 69 S. Ct. 716, 717 (1949), held inadmissible under the hearsay rule a statement by one of defendant's alleged co-conspirators to another that 'it would be better for us two girls to take the blame than Kay [the defendant] because he couldn't stand it, he couldn't stand to take it' (brackets in original). The court held the evidence to be hearsay because the out-of-court declaration 'plainly implied' that Krulewitch 'was guilty of the crime for which he was on trial', and inadmissible because it was not within an exception to the hearsay rule: *ibid* 442–4. Similarly, in *Dutton v Evans*, 400 U.S. 74, 77, 79, 91 S. Ct. 210, 214, 215 (1970), the court regarded the co-conspirator's statement that 'If it hadn't been for that dirty son-of-a-bitch Alex Evans, we wouldn't be in this now', as hearsay subject to the Confrontation Clause when the state offered it as evidence of Evans' guilt.

[54] *Davis v Washington*, above n 53, 2279, stresses that where the witness' statements to police were neither 'a cry for help nor provision of information enabling officers immediately to end a threatening situation', they were testimonial even if the interrogation was an 'initial inquiry'. It also relied on a distinction between provision of information about past events (which would relate to an investigation of a crime, and so tend to be testimonial) and information about ongoing events (which might relate to an emergency for which the declarant was seeking help).

testimonial if not offered to prove the truth of the matter that the statement asserts.[55] The fact that it relied solely on *Tennessee v Street*[56] in doing so suggests that the court did not intend to place implied assertions beyond the reach of the Confrontation Clause. The defendant in *Street* claimed that his own confession was a 'coerced imitation' of the statement of his accomplice. The Court held that the Confrontation Clause did not bar admission of the accomplice's statement for the purposes of comparison, a purpose for which it would not be 'hearsay under traditional rules of evidence'.[57] The most straightforward interpretation of *Crawford*'s reliance on *Street*, then, is that statements are not testimonial under the Confrontation Clause if offered for a purpose for which they present no hearsay dangers, such as to show a statement's effect on the hearer.[58] That would not be true of statements offered to show implied assertions.

The court's opinion in *Crawford* stresses heavily that cross-examination should be the test of the ultimate evidentiary value of statements.[59] In the process, it criticises the *Ohio v Roberts* approach, under which courts not only made an ex ante and often unpredictable determination of the reliability of the evidence in deciding whether to admit it, but also relied on the jury to assess the ultimate value of the evidence in the absence of cross-examination.[60] The problem for those who might wish to place implied assertions beyond the reach of the Confrontation Clause is that there is no good argument that they are free of testimonial or hearsay dangers. Instead, the argument is that they somehow present fewer inferential dangers than explicit out-of-court statements offered to show what they explicate. Most often, the argument is that admission of out-of-court statements to show implied assertions carries less risk of insincerity than admission of normal hearsay does, since deceivers are likely to lie or mislead with direct statements.[61] Yet, deceivers may think they are more likely to be successful by indirection, conveying as much true

---

[55] *Crawford*, above n 1, 59 n 9.

[56] 471 U.S. 409, 414, 105 S. Ct. 2078, 2081–2 (1985).

[57] *Ibid* 412–13.

[58] Eg, *Subramaniam*, above n 35, 965.

[59] *Crawford*, above n 1, 62.

[60] In particular, it pointed out that a significant number of courts admitted accomplice confessions against an accused even though *Lilly v Virginia*, 527 U.S. 116, 117, 119 S. Ct. 1887, 1890–91 (1999), had warned that such evidence was 'highly unlikely' to be admissible under *Ohio v Roberts*: *Crawford*, above n 1, 63–4.

[61] See eg, *Zenni*, above n 21, 466 n 7; *Long*, above n 21, 1580; *McCormick on Evidence*, above n 21, s 250, pp 144–46; Park, above n 5, 129, 137. See also Law Commission Report, above n 14, [7.17]–[7.20] (if declarant did not intend to communicate a matter, there would be no risk of deliberate fabrication with respect to that matter, and in the absence of such a risk, other risks are 'not necessarily sufficient reason to exclude evidence': *ibid* para 7.19).

information—data that suggest the conclusion that they wish their hearers to draw—as they can, and omitting data with contrary implications.[62]

Finally, as Morgan pointed out, cross-examination is often an ineffective test for dishonesty.[63] On the other hand, it would seem to be a very good means for reducing risks of ambiguity. When proponents offer statements to show matters that the statement did not expressly assert, cross-examination could easily dispel or reduce any ambiguity risk. Accordingly, treating statements as non-testimonial when offered to show matters they did not literally assert would rest on a questionable, if not skewed, view of the likely benefits of cross-examination.

Narrowing the reach of the Confrontation Clause by excluding implied assertions from it would have a peculiar effect on future testimony at trial. Were implied assertions not subject to the Confrontation Clause, some police officer witnesses (and other sophisticated repeat players) would simply testify about out-of-court statements by restating them so that a proposition that the proffering party wished to show was only suggested, rather than stated.[64] To the extent such efforts were successful, they would build a trap-door into Confrontation Clause doctrine—the sort of doctrinal flexibility for which the *Crawford* Court criticised decisions following *Ohio v Roberts*.

In sum, the argument for excluding implied assertions from the reach of the Confrontation Clause is simply a categorical judgement about the value or reliability of evidence closely analogous to the reasoning that lower courts earlier employed in admitting hearsay not subjected to cross-examination under *Ohio v Roberts*—reasoning that the Court found so contrary to the intent of the Confrontation Clause in *Crawford*.[65] Placing all implied assertions outside the reach of the Confrontation Clause would seem in tension with the Court's professed goal of being 'faithful to the original meaning of the Confrontation Clause'.[66] In addition, it would conflict with legal history, specifically, *Wright*. *Tennessee v Street* rather obviously did not relate to implied assertions, which *Wright* and other cases held to be hearsay at common law.

Having said that, one cannot be confident that the Court will ultimately hold that some or all implied assertions are within the ambit of the

---

[62]   As Mueller pointed out, 'Deceivers convey very little "false information"': CB Mueller, 'Post-Modern Hearsay Reform: the Importance of Complexity' (1992) 76 *Minnesota LR* 367, 414 n 140.

[63]   Morgan, above n 33, 188; Note, 'The Theoretical Foundation of the Hearsay Rules' (1980) 93 *Harvard L Rev* 1786, 1793.

[64]   See *Park v Huff*, 493 F. 2d 923, 927–28 (5th Cir. 1974), withdrawn on other grounds, 506 F. 2d 849 (5th Cir. 1975) (pre-*Crawford* opinion, noting that, if courts treated implied assertions as non-hearsay, some police officers would reword statements in their testimony to avoid hearsay problems).

[65]   *Crawford*, above n 1, 60.

[66]   *Ibid.*

Confrontation Clause. For example, if the court were to reach the unlikely conclusion that only statements taken during a thorough formal interrogation can be testimonial, interrogators might be so thorough that that they leave no 'implied' loose ends. Or, given *Crawford*'s zeal to distinguish Confrontation Clause jurisprudence from hearsay doctrine, and its reliance on original intent, the courts might eventually conclude that Confrontation Clause doctrine must not reach implied assertions, lest it entangle itself in an issue that would be so reminiscent of hearsay doctrine.

My point here is not to suggest that studies on communication can determine what the court will hold. It is rather to suggest that ideas from research on communication can help us to analyse an important aspect of the issues that the court must face in construing the Confrontation Clause: the extent to which evaluating an out-of-court statement depends on implicit claims that create a need for special procedural precautions.

AN ANALYTICAL MATRIX FOR HEARSAY AND CONFRONTATION

Evidence teachers can introduce interdisciplinary and comparative perspectives into their courses with a relatively simple graphic device. Figure 6.1, overleaf, includes elements derived from research on communication, American and English hearsay law and commentary, and Confrontation Clause doctrine. In order to demonstrate how it can help students (or perplexed lawyers and judges) to understand hearsay and Confrontation doctrine, I will use a hypothetical similar to *R v Kearley*.[67] Suppose that the police arrested club owner C one morning for possession of drugs with intent to sell. The police found a small amount of drugs, consistent with either personal use or possession for sale, in C's possession. C claimed that the drugs were for personal use. Despite C's arrest, the club that C owned held its weekly rock concert later that night, and in a break in the concert S went to the bar-tender at the crowded bar and said, 'Is C here? I'd like to buy the usual'. Police sought to apprehend the speaker, who got away. The question is whether S's utterance should be admissible against C. I will use the matrix to analyse this problem, abbreviating the discussion of points made earlier, and offering contrasting examples to illustrate important distinctions.

Consensus Non-Hearsay

To analyse the issues that C's statement presents, we must identify the purpose for which the evidence is offered—here to show that C would have

---

[67] Above n 9.

intended to sell the drugs. One can then delineate the effects of the various approaches to hearsay and confrontation by asking a set of questions that Figure 6.1 summarises.[68] First, one must ask whether the jury would have to assume or assess S's sincerity, clarity of expression or accuracy in memory or perception in order to appraise the evidence for that purpose. In other words, the question would be whether S's utterance would be non-hearsay under even the broadest views of the common law test, reflected in *Wright*. For example, if one were considering the evidence at issue in *Tennessee v Street*, a written statement of an accomplice, offered to show that it was not the source of the defendant's confession, the evidence would not raise any hearsay risks. The accomplice's statement would be offered to show that it was not similar to the defendant's. For that purpose, it would not matter whether the accomplice's statement was sincere or clear, or whether he perceived or remembered events accurately.

One might wonder why the diagram pays so much attention to the view of the hearsay definition that *Wright* embodied. Few, if any, jurisdictions in the United States now adhere to *Wright*, and the Criminal Justice Act 2003, at a minimum, negates *Wright*. Nor is it likely that the Supreme Court would hold that non-communicative conduct would be testimonial. Nevertheless, it is important to distinguish between those items of evidence that would only be hearsay under *Wright* and those that might be hearsay under narrower interpretations. (To put the point in a slightly different way, it is important to distinguish arguments that could only be correct under *Wright* from those acceptable under more modern interpretations.)

Here, in order to give weight to the evidence on the question of whether C intended to sell the drugs, one would have to make assumptions about the extent to which 'the usual' referred to drugs, and to customary transactions with C. Each of those inferences would involve questions about the clarity of expression, or ambiguity, of S's statement. Moreover, to the extent that S's utterance indicated customary drug purchases from C, jurors would have to make assumptions about S's accuracy in order to assess the weight to which the utterance would be entitled. So, S's utterance would be hearsay under *Wright*. To depict the point graphically, the answer to the question at node 1 of Figure 6.1 for S's utterance would be 'Yes'.

---

[68] It is important to note that Figure 6.1 only addresses one dimension of Confrontation Clause analysis (the extent to which the content of a communication and the purpose for which the prosecution offers it suggest that cross-examination is critical), and omits the other (the extent to which the declarant would have expected the statement to play a role in an arrest or prosecution). See above, text to nn 54–8.

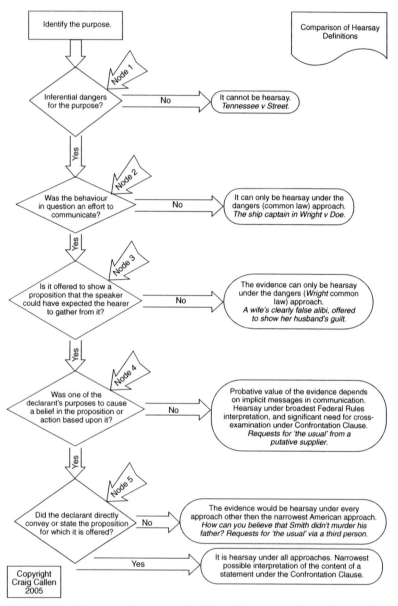

Figure 6.1: Content of communications, hearsay and confrontation

Identifying Communications

If proffered evidence would be hearsay under *Wright*'s broader common law view, the next issue is whether the out-of-court behaviour was a communication, that is, an effort by the speaker, writer or actor to convey or record information[69] or to remind or strengthen another's belief in a fact. Assessment of the probative value of communications offered for a purpose that requires inferences from the messages implicit in that communication is a much more difficult process than evaluation of non-communicative conduct offered to show that a belief on which the actor relied in acting is probably true.[70] *Wright*'s famous ship captain hypothetical would not be communicative behaviour,[71] in that jurors can determine whether the ship captain thoroughly inspected the ship and embarked without relying on any implicit messages or conventions of communication.

Jurors could not, however, determine how to weigh S's statement on the question of whether C intended to sell the drugs without knowing what S's interests in the transaction were and what S believed C's interests to be. In other words, S might have intended to purchase some substance other than the substance found in C's possession, to purchase a service from or through C, or even, if S and C used the same substance, to seek information about where he could obtain that substance. (S's statement does not articulate a desire to buy anything from C). Determining whether those possibilities or others are true would depend on whether S conformed to the conventions of communication. So, the answer to the question at node 2 would be 'Yes' for the hypothetical at hand, but 'No' for *Wright*'s ship captain.

Identification of the Speaker's Intention and the Limit of Confrontation

The next question relates to a relative subtlety in modern hearsay law. Proponents sometimes offer evidence of an out-of-court communication to show that the declarant made a statement we know to be false. Such evidence would tend to suggest a reason why the declarant made the false statement. Suppose, for example, husband is being prosecuted for a bank robbery in Wales, and videotape shows that wife was in Edinburgh at the

---

[69] Speakers, and particularly writers, often communicate to record data for use at another time, even for their own use. The best illustration of a communication intended to create a record that is hearsay is a record of a regularly conducted business activity, which is hearsay, but that is within an exception under Fed R Evid 803(6) and Criminal Justice Act 2003, s 117.

[70] See above, text to nn 36–40.

[71] Under the approach in the Federal Rules and American Evidence law in general, the party objecting to the evidence would have the burden of showing by a preponderance that the declarant intended to communicate, that is, to make an assertion. See Fed R Evid 801(a) advisory committee's note. The Law Commission seems to take the position that the prosecution must show all facts needed for admissibility of evidence beyond a reasonable doubt: Law Commission Report, above n 14, [7.29]–[7.30].

time of the robbery. When police were investigating, they asked wife about husband's whereabouts that day, and she said that they were in Portugal on holiday. The prosecution would not want to offer wife's statement to show they were in Portugal, but, instead, to show that she offered a demonstrably false alibi based on her belief that husband robbed the bank, and, therefore, that husband did rob the bank. Wife's statement would not be hearsay under the Federal Rules[72] or the Criminal Justice Act 2003[73] because the prosecution would not be offering it to show anything she intended to communicate. Jurors would not need to assess the degree to which the messages implicit in her communication were true; they would know that the implicit messages were false. Accordingly, modern rules and statutes treat statements offered to show the reason for their falsity as non-hearsay. If the wife's statement were at issue, the answer at node 3 would be 'No'.

On the other hand, for the drug possession hypothetical, the answer at node 3 would be 'Yes'. S's statement would be offered to show a number of facts that S would typically intend it to convey, either because conveying those facts was part of S's purpose in communicating, or because S would intend to convey any information necessary to accomplish his purpose. At a minimum, on the information in the hypothetical, S would intend to convey that (i) he typically purchased something, (ii) that C was aware of such purchases, and (iii) that C could somehow facilitate such purchases. The prosecution would doubtless believe that S did not articulate what his 'usual' was because stating explicitly that it was a drug could cause trouble for S, C or the bar-tender, as could stating that C was S's source for the drug. In other words, the prosecution's argument about the probative value of the statement would essentially be that S complied with the implicit conventions of communication in making the statement, by putting the statement in a form that would convey as much information as possible that was consistent with S's interest.

Once we have determined that the proponent is offering evidence of out-of-court behaviour that (i) raises hearsay risks for the purpose for which its proponent offers it, (ii) is communicative, that is, an effort to convey information or remind the hearer of something, and (iii) is offered to prove something that the actor could have expected or intended the hearer to gather from it, we know that the proponent is relying on the conventions of communication to prove the proposition for which the evidence is offered.

[72] See RC Park, '*McCormick on Evidence* and the Concept of Hearsay: a Critical Analysis Followed by Suggestions to Law Teachers' (1981) 65 *Minnesota LR* 423, 426.
[73] Law Commission Report, above n 14, [7.3]. See also C Tapper, *Cross and Tapper on Evidence* (10th edn, LexisNexis UK, London, 2004) 596.

That would be enough to make the evidence hearsay in some US jurisdictions, on the ground that S intended to convey that he and C had engaged in prior transactions.[74] It might well be enough to show the utility of cross-examining the statement under *Crawford*. In essence, it would establish that the proponent was offering evidence to prove a proposition that the declarant intended to convey, in the sense that we intend the natural consequences of our actions. It would not, however, establish that the declarant would have intended (or expected) the statement to play a role in the arrest or prosecution of the defendant, which would leave doubt about whether the Confrontation Clause would limit admissibility of the statement in US courts. To return to the two illustrations, in the bank robbery hypothetical, W would have good reason to expect his post-arrest utterance in the presence of the police, 'I didn't tell them anything about you', to be used in a prosecution of D for bank robbery.[75] Accordingly, that utterance might well be subject to the Clause's special limitations. On the other hand, in the drug possession example, S's request for C, and expression of a desire to buy the usual, would probably not be subject to the Confrontation Clause. Even though S might have exhibited some caution in making only minimal references to his reasons for seeking C, S would have had little or no reason to believe that he was providing information to support arrest or prosecution, until the police began to pursue C. In other words, a positive answer at node 3 is insufficient to make an utterance testimonial under *Crawford v Washington*.

Identification of the Speaker's Purpose

The Criminal Justice Act 2003 and a significant share of US rules and cases define hearsay more narrowly. In preparing the recommendations that Parliament incorporated into the Criminal Justice Act 2003, the Law Commission concluded that whether a statement is hearsay should not turn on the form of words that the declarant employs. Rather, the Commission concluded that a statement should be hearsay if causing another person to believe or act on the matter which the statement is being used to prove was one of the declarant's purposes in making the statement.[76] That test would avoid many of the odd conclusions that result from heavy reliance on literal meaning, characteristic of the narrowest American interpretations of the definition of hearsay. For example, the

---

[74] For examples of cases treating implied assertions as hearsay, see *Reynolds*, above n 15, 104; *Dullard*, above n 3, 591; *Morgan*, above n 12, 232–3. A majority of US jurisdictions would be more likely to classify a request for drugs or 'the usual' not involving an intermediary as non-hearsay. See Mueller, above n 62, 413 n 133.

[75] See above, text to nn 15–16.

[76] Law Commission Report, above n 14, [7.24]–[7.27].

Act's test would seem to classify 'How can you believe Smith didn't murder his father?' as hearsay on the assumption that it is likely that the declarant intended to convey that such a belief would be implausible.[77]

Returning to S's utterance 'Is C here? I'd like to buy the usual', the Law Commission's proposed standards (now encapsulated in s 115 of the 2003 Act) suggest that the utterance should be hearsay to show that C possessed the drugs found in his possession for the purpose of sale. That is, one of S's purposes in making the statement would be to cause the bar-tender to believe that he typically purchased 'the usual' from C, or to cause the bar-tender to act on that assumption. It is true that the Law Commission's report preceding the Act argued that a similar statement, requesting the 'usual stuff' from the hearer would not be hearsay. The Commission reasoned that the declarant would simply be requesting drugs from the hearer, without any desire to cause the hearer to believe that the hearer was herself dealing drugs.[78] Accordingly, if the speaker had merely requested drugs from the hearer, the answer at node 4 would be 'No'. Yet, if S were addressing C's bar-tender rather than C, S might refer to the 'usual' in part to suggest S's own trustworthiness as a customer with a course of dealing with C, or, in the Commission's terms, to cause the bar-tender to believe it.[79]

Moreover, the Commission's report says that the prosecution may only succeed in arguing that utterances such as S's are not hearsay if it can show, beyond a reasonable doubt, that causing the bar-tender to believe that S and C had a buyer/seller relationship was not one of S's purposes in communicating with the bar-tender.[80] Proving such facts beyond a reasonable doubt would seem to be very difficult. As a practical matter, then, the Commission's report and the text of the 2003 Act strongly suggest that S's statement should be hearsay if offered to show that S made a number of purchases from C and, in turn, that C possessed drugs for the purpose of

---

[77] For contrary American results see eg, *Bolen v Paragon Plastics*, 754 F. Supp. 221, 225 (D. Mass. 1990). See further above, text to n 82.

[78] Law Commission Report, above n 14, [7.26]–[7.27]. Recently, the Court of Appeal seems to have side-stepped an effort to take a particularly narrow view of the speaker's purpose, in *R v Isichei* [2006] EWCA Crim 1815, [2006] All ER (D) 50, in the judgment of Auld LJ, paras 37–41. Although the precise facts are less than clear, the Crown apparently offered a statement in which an unnamed man said he was going to call 'Marvin' (the defendant's first name), in order to identify the defendant as the recipient of the call. The Crown argued that the statement was not made in order to cause the hearers to believe that the speaker called Marvin, since the speaker would not care whether the hearers believed it. The court said, *ibid* [41], 'The [lower court] judge may have been wrong in concluding that it was not a statement within section 115(3)'.

[79] Law Commission Report, above n 14, [7.32].

[80] *Ibid* [7.30].

sale.[81] That is, they suggest that the answer at node 4 for our drug possession hypothetical should be 'Yes'.[82]

Explicit Communication

Some American decisions define hearsay more narrowly. They would hold that S's request for C, and to buy the 'usual', would not be hearsay. Focusing only on the words S used, such approaches might hold that S's utterance did not literally assert that C had sold drugs in the past, so that the prosecution would not be offering the utterance to prove something that it asserted. Given that S did not directly assert anything about C's previous conduct, they would contend that S's utterance would entail only a mild sincerity risk: declarants cannot lie about something they do not say. Moreover, if declarants are not supplying new information, but only reminding their audience of or referring to something they both know, they are unlikely to intend to deceive. Accordingly, the argument would go, S's reference to 'the usual' would be unlikely to be intended to deceive, since there would be little or no point in referring to a 'usual' transaction that was not customary. (In line with that theory, the answer for our drug possession hypothetical at node 5 would be 'No'.)

---

[81] The Law Commission's own hypothetical based on *Kearley* seems to assume that the speaker asked the defendant, or someone assumed to be the defendant, for the 'usual stuff', concluding that the speaker would not seek to convince anyone that the defendant was a drug dealer: *ibid* [7.26]–[7.27]. On the other hand, a speaker addressing a third person could wish the hearer to believe that the speaker and the defendant engaged in a series of transactions in order to establish himself as someone trustworthy, or to provide the third party with information needed to identify the amount of drugs sought. Each of those would seem to be a purpose for which the declarant was communicating.

[82] While no US statute or case has adopted the Criminal Justice Act 2003's 'purpose' language, some cases and commentary seem to parallel that approach, at least for specific cases. See CB Mueller and LC Kirkpatrick, *Federal Evidence* (3rd edn, St. Paul, MN Thomson/West, 2007) vol 4, s 8:24, pp 155–63, 164–67 (and cases cited therein); Park, above n 5, 137 (requests for illegal activity, as opposed to direct assertions that the hearer is engaged in illegal activity, should not be hearsay; requests reflect lack of doubt that the hearer is engaged in such activity). References in the text to the 'broadest' and 'narrowest' American views are superlatives because courts or commentators may depart from theoretical purity for any number of reasons. For example, Park concludes that 'the decisions classifying implied assertions as nonhearsay generally arise from factual situations in which the circumstances reduce the danger of fabrication by either the declarant or the trial witness', suggesting that courts may use broader interpretations of the hearsay rule when they believe proffered evidence is problematic. RC Park, '"I Didn't Tell Them Anything About You": Implied Assertions as Hearsay under the Federal Rules of Evidence' (1990) 74 *Minnesota LR* 783, 828–9; see also Callen, above n 31, 47 n 18 (includes examples of five Circuit Courts of Appeals whose case law applies inconsistent standards).

Insofar as definitions of hearsay may reflect underlying theories of communication, however, it seems quite plausible that notions of communicative intent (as from Wilson and Sperber), communicative purpose (as in the Criminal Justice Act 2003) and direct or explicit assertion (as in the narrowest American approach) occupy most of the available ground.

Finally, courts and commentators who argue that evidence offered to show implied assertions should not be hearsay conclude that their approach is simpler than a test that relies on the nuances of social practice. That argument has some merit. The interpretation of the hearsay definition that focuses on whether the declarant explicitly stated the proposition for which the proponent offers it can be applied fairly easily.[83] There is also a good argument that communications may be more reliable evidence of facts they seem to take for granted than those they explicitly assert.[84]

Nevertheless, the narrowest interpretation of hearsay yields anomalous results, profoundly inconsistent with both empirical research and intuition. I have already mentioned one illustration: that some cases hold that inquiries cannot be hearsay, since their form of words makes no sufficiently direct assertions.[85] A number of commentators have argued that 'Harold is the finest of my sons' would not be hearsay under that narrow interpretation if offered to show that the declarant was fond of Harold.[86] Further, consider a declarant's statement to a friend, 'I don't see that you have standing to criticise me. At least I never robbed a bank'.[87] If out-of-court statements cannot be hearsay unless offered to show something they directly assert, that statement might well not be hearsay to show that the friend robbed a bank, because all it says directly is that the declarant has not robbed a bank. Finally, the narrow interpretation's approach to non-verbal conduct classifies it as hearsay if the proponent offers it to prove a proposition that the actor intended to assert, yet it would seem to hold that a verbal statement is not hearsay if offered to prove a proposition that the declarant intended to convey unless the declarant did so explicitly. In other words, the narrowest interpretation says that we should consider an actor's intent in deciding what a non-verbal action conveys, but not the

---

[83] See *McCormick on Evidence*, above n 21, s 250, p 146.

[84] See G Weissenberger and JJ Duane, *Federal Rules of Evidence: Rules, Legislative History, Commentary and Authority* (Cincinnati, Ohio Anderson Publishing, 2001) s 801.6, p 418; Park, above n 5, 137.

[85] *Lewis*, above n 21, 1179; *Oguns*, above n 21, 448–9. See also *Long*, above n 21, 1579 (question at issue did not show that declarant intended to convey a message). *McCormick on Evidence* was once the most dependable source of the view that statements should only be hearsay for what they literally or explicitly assert: see eg, E Cleary (ed), *McCormick on Evidence* (3rd edn, St Paul, MN, West, 1972) s 228. The newest edition seems to adhere to that view to some extent: see *McCormick on Evidence* vol 2, above n 21, s 250, pp 144–46. It does, however, seem to conclude that questions can be hearsay if the declarant intends the question to be an assertion: *ibid* s 246, p 129–30 and n 7. That suggests, but only suggests, that McCormick's approach could converge with the Criminal Justice Act's definition of hearsay.

[86] See CT McCormick, *Handbook of the Law of Evidence* (St Paul, MN, West, 1954) s 228, p 446.

[87] Park, above n 5, 125.

speaker's intent in deciding what an utterance conveys. Yet determining the meaning of an utterance is at least as difficult as ascertaining the nature of an act.

CONCLUSION

This chapter has been critical of some interpretations of the hearsay rule. Nevertheless, its aim has not been to determine whether the narrowest American interpretation of the hearsay rule is correct, but to offer an analytical tool that we can use to compare the extant approaches by identifying the effects that those approaches would have in practice. Use of the diagram in Figure 6.1 can help us to develop an understanding of what each seemingly abstract approach means in practice. Of course, adjudication seldom develops or follows a unified theory—courts typically do no more than is necessary to resolve the dispute in front of them, without resolving all the open theoretical questions.[88] But even if we focus on the practical uses of hearsay arguments, that weighs more in favour of exposing students, and others, to alternative theories than against it. Those who learn to use Figure 6.1 will tend to absorb the arguments in favour of each of the interpretations of the hearsay definition that it models. As a result, they will be better able to formulate and assess arguments about whether an item of evidence should be classified as hearsay, or as testimonial evidence.[89] At the least, knowledge of the competing approaches can make the cognitive tools needed to construct or evaluate opposing arguments more accessible.

Among other things, comparative and interdisciplinary scholarship can contribute to evidence pedagogy even in basic Evidence courses, and to more general analysis of evidentiary issues. Introducing comparative and interdisciplinary analysis clearly requires teachers to consider the costs and benefits of those analyses. For an American audience, the Criminal Justice Act 2003's definition of hearsay articulates a new approach to what continues to be a difficult issue for American Evidence law. That Act's approach might be congenial to US courts and commentators who dislike both the broadest and narrowest interpretations of the hearsay rule. For

---

[88]   See CR Sunstein, *Legal Reasoning and Political Conflict* (New York, OUP, 1996) 41–3.

[89]   One might contrast another graphical device that has been fairly popular in the United States, Tribe's triangle: see LH Tribe, 'Triangulating Hearsay' (1974) 87 *Harvard LR* 957, 959. Tribe used a triangular diagram much like that in CK Ogden and IA Richards, *The Meaning of Meaning: a Study of the Influence of Language upon Thought and of the Science of Symbolism* (New York, Harcourt, Brace & Company, 1947) 10–11, to model application of a hearsay definition delineated in accordance with Morgan's theory. Accordingly, Tribe's approach would include even non-communicative conduct in hearsay, contrary to modern rules and statutes. That approach does, however, offer an interesting way of systematising the Federal Rules' exceptions to hearsay. See generally Tribe, above, 961–74.

English Evidence teachers, the competing American interpretations of the definition of hearsay offer useful contrasts. The Law Commission was at pains to distinguish s 115's purpose requirement from tests that turned on the speaker's intent (a standard that the broader American approach adopts) or on the form of words the speaker chose to use (the criterion of the narrower American interpretation). The American standards, then, can illustrate the theoretical limits between which the drafters of s 115 thought they had situated their definition of hearsay.

Research on communication contributes in two ways to the hearsay debates that this chapter summarises. First, it reinforces the rationale for exclusionary rules when the utility of proffered evidence is insufficient to warrant the effort to gather and evaluate it. Secondly, and more specifically, that research provides an understanding of communicative practice. Fact-finders, particularly jurors, will rely on the cognitive strategies that they have learned to use in communicative practice when they assess evidence of out-of-court statements offered to prove facts expressly asserted or suggested by the statements. Evidence law's conception of a speaker's intent may legitimately vary from what communication research suggests is intention in practice. Nevertheless, empirically supported theories about the practical working of communication provide a useful and relatively objective perspective from which to understand and appraise hearsay doctrine.

7

Reasoning, Relevance and Law Reform: the Influence of Empirical Research on Criminal Adjudication

JENNY MCEWAN*

INTRODUCTION

THIS CHAPTER SEEKS to examine the significance of behavioural science (chiefly psychology and sociology) for criminal adjudication and the law of evidence, and its impact on programmes of reform. The relationship between empirical research and fundamental concerns reflecting moral values lies at the heart of the discussion. Failure to understand this relationship has led to profoundly unsatisfactory compromises both at common law and in legislative reforms.

Discussions of Evidence law reform have rarely given empirical evidence central importance. It is, however, becoming increasingly common to make use of it. The discussion of experimental work by psychologists in Sir Robin Auld's *Review of Criminal Courts in England and Wales* has helped to make such studies more familiar to a large circle of criminal practitioners.[1] Indeed, it now seems to be established practice for major inquiries into the criminal justice system to commission their own research.[2] Many lobbyists and pressure groups, too, have made use of empirical studies to

---

* I am grateful to Paul Roberts and Mike Redmayne for comments on drafts.

[1] Auld LJ, *Review of the Criminal Courts of England and Wales: Report* (London, TSO, 2001).

[2] Two successive Royal Commissions on the criminal justice system sponsored empirical research: *Report of the Royal Commission on Criminal Procedure* (Cmnd 8092, London, HMSO, 1981) (Philips Report); *Report of the Royal Commission on Criminal Justice* (Cm 2263, London, HMSO, 1993) (Runciman Report). More recently, the Law Commission did the same, commissioning studies by Sally Lloyd-Bostock into jury and magistrate reactions to bad character evidence. Her findings were published as Appendices to Law Commission, *Evidence in Criminal Proceedings: Previous Misconduct of a Defendant*, Consultation Paper No 141 (London, HMSO, 1996); Law Commission, *Evidence of Bad Character in Criminal Proceedings*, Law Com No 273 (Cm 5257, London, TSO, 2001).

support their arguments. Crusading zeal, however, carries with it the risk of an unconsciously selective or uncritical approach to experimental data. Lawyers have (with some justice) been accused of cherry-picking, espousing social science only when it serves their purposes.[3] And although the debate on the admissibility of the accused's bad character has been increasingly informed by empirical evidence, lawyers have, in typical fashion, managed to use the same research to support both sides of the argument.[4]

Those of us who teach or practice in the law of evidence may all too easily become immersed in an increasingly intricate web of (mainly statutory) reform, obsessed with the interaction of the various exceptions to the rules of exclusion. We may find little time to reflect on the essential nature of the enterprise of criminal adjudication. Yet to gain a full understanding of our subject, it is essential to do so. Having first reviewed the broader context of recent reforms, this chapter considers the implications of behavioural science data for the rules and practices which have traditionally characterised criminal litigation in England and Wales. To draw out these implications the chapter examines a number of examples of issues to which behavioural science appears to be relevant. The overall picture, then, will emerge slowly; this is the only way to do justice to the complex mix of values involved in criminal adjudication.

EVIDENCE AND EMPIRICISM

A continuing process of legislative change has been taking place over the last 30 years, apparently gathering increasing momentum. It is difficult to think of a single rule of evidence that has not been dramatically altered. Trials have become less adversarial and less oral. In addition, there appears to be, at the government level at any rate, greater readiness to allow finders of fact access to the kind of evidence once thought too unreliable or too prejudicial.

Twining has suggested that evidence reform is driven to some extent by 'the Police Morale Problem', 'the New Criminal Class Problem' and 'the Keeping the Right Wing Happy' problem.[5] Not all media criticism, however, has been driven by a conservative agenda. For example, the

---

[3] R Cotterell, 'Why Must Legal Rules be Interpreted Sociologically?' (1998) 25 *British Journal of Law and Society* 171.

[4] Arguing for relaxation of the rules: Auld, n 1 above, 11.119; J McEwan, 'Previous Misconduct at the Crossroads: Which "Way Ahead"?' [2002] *Crim LR* 180. Arguing against: Law Commission (2001), n 2 above, 6.57–6.61; C Tapper, 'Criminal Justice Act 2003' [2004] *Crim LR* 533; R Munday, 'What Constitutes "Other Reprehensible Behaviour" under the Bad Character Provisions of the Criminal Justice Act 2003?' [2005] *Crim LR* 24.

[5] W Twining, *Rethinking Evidence* (Oxford, Blackwell, 1990) 336.

television personality and founder of ChildLine, Esther Rantzen, has consistently campaigned for special measures for child witnesses in criminal cases.[6] The nature of cross-examination in trials of sexual offences became a matter of public debate following Lynn Ferguson's award-winning documentary for Channel 4.[7] Even the modification of the law on identification, which might appear to have been influenced primarily by the empirical findings of psychology, and to have been motivated by the desire to ensure the fairness of trials, followed a dramatic campaign of vocal public disquiet.[8]

Teubner has argued that insofar as law comprises a self-referential set of norms, it must find it difficult to admit the precepts of any other science.[9] The kinds of concepts Teubner gives as examples of peculiarly legal constructs, such as capacity, responsibility and insanity, appear to have developed partly to accomplish pragmatic objectives and partly to ensure compliance with principles derived from morality and conceptions of justice. But I would argue that there is a profound difference between the law of evidence and other areas of law such as Land Law, Torts and even Criminal Law, beyond the obvious contrast that the latter regulate the behaviour of citizens in their everyday lives, whereas the law of evidence is about the conduct of trials (ie the difference between adjectival and substantive law). Substantive law tends not to advance sweeping empirical statements, although the legal formulation of some concepts, such as 'family', for example, is increasingly shaped by knowledge derived from empirical research.[10] Rather than assume that people behave in any particular way, most substantive law sets standards against which actions are to be judged. Such standards prescribe rather than describe, hence empirical challenges tend to reflect the socio-legal tradition that examines the effects of law and legal processes upon particular groupings within

---

[6] Eg *Minutes of Evidence*, House of Commons Joint Committee on Human Rights, 17 June 2002, 331. Ms Rantzen argued for full implementation of the Pigot Report (*Report of the Advisory Group on Video Evidence* (London, Home Office, 1989)), on child witnesses. Videorecorded cross-examination or re-examination is provided for in Youth Justice and Criminal Evidence Act 1999, s 28.

[7] *Dispatches: Getting Away with Rape*, Channel 4, 16 February 1994.

[8] *Report of the Departmental Committee on Evidence of Identification* (Cmnd 338, London, HMSO, 1976) (Devlin Report). In addition to the miscarriage of justice cases cited in the Report, the public became alerted to the 'Free George Davis' campaign in 1975, which culminated in the sabotage of a cricket pitch at Headingly. Also, in 1976 Peter Hain (lately Secretary of State for Northern Ireland, then a high-profile President of the Young Liberals) was prosecuted for bank robbery. He was identified by three schoolboys and a cashier. His alibi led to his acquittal.

[9] G Teubner, *Law as an Autopoeitic System* (Oxford, Blackwell, 1993).

[10] Eg, A Barlow and G James, 'Regulating Marriage and Cohabitation in 21st Century Britain' (2004) 67 *MLR* 143.

society.[11] Criticisms of the content of the law itself usually concentrate on the extent to which law is achieving its own aims.

That is not to say that the rules of evidence—adjectival law—are not heavily preoccupied with morality and conceptions of justice, just as substantive law is. The purpose of a trial goes beyond establishing an accurate picture of the facts.[12] Concerned to provide a peaceful method of dispute resolution through litigation,[13] the legal system holds fast to what Jackson calls 'dearly held process values' which are essential to the system's survival.[14] An obvious example is the exclusion of illegally obtained evidence even when it is reliable,[15] although of course there is debate about just when such evidence should be excluded.

In recent years, perceptions of fairness have widened from a concern with protection of the rights of the accused to recognition that witnesses also have interests deserving of protection, such as the right to be treated with dignity. Arguably, over the last 30 years or so we have seen the emergence of a new process value: the right of a witness to humane treatment in courts of law. Indeed, Roberts and Zuckerman identify this right as one of the foundational values of criminal evidence.[16] Arguments to support reforms in the name of the protection of witnesses carry far greater weight if it can be shown as a matter of empirical fact that they do not interfere with the search for truth. For, as Jackson notes, although lawyers may occasionally take refuge in denying that establishing the truth is the sole aim of trials, few would argue that it is not important.[17]

Even insofar as the trial represents an investigation of the facts, however, it is far from a clinical exercise in scientific detachment. At every stage, legal processes are forced to confront the realities of human behaviour. The law of evidence has developed a complex structure of exclusionary rules and judicial admonishments which impose an approved system of reasoning upon those who must reach a final verdict on the facts. Many of these rules are based on Damaška's 'lay disability rationale',[18] which assumes

---

[11]   CM Campbell and P Wiles, 'The Study of Law in Society in Britain' (1975–76) 10 *Law and Society Review* 547.

[12]   DJ Greer, 'Anything but the Truth? The Reliability of Testimony in Criminal Trials' (1971) *British Journal of Criminology* 131.

[13]   J Jackson, 'Evidence: Legal Perspectives' in R Bull and D Carson, *Handbook of Psychology in Legal Contexts* (Chichester, Wiley, 1995) 167.

[14]   *Ibid.*

[15]   Eg, Police and Criminal Evidence Act 1984 (PACE), s 76(2), which requires the exclusion of any confession obtained by oppression or in consequence of anything said or done which was likely to render it unreliable even if it proves to be true. In s 78, the court is given a discretion to reject prosecution evidence if the admission of the evidence would have an adverse effect on the fairness of the proceedings.

[16]   P Roberts and A Zuckerman, *Criminal Evidence* (Oxford, OUP, 2004) 21.

[17]   J Jackson, 'Law's Truth and Lawyer's Truth: the Representation of Evidence in Adversary Trials' (1992) 3 *Law and Critique* 29.

[18]   MR Damaška, *Evidence Law Adrift* (New Haven, Yale University Press, 1997) 30.

that some evidence is not as helpful as lay people think it is. The inexperience of lay fact-finders may indeed render them less able to unravel complicated evidence or understand difficult legal concepts. However, it does not follow that they have less insight into human behaviour than lawyers or legislators. After all, one of the functions of members of a lay tribunal of fact is to import the benefit of their experience of everyday life into the trial. For example, jurors apparently need no help from expert witnesses 'on matters of human nature and behaviour within the limits of normality' such as how 'ordinary folk who are not suffering from any mental illness are likely to react to the stresses and strains of life'.[19] In *Roberts*,[20] the Court of Appeal went so far as to state that the jury could assess, unaided by any expert opinion, the likely effect of provocation upon a deaf person.

Yet there are exclusionary rules which are entirely based upon the application of a variety of 'common sense' it is assumed that lay people do not share. The whole of 'similar facts' reasoning depends upon judgements about coincidence, in order to assess the probative force of evidence of bad character and to balance that against its prejudicial effect: how many times does it happen that the same man finds his current wife drowned in her bath?[21] The decision in some instances requires an assessment of what is and what is not unusual in human behaviour, and thus becomes an exercise in armchair psychology: how likely is it that a man, found at an agreed rendezvous and with a sexual predilection for young boys, would be identified by mistake by two boys as the man who abused them?[22] How many women would on separate occasions meet the same man in a club, agree to have sexual intercourse with him on the way home and then falsely allege that they had been raped?[23] How likely is it that someone who gets a thrill from slashing the legs of sleeping men in the night might escalate his activities into slashing their throats?[24] In the absence of scientific data, the only source of information on these matters is the individual judge's common sense or life experience. It is a judgement based on perceptions of how many people behave in this way, or how many of these events one would come across by chance. Where, in the judicial view, the similarity between the defendant's past misconduct and the current offence has been deemed not to go beyond the realms of coincidence, evidence of those previous misdeeds has been withheld from the finders of

---

[19] *R v Turner* [1975] QB 834, 841.
[20] [1990] Crim LR 122.
[21] *R v Smith* (1915) 11 Cr App R 229.
[22] *Thompson v R* [1918] AC 221.
[23] *R v Z* [2000] 3 All ER 385; see also *Dispatches*, above n 7; S Lees, *Carnal Knowledge: Rape on Trial* (London, The Women's Press, 2002).
[24] *R v Beggs* [1989] Crim LR 898

fact. And in this area, many judges have tended to be conservative,[25] probably, in part, because of concern that the Court of Appeal might take a different view of the significance of the evidence and quash the conviction.[26] If so, we have an indication that there is less agreement as to the specific content of judicial 'common sense' than might be thought necessary to justify its supremacy over the lay variety. In any event, the traditional approach, that a record of previous bad character requires a 'pattern'[27] in order to be evidentially significant, is now under attack. An illustration may be found in the Home Secretary's classification, for the purposes of the Criminal Justice Act 2003, of those dispositions that are probative in themselves. On the basis that some propensities are more probative than others,[28] a recent statutory instrument prescribes two categories within which prior offences are admissible as evidence of guilt.[29] Thus, someone accused of a sexual offence against a child under the age of 16 may find previous offences within that category adduced as evidence of guilt; the same applies within a range of offences under the Theft Acts.[30] The effect of this appears to be to allow evidence of previous offences within the category even in the absence of 'pattern'.[31]

Assessments of how unusual certain behaviour might be, or whether similar events can be explained as coincidence, are not the sole preserve of legal reasoning. Such judgments are essential to ordinary social interaction, and have to be made frequently during the course of ordinary lives. A great deal of psychological literature exists on the nature of such judgements, for example, in attribution theory.[32] Various mental constructs appear to be

---

[25] Eg, in September 1996, Dennis Chambers was acquitted of causing grievous bodily harm to Margaret Bent through 'stalking'. The jury was not informed of his previous convictions for offences committed against the complainant, even though his record suggested serial obsessive behaviour towards her.

[26] See eg, *R v Cannings* [2004] 1 All ER 725, where the conviction was quashed although expert evidence on the likelihood of coincidence had been adduced. Indeed, given the level of disagreement within the scientific community on the probability of several unexplained infant deaths occurring due to natural causes within the same family, the expert evidence was considered by the Court of Appeal to have rendered the conviction unsafe.

[27] Or 'general similarity': *DPP v P* [1991] 3 All ER 337.

[28] Auld, above n 1, 11.119.

[29] Being evidence of a propensity to commit the kind of crime with which the accused is charged: Criminal Justice Act 2003, ss 101(1)(d), 103(2)(b).

[30] Criminal Justice Act 2003 (Categories of Offences) Order 2004, SI 2004/334.

[31] Although s 103(1) of the 2003 Act provides that the misconduct is not admissible where the defendant's 'having such a propensity makes it no more likely that he is guilty of the offence'. See J Spencer, *Evidence of the Defendant's Bad Character* (Oxford, Hart Publishing, 2006) 65; *R v Hanson; Gilmore* [2005] EWCA Crim 824; [2005] 1 WLR 3169.

[32] HH Kelley, *Attribution in Social Interaction* (Morristown, NJ, General Learning Press, 1971) 1; HH Kelley, 'Attribution Theory in Social Psychology' in D Levine (ed), *Nebraska Symposium on Motivation* (Lincoln, NE, University of Nebraska Press, 1967); R Brown, *Social Psychology* (New York, Free Press, 1986) 137–40; J McEwan, *The Verdict of the Court: Passing Judgment in Law and Psychology* (Oxford, Hart Publishing, 2003) 10–15, 32–6.

essential parts of human thinking, enabling us, through our interpretation of the behaviour of others, to predict what they will do next, and to adjust our own actions accordingly. Work on belief structures has suggested that heuristics[33] are useful in many ways,[34] although they can be misleading, particularly when making judgements of probability and frequency.[35] Lawyers, however, are not immune from statistical error, as may be seen in a series of decisions on the interpretation of DNA evidence.[36]

Script theory in psychology is another way of conceptualising the attribution of meaning or significance to an event. A script is a cognition structure that represents organised knowledge about a given domain. It acts as a means of interpretation for a type of event, such as going out for a meal, or on a first date. Commonplace scripts are shared by members of any given community.[37] In their work on the influence of narrative on jury verdicts, Bennett and Feldman argued that if the plausibility of a story depends on understandings drawn from experience, then jurors who come from different social worlds may disagree about the meaning and the plausibility of the same stories. In contrast to this account, which seems to emphasise divergent interpretations of evidence, Twining argues that simple heuristic assumptions are not the basis of verdicts. Rather than legitimise decisions by anchoring them in vague and possibly misconceived generalisations, 'typically we try to anchor in specific, concrete evidence'; thus, generalisations fill gaps in evidence, justifying 'inferences from particular to particular'.[38] But in fact generalisations have a more fundamental role than this. Inferences from a concrete item of fact may, in law, render that fact relevant or not, as the case may be, and therefore determine its admissibility.[39] Judicially-drawn inferences may depend entirely upon an individual reaction to the conduct or general behaviour of others. Whether at the level of magistrates' court or Crown Court

---

[33] A Tversky and D Kahneman, 'Judgment under Uncertainty: Heuristics and Biases' (1974) 185 *Science* 1124.

[34] HJ Einhorn and RM Hogarth, 'Behavioral Decision Theory: Processes of Judgment and Choice' (1981) 32 *Annual Review of Psychology* 53.

[35] A Tversky and D Kahneman, 'Availability: a Heuristic for Judging Frequency and Probability' (1973) 5 *Cognitive Psychology* 207; D Kahneman, P Slovic and A Tversky, *Judgment under Uncertainty* (Cambridge, CUP, 1982). But see JL Cohen, 'Freedom of Proof' in W Twining (ed), *Facts in Law* (Wiesbaden, Franz Steiner, 1983).

[36] *R v Deen*, The Times, 10 January 1994; *R v Adams* [1996] 2 Cr App R 467; *R v Doheny and Adams* [1997] 1 Cr App R 369; *R v Adams (Denis) (No 2)* [1998] 1 Cr App R 377.

[37] RC Schank and RP Abelson, *Scripts, Plans, Goals and Understanding: an Inquiry into Human Knowledge Structures* (Hillsdale, NJ, Erlbaum, 1977).

[38] W Twining, 'Anchored Narratives: a Comment' (1995) 3 *European Journal of Crime, Criminal Law and Criminal Justice* 106.

[39] Cf the relevance of circumstantial evidence, eg motive, as evidence of intention: see RM Eggleston, 'Generalisations and Experts' in Twining, above n 35, 25.

proceedings, the decision whether or not to admit the evidence is based upon an assessment of the significance or prevalence of that behaviour.

The example of bad character evidence thus begins to show the complexity of interactions between law, common sense and behavioural science. Admissibility rules are based on empirical assumptions about unusual behaviour, and also on assumptions about how lay fact-finders process evidence. But the very criticisms aimed at fact-finders could be turned back on the judges and legislators who craft the rules keeping evidence from fact-finders in the first place. We can see something similar going on in debates about sexual history evidence: here, too, there is disagreement about the scripts and generalisations which are, or should be, used by fact-finders, as well as suspicions about the generalisations that have been relied upon by legislators.

Paul Meehl has usefully referred to the sort of generalisation at issue in these debates as 'fireside inductions'.[40] Meehl acknowledges that fireside inductions can become entrenched in the law, where they may have a legitimate role to play. In his view, where they are concerned with actions, persons or effects that occur frequently and are supported by a substantial proportion of the population at large and by the majority of the legal profession, fireside inductions may be more reliable than conclusions derived from 'a smattering of social science research'.[41] However, Meehl considers that generalisations must give way to statistical evidence where it exists in quantity and is methodologically unassailable. One might suspect that methodological unassailability is unattainable, but Meehl makes a good case for requiring at least convincing research findings before we abandon an induction shared by lay and legal communities. He therefore highlights important questions about the weight the law should place on empirical evidence. In the next section we will see that these questions soon lead us to difficult issues about the extent to which we should assume that lay fact-finders are competent.

FIRESIDES AND LABORATORIES

If evidence is excluded or limited in its effect on the basis that it is unreliable or prejudicial, it is legitimate to ask on what basis it is believed that these dangers exist. The very notion of prejudice assumes that the lay community does not subscribe to the suspicion with which lawyers regard the evidence (if they did, there would be no reason to restrict its use). As it

---

[40] PE Meehl, 'Law and the Fireside Inductions: Some Reflections of a Clinical Psychologist' in JL Tapp and FJ Levine (eds), *Law, Justice and the Individual in Society* (New York, Holt, Rinehart and Winston, 1977).
[41] *Ibid* 28.

is at least unlikely that there should be such a sharp divergence between lawyers and lay people, it is not clear why any empirical challenge to the belief that lay people are less competent than lawyers should be based upon incontrovertible data. Yet many lawyers adopt this position. Roderick Munday, in his discussion of the new provisions on evidence of the accused's bad character, notes that the research findings suggest 'that the effect of revealing certain bad character evidence might not be as deleterious to defendants as had sometimes been assumed'. He goes on to dismiss these results as less than 'definitive' and suffering from 'the usual weaknesses of psychological simulations and statistical rationalisations'.[42] This widespread conviction that bad character evidence must sometimes be excluded is still reflected in the Criminal Justice Act 2003. Although it is not clear whether these new provisions embody an inclusionary or an exclusionary principle,[43] they raise sufficient obstacles to the admission of bad character evidence to suggest a parliamentary reluctance to abandon exclusionary rules altogether until an unassailable empirical case is produced. In the same way, the hearsay provisions in the 2003 Act suffer from an attempted compromise between the more radical, and correspondingly simpler, recommendations of Auld and the reluctance of the legal establishment to undermine rules thought vital for the protection of accused persons. What is curious is that passionate commitment to that latter value is founded on very little, if anything, beyond a traditional belief.

Auld, apparently an agnostic in these matters, seems to take the opposite view,[44] that exclusion of relevant evidence from the tribunal of fact always requires a very solid case.[45] Likewise, L Jonathan Cohen argued that, 'The onus of justification should ... fall on those who wish to restrict freedom of proof rather than on those who wish to defend it'.[46] Similarly, Twining, acknowledging the strength of the argument for a presumption in favour of freedom of proof, considers that it would only have to give way if it were shown empirically that certain kinds of evidence tend regularly to be over-valued or under-valued despite cautionary instructions.[47] This places the burden of persuasion squarely upon those who wish to exclude relevant evidence.

---

[42] Munday, above n 4, 42. The research studies and the methodological weaknesses he refers to are discussed below.

[43] R Fortson, *Criminal Justice Act 2003*, Current Law Statutes (London, Sweet and Maxwell, 2004) 44.14–44.15.

[44] Above n 1 .

[45] J Bentham, *A Treatise on Judicial Evidence* (1825), discussed in W Twining, *Theories of Evidence: Bentham and Wigmore* (London, Weidenfeld & Nicolson, 1985) 66–75.

[46] Cohen, above n 35, 3.

[47] W Twining, 'Rule-Scepticism and Fact-Scepticism' in Twining, above n 35, 81.

Cohen acknowledges that the belief that everyone is capable of rational thought has been attacked by philosophers and by psychologists,[48] but in reply observes that there is some circularity in their arguments: how are we to define competence, if not by the standards we habitually use? He also questions the value of an adjudicative system that bears no relation to 'lay intuition about deducibility': if verdicts are not generally acceptable, the criminal justice system will lose the respect of the public. To avoid the alienation of the community in which it operates, criminal justice should allow as much freedom of proof as possible (as well as encouraging the involvement of lay people in the administration of justice).[49] Cohen is not concerned here with the specific question of the susceptibility of the law of evidence to the conclusions of behavioural scientists: he seems to have no argument with, for example, warning fact-finders about the dangers of eyewitness identification. But his general defence of lay competence in reasoning does underline the need to tread carefully when arguing for a policy of excluding evidence. His arguments emphasise the point that if psychological theory is to be invoked in order to challenge lay competence, psychology must also be allowed a voice on the question of the accuracy of the assumptions underpinning the rules of exclusion.

WITNESSING AND MEMORY

There is a huge volume of empirical work on memory, including the issue of contamination of memory through suggestion. This literature impacts on the issue of witness reliability, both in terms of mistake and of the effect of suggestion through questioning. In the main, these issues are dealt with in experimental work utilising relatively small-scale laboratory studies. These may focus on particular age groups, or may make comparisons between different human subjects in terms of their reliability. Research on memory calls into question the significance lawyers attach to changes in a witness' version of events across successive statements: memory for detail fades over time. Yet the fact that a witness has had to repeat an account a number of times before getting to court provides cross-examiners with a goldmine of potential discrepancies.[50] In pursuit of exposing inconsistency, many cross-examining advocates appear to dwell interminably upon detail

---

[48] RE Nisbett and L Ross, *Human Inference Strategies and Shortcomings of Social Judgment* (Englewood Cliffs, NJ, Prentice Hall, 1980).
[49] Cohen, above n 35, 20.
[50] J Harris and S Grace, *A Question of Evidence: Investigating and Prosecuting Rape in the 1990s* (HORS 196, London, Home Office, 1999) 39; L Frohman, 'Discrediting Victims' Allegations of Sexual Assault' (1991) 38 *Social Problems* 213.

that would appear irrelevant to most observers.[51] Judges, who are by now well aware that most people find it much more difficult to describe than to recognise,[52] seem nevertheless to feel obliged to call attention to any inconsistency between an eyewitness' initial description and the appearance of the person selected at an identification parade.[53] And fact-finders do appear to rely heavily on inconsistency as an indicator of dishonesty.[54] A study in New Zealand found that jurors looked, in the absence of hard facts, for internal consistency within testimony, consistency between the testimony and other evidence, and plausibility in the account. They preferred this to reliance on a witness' demeanour.[55] Mock juror studies made similar observations; indeed, it seems that if any inconsistencies in testimony can be exposed in cross-examination, a witness' entire account will be disbelieved.[56]

Of the psychological literature on memory, the work most well-known to lawyers concerns identification by eyewitnesses. Psychological research was cited in the Devlin Report,[57] which prompted the Court of Appeal's decision in *Turnbull*.[58] Empirical studies challenge the powerful intuitive appeal of positive identification by an eyewitness on oath. Belief in the cogency of such evidence, adhered to by generations of both lawyers and laymen, could be regarded, in Meehl's terms, as a gold-star fireside induction that should give way only to convincing empirical findings derived from a critical mass of research studies. The literature has expanded considerably since the publication of the Devlin Report, but the broad thrust of empirical findings has remained constant. Researchers are virtually unanimous that the sort of eyewitness identification typically

---

[51] Such as, in cross-examination of the complainant in a child abuse case, the question 'what colour was the duvet?' (see G Davies, C Wilson, R Mitchell and J Milsom, *Videotaping Children's Evidence: an Evaluation* (London, Home Office, 1995) 33), and, to a rape complainant, 'did he have a watch on at the time?' (*Heroines of Fortitude: the Experiences of Women in Court as Victims of Sexual Assault* (Woolloomooloo, NSW, Department for Women, 1996). Judicial fear of appeal may explain the considerable freedom afforded to defence advocates in this respect.

[52] See discussion of *Turnbull*, below.

[53] PB Ainsworth, *Psychology, Law and Eyewitness Testimony* (Chichester, Wiley, 1998) 65.

[54] In Jackson and Doran's study of Diplock Courts in Northern Ireland, judges were seen to prefer to rely on the content of testimony, testing it for internal consistency and plausibility, to basing a verdict on the demeanour of witnesses. J Jackson and S Doran, *Judge Without Jury: Diplock Trials and the Adversary System* (Oxford, Clarendon Press, 1995).

[55] See W Young, N Cameron and Y Tinsley, *Juries in Criminal Trials, Part 2*, New Zealand Law Commission Preliminary Paper 37 (Wellington, Law Commission, 1999). See also T Bingham, *The Business of Judging: Selected Essays and Speeches* (Oxford, OUP, 2000) 6.

[56] GL Wells, 'Applied Eyewitness Testimony' in LS Wrightsman, SM Kassin and CE Willis (eds), *In the Jury-Box: Controversies in the Courtroom* (Newbury Park, Sage, 1987).

[57] Above n 8.

[58] [1977] 2 QB 871.

involved in criminal litigation (very often involving brief glimpses of strangers) is much less reliable than commonly thought.[59] Accordingly, in *Turnbull* the Court of Appeal directed that a warning should be given in all identification cases, and that the case should be stopped if the evidence for the prosecution consists primarily of poor quality identifications by eyewitnesses.

Should the law have deferred in this way to the findings of psychology? It is difficult for an experimenter to replicate the conditions affecting a real-life witness to a crime. Ethical standards limit the amount of stress that can be placed upon participants in experiments, and, in any event, the nature of manufactured stress might differ in significant ways from the real thing. On the other hand, not all actual eyewitnesses see the crime being committed; they could be relatively emotionally detached. Another problem is the heavy reliance on university students in laboratory studies. Students are a convenient and inexpensive resource,[60] but hardly constitute a typical cross-section of the population, nor are they likely in an experimental context to regard the consequences of mistaken identification in the same way as an eyewitness who knows a criminal investigation is under way. Where an identification study was designed to replicate a real case, it found eyewitnesses both more reliable and less suggestible than laboratory experiments indicate.[61] However, the research suffered from the problem, common to much real-life investigation into reliability, that the accuracy of the accounts could not be verified objectively. Since the researchers were not present at the crime, they were forced to assume the truth of consensual features among the various witness accounts. Besides, there are some notorious real-life cases which support the psychologists' case. For example, Patrick Murphy was wrongly identified by three witnesses, but saved from a miscarriage of justice by 11 alibi witnesses from his Alcoholics Anonymous meeting.[62] Ronald Cotton was convicted

---

[59] MP Toglia, TM Shlecter and DS Chevalier, 'Memory for Direct and Indirectly Experienced Events' (1992) 6 *Applied Cognitive Psychology* 293; BL Cutler and SD Penrod, *Mistaken Identification: the Eyewitness, Psychology and the Law* (Cambridge, CUP, 1995); J Shepherd, J Ellis and G Davies, *Identification Evidence: a Psychological Evaluation* (Aberdeen, Aberdeen University Press, 1982); PN Shapiro and S Penrod, 'Meta-Analysis of Facial Identification Studies' (1986) 100 *Psychological Bulletin* 139; BR Clifford and R Bull, *Psychology of Person Identification* (London, Routledge, 1988); BR Clifford, 'Eyewitness Testimony: the Bridging of a Credibility Gap' in D Farrington, K Hawkins and S Lloyd-Bostock (eds), *Psychology, Law and Legal Process* (London, Macmillan, 1979).

[60] M King, *Psychology In or Out of Court* (London, Pergamon, 1986); S Lloyd-Bostock, 'Juries and Jury Research in Context' in G Davies, S Lloyd-Bostock, K MacMurran and C Wilson (eds), *Psychology, Law and Criminal Justice* (Berlin, de Gruyter, 1996); R Hastie, S Penrod and N Pennington, *Inside the Jury* (Cambridge, MA, Harvard University Press, 1983).

[61] JC Yuille and JL Cutshall, 'A Field Study of Eyewitness Memory of a Crime' (1986) 71 *Journal of Applied Psychology* 291.

[62] Ainsworth, above n 53, 80.

in the United States of rape, mainly because the victim, Jennifer Thompson, was certain he was her attacker. Yet, in 1995, DNA evidence established that the attack had been carried out by someone else.[63] Mistaken identification has, in fact, been influential in the vast majority of the miscarriage of justice cases identified, using DNA evidence, by the Innocence Project in the United States.[64]

If it is right that the law should have deferred to psychology in *Turnbull*, there remains the question of whether it has deferred sufficiently. A judicial direction under *Turnbull* should include a statement that even confident witnesses may be mistaken. However, the research which inspired this warning insufficiently distinguishes between a confident delivery and being confident that one's identification is correct.[65] It also misses the point that eyewitnesses may legitimately feel confident about the accuracy of some of the details they recall while being less confident about others.[66] In addition, since research shows that some individuals may have a good track record for recognition,[67] it may be unwise to dismiss all eyewitness evidence as equally unreliable. These caveats suggest that the court was wise to require only a warning to the fact-finder, as opposed to a more radical response, such as a requirement of corroborative evidence in every case. However, it is not clear that the accused is sufficiently protected by the warning where the identification evidence is weak. *Weeder*[68] indicates that two poor quality identifications can support each other and ultimately lead to a conviction. A huge quantity of empirical work on identification carried out across the world shows that there is not always safety in numbers. Yet the Court of Appeal finds it difficult to ignore the intuitive appeal of several eyewitnesses in agreement. Indeed, the court held in the Jill Dando murder case that a number of 'fleeting glimpse' cases could support each other, even though it is not clear that all the descriptions related to the same person, and the sightings were four hours apart.[69]

Although in *Turnbull* the Court of Appeal was clearly willing to embrace psychological data, no account was taken of some specific issues that feature in the identification literature. Complications include the greater

---

[63] This man, Robert Poole, had confessed to the crime: A Memon and AT McDaid, 'Factors Influencing Witness Evidence' in J McGuire, T Mason and A O'Kane (eds), *Behaviour, Crime and Legal Processes* (Chichester, Wiley, 2000).

[64] See www.innocenceproject.org/causes.

[65] King, above n 60, 37.

[66] GM Stephenson, 'Accuracy and Confidence in Testimony: a Critical Review and Some Fresh Evidence' in DJ Muller, AE Blackman and A Chapman (eds), *Psychology and Law* (Chichester, Wiley, 1984) 229.

[67] Cutler and Penrod, above n 59, 255–64.

[68] (1980) 71 Cr App R 228.

[69] *George (Barry Michael)*, *The Times*, 30 August 2002.

unreliability of interracial identifications,[70] and also of identifications across genders and age groups.[71] Furthermore, the court's concern about the reliability of eyewitnesses has not been extended to other kinds of non-visual recognition, such as voice recognition.[72] In contrast to the provisions of Code D of PACE on visual identifications, there are no mandatory guidelines on the conduct of a voice identification procedure and there is no statutory obligation to hold one.[73] Yet the dangers of misidentification appear to be more acute in relation to voices than they are in relation to faces, albeit that some voices are more memorable than others.[74] Eyewitnesses have received far more attention. Experimental evidence on identification has affected the drafting of successive Codes of Practice issued under PACE,[75] including the requirement that the police obtain written descriptions immediately, and prevent eyewitness collaboration from contaminating the evidence.[76]

A further cause for concern is that the *Turnbull* warning may be ineffective. There is experimental evidence to suggest that mock jurors disregard judicial warnings on the weaknesses of eyewitness evidence[77] irrespective of the timing and content of judicial instructions.[78] Intuitive beliefs are clearly difficult to displace. Warnings are more effective if an expert witness gives evidence that explains that witness confidence is not an accurate indicator of reliability, and sets out the kind of physical

---

[70] JW Shepherd, JB Deregoswski and MD Ellis, 'A Cross-Cultural Study of Recognition Memory for Faces'(1974) 9 *International Journal of Psychology* 205, but see RCL Lindsay and GL Wells, 'What Do We Really Know about Cross-Race Identification Evidence?' in S Lloyd-Bostock and BR Clifford (eds), *Evaluating Witness Evidence* (Chichester, Wiley, 1983); J Cross, J Cross and J Daly, 'Sex, Race, Age and Beauty as Factors in the Recognition of Faces' (1971) 10 *Perception and Psychophysics* 393.

[71] NL Jalbert and J Getting, 'Race and Gender Issues in Facial Recognition' in F Lösel, D Bender and T Bleisener (eds), *Psychology and Law: International Perspectives* (New York, de Gruyter, 1992).

[72] D Ormerod, 'Sounds Familiar? Voice Identification Evidence' [2001] *Crim LR* 595.

[73] *Ibid*. But see the non-mandatory Home Office Circular 057/2003, *Advice on the Use of Voice Identification Parades*.

[74] AD Yarmey and E Matthys, 'Voice Identification of an Abductor' (1992) 6 *Applied Cognitive Psychology* 367.

[75] IK McKenzie, 'Eyewitness Evidence: Will the United States *Guide to Law Enforcement* Make Any Difference?' (2003) 7 *E & P* 25.

[76] PACE Codes of Practice, Code D 3.2. The memory of eyewitnesses appears to be easily compromisable by time and the influence of stereotypes: FC Bartlett, *Remembering: a Study* (London, CUP, 1932); memory can be contaminated by suggestion from another: EF Loftus, 'Shifting Human Color Memory' (1977) 5 *Memory and Cognition* 696.

[77] WA Wagenaar, PJ van Koppen and HM Crombag, *Anchored Narratives: the Psychology of Criminal Evidence* (Hemel Hempstead, Harvester Wheatsheaf, 1993); KD Williams, EF Loftus and KA Deffenbacher, 'Eyewitness Testimony' in DK Kagehiro and WS Laufer (eds), *Handbook of Psychology and Law* (New York, Springer, 1992).

[78] Cutler and Penrod, above n 59, 255–64.

conditions which reduce the accuracy of identification evidence.[79] The strength of the empirical data suggests that we should consider allowing expert evidence on the identification issue. Also, the *Turnbull* warning should be adapted in appropriate cases, so that the particular problems of certain kinds of recognition, for example, interrace recognition, are indicated. Finally, the 'no case to answer' test should be applied more rigorously where all the identification evidence is of poor quality.

ORALITY AND HEARSAY

Lying and lie detection have been extensively studied by psychologists. Insofar as it focuses on witness demeanour as an indicator of veracity, this research has particular significance for the rule against hearsay. The prominence given by courts to demeanour, and the assumption that the fact-finder is able to interpret it, means that a judge or jury may disregard expert opinion which conflicts with their perception of a witness.[80] The House of Lords has gone so far as to say that where expert witnesses disagree, a court is entitled to resolve the issue by relying on their demeanour.[81] The Criminal Justice Act 2003 contemplates the accused deliberately creating a false impression of himself in the courtroom by means not only of his conduct in the proceedings, but also through his appearance or dress.[82] But faith in the reliability of demeanour cues has been under attack. Auld expressed doubts as to their evidential value as a means of assessing a witness' reliability, and in consequence suggested that the rule against hearsay should be given much less prominence in criminal trials.[83] Although not going as far as Auld, the Law Commission had also recommended substantial reform of hearsay rules.[84] The provisions of the Criminal Justice Act 2003, however, are fairly conservative.[85]

The fact that hearsay evidence is freely admissible in civil trials suggests that retention of an exclusionary rule for criminal proceedings is a

---

[79] *Ibid* 225–51; GL Wells, RCL Lindsay and JP Tousignant, 'Effects of Expert Psychiatric Advice on Human Performance in Judging the Validity of Eyewitness Testimony' (1980) 4 *Law and Human Behavior* 275.

[80] As in *Re DH* [1994] 2 FCR 3.

[81] *Pickford v ICI* [1998] 1 WLR 1189, although there may be other reasons for rejecting expert testimony.

[82] Criminal Justice Act 2003, s 105(4).

[83] Auld, above n 1, 11.79–11.80.

[84] Law Commission, *Evidence in Criminal Proceedings: Hearsay and Related Topics*, Report 245 (London, TSO, 1997).

[85] DJ Birch, 'Hearsay: Same Old Story, Same Old Song?' [2004] *Crim LR* 556.

manifestation of Damaška's 'lay disability rationale'.[86] But the generalisation that laymen cannot accurately assess the value of evidence unless they see it challenged under cross-examination emanates from a distinctly legal fireside. There are, of course, exceptions to the hearsay rule, and when they apply fact-finders are trusted to recognise the limited value of evidence that cannot be directly challenged in cross-examination. The exceptions, too, may rest on armchair psychology. For example, the *res gestae* exception renders admissible a hearsay statement made by a person so emotionally overpowered by an event that the possibility of concoction or distortion can be disregarded. This exception was retained by the Criminal Justice Act 2003 in the absence of any serious analysis of the reliability of statements made in the heat of the moment.[87] The Law Commission complacently remarked that 'nobody was aware of miscarriages of justice caused by the admission of *res gestae*'.[88] A further layer of amateur psychology is added by the requirement that admissibility is dependent on the assessment by judges and magistrates of the level of emotional engagement, and therefore of spontaneity, of the declarant. This is a difficult exercise. Suppose, for instance, that a passer-by observed a bank robbery and described the getaway car to a friend. At the time she made the statement, was she emotionally overpowered by the event, or had she begun to worry about missing her bus home? The answer can be little more than speculation.[89]

Elsewhere in the 2003 Act, reliability of evidence remains a central concern in relation to hearsay. Hearsay is redefined so that implied assertions fall outside the exclusionary rule unless the purpose, or one of the purposes, of the person making the statement appears to the court to have been to cause another person to believe the matter.[90] In such a case the risk of concoction is reduced. The waters become muddied, however, when we look at the Act's catalogue of exceptions to the exclusionary rule.

---

[86] Damaška, above n 18, 30. It is also possible that differential admissibility stems from the different process values underlying civil and criminal trials: see discussion of the right to confrontation, below.

[87] Criminal Justice Act 2003, s 118(1)(4), preserving *R v Andrews* [1987] 1 All ER 513.

[88] Law Commission, above n 84, para 8.119. But see BR Clifford and C Hollin, 'Effects of Type of Incident and the Number of Perpetrators in Eyewitness Testimony' (1981) 66 *Journal of Applied Psychology* 352; cf J Thompson, T Morton and L Fraser, 'Memories for the Marchioness' (1997) 5 *Memory* 615; JC Cutshall and JC Yuille, 'Field Studies of Eyewitness Memory of Actual Crimes' in D Raskin (ed), *Psychological Methods in Criminal Investigation and Evidence* (New York, Springer, 1989); EF Loftus and HJ Burns, 'Mental Shock can Produce Retrograde Amnesia' (1982) 10 *Memory and Cognition* 318; EF Loftus, GR Loftus and J Messo, 'Some Facts about Weapon Focus' (1987) 11 *Law and Human Behavior* 55; NM Steblay, 'A Meta-Analysistic Review of the Weapon Focus Effect' (1992) 16 *Law and Human Behavior* 4.

[89] Although if the witness is unavailable for one of the reasons set out in ss 116 and 117(4) of the 2003 Act, the statement is admissible for that reason.

[90] *Ibid* s 115(3)(a).

The reason for the witness not coming forward suddenly becomes more crucial than the motives he or she may have had for making the statement. For example, s 116 permits the reception of first-hand hearsay where the original maker of the statement is unavailable for one of the reasons set out in a list of qualifying conditions.[91] It seems that the underlying rationale here has more to do with legitimate reasons for departing from the right of the accused to confront the witnesses against him than with reliability. This may be wise. Fact-finders may be reluctant to accept hearsay evidence unless there is a convincing explanation for the witness' absence. The example of hearsay, then, shows how concerns about fairness—here in the form of confrontation rights—need to be taken into account when we draw on behavioural science to inform our evidentiary practices. But things quickly become complex where, as with hearsay, it is difficult to articulate the fairness concerns with precision.

One reading of the hearsay provisions in the 2003 Act is that they really have more to do with an implicit perception of fairness than with fireside assumptions about reliability. The General Council of the Bar, for example, argued that hearsay should be admitted where 'it is just to let it in'.[92] The right to confront one's accusers evolved in an era when the state relied on clandestine denunciations. In an effort to preserve the fairness of the trial, reformers attacked the use of documents and out-of-court accusations (for example, by an alleged accomplice).[93] This rationale for hearsay exclusion has nothing to do with demeanour. The 'strong symbolic function'[94] of the right to confrontation counts against any case by case relaxation of the hearsay prohibition on the basis that the evidence of one particular witness is believed to be reliable. Relaxation might be acceptable in some contexts, but not, Friedman suggests, where a denunciation was intended by its maker for evidentiary use.[95] The business document provisions of the Criminal Justice Act 2003 do recognise the perils of statements made in contemplation of criminal investigations or proceedings, but have conceded admissibility where the declarant is unavailable.[96] Here emphasis is placed not upon reliability but upon having a valid reason for not producing the witness. Echoing similar provisions under the Criminal Justice Act 1988,[97] the court has a discretion to exclude the document in

---

[91] Also *ibid* s 117(4). Section 116 is closely modelled upon Criminal Justice Act 1988, s 23, which shared the same concerns, but was limited to hearsay in documents.

[92] See www.Barcouncil.org.uk/documents/BriefingOntheCriminalJusticeBillMar03.doc.

[93] *Lilly v Virginia*, 527 U.S. 116 (1999).

[94] *Maryland v Craig*, 497 U.S. 836, 846 (1990).

[95] RD Friedman, '"face to face": Rediscovering the Right to Confront Prosecution Witnesses' (2004) *International Journal of Evidence & Proof* 1.

[96] Criminal Justice Act 2003, s 117(4).

[97] Criminal Justice Act 1988, ss 25 and 26.

the interests of justice.[98] Yet other kinds of hearsay admitted under the s 116 exception, which also depends on the unavailability of the witness, are not subject to an interests of justice exclusionary discretion unless the ground relied on is that the witness is in fear.[99] The general exclusionary discretion contained in s 126 applies only to cases where the admission of the statement would result in undue waste of time (though a court anxious about potential unfairness to the defendant might fall back on s 78 of PACE).[100] The 2003 Act supposes that a genuine reason for the witness' absence is sufficient to justify reception even of statements made in full knowledge of their likely use in criminal proceedings.

It is doubtful that we need a hearsay rule simply to protect the tribunal of fact from unreliable evidence. There is experimental work to suggest that laymen consider hearsay to be less reliable than oral testimony, with or without judicial admonishment.[101] Damaška suggests that there might be an argument for excluding evidence where an opposing party has no opportunity to track down the original declarant and check the reliability of the information at source.[102] However, once adversarial procedures are substantially altered, requiring that notice be given to the other side, the difficulty may disappear: 'Doctrines and practices widely associated with Anglo-American fact-finding style are now often deprived of a convincing theoretical basis'.[103] But what is clear is that we will not have a coherent legislative strategy until we decide whether the objection to hearsay evidence rests on doubts about its reliability, or reflects process values that derive their validity from a moral, rather than an empirical, argument.

Hearsay, Lie Detection and Narrative

The legislature's increasing inclination to free criminal trials from dependence on oral sworn testimony is not popular with practitioners, whose experience has given them great respect for cross-examination as an instrument for forensic interrogation. Yet it appears that people who think they can tell when they are being lied to are very likely to be deceiving themselves,[104] whether they be laymen, lawyers or police officers,[105]

---

[98]   Criminal Justice Act 2003, s 117(6) and (7).
[99]   *Ibid* s 116(2)(e), (4).
[100]   See above n 15.
[101]   P Miene, E Borgida and R Park, 'The Evaluation of Hearsay Evidence: a Social Psychological Approach' in NJ Castellan (ed), *Individual and Group Decision-Making: Current Issues* (Hillsdale, NJ, Erlbaum, 1993).
[102]   Damaška, above n 18, 65.
[103]   *Ibid* 142.
[104]   GR Miller and JK Burgoon, 'Factors Affecting Assessments of Witness Credibility' in NL Kear and RM Bray (eds), *The Psychology of the Courtroom* (London, Academic Press, 1982); A Vrij, *Detecting Lies and Deceit* (Chichester, Wiley, 2000) 74.

whether they are questioning children or adults.[106] We are all liable to misinterpret the behaviour of nervous persons,[107] of people whose ethnicity we do not share[108] and of others who tend to employ 'powerless' speech styles, such as women and children.[109] Various research methods have been employed to investigate these issues, from laboratory work on the ability to detect truthfulness, to courtroom observation of the way witnesses behave and are questioned. The study of actual dishonesty presents a considerable methodological challenge: mock jurors are unlikely to be given the amount of time to consider their verdicts that real jurors are allowed; it is difficult to reproduce the weight of responsibility felt by real jurors;[110] there is also a question about whether would-be liars in a laboratory situation are as emotionally engaged as witnesses at a trial, and researchers need to provide them with a powerful incentive to convince observers. There are few real-life studies of lying, because of the difficulty of identifying the exact truth. Nevertheless, interviews with real jurors suggest that they utilise the same indicators of dishonesty as experimental subjects.[111] Since behaviours such as aversion of gaze and fidgeting are not

---

[105] HE Hocking, GR Miller and NE Fontes, 'Videotape in the Courtroom: Witness Deception' (1978) 14 *Trial* 52.

[106] A Vrij and FW Winkel, 'Detection of False Statements in First and Third-Graders: the Development of a Nonverbal Detection Instrument' in G Davies, S Lloyd-Bostock, K MacMurran and C Wilson (eds), *Psychology Law and Criminal Justice* (Berlin, de Gruyter, 1996); HL Westcott, GM Davies and BR Clifford, 'Adults' Perception of Childrens' Videotaped Truthful and Deceptive Statements' (1991) 5 *Children and Society* 123.

[107] A particular problem in courtrooms, given the kind of language and sentence structures lawyers employ: AG Walker, *Handbook on Questioning Children: a Linguistic Perspective* (Washington, Bar Association, 1994); AG Walker, 'Questioning Young Children in Court: a Linguistic Case Study' (1993) 17 *Law and Human Behavior* 39; M Brennan and RE Brennan, *Strange Language: Child Witnesses under Cross-Examination* (Wagga Wagga, NSW, Riverina Murray Institute of Higher Education, 1988); M Brennan, 'The Discourse of Denial: Cross-Examining Child Witnesses' (1999) 23 *Journal of Pragmatics* 71; G Davies and E Noon, *An Evaluation of the Live Link for Child Witnesses* (London, Home Office, 1991); K Murray, *Live Television Link: an Evaluation of its Use in Scottish Criminal Trials* (Edinburgh, HMSO, 1995); *Report of the Interdepartmental Working Group on the Treatment of Vulnerable or Intimidated Witnesses in the Criminal Justice System* (London, Home Office, 1998) para 8.70; A Sanders, J Creaton, S Bird and L Weber, *Victims with Learning Disabilities*, Home Office Research Findings 44 (London, HMSO, 1996); M Kebbell and D Johnson, 'Lawyers' Questioning: the Effect of Confusing Questions on Witness Confidence and Accuracy' (2000) 24 *Law and Human Behavior* 629 .

[108] P Ekman, ER Sorenson and WV Friesen, 'Pan-Cultural Elements in Facial Displays of Emotion' (1969) 164 *Science* 96.

[109] WM O'Barr, *Linguistic Evidence: Language, Power and Strategy in the Courtroom* (New York, Academic Press, 1982).

[110] Young, Cameron and Tinsley, above n 55, paras 10.7–10.26. Although it has been argued that mock jurors become highly involved and take their role very seriously: RM Bray and NL Kerr, *The Psychology of the Courtroom* (New York, Academic Press, 1987) 289–318.

[111] Young, Cameron and Tinsley, above n 55.

indicative of lying in the laboratory, there is no reason to suppose that they indicate lying in the courtroom, notwithstanding conventional wisdom to the contrary.

Fact-finders, in criminal cases at least, appear rightly sceptical of their own ability to spot the liar. The New Zealand jurors were reluctant to rely entirely on demeanour judgements, especially if that would entail finding the accused guilty. They preferred to rely on witness consistency over time, or on the perceived plausibility of the testimony.[112] We know that the probative weight and impact of an item of evidence depends upon the inference(s) to which it gives rise. But it seems that the inference that fact-finders, including judges, will draw from an evidential fact depends partly upon the story they have constructed from the evidence they have heard. Studies of the deliberations of mock jurors,[113] the recollections of actual jurors,[114] and of judicial decisions[115] all converge on this conclusion. The plausibility of this story may dictate which witnesses are believed, and thus have more influence on the outcome than witness demeanour. The important question may be the extent to which the particular testimony fits into a coherent narrative. Lawyers' obsession with whether an item of evidence is or is not hearsay, whether it relates to the issue of guilt or merely to credibility, may miss the point that, to the fact-finder, the important thing is how it relates to the story.

The narrative itself will be convincing only if it complies with common-sense assumptions about the way people behave and events unfold. Would an innocent man joke to his second wife that he had murdered his first?[116] Is it likely that a ship's first officer would, in front of the family of a crewman he does not know, announce his intention to run the ship aground so that he could earn extra overtime?[117] Where the defence story lacks this kind of resonance, as in *Yalman*,[118] aspects of individual performance in the witness-box are less likely to affect the verdict. Yalman had been at Stansted airport waiting for his elderly father's arrival on an incoming flight. However, the defendant made no contact beyond a nod

---

[112]   *Ibid*.

[113]   N Pennington and R Hastie, 'Explanation-based Decision Making: Effects of Memory Structure on Judgement' (1988) 14 *Journal of Experimental Psychology: Learning, Memory and Recognition* 521.

[114]   Young, Cameron and Tinsley, above n 55; WL Bennett and MS Feldman, *Reconstructing Reality in the Courtroom* (London, Tavistock, 1981).

[115]   Wagenaar, van Koppen and Crombag, above n 77. In the Netherlands, criminal court judges have to give reasons for their decisions so it is easier to assess the impact of specific pieces of evidence upon them; see also Jackson and Doran, above n 54.

[116]   *Daily Telegraph*, 6 October 2001. Remarks such as 'I had a hell of job getting the carpet sorted; I must've been at it for an hour', got Nicholas Kay convicted of manslaughter and imprisoned for six years despite the lack of a body, and thus no evidence, other than his wife's disappearance, that she had died or how she died.

[117]   Bingham, above n 55, 14.

[118]   [1988] 2 Cr App R 269.

from a distance, and kept apart from his father as he prepared to leave the airport. Yalman later claimed that they had had a row. The father's suitcase contained heroin, and there was evidence of heroin use at Yalman's flat. The prosecution was therefore able to construct a far more intuitively appealing story than the defence, who had to argue that the accused would ignore his own father on his arrival at the airport. Believing instead that Yalman's apparently unfilial behaviour was part of a prior arrangement designed to avoid attracting suspicion, the jury convicted him of being involved in the importation of a Class A drug.

If narrative is as important as demeanour to the verdict, it may also colour the fact-finder's reaction to hearsay evidence. It is possible that any party who, apparently for no good reason, defeats the fact-finder's expectations that a particular witness would be present will be penalised. In other contexts, lawyers to some extent feed the fact-finder's craving for narrative. For instance, prosecutors routinely adduce into evidence self-serving statements which the defendant made on arrest, even though denials do not assist the prosecution case, and might even assist the defence.[119] Many prosecutors believe that what the defendant said on arrest is so much a part of the narrative that withholding it would appear devious or sinister. There has been behavioural science research on the importance of narrative in jury decision-making;[120] that research, however, tends to be forgotten in debates about jury competence with respect to hearsay. We need to bear narrative more fully in mind as being one piece in the complex hearsay jigsaw.

ASSUMPTIONS OF LAY DISABILITY AND THEIR EVIDENTIARY IMPLICATIONS

One would have to penetrate the magistrates' or jurors' retiring room to assess how real fact-finders cope with instructions on the law. Studies of decision-making by juries in real cases are comparatively rare, and most of these have to rely on post-trial interviews where there is an obvious risk of erroneous reporting, whether due to misunderstanding by the juror or to lapses in memory. Research into jury decision-making tends instead to rely heavily on simulated scenarios, providing an imperfect mirror of the reasoning processes of jurors in real trials. Simulations involve giving mock jurors transcripts or videotapes of a 'witness' giving oral testimony.

---

[119] It presents the risk that the court will mistakenly rely on it as evidence of the defence; in the case of a mixed statement, the self-serving element does constitute evidence for the defence, and discharges the defence evidential burden: *R v Duncan* (1981) 73 Cr App R 359; *R v Sharp* [1988] 1 All ER 65, 68.
[120] Eg R Hastie, S Penrod and N Pennington, *Inside the Jury* (Cambridge, MA, Harvard University Press, 1983).

Testimony in either form is usually edited for brevity and the issues cut down to a minimum, This allows the experimenter the tight control over variables that scientific validity requires. Ironically, the more scientific the approach of the experimenter, in terms of tightly controlled, narrowly focused experiments, the less the results appear generalisable to the world external to the laboratory. The differences between the conditions surrounding the experiment and the realities of the courtroom become more marked.[121] It is generally acknowledged by psychologists that 'internal and external validity are often inversely related'.[122]

Since these methods do not mirror the complexity of the evidence and sheer tedium of many actual criminal trials, some researchers prefer to place shadow jurors in the courtroom itself.[123] The verdict of the real jury can be compared with those of experimental subjects who heard exactly the same evidence under the same conditions. However, although some simulations and shadow studies use volunteer 'jurors' taken from the general pool of people eligible for jury service, expediency often demands that the mock jury consists exclusively of university students. Their intelligence levels are higher than the average, and their reactions may be distorted by anxiety to please the experimenter. A more intractable problem is the difficulty in reproducing the weight of responsibility borne by a real jury. Bray and Kerr argue that mock jurors become highly involved and take their role very seriously. It may be possible to deceive subjects into believing that their decisions will have real consequences, although it is not easy to demonstrate that the deception was successful.[124] It has been pointed out that shadow juries reach decisions very similar, if not identical, to those of the real ones. However, as King observes, similar verdicts may not have involved the same thought processes.[125]

Bray and Kerr argue that laboratory findings are valuable where they appear plausible, despite the differences that exist between the conditions in which they were obtained and the situation to which they are generalised. The issue under investigation may mean that differences in context are not significant.[126] Even King, a notable sceptic in this area, concedes that simulations provide valuable information in relation to very narrowly

[121] S Lloyd-Bostock, 'Psychology and the Law: a Critical Review of Research and Practice' (1981) 8 *British Journal of Law and Society* 1, 16; cf P Rabbitt, 'Applying Human Experimental Psychology to Legal Questions about Evidence' in S Lloyd-Bostock (ed), *Psychology in Legal Contexts* (London, Macmillan, 1981).
[122] Ainsworth, above n 53, 167.
[123] Eg, S McCabe and R Purves, *The Shadow Jury at Work* (Oxford, Blackwell, 1974).
[124] Bray and Kerr, above n 109, 289–318.
[125] King, above n 60, 33.
[126] Bray and Kerr, above n 109, 310; but see VJ Konečni and EB Ebbesen, 'External Validity of Research in Legal Psychology' (1979) 3 *Law and Human Behavior* 39.

defined empirical issues, such as the comprehensibility of jury instructions.[127] Indeed, as will be seen below, there are significant similarities in the reactions of mock jurors and real magistrates (albeit under experimental conditions) to information about the accused's criminal record. Wagenaar's analysis of judicial decisions in the Netherlands is also consistent with a wide range of experimental studies on the issues of narrative, confession evidence and criminal record.[128]

Impact of Judicial Instructions

Investigations into the question whether juries obey judicial instructions to disregard certain evidence have produced mixed results. Data indicating that mock jurors do apply judicial directions[129] are contradicted by studies that suggest that directions are ineffective.[130] Other research suggests that it depends upon the trial stage at which the directions are given.[131] There is some evidence that an instruction to disregard media coverage is effective;[132] on the other hand, some researchers found the opposite.[133] We do know, however, that by the time an explanation is provided of the legal significance of the evidence, the jury will already have heard it.[134] They must recall it to mind and fit it within the legal framework.[135] To non-lawyers, it seems bizarre to describe the rules of the game after people

---

[127] King, above n 60, 35.

[128] Wagenaar, van Koppen and Crombag, above n 77.

[129] TR Carretta and RL Moreland, 'The Direct and Indirect Effects of Inadmissible Evidence' (1983) 13 *Journal of Applied Social Psychology* 291.

[130] Eg, JD Casper, K Bendedict and JL Perry, 'The Tort Remedy in Search and Seizure Cases: a Case Study in Juror Decision Making' (1988) 13 *Law and Social Inquiry* 279.

[131] S Sue, RE Smith and C Caldwell, 'Effects of Inadmissible Evidence and Decisions of Simulated Jurors: a Moral Dilemma' (1973) 3 *Journal of Applied Psychology* 345; S Wolf and DA Montgomery, 'Effect of Inadmissible Evidence and Level of Judicial Admonishment to Disregard on the Judgments of Mock Jurors' (1977) 7 *Journal of Applied Social Psychology* 205; AP Sealy, 'Instructional Sets in Trials of Rape' in PJ van Koppen and G van den Heuvel (eds), *Lawyers on Psychology, and Psychologists on Law* (Amsterdam, Swets and Zeitlinger, 1988); cf Carretta and Moreland, above n 128 .

[132] RJ Simon, 'Murders, Juries and the Press: Does Sensational Reporting Lead to Verdicts of Guilty?' (1966) 3 *Trans-Action* 40.

[133] E Constantini and J King, 'The Potential Juror: Correlate Causes of Judgment' (1980) 15 *Law and Society Review* 9; GP Kramer, NL Kerr and JS Carroll, 'Pre-Trial Publicity, Judicial Remedies and Jury Bias' (1990) 14 *Law and Human Behavior* 409.

[134] One wonders how the jury reacted in a trial for rape observed by Jackson and Doran. Having heard the medical evidence, they passed the judge a note asking whether rape could be committed in the absence of violence, and were told that the judge would explain what rape was at the end of the trial: see Jackson and Doran, above n 54.

[135] J Jackson, 'Juror Decision-Making in the Trial Process' in G Davies, S Lloyd-Bostock, K MacMurran and C Wilson (eds), *Psychology Law and Criminal Justice* (Berlin, de Gruyter, 1996) .

have played it.[136] There is reason to believe that hearing advice on the law before the trial begins is helpful. For example, Heuer and Penrod[137] asked judges to participate in an experiment whereby they would give juries advice on the law at the outset. These judges formed a better impression of the accuracy of the verdicts than judges in trials following the conventional procedure. All parties thought it helpful, in a complicated libel case, for counsel to offer brief interim summaries at regular intervals.[138]

These procedural variations cannot help, of course, if jurors simply do not understand the law that they are expected to apply. Tanford found that people who had sat in real criminal cases knew no more about the legal issues that arose in the cases they had heard than others who had never sat on a jury.[139] Even lawyers who had served on juries got only about 70 per cent of the legal questions right. Compliance by mock jurors rises when judicial instructions are rewritten into simpler language.[140] Charrow and Charrow[141] found that linguistic complexity in the direction to the jury undermined juror comprehension more than conceptual complexity. Once the instructions had been redrafted into simpler language, there was a significant increase in jurors' ability subsequently to recall the law. Although the 'specimen' directions drafted by the Judicial Studies Board of England and Wales employ simpler English language than American written instructions to juries,[142] there remains scope for making them clearer. However, the recommendation in the Auld Review that judges produce guidance in the form of a series of questions and answers, tailored to the law and the issues,[143] has not met with universal judicial enthusiasm. In *Cannings*, Judge LJ warned that it was not to be assumed that the judiciary as a whole supported the idea:

> The proposal overlooks the principle that although each member of the jury participates in the verdict, each must arrive at his or her conclusion by a

---

[136] SM Kassin and LS Wrightsman, *The American Jury on Trial* (New York, Hemisphere, 1988) 144.

[137] L Heuer and SD Penrod, 'Instructing Jurors: a Field Experiment with Written and Preliminary Instructions' (1989) 13 *Law and Human Behavior* 409.

[138] A case brought in 1984–85 by General Westmoreland against CBS. The trial lasted five months: EA Lind and TR Tyler, *The Social Psychology of Procedural Justice* (New York, Plenum, 1988) 136.

[139] JA Tanford, 'The Law and Psychology of Jury Instructions' (1990) 69 *Nebraska Law Review* 71.

[140] BD Sales, A Elwork and J Alfini, 'Improving Comprehension for Jury Instruction' in BD Sales (ed), *Perspectives in Law and Psychology*, vol 1, *The Criminal Justice System* (New York, Plenum, 1977).

[141] RP Charrow and VR Charrow, 'Making Legal Language Understandable: a Psycholinguistic Study of Jury Instructions' (1979) 79 *Colombia Law Review* 1306.

[142] P Darbyshire, A Maugham and A Steward, *What Can the English Legal System Learn from Jury Research Published up to 2001?* (published as an Appendix to Auld, above n 1).

[143] Auld, above n 1, para 8.24.

conscientious personal examination of the evidence in the context of legal principles which have been defined by the trial judge.[144]

Yet one may wonder why, on the issue of the application of the relevant law to the facts in the case, his Lordship is untroubled by a situation where one member of the jury 'may be convinced of guilt for reasons which are different to those of each of the other members who nevertheless, for their own conscientious reasons, are agreed on the result'.[145] Taking an entirely different view, the New Zealand Law Commission suggests providing jurors with flow charts.[146]

Juries who cannot understand what the judge is telling them about the law[147] may resort instead to some version of common-sense justice, that is, proceeding on the basis of what individual jurors think the law should be.[148] Compliance by fact-finders is more likely if a judicial direction is based upon a rationale to which they are sympathetic; therefore the effect of admonishment in a hearsay case might be different from a judicial instruction in a bad character case.[149] The 'forbidden reasoning' from previous convictions admitted as evidence of credibility under Criminal Evidence Act 1898, s 1(f)(ii),[150] and its equivalent in other jurisdictions, does not appear to be manageable by mock juries[151] or actual judges.[152] This may reflect the incoherence of a dichotomy between credibility and guilt rather than an inability or reluctance to comply with legal instructions. Judicial directions may, despite recent reform in England and Wales,

---

[144] Above n 26, 767.

[145] *Ibid.*

[146] But while having copies of the instructions increases jurors' confidence in the verdict it does not appear significantly to increase understanding: Heuer and Penrod, above n 136.

[147] A common state of affairs: A Reifman, SM Gusick and PC Ellsworth, 'Real Jurors' Understanding of the Law in Real Cases' (1992) 16 *Law and Human Behavior* 539; A Elwork, B Sales and JJ Alfini, *Making Jury Instructions Understandable* (Charlottesville, VA, Mitchie, 1982); PC Ellsworth, 'Are Twelve Heads Better than One?' (1989) 52 *Law and Contemporary Problems* 205; R Hastie, SD Penrod and N Pennington, *Inside the Jury* (Cambridge, MA, Harvard University Press, 1983); L Severance and EF Loftus, 'Improving the Ability of Jurors to Comprehend and Apply Jury Instructions' (1982) 17 *Law and Society Review* 153; Young, Cameron and Tinsley, above n 55, para 7.14. Yet several of these studies found mock jurors' grasp of the facts reasonably sound.

[148] NJ Finkel, *Commonsense Justice: Jurors' Notions of the Law* (Cambridge, MA, Harvard University Press, 1995).

[149] KL Pickel, 'Inducing Jurors to Disregard Inadmissible Evidence: a Legal Explanation Does not Help' (1995) 19 *Law and Human Behavior* 407.

[150] Criminal record was not to be used as evidence of guilt, but of the credibility of the defendant on his oath: see *R v Selvey* [1970] AC 304, a distinction to some extent retained under the Criminal Justice Act 2003.

[151] RL Wissler and MJ Saks, 'On the Inefficacy of Limiting Instructions where Jurors use Credibility Evidence to Decide on Guilt' (1985) 9 *Law and Human Behavior* 37; VP Hans and AN Doob 'Section 12 of the Canada Evidence Act and the Deliberations of Simulated Juries' (1975) 18 *Criminal Law Quarterly* 235; S Tanford and M Cox, 'Decision Processes in Civil Cases: the Impact of Impeachment Evidence' (1987) 12 *Social Behavior* 165.

[152] Wagenaar, van Koppen and Crombag, above n 77.

continue to draw the guilt/credibility distinction, but jurors will probably not have to apply it in the rigid manner required formerly.[153]

TAKING ACCOUNT OF BEHAVIOURAL SCIENCE: THE CONDUCT OF TRIALS

The revolutionary changes to the procedures to assist, first children and then other vulnerable witnesses, to give evidence are being extended to further kinds of witness by the Criminal Justice Act 2003. An avalanche of real-life research into the effect of cross-examination on vulnerable witnesses has led to a series of measures to avoid unnecessary stress.[154] Although so far vulnerable witnesses have not been spared cross-examination altogether (unless their evidence is received by way of hearsay) they have at least been granted physical removal from the cauldron that is the courtroom by means of the live link[155] and, increasingly, are being allowed to give evidence in-chief by way of videotaped interview.[156] The emphasis on orality is largely retained, but other fundamental aspects of the adversarial trial have been undermined by these measures. For instance, an unrepresented defendant may have a lawyer (whose client he is not)[157] imposed on him by the court[158] solely for the purpose of ensuring that a particular witness is not cross-examined by the defendant in person.[159] To some critics the new provisions amount to a reversal of the burden of proof.[160] The debate here is complicated by the extra dimension of the witness' right to be protected against degrading

---

[153] Interpreting Criminal Justice Act 2003, s 101(1)(g): *R v Highton* [2005] EWCA Crim 1985, [2005] 1 WLR 3472; *R v Chohan* [2005] EWCA Crim 1813, [2006] 1 Cr App R 3 [31]; Spencer, above n 31, 93–4.

[154] For a summary, see L Ellison, *The Adversarial Process and the Vulnerable Witness* (Oxford, OUP, 2001).

[155] The use of CCTV began with child witnesses in Criminal Justice Act 1988, s 32. Eligibility for the live link has been extended from the vulnerable witnesses identified in the Youth Justice and Criminal Evidence Act 1999 to all witnesses apart from the defendant; Criminal Justice Act 2003, s 51.

[156] Originally introduced in Criminal Justice Act 1991, s 54, for children only; extended to vulnerable witnesses generally by Youth Justice and Criminal Evidence Act 1999, s 27; extended to all eyewitnesses by Criminal Justice Act 2003, s 137.

[157] Youth Justice and Criminal Evidence Act 1999, s 38(5).

[158] *Ibid* s 38(4).

[159] Including complainants in sexual cases, and 'protected witnesses', defined in *ibid* s 35(2). This category, predictably, includes children, who first were protected in Criminal Justice Act 1988, s 34A (as amended by Criminal Justice Act 1991, s55(7)). Other witnesses may be granted immunity from cross-examination by the defendant under Youth Justice and Criminal Evidence Act 1999, s 36 (if it appears to the court that otherwise the quality of evidence given by the witness on cross-examination is likely to be diminished).

[160] Eg, Lord Thomas of Gresford, HL Debs, vol 657, col 1382, 1 February 2003.

treatment in court. The defendant's rights[161] are balanced against,[162] for example, the right of witnesses to protection from cruel and inhuman treatment, and from unwarranted intrusion into their private lives.[163]

Research into criminal court proceedings and the experience of those who participate in them is largely observational, and so does not suffer from the generalisability problems of much psychology and law research. There is a risk of subjective judgements affecting conclusions, but the number of researchers engaged in these large-scale projects reduces this. Many of the studies have been painstakingly thorough and some actually conducted on behalf of government departments.[164] There can be little doubt about the distress undergone by many who give evidence in court, and reform has clearly been to some extent inspired by a desire to encourage witnesses to come forward, as well as by humanitarian concerns. Maintaining a fair balance between these concerns and ensuring a fair trial from the defendant's point of view is the main focus of current debate in this area. But while empirical evidence can inform this debate, it cannot tell us how to weight the values we place in the balance.

CONCLUSION

It is entirely appropriate to question the methodological soundness of empirical research that may have significance for the criminal justice system. To a great extent the research method employed is dictated by the issue under investigation. However, there has been increasing awareness in the psychological community that findings from controlled laboratory experiments that 'reduce jury decision-making, for example, to a few psychology undergraduates reading a paragraph-long, sketchy description of a criminal case'[165] have limited utility in the criminal justice context. Influential psychologists working in the field have commented that it is

---

[161]   The right to examine or have examined witnesses against him: European Convention on Human Rights (ECHR), Art 6(3)(d); or the right to defend himself in person or through legal assistance of his own choosing: Art 6(3)(c) ECHR.

[162]   *Doorson v Netherlands* (1996) 22 EHRR 330; *Croissant v Germany* (1993) 16 EHRR 135.

[163]   Arts 3, 8 ECHR. The complainant in *R v Milton Edwards* had been cross-examined by the defendant in person for six days during the course of his trial for repeatedly raping her. She had been physically sick during this and had to be admitted to hospital after the trial. Her action to the European Court of Human Rights on account of violation of these rights was settled, but the court awarded her £8,000 in recognition of her legal fees and expenses: *JM v United Kingdom*, Decision [Section IV] No 41518/98 (Information Note No 22, September 2000, European Court of Human Rights).

[164]   Eg, Davies and Noon, n 106 above; Murray, above n 106; Davies, Wilson, Mitchell and Milsom, above n 51; Social Services Inspectorate, *The Child, the Court and the Video* (London, Department of Health, 1994).

[165]   A Kapardis, *Psychology and the Law* (Cambridge, CUP, 1997) 8. See also VJ Konečni and EB Ebbesen, 'Methodological Issues in Research in Legal Decision-Making, with Special

'dangerous and bordering on the irresponsible to draw conclusions and make recommendations to the legal system on the basis of simulations which examine effects independently of their real-world contexts'.[166] Accordingly, more recent research makes greater use of real jury interviews, more elaborate simulations or manipulations of real juries,[167] less use of psychology students and more of volunteers from the jury pool.[168] Nevertheless, direct research into the deliberations of juries, as recommended in the Auld review,[169] would be invaluable. The Department for Constitutional Affairs recently published a consultation paper to consider the merits of repealing Contempt of Court Act 1981, s 8, in order to permit meaningful research into how the jury system operates.[170]

Auld's assumption that relevant evidence should be admitted unless it is unfair to do so suggests that fact-finders should have unrestricted access to information that is probative, unless it is demonstrably unreliable or it infringes the rights of either the defendant, the complainant or other witnesses. This was the approach of the legislature to the old corroboration rules that required warnings to fact-finders where children or complainants in sexual cases gave evidence.[171] The mandatory warnings were seen to be unacceptable because there was no empirical evidence to justify them,[172] while at the same time they were counterproductive[173] and

---

Reference to Experimental Simulation' in F Lösel and D Bender (eds), *Psychology and Law: International Perspectives* (New York, Walter de Gruyter, 1992).

[166]   Konečni and Ebbesen, above n 164, 415–16.

[167]   Kapardis, above n 164, 8.

[168]   Eg, E Finch and VE Munro, 'The Sexual Offences Act 2003: Intoxicated Consent and Drug Assisted Rape Revisited' [2004] *Crim LR* 789.

[169]   Auld, above n 1, paras 5.76–5.87.

[170]   Department of Constitutional Affairs, *Jury Research and Impropriety*, Consultation Paper (2005).

[171]   Corroboration requirements for child witnesses were abolished by Criminal Justice Act 1988, s 34, and for sexual complainants by Criminal Justice and Public Order Act 1994, s 32(1).

[172]   In relation to children, see JR Spencer and R Flin, *The Evidence of Children: the Law and the Psychology* (2nd edn, London, Blackstone Press, 1993) 238; DHSS Paper, *Child Abuse: Working Together* (London, 1986). In relation to complainants in sexual cases, see R Walmsley and K White, *Sexual Offences, Consent and Sentencing*, Home Office Research Study No 54 (London, Home Office, 1979); J Temkin, *Rape and the Legal Process* (London, Sweet & Maxwell, 1987); Law Commission, *Corroboration of Evidence in Criminal Trials*, Law Com No 202 (Cmn 1620, London, HMSO, 1991) para 2.19; *Advisory Group on Video Evidence* (Pigot Report) (London, HMSO, 1989) para 5.27.

[173]   The risk of 'backfire effect' increasing the risk of conviction: see AP Sealy, 'Instructional Sets in Trials of Rape' in PJ van Koppen and G van den Heuvel (eds), *Lawyers on Psychology, and Psychologists on Law* (Amsterdam, Swets and Zeitlinger, 1988); CA Insko, 'Primacy versus Recency as a Function of the Timing of Arguments and Measures' (1964) 69 *Journal of Abnormal and Social Psychology* 381; N Miller and DT Campbell, 'Recency and Primacy in Persuasion as a Function of the Timing of Speeches and Measurements' (1959) 59 *Journal of Abnormal and Social Psychology* 1; EA Lind, 'The Psychology of Courtroom Procedure' in NL Kear and RM Bray (eds), *The Psychology of the Courtroom* (London, Academic Press, 1982).

offensive.[174] The legal change may, however, be insufficient to make a real difference to judicial practice; judges are still free to give corroboration warnings if they choose. Abolition of the requirement in New South Wales has not prevented trial judges in 80 per cent of sexual assault trials giving some form of corroboration warning. In 40 per cent of such trials they give the old-style full corroboration warning,[175] even, in some cases, where the complainant had suffered physical injury.[176]

It is beyond dispute that an accused person is entitled to a fair trial. However, objections to receiving certain categories of evidence on the grounds that it is unreliable or prejudicial, in the face of empirical evidence to the contrary, requires some support beyond mere assertion. And, compared with its intense hostility to bad character and hearsay evidence, the legal profession seems relatively untroubled by the use of other kinds of evidence whose reliability is cast into doubt by research data. Neither the legislature nor the Court of Appeal in *Turnbull* have taken sufficient steps to protect accused persons from misidentification. In the same way, a considerable body of empirical work on confession evidence has produced little reaction in legal circles. As well as the behavioural work that suggests that the risk of false confessions is very high in the case of particularly suggestible suspects,[177] there is a large body of literature indicating that false confession is a more common phenomenon than might be thought.[178] There are also some alarming individual cases of false confessions leading to miscarriages of justice, where there was no suggestion of police impropriety, but where the suspect had a low IQ or other form of vulnerable personality.[179] The Court of Appeal has made some concessions to these concerns, as may be seen in *McKenzie*,[180] but there remains a real

---

[174]   Law Commission, above n 171, para 2.19.

[175]   That is, that the corroborative evidence should be independent of the person to be corroborated and must implicate the accused in a material particular: *R v Baskerville* [1916] 2 KB 658.

[176]   *Heroines of Fortitude*, above n 51, 193.

[177]   GH Gudjonsson, 'A New Scale of Interrogative Suggestibility' (1984) 15 *Personality and Individual Differences* 303; GH Gudjonsson, *The Psychology of Interrogations, Confessions, and Testimony* (Chichester, Wiley, 1992); Wagenaar, van Koppen and Crombag, above n 77, 109–10.

[178]   Eg B Irving and L Hilgendorf, *Police Interrogation: the Pyschological Approach*; B Irving, *Police Interrogation: a Case Study of Current Practice*, Royal Commission on Criminal Procedure Research Studies Nos 1 and 2 (London, HMSO, 1980).

[179]   Such as that of Clifton Lawson, an 18-year-old, who confessed on videotape to the brutal rape and murder of an elderly woman. Fingerprints at the scene were not his. He confessed because he wanted to leave the police station and go to choir practice: Kassin SM and Wrightsman LS (1988) *The American Jury on Trial* (New York, Hemisphere) p 87. See also *R v Ward* [1993] 2 All ER 577.

[180]   (1992) 96 Cr App R 98. Where the prosecution case depends wholly upon a confession made by a defendant who suffers from a significant degree of mental handicap and the confession is unconvincing to the point where a jury, properly directed, could not properly convict upon it, then the judge should withdraw the case from the jury.

prospect of defendants being wrongly convicted on the strength of confession evidence. We have no warning requirement, nor a general requirement that there should be additional evidence[181] to support the confession before an accused is convicted. Expert evidence is admissible only when the defendant suffers from a personality disorder or has learning difficulties.[182]

The law of evidence may be unique as a field of law in its dependence on empirical propositions capable of being proved to be true or false. Lawyers may be comfortable with the traditional assumptions embodied in such propositions; without them assessments of relevance would have to be constructed very differently. Possibly in consequence, there has been resistance to some behavioural science challenges. Lawyers have been accused, in a different context, of taking a defensive stance vis-à-vis the contribution social science might make to law and legal process.[183] Similar paranoia might be observed in King's effort to 'hinder the progress of what I believe to be a misguided campaign by psychologists to colonize the law'.[184] It may be that there is no campaign, but it has become apparent that psychology and the law of evidence share much common ground.

Some years ago, Friedman wrote: 'Prestigious law schools offer courses in sociology, history and philosophy; or in psychology or anthropology of law. But everyone knows those are elegant frills, like thick rugs in the dean's office'.[185] His account may not be an entirely fair reflection of the status of other disciplines in the United Kingdom's law schools, where thick rugs are rather less common than interdisciplinary studies. The law of evidence, in particular, cannot afford to treat the findings of behavioural scientists as merely an interesting sideshow. Recognising this, there is an increasing trend amongst writers of textbooks to alert students of Evidence to relevant psychological research.[186] Nonetheless, it remains essential, both in teaching the law of evidence and in debates about its reform, that the issues to which empirical research can make a legitimate contribution are clearly identified. Empirical research can play an important role in debates about the reliability of evidence, and in understanding both the decision-making process and the nature of the difficulties faced by those witnesses upon whose testimony the criminal justice system depends. Where the issue is 'fairness' in some other form, however, arguments must be presented in terms of moral norms or rights. Only when we have

---

[181] Jurisdictions such as Scotland, the Netherlands and some states in the United States require some kind of corroborative evidence.

[182] *R v Ward* [1993] 2 All ER 577; but see *R v Pinfold and MacKenney* [2003] EWCA Crim 3643.

[183] Cotterell, above n 3, 171.

[184] King, above n 60, 102.

[185] LM Friedman, 'The Law and Society Movement' (1988) 38 *Stanford LR* 763, 777.

[186] See eg, IH Dennis, *The Law of Evidence* (2nd edn, London, Sweet & Maxwell, 2002) 179–81, 215–18, 499–501, 662–3.

agreement on what this kind of fairness means can we establish whether and to what extent the fairness of trials is truly at risk from psychology or legislation.

8

Behavioural Science Data in Evidence Teaching and Scholarship

RODERICK BAGSHAW

INTRODUCTION: A SKETCH OF BEHAVIOURAL SCIENCE

WHAT IS BEHAVIOURAL science?[1] For the purposes of this chapter I will define it as 'the branch of science concerned with the advancement of knowledge by the observation of the behaviour of subjects in response to stimuli'. For the avoidance of doubt, I intend the word 'behaviour' to include verbal behaviour, including, in particular, how people describe their assessments of the likelihood that certain events took place in the past.

This brief definition clearly covers a wide range of learning. For convenience, I will concentrate on what might be called 'experimental behavioural science relating to human beings', that is, behavioural science pursued through the use of the following generalised methodology: the experimenter seeks to vary the stimuli given to human subjects and then observes to see if the variance between the behaviour of the subjects forms a pattern which can be correlated to the variance between the stimuli. Thus, when I refer to 'behavioural science data', I am referring to data acquired by the use of this experimental methodology, and often also to the conclusions that are drawn from these data.

The focus described above puts aside, for the time being, research using the following generalised methodology: the scientist observes the behaviour of human beings in uncontrolled settings and seeks to identify the factors which stimulate that behaviour and the relationships between the stimuli

---

[1] The term 'behavioural science' was initially allocated to me at the colloquium where this essay was first presented. By adopting it, I do not intend to commit myself to a position on whether 'mental states' exist, how far they are a proper subject for scientific enquiry, or the consequences for Evidence teaching of the answers to such questions. Personally, I have never raised the question whether intentions exist in an Evidence class. If any readers' concerns about such issues lead them to prefer the term 'experimental psychology' to 'behavioural science', they are welcome to substitute it.

and the behaviour. This side-lining does not reflect an opinion about the utility of such research.[2] Rather, my intention is to focus on a confined class of scientific endeavours in order to progress to the core of my argument, which is about the challenges in teaching students of Evidence law about the value of behavioural science data.

CENTRAL QUESTION: CRITICAL REFLECTION ON THE CLAIMS OF EXPERIMENTAL BEHAVIOURAL SCIENCE

It seems reasonable to assume that many teachers of Evidence law will want to provide their students with some information on the outcomes of relevant behavioural science experiments. But perhaps it is worth pausing to clarify *why* such outcomes are often regarded as an essential element in a student's curriculum.

The simplest explanation is probably that Evidence teachers assume that students ought to be able to evaluate the rules of Evidence law as well as describe them, and propositions about the consequential effects of such rules (and, indeed, the likely consequential effects of alternative rules) play a role in many schemes of justification and criticism. Where those propositions are directly supported by the outcomes of behavioural science experiments, then clearly a teacher has a good reason for drawing those outcomes to the attention of students. Perhaps more often, however, such propositions may be presented in judicial reasoning or academic writing as assertions without reference to supporting evidence or may be openly based on a claim as to how a 'reasonable witness', 'reasonable juror' or 'reasonable judge' can be expected to behave. The prevalence of such propositions in arguments about the law of evidence provides two further good reasons for teaching students about experimental data: the data may tend to support or undermine any specific assertion or any proposition based on the assumed behaviour of a 'reasonable X';[3] further, the data may cast doubt on the utility of some particular version of the 'reasonable X' as an accurate predictor of how real human beings behave in relevant settings.[4]

---

[2] For what it is worth, my opinion is that research using this methodology has produced a wealth of valuable insights (eg, regarding how a case for the prosecution is likely to be constructed and how defence lawyers tend to select defences to advance) that no serious scholar of Evidence law would want to ignore.

[3] To illustrate, if the proposition is that 'when given evidence of type Y a reasonable juror will behave in specific way X', then it seems reasonable to provide students with the information that an experiment designed to determine how 'jurors' behave when given evidence of type Y observed these 'jurors' behaving in specific way Z.

[4] To illustrate, if the proposition in the previous footnote was derived from a model of a 'reasonable juror' that assumed that a 'reasonable juror' processes all evidence using technique R (thus yielding behaviour X from evidence Y), then the experiment just mentioned

To turn now to my primary question: if a teacher of Evidence law feels the need to instruct his or her students about the results of behavioural science experiments in order to help those students reflect critically on Evidence law, then what more must the teacher tell the students to help them to evaluate the results of behavioural science experiments and to decide what conclusions it is legitimate to draw from them?

A JOKE

One evening a mathematician, a physicist, and an engineer were travelling by train through Scotland (having never visited that country before) when they saw a black sheep through the window of the carriage.

'Aha', says the engineer, 'I see that Scottish sheep are black'.

'Hmm', says the physicist, 'you mean that some Scottish sheep are black'.

'No', says the mathematician, 'all we know is that there is at least one sheep in Scotland, and that at least one side of that one sheep is black!'[5]

One odd feature of this joke is that it is unclear who the target is. Online the joke can be found both on sites devoted to cataloguing jokes about engineers and sites devoted to cataloguing jokes about mathematicians. Perhaps this reflects the fact that general knowledge, derived from sources other than a single observation from a moving train, leads even those who have never sought to investigate Caledonian livestock to believe that evidence exists to confirm the physicist's conjecture. But such confirmation does not establish that the conjecture was *warranted* by the observation alone. Clearly the engineer can be criticised for his or her extraordinary eagerness to generalise from a single observation, and no doubt the mathematician's caution unexpectedly leaves out of account widespread beliefs about the minimum number of sheep it might be economic to keep in such a climate and how sheep are likely to be coloured. But the fact that these beliefs might be sufficiently robust to make the mathematician's caution humorous does not, of course, mean that the physicist's perspective would be appropriate when seeking, in other contexts, to draw conclusions from observed data. Indeed, when students are invited to start working with relatively unfamiliar data—such as the results of behavioural science experiments—there may be an advantage in inviting them to adopt the mathematician's perspective, at least until they have discovered something more about the robustness of the beliefs supporting generalisations from

---

would also be useful as tending to cast doubt on the accuracy of the predicated model of the 'reasonable juror', and hence on propositions derived from this model as to how jurors behave when given evidence of type Q, etc.

[5] One can add: 'A barrister overhears the conversation and casually asks if any of the observers are willing to swear that the sheep was not silhouetted against the setting sun'.

those data. Certainly, it is by adopting the mathematician's perspective, even if only temporarily, that we can expose the 'substitutions' that experimental behavioural scientists must inevitably make and the uncertainties that these introduce.

SUBSTITUTIONS IN EXPERIMENTAL BEHAVIOURAL SCIENCE

There are four obvious limits on the discovery of knowledge using the ordinary experimental method which are relevant to Evidence law scholars: the limited availability of subjects to experiment on; the difficulty of synthesising certain types of stimuli; the difficulty of observing patterns in behaviour; and the difficulty of establishing the reliability of *generalisations* based on the data. Experimental behavioural scientists and psychologists are usually well aware of these limits and take them into account in designing their experiments, but students of Evidence law may benefit from having them summarised.

Availability of Subjects

The limited availability of experimental subjects has clearly influenced the aspects of the trial process which have been, and are likely in the future to be, subject to investigation using the experimental method. Generally speaking, lay people are easier to recruit in the numbers necessary for useful experiments than police officers, experienced criminal lawyers, career criminals or appellate judges.[6] Thus, most experimental work investigates the points in the trial process where lay people participate; so experiments tend to focus on witnesses and jurors.

Of course, a constraint on the availability of behavioural science data is the cost of experiments, and this has influenced *which* classes of people tend to be used as generic lay people. For convenience, many experiments have treated university students as fungible representatives of the generic lay population,[7] sometimes administering tests to weed out the apathetic and mischievous. The belief that non-apathetic, non-mischievous university

---

[6] The behaviour of these subjects is *easier* (not easy!) to investigate using the methods associated with empirical survey. But such methods involve loss of control over the stimuli to which subjects are exposed and the consequent uncertainties that arise from having to observe (and interpret) the stimuli as well as the difficulties in observing resulting behaviour.

[7] Two recent examples, drawn from a vast pool of published studies, which used university students to investigate the effect of 'judicial' directions are JM Gray, 'Rape Myth Beliefs and Prejudiced Instructions: Effects on Decisions of Guilt in a Case of Date Rape' (2006) 11 *Legal and Criminological Psychology* 75; and O Nikonova and JRP Ogloff, 'Mock Jurors' Perceptions of Child Witnesses: the Impact of Judicial Warning' (2005) 37 *Canadian Journal of Behavioural Science* 1.

students are an adequate substitute for generic lay people in the contexts being examined can be reinforced, to an extent, by tests designed to investigate whether they perform differently from other groups.[8] Yet a degree of uncertainty inevitably remains. Importantly, it is impossible to *measure* the *likelihood* that weeded university students diverge from generic lay people to any particular extent on any particular task.

Synthesising Stimuli

The difficulty of synthesising certain types of stimuli (or at least doing so ethically) is important because it means that there are many topics which are not amenable to direct experimental investigation. As cartoonish examples, one cannot investigate directly the accuracy of eyewitness identifications made by those woken in the night by an armed intruder in the bedroom, or the truthfulness of dying declarations. Consequently, certain topics are left untouched and others are investigated by the use of substitute stimuli which are believed to be equivalent or similar.

The challenges and pitfalls of employing substitute stimuli are well illustrated by the difficulties of replicating experimentally the experience of participating as a juror in a criminal trial. One sort of substitute is provided by reading a transcript, another by watching a videorecording, a third by watching a live enactment, and a fourth by sitting as a shadow jury. Further variations can be devised by altering the nature and amount of background information provided to substitute jurors, in order to contextualise the dependent and experimental variables.

It may be worth pausing to consider a particular example of the substitutions that even a well-designed and well-resourced experiment can involve.[9] Sally Lloyd-Bostock's study of the effects on juries of information about a defendant's criminal record used specially created videotapes of trial-like events. However, each videotape lasted only approximately half an hour. Where evidence about the defendant's criminal record was presented to the jury this was done by a voiceover on the videotape as the defendant went into the witness-box. The judge in each videotape gave a summing-up based on guideline directions, but did not sum up the evidence. Before deliberating, all the jurors had to fill in questionnaires selecting a verdict and rating the likelihood that the accused committed the offence. They were then allowed half an hour to deliberate before

---

[8] Clearly if non-apathetic, non-mischievous university students are found to exhibit the same patterns of behaviour as other groups of subjects on *some* tasks then this will lend support to the proposition that they are a suitable substitute on *other* tasks as well, but will not provide an *infallible warrant* for that conclusion.

[9] S Lloyd-Bostock, 'The Effects on Juries of Hearing about the Defendant's Previous Criminal Record: a Simulation Study' [2000] *Crim LR* 734.

completing two further questionnaires. Presumably the jurors knew throughout that their behaviour was not going to influence (directly) the welfare of any human being, but rather to produce data of interest to researchers.

Observing Behaviour

Often, the behaviour that the experimenter wishes to study cannot be observed directly. For instance, an experimenter may wish to observe whether a particular stimulus increases the confidence that jurors feel with regard to their verdicts; it is, however, difficult to observe the feeling of confidence directly so the experimenter is likely, instead, to observe how the stimulus effects what jurors *report* about the results of their introspection as to their degree of confidence.[10] In the Lloyd-Bostock study, jurors were asked to report their assessments of the likelihood that the accused was guilty on a scale between 1 and 100. Even such an apparently straightforward substitution can raise concerns because of uncertainty as to variations in people's capacity for introspection and as to how descriptions of their feelings of confidence are calibrated.[11]

A second issue harks back to the difficulties in synthesising stimuli; the stimuli are often contrived in such a way as to make the relevant behaviour more observable. For instance, in the Lloyd-Bostock study:

> the evidence presented in the videos was adjusted so that, in pilot studies, without any evidence of previous convictions the perceived likelihood that the defendant was guilty was just over 50 per cent, and so that between one and three members of a simulated jury of 12 would initially vote for 'guilty'. This was to allow scope for increases in perceived guilt according to different types of previous conviction to be revealed.[12]

---

[10] It may be easier to grasp the point being made by reflecting on the parallel distinction between 'how happy I am' and 'what I report to you about how happy I think I am'.

[11] To spell the point out, there is a difference between being able to experience different degrees of confidence and being able to understand that these are what are being experienced so as to calibrate one's sensations in order to describe them to others. Experimenters who want to observe 'experience of a particular degree of confidence' cannot do so directly by using a questionnaire. Instead, they observe the substitute 'verbal description', which may not be a perfect facsimile of the experience because of its dependence on the additional capacities of understanding, calibration and description. (Obviously, this assumes that a factor which influences a real juror's decision is the 'experience of a particular degree of confidence' rather than any 'verbal description' of it.)

[12] Above n 9, 740.

To paraphrase, the simulated jury was exposed to the stimulus of a knife-edge trial[13] plus, in some cases, the additional stimulus of information about a prior conviction. The knife-edge trial scenario was selected in order to make it easier to observe increases in perceived likelihood of guilt when information about a prior conviction was given.

A third issue is that the mechanism used to observe one sort of behaviour may interfere with another sort of behaviour. For instance, in the Lloyd-Bostock study the juror-substitutes were asked: 'Compared with other men of his age and background is [the accused] more likely or less likely to lie on oath in a court of law?' It seems that this question was intended to detect the jurors' assessments of the accused's general credibility. But the question was administered after the jurors had been asked to determine the likelihood that the accused had committed the crime with which he was charged, after he had testified to his own innocence. Thus, it is difficult to be sure whether for any particular juror their previous assessment of the likelihood that the accused was guilty (and hence 'lying on oath in a court of law' on the videotape) influenced their assessment of the likelihood that he might (in general) lie on oath.

A further issue here is that the starting hypothesis is likely to influence what behaviour the experimenter *seeks* to observe. Suppose, for instance, that an experimenter wanted to observe the influence on juror deliberations of a particular variation in an item of evidence presented to the fact-finder. An experimenter who believed that jurors construct likelihood ratios relating to individual items of evidence would seek to observe one thing, whilst an experimenter who believed that jurors assess the relative plausibility of complete stories or 'trial narratives' would seek to observe something else.

Generalisations Based on the Data

During the House of Commons debates on what is now the Criminal Justice Act 2003, Elfyn Llwyd (the Member of Parliament for Meirionnydd Nant Conwy and a barrister) asked whether Simon Hughes (the Member of Parliament for Southwark and Bermondsey)[14] was aware of the research undertaken by Sally Lloyd-Bostock, professor of law and psychology, which 'showed conclusively that juries are biased by learning about

[13] Albeit the knife-edge used was not that between 'beyond a reasonable doubt' and 'just short of beyond a reasonable doubt'. It would, of course, be interesting to know what proportion of real cases coming to trial involve evidence such as would lead jurors to assess the likelihood of guilt as a fraction over 50 per cent (in the absence of any character evidence).

[14] Mr Hughes was making a speech opposing the provisions in the Bill making evidence of an accused's bad character more easily admissible; the Bill became the Criminal Justice Act 2003.

previous convictions for similar offences'.[15] Clearly, the mathematician in the joke would not describe the conclusions which might be safely drawn from the research in this way. The mathematician might say that the experiment demonstrated that in a case where there was very little evidence, but which was finely balanced overall, the additional information that the accused had a previous conviction affected ordinary people's assessments of the likelihood that the accused had committed the crime, and the effect was greatest when the accused was revealed to have a recent conviction for the same offence as that with which he was now charged. Indeed, the mathematician might be eager to add further qualifications, for instance, that in each case the accused's defence involved admitting the acts alleged by the prosecution but denying the relevant mental state.[16]

Once these qualifications are articulated, it is easier to identify the beliefs that must be accepted in order to justify the conclusion that the results of the experiment demonstrate 'conclusively'(!) that 'juries are biased by learning about previous convictions for similar offences'. These beliefs include that 'what a real jury would do after hearing live evidence can be *reliably* inferred from what the mock jurors did after watching the 30-minute videos' and 'how juries exposed to cases involving very little evidence and a perceived likelihood of guilt just above 50 per cent react to additional character evidence provides a reliable basis for predicting how juries in other types of cases—in particular those where there is far more evidence to assess—will react to character evidence'. Clearly the *experiment* does not itself set out to establish the reliability of such beliefs. Indeed, the second belief, in particular, would be very difficult to test directly by experiment. Instead such beliefs tend to draw their strength from general *theories*, which may themselves have been partially tested by other experiments.

For instance, the belief that 'juries subjected to cases involving very little evidence and a perceived likelihood of guilt just above 50 per cent will use additional character evidence in the same way as juries in other types of cases,in particular those where there is far more evidence to assess' might draw strength from the theory that 'decision-makers make decisions by attaching "weight" to items of evidence'. This theory might tend to suggest

---

[15]   Hansard HC vol 402 col 992 (2 April 2003). Although it does not affect the point being made, the questioner appears to have confused Prof Lloyd-Bostock's study of juries, funded by the Home Office, with her study of magistrates, funded by (what is now) the Ministry of Justice. Mr Hughes answered that he was aware of the research.

[16]   This simplifies somewhat because one case seems to have involved alternative defence stories. As reported, the cases involved: (a) handling stolen goods: accused admits that the goods were stolen but claims that he did not know or believe this to be the case, and was merely storing the goods for payment; (b) indecent assault: accused admits touching but claims it was consensual; (c) wounding with a screwdriver: accused claims that the wounding was accidental or self-defence.

that the results from Lloyd-Bostock's experiment were generalisable because a decision-maker who attaches 'weight' to a particular type of evidence in one context would presumably (absent a good reason for doing otherwise) attach the same 'weight' to that item of evidence in a different context involving greater quantities of evidence. By contrast, to use another cartoonish example, the theory that decision-makers are only capable of taking into account the three most pertinent items of evidence (and proceed by seeking to identify those) would lead to a different view about the generalisability of the results.

One conclusion that it may be particularly worth warning students against is treating the *size* of the measurements as generalisable. For instance, the Lloyd-Bostock study measured the mean jurors' assessment post-deliberation of the likelihood that the accused committed the offence charged at 54 where no information was given about past convictions and 64.5 where the jurors were told of a recent conviction for the same offence. This result clearly does not warrant the claim that, 'evidence of a recent similar conviction makes it on average 10 per cent more likely that the accused will be convicted'.[17] The fact that many experiments are designed to detect the effect of a change in stimulus rather than to measure the significance of that stimulus relative to others is, of course, very significant when it comes to assessing whether experimental results should influence some aspect of public policy, such as a legal rule, which represents a *trade-off* between different values and objectives.[18]

Inducing a New Model

The prevalence in discussions about Evidence law of propositions based on claims as to how a 'reasonable witness', 'reasonable juror' or 'reasonable judge' would behave in particular circumstances has already been noted. Such claims are generally derived, consciously or unconsciously, from

---

[17] Obviously no reputable experimental psychologist would make such an error. My claim is merely that some law students (and perhaps even some of their teachers?) may be susceptible to it.

[18] If, eg, one experiment proved that decision-makers tend to attach too much importance to evidence of previous criminal convictions, a second experiment proved that decision-makers who are told nothing about a defendant's previous convictions sometimes speculate about them and attach weight to their speculations, and a survey proved that members of the public regard the fact that decisions can be reached without reference to a defendant's past behaviour as a strong reason for being sceptical about the accuracy of acquittals, then a policy-maker would find it difficult to forge these elements into a case for a particular rule without some sense of the *relative* significance of the phenomena. For example, a policy-maker convinced that the over-weighing phenomenon would change the outcome of only one in 10,000 *real* cases and that the speculation phenomenon would change the outcome of one in a 100 might clearly formulate a different proposal from a policy-maker who thought that the relative significance was reversed.

models of the reasoning and decision-making processes used by 'reasonable Xs'. Occasionally, the person advancing the proposition will use himself or herself as the model and derive propositions by self-interrogation: 'if I was the X, what would I do in these circumstances?'. But more often the model will be an external construct stipulated to be concerned with maximising some factor or factors and inclined to use some particular processes to do so. A familiar example of such a model might be *homo economicus*, who seeks to maximise fulfilment of his goals in the light of what he knows about incentives and constraints. Common examples of similar models within Evidence law would include the model of the 'reasonable guilty defendant' stipulated to be motivated solely by the goal of minimising the likelihood of being convicted and models of 'reasonable judges' stipulated to be motivated (solely or principally) by the goal of maximising the correspondence between the 'facts' found by a jury (prone to cognitive biases) and 'truth', or the goal of minimising the sum of error-based and other costs.

The reliability of such models as generators of information about the behaviour of participants in the legal process is clearly a topic which can be investigated using the experimental method. Obviously, if a model predicts that jurors dealing with a particular type of evidence will behave in a specific way, then the credibility of the model will be damaged by the revelation that mock jurors subjected to a stimulus intended to replicate dealing with such evidence appear to behave in a distinctly different way. But it may be worth drawing students' attention to the difference between the risks involved in drawing the generalisations necessary to regard the model as hopelessly flawed and the risks involved in reaching the further conclusion that some alternative model is a more accurate, scientifically-validated, model of the 'real X'.[19]

Sympathy for a rather radical-sounding claim lies behind the previous two paragraphs: it would be an error to regard the experimental method as inherently superior to armchair theorising using a simple model of the reasoning processes of the 'reasonable X'. One reason why the experimental method can never wholly overthrow theoretical models is that, as we have seen, experimenters are dependent on theoretical models, for instance, in order to determine what it might be worthwhile to attempt to observe and in order to design further experiments to clarify the explanations for results of previous experiments. A second reason, however, is particularly

---

[19] Since my main theme concerns the assessment of behavioural science data, I will avoid discussing the related, and difficult, question whether the law should be designed to work well when the participants are *real* human beings or when the participants are *partially-idealised* human beings. Obviously, intermediate views are also possible: eg, that the main rules should assume that participants are ideal, but some further rules should be dedicated to increasing the extent to which real participants are capable of acting ideally (eg, rules mandating instructions warning against particular non-ideal reasoning processes).

pertinent in the field of law. Simple models of 'reasonable Xs' can be used to obtain insights far more cheaply and quickly than the experimental method, and, importantly, can be used to design rules for dealing with phenomena that are never likely to be adequately investigated using the experimental method. Of course, the reliability of those insights may be doubtful: it seems trite to state that any insight is only as reliable as the model which produced it. But often lawyers have to decide how to deal with evidential issues of a type or within a timescale which precludes primary reliance on the experimental method.[20]

KEEPING THE LIMITS IN PROPORTION

To say that Evidence law students ought to be made aware of the *limits* of the ordinary experimental method as a generator of knowledge (relevant to Evidence law), is not to invoke these limits as an excuse for blindly ignoring the insights that experimental methods can produce. Indeed, it would be illogical to conclude on methodological grounds that experimental behavioural science data should never be relied on as the basis for drawing inferences in legal contexts, since there is no reason for always treating the risk of a generalisation based on experimental data being erroneous as more significant than the prospect that the generalisation is valid *despite* the risk.

An illustration may help to bring home the point. Imagine that an experimenter wishes to obtain a complete list of the paint colours used by the manufacturers of Ford cars and pursues his goal by standing on a motorway bridge for 12 hours recording the paint colour of every Ford car which passes. Clearly, there is a significant risk that this experiment will not produce a perfect list. But, equally, there is a prospect that it will. My proposition is that there is no reason for *instantly* concluding that the experimenter's list is more likely to be wrong than right.

A somewhat different proposition demands more careful attention. How is it possible to determine when conclusions about Evidence law can safely be derived from experimental data? When, in other words, can the risk of drawing an unsupported inference be dismissed? I suggest that these questions *cannot* be resolved by an appeal to the data themselves. Indeed, the risk that empirically-grounded conclusions are misleading will often be *unquantifiable*. To return to the illustration concerning the colour of Ford cars, we cannot *quantify* the risk that the experimenter's list is incomplete merely by looking at the results of the survey.

Obviously, some risks *can* be quantified. For instance, where the frequency of a particular outcome in the control group is known it is

---

[20]   An easy example might be the reliability of dying declarations.

reasonably straightforward to assess the probability that an increased frequency of this outcome in the group exposed to the stimulus being studied is merely a coincidence. However, it is not possible to *quantify* in a similar way *all* the risks which determine whether a psychology experiment's result is generalisable into a conclusion about participants' behaviour in real trials. For instance, it is not possible to *quantify* the risk that mock juries subjected to short videos containing very little evidence will behave differently to real juries exposed to live trials containing multiple sources of evidence.[21] This is not to claim that all propositions about the *scale* of such risks are meaningless. No doubt if a series of studies seeking to investigate the same feature of real trials utilising different substitute stimuli produced consistent results, we could meaningfully claim that it was now reasonable to regard the risk of non-generalisability as *lower* than it would have been reasonable to regard it immediately after the first such study.[22] But a proposition that a risk is 'lower than previously thought' is manifestly not equivalent to a proposition that it is below 5 per cent.[23]

A student who has followed the argument to this point is likely to be in a state of anxiety: the teacher has suggested that experimental data should be taken into account, but conclusions drawn from those data must not be treated as infallible. Yet the teacher has not offered any positive guidance indicating how to reconcile relevance and potential fallibility.[24] Below, I

---

[21] The closest that one is likely to get to a *quantification of risk* is an expert opinion such as the statement in MJ Saks, 'What do Jury Experiments Tell Us about How Juries (Should) Make Decisions?' (1997) 6 *Southern California Interdisciplinary LJ* 1, 8 n 18, that interactions between such substitutions in the research method and the independent variable of interest are 'pretty rare. And when they are found it usually is not that one finds results going in one direction in the simulation study and in the opposite direction in the correlation field study, for example. It is more usually the case that the simulation setting detects an effect while the real-trial situation finds no difference'.

[22] Similarly, if studies using similar substitute stimuli to investigate some different feature, or features, of real trials were proved to have produced reliable conclusions then it would be reasonable to regard the risk of non-generalisability as *lower* than it would have been reasonable to regard it if such studies had not been undertaken.

[23] Some scholars might be attracted by the idea that if a substantial number of experts share a consistent, intuitive gut reaction that the risk is low then this provides a good reason for regarding it as low (in the absence of any evidence of a higher risk) even when the experts concede that there is no methodologically persuasive route to their conclusions. But it is difficult to commend such an opinion without further information about the aetiology of such gut reactions.

[24] At this stage the chapter departs from the view apparently expressed in RJ Allen and B Leiter, 'Naturalized Epistemology and the Law of Evidence' (2001) 87 *Virginia Law Review* 1491, and it may be worth pausing to point out the extent of the departure. These authors, at 1541–2, note the limits on experimental methods in generating reliable information for Evidence lawyers, but in response suggest: 'The question then is whether these differences [as to subject, stimuli, etc] *vitiate* the value of existing empirical evidence … With respect to proffered empirical evidence bearing on the instrumental value of some evidentiary rule for maximizing veristic value, we must always ask whether the differences … affect the utility of the empirical data for evaluating the evidentiary rules within a social epistemology framework'. I would quarrel with the word *vitiate*, and would prefer to portray the issue as more

will suggest two, admittedly controversial, considerations that might amount to useful guidance. But first it is worth contemplating the merits of leaving Evidence students in a state of anxiety—at least temporarily—and inviting them to reflect on how that anxiety mirrors the experiences of other actors in the legal process.

REFLECTIONS: WHO ELSE IS ANXIOUS?

Law students (and teachers?) may not be the only ones who experience a measure of anxiety in deciding whether or not to rely on inferences drawn from behavioural science data. So perhaps we should introduce students of Evidence to (amongst others) 'the psychologist in the jury' and 'the judge who must balance'.

The Psychologist in the Jury

The experimental psychologist is summoned for jury duty and hears a case where the pivotal evidence against a man accused of a brutal street robbery is that he was picked out of a lawfully conducted parade (line-up) by both the victim and an independent eyewitness. The experimental psychologist is aware that these data suggest that the accused committed the crime, but that there is also a risk that such a conclusion would not be correct, and that risk is unquantifiable. The risk is unquantifiable because although the psychologist may be aware of what proportion of eyewitnesses have made errors of identification in various experiments he will no doubt realise that this figure is not an unassailable measure of the likelihood that any particular eyewitness in any particular circumstances has made an error.[25] At best the psychologist may be able to determine a band of error rates that it seems likely will include the risk that the particular witness' testimony is misleading. But despite uncertainty and anxiety, a decision

often one where a *risk of being misled* ought to be recognised and taken into account. Further, I am unwilling to leave matters at 'we must always ask', because my argument is that the anxiety arises when the student asks 'how can I find an answer to this question?'.

[25] Identification error rates vary in accordance with factors such as the conditions under which the witness perceived the perpetrator and the extent to which the perpetrator had distinctive features. The risk of error in the particular case might appear to be quantifiable if experiments have been conducted on subjects with perceptual and memory abilities identical to the witness, which synthesised opportunities to observe which were similar to those which the witness had, and which involved perpetrators resembling the accused, etc. But even in such cases we could not be sure that the actual witness did not have a higher or lower risk of error because of the influence of some further factor that no one has ever thought to test (or that no one has ever succeeded in designing a method of testing).

must be made today: the option of postponing any decision until further research on the capacities of the particular witnesses has been conducted is not available.

An analogy may be helpful. The experimental psychologist's expertise puts him into a privileged position with regard to assessing the odds, in that he will not mistakenly believe that the testimony of two eyewitnesses who remain confident when cross-examined provides an unshakable basis for a conviction; but his expertise cannot remove the anxiety that comes with being compelled to place a stake (arrive at a definitive verdict), one way or the other, in the particular case.

The Judge Who Must Balance

The well-informed judge in a similar case is told that the victim identified the accused in the street after being driven round local streets by police officers in search of the assailant. The victim was not required to try to identify the accused subsequently despite the accused requesting such a procedure. The accused requested such a procedure because he believed that the victim's identification of him in the street involved recognition of supposedly distinctive clothing rather than facial identification, and the police admit that the failure to accede to this request was the result of a 'mix-up'. The judge is invited to exercise her discretion to exclude the victim's identification evidence in the light of this apparent breach of Police and Criminal Evidence Act 1984 (PACE) Code of Practice D (regulating identification procedures) and, reasonably, assumes that this invitation requires her to assess the probative value of the evidence against the prejudicial effect resulting from the breaches of the Code, taking account of the extent to which prejudice might be neutralised by an appropriate direction. Trial judges in this position must confront the double anxiety of uncertainty as to the 'probative value' of the evidence (similar to the anxiety of the psychologist-juror), *and* as to the magnitude of the risk of irredeemable prejudice: will the jury respond appropriately to a careful direction? Again, a decision cannot be postponed, although it may be possible to revisit an initial determination at later stages in the trial.

Learning to Live with Anxiety

Exposing the ubiquitous nature of anxiety may help to prevent uncertainty becoming an excuse for inertia, for a too ready acceptance of the default position of maintaining the status quo ante. Behavioural science experiments demand attention when Evidence law is being evaluated with regard to its consequences, but it is irresponsible to treat reasoning from experimental data as a process which is free from risk. Doubts about the extent to which it is safe to generalise from experimental data can be progressively diminished: previous experiments can be repeated with modified substitutions and new experiments can often be designed to try to reveal whether the theories that support generalisation beyond the tested substitutes are flawed. But anxiety will never be *entirely eliminated* by a strategy of further experimentation. This strategy must consequently be supplemented by an approach to making decisions *despite* lingering anxiety. Indeed, in contexts where decisions must be made in advance of any reasonable prospect of additional experimental data, the approach to making decisions despite anxiety may be *more important* than the promise of further experiments. Perhaps it is appropriate to go further and to claim that lingering anxiety should be welcomed—provided that it does not become debilitating—as a reassuring indicator that the uncertainties inevitably associated with behavioural science data have been recognised appropriately.

PROGRESS: ELEMENTS IN A POSITIVE GUIDE TO RECONCILING RELEVANCE AND POTENTIAL FALLIBILITY IN CONDITIONS OF ANXIETY

Not everyone will be prepared to accept the revelation that anxiety is widespread as a suitable palliative. However, my further two suggestions are even more contentious. My suggested approach involves, first, detailed analysis of the uncertainties facing the decision-maker, and thus of the risks that particular decisions will carry; and, secondly, the sketch of a process for deciding which risks it is legitimate to take. It should be emphasised that both suggestions proceed from the premise identified above, that there are ineradicable and unquantifiable risks in drawing general conclusions about actors in real settings from experimental data.

Identifying Stakes

There is an important distinction between being able to identify favourable odds and choosing to gamble.[26] Those who are invited to act in reliance on generalisations derived from the results of behavioural science experiments

---

[26] Perhaps I am offered the chance to buy for £1,000 one ticket in a lottery of 100 tickets, with a prize of £1 million for the winner (provided by an eccentric seeking to dispose of his wealth in an original way). My assessment that the price for such a ticket is good clearly cannot predict whether I will accept the offer and buy one.

by, for instance, changing evidential rules or giving verdicts or making rulings, are being asked to gamble, not merely to identify odds.[27] The intellectual and scholarly tasks that students are generally asked to perform, prominently involving the evaluation of legal rules, ought, if performed responsibly, to shadow such gambling: it is difficult to see how it would be appropriate for a student to argue that 'rule f ought to be changed to rule g' unless the student would be willing to effect that change if given power and opportunity to do so.[28] It seems plausible that for many people the move from an identification that the odds are good to a willingness to gamble on them is influenced by what they are being asked to stake.

This insight is significant because in contexts where there is a substantial body of behavioural science data suggesting that existing rules of Evidence law are based on inaccurate suppositions about the behaviour of witnesses, jurors or judges, it might often be thought that the risk of the data being misleading is *low*.[29] But if willingness to gamble is related to the amount that one is asked to stake (as well as to the odds) then perhaps this provides part of the explanation why:

(a) there is a gap between the changes to legal rules of evidence which experimental psychologists regard as warranted by empirical data and the legal reforms that have actually been put into effect by legislators and judges;

(b) some changes to the rules are put into effect and others are not, despite a similar weight of scientific backing;

(c) rules based on theories which are widely conceded to have been discredited nonetheless often persist; and

(d) decision-making may still be improved, notwithstanding unquantifiable uncertainty.

For instance, as an explanation for phenomenon (b) we might note that some proposed changes involve fewer resource implications than others, and thus a lower 'potentially wasted costs' stake. For this reason (if for no others), it is easier to bring about a change in a recommended judicial instruction to juries, than a change in a mandatory instruction, than a

---

[27] Indeed, it has been argued above that, in the particular context under discussion, the odds *cannot* be quantified.

[28] Assuming that the student is writing in his or her own 'voice', adopting the position of a legislator or critic. If the student is merely seeking to describe what he or she imagines that some other actor might 'argue', then clearly such a commitment is not mandatory.

[29] Of course, where an argument takes the form 'behavioural science experiments have demonstrated that an existing legal rule is based on an inaccurate supposition about the behaviour of X, so the rule should be changed in the following way...', it is important to distinguish between the risk that the data do not reliably prove that the supposition is *generally* inaccurate and the risk that the proposed change to the rule will not produce the expected benefits.

change in an admissibility rule or introduction of a mandatory corroboration requirement. Similarly, apart from possible costs within particular trials (for instance, extra time spent on directions, experts, legal points and appeals, etc) there are further transitional costs in adapting the legal system to any alternative rule (for instance, in retraining practitioners, rewriting court guides, dealing with transitional cases, etc) and these costs are yet another element in the stake that a reformer must wager.

To spell out the thinking behind point (d), a useful first step for a person asked to make a decision in the face of uncertainty may be to calculate what he or she is being asked to stake, what will be lost if the available empirical information proves to be deceptive and, importantly, what potential gain will be foregone (the 'opportunity cost') if no change is made because of doubts about the reliability of the generalisations supporting the change. But now it becomes apparent that what a law-maker is being asked to stake cannot be described straightforwardly. What the law-maker may lose on a decision either way is a combination of effects on the rates of wrongful convictions, wrongful acquittals, etc, and simple costs (eg, extra resources). For instance, the proposal that jurors in identification cases should routinely hear expert evidence relating to psychological research on eyewitness accuracy may (and here I am hypothesising in order to provide a simple illustration) carry a possible benefit in terms of a small reduction in the rate of wrongful convictions which will be foregone if the gamble is rejected, but also a risk of significantly increased wrongful acquittals, in addition to the unavoidable costs of the extra resources necessary to pay for the experts, counter-experts and increased usage of lawyer and court time. Thus, when a decision-maker is considering whether to allow such evidence in all cases, the wager pits the sum of simple resource costs and a risk of a significant increase in wrongful acquittals against the prospect that empirical data reliably predict a reduction in wrongful convictions. A further complexity is that the stakes may need discounting to take account of other, less costly methods of furthering the same end. For instance, if the prospect of reducing wrongful convictions by allowing expert testimony is valued at 10 units, it is important to consider whether this valuation ought to be discounted to reflect the fact that some fraction of the anticipated benefit may be obtainable by placing a less costly stake, for instance, by implementing a minor amendment to the standard judicial direction in identification cases.

Despite the previous paragraph's reference to 'units of value', it is essential (at least in my opinion) to stress to students that the decision whether to gamble cannot be reduced to a mathematical formula. One reason why the gamble cannot be converted into a calculation is, as we have noted time and again, the odds will always remain resilient to quantification. A second obstacle, however, is that different elements comprising the stake may not be reducible to a common denominator.

Different people are likely to have different views about the ratio of value between different elements in the stake. Further, and perhaps more importantly, the potential bearers of the costs within the stake are not the same, so each stake has a distributional dimension.

This second obstacle may be worth further exploration. For the purposes of illustration, let us assume that a particular society is contemplating allowing experts to testify about psychology experiments on eyewitness identification in all relevant criminal cases and that experimental data suggest that expert testimony will reduce fact-finders' inappropriate over-confidence in the reliability of eyewitness identifications without increasing the number of wrongful acquittals. Suppose further that this society is made up of only three distinct groups of people. Members of group A regard the threat of wrongful conviction as a very weighty matter and the cost of a significant increase in the rate of wrongful acquittals as regretta-ble, but tolerable. Thus members of group A may lean towards accepting the gamble proposed. By contrast, members of group B regard the threat of being a victim of a violent criminal act as a very weighty matter, and something each of them would be more eager to avoid than an equally likely risk of wrongful conviction. Given what they believe (let us assume correctly) about the relationship between wrongful acquittals and future crime rates, members of group B are more likely than members of group A to reject the gamble. Finally, members of group C regard it as very important not to spend any additional portion of society's wealth on the criminal justice system because they think that the other ways in which such money could be spent (eg, improving education and healthcare) are far more important than reducing the threat of wrongful conviction or reducing the number of wrongful acquittals. Members of group C would be expected to reject any wager on empirical data that did not promise financial cost-savings, or at least appeared to be resource neutral. My suggestion is that even in a society as simple as this one, there is no simple way of 'valuing' the stake which must be placed on the reliability of the data: the different groups do not agree about the ratio of value between the different elements (wrongful convinctions, wrongful acquittals and soci-ety's wealth).

If it is true that the odds cannot be quantified and that there is no common metric which will produce an authoritative 'valuation' of the stake which could be used in some 'cost-benefit' calculation, then alter-native mechanisms or processes for making decisions must be employed. Nonetheless, modelling the stake in all its complexity of value and distribution is likely to be a useful step in reaching a decision. Indeed, standing back, it seems obvious that a decision-maker contemplating relying on scientific data which may be deceptive will benefit from knowing what the cost of a decision could be if those data prove to be misleading, and also the cost of refusing to rely on a generalisation from empirical data which might, after all, be valid and reliable.

It may be worth underlining the fact that the previous paragraphs *have not* advocated the recognition of a principle governing reform of the law of evidence (even a principle confined to criminal cases) which demands that *everything possible* must be done to reduce the risk of wrongful convictions. If such a principle were adopted, that would certainly simplify the decision-making processes of those attempting to design and evaluate Evidence law. But there is no obvious reason for making reduction of the risk of wrongful convictions an absolute goal which must be pursued regardless of its impact on other important goals, that is, regardless of cost. Moreover, it is clear that no such principle is currently recognised: there are many *possible* trial strategies[30] and reform proposals which would reduce the risk of wrongful convictions which are consciously not pursued.

Representation

Encouraging decision-makers to take the time to identify the stakes involved in decisions whether to rely on experimental data despite the risks, or to reject it despite the prospect that it is reliable, strikes me as a good way of making progress despite anxiety. My second suggestion for moving forward is that the decision whether to gamble should be made by a collection of persons *representing* the range of interested parties, or by a decision-maker who attempts to incorporate the perspectives of such a range of representatives. This suggestion does not, of course, take us very far—it does not, for instance, tell us what process this collective enterprise should adopt.[31] But it is a suggestion which provides an interesting standard against which to assess juries, judges, legislators and others who make regulations relating to Evidence law.

How representative groups make decisions in the face of incomplete information and unquantifiable risks is clearly *itself* an important topic for research, including research using the experimental method. But the question how Evidence scholars ought to go about making such a decision despite lingering anxiety is obviously not identical to the question how groups commonly make such decisions. In suggesting that the gambles

---

[30] To give a simple example, it is not generally thought *unprincipled* to allow expert evidence to be adduced by the prosecution which has not been double-checked and peer-reviewed in advance.

[31] I hope that no reader will feel short-changed by my failure to provide a prototype for a process for making legitimate *political* decisions about uncertain risks. I am not qualified to perform the task and any opinions which I might offer about the relative merits of possible processes would merely distract from my primary theme, that behavioural science cannot *itself* determine whether it is legitimate to gamble on the reliability of experimental data.

required by decisions whether to rely on the generalisability of experimental data should be made by groups of representatives, or by decision-makers who attempt to incorporate the perspectives of a range of representatives, I am not seeking to claim that any perfect model for such decision-making exists. Indeed, one notable oddity of debates about whether Evidence law scholars misuse or marginalise behavioural science data is that so many participants *assume that there is* some simple standard which can be used to define proper use of such data. Perhaps the oddity of such an assumption can best be seen by generalising, and asking whether we would be equally ready to assume that there is a general standard for determining whether it is legitimate and appropriate for a community to take a particular risk. The two suggestions that I have put forward do not depend on the existence of any simple standards. Indeed, the two suggestions could be combined and summarised as follows: *because* there is no simple standard for determining whether it is legitimate and appropriate for a community to act on experimental data despite the lingering risk that the data may be misleading, the best way forward is to analyse the risks as carefully as possible (accepting that they are unlikely to be quantifiable) and then to allow a representative body to determine how to proceed (whether to gamble).

CONCLUSIONS

In the light of the preceding discussion, modest conclusions seem best. This chapter does not purport to dent the claim that experimental behavioural science provides very useful evidence for Evidence scholars. But it has sought to puncture any extravagantly inflated beliefs about the omniscience of scientists. The limits inherent in the substitutions used within the basic experimental method introduce risks that it will be misleading to generalise from experimental results. Moreover, these risks will often be impossible to eradicate or even to measure. The constant presence of unquantifiable risks will probably mean that practical decision-making in the light of available empirical data will be attended by anxiety. There is no simple method for decision-makers to dispel their anxieties, but uncertainty need not become debilitating.

In practical terms, anxiety may be neutralised by reflecting on the other evidential contexts where similar anxieties arise and on the steps which can be taken to clarify what decision-makers are being asked to stake and whether particular gambles seem legitimate, in the light of their understanding of society's expectations and values. Students and scholars trying to understand the dynamics of law reform (including its reliance on empirical data), and to evaluate legislation and judicial decision-making, might profitably attend to the same considerations.

9

Teaching Evidence Scholarship: Evidence and the Practical Process of Proof

ANDREW LIGERTWOOD

INTRODUCTION

THE COLLOQUIUM GIVING rise to this collection of essays was entitled 'Teaching Evidence Scholarship', not 'Teaching the Law of Evidence Scholarship'. Yet, as a colloquium of lawyers, it was a fair assumption that its focus would be Evidence scholarship within the discipline of law. Within that discipline it is the practising lawyer who instinctively understands that the foundations for laws of evidence are not primarily legal and that rules of evidence build upon something else, a 'something else' which can be conceptualised as epistemological. But whilst the legal academic might seek justification for these foundations in the philosophical or the scientific or the logical, the legal practitioner is more likely to see the influence of the cognitive and the psychological and the sociological and the economic.

It is always dangerous for a legal academic to seek explanations in legal practice, for appeals to practice can be seen by other academics as an apology for rigorous analysis or, by practitioners, as naïve or uninformed. Notwithstanding these risks, this chapter emphasises the notion of law as a practical discipline. Within that context its objectives are twofold: first, to explain the complexity of common law evidential issues and, secondly, to propound a particular pedagogical approach to introducing students to that complexity and the need for its scholarly analysis. Later sections of the chapter describe in detail how this practical orientation has shaped the compulsory undergraduate (LLB) Evidence course currently taught at the University of Adelaide.

My thesis is that, within the discipline of law, evidential issues are most effectively analysed and understood in the context of the practical legal process within which they arise. An analysis of this process is consequently the most effective starting point for evidential scholarship. Ultimately, it is the instrumental ends of that legal process which determine when evidential issues arise, and the content of any applicable evidentiary rules.

Evidential issues arise because decisions about facts[1] are made as a consequence of considering evidence.[2] Indeed it is assumed that factual decisions necessarily involve, to some degree, the consideration of evidence.[3] Evidential issues of concern to lawyers arise when decisions within the legal process[4] are to some extent dependent upon determinations of fact. It is the consideration of such decisions which, it will be argued, provides the starting-point for Evidence scholarship within the discipline of law. The regulation of evidential issues through rules of evidence can then be seen as merely one manifestation of the larger practical and instrumental enterprise of legal process.

I am conscious that in England legal process, centrally comprising subjects traditionally described as Civil Procedure, Criminal Procedure and the Law of Evidence, is not generally a compulsory part of the undergraduate degree. This differs from the position in Australia, where professional training requirements have made the study of legal process de facto compulsory in most university law degrees. While the reason for this is essentially pragmatic and imposed by those outside academia, this chapter makes a principled argument for the centrality of legal process, including matters evidential, to an understanding of law and its instrumental ends, and presents a detailed syllabus for translating this pedagogical aspiration into classroom practice.

CONTEXT AND STANDPOINT: LEGAL PROCESS

Evidential issues arise in a variety of contexts and can be looked at from a variety of standpoints. The contexts within which an historian or journalist

---

[1] For the purposes of this discussion, it is assumed that facts are states and events that exist or have existed in the world; that is, a correspondence theory of knowledge is assumed.

[2] Cf P Roberts and A Zuckerman, *Criminal Evidence* (Oxford, OUP, 2004) 2: 'A more informative definition is that the "Law of Evidence" regulates the generation, collection, organization, presentation and evaluation of information ("evidence") for the purposes of resolving disputes about past events in legal adjudication. Less technically we might say in broad terms that the law of evidence governs fact-finding in legal proceedings'.

[3] This assumption can be made on normative and/or positive grounds. Rationalists strive for normative truth based on evidence but, for whatever reason, decisions of fact made in the world have always been based upon evidence of some kind.

[4] Decisions affecting the outcome of legal process are made by all its participants. For example, the outcome of adjudication is affected by decisions made by police investigators, parties, lawyers, witnesses, judges, juries, etc and, if legal process is taken to extend beyond adjudication to embrace the enactment of legislation, the content of legislation is affected by decisions made by all involved in the legislative process. All these decisions involve the determination of facts to some degree or other.

draws conclusions of fact are different from the context in which a court draws factual conclusions. And the approach each might take to the consideration of evidence, and its support for certain factual conclusions, will undoubtedly differ from the approach that a philosopher might take in analysing the justifications for drawing conclusions of fact from particular evidence. Common evidential questions and issues arise in differing contexts, and there may be much to learn from approaches taken in different contexts and from different standpoints. But in the final analysis, it is the particular context and standpoint and its instrumental end that must necessarily determine the approach to be taken to matters evidential.

The question then becomes: in what context and from what standpoint or standpoints do those involved with the discipline of law look at evidential issues? More particularly, as a scholar of that discipline, what is the appropriate context and standpoint from which to commence one's scholarship?

One could commence in an abstract way with the whole problem of human knowledge, and look to philosophical analyses of what knowledge is and how we come to have it. But what then are the *legal* connections? Why are these matters of concern for a scholar of *law*? What contexts are appropriately regarded as *legal*? What standpoints within that context are decisive? Again, it may be possible in an abstract way to seek to describe and explain the nature and scope of legal systems and the various categories of norms that comprise those legal systems, including any categorisation that might be described as evidential. We might in that way seek to analyse the law of evidence. But that analysis will itself be limited if it ignores the standpoint of those who create and enforce the laws within the legal system. Why are legal systems created? What drives law-makers to create particular norms, including those comprising the rules of evidence? Without an appreciation of these instrumental questions, any conceivable analysis fails to capture the very human reasons for having legal systems and laws, and a scholar's quest would seem to be seriously deficient if those reasons, and the standpoints implicit in them, are ignored.

My contention is that law is fundamentally a practical discipline, and also an instrumental discipline: the parameters of the discipline are defined by what those appealing to legal norms are attempting to achieve. A 'top-down' approach to questions of legal evidence, beginning with abstract philosophical questions, is therefore inappropriate. Legal questions need to be understood instrumentally.

The essence of the practice of law is an appeal to normative decision-making. Legal norms function to regulate the conduct of citizens within society. This regulation is achieved by society's empowered legislators[5] laying down in advance norms to which citizens can refer in order to guide their own conduct, and through legislation[6] creating processes which the state or citizens can follow where the applicable norms have apparently been ignored. These processes ultimately result in an authoritative judicial determination of what conduct is appropriate, having regard to the applicable norms. Of course, many difficult questions arise in the context of law's enforcement, since legal rules may be unclear, obscure, apparently contradictory or inapt to cover the instant case.

Bearing all this in mind, one might conceptualise the legal system as ultimately providing a practical process whereby judges authoritatively determine the outcome of disputes between citizens. Legal norms must be looked to as the source of those principles which ultimately provide the reasons for authoritative decision.[7] Seen in this light, the virtues of law and legal process are essentially instrumental.

At one level, legal process involves those citizens who have either been accused of misconduct by the state, or those who are in dispute with fellow citizens and are seeking an appropriate and, if agreement is impossible, authoritative outcome to that dispute. Viewed in this way, adjudicative process is placed centre-stage, and the standpoints of those involved in the adjudicative process become important—investigators, accused and parties, lawyers, mediators, witnesses, judges and jurors. At another level, legislators aspire to lay down guidelines for appropriate conduct by providing norms citizens can follow and by which judges may ultimately and authoritatively determine the outcome of litigated disputes. At a more abstract level one might see electors as somehow involved in this instrumental process, providing authority for legislators and independent judges to set up and administer the legal system.

Evidential issues arise at every level of instrumental legal activity. In every procedural context, participants are obliged to make decisions involving determinations of fact, which in turn involve the consideration of

---

[5] The notion of 'legislator' employed here is broad, ranging from elected Parliament to judges empowered to create precedents in individual cases. At common law the latter form of 'legislation' has always been a fundamentally important supplement to parliamentary legislation and any understanding of the nature and extent of judicial precedent requires an understanding of the processes by which the precedential decision came about.

[6] Whilst process is now often governed by parliamentary legislation and rules of court, at common law process was the very foundation of law, with courts evolving processes (forms of action) through which litigants could seek to enforce their particular interests: FW Maitland, *The Forms of Action at Common Law: a Course of Lectures* (AH Chaytor and WJ Whittaker (eds), Cambridge, CUP, 1962). Adversarial process in criminal cases was also evolved by judges, influenced by the increased involvement of lawyers in process: see generally, JH Langbein, *The Origins of Adversary Criminal Trial* (Oxford, OUP, 2003).

[7] R Dworkin, *Taking Rights Seriously* (London, Duckworth, 1977) ch 4; M Detmold, *The Unity of Law and Morality: a Refutation of Legal Positivism* (London, Routledge & Kegan Paul, 1984).

evidence. In terms of accusation and dispute resolution, evidential issues arise when alleged (mis)conduct is disputed and the court must determine what actually happened. At the legislative level, evidential issues arise as legislators seek to calculate the consequences of formulating laws in one way or another. In broader terms of democratic participation, voters must seek evidence upon which to predict the policies and conduct of their elected representatives. The standpoint of those involved at these various levels of legal process provides the scholar with an obvious starting-point for enquiry. It is with evidential issues that arise within this instrumental process that legal scholars are primarily concerned. And, of course, one must recognise that instrumental legal process itself necessarily imposes normative parameters upon how evidential issues arise and should be resolved.[8]

ISOLATING EVIDENTIAL ISSUES WITHIN LEGAL PROCESS

Having explained the overall legal context and emphasised the fundamental importance of instrumental objectives to evidential issues, the next step is to look more closely at the nature of legal process in order to see where such issues arise. This chapter focuses specifically on common law jurisdictions, but evidential issues necessarily arise within every legal system.[9]

Traditional common law Evidence scholarship, driven by the desire to analyse rules, focused only upon evidential issues arising as part of the adjudicative process. For it is here that one finds a sophisticated system of rules governing evidential issues. But one might see the process that applies at the legislative level as also involving evidential issues. Relatively little attention has been paid to the facts which become influential in determining the content of legislation. One might also argue that more consideration should be given to evidential issues arising in the legislative process where judges are involved.[10] Nonetheless, rigorous analysis of adjudication presents itself as an obvious starting point for the Evidence scholar, if only

---

[8] This is seen, eg, in modern civil rules of court which define a just outcome not simply in terms of reaching a correct decision in a particular case, but in terms of the cost-effectiveness and availability of the system for administering civil justice as a whole: see eg, *Zuckerman on Civil Procedure: Principles of Practice* (London, Sweet and Maxwell, 2006) ch 1.

[9] Evidential issues necessarily arise in all legal systems and must be dealt with appropriately, even in those civil law jurisdictions which have no separate law of evidence. For example, codes of criminal and civil procedure regulate evidential issues where they arise at that level of process which resolves accusation and civil dispute through authoritative determination.

[10] See KC Davis, 'Judicial Notice' (1955) 55 *Columbia Law Review* 945, where the distinction between judges finding 'adjudicative facts' and 'legislative facts' is drawn to emphasise that rules of evidence appear to apply more centrally to the former than the latter. See also A Ligertwood, *Australian Evidence* (4th edn, Sydney, Lexis-Nexis/Butterworths, 2004) paras 6.71–6.73.

because it is here that lawyers and judges are centrally involved and sophisticated rules have been evolved to control evidential issues.

The law of evidence is traditionally conceptualised as regulating only the process of trial. However, as Evidence scholars have now pointed out,[11] well before formal resolution at trial, many evidential decisions must be made which may have a decisive influence upon the adjudicative process. For example, accusation of criminal misconduct generally has its origins in police investigation and police carry the responsibility for collecting and preserving evidence capable of sustaining the accusation at trial. What evidence they collect and preserve may be decisive of authoritative resolution following trial.[12] Civil litigation similarly requires the parties to consider potentially decisive evidential issues from the outset. Few civil disputes reach formal trial and most are settled through agreement without the assistance of outsiders, but before reaching settlement the parties would normally investigate carefully the factual circumstances which have apparently given rise to their differences. Parties must decide where they stand on these factual issues when their differences are negotiated or mediated. Once formal proceedings become more imminent, the parties are likely to focus on evidential issues in deciding whether to seek legal advice concerning more formal process. When lawyers are then consulted, the evidential focus will sharpen as, like the police investigator, lawyers will ensure that they collect and preserve evidence capable of establishing at trial the material facts upon which formal claims are likely to depend. Indeed, there will be a myriad of other factual decisions that will have to be made before advising the client whether to proceed, from determining the attitude of the opponent towards settlement, to determining the depth of the client's pocket if the matter does proceed to judgment and damages. The lawyer must consider all these evidential issues in advising the client about commencing or defending formal proceedings. How these issues are resolved will determine how the lawyer advises the client and assesses the risks involved in formal process. Following the issue of formal process, evidential issues are brought into even sharper relief.

Party responsibility for evidence-gathering and presentation, which gives rise to the nomenclature of adversarial trial, exerts a strong influence upon the consideration of evidential issues throughout the adjudicative process at common law.[13] The other strong influence, which manifests itself

---

[11] Most famously in W Twining, *Rethinking Evidence: Exploratory Essays* (Oxford, Blackwell, 1990; 2nd edn, Cambridge, CUP, 2006); but see also Paul Roberts, Chapter 1.

[12] Other decisions of fact by police, eg, resolving a decision to arrest rather than proceed by summons, are less relevant to later authoritative resolution of the charges brought, although they may give rise to further disputation (eg, in an action for false imprisonment).

[13] Whilst courts in most common law jurisdictions now have extensive powers to ensure that cases are managed efficiently, the responsibility for civil actions still lies primarily with individual litigants. The parties formulate claims and collect evidence and make appropriate

centrally at trial, is the traditional use of the lay jury to decide material facts in issue. Although in most common law jurisdictions juries now sit only to decide serious criminal accusations, the influence of jury trial continues in the common law's demand that evidence be given orally to the court at one continuous hearing. This demand applies whether the trial is before a jury or a judge sitting alone, and has evolved as one of the fundamental characteristics of the common law adversarial trial. The demand for oral testimony coupled with party control at trial has led to that process of oral examination and cross-examination that is now regarded as so central to the common law trial. As a result of these influences, the common law trial has evolved a quite distinct approach to evidential issues. The hearsay rule is justified by the demand for oral process. Whilst in all legal systems accusations and pleadings allege material facts which must be proved if the prosecution or plaintiff's claim is to succeed, at common law these material facts are established through parties calling witnesses to testify orally to the court through a process of examination-in-chief and cross-examination. The court is asked to sit back and decide the facts upon the evidence so presented by the parties.[14] In civil cases, interlocutory steps have diluted the requirement of one continuous hearing, and documentary evidence (extending to witness statements in England) combined with compulsory pre-trial disclosure, have come to dominate civil trials in the interests of efficiency. Still, when issues of fact come to a head, common lawyers continue to turn to what they know, the oral examination and cross-examination of witnesses, to determine factual disputes.

There is a rich complexity of evidential issues that arise during the common law adjudicative process. Much of this is driven by the structure of adversarial trial which lies at the very heart of that process. By analysing evidential issues at trial one can begin to understand their complexity, to understand what need there is for regulation, and to understand what sort of considerations might determine the nature of regulatory supervision. By exposing the difficult and elusive evidential issues inherent in adjudication, and critically at trial, the need for scholarship becomes immediately apparent.

---

applications in carriage of litigation. In common law jurisdictions, court management has not reached the point where judges may have decisive influence in determining the parameters of a case (as they do in civilian law jurisdictions): see Zuckerman, above n 8, para 10.6ff.

[14] See generally MR Damaška, *Evidence Law Adrift* (New Haven, Yale UP, 1997); Langbein, above n 6.

ROOT OF PROCEDURAL COMPLEXITY: FACTUAL UNCERTAINTY

Adjudicative process, particularly at trial, but also encompassing pre-trial procedure and criminal investigations, is notorious for its complexity and sophistry. Many legal rules and procedures were ostensibly devised to facilitate settling disputes about facts. Yet, certainly at common law, legal processes often seem to provide smokescreens to conceal subjective judgements about facts by persons with particular interests in the outcome of proceedings. Police use their position of authority to collect evidence supporting the charges against the accused and to coerce evidence from accused and witnesses, and then use this at trial to achieve their desired conviction.[15] In similar fashion, parties to civil cases posture and manoeuvre prior to trial in order to pressure opponents to make concessions or to settle. They seem only concerned with tactics and evidence in support of their case. Then, the common law trial itself appears to lend itself to party tactics and persuasion. Trial outcomes often appear more dependent upon the interests of the parties and the psychological and sociological idiosyncrasies of jurors, party-selected witnesses and counsel's powers of persuasion, rather than any more objective or normative basis.[16]

An instinctive reaction is to say that there must be a more rational and normative way of determining facts, an approach which could do away with the complexity and sophistry that encourages subjective decisions. If this subjectivity is what 'free proof' comes to, one must question its wisdom and seek more rational procedures.[17] Truly rational fact-finding at trial might permeate into pre-trial process, and progressively eliminate the subjective basis of adjudication.

It is in the realms of probability theory that normative solutions to fact-finding are most readily sought. Evidence scholars from the 1970s have hotly debated whether probability theories can adequately provide a normative guide to fact-finding in the courts. Whilst most scholars have turned to established mathematical notions to develop a normative theory (in particular the self-styled Bayesians),[18] others have sought to use the

---

[15]   The miscarriages of justice that occurred in England in the later years of the twentieth century are extreme examples of how the purpose of the investigators can influence the collection and assembly of evidence, but the same purpose exercises its influence upon the investigation of every crime.

[16]   Books on trial advocacy appear to endorse these techniques: see, eg, TA Mauet and LA McCrimmon, *Fundamentals of Trial Techniques* (2nd edn, Sydney, LBC Information Services, 2001).

[17]   Some intuitive concept of free proof arguably lies at the heart of all legal systems dependent upon the proof of facts: LJ Cohen, 'Freedom of Proof' (1983) 16 *Archiv für Rechts und Socialphilosophie* 1.

[18]   Whilst Prof Tribe warned in 1971 of the pitfalls of mathematical analysis in determining facts (LH Tribe, 'Trial by Mathematics: Precision and Ritual in the Legal Process' (1971) 84 *Harvard Law Review* 1329) the effect was rather to stimulate interest in the use of

reasoning of the courts to justify a different, albeit still apparently normative, 'inductive' approach.[19] But the normative justifications of the inductive approach are doubtful, and orthodox probability theory seems in most cases beyond the competence of those participating in the trial process.[20] Moreover, where a consideration of probabilistic reasoning has been forced upon courts as a result of the presentation of evidence in probabilistic terms, as occurs when DNA evidence is presented as a 'likelihood ratio', courts have refused to encourage juries, for fear of confusion, to employ mathematical analysis (in particular, Bayesian analysis) in determining evidential weight. The Court of Appeal in *R v Denis Adams*[21] gave short shrift to such analysis, and Australian courts are similarly reluctant to direct juries on the logic of Bayesian inference (although not reluctant to permit DNA evidence to be presented in terms of a likelihood ratio).[22]

From the perspective of an instrumentally-orientated adjudicative process, such reluctance is understandable. Even the committed Bayesians appear to recognise the practical impossibility of humans utilising a normative mathematical probability analysis. Even if jurors were replaced with triers of sufficient intelligence and training to understand the application of probabilistic norms, the required number of computations cannot be cognitively achieved by a human being; and even if they could be achieved with the assistance of computers, these mathematically adept triers would be hard-pressed to provide even roughly accurate subjective assessments of frequencies or chances to which the canons of mathematical probability could be applied. In the end, one could have little confidence

---

mathematical analysis in determining facts. The end result was a school of jurists who advocated Bayesian logic as the appropriate method for determining the probability of facts in relationship to tendered evidence: DH Kaye, 'What is Bayesianism? A Guide for the Perplexed' (1988) 28 *Jurimetrics J* 161; DH Kaye, 'The Laws of Probability and the Law of the Land' (1979) 47 *University of Chicago Law Review* 34; B Robertson and GA Vignaux, 'Probability: the Logic of the Law' (1993) 13 *Oxford Journal of Legal Studies* 457; B Robertson and GA Vignaux, *Interpreting Evidence: Evaluating Forensic Science in the Courtroom* (London, Wiley, 1995); R Friedman, 'Assessing Evidence' (1996) 94 *Michigan Law Review* 1810; RJ Allen and M Redmayne (eds), *Bayesianism and Juridical Proof, E & P* Special Issue 1(6) (London, Blackstone Press, 1997).

[19] LJ Cohen, *The Probable and the Provable* (Oxford, Clarendon Press, 1977). It might be argued that Cohen was concerned simply to explain the logic employed by courts in finding facts rather than advocating a normative system.

[20] See CR Callen, 'Notes on a Grand Illusion: Some Limits on the Use of a Bayesian Theory in Evidence Law' (1982) 57 *Indiana Law Journal* 1, 10–15; CR Callen, 'Second Order Considerations, Weight, Sufficiency and Schema Theory: a Comment on Professor Brilmayer's Theory' (1986) 66 *Buffalo University Law Review* 715, 726 n 72: 'for the consistent use of Bayesian theory for the updating of probabilities by conditionalization, where thirty items of evidence are introduced relevant to an inference, one must record a billion probabilities'.

[21] [1996] 2 Cr App R 467.

[22] See A Ligertwood, 'Avoiding Bayes in DNA Cases' (2003) 77 *Australian Law Journal* 317.

that experts in probability analysis would make determinations of fact significantly closer to the truth than lay juries and judges. And their reasoning processes would be a mystery to litigants, parties and other participants in the trial process.

Consequently it appears that the probability debate is dead in the water, in the sense that the aspiration to a normative approach to fact-finding seems utterly impractical. Mathematical probabilities may be used as an heuristic against which some decisions of fact may be analysed and criticised but they are inappropriate for practical application in a court of law.[23] We appear, therefore, to be thrown back on a process that, even if it aspires for objective truth, remains dependent upon the vagaries of human nature and the fallible methods by which 'ordinary' humans go about their business, rather than having any normative justification for its factual conclusions. Many researchers now concentrate on explaining how human beings go about determining past events through the construction of consistent narratives.[24]

NORMATIVE GOALS OF PROCESS

Even if one accepts the aspiration to objectivity in fact-finding, one must at the same time face the practical limitations of any normative approach and seek in consequence a process able to accommodate these limitations. More radically, one might question whether competing values or objectives trump normative truth-finding or, less radically, provide protections against the practical limits of our current theories of fact-finding. By returning to the ultimate purpose of legal process, the enquiry takes on a perspective which is lost on the mathematician seeking only a normative solution to the discovery of facts, and equally lost on the sociologist or psychologist who sees only a perplexing plurality of influences determining the actions of humans within that process.

Serious analysis of process must first seek to distinguish the various matters which give rise to the need for process. One only has to recall the number of distinct courts and their characteristic procedures to realise that there cannot be one idealised process model that fits all.

---

[23] See RJ Allen, 'The Nature of Juridical Proof' (1991) 13 *Cardozo Law Review* 373; RJ Allen, 'Factual Ambiguity and a Theory of Evidence' (1994) 88 *Northwestern University Law Review* 604.

[24] See eg, N Pennington and R Hastie, 'Juror Decision-Making Models: the Generalisation Gap' (1981) 89 *Psychology Bulletin* 246, 251; N Pennington and R Hastie, 'Evidence Evaluation in Complex Decision Making' (1986) 51 *J Personality and Soc Psychology* 242, 244; WL Bennett and MS Feldman, *Reconstructing Reality in the Courtroom* (New Jersey, Rutgers University Press, 1984).

Most fundamentally, a distinction can be drawn between process existing to enable autonomous citizens to determine through settlement or judgment the differences between them (civil process) and process existing to determine whether alleged law-breakers should be punished (criminal process).[25] The starting-point in each case is fundamentally different and the results of each process are distinct: the civil case is determined by agreement or appropriate adjustment of the situation between the parties; the criminal case starts with an accusation of misconduct by the state against a citizen and is determined through the imposition of punishment by the state or the dismissal of the accusation. The civil dispute may be resolved without any definitive determination of the facts giving rise to the dispute; the parties may agree upon a solution or opt for mediation, arbitration or some other private settlement in preference to seeking a judgment from the court. It is less easy to see how the criminal accusation can avoid judicial determination, although the accused may concede the truth of the allegation by pleading guilty.[26] However, once civil cases go to trial they also assume the appearance of accusations, with one party, the 'plaintiff' or 'claimant', alleging that a certain state of affairs created by his opponent, the defendant, gives rise to a legal remedy. Many civil suits are from the outset really a set of accusations of more widely anti-social behaviour (for example, class actions alleging toxic torts).

It would be completely unrealistic to assert that the determination of facts did not play a major part in deciding the outcome of both civil and criminal cases. But the important question is the extent to which the aims of process impose further normative requirements, demanding that other interests be taken into consideration, and the extent to which these other interests affect matters evidential. One also needs to ask whether these interests are the same in civil and criminal cases and whether different procedural aims produce normative differences in evidential process.[27]

In neither civil nor criminal cases does the common law aspire to factual rectitude at all costs. Neither are the resources for factual enquiry unlimited, nor the range of appropriate techniques for fact-finding. At common law there are many similarities in civil and criminal process but the inherent nature of each proceeding must lead to some differences in approach. The criminal case, as an accusation which might lead to the loss of liberty, demands strict proof of the facts constituting the accusation and some guarantee that the innocent will not be wrongly convicted. Hence the requirement that material facts be proved beyond reasonable doubt. As a

---

[25] See Roberts and Zuckerman, above n 2, 5–9.
[26] Even following a guilty plea, factual decisions can hardly be avoided in the determination of the appropriate punishment by the court.
[27] Roberts and Zuckerman, above n 2, 5–9, are in agreement that criminal and civil evidence should receive separate treatment. Also see Paul Roberts, Chapter 1.

practical adjustment of the situation between the parties, civil judgment may be rendered on the basis of less certain factual conclusions. Hence the requirement that facts need only be proved on the balance of probabilities. Moreover, in civil cases subject to the principle of proportionality, the rationing of resources may require the case to be settled out of court or that it proceed to trial before there is time fully and comprehensively to compile all the evidence of material facts.

Some argue that civil and criminal evidence should be analysed separately.[28] In response, it might be argued that whilst criminal and civil processes do impose different normative constraints, their approach to decisions of fact—the central notion of matters evidential—is consistent. From a strictly evidential point of view, it is preferable not to hive off evidential issues into separate criminal and civil compartments. A unified approach to the law of evidence facilitates comparative investigation of matters evidential across different procedural contexts. In this way, it should be possible to isolate the distinctive normative restraints imposed on the determination of facts by particular forms of procedure.

TEACHING EVIDENCE TO EMPHASISE THE COMPLEXITY OF EVIDENTIAL ISSUES IN LEGAL PROCESS

Evidential issues are part of a complex and sophisticated human process. As a human process, in the absence of any acceptable normative approach to fact-finding, Evidence scholarship seeks an understanding of the participation of persons in that process and how, in the context of determining matters evidential, their behaviour might be modified to achieve its instrumental ends.

How, then, to begin teaching students about evidential issues as they arise within this adjudicative process and centrally at trial? I always begin by attempting to provide students with an appreciation of the wider procedural context. Anecdotal personal experience of criminal litigation as a practising lawyer subsequently provided the foundation for a course devoted to more abstract analysis of the procedural context within which evidential issues arise, including examination of the epistemological

---

[28] Indeed this belief is acted upon by Paul Roberts and Adrian Zuckerman in Roberts taking primary responsibility for *Criminal Evidence*, above n 2, whilst Zuckerman now focuses his work on civil procedure: see above n 8. Evidential issues receive little prominence in books on civil procedure, which tend to focus on the objects of the civil justice system as a whole. In Australia the essential unity of Evidence law is assumed and encouraged by the Evidence Act 1995 (Cth) which now forms the basis for 'uniform' legislation in New South Wales and Tasmania. Other states may join this uniform scheme: see the joint report of 2005 of the Australian Law Reform Commission (Report 102), the New South Wales Law Reform Commission (Report 112) and the Victorian Law Reform Commission (Final Report) on *Uniform Evidence Law*.

assumptions that appear to underlie that process. The lessons of this experience were two-fold. First, even when one merely scratches the epistemological surface, the nature of fact-finding is extremely elusive. Secondly, this elusiveness itself provides a justification for common law procedural process which leaves it to parties to define issues and control the collection and presentation of evidence at trial. It also underpins the assumption that the oral testimony of eyewitnesses, which gives the opportunity for opponents to cross-examine, is the most appropriate way to present and test evidence. Ceding control to the parties in this way, on the one hand, gives them the greatest opportunity to invoke those epistemological and other arguments they regard as favourable to their cause, and on the other hand, invokes ideas of equality and procedural fairness (widely construed to imply protections against unreliable evidence whenever and however generated) which might somehow be regarded as making up for the inherent uncertainty of the fact-finding process.[29] In my teaching, the elusiveness of proof and the common law's acceptance of an adversarial oral process are prominent in providing a coherent explanation of the common law rules of evidence. Furthermore, my treatise on *Australian Evidence*[30] is organised around these principles of adversarial proof. In theory these principles provide a powerful explanation of how evidential issues arise in legal proceedings and inform the underlying rationales of the common law's evidentiary rules.[31]

Yet abstract exposition does not really capture the complexity of the situations in which evidential decisions are made. Nor does abstract exposition ever really convey why the proof of facts within the common law adversarial oral trial is so elusive. These complexities are best and most profoundly appreciated by first-hand exposure to the practical processes of adjudication, or to the next-best-thing in the classroom: student role-play in mock trials.

Many academic lawyers of my generation remain sceptical of the practical. University scholars for the most part replaced practitioner-teachers, who lectured, after-hours, to students who were primarily seeking admission to professional legal practice. Whilst such teachers might show students 'the ropes' of legal practice at a relatively superficial level, the bigger and more critical picture necessary to understand the discipline of law is unlikely to emerge from a predominantly practice-orientated train-ing. Hence the need for professional law teachers with time to develop

---

[29] See Ligertwood, above n 10, esp ch 1.
[30] *Ibid.*
[31] Whether these principles should continue to dominate the formulation of evidential rules is, of course, a separate question.

more coherent, broader and critical perspectives, today regarded as central to the notion of a university education.[32]

Global scepticism of the practical is not necessarily the appropriate conclusion to be drawn from the evident limitations of the practitioner-teacher. One might criticise the practitioner-teacher who has little training, experience or, more crucially, time, to develop reflective courses and teaching skills. Yet, if one takes the view that law remains a practical and instrumental discipline, then critical perspectives need to be developed in the light of what the law and its legal practitioners are trying to do. As participants in this instrumental discipline, practitioners must have insights beyond those of academics who have never practised law in this instrumental way. I would argue that all lawyers are involved in legal process at some level, such that an understanding of any area of law can only be enhanced through consideration of the practitioner's inside view. But for present purposes it is enough to assert that the insights of practitioners involved in the formal administration of adjudicative justice, in particular at trial, are crucial to an understanding of the evidential issues that arise, and the rules of evidence that apply, within that process.

How does a university-based scholar communicate the insights of the legal practitioner effectively? An obvious method is to invite friendly practitioners to come to class and provide anecdotal examples of their work. One might also show students films of trials. One might have students attend the courts. These are all useful methods. But I have reached the conclusion that the most effective way to communicate the inside view is to have students themselves participate in the process.

This conclusion was reached after the curriculum for the LLB at the University of Adelaide was changed to teach subjects over one semester and to incorporate (so-called) legal skills. Whilst my experience with legal skills courses run in satisfaction of admission requirements had made me sceptical of their intellectual content and hence suitability for teaching at a university, I was at the same time much concerned that teaching Evidence in a single semester would be too constrained. From a tactical point of view, by associating Evidence with one of the legal skills subjects taught in the same semester, some curriculum pressure might be relieved. I consequently developed a course combining the law of evidence ('Evidence') with an Introduction to Advocacy ('Advocacy') with the object of using the

---

[32] Paul Roberts, Chapter 1, formulates this 'foundational principle' for university Evidence teachers: 'The Law of Evidence should make its contribution to the overarching goals and values of university education, by inculcating relevant, robust and adaptable (more or less) transferable skills, helping students to become life-long learners (self-teachers), and promoting responsible citizenship. Evidence courses will naturally develop skills and provide information that will be useful to the minority of students entering pertinent areas of legal practice. But this instrumental objective is only a subsidiary, component part of the broader remit of Evidence teaching'.

'skills' teaching to provide intellectual insight into evidential issues.[33] Four years of teaching these combined courses have convinced me that student participation in evidence marshalling exercises and mock trials has not just resulted in a much greater appreciation by students of evidential rules, but has also given them a greater appreciation of the complexity of the process and its influence upon matters evidential and legal decisions generally.

Before describing the detailed content of these courses and indicating their potential for generating insights into evidential issues, I should explain (for the benefit of Evidence teachers who might wish to experiment along similar lines) how these courses are administered and assessed at Adelaide.[34] There are a number of common features: each course is compulsory; they must be taken together and in the same 12-week semester; the teaching is primarily through participatory seminar rather than by expositional lecture; to facilitate teaching by seminar the class is divided into groups of 24 students who stay together and with the same teacher for seminars in both subjects (we usually have eight seminar groups in any one year); each week students have a lecture and a two-hour seminar in each subject; and students are required to attend and prepare thoroughly for at least 10 of the 12 seminars in each subject. There are also many differences: Evidence is weighted at four contact hours a week and Advocacy at two, reflecting the fact that the reading and analysis in Evidence is more extensive and provides the basis for follow-up Advocacy exercises; Evidence seminars consist of the discussion of problems based upon set materials, whereas in Advocacy seminars teams of students conduct a trial before the teacher acting as judge; Evidence is assessed individually on the basis of assignments and exams whereas Advocacy assessment is based upon each team's capacity to conduct a trial, measured by a trial notebook memorialising the preparation, presentation, evidence and argument in the case (a group mark), together with an assessment of each individual student's performance in examining witnesses and present-ing oral argument (a personalised mark). Each week commences with a lecture introducing the evidence topic for the week. Where appropriate, a practitioner will lecture on a related point of advocacy. In Wednesday seminars students discuss materials and problems dealing with that topic; and then on the Friday students enact an aspect of trial in which it figures.

---

[33] At the same time we set up a course teaching Civil and Criminal Procedure (CCP) in association with a legal skills course (Litigation Practice). This combined course is taken in the first semester as a prerequisite to the Evidence/Advocacy course offered in the second semester. Both combined courses share the same philosophy and approach, and the cases developed procedurally by students in first semester are subsequently taken to trial in Introduction to Advocacy in second semester.

[34] The same features define the approach to the combined CCP/Litigation Practice courses taken in first semester as a prerequisite to Evidence/Advocacy courses in second semester.

Integration of the evidence and advocacy components is facilitated through the conceptual orientation of the Evidence course, founded on the organising concept of proof through adversarial trial. Rules in civil and criminal cases are dealt with together in the light of this organising concept, although in the final four weeks the focus turns to those rules peculiar to criminal cases which seek to protect the accused against possibly prejudicial or unreliable evidence consistent with the strict standard of proof in a criminal trial. This curriculum might appear narrower than that of many comparable Evidence courses, in that it excludes privileges and immunities and pre-trial criminal process. However, in Adelaide these topics are taught as part of the procedure course held in first semester, which is a prerequisite for the second-semester Evidence course.[35] This still leaves a substantial amount of material to be covered in Evidence. Progression is facilitated by providing lecture notes and materials to students in advance of the seminars on the University's intranet.

The trial advocacy exercises are organised around two student-led trials.[36] The first is a civil trial which focuses on the presentation of evidence, the way evidential rules affect that presentation and the need to persuade the court to find the case proved (Weeks 1 to 8). This is followed by a criminal trial exercise where the focus is upon rules unique to criminal cases and features the presentation of persuasive argument for or against the reception of particular evidence in the light of those rules (Weeks 9 to 12). Students work in teams of three and assume responsibility for running a case for a nominated party. Paired teams become opponents in mock trial scenarios, taking turns to conduct advocacy exercises.[37] These exercises are supported by an introductory text which explains, with examples, how the various advocacy exercises are in practice approached.[38]

Week 1 introduces the concept of proving material facts in issue through reliance on relevant and admissible evidence. The emphasis is upon isolating the material facts in issue with precision, and pinpointing the evidence that is being considered to establish one or more of those material facts. This at once underscores the very single-minded instrumental ends of the evidential process, explains concepts of relevance and admissibility and

---

[35]   See above nn 33 and 34.

[36]   These are based upon cases which students have been developing procedurally in first semester in CCP and Litigation Practice (see above n 33).

[37]   In each seminar group of 24 students there are eight teams, four acting for plaintiffs (or the DPP) and four for defendants. One could simply pair up a plaintiff and a defendant and let them run their own trial, but this is a learning exercise and it is important for students to see how their classmates perform and to receive feedback from teacher-judges. Resources permitting, two judges are provided for each seminar group allowing two trials to be run in parallel for each group. While each team opens and closes, teams take turns in presenting the evidence. Thus, each team remains obliged to keep track of their trial as a whole and to maintain a record for their (assessed) trial notebooks.

[38]   Mauet and McCrimmon, above n 16.

proof, and raises practical questions about collecting and organising evidence to meet the applicable standard of proof. This approach also emphasises the dependence of proof upon the evidence collected and presented. Inferential analysis is introduced, with reference to Wigmorean charts. Brief mention is made of the presentation of DNA evidence and the problem of combining statistical information with other evidence.

Advocacy teaching invites students to organise evidence in relation to a civil 'case' prepared for trial over the ensuing seven weeks. In order to ensure that these advocacy exercises proceed in an orderly fashion and reflect the evidential issues selected for discussion each week, the material facts in issue and the available evidence (documents, exhibits and witness proofs) are stipulated. On the basis of these stipulations, students are encouraged to use the analysis introduced in Evidence to determine what evidential information to tender in proof (or disproof) of the material facts in issue.

In Week 2 the adversarial nature of the common law trial and the primary responsibility of the parties to carry the case forward are highlighted. Burdens of proof (evidential and legal) and the effect of presumptions, the requirements of a case to answer and the need for courts to act only upon the evidence presented by the parties, rather than themselves calling witnesses or acting upon their own knowledge, are explained. Whilst in Evidence these notions are introduced through case analysis and problems, in Advocacy the responsibilities of the parties in running the case are emphasised. Students must compose their opening addresses and outline exactly what evidence they will be calling to fulfil their adversarial obligations.

Week 3 in Evidence focuses upon the different forms of evidence available to litigants, distinguishing between testimonial evidence, documentary evidence and real evidence. Emphasis is placed on the primacy of oral testimony and the hearsay prohibition against presenting testimony through the tender of documents. At the same time, the importance of authenticating documents and physical objects ('real evidence') tendered as original evidence or in exception to the hearsay rule is stressed. In Advocacy, the trial proper begins. Four 'witnesses' (students equipped with stock scripts) are called, two for the plaintiff and two for the defendant.[39] The exercise comprises a simple examination-in-chief and procedures for tendering and authenticating documents, photographs and real evidence.[40]

---

[39] In this respect our civil trial does not reflect what happens in practice where the defendant's case follows the plaintiff's. The progression of exercises could not be controlled if our trial adopted this more realistic format.

[40] The advocacy text provides examples: Mauet and McCrimmon, above n 16, chs 4 and 5.

Oral adversarial presentation of testimony through the examination and cross-examination of witnesses and the exclusion of hearsay evidence occupy Weeks 4 to 8 of the Evidence course. These topics are all central to the common law adversarial trial and the general rules apply in both civil and criminal cases. Advocacy classes for these components of the course feature student witnesses primed with confidential instructions. Week 4 focuses upon issues arising from examination-in-chief, for example, the use of documents to refresh memory and dealing with adverse or hostile witnesses. Week 5 considers issues arising during cross-examination, for example, the need to comply with the rule in *Browne v Dunn*,[41] the limits of cross-examination as to credit, the finality of answers to collateral questions and cross-examination on documents. Week 6 explores the admissibility and presentation of expert evidence. In Week 7, students are permitted to call a witness of their choice to complete the evidence in their case (to focus attention back on the need to ensure evidence in support of their overall case). Final addresses are made by each side in Week 8. Although hearsay points arise intermittently throughout these various exercises, the hearsay rule and its exceptions are dealt with in some depth in Evidence classes in Weeks 7 and 8.

Weeks 9 to 12 concentrate upon those evidential rules which apply specifically in criminal cases: the silence of the accused and confessional evidence in Week 9; evidence revealing the character of the accused in Weeks 10 (in-chief) and 11 (in cross-examination); and other testimony carrying risks of unreliability which might require some judicial direction or warning in Week 12. In Advocacy, we devise *voir dire* applications which give rise to these issues in the context of a criminal case. Students argue for and against the application. Whilst more limited than the earlier civil procedure exercises, these role-plays continue to emphasise orality, powers of persuasion, analytic rigour and the virtues of thorough preparation. With exams in Evidence fast approaching, students are now permitted to concentrate upon understanding evidential rules and their application rather than grappling with the complexities arising from the presentation of evidence.

The primary objective of this course is to teach Evidence in a practical context which demonstrates the complexity of evidential issues and the delicate contingencies which make the application of evidential rules often so difficult to predict. This lays a foundation for more ambitious forays into Evidence scholarship. One can then examine evidential complexity from various perspectives, from the normative to the positive, from the cognitive and psychological to the sociological, from the view of law enforcement to the protection of the rights and dignity of the participants

---

[41] (1894) 6 R 67, HL.

in the process. Evidence scholarship injects all these things into the analysis of evidential process. Although the proof of facts within an adversarial trial structure is the course's organising principle, this principle and its normative implications are themselves opened up to critical scrutiny.

Until one has actually played the role of the lawyer, one cannot begin to appreciate what an integral (and powerful) part the lawyer plays within the adversarial process, nor comprehend the significance of the lawyer's ethical responsibilities. The lawyer defines issues, develops hypotheses and themes, collects evidence and adduces testimony through examination-in-chief and cross-examination. In role-play scenarios, the emphasis of the common law trial upon testimonial evidence and the effects of this emphasis become immediately apparent. The contingency of testimony on the questions asked, the words chosen in answer, witnesses' memory for detail, the relative articulacy of individual witnesses, and so forth, are experienced at first-hand. One soon appreciates that theories of probability are little help in accepting the testimony of eyewitnesses and that there are sociological and psychological and cognitive issues that are much more important. By the same token, students playing the roles of witnesses can see the contingencies of evidence from the other side, and can appreciate the intricate detail required if testimony is to be put forward convincingly.[42] Although full-time and part-time (practitioner-)teachers generally act as judges, in the advocacy exercises students are asked at some stage to join the bench to appreciate the communicative trial process from the other side of the courtroom.

There is much talk these days of universities becoming more vocationally-orientated. In an immediate sense, advocacy role-play involves teaching lawyerly skills to students. Yet the rationale of the pedagogical innovations discussed in this chapter goes much deeper. Teaching trial advocacy as such is not the point of my course. It does not aspire to impart the techniques and tricks of persuasion or to equip would-be advocates to push the informational envelope at trial. Rather, the course is a medium for demonstrating the deeper issues of process and evidence in order to develop students' critical interest and understanding of these issues.

Experimentation with role-play also contains valuable lessons for educa-tors. Many law teachers are reluctant to involve themselves in practical exercises, fearing that they lack the practical training or experience to carry it off.[43] But the potential benefits and challenges of pedagogical innovation

---

[42] Experts are, however, virtually impossible to role-play effectively. No prepared script can be a proper substitute for the detailed knowledge and experience constituting genuine scientific or other expertise.

[43] The reticence of academics to enter pastures beyond black-letter law is adverted to by Paul Roberts, Chapter 1.

must be understood in terms of the teacher's overriding objectives. First, to repeat, the role-play exercises advocated here are not conducted to teach practical skills in any simple, vocational sense, but to develop an intelligent and critical approach to problems of process and evidence, the traditional staples of Evidence teaching. Secondly, the experience of teachers at Adelaide suggests that it does not take long for experienced academics to feel comfortable with the nature and skills of the practical process, particularly when assuming the role of trial judge. It should be remembered that in practice a trial judge is always personally in charge of what happens in his or her court, albeit subject to possible appeal. Seldom do trial judges observe their judicial colleagues in action during trial.

The principal shortcoming of role-playing exercises lies in their apparent superficiality. One merely has an opportunity to raise questions about process and evidence, not to develop complex strategies in relation to those problems, although supplementary advanced courses might develop the analysis. It must also be admitted that the combined course is fairly resource intensive.[44] Devising mock trials and ensuring that each case proceeds coherently week by week can be relatively onerous for instructors. However, the predictable criticism that such a course is too orientated to practical vocational training simply misses the point. As I have emphasised from the start, law is a practical discipline, to be understood, ultimately, through its complex procedural practices. Every judgment studied in a substantive law subject is a consequence of the contingencies of legal process. This is an important insight for anyone seriously interested in studying and understanding law.

CONCLUSION

William Twining has long argued that the perspectives adopted by Evidence scholars are too narrow. Rules of evidence should instead be seen in their wider context. This chapter has argued that the relevant context is process, and that process is instrumental and practical. If one approaches law as a practical and instrumental discipline one cannot avoid exposing the complexity of evidential issues. This throws open the doors to a wide-ranging Evidence scholarship. Whilst some might think it ironic that Evidence scholarship has been nudged towards the practical by a legal philosopher, this chapter maintains that a practical orientation is essential if we are to begin to understand matters evidential within the discipline of law.

---

[44] In Evidence, eight seminar groups meet for two hours each week; in Advocacy there are 16 trial sessions each running for two hours each week. Half the trial sessions are led by practitioners.

Viewed in their practical procedural context, the wider issues of Evidence scholarship necessarily arise. By focusing upon common law adjudicative process as it manifests itself at trial, inferential analysis becomes important when counsel provides an advice bearing on questions of fact, or when the advocate first attempts to marshal the available evidence in order to devise a persuasive trial strategy. The relationship between probabilistic proof and persuasive proof immediately asserts itself in adjudication, as do pressing ethical considerations. How far can the trial envelope be pushed from an ethical perspective? Lawyers are also obliged to grapple with issues arising from the ways in which evidence has been collected by law enforcement authorities, including possible breaches of protective procedural standards. An additional comparative dimension can be introduced into the analysis by explaining that civil law jurisdictions do not accept such partisan control of the process nor the supremacy of oral testimony.

Role-plays and advocacy exercises bring Evidence doctrine to life. This chapter has set out in detail one tried-and-tested model for an Evidence course incorporating a pronounced practical orientation. Having introduced students to this insider-perspective, lawyers' control over the common law evidential process during adjudication, particularly at trial, becomes all too apparent. This is a fundamental insight not only for the student of Evidence who aspires to practice but also for anyone seeking scholarly understanding of evidential issues within common law process.

10

Battling a Good Story: Cross-examining the Failure of the Law of Evidence

JILL HUNTER*

INTRODUCTION: LIMITED IMPACT OF LEGAL REFORMS ON CROSS-EXAMINATION

The way to find out whether a witness is lying is to basically confront that witness', Mr [S] said. 'Does the witness squirm, does the witness sweat, does the witness not have a ready answer? It''s that moment that's at the heart of the trial.[1]

THIS CHAPTER EXPLORES the common law's 200-year-old love affair with lawyers' cross-examination. It examines the law of evidence regulating witness impeachment, a law that operates with immense technicality and legalism. It examines also the inequality of the cross-examiner and the witness, and the major dynamic impacting upon witness impeachment, that is, advocacy in cross-examination. Despite the fact that cross-examination is central to the common law criminal trial this dynamic is barely touched by legal regulation.[2]

Cross-examination is founded on a mindset of profound mistrust of witnesses. Wigmore illustrates law's suspicion of witnesses in his *Treatise*

---

* Thanks to Jill Anderson, Mark Aronson, Dorne Boniface, Terese Henning and Paul Roberts for their comments and suggestions.
[1] P Belluck, 'Court Ruling May Remove Some of the Drama from Massachusetts Criminal Trials', *New York Times*, 2 April 2006.
[2] It enjoys a particularly privileged status in the United States by virtue of the Sixth Amendment's confrontation clause which provides that '[i]n all criminal prosecutions, the accused shall enjoy the right . . . to be confronted with the witnesses against him'. See also *Crawford v Washington*, 124 S. Ct. 1354, 158 L. Ed. 2d 177 (2004); *R(D) v Camberwell Green Youth Court* [2005] 1 WLR 393, HL; and *Grant v R* [2006] UKPC (Jamaica) 2.

where he refers to 'false claimants and pretended victims of wrongs'.[3] But suspicion of witnesses persists today. For example, in 2005 Lord Rodger in *R(D) v Camberwell Green Youth Court* observed:[4]

> Relatively few crimes are committed ... in front of disinterested, sober, upright members of the public ... [Certain] witnesses will give deliberately false evidence that is designed to conceal the actual course of events ... many witnesses of this kind [youths under the age of 17 years] are only too little affected by the formality of the trial proceedings or by any judicial sanctions which might be imposed for their failure to speak up or for their perjury ... The unenviable task of the jury in such cases is to assess the witnesses and to try to pick out those parts of their evidence that are truthful and reliable.

Such sentiments reinforce cross-examination's primacy in the process of testing evidence, a primacy that was arguably justified in the early days of the common law criminal trial when the investigation and prosecution of crime were not professionalised. But times *have* changed. In his *Treatise* Wigmore referred to cross-examination as 'the greatest legal engine ever invented for the discovery of truth'.[5] However preceding this aphorism are two sentences that are quoted far less often. It is timely to redress this imbalance:

> Not even the abuses, mishandlings, and the puerilities which are so often found associated with cross-examination have availed to nullify its value. It may be that in more than one sense it takes the place in our system which torture occupied in the medieval system of the civilians.

As revealed by Wigmore's observation of cross-examination's dark side, it can be a force that damages witnesses. Modern statutory protections for witnesses have developed in a piecemeal fashion,[6] with an initial focus on rape trials.[7] Here, historically embedded misogyny in the law and in the legal profession facilitated an almost unbounded cultural lack of constraint over cross-examiners. Rape shield laws heralded the acknowledgment that sexual assault complainant witnesses should and could be protected from degrading, diminishing and functionally deficient cross-examination. They

---

[3] Uttered in opposition to fettering the cross-examination of witnesses, see JH Wigmore, *A Treatise on the Anglo-American System of Evidence in Trials at Common Law* (Boston, Little, Brown & Co, 1940) vol 3, para 963, p 523; and see below n 98.

[4] In relation to an application for 'special measures' to accommodate the needs of vulnerable witnesses: [2005] 1 WLR 393 [6].

[5] Wigmore, above n 3, vol 5, para 1367, p 29.

[6] See Youth Justice and Criminal Evidence Act 1999, s 41: any evidence of the complainant's sexual behaviour is deemed irrelevant, 'if it appears to the court to be reasonable to assume that the purpose (or main purpose) for which it would be adduced or asked is to establish or elicit material for impugning the credibility of the complainant as a witness'. See also S Easton, 'The Use of Sexual History Evidence in Rape Trials' in M Childs and L Ellison (eds), *Feminist Perspectives on Evidence* (London, Cavendish, 2000).

[7] See *R(D) v Camberwell Green Youth Court* [2005] 1 WLR 393.

did so chiefly by demanding cross-examiners adhere to the requirement of relevance. Yet experience transcending national boundaries[8] unfortunately demonstrates that the machismo adversarial legal culture of cross-examination of sexual assault complainants is difficult to displace or even reduce to any significant extent.

A second wave of law reform focuses on ameliorating the emotional impact of in-court questioning by extending protection beyond sexual assault complainant witnesses to vulnerable and intimidated witnesses. These may be victims, parties or bystanders.[9] For these witnesses, special measures[10] offer physical protection from the brutality of the court process by making the cross-examiner's verbal attacks on witnesses' dignity and privacy less immediate and consequently less emotionally punitive. Cooper and Roberts' study, *Special Measures for Vulnerable and Intimidated Witnesses: an Analysis of Crown Prosecution Service Monitoring Data*,[11] provides indicative figures on the use of, and arguably by implication the need for, special measures for vulnerable and intimidated prosecution witnesses across a major sector of the Crown Prosecution Service during 2003/04. This study showed that in this 12-month period 6,064 witnesses were identified as vulnerable and intimidated (4,500 children and 1,500 adults). Almost three-quarters of the adults were female, with the 'child witness' category roughly gender-balanced; 64 per cent were 'victim' (complainant) witnesses.

The latest generation of reforms have built on these progressively victim-centred initiatives, but extended the reform reach to all witnesses, not just those deemed 'vulnerable'. Criminal Justice Act 2003, s 100, creates a potentially significant bar for the admission of evidence of a

---

[8] See C Eastwood and W Paton, *The Experiences of Child Complainants of Sexual Abuse in the Criminal Justice System* (Brisbane, Queensland University of Technology, 2002); New Zealand Law Commission, *Evidence: Total Recall? The Reliability of Witness Testimony*, Miscellaneous Paper 13 (1999); *Heroines of Fortitude: the Experiences of Women in Court as Victims of Sexual Assault* (Woolloomooloo, NSW Office for Women, 1996); T Henning, *Sexual Reputation and Sexual Experience Evidence in Tasmanian Proceedings relating to Sexual Offences*, Occasional Paper No 4 (University of Tasmania, Law Press, 1996).

[9] In England, these protections did not originally extend to the accused, see Youth Justice and Criminal Evidence Act (YJCEA) 1999, ss 16 and 17; see now YJCEA 1999, s 33A, as inserted by Police and Justice Act 2006, s 47. Cf Evidence (Children) Act 1997 (NSW), s 19, for the accused child's right to give evidence via CCTV in New South Wales.

[10] For witnesses under the age of 17 years, those with a physical disability or disorder, a learning disability or mental disorder, or witnesses 'experiencing fear or distress likely to diminish the quality of the witness's evidence', protections include screens, closed circuit TV, a closed court, mufti dress for legal personnel, videotaped examination-in-chief, videotaped cross-examination (not yet brought into force) and replacing the unrepresented accused cross-examiner with a legal representative to act on his or her behalf: see YJCEA 1999, ss 16–18, 23–30 and *R(D) v Camberwell Green Youth Court* [2005] 1 WLR 393, HL.

[11] London, CPS, 2005. Defence witnesses were outside the research design.

non-defendant witness' bad character.[12] Under s 100, evidence of a witness' bad character is only admissible if it is 'important explanatory
evidence'[13] that possesses 'substantial probative value'[14] to a matter in
issue. In addition, it must be substantially important in the case as a whole.
Section 100 sets a potentially higher standard than its Australian approximate equivalent, Evidence Act 1995 (Cth) and (NSW), s 103.[15] However,
both provisions betray serious limitations by virtue of their legalism, since
they cover only a small subset of topics that a cross-examiner might draw
upon in pursuing a gratuitously damaging cross-examination.[16]

Section 100 requires leave from the court.[17] The technique of utilising a
leave requirement to prevent abhorrent questioning offers a potential
procedural and educative advance because it creates a judicial obligation to
assess lines of questioning before damage occurs. Whilst it remains early
days for determining how effectively s 100 might curb insufficiently
relevant questioning of witnesses,[18] it seems safe to predict that embedded
cultural norms and practices will not be altered by isolated statutory
interventions. In Tasmania, Henning has revealed that law reform establishing an admissibility standard of 'substantial relevance to facts in issue'
for evidence of past sexual experience in relation to sexual assault
complainants had little impact on the cases in her empirical study.[19]
Depressingly, there was poor compliance with the statutory leave requirement as well.

---

[12] Broadly, this is 'evidence of, or of a disposition towards, misconduct on his [the
witness'] part'. This is evidence that would be used by cross-examiners to impeach witnesses,
mindful of the obligation expressed in the rule in *Browne v Dunn* (1894) 6 R 67, HL.

[13] That is, 'without it, the court or jury would find it impossible or difficult properly to
understand other evidence in the case, and ... its value for understanding the case as a whole
is substantial': Criminal Justice Act (CJA) 2003, s 100(2).

[14] *Ibid* s 100(3) lists factors that must be taken into account to determine whether
evidence is of substantial probative value.

[15] *Ibid* s 103 requires evidence relevant solely to the witness' credibility to be of
substantial probative value if it is to be used in cross-examination. See also Evidence Act 2001
(Tas), s 103.

[16] For example, case law from the High Court of Australia has indicated that most prior
inconsistent statements are beyond the purview of *ibid* s 103: *Adam v R* (2001) 207 CLR 96.

[17] CJA 2003, s 100(4).

[18] Some applications of *ibid* s 100 have been considered by appellate courts, eg in *R v V*
[2006] EWCA Crim 1901.

[19] See Evidence Act 2001 (Tas), s 194M(2)(a). A study of 94 committal, 77 trial and 51
sentencing transcripts (1987–94) by Henning, above n 8, shows that the forerunner of the
current provision, Evidence Act 1910 (Tas), s 102A, had little impact. Judges admitted
evidence with highly problematic probative value, eg, that the complainant had kissed, flirted,
engaged in sexual horseplay or in sexually suggestive conversation (in one case only in the
presence of the accused; in seven other cases in his absence). In 65 out of the 72 cases
monitored, evidence of sexual experience was admitted directly contrary to s 102A(1)(b) of
the 1910 Act, that is, without the required prior application to the trial judge. See also
Heroines of Fortitude, above n 8; J Hunter, C Cameron and T Henning, *Litigation II:
Evidence and Procedure* (7th edn, Australia, LexisNexis, 2005) ch 23.

In 2005 the New South Wales legislature moved to address trial judges' passivity in the face of improper questioning by counsel. Criminal Procedure Act 1986, s 275A, as amended, now obliges the trial judge in all New South Wales criminal trials, irrespective of the absence of objection, to disallow questions put to a witness in cross-examination if the court considers the questions 'misleading or confusing', 'unduly annoying, harassing, intimidating, offensive, oppressive, humiliating or repetitive', or that they have been put to the witness 'in a manner or tone that is belittling, insulting or otherwise inappropriate', or with 'no basis other than a sexist, racial, cultural or ethnic stereotype'.[20] Anecdotally, s 275A seems to have assisted already well-motivated trial judges to intervene within its terms, but real success will be achieved only if the section can energise trial judges resistant to challenging counsel's improper questioning of witnesses. Symbolically, it is a provision ripe with potential for effecting timely redistribution of power from the Bar to the Bench. That said, s 275A's symbolism, educative potential and practical operation would be enhanced significantly if it did not invite the negative inference that it is permissible for a cross-examiner to be *duly* 'annoying, harassing, intimidating, offensive, oppressive, humiliating or repetitive'. This ambivalence crystallises the essential problem of regulating cross-examination, namely, the difficulty of articulating and policing a defensible line between acceptable and unacceptable cross-examination.

Drawing this line is no easy task for legislators, judges or commentators. To do so one must confront the inherent tensions of an adversarial dynamic that obliges counsel to 'promote and protect fearlessly and by all proper and lawful means the lay client's best interests', whilst simultaneously imposing the somewhat amorphous obligation to ensure that all participants are treated humanely.[21] What Mr S describes in this chapter's masthead quotation as 'that moment that's at the heart of the trial' is truly, by extension, at the heart of adversarialism. This is not deviant or aberrant behaviour. It is what lawyers are expected to do. In other words, poor treatment of witnesses has more to do with adversarial norms and cultures of advocacy than with the strict letter of the law. Dignity and humanity must struggle to reassert themselves in the interstitial spaces.

On the topic of reform, this chapter concludes with some observations for ameliorating the negative impact of adversarialism upon witnesses, particularly in relation to overbearing cross-examination. Much more than

---

[20]   Challenging a witness merely through inconsistency or inaccuracy of their statements is expressly outside the ambit of Criminal Procedure Act 1986, s 275A. For an application of Uniform Evidence Act 1995 (NSW), s 41, the precursor to s 275A of the 1986 Act (but without the requirement of judicial proactivity), see *R v Ta* (2003) 57 NSWLR 444, (2003) 139 A Crim R 30. Spigelman CJ ruled that questioning (which was in fact irrelevant) was not permitted because it was 'unduly harassing, offensive and oppressive'.

[21]   Bar Council, Code of Conduct, cl 303(a).

the dignity and wellbeing of witnesses themselves hang on these issues, though these are sufficiently weighty considerations in their own right to demand redress. As we shall see, the public credibility and moral integrity of the criminal process are jeopardised by lawyers' abuses. Sound solutions require a strong appreciation of the historical roots of adversarial behaviour and the extent to which it has become embedded in contemporary legal culture and professional practice. For our purposes, history has a dual relevance. When we examine law's protective role regarding witnesses, we see 150 years of entrenched legalism and technicality.

CROSS-EXAMINATION, LAWYERISATION AND THE CRIMINAL TRIAL

It is tempting to see the ills that we derive from lawyers' role in questioning witnesses as a recent phenomenon.[22] The reality is quite different. History reveals that centuries of adversarial litigation have elevated a culture of lawyers' cross-examination into an art form. Once lawyers (for both sides) gained dominance in court, advocacy's impact on the trial burgeoned and flourished. The late eighteenth and early nineteenth century marked the beginning of what Langbein[23] describes as 'lawyerisation', the ascendancy of defence counsel in the trial process. Today, lawyerisation is a major defining element of the modern criminal trial.[24] Prior to lawyerisation, the criminal trial was inquisitorial in style. The underlying philosophy of the trial process was simple. It was described by Hawkins as requiring 'no manner of Skill to make a plain and honest Defence. The Simplicity and Innocence, artless and ingenuous Behaviour of one whose Conscience acquits him ... [is] more moving and convincing than the highest Eloquence of Persons speaking in a Case not their own'.[25] Within a hundred years the trial was no longer shaped by these sentiments. They were displaced by views synonymous with those expressed by Mr S.

By the end of the eighteenth century it was patent that defence counsel could achieve what the uneducated and disempowered defendant could not do alone: he could expose corrupt prosecution witnesses, particularly professional thief-takers whose motivation ('blood money') supported unmeritorious prosecutions. A flavour of Garrow's celebrated prowess in

---

[22] Comprehensive legal representation of defendants occurred with the passing of the Prisoner's Counsel Act 1836.

[23] JH Langbein, *The Origins of the Adversary Criminal Trial* (Oxford, OUP, 2003) ch 5.

[24] *Ibid.*

[25] JM Beattie, 'Scales of Justice: Defense Counsel and the English Criminal Trial in the Eighteenth and Nineteenth Centuries' (1991) *Law and History Review* 221, 223, quoting W Hawkins, *A Treatise of the Pleas of the Crown* (1716–21) vol 2, 400; and see Beattie, above, 263.

cross-examination during the late eighteenth century usefully illustrates the reason why defence lawyers were so successful:[26]

> Q: You know it is not every day that one gets forty pounds for hanging a man ...
>
> [and of another witness]
>
> Q: Perhaps you do not know that there is a reward for these men if they are convicted?
>
> A: How should I know?
>
> Q: What is the price of the blood of these men, if they are convicted?
>
> A: I shall not tell you.

As these exchanges illustrate, drama and effect were mustered to generate powerful emotional responses with persuasive appeal. Perhaps it was no accident that advocacy developed when debating was popular sport.[27] By the nineteenth century cross-examination garnered awe and deprecation.[28] As Charles Dickens was later to illustrate, lawyers' presentational creativity in court quickly became an art form.[29] Lawyerly cross-examination was not the sole prerogative of defence counsel, nor was it solely the craft of the criminal Bar. Lawyers' increasing dominance in the courtroom meant evidence and procedural doctrine were hammered out. Lawyerisation arrived with the ascendancy of rationalism and, as Beattie notes, 'defense counsel were swimming with not against the intellectual tide'.[30] Restrictive and rigid competency rules were no longer sustainable in an environment where the law of evidence was informed and stimulated by an intellectual rationalist culture infused with post-Enlightenment thinking.

It is hardly surprising that the number of defendants legally represented at the Old Bailey doubled in the last 20 years of the eighteenth century. By that century's end, between one-quarter and one-third of defendants were legally represented.[31] With defence counsel's right to speak and question on his client's behalf, the accused became silent by choice and the judge lost

---

[26] Beattie, above n 25, 263. Like many leading statesmen, judges and lawyers of his day, Garrow belonged to a debating club.

[27] *Ibid* 263.

[28] In 1819 John Payne Collier spoke of the 'abuses of the Bar' in cross-examining witnesses, which cause truthful testimony to 'be defeated by those who have attained such skill in confusing what is clear, and involving [that is, making complex] what is simple': John Payne Collier, *Criticisms on the Bar* 109–10, quoted by Langbein, above n 23, 247.

[29] See eg, Charles Dickens, *The Pickwick Papers* (1st edn 1837; London, Penguin Classics Reissue, 2000) ch 34.

[30] Beattie, above n 25, 236. See also D Lemmings, 'Ritual, Majesty and Mystery: Collective Life and Culture among English Barristers, Serjeants and Judges, c 1500–1830' in WW Pue and D Sugarman (eds), *Lawyers and Vampires: Cultural Histories of Legal Professions* (Oxford, Hart Publishing, 2003).

[31] Beattie, above n 25, shows that legal representation at the Old Bailey doubled in the last 20 years of the eighteenth century.

his role as dominant questioner. The accused was no longer the primary informational resource of Hawkins' era. Backlit against the vocal stance of the lawyer, the right to silence speaks volumes about those who do the talking—or more precisely the questioning—for the accused. A marginalised Bench meant that victims who personally prosecuted criminal charges needed legal representation to meet the newly professionalised defence case. During the course of the eighteenth century the criminal trial moved from something akin to cottage industry dispute resolution, with the judge the sole professionally skilled participant, to a thoroughly professionalised process with lawyers placed centre-stage.

Advocacy created[32] and framed the law of evidence, pressing seventeenth century practice and procedure into concrete rules. With lawyers came cross-examination, oral process and its various normative manifestations, such as the rule against hearsay. The very force of cross-examination, and its soon-recognised potential for abuse, led to the creation of a now obsolete witness privilege[33] which precluded a witness from being cross-examined in a manner that degraded him or her as 'infamous' or 'disgraceful'.[34] Yet, as we shall see, neither formal legal categories nor tightly-drawn rules can be relied upon to provide witnesses with much protection in practice.

A most striking feature of the criminal trial process is that, despite fundamental changes in the values and philosophical bases underpinning criminal justice, little has changed in the passage of 150 years in the power relationships defining personnel within the criminal trial. Not so civil litigation, which nowadays is informed by the language of managerialism, resources, costs, delay and the prevalence of episodic hearings rather than 'main event' summative trials. The abolition or, in some jurisdictions, the

---

[32] As Langbein, above n 23, observes, '[t]he law of evidence may have been a judicial creation, but it had the effect of empowering counsel ... [I]n the new setting of adversary combat the quest for advantage in the particular case would cause counsel to press to extend such potentially expansive principles ... as suited his client's case'.

[33] A formal protection for the dignity of witnesses, described in Langbein, above n 23, 284.

[34] Langbein, above n 23, 283–4, describes the witness privilege as protecting the 'dignity or reputational interest [of a witness] against shameful disclosures'. He quotes from an 1874 murder case where the trial judge stopped a line of cross-examination, saying, 'I have always understood that no man or woman is to be asked a question that tends to disgrace themselves. I have known a woman asked whether she ever had a bastard child, and it has always been stopped'. In *Wigmore on Evidence* it was pointed out that a privilege against 'disgracing answers' clearly existed in the early 1700s, 'but in some obscure way the privilege fell into disuse, and its exercise was not revived again till the beginning of the 1800s'. Cf *Cundell v Pratt* (1827) Moo and M 108, 173 ER 1098, per Best CJ: 'I do not forbid the question [as to whether the witness was living in an incestuous relationship] ... I for one will never go that length ... [T]he rule I shall always act upon, is to protect witnesses from questions the answers to which may expose them to punishment. If they are protected beyond this, from questions that tend to degrade them, many an innocent man may suffer'. For general discussion, see *R v Noud, ex p McNamara* [1991] 2 Qd R 86, 94–6, per McPherson J.

relaxation of the hearsay rule has made civil actions far less dependent on oral evidence, thus reducing the market for the cut-and-thrust of witness-testing by cross-examination. Most dramatically of all, there is a declining incidence in both numbers and rates of civil trials in England and in other jurisdictions where procedural rules have incorporated Bench-focused managerialism.[35]

RATIONAL PROCESS OR TOURNAMENT?[36] THE FAILURES OF CROSS-EXAMINATION

What Wigmore's 'legal engine' aphorism fails to identify is that cross-examination can be totally ineffective in 'truth'-seeking. Human beings have in-built imperfections as fact-finders. We make assumptions based on class, culture,[37] age, intellectual functioning and gender, when evaluating a witness and his or her responses in court. The practised and impressive, but deceptive or misleading, witness can be impenetrable. The most prominent recent example is Professor Sir Roy Meadow.[38] Further, it is a notorious fact that cross-examination is a weak truth-testing device against the confident, honest but mistaken identification witness.[39] In terms of assumptions based on class and education, consider this illustration of the impact of class and self-expression in the Guildford Four case described by Kee:

> For, of course, judgment on the quality of a person's evidence, and of his or her stand under cross-examination, is not easy to separate from judgment of their quality as a class of person. Armstrong's 'I never done no bombs at all' inevitably

---

[35] HM Kritzer, 'Disappearing Trials? A Comparative Perspective' (2004) 1 *Journal of Empirical Legal Studies* 735, 752.

[36] *Whisprun Pty Ltd v Dixon* (2003) 200 ALR 447, per Kirby J.

[37] See eg, D Eades, 'A Case of Communicative Clash: Aboriginal English and the Legal System' in J Gibbons (ed), *Language in the Law* (London, Longman, 1994); D Eades (ed), *Language in Evidence: Issues Confronting Aboriginal and Multicultural Australia* (Sydney, UNSW Press, 1995). See also *Heroines of Fortitude*, above n 8; P Greer, 'They Throw the Rule Book Away: Sexual Assault in Aboriginal Communities' in J Breckenridge and M Carmody (eds), *Crimes of Violence: Australian Responses to Rape and Sexual Assault* (Australia, Allen & Unwin, 1992); *Minister for Immigration and Multicultural and Indigenous Affairs v SGLB* [2004] HCA 32.

[38] See eg, *R v Clark* [2003] EWCA Crim 1020; *R v Cannings* [2004] EWCA Crim 1, [2004] 1 FCR 193; *Kent County Council v B* [2004] EWHC 411 (Fam); T Ward, 'Experts, Juries, and Witch-hunts: from Fitzjames Stephen to Angela Cannings' (2004) 31 *Journal of Law and Society* 369, 385. The High Court of Australia has long recognised the difficulty of cross-examining the prison informant witness effectively: *Pollitt v R* (1992) 63 ALJR 613.

[39] *Report to the Secretary of State for the Home Department* (*Devlin Report*) (London, HMSO, 1976) paras 1.24 and 2.5, quoted in ALRC, *Evidence* (Interim) Report, para 827: 'A witness says that he recognises the man, and that is that or almost that. There is no story to be dissected, just a simple assertion to be accepted or rejected. If a witness thinks that he has a good memory for faces when in fact he has a poor one, there is no way of detecting the failing'.

contrasted unfavourably with the 'Certainly not, my Lord' of police officers responding to the allegations made against them.[40]

Misinterpretation is potentially pervasive. Witnesses (and jurors) are drawn from communities that are far more culturally diverse than they were 20, 50 or 100 years ago. Different political, legal and religious traditions may struggle with Anglo-based processes. In many cultures swearing an oath in a secular context is inappropriate and choosing between an oath and an affirmation baffling.[41] Observers can completely misinterpret avoidance of eye contact where a witness speaks to counsel, a professional garbed and positioned in authority. Social science research indicates that features of women's speech, such as intonation and hesitancy, are associated with perceptions of lack of credibility.[42] A number of US studies indicate that women litigants and witnesses are accorded less respect than men. In court they are more likely to be addressed informally, spoken to with a condescending tone, be patronised with endearments, receive comments on their appearance, be intimidated and badgered.[43]

Research by psychologists on deception and its detection further problematises the common law's strong preference for oral evidence. The work of Ekman, Vrij and other psychologists[44] indicates that the general population has deceit detection abilities that barely improve upon chance. Psychologists indicate that training *may* assist deceit detection. Ekman claims that:

> [t]he criminal justice system must have been designed by someone who wanted to make it impossible to detect deceit from demeanour. The guilty suspect is given many chances to prepare and rehearse her replies before her truthfulness is evaluated by jury or judge, thus increasing her confidence and decreasing her fear of being detected..... [Examination in court takes] place months, if not

---

[40] R Kee, *Trial And Error: the Maguires, the Guildford Pub Bombings and British Justice* (London, Hamish Hamilton, 1986).

[41] See Victorian Parliament Law Reform Committee, *Inquiry into Oaths and Affirmations with reference to the Multicultural Community* (2002) 79–62, discussed in Hunter *et al*, above n 19.

[42] See K Mack, 'Continuing Barriers to Women's Credibility: a Feminist Perspective on the Proof Process' (1993) 4 *Criminal Law Forum* 327; and also JA Blumenthal, 'A Wipe of the Hands, a Lick of the Lips: the Validity of Demeanor Evidence in Assessing Witness Credibility' (1993) 72 *Nebraska Law Review* 1157.

[43] R Hunter, 'Gender in Evidence: Masculine Norms vs Feminist Reforms' (1996) 19 *Harvard Women's Law Journal* 127.

[44] See P Ekman, 'Lie Catching in the 1990s' in P Ekman, *Telling Lies: Clues to Deceit in the Marketplace, Politics and Marriage* (New York, WW Norton & Co, 1991) 287–92; KL Landry and JC Brigham, 'The Effect of Training in Criteria-Based Content Analysis on the Ability to Detect Deception in Adults' (1992) 16 *Law and Human Behavior* 663; A Vrij, K Edward, K Roberts and R Bull, 'Detecting Deceit via Analysis of Verbal and Nonverbal Behavior' (2000) 24 *Journal of Nonverbal Behavior* 239; J Masip *et al*, 'The Non-Verbal Approach to the Detection of Deception: Judgemental Accuracy' (2004) 8 *Psychology in Spain* 48.

years, after the incident, thereby blunting emotions associated with the criminal event... And then there is the *innocent* defendant who comes to trial terrified of being disbelieved... The signs of fear of being disbelieved can be misinterpreted as a guilty person's fear of being caught.[45]

It is 80 years since Atkin LJ observed that 'an ounce of intrinsic merit or demerit in the evidence, that is to say, the value of the comparison of evidence with known facts, is worth pounds of demeanour'.[46] His Lordship's admonition has been increasingly acknowledged by the High Court of Australia as an appropriate rule-of-thumb for trial judges and appellate courts.[47] Yet advocates are allowed to persist with adversarial techniques that play upon discredited assumptions of credibility assessment and witness testing.

CROSS-EXAMINATION: ADVOCACY NOT EVIDENCE RULES

A study of advocacy techniques combined with the research of social and behavioural scientists suggests that victory for the cross-examiner is too often the work of the trained curial assassin ambushing an easy target. As any practising lawyer would expect, yes/no closed questions, leading questions and double negative questions dominate cross-examination. These formats constrain witness responses, which of course is why they are adopted. The research of Kebbell *et al*[48] highlights the impact of cross-examination on witnesses with intellectual disability. According to Kebbell *et al*, constraining questions distort, with varying levels of severity, the accuracy of witnesses with an intellectual disability. These researchers question why cross-examination is allowed to be so distorting. After responding to the question with a modern version of Wigmore's 'greatest legal engine' canard, Kebbell draws four conclusions:

> First, the way in which witnesses are examined does little to ensure that their memories are as accurate as possible. Second, the questioning of witnesses with intellectual disabilities was almost identical to that of witnesses from the general population, indicating that lawyers are not altering their questioning behaviour for witnesses with intellectual disabilities, either positively or negatively. Third, cross-examination as currently practised is particularly poor for eliciting accurate memory reports, a problem that is likely to compound the general memory

---

[45] Ekman, above n 44.

[46] *Societe D'Avances Commerciales (Societe Anonyme Egyptienne) v Merchants' Marine Insurance Co (The 'Palitana')* (1924) 20 Ll L Rep 140 at 152.

[47] See *Fox v Percy* (2003) 77 ALJR 989, 197 ALR 201; *State Rail Authority (NSW) v Earthline Constructions Pty Ltd (In Liq)* (1999) 73 ALJR 306, 160 ALR 588; Kirby and Callinan JJ, dissenting, in *Whisprun Pty Ltd v Dixon*, above n 36.

[48] MR Kebbell, C Hatton and SD Johnson, 'Witnesses with Intellectual Disabilities in Court: What Questions are Asked and What Influence do They Have?' (2004) 13 *Legal and Criminological Psychology* 23.

problems associated with people with intellectual disabilities. Fourth, the accounts of witnesses with intellectual disabilities are shorter and more likely to agree with a leading question than are accounts of witnesses from the general population.[49]

It is not only vulnerable witnesses who may find their account reconstructed by the process of questioning in court. Narratologists help us to understand the force of the advocate's techniques in the context of the adversarial trial and lawyers' performances before clients, for clients. Advocacy embraces the art of story-telling, using rhetorical devices that advance and protect the client's interests.[50] Story-telling has been examined in relation to the building of prosecution cases,[51] to decision-making and juror comprehension,[52] to police questioning, in advocacy,[53] to conflicts of scientific evidence in the courtroom,[54] and also with respect to its ethical[55] dimensions. Story-telling for ordering, and reordering, information travels far beyond the courtroom. Arranging and telling stories helps us to explain 'our sense of history, like our sense of memory and self-identity'.[56] The qualities of story-telling that bear upon witness questioning relate to its attraction as the listener-friendly art of constructing, framing and reconstructing information.

A lawyer's theory of case[57] is framed and supported evidentially for maximum effect. Novice advocates learn that a case theory requires a

[49]   *Ibid.*

[50]   W Twining, *Rethinking Evidence* (Oxford, Blackwell, 1990) 219–61; WL Bennett and MS Feldman, *Reconstructing Reality in the Courtroom: Justice and Judgment in American Culture* (New Brunswick, NJ, Rutgers University, 1981); WL Bennett, 'Legal Fictions: Telling Stories and Doing Justice' in ML McLaughlin, MJ Cody and S Reed (eds), *Explaining One's Self to Others* (Hillsdale, NJ, Erlbaum, 1992); L Sarmas, 'Storytelling and the Law: a Case Study of Louth v Diprose' (1994) 19 *Melbourne University Law Review* 701; K Abrams, 'Hearing the Call of Stories' (1991) 79 *California Law Review* 971; G Edmond, 'Negotiating the Meaning of a "Scientific" Experiment during a Murder Trial and Some Limits to Legal Deconstruction for the Public Understanding of Law and Science' (1998) 20 *Sydney Law Review* 361.

[51]   D McBarnet, *Conviction: Law, the State and the Construction of Justice* (London, Macmillan, 1981) 1–11, 79; M McConville, A Sanders and R Leng, *The Case for the Prosecution* (Routledge, London, 1991); A Sanders, 'Constructing the Case for the Prosecution' (1987) 14 *Journal of Law and Society* 229.

[52]   N Pennington and R Hastie, 'A Cognitive Theory of Juror Decision-making: the Story Model' (1991) 13 *Cardozo Law Review* 519.

[53]   Eg, BJ Foley and RA Robbins, 'Fiction 101: a Primer for Lawyers on How to Use Fiction Writing Techniques to Write Persuasive Facts Sections' (2001) 32 *Rutgers Law Journal* 459.

[54]   Edmond, above n 50.

[55]   'Stories … excellent vehicles for cheating': W Twining, *The Great Juristic Bazaar: Jurists' Texts and Lawyers' Stories* (Aldershot, Ashgate, 2002) 12.

[56]   RK Sherwin, 'Symposium Introduction: Picturing Justice: Images of Law and Lawyers in the Visual Media' (1996) 30 *University of San Francisco Law Review* 891.

[57]   Case theory isolates 'that aspect of advocacy which is concerned with rational arguments from other aspects, such as commanding attention, communication, questioning,

logical accounting of all incontrovertible evidence into a story that explains why their side should win. A case theory must have a persuasive theme. This is typically a moral framework that makes it compelling. For example, a party seeking to enforce a contract may have 'keeping promises' as a theme for his or her case. The opponent's case may be organised around a competing moral theme, for example, the rejoinder that enforcing a contract places 'profits over people'.[58] Crucially, framing the 'story' can exploit an audience's prejudices.[59] When the cross-examiner's mission requires a witness' story to be challenged, the advocate's repertoire of standard techniques includes milking the marginal point for much more than it is really worth. Drama and emotional appeal, ripe since Garrow's day, are the essential ingredients of successful advocates' stories.

Few witnesses know how to play an audience better than lawyers. For example, prosecution counsel relying on an eyewitness may portray her as independent and confident. The prosecutor may present an accomplice prosecution witness as a direct witness of criminality, a person who saw and can tell everything. For defence counsel, a sexual assault complainant may be described as a liar, guileful, maybe confused, perhaps a temptress. Case construction is not static. Cases with one construct can be revised and reconstructed before and during a trial as the need arises. A striking Australian example of the evolving prosecution case is *R v Anderson*, the Hilton Hotel Bombing case.[60] In a trial that took place in highly politicised circumstances the prosecution relied heavily on the testimony of an accomplice witness. As holes were punched in the accomplice's account the prosecution reconstructed its case, repairing each new case theory around ever-changing key facts. The multiplicity of revisions per se attracted no appellate criticism. It was only the last revised version of the prosecution case, put to the jury in the prosecutor's final address, that crossed the ethical boundary line.[61] It did so not because it reflected an unethical vacillation by the prosecutor of its case against the defendant, but because it occurred so late in the trial that the defence had no fair opportunity to respond. Law's tolerance for such advocacy techniques is intrinsic to the adversarial tradition.

persuasive presentation and various courtroom tactics': W Twining, 'Lawyers' Stories' in *Rethinking Evidence: Exploratory Essays* (London, Blackwell, 1990) 222.

[58] See S Lubet, *Nothing But the Truth: Why Trial Lawyers Don't, Can't, and Shouldn't Have to tell the Whole Truth* (New York, New York UP, 2001).

[59] Xenophobia was used to great effect in *Benedetto v R* [2003] UKPC 27. Lubet, above n 58, provides an example from the OJ Simpson criminal trial: the prosecution framed its case as one of domestic violence, whilst the defence drew on the United States' history of racial injustice exemplified by (disenfranchised) black men being falsely accused of murdering whites and developed a counter-story of police prejudice and fraud.

[60] (1991) 53 A Crim R 421 (NSW CCA).

[61] See also Edmond, above n 50, for a masterly dissection of prosecution reconstruction in the Lindy Chamberlain prosecution.

Advocates do not start with a blank slate. Narrative case construction proceeds from the parties' pleadings, and a crucial aspect of the parties' pleadings is that they represent carefully crafted ambit claims—not disinterested claims to truth.[62] As Deane and Dawson JJ once observed:

> to characterise the factual assertions in a plaintiff's unverified pleading as positive representations of the truth of their content would be to misunderstand or ignore the traditional nature and function of a... statement of claim [which is not]... a representation or warranty of the objective accuracy of the assertions of fact.... [but] a written identification and communication of the extent of the plaintiff's claim.[63]

The parties' contentions in criminal proceedings are no different to civil pleadings in this respect. Prosecutors' pleadings can form the cornerstone of the plea bargain. In this context, an ambit claim may take the form of overcharging in order to strike deals on sentence in return for valuable criminal intelligence or naming other suspects. In contested trials a party's case rises or falls according to the presentation of evidence and disputed counternarratives. Combine the skills of narration with the advocate's licence to construct a case, and even allowing for ethical obligations to 'the court' (conflicting, as they often do, with the client's interests), the prospects for ethical witness examination, and consequently for accurate decision-making, are not especially encouraging.

In sum, whenever a party adduces witness testimony, and especially in front of a jury, the opposing party's task of testing the witness' account and pressing its own case is intrinsically confrontational and emotive. The guile, stealth or open challenge of adversarial tactics may vary from case to case, but the underlying technique is always the same. Claims are packaged into the most compelling trial stories that the incontrovertible evidence, and lawyers' powers of abductive imagination, will permit. In the Anglo-adversarial tradition this is normative behaviour for lawyers. By legal standards, counsel who employ such tactics are not rogues or deviants.

Cultural variations create some procedural differences across Anglophone jurisdictions, but the core structural features of the common law trial remain constant. These variations do not remove the fundamental premise that advocacy is about presenting a persuasive case constructed from an ambit claim. It is not about defending a position of truth. It is about a *good* story (but not necessarily a *true* story).[64] A central feature of a good story is to know one's audience. Take, for example, the prosecution of Lindy Chamberlain, the young woman who in the 1980s was prosecuted in the Northern Territory of Australia for the murder of her baby,

---

[62]   *Jamieson v R* (1993) 177 CLR 574.
[63]   *Ibid* (citations omitted) Deane and Dawson JJ.
[64]   W Twining, 'Good Stories and True Stories' in Twining, above n 55.

Azaria. Lindy claimed that a dingo had taken Azaria. Barker, as counsel for the prosecution, spoke to a Northern Territory jury, playing to character-istics in the local community that had been opened up in the media frenzy surrounding the case. At this time and in this location, the community from where the jury was drawn was conservative and unsophisticated. It looked upon outsiders with suspicion. The Chamberlains were outsiders from the south east. Michael Chamberlain was a Seventh Day Adventist pastor. He and Lindy behaved in a manner perceived by locals as oddly spiritual and stoic, given that, on their own account, they had just lost their baby to a wild carnivorous beast. The Chamberlains' spirituality was juxtaposed against a prosecution case founded on science. For example, a key issue in the trial was whether the prosecution's scientists had correctly identified traces of foetal blood on the front passenger seat of the Chamberlains' car. This evidence was significant in exonerating the dingo and in linking Lindy to the death of her baby. The prosecution's 'foetal blood' theory fitted comfortably with the values of the Northern Territory. The prosecution's expert scientist testified clearly, convincingly and with-out equivocation in the witness-box. She had spent her professional life working in a scientific laboratory. The defence produced an academically well-credentialed scientist, a southerner and a professor who saw compli-cations and qualifications in the prosecution's scientific evidence. In his closing speech, Barker painted this scientist to the jury as an academic interloper who had:

> never been actively engaged in the day to day routine work of testing blood stains … [H]e teaches and engages in pleasant research and writes for learned journals, … never about forensic biology. Never about the dirty side of the profession … [T]here are scientists who work at teaching, and there are scientists that work at testing blood, and they should leave the field to the professionals.[65]

As Edmond reports, 'Barker insisted … that only two alternative findings were available to the jury: dingo abduction or infanticide'.[66] The jury found the infanticide option the more compelling alternative. After all, infanticide occurs more often than dingo abduction. Yet with hindsight, we now know that it was dingo abduction.[67]

The Chamberlain case raises another formative issue, namely, the ways in which jurors' understanding of legal narratives may be influenced heavily by meanings inculcated by the media. The media and the law

---

[65] G Andrewartha, 'Psychological Communication in the Courtroom' in G Eames, *Criminal Law Advocacy* (South Australia, Legal Services Commission, 1984) 62–3, quoting from Barker's closing speech.

[66] Edmond, above n 50.

[67] Lindy Chamberlain was convicted and gaoled for her daughter's murder in 1982, but released in 1986. All told, there were two inquests, a criminal trial, two appeals, a Royal Commission and ultimately a pardon.

operate in different discursive registers. The media uses its own devices to construct and reconstruct as it reports on a trial.[68] It simplifies legal 'facts', removing detail and complexity and injecting information-bites that mingle with stories of human tragedy, intrigue and salacious detail. The media's depiction of the contest in a trial may conflate evidence from the trial with out-of-court opinion. The mingling of the two allows a complex contest to be reduced to a few simple but engaging themes.[69] Media misreporting of real crime and real cases[70] reinforces interpretative messages derived from fictional portrayals of criminal trials in television serials such as *Law and Order*, *LA Law* or *CSI: Crime Scene Investigation*. In the fictional celluloid world, good and evil can be distinguished by invoking a few ready-packaged conclusions. There is no need to wade through detail.[71]

CROSS-EXAMINATION: STEREOTYPES AND LYING

A favourite and deeply embedded stereotype in the legal psyche is the witness whose account deviates from her prior out-of-court statements. The law of evidence treats the revelation that a witness has been inconsistent, or that he or she has lied, as a glittering credibility prize.[72] Yet is an exposed lie or inconsistency truly and consistently indicative of mendacity? Richard Eggleston[73] was a strong proponent of carefully extracting the nuanced meaning from a lie told in court. According to Eggleston, when a question is perceived by a witness to have little bearing on the case,

---

[68] In *Sally Clark*, eg, the narrative shifted from 'solicitor' to 'wronged mother': see R Nobles and D Schiff, 'A Story of Miscarriage: Law in the Media' (2004) 31 *Journal of Law and Society* 221, 238.

[69] *Ibid.*

[70] Consider, eg, the media's problematic treatment of the '73 million to one' statistic presented in the trial of Sally Clark: Nobles and Schiff, above n 68, 232, 239, 241. See generally R Nobles and D Schiff, Understanding Miscarriages of Justice: Law, the Media, and the Inevitability of Crisis (Oxford, OUP, 2000). See also RK Sherwin, *When Law Goes Pop* (Chicago, University of Chicago Press, 2000) ch 3.

[71] 'To do justice to both parties, the decision-maker was therefore obliged to enter upon a more detailed analysis: not to treat the case as a kind of sport, where a player whose credibility is damaged is inevitably judged the loser. Engaging in this kind of tournament can be comparatively easy for skilled, repeat players. The obligation to assess the claim justly, according to the entirety of the evidence and according to law, is rather more difficult, tedious and time consuming': *Whisprun Pty Ltd v Dixon*, above n 36, para 123 per Kirby J. See also, M Kirby, *Speaking to the Modern Jury: New Challenges for Judges and Advocates*, www.hcourt.gov.au/speeches/kirbyj/kirbyj_genx.htm.

[72] See J Temkin, 'Prosecuting and Defending Rape: Perspectives from the Bar' (2000) 27 *Journal of Law and Society* 219; D Brereton, 'How Different are Rape Trials? A Comparison of the Cross-Examination of Complainants in Rape and Assault Trials' (1997) 37 *British Journal of Criminology* 242.

[73] R Eggleston, *Evidence, Proof and Probability* (2nd edn, London, Weidenfeld & Nicolson, 1983).

witnesses routinely prevaricate and evade the issue for all sorts of extraneous and not necessarily immoral reasons. Witnesses balance the value they attribute to an answer against other values, such as the damage to a person's reputation which might be caused by giving a completely truthful reply. Eggleston argued persuasively that all witnesses can find themselves exposed as liars, even to the extent of intentionally misleading the court:

> [M]ost witnesses will lie if the motive is strong enough, and many will lie merely to save lengthy explanations about matters which they think have nothing to do with the case. I do not regard the demonstration that a witness had lied about some irrelevant matter as affording much help in deciding whether he is telling the truth about the facts in issue.[74]

For a lie to be clear, the truth must be correspondingly unambiguous and also accessible to the court.[75] A lawyer who questions a witness with an unreliable memory, mistaken perception, loose expression, or recollection impaired by subjective bias, illness or the passage of time does not necessarily expose a liar. A witness' account may be flawed in part whilst still containing relevant and reliable information bearing on the main points in issue.

In *Whisprun v Dixon*,[76] Kirby J illustrates Eggleston's point and underscores the continuing significance of class, education and cultural sophistication in credibility contests. The plaintiff, Dixon, was an abattoir worker who had been employed to suck foetal blood from unborn calves' hearts into a pipette. To sustain her claim for damages for chronic disability she had to prove that she had developed chronic Q-fever after an acute episode of Q-fever.[77] There was no dispute that she had contracted Q-fever. The question for the court was whether she was one of the 10 to 20 per cent of sufferers who had developed the chronic complaint as well. Cross-examination of Dixon revealed that she had exaggerated (ie lied) about the extent of her disability. Yet as Kirby J pointed out, these lies did not automatically mean that she was not a chronic Q-fever sufferer. Parts of her evidence were not directly about her incapacity. For example, what was the status and significance of her testimony regarding her accommodation arrangements? Was it mere oversight, or a shorthand way of

---

[74] *Ibid* 77. See also R Eggleston, 'What is Wrong with the Adversary System?' (1975) 49 *Australian Law Journal* 428; *Minister for Immigration and Multicultural and Indigenous Affairs v SGLB* (2004) 207 *ALR* 12: 'There is no necessary correlation between inconsistency and credibility in [claims for refugee status]'.

[75] See G Loughton, 'Truth and Fictions: Lying and the Law' in L Dobrez *et al* (eds), *An ABC of Lying: Taking Stock in Interesting Times* (Melbourne, Australian Scholarly Publishing, 2004); B Tversky and E Marsh 'Biased Retellings of Events Yield Biased Memories' (2000) 40 *Cognitive Psychology* 1.

[76] (2003) 200 ALR 447

[77] Q-fever is an infectious disease that is prevalent in animals and can be transmitted to humans.

avoiding a lengthy explanation of matters regarded by the witness as peripheral to the trial? Dixon agreed with counsel in her evidence-in-chief that she lived on her parents' property. However, subsequently (as Kirby J recounts):

> [i]t transpired that she was housed in a shed which stands on land that she herself owns. She was asked why she had not corrected the questioner and stated that the shed was on her own property. Her answer was that she had 'no idea'. Perhaps, like not a few lawyers before and since, she was not quite sure what 'property' meant. Perhaps she did not think the ownership of the land on which her shed stood really mattered enough to make a fuss so as to correct the questioner's assumption.

A High Court majority found that the trial judge had rightly decided against Dixon. The minority, however, concluded that the trial judge's determination was flawed because the judge had attached inflated importance to Dixon's poor performance under cross-examination. Callinan J emphasised the unlikelihood that a previously healthy and hard-working young woman would resolve 'to live a complete lie and maintain a consistent but wholly or largely mendacious story to be told to her family, her friends, her doctors, her lawyers and ultimately the court over a period of six years'.[78] He found objective evidence that supported her case. To similar effect, Kirby J was influenced by the very strong medical evidence adduced on the behalf of the plaintiff, adding:

> [Dixon] was a soft target: a former abattoir worker, of limited education, inarticulate, living in a country town, with an alleged medical condition one feature of which was its possible impact upon her powers of concentration and memory. In the old days of civil jury trials, parties would fight such cases with as much bluster and prejudice as they could respectively get away with. In this trial, considerable latitude was allowed. But, in the end, objectively at least, what did the attack prove?[79]

Irrespective of where the truth actually lay in *Dixon v Whisprun*, the case amply demonstrates how the tournament of questioning is one-sided where the witness lacks the verbal prowess of the questioner. Some witnesses are patently ill-equipped to spar on anything approximating equal terms with counsel. Child complainant witnesses are the most obvious example,[80] though gross inequality in adversarial combat is pervasive, as *Dixon* shows. Brennan and Brennan quote a magistrate interviewed in their research:

---

[78] *Dixon v Whisprun Pty Ltd (formerly known as Northwest Exports Pty Ltd)* [2001] NSWCA 344, per Heydon JA (quoted by Callinan J in the High Court).
[79] Kirby J, dissenting, in *Whisprun Pty Ltd v Dixon*, above n 36.
[80] Eastwood and Paton, above n 8; New Zealand Law Commission, above n 8.

> The evidence from ... police ... doctors [and other criminal justice professionals] ... is that because of the rigours of the adversarial, adult court procedures, those responsible are reluctant to prosecute offenders whose victims are either young, unconfident, slow or passive ... [C]ross-examining children is '... like shooting rats in a barrel ... it's easy to confuse them and make out they're telling lies'.[81]

Observers may think that they understand the child witness frailties, but in reality it is very difficult for a researcher or lawyer or juror to step into the shoes and appreciate the mindset of a rape victim, a child witness or a chronically ill plaintiff like Ms Dixon. The complexities of the situation are elaborated by Brennan and Brennan, specifically in relation to child complainant witnesses:[82]

> [D]ifferences between children and adults are considered by the community to be quantitative rather than qualitative ... Children are thought of as socially, emotionally and intellectually inferior to their adult models and their validity and reliability as individuals is reduced in direct proportion to their age. This way of thinking precludes any serious consideration being given to the issue of child credibility ... To elevate child credibility it is necessary for the community as a whole to appreciate the many stages and faces of child development ... [RC Summit, 'The Child Sexual Abuse Accommodation Syndrome' (1983) 7 *Child Abuse and Neglect* 177 maintains that] society's values are stacked in several ways heavily against the child victim witness. First, the child has a great deal of difficulty accepting the abuse of love and power by a trusted adult. Second, the translation of this abuse, during disclosure, is restricted by the likely absence of language and concepts to express the necessary details in a convincing and credible way. Third, the legal system bolstered by community attitudes [in Summit's words] 'allows the child one acceptable set of reactions to such an experience. Like the adult victim of rape, the child victim is expected to forcibly resist, to cry for help and attempt to escape the intrusion. By that standard almost every child fails. The normal reaction is to play possum, that is to feign sleep, to shift position and pull up the covers ... It is sad to hear children attacked by attorneys and discredited by juries because they claimed to be molested yet admitted they made no protest or outcry ... Adults must be reminded that ... the threat of loss of love, or loss of family security is more frightening to the child than any threat of violence'.

This brief summary of a wealth of empirical data and practical experience should suffice to indicate the realities of litigation for witnesses who must endure the consequences of lawyers' adversarial strategies. It is against this

---

[81] M Brennan and RE Brennan, *Strange Language: Child Victims under Cross Examination* (3rd edn, Wagga Wagga, NSW, Centre for Teaching and Research in Literacy, 1990) 3.

[82] *Ibid* 89. Also see J Hunter and K Cronin, *Evidence, Advocacy and Ethical Practice: a Criminal Trial Commentary* (Sydney, Butterworths, 1995) ch 6. For discussion and recommendations arising from the first (abortive) Damilola Taylor murder trial, see J Sentamu, *The Review of the Investigation and Prosecution arising from the Murder of Damilola Taylor* (2002).

backdrop, rather than against the abstractions of legal theory, that the law of evidence and court process should be evaluated.

LAW'S TIRED, SAD AND INADEQUATE RULES

Legal adjudication is located in a 'rationalist tradition' that arranges and mediates information by hierarchies and privileged processes conforming to specifically legal conceptions of rationality. At the same time, legal process affords some limited traction to insights from other disciplines. As we have noted, it attempts to address witnesses' vulnerabilities primarily by the 'special measures' reforms mentioned in this chapter's introduction. In addition, over the years we have seen the door open a little to allow experts from the soft sciences to testify on matters such as children's behaviour.[83] The legal admissibility of information derived from new fields of expertise is by no means uncontentious, and the door in many jurisdictions is merely ajar, not flung open wide.

Law's rationalist methodology remains strongly resistant to embracing disciplines seeking to challenge embedded procedures, including (lightly regulated) cross-examination. But does law, abetted by orthodox adversarial procedure, always know best? The eminent Australian jurist Hal Wootten once remarked:

> [T]he last thing I would wish to encourage in humanist witnesses is obsequiousness toward lawyers, either practitioners or judges. There are good social reasons for treating the legal system's normative and adjudicatory authority with respect, but none for endowing it with intellectual authority.[84]

Law's failings in this regard may be attributed to two further sources, above and beyond the deleterious effects of embedded adversarial cultures. First, soft-law regulation through professional codes of conduct has been an abject failure so far as the protection of witnesses is concerned. Secondly, judges and lawyers have clung to rigid normative frameworks and outmoded conceptual dichotomies which serve only to introduce needless complexity into legal adjudication whilst further eroding protection for witnesses. The collateral evidence rule, with its underpinning of a (supposed) dichotomy between evidence going directly to the issue and evidence going merely to collateral matters (prominently including witness credibility), is the epitome of such fossilised thinking. The rule operates not

---

[83] See eg, Evidence Act 2001 (Tas), s 79A (specialised knowledge of child behaviour); *HG v R* (1999) 197 CLR 414.

[84] H Wootten, 'Conflicting Imperatives: Pursuing Truth in the Courts' in I McCalman and A McGrath (eds), *Proof and Truth: the Humanist as Expert* (Canberra, Australian Academy of the Humanities, 2003), quoted by G Edmond, 'Thick Decisions: Expertise, Advocacy and Reasonableness in the Federal Court of Australia' (2004) 74 *Oceania* 190.

only to the detriment of individual witnesses, but also imperils the moral legitimacy and public credibility of legal verdicts.

Professional Codes of Conduct

The notion of 'respect' for witnesses is most directly addressed for England and Wales by the Bar Council's Code of Conduct. Clauses 701(a) and 708(g), respectively, commend the virtue of courtesy and require that counsel avoid 'questions which are merely scandalous or intended or calculated only to vilify insult or annoy either a witness or some other person'.[85] Whilst these are eminently laudable sentiments, the Code is not an effective form of regulation in practice.

A principal limitation is that the Code is not strictly binding in court. In the scheme of things, exhortatory professional conduct rules are a 'light touch' form of regulation, highly dependent on judge and counsel for their further elucidation and implementation. In practice, judges typically intervene to protect witnesses from improper questioning only in extreme cases, and sometimes not even then. And the contradictory nature of the guidance given to counsel, who must also advance the client's best interests almost irrespective of any unfortunate consequences for other people, including him- or herself, has already been noted.

Of course, judicial resistance to intervention reflects the orthodox adversarial paradigm. A trial judge knows that 'good' cross-examination may require key issues to be broached indirectly. Consequently, leeway and deference are conceded to the cross-examiner's professional judgement, with the rider—almost an afterthought—to be mindful of 'the burden that is imposed upon the witness'.[86]

Collateral Evidence Rule[87]

Legal approaches to witness credibility derive from the conjunction of several critical axes or fault lines, articulated with varying degrees of

---

[85] Bar Council, Code of Conduct (8th edn, October 2004) available at www.barcouncil.org.uk. Also see CPS, *Care and Treatment of Victims and Witnesses*, Annex C 'The Prosecutors' Pledge', cl 17 ('Protect victims from unwarranted or irrelevant attacks on their character ... seek the court's intervention where cross-examination is considered to be inappropriate or oppressive').

[86] *Mechanical and General Inventions Co v Austin and the Austin Motor Co* [1935] AC 346, 359–60, HL, per Lord Hanworth MR in the Court of Appeal (endorsed in the House of Lords by Lord Sankey LC). In Australia, Hope JA made similar observations in *Albrighton v Royal Prince Alfred Hospital* (1980) 2 NSWLR 542.

[87] See also GTG Seniuk, 'Judicial Fact-Finding and Contradictory Witnesses' (1994) 37 *Criminal Law Quarterly* 70. For Australia, see the Evidence Acts 1995 (Cth) and (NSW) and Evidence Act 2001 (Tas). The collateral evidence/finality rule is embodied in s 102.

clarity and coherence through a hierarchy of rules.[88] Principles of accusatorial justice figure prominently in criminal cases. Low priority is given to
marginally relevant evidence. Traditional dichotomies based upon out-
moded logic tend to persist and the collateral evidence (or collateral
finality) rule typifies Anglo-based Evidence law's obsession with drawing
increasingly obsolescent boundaries and distinctions.

The collateral evidence/finality rule limits a party's right to call evidence
that is admissible[89] solely to credibility. The rule's application can be
complex and it is subject to exceptions.[90] The evergreen Australian classic,
Piddington v Bennett & Wood Pty Ltd,[91] a running down case arising
from an incident in Phillip Street, Sydney, in 1939, illustrates the rule's
technical operation. An eyewitness, Donellan, gave evidence supporting the
plaintiff's case. He testified that he was in Phillip Street after attending to
banking business on behalf of a Major Jarvie. The defendant challenged
Donellan's account that he was in Phillip Street at all. He supported this
challenge by calling the bank manager to show that there was no record of
a banking transaction for Major Jarvie on the day in question. The
majority of the High Court held that the bank manager's testimony was
relevant, at best, only to Donellan's credit, and so its admission into
evidence offended the collateral evidence/finality rule and justified setting
aside the jury's verdict and ordering a new trial. Within the court, judicial
opinion on the propriety of admitting the bank manager's evidence was
deeply divided.

A striking feature of the collateral evidence/finality rule is the regularity
with which precedents and law books recite the same 150-year-old
authorities[92] in support of the orthodox rule. With such a dated pedigree,
the collateral evidence/finality rule is predictably dense with technicality. A
major basis for this technicality derives from the dichotomous distinction[93]

---

[88]   For five foundational principles of criminal evidence, elegantly expressed, see P Roberts
and A Zuckerman, *Criminal Evidence* (OUP, 2004) 18–25.

[89]   In Australia, the uniform Evidence Act 1995, s 102 creates a rule defined by the
relevance of evidence solely to credibility, not its admissibility.

[90]   The exceptions permit a witness' credibility to be challenged by adducing a prior
inconsistent statement, showing a motive to lie or bias (*R v Busby* (1981) 75 Cr App R 79);
proving that the witness has a conviction (*Clifford v Clifford* [1961] 1 WLR 1274;
demonstrating that the witness is incapable of telling the truth in the *Toohey v Metropolitan
Police Commissioner* [1965] AC 595 sense; or a general reputation for lying (*R v Richardson*
[1969] 1 QB 299). For recent discussion of whether the rule should have a bright or blurry
line, see *Nicholls v R* (2005) 219 CLR 196.

[91]   (1940) 63 CLR 533. See also *Goldsmith v Sandilands* (2002) 190 ALR 370, HCA.

[92]   *Harris v Tippett* (1811) 2 Camp 637, 170 ER 1277 is credited with giving the rule
modern form. Lawrence J rejected evidence contradicting the defence witness' denial that he
had attempted to dissuade a witness for the plaintiff from attending the trial, saying '[n]o
witness can be prepared to support his character as to particular facts, and such collateral
inquiries would lead to endless confusion'. In the same year the motive to lie/bias exception to
the finality rule was established: *R v Yewin* (1811) 2 Camp 638, 170 ER 1278.

[93]   *Attorney-General v Hitchcock* (1847) 1 Ex 91, 154 ER 38.

between matters relevant to a fact in issue and collateral matters (generally meaning information relevant only to credit). This reliance has entrenched an obsession with drawing a bright line when often only a blurry line, if any, would be justifiable. In 1847, *Attorney-General v Hitchcock*[94] confirmed the rule's existence and fatally connected it to the credit/fact-in-issue pivot. The rule's rationale is grounded in the primacy of orality in the common law trial[95] and the notion that trials should focus on illuminating contentious facts, not on pursuing matters collateral to the dispute. But the dichotomy between facts in issue and witness credibility is indefensibly slippery and elusive. A concern for the ease and dignity of witnesses was integral to the rule in its early form, but this consideration neither drives nor defines it today. It is generally acknowledged[96] that in modern times the rule is an expression of the policy imperatives of trial management and efficiency. But if it does conserve court time (which is open to argument), it simultaneously inflates, intensifies and extends cross-examination by funnelling parties' energies into challenging a witness' oral testimony. The rule, in other words, aids and abets the dominance of cross-examination in the common law trial.[97]

In prevailing legal opinion, the collateral evidence rule is not regarded as a flexible rule of convenience. It is typically viewed as a rule of strict and technical application. This strictness has courted controversy by mandating judicial decisions perceived as risking injustice.[98] Some modern authorities have responded to these technical legal strictures by preferring to view the rule as one of convenience rather than principle.[99] In England, some

---

[94] *Ibid.*

[95] Of course, the traditional operation of the hearsay rule prevented the admission of most out-of-court statements. An out-of-court statement inconsistent with a witness' evidence bypasses the rule.

[96] *Attorney-General v Hitchcock*, above n 93, per Rolfe B; *R v Burke* (1858) 8 Cox CC 44, 53, 54 per Christian J; *Piddington v Bennett & Wood Pty Ltd* (1940) 63 CLR 533, per Starke J; *Nicholls v R*, above n 90.

[97] Cf *Attorney-General v Hitchcock*, above n 93, 44, per Alderson B.

[98] For frustration with the rule's limitations see Wigmore, above n 3, para 963, p 523, describing the collateral evidence/finality rule as a 'maddening prohibition' facilitating injustice by making it even harder to detect and expose 'false claimants and pretended victims of wrongs'. Wigmore cites as examples, 'children, some eccentrics, some hysterics, some insane, some nymphomaniacs, some conscious blackmailers'. And see *Nicholls v R*, above n 90, per Gummow and Callinan JJ.

[99] 'To elevate the finality rule and the prohibition on bolstering to fixed rules of law rather than rules of convenience would be a mistake, particularly as the finality rule has been strongly criticised': *Piddington v Bennett and Wood Pty Ltd* (1940) 63 CLR 533. In *Palmer v R* (1999) 193 CLR 1, 23, it was said that the finality principle 'should not be regarded as hard and fast rules but should instead be seen "as a well established guide to the exercise of judicial regulation of the litigation process"'. And see *Smith v R* (1993) 9 WAR 99; *Natta v Canham* (1991) 32 FCR 282, 300: 'the court is not bound to the view that the exclusionary rule is absolute or that the categories of exceptions to it are closed. It is a rule of practice related to the proper management of litigation. A trial judge should not be precluded from determining in an appropriate case that the matter on which the witness' credit is tested is sufficiently

flexibility in the application of the rule was discernible from 1981,[100] but this tendency caught a tailwind in 1990 with the well-known decision in *R v Funderburk*.[101] In Australia, the judgment of McHugh J in *Palmer v R* (1990)[102] embraced *Funderburkian* flexibility, but in 2005 a majority of the High Court of Australia in *Nicholls v R* displayed no enthusiasm for abandoning the rule's venerable technicalities.[103] To the contrary, the court explicitly drew attention to factual similarities between the instant appeal and *Lord Stafford's Case*,[104] a treason trial of 1680 endorsed by Pollock CB in *A-G v Hitchcock*.

McHugh J in *Palmer v R* championed pragmatism, observing that, 'the answer is an instinctive one based on the prosecutor's and the court's sense of fair play rather than any philosophic or analytic process'.[105] Dissenting in *Nicholls v R* six years later, McHugh J spelt out the implications of this perspective:

> Given the problems with the finality rule and the cases that are not explicable in terms of the rule, common law courts should now regard that rule as a rule of convenience—a rule for the management of cases—rather than a fixed rule or principle.[106]

Despite these progressive voices, judicial discontent with the rule still remains confined to dissenting judgments and isolated dicta. Alternative remedies for the rule's excessive rigidity have ranged from widening existing categories of exceptions, to creating entirely new exceptions (for example, a special category for corrupt police officers),[107] and even to non-jury trials.[108] In the United States, McCormick[109] advocated elevating

---

relevant to that credit as it bears upon issues in the case that such evidence may be admitted'; *Urban Transport Authority v Nweiser* (1992) 28 NSWLR 471; *R v Lawrence* [2001] QCA 441. For commentary, see M Newark, 'Opening up the Collateral Issue Rule' (1992) 43 *Northern Ireland Legal Quarterly* 166.

[100]   *R v Busby*, above n 90, per Eveleigh LJ.

[101]   *R v Funderburk* [1990] 1 WLR 587, CA; and see *R v Nagrecha* [1997] 2 Cr App R 401. For the United States, see *Covington v State*, 703 P. 2d 436 (Alaska CA, 1985); *State v Boiter*, 396 S.E. 2d 364 (S.C. 1990).

[102]   (1999) 193 CLR 1.

[103]   *Nicholls v R*, above n 90, by majority (McHugh J dissenting).

[104]   (1680) 7 How St Tr 1293.

[105]   *Palmer v R*, above n 99.

[106]   *Nicholls v R*, above n 90, para 53, per McHugh J (dissenting).

[107]   See eg, *R v Lawrence* [2001] QCA 441, per Thomas AJ; possibly where a witness has 'garnished his account . . . with associated details designed to give verisimilitude': *Piddington v Bennett and Wood Pty Ltd* (1940) 63 CLR 533, 558; *Goldsmith v Sandilands* (2002) 190 ALR 370, per Kirby, para 67; *R v Busby*, above n 90 (arguably also within the bias exception).

[108]   *Natta v Canham* (1992) 104 ALR 143; *Urban Transport Authority v Nweiser* (1992) 28 NSWLR 471.

[109]   EW Cleary *et al* (eds), *McCormick on Evidence* (3rd edn, St Paul, MN, West Publishing, 1984) paras 47, 112. See eg, *Stephens v People*, 19 N.Y. 549, 572 (1859) where, in a prosecution for murder by arsenic poisoning, the defendant's witnesses testified that the

the 'linchpin' of any witness' account into a new exception to the collateral evidence/finality rule. Such proposals sound a lot like conditioning admissibility on the probative value of testimony, dressed up as a new exceptional category. As Roberts and Zuckerman observe, 'candid judicial admissions of uncertainty [about the rule's operation] reflect a profound instability, or radical indeterminacy, in the application of the collateral-finality rule'.[110]

Well-resourced litigants can still invoke a handful of 'rogue' precedents, combined with the force of a good story and counsel's powers of persuasion, to outflank supposedly strict rules of evidence with creative strategies for cross-examination.[111] Prominent amongst those instances where the court has been persuaded to relax the collateral evidence/finality rule is the theme that a sexual assault complainant's credibility may be explored beyond the bounds of recognised exceptions. One might be forgiven for wondering whether Wigmore's[112] misogynist babble about 'nymphomaniacs', 'hysterics' and 'false victims' has found a receptive legal audience.

In sum, 150 years of jurisprudential anguish over the collateral evidence rule's operation, scope and focus reveals little more than disputation over moribund legal technicalities. Occasionally, as in the *Funderburk* line of decisions, the authorities raise important social questions, but in broad terms, the rule's technicalities have transfixed courts, practitioners and commentators for little real purpose. Worse than pointless, this concentration has arguably distracted attention away from far more pressing issues.

THE LAW OF EVIDENCE AND WITNESS RIGHTS: THE WAY FORWARD

Before considering reform which might ameliorate the position of individual witnesses, and in the process buttress the moral integrity and public credibility of the criminal trial process, let us first recap and underscore this chapter's principal conclusions.

First, common law rules purporting to regulate cross-examination operate inadequately. They systematically permit cross-examination that obscures, distorts and inadequately tests the accounts given by witnesses in court. Cross-examination has become a relatively unfettered vehicle for advocacy's highly refined devices that strategically utilise witnesses' weaknesses and in so doing damage witnesses and obscure and distort their

---

arsenic was administered to rats in a cellar where provisions were kept. The court held that it was proper to call another witness to prove that no provisions were kept in the cellar.

[110]   Roberts and Zuckerman, above n 88, 265–9.

[111]   See J Braithwaite, 'Rules and Principles: a Theory of Legal Certainty' (2002) *Australian Journal of Legal Philosophy* 27, 47–82.

[112]   Above, n 98.

evidence. The narrow preoccupations of the common law's adjectival rules stand in stark contrast to the deft and apparently instinctive powers of cross-examiners to undermine lay witnesses, who are no match for them under cross-examination.

Secondly, these rules cultivate the misperception that cross-examination is a vital and effective vehicle for testing information before the court. They do this by affirming and reinforcing the false and simplistic perception that witness credibility can and should be tested by hearing and seeing witnesses respond to a lawyer's probing questions.

Thirdly, like a lightning rod the law directs attention away from a major source of procedural malaise: the advocate's arsenal of weaponry, exploiting emotion, narrative and case construction. Similarly, while reformers, academics and practitioners tinker with new or variously conceived exceptions or conceptions of the collateral evidence/finality rule—bright line, blurry line or anything in between—the socio-political context escapes critical gaze. This is most prominent with respect to the impact of cross-examination upon young sexual assault complainant witnesses.[113] One is left to wonder whether the law offers the young sexual assault complainant video pre-recording, screens and CCTV to dull the pain of bearing witness yet simultaneously does far too little to curb the excesses of opposing counsel's verbal assault upon these most vulnerable of witnesses.

Fourthly, law's inadequacy in permitting the humiliation and denigration of witnesses creates deleterious ripple effects extending far beyond the plight of individual witnesses. Notoriously, crime victims, and particularly victims of sexual assault, are discouraged by the anticipated ordeal of testimony from participating in the prosecution process.[114] Further, law's inadequacy at tempering the excesses of advocacy has fanned community denigration of the criminal trial process and its lawyer-participants. This in turn has delivered very mixed blessings for the law reform agenda.[115]

Finally, however, there is no magic bullet and no perfect trial process. Our goals of accurate fact-finding are inevitably aspirational because interpreting the past is inevitably replete with uncertainty. We must consequently rest content with arriving at the best possible understanding of a disputed past event with optimum adherence to the values of dignity and humanity, consistent with procedural integrity and resources constraints.

---

[113]   See *R v Funderburk*, above n 101; *R v Nagrecha*, above n 101; *R v Gibson* [1993] Crim LR 453; and the Australian case of *Palmer v R*, above n 99.

[114]   Cooper and Roberts, above n 11, 13 n 8, quote CPS figures for 2002/03 indicating that 22 and 26 per cent (respectively) of all ineffective trials in the Crown Court and in the magistrates' courts suffered from the non-attendance of witnesses.

[115]   JD Jackson, 'Justice for All: Putting Victims at the Heart of Criminal Justice?' (2003) 30 *Journal of Law and Society* 309.

Can we realistically expect judges to step in to protect witnesses? Common law judges by their very appointment are wise to the courtroom clash of case-constructed stories; indeed they utilise similar devices in their own professional narrative, the judgment.[116] If they step into the fray in front of the jury they risk compromising judicial impartiality, and in any case the advocate's creativity is part of the taken-for-granted scenery of the common law trial. Cultural attachment to adversarialism is psycho-politically embedded in the symbolism of the accused's right (through his agent) to conduct his own defence in answer to criminal charges. Culturally-embedded practice does not vanish overnight. Legal culture is tenacious, as Pizzi and Marafioti have shown in their study of Italy's faltering attempts to shake off its inquisitorial traditions in favour of a common law adversarial-style trial.[117] Without a profession already blooded for battle, it turns out to be very difficult to import a culture of genuine adversarialism into criminal adjudication. Conversely, where the legal profession is already battle-hardened, as it is in the traditional heartlands of adversarialism, it will take more than a series of polite requests to persuade the champions of adversarial combat to lay down their swords.

Any even remotely plausible attempt to ameliorate the current plight of witnesses testifying in criminal trials must recognise that adversarialism will remain our dominant paradigm for the foreseeable future. The challenge for reformers is to accommodate the values of respect, humanity and dignity within an appropriately modified adversarial framework. Two practical suggestions spring to mind.

First, the time is long overdue for purging the law of unnecessary, out-dated and distracting technicality. Impenetrable procedural law and evidentiary requirements can no longer masquerade as pronounced intellectualism. Lawyers will always be to some extent specialists in arcane court language and practices, but the cloak of unquestioned legal authority is now threadbare. Step one in this programme of conceptual decluttering and modernisation would be to replace the largely unworkable collateral evidence/finality rule with a well-informed case management principle, leaving judges to make balanced admissibility rulings according to the contextualised facts of individual cases.

My second proposal seeks to exploit untapped resources for testing and authenticating evidence in the pre-trial process, rather than relying almost exclusively on a continuous, 'main event' trial. Our focus should shift downstream to consider the quality of pre-trial information. A well-resourced, well-managed investigation process with a properly functioning

---

[116] See eg, Edmond, above n 84.

[117] See WT Pizzi and L Marafioti 'The New Italian Code of Criminal Procedure: The Difficulties of Building An Adversarial Trial System on a Civil Law Foundation' (1992) *Yale Journal of International Law* 1. Also see WT Pizzi and M Montagna, 'The Battle to Establish an Adversarial Trial System in Italy' (2004) 25 *Michigan Journal of International Law* 429.

culture of disclosure and transparency can provide trials with improved pre-testing of information, and thus reduce the temptation to cast a prosecution case solely on the oath of a witness. Indeed, modern criminal justice processes are already moving in this direction. Criminal procedure already straddles the trial/pre-trial divide by regulating police interviews, official evidence-gathering activities (including special measures for vulnerable witnesses), expert witness reports, scientific examination and identification procedures. In England, the Police and Criminal Evidence Act 1984 and subsequent waves of statutory reform, professional police forces and the development of the Crown Prosecution Service, epitomise the dramatic changes that have occurred in pre-trial criminal process since Garrow's day, when cross-examination was the only procedural mechanism for authenticating testimony and dissembling thief-takers plied their crooked trade. Elements of inquisitorialism are increasingly being introduced;[118] and incremental professionalisation of pre-trial proceedings continues under the Criminal Justice Act 2003, which gives prosecutors an enhanced role in the charging process and extends their involvement in case construction into areas previously inaccessible to lawyers.[119] Though significant strides have already been made, our pre-trial processes are still far from perfect. The Sentamu Report[120] into the flawed investigation of the murder of Damilola Taylor provides a detailed illustration of lost opportunities for pre-trial evidence gathering and testing.

There is scope for pre-trial determinations and videotaped witness questioning to play an expanded role in controlling the theatre of the trial. For example, technology allows pre-recorded questioning to be edited in a way that mediates the tension between testing witness testimony in court and protecting witnesses from improper questioning. Cross-examination can be punctuated by objection and debate without the need to tiptoe around the jury. Counsel's fear that objecting to aggressive cross-examination might expose a witness' 'weaknesses' in front of the jury would no longer be a barrier to effective witness protection. Conspicuously, this approach harnesses the important cultural attribute of the warrior lawyer by encouraging their defensive capabilities rather than only prowess in attack.

The public manifestation of our justice system is as important as its operational truths. A community's deference to the integrity of a jury

---

[118] Exemplified by para 3.5 of the Code of Conduct issued pursuant to Criminal Procedure and Investigations Act 1996, s 23, which requires police and other investigators 'to pursue all reasonable lines of inquiry, whether these point towards or away from the suspect'.

[119] Consider, further, the announced pilot scheme to put aside a centuries old law preventing prosecutors from interviewing witnesses before trial: see C Dyer, 'Criminal Justice Revolution to Secure More Convictions', *The Guardian*, 11 November 2005.

[120] *The Review of the Investigation and Prosecution arising from the Murder of Damilola Taylor* (2002) esp. paras 4.1.8–4.1.9, 6.15, 6.16.

verdict requires the justice system to display procedural integrity.[121] Often the criminal justice system has bad press for bad reasons, but it also has bad press for good reasons. Functionally, the nineteenth century English criminal trial could rely far more on authoritarian precepts than the criminal trial of the twenty-first century. Nowadays the community is in relative terms highly educated, the media already promotes a cynical perception of the justice system, and 'consumers' vocally demand their rights. Community respect may not be readily gauged according to the content of the tabloid press but nor is it gauged solely by lawyers' views and values. Both ethical and instrumental considerations therefore reinforce the need for witness questioning practices to accord with a civilised society's obligation to provide a humane justice system.[122] Victim perspectives in law reform have moved centre-stage. It is imperative that we place greater emphasis on pre-trial process and apply strategic conceptual renovation to our current technical adjectival law. This approach should replace simplistic and potentially damaging tinkering with the trial system reflected in slogans about 'creating a level playing field' and 'equal justice for all', which can be antithetical to the fundamental precepts of accusatorial justice. Of course, simplistic and damaging tinkering with pre-trial criminal process must be resisted as well.

---

[121] C Nesson, 'The Evidence or the Event? On Judicial Proof and the Acceptability of Verdicts' (1985) 98 *Harvard Law Review* 1357.

[122] Roberts and Zuckerman, above n 88, 20–1. See also *Doorson v The Netherlands* (1996) 22 EHRR 330; *R(D) v Camberwell Green Youth Court* [2005] 1 WLR 393, HL; and *Grant v R* [2006] UKPC (Jamaica) 2.

11

*Taking Comparative Evidence Seriously**

JOHN JACKSON

INTRODUCTION

IN A SYMPOSIUM dedicated to Evidence teaching organised a few years ago by the American Association of Law Schools,[1] I commented that the advent of the so-called 'new' Evidence scholarship had done much to answer the charges levelled by William Twining against orthodox legal scholarship on evidence and proof.[2] Since the early days of Twining's critique, Evidence scholarship has ranged far beyond the narrow confines of legal doctrine. It has become much concerned with theory, particularly theoretical models, and has been informed by a wide range of disciplines from social psychology, forensic philosophy, mathematics, linguistics and most recently economics. I argued that these influences have had an enriching effect on Evidence scholarship, and added that comparative and historical approaches also had much to offer.[3]

When it comes to Evidence teaching, however, much of it still apparently conforms to the dated orthodoxy that evidence and proof scholarship has

---

* This chapter is derived substantially from my previous article, 'The Effect of Human Rights on Criminal Evidentiary Processes: Towards Convergence, Divergence or Realignment?' (2005) 68 *Modern Law Review* 737. I am grateful to all the participants at the 'Teaching Evidence Scholarship' colloquium for stimulating my thoughts on the subject of comparative evidence and in particular to Maximo Langer, Bill Pizzi, Paul Roberts and Sarah Summers for commenting on earlier drafts.
[1] EW Marsh, 'Teachers of Evidence and their Jeweled Mosaic' (2003) 21 *Quinnipiac Law Review* i and succeeding articles.
[2] Twining originally levelled his charges in W Twining, 'Goodbye to Lewis Elliott: the Academic Lawyer as Scholar' (1980) 15 *Journal of the Society of Public Teachers of Law* 2. The term 'new Evidence scholarship' derives from R Lempert, 'The New Evidence Scholarship: Analysing the Process of Proof' (1986) 66 *Boston University Law Review* 439. See also J Jackson, 'Analysing the New Evidence Scholarship: Towards a New Conception of the Law of Evidence' (1996) 16 *Oxford Journal of Legal Studies* 309.
[3] J Jackson, 'Modern Trends in Evidence Scholarship: Is All Rosy in the Garden?' (2003) 21 *Quinnipiac Law Review* 893.

left behind. It is true that a number of articles in the US symposium reflected a variety of imaginative approaches towards Evidence teaching, making use of cross-disciplinary materials on rhetoric, ethics, social psychology, and literature and popular culture. And as Roger Park said in his contribution to the symposium, even when a case method approach is taught, it is still possible to introduce a range of non-law materials, for example by drawing upon psychological personality theory when teaching character evidence, feminist theory and criminology when discussing rape shield laws, and scientific method and statistics when discussing expert evidence.[4] But if Judge Posner can be treated as an authority on the matter, Evidence teaching in the United States remains dominated by doctrine. The result is that students get neither practical insight into the handling of real-life evidentiary issues nor much theoretical insight into Evidence law. Instead they are subjected to a course that many students find 'boring and useless'.[5] Across the Atlantic, Paul Roberts' critique of Evidence teaching in the United Kingdom, published in the year preceding the US symposium, was hardly more flattering.[6] Roberts concluded that Evidence teachers have complacently accepted a standard nineteenth century conception, distilled by Thayer and popularised by Wigmore and Cross, which sees the law of evidence as limited to a set of rules for excluding evidence at trial developed by statute and case law. To substantiate this assertion, Roberts draws attention to the proliferation of Evidence texts devoted to this model of the subject.

This chapter does not explore the reasons why Evidence teaching appears to have lagged behind the innovative strides that have been taken within Evidence scholarship. Nor does it attempt to evaluate the extent to which such perceptions are well-founded in fact. A number of innovative teaching texts have appeared in recent years across a range of jurisdictions, of which Roberts' own *Criminal Evidence*, written with Adrian Zuckerman, is one.[7] Even if Evidence teaching is not in such an impoverished state as Posner and Roberts say it is, however, there is always room for improvement. Posner's solution has been to dispense with doctrine almost entirely and replace the teaching of evidentiary rules with a clinical course giving students experience in trial advocacy. While this is no doubt an

---

[4] R Park, 'Posner on Teaching Evidence' (2003) 21 *Quinnipiac Law Review* 741, 744.

[5] RA Posner, 'Clinical and Theoretical Approaches to the Teaching of Evidence and Trial Advocacy' (2003) 21 *Quinnipiac Law Review* 731, 736.

[6] P Roberts, 'Rethinking the Law of Evidence: a Twenty-First Century Agenda for Teaching and Research' (2002) 55 *Current Legal Problems* 297. Now see Paul Roberts, Chapter 1.

[7] P Roberts and AAS Zuckerman, *Criminal Evidence* (Oxford, Oxford University Press, 2004). See also J Hunter and K Cronin, *Evidence, Advocacy and Ethical Practice* (Sydney, Butterworths, 1995); C Boyle, M MacCrimmon and D Martin, *The Law of Evidence: Fact Finding, Fairness and Advocacy* (Toronto, Edmond Montgomery Publications, 1999) and R O Lempert (ed), *Evidence Stories* (New York, Foundation Press, 2006).

excellent pedagogical way in which to encourage students to take facts seriously in accordance with Twining's longstanding agenda,[8] it is less clear that this alone will help students to think more deeply about the variety of ways in which legal processes regulate fact-finding and constitute proof. Concentration on trial advocacy risks subordinating other proof-generating processes such as police questioning, discovery, plea bargaining, negotiation and settlement, which often determine case outcomes.

Roberts eschews any attempt to set out an alternative conception of the law of evidence to replace what he calls the 'one-dimensional, anachronistic and prescriptive' version bequeathed by 'Thayer & Co'.[9] But he makes two proposals to help differentiate Evidence from related legal disciplines. First of all, he argues that the law of evidence needs to expand temporally and develop away from its traditional near exclusive focus on the trial stage of legal process and take a much greater interest in pre-trial proceedings. Secondly, he argues that there is a need to rethink the conception of a unified law of evidence and move more in the continental direction by splitting the subject into two: Criminal Evidence and Procedure and Civil Procedure.

My proposal builds on Roberts' suggestions to argue for a whole-heartedly comparative approach toward Evidence. I agree entirely with the first of his proposals, and would add that there is also a need to look at post-trial evidentiary procedures such as sentencing, parole and early-release hearings established to determine whether prisoners any longer pose a risk to the public.[10] The second proposal also makes sense insofar as it would provide a much needed boost within the law curriculum for the study of civil processes. The danger, however, is that rigidly differentiating between civil and criminal litigation may preclude interesting comparisons being made between civil and criminal procedures, and between these processes and other, less prominent forms of adjudication such as the numerous tribunal hearings and public inquiries which have proliferated in scope and frequency in a number of jurisdictions. There is also a danger that dichotomous treatment may tend to divert attention away from core evidentiary questions about proof and its management, towards more theoretical questions, such as the purpose of criminal justice or civil justice which, though immensely important in their own right, might just as suitably be tackled in substantive law courses on crime, contracts, torts, etc, rather than colonising specialist courses devoted to Evidence.

---

[8]   W Twining, 'Taking Facts Seriously' (1984) 34 *Journal of Legal Education* 22.
[9]   Roberts, n 6 above, 339–40.
[10]   For a discussion of how judges are developing these procedures, see J Jackson, 'Criminal Justice, Human Rights and the Future of the Common Law' (2006) 57 *Northern Ireland Legal Quarterly* 352.

Although there is much to be said for organising an Evidence course within the particular context of criminal evidence, or indeed civil evidence, it is essential, in my view, to introduce students to a range of contrasting modes of legal proof. The first section of this chapter explains why this is particularly important today, and the following section examines the legal materials and other resources that can be used to implement this comparative approach. Although there is some interesting case study material, much of the literature continues to suffer from a slavish adherence to two dominant models of proof: the 'adversarial' and the 'inquisitorial'. The chapter proceeds to analyse these two models of proof. Taking the jurisprudence of the European Court of Human Rights by way of illustration, I argue that recent signs of harmonisation in European human rights law are better interpreted, not as incipient convergence in existing procedural models, but as an attempt to move beyond them towards a vision of proof rooted in rights of participation that is genuinely sui generis.

WHY COMPARATIVE EVIDENCE?

Before coming to the reasons why it is important to take a comparative approach toward Evidence teaching, the sense in which the term 'comparative' is being used should be clarified. References to comparative law tend to take rules and procedures across a range of jurisdictions as their subject matter. There are indeed good reasons (as we shall soon see) why it is important to take a transjurisdictional approach to Evidence. But there are many types of comparisons that can be made even within a single national jurisdiction. We have already touched upon the contrast between civil and criminal proceedings, but we could also compare processes of proof in public law and private law settings. Then there are different processes of proof according to the way in which cases are categorised within a particular type of proceeding. So, for example, in England and Wales there have been considerable differences between the way in which the more serious indictable cases are handled as opposed to summary cases, the former meriting extra layers of process such as committal proceedings and special tribunals, composed of judge and jury, to determine the ultimate verdict. Even the institutionalised division between summary and indictable cases obscures the fact that not all summary and indictable cases are handled in the same way. In England and Wales, summary cases may be heard by lay magistrates, professional magistrates or in the case of young persons, a combination of lay and professional magistrates. Even when we consider a single case, there are, as Roberts points out, different temporal phases that may apply very different models of proof. In criminal proceedings, for example, there are police interviews, bail hearings, committal proceedings, pre-trial hearings and post-conviction sentencing and parole hearings.

Straying beyond contemporary processes of proof, one could also decide to examine processes of proof historically, looking at how criminal or civil processes have evolved over time to become what they are today. Then there are the range of extra-legal dispute resolution processes that have come to the fore in the late twentieth century such as negotiation, conciliation, arbitration and, in the criminal context, restorative justice processes.[11] In a number of jurisdictions there has also recently been a proliferation of judicial inquiries established to determine events that have given rise to matters of public concern.[12] Finally, one can compare various legal modes of proof with the manner in which evidence is processed and evaluated in other disciplines. Scientists, doctors and historians, for example, handle evidence in a very different manner from legal tribunals.[13]

Of course, it would be impossible within the confines of one Evidence course to cover anything like this range of comparisons. My point is simply that an Evidence course should attempt to highlight some of these comparisons for sound pedagogical reasons. Legal education in the United Kingdom often finds itself straddled between providing students with transferable skills that equip them to become life-long learners and responsible citizens and providing students with the information and skills peculiarly relevant to legal practice.[14] I would argue that a study of comparative evidence can contribute positively to both these strands of legal education.

Most Evidence courses in the United Kingdom content themselves with studying the rules of evidence that operate at trial. But it is seriously misleading to present the law of evidence as one set of unified rules that

---

[11] Twining has discussed some of these in W Twining, *Rethinking Evidence* (Oxford, Blackwell, 1990) 354. For a discussion of the relationships between alternative dispute resolution and trial processes, see ML Seigel, 'Pragmatism Applied: Imagining a Solution to the Problem of Court Congestion' (1994) 22 *Hofstra Law Review* 567. For introductions to the burgeoning literature on restorative justice processes, see G Johnstone, *Restorative Justice: Ideas Values, Debates* (Cullompton, Willan, 2002) and the special issue on 'Practice, Performance and Prospects for Restorative Justice' (2002) 42 *British Journal of Criminology* 469. On restorative justice in the international arena, see P Roberts, 'Restoration and Retribution in International Criminal Justice: an Exploratory Analysis' in A von Hirsch *et al* (eds), *Restorative Justice and Criminal Justice* (Oxford, Hart, 2003).

[12] See eg, the recent Inquiries Act 2005 in the United Kingdom.

[13] See eg, S Haack, 'Epistemology Legalised: Or, Truth, Justice, and the American Way' (2004) 49 *American Journal of Jurisprudence* 43. For interesting contrasts drawn between historical and legal inquiries, see R Evans, *Telling Lies about Hitler* (London, Heinemann, 2002).

[14] On the role that legal academics have played in UK legal education, see F Cownie, *Legal Academics: Cultures and Identities* (Oxford, Hart, 2004).

operate, come what may, in all trial contexts. Roberts has pointed out that there has been a divergence between criminal and civil proceedings in the last 20 years, with (as he puts it) criminal evidence expanding and the civil law of evidence 'withering on the vine'.[15] This poses interesting questions. Why has the civil law of hearsay all but vanished while the criminal law of hearsay continues to remain very much alive? Are different values and objectives in play in different types of proceeding? Exploring such questions could lead to a more general comparison of evidence and proof in civil and criminal contexts.[16] But instead of analysing the differences between civil evidence and criminal evidence, most texts continue to refer to a unified law of evidence while giving most weight to criminal evidence. Even to represent the law of criminal evidence as one set of rules for criminal cases is misleading, however, since the extent to which the rules are rigorously applied in practice will depend on the level and composition of the court, and especially on whether the fact-finder is a professional judge or magistrate, or a lay jury.[17]

It follows that in order to present an accurate portrayal of the operation of the rules of evidence it is necessary to draw comparisons and contrasts between different kinds of proceedings. Moving beyond the rather limited pedagogical aim of analysing legal rules, the more ambitious aim of taking facts seriously, as urged by Twining, would introduce students to important transferable skills such as handling and evaluating evidence. It would also seem important to draw attention to the different contexts in which fact-finding takes place. Twining himself has emphasised the importance of standpoint or role when it comes to fact-finding, suggesting that each actor at each stage of the process may occupy a particular role with different objectives influencing their decision-making and conclusions.[18] When introducing students to the varieties of probability theory, for example, it is important to ground theorising in specific litigation contexts. Of course, it may be argued that there are pedagogical virtues in studying Bayes' theorem and other probabilistic concepts for their own sake. Student response is likely to be much more enthusiastic, however, if students are encouraged to compare and contrast the different concrete contexts in which the various theories are most appropriately applied.

---

[15]   Roberts, above n 6, 317.

[16]   For discussion of justifications of the hearsay rule in the different institutional contexts of civil and criminal processes, see J Jackson, 'Hearsay: the Sacred Cow that Won't be Slaughtered' (1998) 2 *E & P* 166.

[17]   For an interesting insight into the use of character evidence in magistrates' courts see P Darbyshire, 'Previous Misconduct and Magistrates' Courts' [1997] *Crim LR* 105. For contrasts between jury trials and trials without jury, see J Jackson and S Doran, *Judge Without Jury: Diplock Trials in the Adversary System* (Oxford, OUP, 1995).

[18]   See eg, W Twining and T Anderson, *Analysis of Evidence* (London, Weidenfeld, 1991) 120–1.

Comparative evidence can also be a very useful means of injecting critical thinking skills into the curriculum. It would be difficult for students to make any critical assessment of existing processes of proof unless they were given a context in which to compare and contrast them. As the German novelist Thomas Mann once remarked, it is only by making comparisons that we can distinguish who we are, in order to become all that we are meant to be.[19] Bill Pizzi has previously extended this insight to trial systems, and we might also apply it to processes of proof. If students are to be encouraged to engage in critical analysis of our present processes of proof, whether from the standpoint of promoting accuracy or to promote other values, then we need to suggest suitable alternatives as possible points of comparison.

Since lawyers in practice find themselves having to grapple with an increasingly varied set of procedures, it is helpful to expose law students to some of this variety at an early stage of their vocational training. Procedural variations in summary trial have already been mentioned. At the level of more serious crime, the tradition of jury trial would appear to be breaking down. Sheriff courts in Scotland have long sat without a jury. In Northern Ireland it is proposed to make so-called 'Diplock' trials, tried by judge alone, an established feature of the legal landscape, albeit in exceptional circumstances,[20] and even in England and Wales, the traditional home of the jury, lay juries look set to disappear in serious fraud trials and in other trials where there is a real risk of juror intimidation.[21] Beyond court practice, it used to be very rare for lawyers to be asked to consult or advise their clients in the police station prior to charge. Since the advent of the Police and Criminal Evidence Act 1984 (PACE) in the mid-1980s, however, there is hardly a criminal law practice in the country that does not provide some custodial legal advice under PACE. This involves not only advising clients who have been arrested and held in police custody, but also being present at the police interview and keeping a watchful eye over the way police officers are questioning their clients. What is said in these interviews will often determine whether suspects are charged or released and, if charged, will materially affect the strength of the case against them. There has been a proliferation of legal handbooks on how lawyers should advise clients during the interview and on how to

---

[19] Quoted in WT Pizzi, *Trials Without Truth* (New York, New York UP, 1999) 89.
[20] See the Justice and Security (Northern Ireland) Act 2006.
[21] See Criminal Justice Act 2003, ss 43 and 44 and the Fraud (Trials Without a Jury) Act 2006.

conduct themselves at these interviews.[22] However, most Evidence text-books only pay attention to these crucial pre-trial processes in relation to the admissibility of confessions and when discussing inferences form silence.

Turning to the international arena, it used to be that outside specialist practices there was little need for lawyers to look beyond the processes of proof in their own country. In his classic text on comparative law, Professor Schlesinger used the example of military lawyers having to immerse themselves in the criminal procedure of civil law countries when military personnel became subject to prosecution in the courts of 'receiving states'.[23] Today in the United Kingdom, however, the incorporation of the European Convention on Human Rights (ECHR) has required lawyers to acquaint themselves with the rulings of the European Court of Human Rights (ECtHR) and the increasing willingness of the ECtHR to pronounce on matters of criminal procedure and evidence is leading to the arrival of pan-European norms of criminal process which can no longer be ignored. The need for the European Union to tackle crime on a more global level and the measures that are being taken for strengthening co-operation, such as the European Arrest Warrant and the European Evidence Warrant, are also requiring lawyers to become conversant with European criminal procedures.[24] Beyond Europe, the emergence of the ad hoc criminal tribunals for the former Yugoslavia and Rwanda and of the International Criminal Court has led to the development of truly international rules of evidence and procedures. The statutes of the international tribunals, which contain detailed fair trial standards that go beyond the general principles of the European Convention on Human Rights, may in time have major repercussions for legal practice.[25]

If we are to produce lawyers who are reflective about existing legal practice, it is also important to employ different procedural contexts as a means of thinking about the ways of improving processes of proof. Much has been written about the dangers of transplanting foreign procedures

---

[22] See eg, E Cape and J Luqmani (eds), *Defending Suspects at Police Stations: the Practitioner's Guide to Advice and Representation* (5th edn, London, Legal Action Group, 2006).

[23] RB Schlesinger, HW Baade, PE Herzog and EM Wine, *Comparative Criminal Procedure* (6th edn, New York, Foundation Press, 1998) 508.

[24] As Roberts has commented: 'As legal norms and concepts generated by the Court of Justice in Luxembourg and the European Court of Human Rights in Strasbourg increasingly bear upon English criminal litigation, legislators, judges and legal practitioners are going to have to get to grips with new ways of formulating, developing and thinking about the law': see P Roberts, 'On Method: the Ascent of Comparative Criminal Justice' (2002) 22 *Oxford Journal of Legal Studies* 539, 561; and see generally, M Delmas-Marty and J Spencer (eds), *European Criminal Procedures* (Cambridge, CUP, 2002).

[25] See Paul Roberts, Chapter 13; R May and M Wierda, *International Criminal Evidence* (New York, Transnational Publishers, 2002); *Archbold International Criminal Courts* (3rd edn, London, Sweet & Maxwell, 2006).

into local soil.[26] But this is not an argument for refusing to look at other procedures with a view to understanding how things are done differently elsewhere. Rather it is an argument *for* looking at other procedures, *provided* this is done by giving detailed attention to the institutional context in which particular processes are administered. Critical comparativism can help as much to guard against the temptation to adopt superficially attractive foreign solutions as to suggest positive ways forward and models for reform. For example, concern has been growing in a number of common law countries at the way in which victims and witnesses are required to give evidence in adversarial processes. This has prompted critics to look at civil law processes, where various procedures are thought to ameliorate the plight of the victim.[27] The procedure whereby certain victims may participate at trial through their own counsel is particularly notable from a common lawyers' perspective. A few years ago, the Irish Law Reform Commission picked up on this idea and proposed that rape complainants be able to be represented at applications by the defence to ask questions or adduce evidence in relation to sexual history evidence.[28] Although it is too early to say whether this provision has assisted rape complainants in arguing to have such evidence excluded, this type of continental transplant is liable to intrude awkwardly into the adversarial trial which is structured around a two-party, not a three-party, contest. A close examination of civil law trials would illustrate how party interventions on behalf of victims are less intrusive in continental settings, since the judge exercises a much more commanding role over the entire proof process.[29]

More positively, however, a study of comparative proof processes may help to throw up imaginative solutions that have not been encountered within indigenous processes. One of the problems that is vexing a number of countries at present is the extent to which it is possible to amend trial procedures consistently with human rights norms to deal more effectively with terrorist suspects. In the first Belmarsh case, in which the applicants challenged their indefinite detention without trial, the House of Lords ruled out the option of indefinitely detaining non-British nationals who cannot be deported without breaching the ECHR.[30] The alternative

---

[26] See eg, N Boaria, 'On the Efficiency of Penal Systems: Several Lessons from the Italian Experience' (1997) 17 *International Review of Law and Economics* 115; O Chase, 'Legal Processes and National Culture' (1997) 5 *Cardozo Journal of International and Comparative Law* 1.

[27] See eg, L Ellison, *The Adversarial Process and the Vulnerable Witness* (Oxford, OUP, 2001).

[28] See Criminal Law (Rape) Act 1981, s 4A, as amended by Sex Offenders Act 2001, s 34.

[29] For an excellent analysis of the treatment of victims in German trials, see WT Pizzi and W Perron, 'Crime Victims in German Courtrooms: a Comparative Perspective on American Problems' (1996) 32 *Stanford Journal of International Law* 37.

[30] *A v Secretary of State for the Home Department* [2005] 2 AC 68.

approach of subjecting them to stringent control measures short of detention is also problematic from a human rights point of view.[31] Short of these measures, the only option for dealing with such persons would seem to be to bring them to trial, and for this purpose it may be necessary to revisit the experience in Northern Ireland and Germany in the 1970s when resort was made to special procedures such as non-jury courts and the appointment of special counsel in order to combat terrorism. One concern is that public trials might reveal the state's knowledge of terrorist networks and information about informants. It is for this reason that the security services in the United Kingdom have traditionally opposed making evidence resulting from surveillance, such as telephone taps, admissible at trial.[32] But the recent guidelines of the Committee of Ministers of the Council of Europe on Human Rights and the Fight against Terrorism contemplate legitimate restrictions on access to and contacts with counsel, partly sealed case files, and the use of anonymous testimony, provided that such restrictions are strictly proportionate to the threat and compensatory measures are taken to protect the interests of the accused.[33]

Experience in Northern Ireland shows how such restrictions might be implemented through, for example, the appointment of a special judge to consider the extent to which security information may be relevant to an accused's defence.[34] Special counsel could also be appointed to represent the defence during review hearings under similar conditions to that of special counsel appointed to represent the applicant in detention proceedings before the Special Immigration Appeals Committee (SIAC).[35] There have even been suggestions contemplating the appointment of a French-style investigating judge in terrorism cases who could be responsible for gathering evidence and assembling a case, which would then be presented at trial in the conventional manner.[36]

---

[31] See *Secretary of State for the Home Department v JJ and others* [2006] EWCA Civ 1141.

[32] It would seem, however, that attitudes towards the inadmissibility of this evidence may be changing: see 'Goldsmith Backs the Use of Phone Tap Evidence', *Daily Telegraph*, 22 September 2006.

[33] Council of Ministers, Guidelines of the Committee of Ministers of the Council of Europe on Human Rights and the Fight against Terrorism (2002) 35 EHRR CD 214.

[34] The procedures have most recently been summarised by the Attorney General in a reply to the Northern Ireland Affairs Committee following a high profile case in which charges of spying in the Northern Ireland Assembly against a number of defendants were dropped. See House of Commons Northern Ireland Committee, *Eighth Special Report of Session 2005-06*, HC 814.

[35] The House of Lords has given cautious approval to the use of special advocates in claims for public interest immunity in exceptional circumstances: see *R v H* [2004] 2 AC 134.

[36] See eg, Privy Counsellor Review Committee, *Anti-Terrorism, Crime and Security Act 2001 Review: Report* (2004); House of Lords and House of Commons Joint Committee on Human Rights, *Review of Counter-Terrorism Powers* (2004); Eighteenth Report of the Session 2003–2004.

COMPARATIVE EVIDENCE SCHOLARSHIP

Enough has been said to justify the study of comparative proof processes. The question remains whether there is enough literature available to make this study rewarding and interesting for students. It has already been indicated that there is very little comparative material in any of the standard Evidence textbooks. There has also traditionally been a dearth of English language literature on comparative evidence. However, the last 30 years or so have witnessed a renaissance of interest in 'foreign' processes, as disenchantment grew with 'home' solutions to the problems of combating serious crime and terrorism.

Renée Lerner has referred to two waves of literature on comparative criminal procedure during this period.[37] In the first wave in the 1970s and early 1980s, a growing dissatisfaction with 'adversarial' processes in Anglo-American systems caused many for the first time to look towards 'foreign' systems, but much of the literature that emerged was theoretically and methodologically flawed. One of the difficulties with comparative scholarship generally is that foreign processes have tended to be viewed through a local lens, producing misleading caricatures rather than faithful descriptions of legal practice. One mistake which was particularly prevalent in this first wave of comparative criminal procedure literature is the tendency to adopt the values of one's own system uncritically.[38] Those who are most familiar with adversary values have tended to portray continental systems as being endowed with opposing 'inquisitorial' features such as reliance on written statements, a presumption of guilt and the absence of any privilege against self-incrimination. Damaška has described this tendency as succumbing to a Manichean dichotomy whereby the Anglo-American system predicated on a presumption of innocence is contrasted with a continental system predicated on a presumption of guilt.[39] Others, alternatively, have tended to 'play the culture card': turning their face against any foreign change on the grounds that it would conflict with traditional local legal values.[40] On the other hand, intuitive critics of adversarial process had a tendency to view continental systems through rose-tinted spectacles, and freely advocated transplants from the supposedly superior continental tradition as palliatives for what they regarded as

---

[37] RL Lerner, 'The Intersection of Two Systems: an American on Trial for an American Murder in the French *Cour d' Assises*' (2001) *University of Illinois Law Review* 791, 796.

[38] For a critical review of some of this literature, see J Jackson, 'Theories of Truth Finding in Criminal Procedure: an Evolutionary Approach' (1988) 10 *Cardozo law Review* 475, 481–6.

[39] MR Damaška, 'Evidentiary Barriers to Conviction and Two Models of Criminal Procedure: a Comparative Study' (1973) 121 *University of Pennsylvania Law Review* 506.

[40] See J Jackson, 'Playing the Culture Card in Resisting Cross-Jurisdictional Transplants' (1997) 5 *Cardozo Journal of International and Comparative Law* 51.

the excesses of adversarial procedure.[41] Another mistake is the tendency to lump 'foreign' systems into models which do not do justice to the variety of approaches that can be seen in different systems. In the past, as we shall see, comparative literature on evidence has rarely risen much above the level of classifying systems into being either adversarial or inquisitorial, as a preliminary to considering which model is better suited to finding the truth.

If much of the first wave of comparative evidence literature was somewhat fixated by insubstantial caricatures, the second wave which began in the early 1990s proved more sensitive to the realities of practice and the institutional and cultural context in which processes evolve. There are three noteworthy features of this literature. First of all, it took a much more critical approach towards the possibility of 'transplanting' process from one legal culture to another. A number of studies concluded that it was not realistic to transplant wholesale civil law processes into common law systems and vice versa,[42] although it may be possible to import changes incrementally.[43] Secondly, this literature was less attached to abstract models and more sensitive to the variation in procedures between different countries, building into a substantial corpus of information about foreign legal process which is very good source material for students.[44] Finally, this literature has closely examined the manner in which cases are processed through successive procedural stages rather than perpetuating the theoretical models and principles that are assumed to operate. In her recent empirical study of the role of investigating magistrates and prosecutors in France, for example, Jackie Hodgson concluded that although magistrates and prosecutors are notionally responsible for criminal investigation, in practice investigations largely remain in the hands of the police, as they do in England and Wales.[45] An expanding empirically-based literature on actual trial and pre-trial practices has brought to light differences of process within particular courts as well as highlighting contrasts between trial processes, for example, between French procedures

---

[41] On the notion of 'transplants' from one system to another, see A Watson, *Legal Transplants: an Approach to Comparative Law* (2nd edn, Athens, GA, University of Georgia Press, 1993).

[42] See L Leigh and L Zedner, *A Report on the Administration of Justice in the Pre-Trial Phase in France and Germany* (London, HMSO, 1993); Lerner, above n 37.

[43] RS Frase, 'Comparative Criminal Justice as a Guide to American Law Reform: How Do the French Do It, How Can We Find Out and Why Should We Care?' (1990) 78 *California Law Review* 542; RS Frase and T Weigend, 'German Criminal Procedure as a Guide to American Law Reform: Similar Problems, Better Solutions?' (1995) 18 *Boston College International and Comparative Law Review* 317.

[44] See eg, B McKillop, 'Anatomy of a French Murder Case' (1997) 45 *American Journal of Comparative Law* 527; Lerner, above n 37.

[45] J Hodgson, *French Criminal Justice: a Comparative Account of the Investigation and Prosecution of Crime in France* (Oxford, Hart Publishing, 2005).

in the intermediate tribunal *correctionnel* and more serious matters prosecuted before the *cours d'assises*.[46] Within the *cours d'assises* the President of the court occupies a commanding role, but it appears that, in practice, there can be considerable differences in the extent to which juries and lawyers actively participate in the proceedings.

Much of this material can readily be made available to students. Detailed accounts of actual trials in foreign systems are a vivid source of contrasts with more familiar trial procedures. Exercises can be set, for example, which ask whether evidence would have been more or less straightforwardly admissible in Anglo-American trials, and students can be invited to discuss whether the outcome of the trial would have been different under an alternative procedural regime. At the same time it should be recognised that significant gaps in the literature still remain. First of all, there is a tendency to focus on the processes of proof at trial to the neglect of pre-trial processes.[47] Secondly, there has been a tendency to neglect the role that evidence norms and standards are playing in the international arena. In her critique of the rules of evidence adopted by the Yugoslav war crimes tribunal (ICTY), Patricia Wald observes that scholars and commentators have paid much more attention to developments in substantive law than to procedure and process, and calls on Evidence scholars to draw up rules of evidence for international tribunals combining civil and common law approaches.[48] Thirdly and most significantly, although second wave comparative literature has in general paid less attention to abstract models of proof, the dichotomy between adversarial and inquisitorial processes continues to be invoked or assumed as the normative conceptual framework, both for describing and explaining, and for comparing and contrasting, processes of proof.[49] This can be seen, for example, in debates about the extent to which we are witnessing a gradual convergence in the evidentiary processes of common law and civil law systems, which have been conducted largely through the lens of this dichotomy.[50]

---

[46] B McKillop, 'Readings and Hearings in French Criminal Justice: Five Cases in the Tribunal Correctionnel' (1998) 46 *American Journal of Comparative Law* 757.

[47] There are exceptions: see S Field and A West, 'Dialogue and the Inquisitorial Tradition: French Defence Lawyers in the Pre-trial Criminal Process' (2003) 14 *Criminal Law Forum* 261; and Hodgson, above n 45.

[48] P Wald, 'Rules of Evidence in the Yugoslav War Tribunal' (2003) 21 *Quinnipiac Law Review* 761. See also Paul Roberts, Chapter 13.

[49] See eg, the recent collection of essays in A Duff, L Farmer, S Marshall and V Tadros (eds), *The Trial on Trial: Truth and Due Process* (Oxford, Hart, 2004).

[50] See eg, C Bradley, 'The Convergence of the Continental and the Common Law Model of Criminal Procedure' (1996) 7 *Criminal Law Forum* 471, 475; CM Bradley (ed), *Criminal Procedure: a Worldwide Study* (Durham, NC, Carolina Academic Press, 1999); and the essays in P Fennell, C Harding, N Jörg and B Swart (eds), *Criminal Justice in Europe: a Comparative Study* (Oxford, OUP, 1995); and in M Feeley and S Miyazawa (eds), *The Japanese Adversary System in Context* (Basingstoke, Palgrave Macmillan, 2002). On the convergence thesis

Although the familiar adversarial-inquisitorial opposition continues to have some explanatory power, however, it cannot provide a comprehensive picture of all evidentiary processes, and therefore threatens to skew our understanding of the manner in which processes of proof are changing and to impede attempts to conceptualise desirable reforms. In order to maximise the benefits of studying Evidence comparatively, as well as making comparative literature safe for law reformers and domestically-focused scholars and teachers, it is therefore necessary to consider the extent to which traditional models of legal process remain fit for purpose. My argument will be that developments in international human rights law require traditional conceptual frameworks, and their associated procedural models and forms of analysis, to be rethought and recalibrated.

THE ADVERSARIAL AND INQUISITORIAL DICHOTOMY

Comparative legal scholars have drawn attention over the years to the dangers of using adversarial or inquisitorial labels to characterise legal processes in the common law and civil law traditions. An immediate problem is that across the common law-civil law divide, basic terms have been used inconsistently and with no agreed meaning. For example, scholars interpret the term 'accusatorial', often used interchangeably with 'adversarial', quite differently. Within the Anglo-American tradition, there has been a tendency to use this term in an ideological manner to refer to a series of idealised features of common law proceedings, including the presumption of innocence, the privilege against self-incrimination and the use of oral testimony, which are then contrasted with countertendencies supposedly to be found in continental proceedings.[51] Within the continental tradition, on the other hand, the term 'accusatorial' has at times been used to describe the reformed continental procedures of the nineteenth century characterised by separate functions of prosecuting and ascertaining facts, with the former entrusted to the prosecutor and the latter to the

---

generally, see BS Markesinis (ed), *The Gradual Convergence* (Oxford, OUP, 1994) 30, observing that '[t]he convergence is gradual and, indeed patchy'. Cf P Legrand, 'European Legal Systems are Not Converging' (1996) 45 *International and Comparative Legal Quarterly* 52.

[51] MR Damaška, 'Evidentiary Barriers to Conviction and Two Models of Criminal Procedure: a Comparative Study' (1973) 121 *University of Pennsylvania Law Review* 506, 569. A recent example of this 'Manichean' tendency is to be seen in *Crawford v Washington*, 124 S. Ct. 1354 (2004), where the US Supreme Court stated that English common law has long differed from continental civil law in regard to the manner in which witnesses give evidence in criminal trials: 'The common law tradition is one of oral testimony in court subject to adversarial testing, while the civil law condones examination in private by judicial officers'. For comment see SJ Summers, 'The Right to Confrontation after *Crawford v Washington*: a "Continental European" Perspective' (2004) 2 *International Commentary on Evidence*, Art 3 (see www.bepress.com/ice).

investigating judge.[52] Similarly, the term 'inquisitorial' is more frequently used by Anglo-American commentators to characterise continental procedures. Continental commentators have considered the term 'inquisitorial' too reductive to cover divergent European continental legal jurisdictions,[53] preferring instead to see modern continental procedures as 'mixed' systems which ought to be placed midway between the accusatorial and inquisitorial models. Recent reforms such as those in Italy have even caused some commentators to claim that particular continental jurisdictions have 'crossed the Rubicon' into the zone of accusatorial systems.[54] Conversely, certain American commentators have taken such a pure view of adversarial procedures that they have been unwilling to concede that even common law countries such as England truly belong within the adversarial camp.[55]

In his path-breaking work on comparative criminal procedure, Mirjan Damaška has illustrated how problematic it can be to use historically-based taxonomies in order to determine whether a system is adversarial or inquisitorial.[56] In his view, the concepts of continental and Anglo-American legal traditions are too vague and open-ended to determine what is fundamental to the accusatorial and inquisitorial ideal-type.[57] Some commentators have adopted a common denominator approach to specifying those features which are universal within each tradition. Yet this proposed test of pedigree appears circular: we call a common denominator 'adversarial' or 'inquisitorial' simply because we find it across a number of systems and we then label those systems adversarial or inquisitorial.[58] Another problem is that it is difficult to explain what should happen when one of the common denominators no longer inhabits a particular jurisdiction. Do we say that the parent system no longer belongs within the adversarial or inquisitorial camp, or do we conclude that this denominator

---

[52]   Damaška, above n 51, 558–9.

[53]   Nijboer has challenged use of the label 'inquisitorial' to describe the 'more than 25 different European continental legal cultures': see JF Nijboer, 'Common Law Tradition in Evidence Scholarship Observed from a Continental Perspective' (1993) 41 *American Journal of Comparative Law* 299, 305. Damaška, above n 51, 559, observed that it seems unfair to continentals to describe their contemporary criminal proceedings as 'inquisitorial'.

[54]   MR Damaška, 'Models of Criminal Procedure' (2001) 51 *Zbornik* 477, 485.

[55]   See eg, RA Posner, 'An Economic Approach to the Law of Evidence' (1999) 51 *Stanford Law Review* 1477, 1500 n 49: 'functionally, the English legal system is closer to the legal systems of the Continent than to the US system'.

[56]   See eg, MR Damaška, 'Adversary System' in SH Kadish (ed), *Encyclopedia of Crime and Justice* (London, Macmillan, 1983) vol 1, 24; MR Damaška, *The Faces of Justice and State Authority* (New Haven, Yale UP, 1986) 4–6; Damaška, above n 54, 478–82.

[57]   Damaška, above n 54, 481.

[58]   *Ibid.*

is no longer common? As Damaška says, the meaning of adversarial or inquisitorial remains 'hostage' to procedural change in a single country assigned to the relevant tradition.[59]

In the second part of the twentieth century, the historical approach was superseded by an approach which tried to find a series of ideal-type features that may be classified as adversarial or inquisitorial. These are not abbreviated descriptions of actual procedures. They are opposed ideal-types, in the Weberian sense, depicting patterns that can be found within the generality of Anglo-American and continental procedures, respectively. Ideal-typical models summarise particularly distinctive trends and features that contain enough essential elements of Anglo-American or continental processes to enable any particular system to be located somewhere along a spectrum between the two polar extremes. Although these models are simplistic, it is widely assumed that this approach is not only a valuable heuristic tool for theorising about different influences at play in Anglo-American and continental processes but that it also provides a useful independent standard for comparing different systems and determining how convergent or divergent they are.[60] The difficulty once again, however, lies in determining how these ideal types should be constructed and what level of detail should go into them.

There is broad consensus that the essence of the contrast in criminal procedure lies in the notion of a dispute or contest between two sides—prosecution and defence—in a position of theoretical equality before a court which must decide on the outcome, and the contrasting notion of an official and thorough inquiry driven by court officials.[61] From this essential contrast two different models of proof can be extrapolated. In the 'contest model' the prosecution prepares the case, brings the charge and is responsible for presenting the evidence and proving the offence charged. In contested cases, the defendant attempts to rebut the charge by presenting evidence and arguments against the prosecution. The proceedings are presided over by a neutral adjudicator whose function is to see that the parties play by the rules of the contest, but not to take an active part in the presentation of the evidence or to decide the outcome of the case. In the 'inquest model', to which the 'contest model' is conventionally counter-posed, the court takes centre-stage in the handling of the evidence. The

---

[59]   *Ibid*. For other difficulties with this approach, see M Langer, 'From Legal Transplants to Legal Translations: the Globalisation of Plea Bargaining and the Americanisation Thesis in Criminal Procedure' (2004) 45 *Harvard International Law Journal* 1.

[60]   For defences of the use of adversarial and inquisitorial models in order to analyse criminal procedure systems, see N Jörg, S Field and C Brants, 'Are Inquisitorial and Adversarial Systems Converging?' in Fennell *et al*, above n 50, 41; Ellison, above n 27; Langer, above n 59, 5; P Duff, 'Changing Conceptions of the Scottish Criminal Trial: the Duty to Agree Uncontroversial Evidence' in Duff *et al*, above n 49, 31.

[61]   See eg, Damaška, above n 51, 563–5; Roberts and Zuckerman, above n 7, 45.

prosecution may first decide the charge but officials of the court then have the responsibility for gathering, testing and evaluating the evidence. Any role the prosecution and defence play in the proof process is minimal and subordinate to the court's function of finding the truth.

Although these simple models give rise to familiar contrasts, there is considerable uncertainty whether additional features commonly associated with each model should also be included within its specification. Some features are commonly included: for example, the notion of the contest model is said to require a continuous trial while the inquest model is said to require a series of inquiries; oral evidence is a feature of the contest model, while written evidence is a more common feature of the inquest model.[62] Further contrasts, on the other hand, are not usually considered essential characteristics of the models. These include the fact that in the contest model the proceedings are in public whereas in the inquest model they are more often conducted in private; and also the observation that a lay jury sitting separately from the professional judge in a divided trial court will often decide the outcome of the case in the contest model, whereas in the inquest model judges sitting in a unitary court will decide the case, with or without lay assistance.[63] Decisions as to what factors should and should not be included are not easy to make on the basis of logic.[64] Logic does not dictate that we should include a continuous trial as a necessary feature of the contest model but conclude that a jury system is not necessary. It would be possible to divide proceedings arranged around the notion of a contest into a series of phases of proof. Conversely, it could be argued that a jury is a more essential feature of the contest model, as the involvement of lay jurors imposes constraints on judicial fact-finding without which the principle of party presentation might otherwise be overwhelmed.

Another feature which is commonly considered to be an essential characteristic of the contest model, and a point of contrast with the inquest model, is the need for rules of evidence. Logic may dictate that in a party-dominated system there is a need for rules to allocate the burden of proof and to regulate the contest. But beyond this it is unclear how essential other rules are. Disclosure rules are commonly justified in the contest model in order to ensure 'equality of arms' between the parties, particularly in the criminal context where there is such an imbalance of resources between prosecution and defence.[65] But there is a natural

---

[62] See eg, Roberts and Zuckerman, above n 7, 47.

[63] *Ibid*. Others, however, would include the jury within the adversarial system: see eg, Jörg, Field and Brants, above n 60, 42; Langer, above n 59, 10.

[64] Damaška, above n 54, 483.

[65] AS Goldstein, 'The State and the Accused: Balance of Advantage in Criminal Procedure' (1960) 69 *Yale Law Journal* 1149; RJ Traynor, 'Ground Lost and Found in Criminal

tendency in a contest model for parties to be reluctant to disclose all evidence material to the case, and rules mandating disclosure inevitably rub up against this more natural inclination to hold one's cards close to one's chest. Other means of redressing the imbalance, such as providing for strong defence representation, might prove just as effective.[66] A number of exclusionary rules, including the hearsay prohibition and its exceptions, are also sometimes said to be justified by the adversary system as they provide incentives for parties to adduce the best evidence.[67] But there are structural difficulties in making these rules effective, unless we import into the procedural system a bifurcated structure of decision-making, allowing judges as the tribunal of law to screen the evidence from a differently-constituted tribunal of fact. Mandatory directions can also be used to try to influence the manner in which fact-finders reason, but again it is not so clear that these need be reserved exclusively for fact-finders in the contest model. Although freedom of proof is closely associated with continental fact-finding,[68] there is no reason why this need be a necessary feature of an inquest model.

All this serves to make the point that it is very difficult to add features to the core contrast between proof by contest and proof by inquest that can be said to be essential characteristics of the two models. As soon as we start to flesh out the models, we tend to ascribe features to them either on an empirical basis from what we see happening in the Anglo-American or continental traditions or on a normative basis from what we believe ought to be included within each model. But this inevitably leaves scope for different views as to what should or should not be included within each model, with the result that locating particular systems along the spectrum of procedural types will always be controversial.

Even if we could agree on the core features of adversarialism and inquisitorialism, difficulties of application remain. Certain non-common law countries, for example, insist that they now have adversary systems.[69] But Anglo-American commentators are much less likely to view the recent

---

Discovery' (1962) 39 *New York University Law Review* 228, 249; Jackson and Doran, above n 17, 62; Roberts and Zuckerman, above n 7, 52–6.

[66] In Scotland, for example, there has been a tradition (which is now changing) of non-disclosure by the Crown of any evidence helpful to the defence case: see AV Sheehan and DJ Dickson, *Criminal Procedure* (2nd edn, Edinburgh, Butterworths, 2003) para 164.

[67] See eg, D Nance, 'The Best Evidence Principle' (1988) 73 *Iowa Law Review* 227. On the wider relationship between rules of evidence and the adversary system, see MR Damaška, *Evidence Law Adrift* (New Haven, Yale UP, 1997) ch 3.

[68] MR Damaška, 'Free Proof and its Detractors' (1995) 43 *American Journal of Comparative Law* 343.

[69] WT Pizzi, 'The American "Adversary System"' (1998) 100 *University of West Virginia Law Review* 847, 848. See also C Brants and S Field, 'Legal Cultures, Political Cultures and Procedural Traditions: Towards a Comparative Interpretation of Overt and Proactive Policing in England and Wales and the Netherlands' in D Nelken (ed), *Contrasting Criminal Justice* (Aldershot, Dartmouth, 2000) 77, 79.

changes in a number of reformed continental processes as truly 'Coperni-
can'.[70] Pizzi has observed that there are features of German trials that are
deeply adversarial, in the sense that witnesses' versions of events are
strongly contested by defence lawyers, yet judges retain considerable
procedural control.[71] Are these trials adversarial or non-adversarial? He
also invokes the example of Norway, where the parties have the responsibility for presenting the evidence, yet at the beginning of the trial
defendants are asked to respond to the charges, quite unlike Anglo-
American trials. Again, are these trials adversarial or non-adversarial?

Variations within systems on particular aspects of procedural organisation make it even more difficult to locate the system as a whole on the
adversarial/inquisitorial spectrum. It is commonly said, for example, that
many of the pre-trial proof processes in the Anglo-American criminal
systems are just as inquisitorial as those found in continental systems.[72]
How, then, are we to characterise systems which manifest pronounced
features of inquest in pre-trial procedures, followed by extreme characteristics of contest at trial? The prominence of 'adversarial' and inquisitorial'
features may also vary within a single national jurisdiction. Although there
are similarities between the process of proof in the tribunaux correction-
nels and the cours d'assises in France, in practice more oral testimony is
heard in the proceedings of the higher court.[73] Similarly, in Anglo-
American trials it has been suggested that the absence of the jury causes an
adversarial deficit even though the rules of procedure and evidence remain
the same in both jury and non-jury trials.[74] Some have even detected
conflicting forces at work within the same trial, with judges simultaneously
taking both passive and active stances towards the evidence presented at
various stages of the process.[75]

All this does not mean that 'adversarial' and 'inquisitorial' models of
proof have been entirely unilluminating. If we limit our definition of these
terms to those features that flow logically from the contest-inquest polarity,
the contrast would seem to be incapable of encompassing the diversity of
processes of proof that are evident across the many Anglo-American and
European systems. But if we take a more expansionist view, the models can
be used to cover quite a wide variety of practices, ranging beyond party

[70] Damaška, above n 54, 491.
[71] Above n 69.
[72] See eg, AS Goldstein, 'Reflections on Two Models: Inquisitorial Themes in American Criminal Procedure' (1974) 26 *Stanford Law Review* 1009.
[73] McKillop, above n 46, 779.
[74] S Doran, J Jackson and ML Seigel, 'Rethinking Adversariness in Non-Jury Criminal Trials' (1995) 23 *American Journal of Criminal Law* 1.
[75] See eg, Pizzi, above n 69.

contest and court official inquest, to other factors such as: the concentration of criminal proceedings on the trial stage as opposed to the proceedings being spread over successive steps or phases; reliance at trial on oral as opposed to written testimony; the extent to which decision-making is organised in a bifurcated or unitary manner; and the use of exclusionary rules of evidence as opposed to mechanisms promoting free proof.

In recent times, scholars have drawn more expansive parallels with other typologies, which are less preoccupied with rules of procedure and proof and more attentive to the positions that key actors such as police officers, prosecutors and judges occupy within organisational structures and their distinctive roles in the processes of proof. Damaška's classic analysis contrasted two ideals of officialdom. The 'hierarchical' model emphasised certain features of continental procedure, with its emphasis on officials organised in a hierarchy applying technical norms, whilst the 'co-ordinate' model reflected certain tendencies within Anglo-American criminal process to hand over decision-making to lay persons applying community norms with considerable discretion.[76] More recently, a number of scholars have explored whether police officers and prosecutors are motivated by considerations of case-building or truth-finding.[77] 'Co-ordinate' and 'case construction' models have tended to be associated with adversarial processes, 'hierarchical' and 'truth-finding' models with inquisitorial processes, although opinions may differ regarding the appropriate categorisation of particular stages of a criminal investigation. When we probe the processes of proof in Anglo-American justice, for example, we find that at a certain stage of an inquiry a process can be transformed from one in which actors are primarily interested in truth-finding to an exercise in constructing a case against the suspect. But it may not be easy to determine at what point a process moves from the 'inquisitorial' zone into the 'adversarial' one.[78]

The imposition of these extra dimensions on procedural models already laden with opaque meaning predictably exacerbates disagreements as to

---

[76] MR Damaška, 'Structures of Authority and Comparative Criminal Procedure' (1975) 84 *Yale Law Journal* 480.

[77] For case construction in England, see M McConville, A Sanders and R Leng, *The Case for the Prosecution* (London, Routledge, 1991). For an analysis of the roles of police officers, prosecutors and judges in the French criminal justice system, see J Hodgson, 'The Police, the Prosecutor and the Juge d'Instruction' (2001) 41 *British Journal of Criminology* 342; and J Hodgson, *French Criminal Justice* (Oxford, Hart Publishing, 2005). For a comparative analysis of the role of prosecutors in evidentiary processes, see J Jackson, 'Legal Culture and Proof in Decisions to Prosecute' (2004) 3 *Law, Probability and Risk* 109.

[78] Commentators have differed as to how to characterise police questioning in England and Wales, some referring to it as an 'adversarial' process and others as 'inquisitorial': cf R Evans, *The Conduct of Police Interviews with Juveniles* (London, HMSO, 1993) and E Cape, 'The Revised PACE Codes of Practice: a Further Step towards Inquisitorialism' [2003] *Crim LR* 355.

whether systems are converging or diverging. An analysis focused exclusively on the rules and procedures of proof is more likely to accept at face value the 'transplants' or deviations away from the extreme pole of either model, and more likely to detect convergence in proof processes somewhere closer to the centre of the spectrum. Analyses which probe deeper into what the rules mean to the actors themselves, on the other hand, are more likely to detect cultural resistance to the changes that are being made. When it is understood that legal reforms are mediated by local culture, the story tends to become one of institutional resistance, innovation and diversity in procedural forms rather than a tale of transnational convergence.

Risks of over-generalisation and the absence of agreed terminology are endemic to any exercise which attempts to make cross-cultural comparisons between legal systems. So long as we are careful to explain what we mean by the terms 'adversarial' and 'inquisitorial', they can still be useful concepts in analysing shifts in direction within and between systems. But if we use the terms inappropriately, as though they were comprehensive, all-inclusive categories, we may lose sight of important aspects of legal process which cannot be categorised as either 'adversarial' or 'inquisitorial' at all, no matter how broad or deep our perspective. It has been argued, for example, that some of the developments that have taken place within US civil processes in the last 20 years and, more latterly, within the procedures of the ICTY, are better described in terms of a third procedural model, labelled 'managerial' by Langer.[79] Similar trends may be discerned within English civil process in the aftermath of the Woolf reforms and increasingly also within English criminal procedure.[80] Developments at work at the sentencing stage of common law processes are also hard to categorise within either traditional model.[81] Restorative justice processes, in which offenders are brought face to face with victims in order to find ways of addressing offending behaviour,[82] involve trying to reach a consensus covering the circumstances of the offence. This process of factual inquiry is not easily categorised as 'adversarial' or 'inquisitorial', and might be better described as 'problem solving'.[83] Such developments further underscore the limitations of the traditional adversarial/inquisitorial dichotomy as a

[79] M Langer, 'The Rise of Managerial Judging in International Criminal Law' (2004) 52 *American Journal of Comparative Law* 835.

[80] See *Access to Justice: Final Report by Lord Woolf MR to the Lord Chancellor on the Civil Justice System in England and Wales* (1996). On the rise of managerialism in English criminal procedure, see J McEwan, 'Cooperative Justice and the Adversarial Criminal Trial: Lessons from the Woolf Report' in S Doran and J Jackson (eds), *The Judicial Role in Criminal Proceedings* (Oxford, Hart, 2000) 17.

[81] J Shapland, *Between Conviction and Sentence: the Process of Mitigation* (Oxford, OUP, 1981).

[82] See above n 11.

[83] Shapland, above n 81, 141.

framework for analysing the complexity of real-life processes of proof. As one critic has put it, 'dichotomies provide only two-dimensional slices through reality: they give us black and white and—depending upon their degree of refinement—innumerable shades of grey ... But they do not give us the reds and greens and blues'.[84] As well as distorting our perception of real-life processes, dichotomies can also serve to stifle imaginative thinking about how these processes might be improved, insisting that any solution be categorised within their cramped conceptual framework.

A further important illustration of the limitations of the adversarial/inquisitorial dichotomy may be found in the way in which the European Court of Human Rights has been developing its concept of 'adversarial rights'. Although the ECtHR has commonly referred to 'adversarial' rights and principles and has not been able to abandon entirely the adversarial/inquisitorial dichotomy, its conceptions do not match existing practices within the adversarial tradition and it is therefore misleading to regard the ECtHR's jurisprudence as a concrete manifestation of convergence in the direction of traditional adversarial processes. We have seen that on the broadest interpretation of the adversarial model, we would expect to see one or more of the following characteristics: party control of the proof process, concentration on a climactic trial, reliance on oral testimony, trial by jury and exclusionary rules of evidence. Yet the ECtHR has not required states parties to adopt any of these practices. In fact, the main thrust of its rulings has been to realign national trial processes in accordance with what is best conceptualised as an entirely new model of proof.

EVOLUTION OF EVIDENTIARY HUMAN RIGHTS NORMS

The primary vehicle in the development of evidentiary human rights norms has been the right to a fair trial encapsulated in Article 6 of the European Convention on Human Rights. The right to a fair trial has deep roots in the history of human rights law, and finds expression in the UN Universal Declaration of Human Rights.[85] Article 6(1) ECHR contains a general definition of the right which closely follows Article 10 of the Declaration, whilst Article 6(2) enshrines the presumption of innocence which is contained in Article 11 of the Declaration. But Article 6 ECHR goes further than the Declaration by enumerating a number of other specific safeguards, including in Article 6(1) the right to be brought to trial within a reasonable time and in Article 6(3) a number of defence rights for those

---

[84] I Markovits, 'Playing the Opposites Game: On Mirjan Damaška's *The Faces of Justice and State Authority*' (1989) 41 *Stanford Law Review* 1313, 1340–1.

[85] AH Robertson and JG Merrills, *Human Rights in Europe* (3rd edn, Manchester, Manchester UP, 1993) 87.

charged with a criminal offence, including the right to have adequate time and facilities for the preparation of the defence, the right to legal assistance, the right to examine or have examined witnesses against the defence and to obtain the attendance and examination of witnesses under the same conditions as prosecution witnesses.

In many respects, the inclusion of these specific rights may be seen as a triumph for those British lawyers steeped in the common law tradition who argued in favour of a more specific set of rights during the drafting process. In his masterly account of the ECHR's origins, Simpson has shown how the final draft was a compromise between civil law and common law approaches towards the protection of individual rights.[86] The civil law approach favoured setting out the enumerated rights in brief general terms, leaving the detailed working out to be done by member states with a Court of Human Rights responsible for elaborating a jurisprudence of rights. The common law approach, on the other hand, was distrustful of bills of rights and reluctant to place its trust in the evolution of a jurisprudence derived from very general principles of law. Instead it put its weight behind a more precise specification of the rights and their exceptions, and in the provision of effective remedies. The resulting compromise was one which appeared to favour both sides. On the one hand, the agreed final text appeared to reflect the common law approach of a more specific delineation of particular rights than are outlined in the Universal Declaration. On the other hand, the establishment of a Commission and Court to enforce the rights was a victory for the civil law approach, albeit that the Convention did not require states parties to accept either the right of individual petition or the jurisdiction of the ECtHR.

Taken at face value, the specific rights incorporated in Article 6 ECHR, drafted as they were largely by the British, not unnaturally appeared to resonate more with the common law than the civil law tradition. Although the right to a trial within a reasonable time has not been independently recognised in either, Article 6(3)'s emphasis on the rights of the defence and in particular its concern to buttress the role of the parties in presenting and challenging evidence, appears to give the ECHR a decidedly adversarial flavour.[87] Any victory which the common law tradition might claim from the enumeration of specific defence rights was, however, reined-in over time by the interpretation that came to be placed on those rights by the Commission and the ECtHR in their subsequent jurisprudence. The very development that the British drafters had resisted, namely that Convention

---

[86] AWB Simpson, *Human Rights and the End of Empire* (Oxford, OUP, 2001) chs 13 and 14.

[87] B Swart and J Young, 'The ECHR and Criminal Justice in the Netherlands and the UK' in Fennell, Harding, Jorg and Swart, above n 50, 57; Nijboer, above n 53, 311; JF Nijboer, 'Vision, Abstraction and Socio-Economic Reality' (1998) 49 *Hastings Law Journal* 387, 394.

rights would come to be interpreted by an international court with binding effect on national law, has come to pass. In the process, some of the adversarial purity of the written text was sacrificed.

Although the European Commission and ECtHR have emphasised that the right to a fair trial holds a prominent place in a democratic society, with the result that Article 6 must be given a broad construction,[88] a number of limiting principles have prevented the Strasbourg authorities from being over-prescriptive about the evidentiary procedures that should be adopted in the member states. First of all, from the beginning the Commission established that the Strasbourg authorities do not constitute a further court of appeal from the national courts.[89] This 'no fourth instance' doctrine together with international tribunals' respect for the 'margin of appreciation' has meant that national courts are given considerable latitude concerning the evaluation of evidence. Secondly, as a general principle states parties enjoy considerable freedom in their choice of the appropriate means for ensuring that their judicial systems comply with the requirements of Article 6 ECHR.[90] The ECtHR does not require states to adopt any particular rules governing the admissibility of evidence, although (as we shall see) it has embraced certain evidentiary principles that have had to be translated into national systems. The competent national authorities have been left to determine the relevance of proposed evidence, whilst rules governing the admissibility of evidence are 'primarily a matter for regulation under national law'.[91] The ECtHR's unwillingness to prescribe rules of evidence or concepts such as admissibility was a clear signal that it had no wish to impose a common law system of evidence on signatory states. Thirdly, the Commission and ECtHR both said at an early stage that their task is to determine whether the proceedings taken 'as a whole' were fair.[92] On the one hand, this has enabled the ECtHR to give an expansive interpretation to Article 6, declaring that the rights accorded to defendants in Article 6(2) and (3) are 'specific aspects of the general principle stated in paragraph 1 and are to be regarded as a non-exhaustive list of "minimum rights" which form constituent elements amongst others, of the notion of a fair trial in criminal proceedings'.[93] This expansionist interpretation has enabled the ECtHR to read other important protective

---

[88] *Delcourt v Belgium* (1979–80) 1 EHRR 355; *Moreira de Azevedo v Portugal* (1992) 13 EHRR 731, para 66.

[89] *X v Federal Republic of Germany* (1957) 1 Yearbook 150, 152.

[90] *Hadjianastassiou v Greece* (1993) 16 EHRR 219, para 33.

[91] *Engel v Netherlands* (1979–80) 1 EHRR 647, para 46; *Schenk v Switzerland* (1991) 13 EHRR 242; *Delta v France* (1993) 16 EHRR 574, para 35.

[92] *Nielson v Denmark* (1957) 4 Yearbook 518; *Barberà, Messegué and Jabardo v Spain* (1989) 11 EHRR 360; *Delta v France*, above n 91.

[93] *Deweer v Belgium* (1979–80) 2 EHRR 439, para 56.

rights into Article 6, such as the privilege against self-incrimination.[94] On the other hand, however, it has given the ECtHR leeway to conclude that particular rights need not be respected in every case if measures restricting the rights of the defence are 'strictly necessary' and there are adequate compensating measures taken to protect the accused at trial.[95] This has permitted inroads to be made into the specific rights by domestic jurisdictions, provided that the trial as a whole may still be considered fair.[96] Finally, the ECtHR has given the ECHR an evolutive interpretation according to which the Convention is 'a living instrument which must be interpreted in the light of present day conditions'.[97] This has enabled some of the rights and principles developed under Article 6 to be given an expansionist interpretation 'in the light of present day conditions'; but at the same time it has also enabled rights to be traded-off against competing concerns that have come to dominate the criminal process landscape.[98]

These limiting principles have enabled the ECtHR to be quite flexible about the evidentiary principles and processes that are compatible with Article 6, departing when necessary from the straitjacket of the specific rights in Article 6(2) and (3) and developing its own distinctive principles of fairness. Instead of adopting a fully-fledged adversarial position requiring party control over the presentation of evidence, the Commission and ECtHR from an early stage chose to develop the principle of 'equality of arms', an old idea with roots in both common law and civil law traditions.[99] The principle of equality of arms has been expressed in terms of affording every party to the proceedings 'a reasonable opportunity to present his case in conditions that do not place him at substantial disadvantage vis-à-vis his opponent'.[100] Although this principle was enunciated in the formative jurisprudence of the Commission and ECtHR,[101] it has undergone development and refinement over the years. In 1970, for

---

[94] See eg, *Funke v France* (1993) 16 EHRR 297.

[95] See eg, *Van Mechelen v Netherlands* (1998) 25 EHRR 647, para 58.

[96] As Lord Bingham put it in *Brown v Stott* [2001] 2 All ER 97, 115, 'the jurisprudence of the European Court very clearly establishes that while the overall fairness of the criminal trial cannot be compromised, the constituent rights comprised, whether explicitly or implicitly, within Article 6 are not themselves absolute. Limited qualification of these rights is acceptable if reasonably directed by national authorities towards a clear and proper public objective and if representing no greater qualification than the situation calls for'.

[97] *Tyrer v United Kingdom* (1979–80) 2 EHRR 1, para 31.

[98] This balancing approach has been evident when the court has come to balance the interests of victims and witnesses against the interests of a defendant in a fair trial: see below text accompanying nn 128–136.

[99] The principle is an expression of the old natural law principle, *audi alteram partem*, which was first formulated by St Augustine: see JR Lucas, *On Justice* (Oxford, OUP, 1980) 84.

[100] *Kaufman v Belgium* (1986) 50 DR 98, 115; *Foucher v France* (1998) 25 EHRR 234, para 34.

[101] See eg, *X v FRG*, above n 89.

instance, the ECtHR upheld an old Belgian practice whereby the procureur général would retire with the court after expressing a view as to whether the appellant's appeal should be heard.[102] Over 20 years later, however, the ECtHR reached a different conclusion. Once the procureur général had expressed an opinion on the merits of the appeal, he became (said the ECtHR) the applicant's opponent and the procureur général's participation in the judges' private deliberations gave him an unfair advantage over the appellant.[103] Emphasising the importance of appearances, the ECtHR drew attention to the increased sensitivity of the public to the fair administration of justice. Equal participation by the parties makes it important to distinguish between those responsible for prosecuting or appearing to be prosecuting and those responsible for judging. This ruling marked a decisive break with the old continental practices which tended to blur the distinction.

It is not only equality in presenting arguments that is required, but also equality in being able to present evidence as well. Thus in *Bonisch v Austria*,[104] a court-appointed expert provided a report that meat prepared by the applicant contained an excessive concentration of a carcinogenic substance called bezopyrene. The ECtHR considered that this expert was more like a witness against the accused than an impartial advisor. As a court witness, the expert could attend throughout the hearings, put questions to the accused and to witnesses with the leave of the court, and comment on the evidence. Since he was given much greater control over the proceedings than a defence expert witness would have been given, Bonisch had not been accorded equal treatment.

The principle extends beyond formal equality during the presentation of evidence at trial and during the appeals process. In order for prosecution and defence to be able to contest on equal terms, despite their markedly unequal resources, the Commission and ECtHR have recognised that the principle of equality of arms requires that everyone charged with a criminal offence should, pursuant to Article 6(3)(b), have access to all relevant information that has been or could be collected by the competent authorities.[105] Since the prosecution enjoys considerable facilities derived from its powers of investigation, equality demands that the results of these investigations be shared with the defence.

Despite the significance that the principle of equality of arms attaches to party information and party presentation of evidence, however, it cannot be equated with adversarial preferences. This is illustrated by the civil case

---

[102] *Delcourt v Belgium*, above n 88.
[103] *Borgers v Belgium* (1993) 15 EHRR 92.
[104] *Bonisch v Austria* (1987) 9 EHRR 191.
[105] *Jespers v Belgium* (1981) 27 DR 61.

of *Feldbrugge v Netherlands*,[106] where the applicant was denied any opportunity to appear either in person or through her lawyer in making her claim for health insurance benefits. The ECtHR held that there had been no breach of the principle of equality of arms because Mrs Feldbrugge's opponents were equally disadvantaged under the procedures of the Appeals Board. It is true, of course, that Article 6(3) specifically guarantees certain defence rights in criminal cases such as the right to call witnesses, but even here equality of arms may serve to limit adversarialism as Article 6(3) provides that parties have the right to obtain the attendance and examination of witnesses on their behalf only 'under the same conditions' as their opponent. It follows that the defence have no right under this principle to call any witness of its choosing. The competent national authorities are therefore entitled to determine the relevance of the proposed evidence of each witness.[107] In addition, it would seem that in a legal system utilising court-appointed experts, parties have no right to call their own expert in rebuttal unless there are objectively justified fears concerning the court expert's impartiality.[108]

Although there was no inequality of arms in the *Felbrugge* case, the ECtHR went on to hold that there had nevertheless been a breach of Article 6(1) ECHR because the failure to hear Mrs Feldbrugge meant she had not been allowed proper participation in the proceedings. Towards the end of the 1980s, the ECtHR began to develop this right to be heard, articulating not merely the principle of equality of arms but also the principle that 'all the evidence must be produced in the presence of the accused at a public hearing with a view to adversarial argument'.[109] Subsequent decisions indicated that the right to an adversarial trial means, in a criminal case, that the prosecution and defence must be given the opportunity to inspect and comment on the observations filed and the evidence adduced by the other party.[110] It is important to appreciate, however, that in developing this adversarial right, the ECtHR stopped short of prescribing the kind of adversarial trial that is associated with common law jurisdictions where procedural control is largely in the hands of the parties rather than the judge. Under the rubric of *une procédure contradictoire*, it has long been considered important in continental procedure that the defendant should be present when procedural activities are under way and should be entitled to offer counterproofs and counterarguments.[111] The Commission and ECtHR sought to 'translate' the

---

[106] (1986) Series A 99.

[107] *Engel v Netherlands*, above n 91, para 91; *Vidal v Belgium* (1992) Series A 235-B.

[108] *Brandstetter v Austria* (1993) 15 EHRR 378.

[109] *Barberà, Messegué and Jabardo*, above n 92, para 78.

[110] *Brandstetter v Austria*, above n 108, para 67; *Rowe and Davis v United Kingdom* (2000) 30 EHRR 1, para 60.

[111] Damaška, above n 39, 561.

defence rights prescribed in Article 6 ECHR into a vision of trial procedure that was as compatible with the continental notion of *une procédure contradictoire* as with the common law adversary trial. Defendants have to be guaranteed rights to legal representation, to relevant information, to be present in person, and to present arguments and evidence at trial. But this does not rule out considerable participation by judges in asking questions or even calling witnesses.

The Strasbourg authorities have not self-consciously tried to squeeze Article 6 defence rights into a continental mould to be imposed on all states parties regardless of their procedural heritage. The one right that would seem to stretch the notion of *une procédure contradictoire* is the right to examine witnesses, expressly safeguarded in Article 6(3)(d). In a series of decisions beginning in 1986,[112] the ECtHR began to interpret Article 6(3)(d) to mean that convictions should not be substantially based upon the statements of witnesses whom the defence were unable to cross-examine. There would seem to be little doubt that these decisions, although not always consistent with one another,[113] were a major factor in some of the changes that began to take effect in several continental jurisdictions firmly associated with the old inquisitorial tradition.[114] As a result of the *Kostovski* decision against the Netherlands, for example, in which the ECtHR ruled that there was a breach of Article 6 where the conviction was based to a decisive extent on the statements of two anonymous witnesses who gave evidence in the absence of the accused, the Dutch Supreme Court was forced to retreat from earlier case law that had permitted the use of anonymous hearsay evidence.[115] In France, the Court of Cassation held that Article 6(3)(d) requires the trial court to grant the defendant's request to summon and question a witness unless the witness is clearly unavailable, or his testimony would be irrelevant, or the accused has had an adequate opportunity to confront and question the witness in prior proceedings, or there is a serious risk of witness intimidation or

---

[112] See eg, *Unterpertinger v Austria* (1991) 13 EHRR 175; *Kostovski v Netherlands* (1990) 12 EHRR 434; *Windisch v Austria* (1991) 13 EHRR 281; *Delta v France* (1993) 16 EHRR 574.

[113] Although the court has generally considered that cross-examination must be permitted where the evidence plays a substantial, or a decisive, or main part in the conviction, on occasions it has varied this standard, narrowing it at times to apply where the evidence is the only item of evidence (see eg, *Asch v Austria* (1991) 15 EHRR 597 and *Artner v Austria* (1992) 242 Series A 3) and widening it in other cases to apply where the evidence has 'played a part' in the conviction (see eg, *Ludi v Switzerland* (1993) 15 EHRR 173). See DJ Harris, M O'Boyle and C Warbrick, *Law of the European Convention on Human Rights* (London, Butterworths, 1995) 212.

[114] Nijboer, above n 53, 311, has singled out Spain, France, Belgium and the Netherlands in this category. See also M Chiavario, 'The Rights of the Defendant and the Victim' in Delmas-Marty and Spencer, above n 24, 548.

[115] See PTC van Kampen, *Expert Evidence Compared* (Leiden, E M Meijers Institute, 1998) 105–6.

retaliation.[116] The adversarial defence rights in Article 6 ECHR strongly influenced the Delmas-Marty Commission, which proposed that a list of basic principles should be placed at the head of a new Code of Criminal Procedure. In legislative reforms enacted in 2000, the principle that criminal procedure should be fair and *'contradictoire'* was given pride of place in the list of guiding principles.[117] In Italy the new Code of Criminal Procedure in 1988 gave expression to similar principles and Article 111 of the Italian Constitution was amended to provide that every trial should be based on giving the parties the right to offer counterproofs and counterarguments against unfavourable evidence (including *contradittorio tra le partii*) on an equal standing in front of an impartial judge.[118]

Although the ECtHR seems to have played a significant role in prompting these changes, none of its pronouncements enjoin anything like a fully fledged common law adversarial trial.[119] First of all, as we have seen, the ECtHR has steered well clear of imposing any common law concepts on states parties such as admissibility or hearsay. It has put much more emphasis on the *use* that is made of evidence rather than posing the question of its admissibility. Thus, in the first major decision on Article 6(3)(d), the ECtHR stressed that written statements cannot per se be regarded as inconsistent with Article 6 but the *use* made of the statements as evidence must nevertheless comply with the rights of the defence.[120]

Secondly, it would seem that it is not necessary for the right to examine witnesses to be exercised at the trial. In the *Kostovski* case the ECtHR made it clear that the right to confrontation does not mean that in order to be used as evidence, statements of witnesses should always be made at a public hearing:

> [T]o use as evidence such statements obtained at the pre-trial stage is not in itself inconsistent with paragraphs (3)(d) and (1) of Article 6, provided that the right of the defence has been respected.

> As a rule, these rights require that an accused should be given an adequate and proper opportunity to challenge a witness against him, either at the time the witness was making his statement *or at some later stage in the proceedings*.[121]

This is a further illustration of accommodation with civil law procedures, which are generally more receptive towards the idea of reviewing evidence

---

[116] J Pradel, 'France' in C van den Wyngaert (ed), *Criminal Procedure Systems in the European Community* (London, Butterworths, 1993) 120.

[117] See V Dervieux, 'The French System' in Delmas-Marty and Spencer, above n 24, 218, 220–2.

[118] A Perrodet, 'The Italian System' in *ibid*, 348, 368–9.

[119] J R Spencer, 'Introduction' in *ibid*, 45.

[120] *Unterpertinger v Austria*, above n 112, para 31 (emphasis added).

[121] *Ibid* para 41 (emphasis added).

before trial.[122] So long as opportunities exist for challenging witnesses before trial, the absence of an opportunity to examine them at trial is not fatal to compliance with Article 6 standards. This could pose difficulties for common law processes where there is no properly organised pre-trial phase of procedure taking place under judicial control at which witnesses may be examined.[123] Where vital witnesses become unavailable at trial and there has been no pre-trial opportunity for cross-examination, the European jurisprudence suggests that prosecution cases may fail in the absence of other evidence against the accused.[124]

Thirdly, not all witnesses need to be examined on the defence's request in order to meet the fair trial standards of Article 6. In some cases, the ECtHR would seem to have taken into account the difficulty of producing witnesses who have gone missing or where the witnesses exercise their right not to testify.[125] In these instances, the court will look for any compensating safeguards, which might include the fact that the witness has already been questioned by a judge or that the defence have had another opportunity to view the demeanour of the witness or an opportunity to cast doubt on the witness' credibility.[126] Whatever the compensating safeguards, however, the ECtHR has tended to insist that the right to examination should be available where the testimony concerned constitutes the 'main',[127] 'decisive',[128] 'only'[129] or 'sole'[130] basis for the conviction.

This again implies that the ECtHR has construed the right as much to accommodate continental systems of justice as common law systems. Indeed it may be argued that it is common law judges rather than their civil law counterparts who are likely to have to change their perspective in the light of these standards. Judges in the common law tradition are used to ruling on the admissibility of evidence in a piecemeal, 'atomistic' manner, although once the prosecution case is completed, they have had a role in

---

[122]   Note, however, that the German immediacy principle attempts to put a fetter on the use of derivative sources at trial by restricting the use of hearsay evidence when better sources of information are easily accessible. See MR Damaška, 'Of Hearsay and its Analogues' (1992) 76 *Minnesota Law Review* 425.

[123]   JR Spencer, 'French and English Criminal Procedure: a Brief Comparison' in Markesinis, above n 50, 33.

[124]   For recent case law see *Mayali v France* (2005) App no 69116/01; *Guilloury v France* (2006) App no 62236/00; and *Balsan v Czech Republic* (2006) App no 1993/02.But see, *R v Sellick* [2005] 1 WLR 327, CA, suggesting that there is no automatic prohibition on the admissibility of hearsay evidence from a non-cross-examined absent witness, even if that witness provides the sole or decisive evidence.

[125]   See eg, *Asch v Austria* and *Artner v Austra*, above n 113, cited by B Emmerson and A Ashworth, *Human Rights and Criminal Justice* (London, Sweet & Maxwell, 2000) para 5–115.

[126]   See eg, *Van Mechelen v Netherlands*, above n 95, para 62.

[127]   See eg, *Unterpertinger*, above n 112, para 33.

[128]   See eg, *Kostovski*, above n 112, para 44.

[129]   See eg, *Asch v Austria*, above n 113, para 30; *Artner v Austria*, above n 113, para 24.

[130]   See eg, *Saidi v France* (1994) 17 EHRR 251, para 44.

screening out weak cases before factual disputes are sent to the jury for decision. By contrast, the ECtHR has favoured a much more 'holistic' approach towards the assessment of evidence, turning on how decisive or substantial the unexamined witness evidence is to the case as a whole.[131] Judges consequently need to be in a position to make some assessment of the strength of the other evidence against the accused, and it has been argued that this is likely to bring about a considerable change of perspective and practice in the English criminal process.[132] It would seem to mark a shift away from the traditional focus on determining the admissibility of individual pieces of evidence towards considering whether there is a sufficient basis under Article 6 ECHR for sending a case to the jury. Such judgements of sufficiency would require a much more probing assessment of the evidence as a whole than the traditional approach taken at the end of the prosecution case, which has been to consider whether *on one possible view* of the facts there is evidence on which a jury could conclude that the defendant is guilty.[133] This in turn points towards a more active fact-finding role for the common law judge. The trial judge is there not just to referee a contest in the traditional common law mould, making atomistic rulings of evidence, but to take a more proactive and dominant role in the proceedings in deciding whether fairness requires that particular witnesses need to be examined.[134]

The upshot of all this is that the adversarial principle of defence examination of witnesses has been accommodated by the ECtHR to meet continental processes without too much disturbance. Although the right to examine witnesses would seem to have stretched the continental notion of *une procédure contradictoire* beyond its traditional boundaries, this right has not required any full-scale transition towards a party-controlled trial. Indeed, so great has been the accommodation that it may be argued that traditional common law approaches, so long associated with the adversarial right of cross-examination,[135] have been as much disturbed by the ECtHR's jurisprudence as civil law traditions. There are other respects as well in which it may be said that the 'adversarial' requirements that have

---

[131] For the contrast between 'atomistic' and 'holistic' approaches to evidence, see MR Damaška, 'Atomistic and Holistic Evaluation of Evidence' in R Clark (ed), *Comparative and Private International Law: Essays in Honour of John Merryman* (Berlin, Duncken and Humblot, 1990).

[132] A Ashworth, 'Article 6 and the Fairness of Trials' [1999] *Crim LR* 261, 272.

[133] See eg, *R v Galbraith* [1981] 1 WLR 1039, CA.

[134] J Jackson, 'The Impact of Human Rights on Judicial Decision Making' in Doran and Jackson, above n 80, 109, 118.

[135] Although the modern adversary trial involving the presentation of cases by lawyers only dates back to the eighteenth century, the idea of the criminal trial as an 'altercation' between accused and accusing witnesses goes back much earlier: see JH Langbein, *The Origins of Adversary Criminal Trial* (Oxford, OUP, 2003).

been interpreted by the ECtHR as necessary in the light of Article 6 standards of fairness have stretched common law adversary traditions beyond their comfort zone.

We have seen that one of the conditions for meeting the principle of equality of arms is the right of the defence to have access to relevant information before the trial. This effectively predicates fairness at the trial upon fair disclosure before trial and once again elevates the significance of pre-trial procedures. In continental eyes, the principle of disclosure of evidence through a shared dossier which is constructed by judicial or prosecutorial officials charged with gathering evidence in an impartial fashion, whether tending to implicate or exonerate the accused, is an essential precondition for the defence meaningfully to exercise 'adversarial rights' because there is no tradition of the defence having the resources to find evidence for itself.[136] But the notion of sharing information is not so easy to assimilate into the common law tradition, with its emphasis on each side gathering and presenting 'its own' evidence. Whilst the ECtHR has claimed that the disclosure requirements mandated by Article 6 are recognised under English law,[137] the prosecutor's duty to disclose all material—inculpatory or exculpatory—evidence to the defence is not deeply embedded in the English tradition. Although an opportunity to inspect the depositions on which the accused was to be committed for trial dates back to the nineteenth century,[138] it has taken much longer for the principle of disclosure to be extended to 'unused' prosecution material. Indeed, it was not until the Judith Ward case that this principle of disclosure was clearly established.[139] Even today, the notion that evidence is used by one side or the other, rather than pooled before the court, holds sway. Meanwhile English procedure has fallen foul of the ECtHR on issues of disclosure in a number of cases.[140] Disclosure is now governed by a statutory regime which determines what material needs to be disclosed by each side in a two-stage process.[141] But it has been pointed out that these arrangements fall short of European jurisprudence, both in failing to require the prosecution to disclose all material evidence and in failing to provide the defence with recourse to judicial review at the first stage of

---

[136] *Jespers v Belgium*, above n 105, 87–8.

[137] *Edwards v United Kingdom* (1993) 15 EHRR 417, para 36.

[138] P Devlin, *The Criminal Prosecution in England* (London, Stevens, 1960) 6.

[139] *R v Ward* (1993) 1 WLR 619, CA. Earlier Attorney General's guidelines, stating that all unused material was to be made available to the defence if it had some bearing on the offences charged, never had the force of law: see (1981) 74 Cr App R 302.

[140] See eg, *Rowe and Davis v United Kingdom*, above n 110; *Atlan v United Kingdom* (2001) App no 36533/97; *Edwards and Lewis v United Kingdom* (2003) App nos 39647/98 and 40461/98.

[141] See Criminal Procedure and Investigations Act 1996.

prosecution disclosure.[142] Besides, the disclosure obligations only come into play at the stage when a case has been investigated. There is no obligation on the prosecution to disclose information while investigations are ongoing.[143]

TOWARDS CONVERGENCE OR REALIGNMENT?

It has been seen that traditional common law and civil law approaches to evidence have been challenged by some of the rulings of the Strasbourg authorities. The principle of equality of arms has required civil law countries to make a sharper differentiation between those exercising judicial functions and those exercising 'party' functions. The principle of an adversarial trial has also required such systems to give greater weight to defence rights to examine witnesses. Although some commentators have argued that this move towards adversarialism is promoting some sort of convergence between the two legal traditions, it is clear that the ECtHR's idea of adversarial proceedings does not correspond in every respect with common law practice. The ECtHR itself did not set out with any presumption that the common law concept of a fair trial is superior to the civil law concept, or vice versa.[144] The ECtHR has steered clear of imposing any abstract model of proof on contracting parties.[145] Instead, as we have seen, it has tried to 'translate' the principles in Article 6 ECHR in such a manner as to make them amenable to accommodation within both common law and civil law traditions.

It is tempting to infer from these developments some sort of gradual convergence of party- and court-dominated procedures towards a mixed model of proof, more party-orientated than traditional continental criminal procedure but falling short of the party control exercised in the common law adversarial trial. Rather than attempting to piece together the various strands of both traditions, borrowing from each tradition where possible to reach a compromise between the two, the ECtHR should be seen as developing its own distinctive brand of jurisprudence through the principles of the equality of arms and the right to an adversarial trial which

---

[142] SD Sharpe, 'Article 6 and the Disclosure of Evidence in Criminal Cases' [1999] *Crim LR* 273. Further changes to the regime enacted in the Criminal Justice Act 2003 remedy some of these defects: see M Redmayne, 'Criminal Justice Act 2003: Disclosure and its Discontents' [2004] *Crim LR* 441, 444–5.

[143] According to Spencer, '[i]n England, the battle is barely yet won to ensure that the prosecution communicates its evidence to the defence before trial: although ... the prosecution is now generally obliged to disclose to the defence, at some point before the trial, "unused material" that might be helpful to their case': see JR Spencer, 'Evidence' in Delmas-Marty and Spencer, above n 24, 594, 632.

[144] Swart and Young, above n 87, 86.

[145] Chiavario, above n 114, 542.

is transforming rather than merely mixing together the two established traditions. Delmas-Marty has argued that the great lesson of the European jurisprudence is that *no* model of criminal procedure—accusatory, inquisitorial or mixed—has escaped censure by the Strasbourg judicial organs.[146] Instead the Commission and ECtHR have over the years developed a vision of participation in the decision-making of the justice system which is rooted both in common law principles of natural justice and due process and in the continental *theorie de la procédure contradictoire*. At the heart of this vision is what Delmas-Marty has called the 'contradictory debate': the rejection, as she has put it, 'of revealed, uncontested truth replaced by facts which are contested and only then established as truths'.[147] Her own Commission in France went some way towards attempting to realise this ideal in practice when it recommended that defence lawyers be given enhanced rights of access to their clients in custody, access to the official dossier, a right of attendance at judicial hearings and the power to request investigative acts of the juge d'instruction.[148]

But if this vision is rooted in both common law and civil law traditions of criminal justice, the ECtHR's jurisprudence has shown that it has not always been evident in the practice and procedure of national systems. In drawing attention to shortcomings in states parties' criminal procedures, the ECtHR has had to develop its vision in a piecemeal fashion, case by case, proceeding on the basis, as the ECtHR has done throughout its jurisprudence, that the ECHR is a living instrument that requires adaptation as circumstances change. Nevertheless, it is possible to identify four broad strands in the development of its vision of defence participation in the criminal processes of proof that require to be accommodated within national systems. First, defendants cannot be required to participate in the proof process. Although Article 6 makes no mention of the privilege against self-incrimination, the ECtHR made it clear in 1993 that the right of anyone charged with a criminal offence to remain silent and not contribute to incriminating himself flowed directly from Article 6 ECHR.[149] At first glance it may seem that the principle of participation sits uneasily with a principle that permits defendants to refuse to participate.

---

[146] M Delmas-Marty, 'Toward a European Model of the Criminal Trial' in M Delmas-Marty (ed), *The Criminal Process and Human Rights* (Dordrecht, Martinus Nijhoff, 1995) 191, 196. Fennell *et al*, above n 50, 384, also argue that the ECHR does not make a choice between inquisitorial and adversarial systems; rather its role as developed by the Commission and the ECtHR has been to confirm and develop further existing fundamental notions of fairness which have to be respected by both common law and civil law systems.

[147] *Ibid* 197.

[148] For recent studies on how far these participatory principles are challenging and reforming pre-trial practice in France, see J Hodgson, 'Constructing the Pre-trial Role of the Defence in French Criminal Procedure: an Adversarial Outsider in an Inquisitorial Process' (2002) 6 *E & P* 1; Field and West, above n 47.

[149] *Funke v France*, above n 94.

But if participation is viewed broadly as the right of the individual to choose to participate in the fact-finding process, then this must be compatible with a right to choose not to do so.[150] This does not mean, however, that in situations which clearly call for an explanation from the accused, accused persons should not be strongly encouraged to answer questions provided appropriate safeguards are put in place.[151] This analysis implies a second principle: that any participation must be on an informed basis. This would seem to require the assistance of counsel at pre-trial stages when the accused is being questioned, full disclosure of relevant information to the defence and the right to comment on the evidence.[152] Thirdly, the defence must be given an opportunity to challenge this evidence, including, as we have seen, the right to examine decisive witnesses at some stage during the proceedings. Finally, the national courts must indicate with sufficient clarity the grounds on which they base their decisions. This requires some form of reasoned judgment which can be challenged by the defence.[153]

The ECtHR has given states parties considerable leeway in translating these principles into national law in an attempt to accommodate established procedures within the two prevailing traditions. It may seem, for example, that jury trial offends against the principle of a reasoned judgment, but the ECtHR has accepted that one way of compensating for the lack of a reasoned judgment is by a carefully framed direction from the judge.[154] It is also true that each principle may not in isolation measure up to the degree of participation permitted in one or other of the established traditions. For example, the right to examine witnesses in the adversarial tradition has not been confined only to decisive witnesses. By contrast, however, the second principle requiring informed defence participation before trial goes much further than traditional adversarial or inquisitorial procedure. Collectively, it may be said that the principles extend the boundaries of participation beyond the parameters of either tradition, so that established procedures in domestic criminal process have had to be realigned upon a more participatory footing.

---

[150] Chiavario, above n 114, 570. Paul Roberts has pointed out to me, in correspondence, that the right to participate does not always go together with the right *not* to participate. Defendants are given a right to participate in certain procedures, such as a right to enter a plea on arraignment, but are also required to participate in entering a plea. The key principle that is being advanced here is that defendants have a right to choose to participate in the fact-finding process, and it follows from this being a matter of the defendant's choice that they have a right to choose not to participate in it.

[151] *Murray v United Kingdom* (1996) 22 EHRR 29.

[152] The precise parameters of the right of access to counsel before trial, like the right of silence, remain uncertain. Cf *Murray v United Kingdom*, above n 151; *Brennan v United Kingdom* (2002) 34 EHRR 507; *Öcalan v Turkey* (2003) App no 46221/99.

[153] *Hadjianastassiou v Greece* (1993) 16 EHRR 219, para 33.

[154] *Saric v Denmark* (1999) App no 31913/96.

It is no longer possible for proof processes to be dominated entirely by judicial inquiry but neither is it possible for them to be dominated entirely by a trial contest between partisan parties refereed by a passive judge. Instead, defence participation has come to enable defendants to play an active role in the proof process throughout the course of the proceedings, with access to legal advice when suspects are being questioned and material evidence disclosed to the defence well before trial. This seems to call for more than just a realignment of procedures. It requires a change in legal culture on the part of public authorities. In the common law tradition, judges have long shouldered the responsibility to guarantee a fair trial, but what is now required is a much more protective stance towards defendants on the part of those acting on behalf of public authorities, including police officers and prosecutors, as well as judges, throughout the criminal process. Those responsible for examining defendants in the preparatory phase of procedure must ensure that rights to legal access are safeguarded. In the course of criminal investigations, police and prosecutors are called upon to search for evidence *à charge et à décharge*, and then share this information with the defence.[155] Then, during the course of the trial itself, prosecutors must consider whether to rely on evidence that has been tainted by coercion or illegality and judges must be vigilant to ensure that convictions are not based substantially on unexamined or otherwise suspect evidence. Although all this requires a considerable change of culture on the part of public authorities, particularly where prosecutors and judges are unused to monitoring investigative activities,[156] it would also seem to entail a change of culture on the part of defence lawyers who have been accustomed within the common law tradition to focus their proof-gathering activities on the trial. In this evolving model of criminal procedure they are obliged to represent their clients at vital earlier stages of the proof process and, with greater rights to disclosure, they are being encouraged to participate in this process at a much earlier stage.[157]

The culture change necessary to align procedures towards a participatory model of proof is not limited to active protection of defence rights. Although the ECtHR has been incrementally widening the scope of defence

---

[155] This has not traditionally been a requirement on the police conducting criminal investigations in the United Kingdom. However, the Code of Practice under Criminal Procedure and Investigations Act 1996, s 23(1), provides that the police are now expected 'to pursue all reasonable lines of inquiry, whether these point towards or away from the suspect' (para 3(4)).

[156] In the United Kingdom, prosecutors have been said to occupy a quasi-judicial role but this has fallen far short of becoming actively involved in monitoring criminal investigations: see S Field, P Alldridge and N Jörg, 'Prosecutors, Examining Judges and Control of Police Investigations' in Fennell *et al*, above n 50, 227; Jackson, above n 77.

[157] For the different role that defence lawyers play in the Netherlands and England and Wales, see Field, Alldridge and Jörg, above n 156, 246–7.

participation, the court has also had to take cognisance of other Convention rights. One issue that has come to exercise the ECtHR in recent years has been how to protect the interests of particularly vulnerable witnesses and victims in the course of criminal proceedings. In the landmark decision of *Doorson v Netherlands*[158] in 1996, the ECtHR accepted that although Article 6(3)(d) guarantees the right of a defendant to examine or have examined witnesses against him, steps may be taken to limit this guarantee in the interests of witnesses where, for example, their life, liberty, security of person or privacy interests within the ambit of Article 8 ECHR may be threatened. The ECtHR concluded that contracting states should organise their criminal proceedings in such a way that witnesses' interests are not unjustifiably imperilled, formulating the following important statement of principle:

> Against this background, principles of fair trial also require that in appropriate cases the interests of the defence are balanced against those of witnesses or victims called upon to testify.[159]

This statement appears to demand that the interests of victims and witnesses are built into the ECHR concept of fair trial. The ECtHR is not suggesting that the principles of fair trial be balanced against other Convention rights. The principle of a fair trial remains absolute. However, the principles of fairness enshrined in Article 6 need to take account of the interests of victims and witnesses as well as defendants. To date, whilst cognisance must be taken of enumerated Convention rights to life, liberty, security and privacy, the ECtHR has not explicitly stated that victims are entitled to any direct rights of participation in the criminal process.[160] Nonetheless, the effect of some of the decisions since *Doorson* has been to assist vulnerable witnesses to participate in the process of giving evidence without undue coercion on the part of the defence.

In *Doorson* itself, the identity of two witnesses was withheld from the defence in a drugs case where there was concern about threats of violent reprisals. A number of counterbalancing safeguards had been put in place. Witnesses had been questioned in the presence of counsel by an investigating judge, and the defence were allowed to put certain questions to the witnesses. Consistent with its previous jurisprudence, however, the ECtHR held that even when counterbalancing procedures were found to compensate the handicaps experienced by the defence, a conviction should not be based either wholly or to a decisive extent on anonymous witnesses.

---

[158] (1997) 23 EHRR 330.
[159] *Ibid* para 70.
[160] On the rights of victims within the ECHR, see J Doak, 'The Victim and the Criminal Process: an Analysis of Recent Trends in Regional and International Tribunals' (2003) 23 *Legal Studies* 1; F Leverick, 'What has the ECHR Done for Victims? A United Kingdom Perspective' (2004) 11 *International Review of Victimology* 177.

More recent cases involving allegations of sexual abuse, however, have severely tested the principle that convictions should not be based on 'decisive' testimony, anonymous or otherwise, that has not been examined by the defence.[161] Whilst certain decisions have reiterated the orthodox principle,[162] other rulings appear to dilute the significance of defence cross-examination as an essential component of a fair trial. One approach involves reinterpreting the meaning of 'decisive evidence', so that the complainant's evidence is not regarded as decisive where there is some supporting evidence against the accused.[163] A more direct inroad into the principle was made in *SN v Sweden*[164] where a conviction was based on the 'decisive' but unexamined evidence of a child. The child had initially been videotaped in the absence of the defence. At his request, the defendant's counsel was given an opportunity to attend a second interview with the child, but in the event was unable to attend. Instead, counsel agreed to the interview going ahead in his absence and certain questions were drafted by him which were put to the child by the police. The ECtHR considered that the criminal proceedings were fair and laid much store by the fact that defence counsel had been given an opportunity to attend an interview with the child before trial and that he was able to have questions put to the child. The court appeared to be suggesting that defence rights are satisfied by counsel being allowed to put questions indirectly to the witness. The two dissenting judges appeared to agree that the interests of minors may require that the principle of cross-examination can be 'left aside', but insisted that this should be possible only in cases where there is independent corroborating evidence.[165] The authorities had not done everything that could have been done in this case to offset the risk of unfairness. One additional step that might, in the dissentients' view, have served sufficiently to compensate the defence for the disadvantage under which it laboured would have been to call for forensic psychology experts to assist in the assessment of the victim's behaviour and testimony.

The emphasis given to the needs of particularly vulnerable witnesses in the light of modern day concerns about the efficacy of sexual abuse prosecutions is an example of Article 6 ECHR being interpreted as a living instrument. The ECtHR seems to accept that in these cases direct examination by counsel may not be appropriate. Critics have charged that the court has succumbed to a zero sum calculation according to which safeguarding the interests of witnesses must mean diminishing the rights of

---

[161] For recent commentary, see Summers, above n 51.

[162] See eg, *PS v Germany* (2003) 36 EHRR 61.

[163] See eg, *Verdam v Netherlands* (1999) App no 35353/97; *NFB v Germany* (2001) App no 37225/97.

[164] (2004) 39 EHRR 13.

[165] *Ibid* (dissenting opinion of Judges Türmen and Maruste).

the defence.[166] But the principle of the need for compensating safeguards, such as the involvement of independent experts in the assessment of witness evidence, has meant that the ECtHR has not lightly sacrificed the rights of the defence. These requirements place a heavy onus on public authorities to arbitrate fairly between the interests of witnesses and the interests of the accused. A culture of safeguarding witness and defence participation would seem to be required, but this need not translate itself into common procedures across the European systems. On the contrary, the flexibility which the ECtHR has preserved in the design of procedures capable of satisfying Article 6 means that states are encouraged to think imaginatively of the various ways in which the rights of defendants and witnesses might be respected in their indigenous systems. This may require some significant modification to traditional approaches. The attendance of defence lawyers at pre-trial witness interviews in order that the demeanour of the witness may be observed and questions may be put indirectly, pre-trial questioning of the witness by a judge, and the involvement of court-appointed or independent forensic psychology experts, are all procedures that are alien to the common law tradition. Yet it may be that these and other measures will have to be contemplated if the authorities wish to find ways of protecting particularly vulnerable witnesses from direct cross-examination.

As the ECtHR refines and develops its vision of participatory proof in the light of modern day conditions and takes criminal procedure beyond the traditional boundaries of adversarial/inquisitorial discourse, the states parties to the ECHR are being afforded considerable freedom of manoeuvre in realigning their procedures in a manner that respects the rights of the defence. It is perhaps only natural that individual states will be inclined to cling to their indigenous procedural traditions, but pressure is mounting for them to develop distinctive processes which diverge from the traditional norm for particular kinds of case. It follows that there may be considerable divergence in the manner in which the participatory principles developed by the ECtHR are translated from one system to another, and even from one category of case to another within the same system.

CONCLUSION

This chapter has argued that there are sound pedagogical reasons for taking comparative evidence seriously. Indeed, comparison might be regarded as the quintessential mode of legal scholarship. Evidence teachers can expand their subject by drawing comparisons between legal and

---

[166] RK Kirst, 'Hearsay and the Right of Confrontation in the European Court of Human Rights' (2003) 21 *Quinnipiac Law Review* 777, 806–7.

extra-legal factual inquiries, between different types and stages of legal process, and (of course) between the legal processes of different legal systems, both municipal and international. There is a growing corpus of empirical literature on which to draw, incorporating the sophisticated theoretical and methodological reflections which today characterise comparative legal scholarship. Of course, to say that Evidence teachers might profitably utilise such material is not to advocate an uncritical approach. Successive waves of comparative legal writing have found plenty to criticise in their predecessors' methods and conclusions. Specifically in relation to evidence and proof, the standard 'models' of legal procedure which appear, for example, in debates about transjurisdictional convergence seem increasingly problematic. This chapter has argued that continuing use of the adversarial and inquisitorial models as the conceptual framework for describing and explaining criminal processes of proof has become an obstacle to better understanding.

Taking the example of the jurisprudence of the ECtHR, it has been argued that the continuing debate as to whether European systems of criminal proof are converging or diverging by reference to these models is obscuring the reality of the situation. Although the court has itself referred to 'adversarial' rights and therefore to some extent remains in thrall to the adversarial/inquisitorial dichotomy, the model of proof that has been developed is better characterised as 'participatory' than as 'adversarial' or 'inquisitorial'. It has been shown that various features of this model are just as compatible with the continental notion of *procédure contradictoire* as with the common law adversary trial. Albeit not self-consciously, the ECtHR has been developing a model of criminal procedure that has secure roots in both traditions but is simultaneously transcending them. As contracting parties to the ECHR are progressively obliged to realign their processes and procedures to meet the standards of fairness that this model entails, across the whole spectrum of criminal process from police interviews with suspects through to parole hearings, practitioners and commentators will have to find a new vocabulary for describing and explaining what is taking place. Evidence teachers, too, will need to learn this new jurisprudential language if they are serious about participating in the comparative study of evidence and proof.

12

Convergence, Appropriate Fit and Values in Criminal Process

INTRODUCTION

L
AW TEACHERS AND law reformers concerned with criminal
evidence cannot avoid grappling with the broader context in which
the criminal process is situated. The establishment of international
courts, the phenomenon of crime that does not recognise international
boundaries and a global environment that makes the transfer of ideas
inevitable, have all contributed towards a growing body of research
interrogating the feasibility of convergence in procedural systems and the
usefulness of the 'inquisitorial' and 'adversarial' procedural models as
analytical tools.[1] It is against this discursive background that this chapter
attempts to locate 'values' in the intersecting functional circles of accurate
decision-making and legitimacy constrained by socio-economic conditions.

By 'values' I mean shared beliefs held by a society in a normative ideal
that the state is required to promote. These might pertain to the relationship between the state and the individual as well as to relationships
between individuals. Values are not rules of law, although they may inform
and be reflected in rules of law. For example, a constitution may specifically identify the values on which the state is founded and then reflect these
values in the entrenchment of corresponding rights. Thus, section 1(a) of
the South African Constitution 1996 explicitly articulates that the South
African State is founded on the values of human dignity, equality and the
advancement of human rights and freedoms. These values are then
promoted and protected by entrenching various corresponding rights
enumerated in the Bill of Rights.

* I would like to thank Paul Roberts and Mike Redmayne for their extremely useful
editorial comments, and Kelly Phelps for finding me lots of interesting material to read.
[1] See J Jackson, 'The Effect of Human Rights on Criminal Evidentiary Processes: Towards,
Convergence, Divergence, or Realignment?' (2005) 68 *Modern Law Review* 737.

This chapter argues that identifying the values shaping evidence rules has the potential to inform assessments of the extent of convergence in national and international Evidence law, as well as providing a basis for evaluating the merits of importing or exporting rules between jurisdictions. The success, or otherwise, of transnational transplants will be conceptualised in terms of 'appropriate fit' between the exported rule and the receiving 'host' system.[2] Crucially, the focus of this analysis is not the degree of convergence between abstract models of inquisitorial and adversarial procedures, conceived in the traditional way, but convergence between underlying values.[3] I will not attempt to identify which values should be given precedence as a normative ideal. My more modest aim is to demonstrate a novel approach to measuring convergence and assessing the appropriateness of jurisprudential borrowing from foreign jurisdictions.

FUNCTIONALITY

In accordance with the precepts of the rationalist tradition, the promotion of accuracy in decision-making remains widely recognised as a primary function of the Law of Evidence.[4] However, evidence rules are also shaped by 'non-rationalist values such as the acceptability of verdicts and the need for efficient resolution of disputes'.[5] Ian Dennis[6] has argued that an essential function of the rules of evidence in a criminal trial is to promote

[2] Jackson, above n 1, 738, notes that 'there is a growing scepticism in much recent comparative scholarship about the effects of transplanting processes and procedures from one national and legal culture into another. Many transplants may not have the effects that are intended'. Also see P Roberts, 'Rethinking the Law of Evidence: a Twenty-First Century Agenda for Teaching and Research' (2002) 55 *Current Legal Problems* 297, 329, who asks: 'How are rules to be applied and extended to new situations, as part of the process of identifying and resolving (or at least managing) normative conflict, without an appreciation of the values they instantiate?'; C Bradley, 'The Convergence of the Continental and the Common Law Model of Criminal Procedure' (1996) 7 *Criminal Law Forum* 471.

[3] K Roach, 'Criminal Process' in P Cane and M Tushnet (eds), *The Oxford Handbook of Legal Studies* (Oxford, OUP, 2003) 773, 776, notes that models such as due process, crime control and victim's rights can be used to articulate conflicting values, but it is extremely difficult to make a correlation between a specific set of values and adversarial and inquisitorial models, the two models in many instances sharing an identity of values. See also P Van Koppen and S Penrod, *Adversarial versus Inquisitorial Justice: Psychological Perspectives on Criminal Justice Systems* (New York, Kluwer Academic, 2003) 2.

[4] See ML Siegel, 'A Pragmatic Critique of Modern Evidence Scholarship' (1994) 88 *Northwestern. University Law Review* 995, 996. On the rationalist tradition generally, see W Twining, *Rethinking Evidence, Exploratory Essays* (2nd edn, Cambridge, CUP, 2006); CR Nesson, 'The Evidence of the Event? On Judicial Proof and the Acceptability of Verdicts' (1985) 98 *Harvard Law Review* 1357.

[5] JD Jackson, 'Modern Trends in Evidence Scholarship: Is All Rosy in the Garden?' (2003) 21 *Quinnipiac Law Review* 893, 899.

[6] IH Dennis, 'Reconstructing the Law of Criminal Evidence' (1989) 42 *Current Legal Problems* 21.

legitimacy in decision-making. This requires rules that are not only directed at maximising factual accuracy but also at giving 'moral and expressive authority'[7] to verdicts.[8] Evidence rules do this by excluding inherently unreliable evidence, and also reliable evidence 'if it carries significant risks of impairing the moral authority of the verdict'.[9]

If we follow Dennis' approach, factual accuracy is merely one, albeit extremely important, component of legitimacy.[10] A legitimate verdict also requires moral authority. In order to have moral authority the process of obtaining the verdict needs to be consistent with the 'core principle of criminal law',[11] namely, recognition of individual autonomy and dignity.[12] Although Dennis specifically addresses criminal law as his contextual point of reference,[13] he clearly situates criminal litigation in the broader context of societal values which go beyond the narrower confines of criminal responsibility and punishment, to embrace the set of values enshrined in the European Convention on Human Rights (ECHR).[14] Ashworth and Redmayne suggest that 'legitimacy', as invoked by Dennis, amounts to no more than 'accuracy and respect for rights'.[15] However, the advantage of Dennis' concept of legitimacy is that it augments rationality in fact-finding as a foundational principle without implying the wholesale rejection of

---

[7] IH Dennis, 'Rectitude Rights and Legitimacy: Reassessing and Reforming the Privilege against Self-incrimination in English Law' (1997) 31 *Israel Law Review* 24, 36.

[8] A Ashworth and M Redmayne, *The Criminal Process* (3rd edn, Oxford, OUP, 2005) 25 are sceptical of 'the legitimacy-based account of the criminal trial', preferring to ground their own theory in retributive justice. Despite these plausible reservations, I find Dennis' functional account emphasising legitimacy extremely useful in so far as it is restricted to *the Law of Evidence*.

[9] Dennis, above n 7, 36. Both inquisitorial and adversarial procedural models exclude reliable evidence on grounds of policy: see C Bradley, 'The Emerging International Consensus as to Criminal Procedure Rules' (1993) 14 *Michigan Journal of International Law* 171, who gives examples of the exclusion of evidence in German courts on the basis of privacy and personality rights. See also M Damaška, 'Evidentiary Barriers to Conviction and Two Modes of Criminal Procedure: a Comparative Study' (1973) 121 *University of Pennsylvania Law Review* 506.

[10] Dennis, above n 6, 38.

[11] *Ibid* 37.

[12] *Ibid* 42.

[13] *Ibid* 35. He also explicitly rejects the notion that the Law of Evidence should be primarily concerned with enforcing human rights, whilst acknowledging that 'in many cases public and individual interest will coincide in demanding the exclusion of certain evidence': *ibid* 39.

[14] Dennis continues: 'The moral authority of a verdict is a function of a combination of its factual accuracy and its consistency with other fundamental values embedded in the criminal justice system. These may be of a substantive or a procedural nature, and are to be discovered by analysis of legal materials and relevant moral and political discourses. Examples of substantive values include respect for human autonomy and dignity, security of person and property from unjustified interference, privacy, freedom from discrimination. Examples, of procedural values include the presumption of innocence, fair trial according to principles of natural justice and probity on the part of state agencies entrusted with coercive powers'.

[15] Ashworth and Redmayne, above n 8, 25.

optimistic rationalism and the search for 'truth' in legal adjudication. It also dispenses with the need to distinguish between rights and values at this relatively abstract level of analysis. However, it is not entirely clear whether the promotion of legitimacy can also explain those evidence rules based on the utilitarian function of avoiding undue delay and expense. In order to bring these utilitarian considerations under the legitimacy umbrella it might be necessary to extend the components of legitimacy to include the broader, redistributive demands of social justice.

LEGITIMACY AND CONTEXT

The appropriate contextual reference points for determining the legitimacy of legal verdicts will inevitably vary between jurisdictions. This requires us to navigate layered and intersecting contexts. For example, the requirement of proof beyond reasonable doubt in a criminal trial is a direct product of the presumption of innocence; the absence of the presumption of innocence from civil procedure legitimates a standard of proof expressed as a balance of probabilities.

Civil and criminal proceedings[16] are distinguished not only by their different process values, but also by their broader procedural context. This is obvious if we consider the different evidence regimes operating in adversarial and inquisitorial systems, with their familiar contrasts between party-orchestrated and judge-dominated trials, preferences for oral or documentary evidence, lay versus professional fact-finding, and so forth. Procedural contours are in turn constrained and shaped by social, economic, historical and political context.[17] Consequently, it is possible that a similarly, or even identically, articulated rule applied in different jurisdictions have a very different impact on the process of proof, the interests of the parties and the outcomes of proceedings in each jurisdiction.[18] Conversely, differently-formulated rules may nonetheless share similar functional objectives and reflect the same set of values.[19]

---

[16] For a fuller discussion of the functional differences between the Law of Evidence in civil and criminal proceedings, see Jackson, above n 5, 901.

[17] The correlation between procedural systems and political organisations has been made by M Damaška, *The Faces of Justice and State Authority* (New Haven, Yale UP, 1986). See also R Kagan, *Adversarial Legalism: the American Way of Law* (Cambridge MA, Harvard UP, 2002); H Crombag, 'Adversarial or Inquisitorial: Do We have a Choice?' in van Koppen and Penrod, above n 3, 21; M Zhou, 'A Comparative Analysis of Contemporary Constitutional Procedure' (1998) 30 *Case Western Reserve Journal of International Law* 149.

[18] See Jackson, above n 1, 739.

[19] Damaška, above n 9, 526.

SUBSTANCE AND FORM

John Jackson in Chapter 11[20] examines the convergence debate in respect of European systems of criminal proof, and concludes that a sui generis system is emerging as contracting parties to the ECHR are required to realign their criminal processes to accommodate the standards of fairness set by the Convention. This 'new system' Jackson characterises as participatory 'on the ground that it seeks to enable all those capable of giving relevant evidence in the proceedings to do so in as least a coercive manner as possible'.[21] Jackson's analysis of the European Court of Human Rights (ECtHR) jurisprudence identifies four broad strands, derived from Article 6 ECHR's right to a fair trial, as the standards against which the ECtHR has evaluated national criminal procedures. These sui generis standards have enabled the court to avoid imposing either inquisitorial or adversarial models of proof on the parties to the ECHR.[22]

Jackson's analysis provides a useful tool both for measuring convergence within, and the merits of normative transplantation beyond, the Council of Europe. Although the convergence debate is far more prominent in Europe, interrogating systems of proof is a favourite pastime of academics and politicians (the latter generally seeking greater efficiency in criminal law enforcement) worldwide. If we focus on the convergence and divergence of values, rather than specific forms of procedure, consistency with values becomes the key criterion of convergence, irrespective of formal legal label or juridical form. This reconceptualisation suggests a conclusion somewhat at odds with Jackson's assertion that it is 'unlikely that human rights law will lead to any clear convergence of evidentiary practices'.[23] I contend, by contrast, that values should be the true measure of convergence, and not the formal linguistic and structural properties of particular rules or procedures.

It is not merely a rhetorical expression of commitment to certain values that should inform an assessment of convergence, but rather the genuine promotion and protection of specified values in practical contexts. For example, in a country with a low socio-economic base, respect for

---

[20]   John Jackson, Chapter 11.

[21]   Jackson, above n 1, 740.

[22]   *Ibid* 758–9 identifies the following 'strands': (1) 'defendants cannot be required to participate in the proof process'; (2) 'any participation must be on an informed basis'; (3) 'the defence must be given an opportunity to challenge … evidence'; (4) 'the national courts must indicate with sufficient clarity the grounds on which they base their decisions'.

[23]   *Ibid* 764. Cf DM Amann, 'Harmonic Convergence? Constitutional Criminal Procedure in an International Context' (2000) 75 *Indiana Law Journal* 809, who identifies, as a necessary condition for convergence, 'the acceptance of a shared norm, of a body of internationally recognised rights, as a fundamental component of civil society'. However, she also notes that 'states will reject components of convergence that they believe threaten their security or position within the world community'.

individual autonomy and dignity may be constitutionally protected, the participatory values outlined by Jackson may be endorsed as prerequisites for the realisation of these ideals, yet economic reality may dictate that the state cannot afford to pay for legal representation or muster the professional skills or resources to meet disclosure requirements. Economic strictures, and their further implications for legal process, could impact directly on the practical realisation—or otherwise—of the value in comparison to an identically specified rule in another jurisdiction. A rule that permits inferences from pre-trial silence will make very different inroads on suspects' rights to silence and the privilege against self-incrimination where legal representation for accused persons cannot be assumed. The degree of genuine convergence must be measured in terms of the extent to which an identified value is protected in a specified practical context, rather than in the ostensible commitments of formal legal standards.

INTERNAL AND EXTERNAL VALUES

Ashworth and Redmayne's account of the criminal process distinguishes between internal and external values.[24] The internal value underpinning the primary objectives of the criminal process, accurate fact-finding and fair procedures, is respect for human rights. External values are shaped partially by political history and in some instances are jurisdictionally specific.[25] Ashworth and Redmayne cite adversarialism and the use of lay fact-finders as examples of external values. Damaška demonstrates how these procedural characteristics shape the content of the rules of evidence, establishing a correlation between procedural models and political philosophy.[26] If we accept such a correlation, it follows that both internal and external values could be jurisdiction-specific. Consequently, convergence can only be established by interrogating both the internal and external values underlying the content of evidentiary rules, principles and procedures. A concrete example will make this point clearer.

   A distinctively adversarial rule of evidence is the prohibition on hearsay (albeit subject to a long list of exceptions). The rationales underlying the hearsay rule relate both to accuracy and to fairness. A rationale that is frequently repeated is the fear that the trier of fact may place undue weight on hearsay despite its inherent weaknesses. However, this 'frailty' argument is itself very frail in the light of social science evidence that disputes

---

[24]   Ashworth and Redmayne, above n 8, 26.
[25]   *Ibid.*
[26]   See Damaška, above n 17; M Damaška, *Evidence Law Adrift* (New Haven, Yale UP 1997); Ashworth and Redmayne, above n 8, 27.

the naivety of fact-finders, be they jurors or professional judges.[27] It also does not explain the retention of the hearsay rule in adversarial systems that have dispensed with lay juries and require professional triers of fact to state reasons for their factual conclusions.

Adversarial procedures themselves provide a far stronger justification for the hearsay rule. The dominant and partisan role of the parties in adversarial proceedings increases the possibility of misleading evidence being introduced. Consequently, there needs to be an immediate mechanism for testing evidence, and this mechanism is cross-examination. The admission of hearsay evidence would circumvent this safeguard.[28] Furthermore, concentrated trial proceedings placing emphasis on orality preclude other means of testing 'hearsay' evidence.[29] These rationales are articulated in a form that is solely concerned with the accuracy of fact-finding in a specified procedural context; and it follows that admitting hearsay should not impact adversely on the accuracy or legitimacy of criminal verdicts provided that the safeguard of cross-examination is replaced by some other mechanism, such as pre-trial investigation accompanied by extensive disclosure.[30] This conclusion suggests that continued enthusiasm for the hearsay prohibition in many Anglo-American jurisdictions, especially in criminal proceedings, might be better explained by another internal component of legitimacy, namely, respect for rights and moral and political values.[31]

Respect for personal dignity and autonomy requires that the individual be protected from abuse of state power. Unrestricted admission of hearsay might negatively influence 'the conduct of police and prosecutors in the

---

[27] CB Mueller, 'Post-Modern Hearsay Reform: the Importance of Complexity' (1992) 76 *Minnesota Law Review* 367, 380. DA Nance, 'Commentary: a Response to Professor Damaška: Understanding Responses to Hearsay: an Extension of Comparative Analysis' (1992) 76 *Minnesota Law Review* 459, 463, expresses his scepticism as follows: 'The difficulty for a taint theory is explaining why being exposed to admittedly relevant information, what may be very probative, should lead to greater inaccuracy, especially when the information carries on its face a consumer warning ... by virtue of its derivative status'. See also P Miene, RC Park and E Borgida, 'Juror Decision Making and the Evaluation of Hearsay Evidence' (1992) 76 *Minnesota Law Review* 683.

[28] Damaška, above n 26, 79–80.

[29] *Ibid* 64–5.

[30] RC Park, 'Adversarial Influences on the Interrogation of Trial Witnesses' in van Koppen and Penrod, above n 3, 131.

[31] Given that there is significant scepticism as regards the strength of cross-examination as a truth-seeking mechanism (see A Choo, *Hearsay and Confrontation in Criminal Trials* (Oxford, OUP, 1996) 43) one would think that the hearsay rule is perhaps over-emphasised as a prerequisite for accurate decision-making. This is perhaps reflected in the declining role of the hearsay rule in civil proceedings in a number of traditionally adversarial jurisdictions. It can also plausibly be argued that accuracy could equally be attained without a rule excluding hearsay provided that the party against whom it was sought to be admitted was given notice and sufficient opportunity to lead contradictory evidence.

process of preparing and preserving evidence',[32] by operating as a disincentive to thorough and fair investigation. Respect for dignity and autonomy also requires that accused persons be active participants in the criminal process and confrontation and cross-examination are important expressions of the accused's capacity and opportunity for participation.[33] However, if the lens of procedural context is refocused, the hearsay rule need not be necessary to achieve these ends. Indeed, it does not require much imagination to envisage different safeguards against police abuse and other ways of designing participatory process. For example, the recording of police interviews and the requirement that sufficient notice be given of a party's intention to introduce hearsay ensure more substantial participation without resorting to the blunderbuss remedy of inadmissibility.

Once the values underlying legal doctrine are recognised, it may be possible to imagine their promotion within different normative structures and models of proof. This might lead to the conclusion that the hearsay rule, for example, is not an inalienable prerequisite of a fair trial. Its instrumental value in promoting trial fairness may turn out to be contextually specific. The hearsay example also demonstrates the close relationship between internal and external values. The internal values, which constitute the prerequisites for legitimacy, can be diminished or enhanced by procedural design (which is extraneous to the internal values of accurate fact-finding and moral legitimacy). External values may be viewed as the vehicles for the promotion and protection of values internal to legal process. In order to be effective conduits for internal values, external values must be responsive to broader social, economic, historical and political context.

THE BROADER SOCIETAL CONTEXT

The role of procedural context in giving expression to an identified value is crucial, but this is not the only important consideration. For example, prevalent police culture and public confidence in the police may play a significant role in determining whether the hearsay prohibition can safely

---

[32]   RC Park, 'The New Wave of Hearsay Reform Scholarship' (1992) 76 *Minnesota Law Review* 363, 365. See also Choo, above n 31; RD Friedman, 'Face to Face: Rediscovering the Right to Confront Prosecution Witnesses' (2004) 8 *E & P* 1; HL Ho, 'Confrontation and Hearsay: a Critique of *Crawford*' (2004) 8 *E & P* 147, 156. Mueller, above n 27, 384, notes that other grounds for objecting to hearsay include 'concerns about ... concocted or exaggerated statements, and the use of trained investigators to exact statements by trickery and offers of immunity or leniency'.

[33]   See generally, EA Scallen, 'Constitutional Dimensions of Hearsay Reform: Toward a Three Dimensional Confrontation Clause' (1992) 76 *Minnesota Law Review* 623.

be dispensed with as a restraint on abuses of power by officials.[34] The availability of state-sponsored legal representation may also determine whether an accused is able to participate fully in legal proceedings.

In developing countries, the provision of legal representation at state expense will almost inevitably, at least to some extent, be the victim of competing socio-economic demands. Those values reflected in adversarial procedures which are dependent on approximating 'equality of arms' will be severely compromised in the absence of legal representation. It may well be that participatory and equality values are better pursued by a pro-active inquisitorial judge in the absence of an enforceable substantive right to legal representation.[35]

The influences of broader political context are pervasive and can be detected across the board, from theorists' abstract conceptualisations of the criminal process to the reformulation of particularistic evidentiary rules in criminal trials. Commenting on the dated appearance of Packer's crime control and due process models,[36] for example, Roach observes that '[f]eminism only emerged as a powerful intellectual and political force after Packer had articulated his models'.[37] The emergence of 'victims' rights' models has clearly impacted on rules of proof in prosecutions of sexual offences and in other cases where witnesses are viewed as vulnerable.[38] There have been significant reforms in respect of the rules of corroboration and the use of sexual history evidence in a number of jurisdictions.[39] These developments reflect an evolving commitment to gender equality. This shared value has precipitated broad convergence regarding the underlying rationales of procedural rules and their formal legal expression.

However, far less convergence may be apparent once the application of legal norms is examined in their practical context. In South Africa, for

---

[34] See C Slobogin, 'An Empirically Based Comparison of American and European Regulatory Approaches to Police Investigation' in van Koppen and Penrod, above n 3, 27, who explores the relationship between the impact of rules, such as the exclusionary rule, and cultural, systemic and legal differences. On variance in police techniques and culture, see also, A Vrij, '"We will Protect your Wife and Child, but Only if You Confess": Police Interrogation in England and the Netherlands' in van Koppen and Penrod, above n 3, 55; H Quirk, 'The Significance of Culture in Criminal Procedure Reform: Why the Revised Disclosure Scheme Cannot Work' (2006) 10 *E & P* 42.

[35] See N Steytler, *The Undefended Accused on Trial* (Cape Town, Juta, 1988); N Steytler, *Constitutional Criminal Procedure* (Durban, Butterworths, 1998) 302.

[36] HL Packer, *The Limits of the Criminal Sanction* (Stanford, Stanford UP, 1968).

[37] K Roach, 'Four Models of the Criminal Process' (1999) 89 *Journal of Criminal Law and Criminology* 671, 686. The observation made by Roach in respect of feminism is only a small part of a multifaceted argument.

[38] See eg, J Doak, 'Child Witnesses: Do Special Measures Directions Prejudice the Accused's Right to Fair Hearing? *R v Camberwell Green Youth Court, ex .p. D; R v Camberwell Green Youth Court, ex. p. G*' (2005) 9 *E & P* 291; PJ Schwikkard, 'The Abused Child: a Few Rules of Evidence Considered' [1996] *Acta Juridica* 148.

[39] Eg Canadian Criminal Code, ss 276 and 277; and in England, Youth Justice and Criminal Evidence Act 1999, s 41.

example, the lack of institutional support for the complainant and an under-resourced prosecutorial service have conspired to neutralise provisions purporting to regulate the use of complainants' sexual history evidence. Although the relevant provision was introduced in 1989,[40] in 2002 the South African Supreme Court of Appeal[41] confessed that it was unaware of the section's ever having been invoked. During the last eight years, South Africa has engaged in a law reform process with the potential to clarify and entrench progressive changes in the common law, including accommodating the rights of victims. However, budgetary constraints have been cited for the legislature's failure to adopt the full range of recommendations made by the South African Law Commission and then blamed for delays in implementing the parts that have been adopted. Here is an example of deliberately crafted law reform, rooted in a coherent set of internationally shared values, being frustrated by a failure to take socio-economic conditions with the potential to block or derail the implementation of formal legislation sufficiently into account. (Of course, a more cynical view might see the real stumbling-block as the absence of political will.)

LEGITIMACY AND POPULISM

Although the rules of evidence need to be aligned with prevailing societal values in order to promote legitimate decision-making, this does not mean equating legitimacy with populism. Legitimacy requires respect for entrenched values, and it is these values that shape exclusionary rules, not all of which adopt accuracy in fact-finding as their underlying rationale. Until the 1980s, Packer's due process and crime control models constituted the dominant theoretical framework in which the tensions between competing values were explored. More recently, however, another set of enduring values has entered criminal justice debates. Respect for victims' rights has generated a discourse centred on balancing the competing rights-claims of victims and defendants. Ashworth and Redmayne[42] warn that the balancing metaphor can be misleading: increasing institutional support for the victim does not necessarily require any detraction from the rights accruing to the accused. They concede that sometimes a balance does have to be struck, for example, protections afforded to vulnerable witnesses may place constraints on cross-examination. But even here the

---

[40]   Criminal Procedure Amendment Act 39 of 1989, s 2, amending Criminal Procedure Act 51 of 1977, s 227.
[41]   *S v M* 2002 (2) SACR 411 (SCA), para [17].
[42]   Ashworth and Redmayne, above n 8, 42.

balancing metaphor may be inappropriate, as the purpose of cross-examination and the protection afforded to vulnerable witnesses share, in some respects, the same goal of maximising accuracy. There need not be any contradiction between this rationalist objective and the additional goal of ensuring the dignity and security of the complainant.

There is always the further danger that vote-winning populism may assume the guise of protecting victims' rights.[43] As Andrew Ashworth gently warns:

> Greater protection from harm is much desired, but it should not be pursued without respect for other fundamental values, and it should not be pursued by measures that may have popular appeal but which are unlikely to achieve the hoped-for effect.[44]

In seeking to determine the extent of convergence in values across procedural systems, the influence of the victims' rights model in any particular jurisdiction needs to be taken into account. If evidence rules are to fulfil their function of legitimating decision-making they need to cohere with specific jurisdictional values. Successful convergence will only occur when there is a coincidence of general and specific values.

From this analytical perspective, it becomes possible to identify rules that are merely the product of expedient political rhetoric. Garland has noted the political dilemma in a state's recognition of its limited ability to guarantee its citizens' security, and the consequent resort by governments to the mythical rhetoric of crime control.[45] This manipulation of public fears may be translated into legislation that is not the product of research or rational analysis. And because the 'limits of the sovereign state' have global resonance and repercussions it is not surprising that politically expedient legislation crosses state boundaries with ease.

For an example we may look to the constraints placed on the right to remain silent, originally contained in the Criminal Evidence (Northern Ireland) Order 1988. These provisions were subsequently replicated for England and Wales in the Criminal Justice and Public Order Act 1994, and thereafter embraced with enthusiasm by the Law Commissions of a

---

[43] For a general discussion of political expediency versus respect for rights in the context of recent criminal justice reform in England and Wales, see A Ashworth, 'Criminal Justice Act 2003 (2): Criminal Justice Reform: Principles, Human Rights and Public Protection' [2004] *Crim LR* 516.

[44] *Ibid* 530.

[45] Cf D Garland, 'The Limits of the Sovereign State' (1996) 36 *British Journal of Criminology* 445, 460: 'A show of punitive force against individuals is used to repress any acknowledgement of the state's inability to control crime to acceptable levels. A willingness to deliver harsh punishments to convicted offenders magically compensates a failure to deliver security to the population at large. This punitiveness has complex roots. It is by now a deep-rooted aspect of our culture, embedded in the common-sense of the public, the police and the judiciary'. See also Ashworth and Redmayne, above n 8, 9–16.

number of Commonwealth countries, notwithstanding the absence of any evidence to demonstrate that this departure from embedded values will actually improve the efficiency of criminal adjudication.[46] The far-flung appeal of these repressive measures in jurisdictions as varied as Namibia, South Africa and Australia may readily be explained in terms of the growing prevalence, domestically and internationally, of crime control rhetoric, coupled with their ease of transmission.[47] Models for procedural transplants can today be generated at the touch of a button, utilising the cut-and-paste function on an Internet browser to exploit the bounteous resources of the World Wide Web.

RECOGNISING LIMITATIONS

Interrogating values also helps to determine the parameters of convergence and their pragmatic limits. Values reflect political and philosophical choices and processes of proof are inevitably influenced by these choices. For example, commitment to gender equality may be high in a particular secular state and significantly lower in a particular theocratic state,[48] with the consequence that rules applicable to the evaluation of the testimony of women may be disparate and convergence could only occur if there was a radical shift in values in one or other of the two jurisdictions. Similarly, the rules relating to silence and self-incrimination may have a substantially different form and impact in a state that reveres individual autonomy as opposed to the interests of the collectivity.[49] The dynamic relationship

[46] There is an extensive body of literature considering the merits of provisions such as those contained in Criminal Justice and Public Order Act 1994, s 34: see eg, D Birch, 'Suffering in Silence: a Cost-benefit Analysis of Section 43 of the Criminal Justice and Public Order Act 1994' [1999] *Crim LR* 769, S Easton, *The Case for the Right to Silence* (2nd edn, Aldershot, Ashgate, 1999); I Dennis, 'Silence in the Police Station: the Marginalisation of Section 43' [2002] *Crim LR* 25; J Jackson, M Wolfe and K Quinn, *Legislating Against Silence: the Northern Ireland Experience*, Northern Ireland Office Research and Statistical Series Report No 1 (2000); J Jackson, 'Silence and Proof: Extending the Boundaries of Criminal Proceedings in the United Kingdom' (2001) 5 *E & P* 145; PJ Schwikkard, 'Silence and Common Sense' [2003] *Acta Juridica* 92.

[47] See South African Law Commission, Project 73 Report, *A More Inquisitorial Approach to Criminal Procedure: Police Questioning, Defence Disclosure, the Role of Judicial Officers and Judicial Management of Trials* (2002); New South Wales Law Commission, Report, *Right to Silence* (2000); Australian Law Council, *Draft Principles relating to the Reform of Pre-trial Criminal Procedure* (1998).

[48] Cf SS Ali, 'The Conceptual Foundations of Human Rights: a Comparative Perspective' (1997) 3 *European Public Law* 261, who disputes the significance of a divergent normative basis for conceptualisations of human rights.

[49] See D Huan, 'The Right to a Fair Trial in China' (1998) 7 *Pacific Rim Law and Policy Journal* 171.

between values and context makes it inevitable that values may display an element of fluidity, and consequently convergence may be a function of time as well as place.

Societal values change, effecting a corresponding shift in the content of rights. Less than a century ago, the notion of equality in Western democracies was restricted to equality between 'white men'. The cautionary rule applicable to complainants in sexual offence cases provides a telling example of the responsiveness (albeit belated) of the rules of evidence to changes in social values.

South Africa is still experiencing the aftershock of a revolutionary political transformation from oppressive minority rule based on race distinctions to a multicultural democracy.[50] Prior to 1998, the South African courts, with one honourable exception,[51] vigorously upheld the rule that required the testimony of complainants in sexual offence cases to be treated with caution on the basis that these complainants were inherently less reliable.[52] In 1998, the Supreme Court of Appeal rejected this rule as 'irrational'[53] and held that its historical justification lacked 'any factual or reality-based foundation'.[54] A year later the Constitutional Court noted that the rejection of the cautionary rule was 'a reminder that today's received wisdom regarding human behaviour and the ability of a lay person to correctly interpret it, may tomorrow be discarded as irrational and out of date'.[55] However, the Supreme Court of Appeal's judgment was not based on new social science data. It drew on research that had been available for at least two decades. The crucial distinction was that it was now viewing those data, and the disreputable evidentiary rule hitherto sustained in their defiance, in a value context that prioritised equality and dignity and the specific values of non-racialism and non-sexism.[56]

A change in political context can lead to an expansion of civil liberties, as it has done in South Africa, but it can also have the converse effect. The risk is perhaps greatest when a nation perceives itself to be under threat.[57]

---

[50]   South Africa's first democratic election was held on 27 April 1994, with victory for the African National Congress led by Nelson Mandela.

[51]   See the judgment of Davis AJ in *S v M* 1997 (2) SACR 682 (C).

[52]   See PJ Schwikkard, 'A Critical Overview of the Rules of Evidence relevant to Rape Trials in South African Law' in S Jagwanth, PJ Schwikkard and B Grant (eds), *Women and the Law* (Pretoria, Human Sciences Research Council, 1994) 198.

[53]   *S v Jackson* 1998 (1) SACR 470 (SCA), 476.

[54]   *Ibid* 474–5.

[55]   *President of the Republic of South Africa v South African Rugby and Football Union* 1999 (10) BCLR 1059 (CC), para 79 n 57.

[56]   South African Constitution 1996, s 1(b).

[57]   See eg, K Anderson, 'What to Do with Bin Laden and Al Qaeda Terrorists? A Qualified Defense of Military Commissions and United States Policy on Detainees at Guantanomo Bay Naval Base' (2002) 25 *Harvard Journal of Law and Public Policy* 616. Cf CN Belk, 'Next Friend Standing and the War on Terror' (2004) 53 *Duke Law Journal* 1747; A Elgart, '*Hamdi*

For example, shortly after the terrorist attacks of 11 September 2001, the United States Congress passed the 'Patriot Act'[58] significantly extending powers to monitor, search and detain persons suspected of terrorism. Military commissions, not bound by the rules of criminal law and evidence applicable in regular criminal trials, were hurriedly established to try suspected foreign terrorists. Recognising such contextual pressures on values, and their consequent impact on the formulation and interpretation of legal rules, should encourage continual reconsideration and re-evaluation of convergence and appropriate fit across jurisdictions. The impact of broader political, social and cultural forces on rules of evidence and procedure is often particularly pronounced. Evidentiary rules and doctrines may consequently serve as a tangible index, both of social progress within a particular legal jurisdiction and of international convergence upon a shared set of values.

CONCLUSION

Whilst in Europe administrative convenience may make a degree of formal legal convergence desirable, formal convergence in itself should not be viewed as an aspirational ideal. In measuring whether a rule is good or bad, in the context of any particular jurisdiction, it must surely be the values to which the rule gives expression that are ultimately decisive.[59] This suggests a values-based alternative to orthodox analyses of 'convergence' in international criminal procedures, which usually take idealised models of process as their basic unit of analysis.

If substance is to be preferred over form, the internal values of accurate fact- finding, procedural integrity and (in jurisdictions such as South Africa, with explicit constitutional commitments to redistribution) social justice should be the measure of convergence in legal process. A fully functional justice system requires a critical level of popular legitimacy. It is the internal values that ultimately legitimate decision-making, and it is therefore appropriate to focus on these values in measuring the extent of procedural convergence and in assessing the success, or otherwise, of interjurisdictional transplants. External procedural values can be viewed instrumentally, as vehicles for the expression of internal values. External

v *Rumsfeld*: Due Process Requires that Detainees Receive Notice and Opportunity to Contest Basis for Detention' (2005) 40 *Harvard Civil Rights-Civil Liberties Law Review* 239; M Osborn, '*Rasul v Bush*: Federal Courts have Jurisdiction over Habeas Challenges and Other Claims Brought by Guantanomo Detainees' (2005) 40 *Harvard Civil Rights-Civil Liberties Law Review* 265.

[58] The Uniting and Strengthening by Providing Appropriate Tools Required to Intercept and Obstruct Terrorism Act of 2001.

[59] See Roberts, above n 2, 329, and Chapter 1.

values are shaped by historical and cultural contingencies, giving idiosyncratic local expression to internal values that may be served by different institutional forms in other legal systems. Convergence, on this view, is therefore not a measure of superficial similarities between legal doctrine or process in different jurisdictions, but a search for a deeper underlying unity of moral and political values.

The broader socio-economic context must also be taken into account in measuring the extent to which internal values are promoted and protected in different jurisdictions. For as we have seen, the fact that particular values find expression in similarly formulated rules is no guarantee of their identical impact in practice. Far less convergence may be apparent once the application of legal norms is examined in their practical settings. Any state can pass a law enshrining particular internal values, but not all states are equally well-equipped, or indeed equally well-motivated, to turn these paper guarantees into practically enforceable rights and obligations.

13

Why International Criminal Evidence?

PAUL ROBERTS*

C HAPTER 1 IDENTIFIED 'COSMOPOLITANISM' as an essential dimension of the law of evidence in the twenty-first century, and briefly made the link between Evidence teaching and scholarship and the emerging field of International Criminal Justice (ICrimJ).[1] This chapter will expand on those observations and attempt to substantiate the argument with detailed illustrations.

A preliminary task is definitional and taxonomic. The question 'Why (should Evidence scholars be interested in) International Criminal Justice?' is utterly vacuous until we have at least a rough sense of what ICrimJ encompasses. What are the boundaries, content and methodologies of the discipline? How does it relate to cognate fields, or divide into subspecialisms? Has attention been devoted to conceptualising the relationship between academic theory and legal practice in this context, and if so, are there any pedagogical implications for legal education? These questions, though in many ways elementary, are more difficult to answer than might be imagined, for at least two reasons. First, as a newly emerging discipline, ICrimJ remains rather ill-defined and eminently contestable disciplinary territory. Even confining our attention to the much narrower concept of international criminal *law* (ICrimL), the extent to which the first rash of ICrimL textbooks have elaborated contrasting disciplinary taxonomies around notably disparate content implicitly attests to ICrimJ's fledgling

---

* I am grateful to the participants at the Nottingham colloquium for positive feedback on the original presentation, and to Mike Redmayne for detailed written comments on a working draft.
[1] Also see P Roberts, 'Rethinking the Law of Evidence: a Twenty-First Century Agenda for Teaching and Research' (2002) 55 *Current Legal Problems* 297, Part 6.

character.[2] Of course, this initial experimentation is likely to be a transitory phase in a new subject's growth to full maturity; and in any case such variety is more refreshing than disorientating at any stage of a discipline's evolution. But a second obstacle to presenting a satisfactory disciplinary taxonomy of ICrimJ is more intractable, arising as it does from the invariable connection between conceptual definition and its underlying motivation. Simply put, definitions are conditioned by the values and objectives of those doing the defining; and it follows that there is no such thing as a value-free taxonomy of an academic discipline, ancient or modern. Definition involves a process of selection. Some things are emphasised, whilst others are relegated to the margins, or excluded altogether. In view of their theoretical and practical significance, the selections involved in disciplinary taxonomy and conceptual definition should be undertaken openly and self-consciously, and the inherently controversial nature of the exercise should be recognised candidly at the outset.

In my view, ICrimJ is best conceptualised in broad terms, as a discipline comprising seven concentric circles of dynamically interactive institutional activity.[3] At its core is the law and practice of the International Criminal Court (ICC), created by the Rome Statute signed in 1998 and fully operational since 2002. This is now ICrimJ's centre of gravity, around which radiate six further jurisprudential 'circles' constituted by: the United Nations' ad hoc Tribunals for the former Yugoslavia and Rwanda; so-called 'hybrid' or internationalised tribunals, such as the Special Court for Sierra Leone;[4] the post-1945 international military tribunals which sat

---

[2] The most straightforward approaches closely follow the provisions of relevant treaties, especially the International Criminal Court's Rome Statute: eg K Kittichaisaree, *International Criminal Law* (Oxford, OUP, 2001). More sophisticated conceptualisations, such as market-leader A Cassese, *International Criminal Law* (Oxford, OUP, 2003), afford individualised treatment to substantive law and questions of institutions and process. A third variant, represented by I Bantekas and S Nash, *International Criminal Law* (2nd edn, London, Cavendish, 2003), gives prominent coverage to 'transnational' topics such as mutual legal assistance, extradition and international policing co-operation, in addition to the 'core crimes'. A fourth approach elevating human rights to headline billing with international criminal law, and, partly in consequence, encompassing extended discussion of topics such as terrorism and violence against women, can be seen in C de Than and E Shorts, *International Criminal Law and Human Rights* (London, Sweet & Maxwell, 2003).

[3] The argument is more fully developed in P Roberts, 'Comparative Law for International Criminal Justice' in E Örücü and D Nelken (eds), *Comparative Law: a Hart Handbook* (Oxford, Hart, 2007).

[4] The Special Court maintains a website at www.sc-sl.org/. Also see A Smith, 'Sierra Leone: the Intersection of Law, Policy, and Practice', P Mochochoko and G Tortora, 'The Management Committee for the Special Court for Sierra Leone' and WA Schabas, 'Internationalized Courts and their Relationship with Alternative Accountability Mechanisms: the Case of Sierra Leone', all in CPR Romano, A Nollkaemper and JK Kleffner (eds), *Internationalized Criminal Courts: Sierra Leone, East Timor, Kosovo, and Cambodia* (Oxford, OUP, 2004).

in Nuremberg and Tokyo; transnational and intergovernmental criminal legislation, law enforcement and mutual judicial assistance (including regional initiatives, such as EU criminal justice policy); international criminal law enforcement at the domestic level; and finally, the seventh 'concentric' circle comprising scholarly research, analysis and critical evaluation, which is perhaps better described as a chord bisecting the first six orbits and running through the entire enterprise of ICrimJ as a self-consciously theorised discipline. Other commentators, including most of the international lawyers who have made this field their own, advocate narrower conceptualisations, and tend to regard the ICC's 'core crimes' as marking the territorial limits, rather than the interior centre-ground, of ICrimL. Fortunately, we can set such controversies aside for present purposes. This chapter seeks to demonstrate the salience of ICrimJ for Evidence teaching and scholarship. Any critic minded to argue the contrary would need to show that ICrimJ, *however broadly defined and inclusive*, has nothing to offer Evidence scholars. Demonstrating that this or that particular aspect of ICrimJ has no bearing on evidence and proof would barely serve the critic's global purpose if other, potentially more promising, features of the subject were being left out of account. The broad conception of ICrimJ which I happen to favour is therefore ideally suited to serve as a test-bed for the general proposition, regardless of its perceived shortcomings in other contexts and for other purposes.

Inviting Evidence scholars to take a greater interest in ICrimJ will predictably be met with ambivalence, if not open hostility, in some quarters. 'Haven't I already got enough material to cover in researching and teaching Evidence?' would be one understandable reaction. 'Am I now being told that I have to become a public international lawyer as well as an Evidence specialist?' would be another. Evidence teaching and scholarship, it might be felt, are already at saturation point and cannot be expected to absorb major new streams of information in addition to their established sources. So says the Reluctant Cosmopolitan. However, the broad conception of ICrimJ adopted in this chapter necessarily implies that such reactions, though meriting a measure of empathetic collegial solidarity, are fundamentally misconceived, for at least two reasons.

The Reluctant Cosmopolitan's first mistake lies in his or her implicit assumption that Evidence scholars have a choice in the matter. This, I contend, is simply false. ICrimJ *is already here* in various guises, most tangibly in the impact of international human rights law (IHRL) on domestic criminal procedure.[5] England and Wales held out longer than most Western jurisdictions in this regard, but since 2 October 2000 when

---

[5] See Paul Roberts, Chapter 1, and John Jackson, Chapter 11; JD Jackson, 'The Effect of Human Rights on Criminal Evidentiary Processes: Towards Convergence, Divergence or Realignment?' (2005) 68 *MLR* 737; AL-T Choo and S Nash, 'Evidence Law in England and

our Human Rights Act 1998 came fully into force, we have joined the international family of jurisdictions in which IHRL standards establish a floor of minimum rights for suspects, the accused, complainants and witnesses in criminal trials. John Jackson has already provided detailed examples in his contribution to this volume.[6] Such developments, which simultaneously transform the character of English law in the process of their domestic assimilation, can no more be ignored by the Evidence scholar than a new Act of Parliament or the latest pronouncement of the Court of Appeal. Similar supra-national stirrings may be detected within the EU system of penal law, which is still relatively under-developed at the present time,[7] but has enormous potential for shaping the domestic criminal process of Members States, not least within the ideological framework of the 'war on terror'.[8]

A second fundamental misconception embedded in the Reluctant Cosmopolitan's plea of information-overload is the failure to appreciate the extent to which Evidence teaching is already highly selective. English law constantly generates a torrent of new legislative provisions and common law precedents, only a small fraction of which finds its way into Evidence textbooks and syllabi. Readers who do not trust their intuitions on this point will readily find reassurance by typing 'evidence' or 'proof' into the search facility of any of the standard legal databases. The number of 'hits' will be mind-boggling; and far in excess of searches for broadly equivalent discipline-defining terms such as 'crime', 'contract', tort' or 'property'. Of course, a proportion of the selectivity characterising Evidence books and courses is easily justified in terms of pertinence and importance: some legislation is not very interesting and some judicial pronouncements are, from the Evidence teacher's perspective, irrelevant, obscure or just plain wrong. Many such choices, nonetheless, necessarily have to be made in the light of pedagogic goals and values, whether self-consciously articulated and examined or otherwise. If this truism is accepted (and it can barely be denied), one is prompted to pose a further question: is it not at least

---

Wales: the Impact of the Human Rights Act 1998' (2003) 7 *E & P* 31; P Roberts and A Zuckerman, *Criminal Evidence* (Oxford, OUP, 2004) § 1.6.

   [6] John Jackson, Chapter 11.
   [7] Cf *International Transport Roth GmbH v Home Secretary* [2003] QB 728, [2002] EWCA Civ 158; *R v Chief Constable of Sussex, ex p International Trader's Ferry Ltd* [1999] 2 AC 418, HL.
   [8] See, in particular, the Council Framework Decision 2002/475/JHA, 13 June 2002, on combating terrorism, which is summarised at http://europa.eu/scadplus/leg/en/lvb/ l33168.htm. 'Since the attacks of 11 September 2001', we are informed under the headline 'Fight Against Terrorism', 'the European Union has been determined to step up the fight against terrorism. With this in mind, it has adopted a Framework Decision urging Member States to align their legislation and setting out minimum rules on terrorist offences. After defining such terrorist offences, the Framework Decision lays down the penalties that Member States must incorporate in their national legislation'.

conceivable that evidentiary aspects of ICrimJ would serve at least some pedagogic goals and values better than existing choices? Needless to add, uncritical adherence to traditional teaching habits and conventions of textbook-writing will never answer that question satisfactorily. The only way to make progress is to investigate for oneself.

This chapter aims to provide some initial pointers for the curious, and to whet Evidence teachers' appetites for more extensive engagement with the international dimensions of their subject. It will be argued that Evidence specialists have important things to teach, as well as much to learn, from ICrimJ. Through concrete illustrations, I will try to demonstrate how a two-way process of teaching and learning might contribute to Evidence teachers' pedagogic agendas, and much more besides.

JUSTICE UNDER CONSTRUCTION

The first thing to emphasise about ICrimJ is that its normative and institutional structures are very much works in progress. If this is always to some extent true even of domestic systems of criminal justice (especially common law systems which sanction judicial law-making through *stare decisis*), it is all the more apt as a description of international criminal proceedings, which are still in their formative years. Rapid innovation and extension characterise discrete strands, institutions and normative systems of ICrimJ, as well as the discipline as a whole.

Although the European Convention on Human Rights (ECHR) is over 50 years old, in the last two post-Cold War decades membership of the Council of Europe has more than doubled (increasing from 23 members in 1989 to 47 today) and the flow of the European Court of Human Rights (ECtHR)'s jurisprudence has swollen from a trickle to a torrent, precipitating major institutional reform. For English lawyers, the growing influence of international human rights law on domestic criminal proceedings was of course taken to a new level of priority by the introduction of the Human Rights Act 1998. ECHR fair trial jurisprudence has exerted an almost immediate (albeit uneven) impact on a range of core evidentiary topics, from 'entrapment' and the exclusion of improperly obtained evidence,[9] public interest immunity[10] and the privilege against self-incrimination,[11] to

---

[9] *R v Looseley; Attorney-General's Reference (No 3 of 2000)* [2001] 1 WLR 2060, HL; *Teixeira de Castro v Portugal* (1998) 28 EHRR 101. See AL-T Choo and S Nash, 'Improperly Obtained Evidence in the Commonwealth: Lessons for England and Wales?' (2007) 11 *E & P* 75; A Ashworth, 'Redrawing the Boundaries of Entrapment' [2002] *Crim LR* 161.

[10] *R v H* [2004] 2 AC 134, HL; *R v Botmeh* [2002] 1 Cr App R 28, CA; *Edwards and Lewis v United Kingdom* (2005) 40 EHRR 24, ECtHR (Grand Chamber).

[11] *Brown (Margaret) v Stott* [2003] 1 AC 681, PC; *Allan v United Kingdom* (2003) 36 EHRR 143; *Saunders v United Kingdom* (1996) 23 EHRR 313.

hearsay,[12] disclosure[13] and—precipitating serial visits to the House of Lords—burdens of proof and the presumption of innocence.[14] EU law lags behind the Council of Europe system in this respect, but has recently been branching out into criminal justice policy with accumulating concrete applications.[15] Most spectacularly of all, international penal norms and procedures addressing the 'core' international crimes have been reclaimed from their post-Nuremberg mothballing, and developed apace through the work of the ad hoc Tribunals for former Yugoslavia and Rwanda (the ICTY and ICTR) and the now fully operational International Criminal Court. The development and refinement of procedural and evidentiary norms, processes and practices has been a major dimension of all of these diverse, and largely unco-ordinated, efforts to advance the cause of ICrimJ.

One obvious implication of ICrimJ's being actively under construction is that Evidence scholars ought to be contributing their skills and expertise in the design and implementation of international criminal procedures, providing specialist advice and assistance to their Public International Law (PIL) colleagues, who have tended thus far to take the lead in the normative and institutional development of ICrimJ. With a handful of notable exceptions,[16] Evidence specialists (or for that matter, Criminal Law scholars of any description) have not been well-represented amongst the architects or personnel of international criminal adjudication.[17] As far as I can tell, this lopsided division of labour has occurred for reasons of professional habit and traditional disciplinary taxonomy lacking any intrinsic merit. ICrimJ may have fallen into the laps of PIL and International Relations (IR) scholars and practitioners, but they represent only

---

[12]   *Grant v R* [2006] 2 WLR 835, PC; *R v Al-Khawaja* [2006] 1 WLR 1078, CA; *R v Sellick* [2005] 1 WLR 3257, CA.

[13]   *R v D* [2004] EWCA Crim 1022; *Rowe and Davis v United Kingdom* (2000) 30 EHRR 1; *Edwards v United Kingdom* (1993) 15 EHRR 417.

[14]   *Sheldrake v DPP* [2005] 1 AC 264, HL; *R v Johnstone* [2003] 1 WLR 1736, HL; *R v Lambert* [2002] 2 AC 545, HL: see P Roberts, 'Criminal Procedure, the Presumption of Innocence and Judicial Reasoning under the Human Rights Act' in H Fenwick, R Masterman and G Phillipson (eds), *Judicial Reasoning under the UK Human Rights Act* (Cambridge, CUP, 2007); A Ashworth, 'Four Threats to the Presumption of Innocence' (2006) 10 *E & P* 241.

[15]   For general information and documentation on the EU's 'Freedom, Security and Justice' agenda, see www.ec.europa.eu/justice_home/index_en.htm.

[16]   Including the late Sir Richard May who served as a judge of the ICTY: see R May, D Tolbert, J Hocking, K Roberts, BB Jia, D Mundis and G Oosthuizen (eds), *Essays on ICTY Procedure and Evidence in Honour of Gabrielle Kirk McDonald* (The Hague, Kluwer, 2001); R May and M Wierda, 'Trends in International Criminal Evidence: Nuremberg, Tokyo, the Hague and Arusha' (1999) 37 *Columbia Journal of Transnational Law* 725; and Peter Murphy, who has combined editing *Blackstone's Criminal Practice* with criminal defence work before the Yugoslav Tribunal.

[17]   Also see PM Wald, 'Rules of Evidence in the Yugoslav War Tribunal' (2003) 21 *Quinnipiac Law Review* 761, 763, commenting that 'scholars and commentators on the Tribunals appear to pay much more attention to substantive law developments than to procedure and process'.

one-half of the conjunction between international and criminal laws; and neither party can legitimately claim intellectual property in the unified discipline or a monopoly of wisdom in its normative conception and practical implementation.

In relation to the core crimes, it might be said that Evidence scholars have already missed the boat. The ad hoc Tribunals have entered into their winding-down phase, with published 'completion strategies' anticipating that all trials should be finalised by 2008, and appeal hearings concluded by 2010.[18] Moreover, the Rules of Procedure and Evidence for the ICC, not to mention procedural aspects of the Rome Statute itself, have already been agreed and adopted.[19] Perhaps the drafting and implementation of these norms would have benefited from greater input from Evidence scholars at an earlier stage, but it is far too pessimistic to conclude that ICrimJ has already passed us by. For one thing, new 'internationalised' or 'hybrid' tribunals are being created or proposed all the time – eg, for Sierra Leone, East Timor and Cambodia[20] – presenting fresh opportunities for active participation. For another, whilst the politics of multilateral treaty-making generally dictate that international instruments must be drafted in relatively open-ended language, and incorporate established norms which have already garnered the international community's broadly-based assent,[21] the Evidence scholar's special sphere of knowledge and expertise concerns the translation of these general, aspirational standards into the pragmatic realities of criminal adjudication. The international community has managed to agree on a skeletal definition of 'fair trial', and this is a practical achievement of no little significance. Thus, the ICTY, ICTR and ICC Statutes all took their basic 'fair trial' provisions off-the-peg from

---

[18] Security Council Res 1503/2003. In fact, this timetable has experienced some slippage, and it now appears that first instance trials before the ICTY will not be completed until 2009 at the earliest: see *Assessment and Report of Judge Fausto Pocar, President of the International Tribunal for the Former Yugoslavia, provided to the Security Council pursuant to paragraph 6 of Council Resolution 1534/2004* (S/2006/898, 16 November 2006) para. 38, remarking that '[w]hile the International Tribunal will remain steadfast in its efforts to increase the efficiency of its proceedings ... its success in meeting the completion strategy hinges on several factors beyond its control including the arrest of the remaining fugitives'.

[19] ICC Rules of Evidence and Procedure, ICC-ASP/1/3, available at www.icc-cpi.int/about/ ataglance/establishment.html.

[20] For valuable overviews, see CPR Romano, A Nollkaemper and JK Kleffner (eds), *Internationalized Criminal Courts: Sierra Leone, East Timor, Kosovo, and Cambodia* (Oxford, OUP, 2004).

[21] The drafting style of treaties is also dictated by other factors, including the inherent structural constraints on any such drafting exercise (it is impossible to foresee *every* contingency; comprehensiveness must always be traded off against intelligibility and practical utility, etc) and applicable moral principles, eg the non-retroactivity constraint on criminal legislation, itself guaranteed by IHRL. But all these factors only tend to reinforce the pragmatic diplomat's preference for a relatively conservative approach to the development of international criminal law couched in suitably flexible, even deliberately ambiguous, language.

Article 14 of the International Covenant on Civil and Political Rights (ICCPR) (which in turn was modelled on Article 6 of the ECHR).[22] But it still remains for criminal justice professionals to graft flesh, skin and sinew onto these normative bare bones through their legal advice and advocacy, trial adjudication, appellate precedent, academic commentary and executive policy-making. It would consequently seem perverse for Evidence scholars to disqualify themselves from contributing to the practical realisation of ICrimJ before the ICC has even completed a single trial. We should, instead, be actively seeking out opportunities to communicate evidentiary learning to ICrimJ scholars and practitioners.

Whilst Evidence scholars might in these ways advance the ideals of international justice, the novelty and fragility of ICrimJ also afford significant pedagogic potential for Evidence teachers. Domestic systems of criminal justice tend to be embedded within historically-conditioned professional legal and national cultures which sometimes serve to distort or obscure the objectives, values, conduct and social meaning of criminal proceedings.[23] Being part of a particular system of justice is simultaneously both a guarantee of privileged 'insider' access to information, and a recipe for distortion, partiality and oversight. That which is up-close-and-personal is sometimes hardest to view dispassionately; that which is most familiar is often overlooked or taken-for-granted. The paradox[24] of understanding one's own system of justice lies in the need to achieve a certain critical distance from matters with which one is intimately acquainted. And mirror-image problems of standpoint frustrate attempts to become better acquainted with foreign legal systems, not least because indigenous experts on foreign laws and legal culture tend to be 'interested as well as interesting', as David Nelken has pithily observed.[25]

ICrimJ, by contrast, is relatively untouched by the contempt of familiarity. In its unique conjunction of novelty and universality, ICrimJ potentially offers all the enlightenment of comparative legal study,[26] without reproducing the nationalistic competition or alienation which often infect

---

[22]   ICTY Statute, Art 21; ICTR Statute, Art 20; ICC Statute, Arts 66 and 67.

[23]   These themes are further developed in P Roberts, 'Theorising Procedural Tradition: Subjects, Objects and Values in Criminal Adjudication' in A Duff, L Farmer, S Marshall and V Tadros (eds), *The Trial on Trial*, Vol 2: *Judgment and Calling to Account* (Oxford, Hart, 2006).

[24]   'Paradox' is admittedly a strong claim; and readers may substitute more modest alternatives ('deep tension'? 'fundamental challenge'?) if they wish. But it seems to me that the desire to be simultaneously inside and outside one's system of justice may be genuinely paradoxical, and at some level methodologically intractable.

[25]   D Nelken, 'Just Comparing' in Nelken (ed), *Contrasting Criminal Justice: Getting from Here to There* (Aldershot, Ashgate, 2000) 9.

[26]   Generally, see E Örücü and D Nelken (eds), *Comparative Legal Studies: a Handbook* (Oxford, Hart, 2007); G Samuel, 'Comparative Law as a Core Subject' (2001) 21 *Legal*

analyses of foreign legal systems. At least, chauvinistic confidence in the inevitable superiority of one's own national traditions is not so easily externalised to a sui generis international system of justice, in which all nations and all peoples have a direct stake through their formal equal membership of the international community. More specifically for the purposes of this chapter, we will explore ICrimJ's pedagogic merits in relation to (a) normative values and objectives; (b) procedural and institutional design; and (c) cultural influences on evidence, proof and fact-finding.

NORMATIVE VALUES AND OBJECTIVES

Doctrinal analyses of procedural law and adjudication in the domestic context generally assume that we already know what criminal trials are *for*. The basic rationale and purpose of criminal proceedings are largely taken for granted. Thus, English law Evidence texts typically[27] open with some reflections on the concept of 'evidence' and its cognates ('judicial evidence', 'rules of evidence', 'proof', etc), present a definitional taxonomy of judicial evidence in 'glossary of terms' format ('real evidence', 'testimonial evidence', 'documentary evidence', 'circumstantial evidence' etc),[28] and then proceed immediately to explore the law's engagement with evidence in different institutional contexts. Pride of place may be given to trials on indictment in the Crown Court, but—nowadays—care is usually taken to emphasise that evidential issues arise in all types, and at every stage, of a variety of adjudicative processes.

There is nothing intrinsically wrong with an approach to the subject founded on conceptual analysis. Rupert Cross, Colin Tapper and Ian Dennis are prominent amongst those scholars who have developed this approach to the law of evidence in distinctive ways and with conspicuous success.[29] William Twining has also been intensely preoccupied with the concept of 'evidence' over a sustained period,[30] although Twining's project

---

Studies 444; W Ewald, 'The Jurisprudential Approach to Comparative Law: a Field Guide to "Rats"' (1998) 46 *American Journal of Comparative Law* 701; HP Glenn, *Legal Traditions of the World* (2nd edn, Oxford, OUP, 2004).

[27] I am thinking of the best examples of the genre. Lesser specimens are in too much of a hurry to dissect legal judgments to be overly concerned with basic conceptual elaboration.

[28] J Doak and C McGourlay, *Criminal Evidence in Context* (Exeter, Law Matters Publishing, 2005) 12–22, actually contains a 'Glossary of Terms'. Other authors refer to 'Key Concepts', 'Basic Terminology', and the like.

[29] C Tapper, *Cross and Tapper on Evidence* (10th edn, London, Butterworths, 2004); IH Dennis, *The Law of Evidence* (2nd edn, London, Sweet & Maxwell, 2002).

[30] Eg W Twining, *Rethinking Evidence: Exploratory Essays* (Oxford, Blackwell, 1990; 2nd edn, Cambridge, CUP, 2006).

quickly takes a distinctive turn by eschewing traditional doctrinal exposition in favour of explicating the forms of practical reasoning involved in presenting, analysing and evaluating evidence.[31] Those who adopt the concept of 'evidence' as their starting-point for theoretical or doctrinal exposition, however, need to take care that they do not fall into the vice of *conceptualism*, which is my name for the fallacy of thinking that moral and political questions are capable of being settled by conceptual taxonomy or definition.[32] Such resolution is impossible, because moral and political questions can only ever be settled (to the extent that they ever are) by moral and political argument employing normative reasoning of the appropriate kind. Conceptual analysis is therefore never entirely innocent, inasmuch as it always at least *defers* moral and political questions to another time and place, even when it does not self-deludingly purport to settle them directly, or give this misleading appearance. But if conceptual analysis is always morally and politically loaded in this methodological sense, the conceptual approach to Evidence should be interrogated a little more searchingly than it usually is. What is being assumed by this approach? What is being left out of account? Perhaps if we began instead by treating the law of evidence as one component of an explicitly normative theory of adjudication, or as incidental to a normative theory of one particular adjudicative context such as criminal trials,[33] our conceptualisations and appraisal of the subject might be somewhat different. Which brings us back to the neglected questions of the basic rationale and purposes of criminal adjudication.

At the domestic level, even the ostensibly more substantive discipline of Criminal Law has for the most part succeeded in shunting off serious reflection on the underlying rationales and objectives of criminal trial and punishment to the nether-regions of penal philosophy. Whilst textbooks on

---

[31]   T Anderson, D Schum and W Twining, *Analysis of Evidence* (2nd edn, Cambridge, CUP, 2005).

[32]   For the avoidance of doubt, let me stress that paying close attention to the concept of 'evidence' is by no means bound to degenerate into conceptualism. Thus, as previously stated in Chapter 1, Ian Dennis was one of the first British scholars to emphasise the moral and political foundations of evidentiary doctrine: see eg, IH Dennis 'Reconstructing the Law of Criminal Evidence' [1989] *CLP* 21. I am drawing attention to *a potential risk* of approaches to Evidence that proceed from conceptual taxonomy, not to any inevitable or unavoidable pitfalls in conventional analysis.

[33]   No prizes for noticing that this is the approach adopted by P Roberts and A Zuckerman, *Criminal Evidence* (Oxford, OUP, 2004). What differentiates our text from most others at a fundamental level, at least as much as its more obviously restricted focus on criminal trials, is the very first question articulated in the opening paragraphs: not, 'What is "evidence"?', as in the concept-driven expository tradition, but 'What is the disciplinary scope, method and content of Evidence?', a question that cannot be answered by conceptual analysis. (To think otherwise would be a compounded form of meta-conceptualism: the fallacy of thinking that the scope of a disciplinary inquiry into a subject with moral and political dimensions can be settled merely by conceptual-taxonomic fiat.)

criminal process and criminal justice admittedly do somewhat better (especially those including extensive commentary on sentencing law and practice),[34] few Criminal Law books accommodate more than a perfunctory nod to the standard list of penal objectives—retribution, deterrence and rehabilitation—before getting down to the real business of analysing doctrine in minute detail. For those steeped in this tradition of Criminal Law scholarship and teaching,[35] criminal justice at the international level presents a startlingly different proposition.

The moral and political foundations of ICrimJ, as an extension of international relations, are unmistakably vivid and inescapably acrimonious. Coupled with the recent novelty of the enterprise, it is hardly surprising that ICrimJ policy-makers, practitioners and commentators concern themselves intensely with basic questions of moral and political legitimacy, values, objectives and underlying rationales for penal enforcement. An important source of value derives from the humanitarian impulses which have inspired the laws of armed conflict ('International Humanitarian Law') over the last 150 years. A second strand is contributed by the values of the post-1945 human rights movement, which are explicitly founded on the notion of human dignity and institutionalised by the United Nations' Universal Declaration (UDHR), the ICCPR and associated regional human rights regimes (including the ECHR). Penal philosophy supplies a third essential dimension. ICrimJ scholars have rightly emphasised the plurality of objectives to be taken into account in appraising the conduct of international criminal tribunals, including retributive punishment, deterrence, reaffirmation of values, maintaining international peace and security, national reconciliation, post-conflict reconstruction, promoting democracy and the Rule of Law, institution-building, and so on. To the extent that the Statutes and founding instruments of international criminal tribunals often specify a range of potentially conflicting objectives and values, some attempt to clarify and, where necessary, rank these competing considerations is unavoidable. Several commentators have persuasively argued that the traditional demands of punishment, which without much reflection tend to dominate prosecutions and sentencing at the domestic level, cannot simply be

---

[34] Eg A Ashworth, *Sentencing and Criminal Justice* (4th edn, Cambridge, CUP, 2005); L Zedner, *Criminal Justice* (Oxford, OUP, 2004).

[35] For criticism, see P Alldridge, 'What's Wrong with the Traditional Criminal Law Course?' (1990) 10 *Legal Studies* 38. As always, there are exceptions. More theoretically astute textbook treatments include AP Simester and GR Sullivan, *Criminal Law: Theory and Doctrine* (3rd edn, Oxford, Hart Publishing, 2007); A Ashworth, *Principles of Criminal Law* (5th edn, Oxford, OUP, 2006). CMV Clarkson and HM Keating, *Criminal Law: Text and Materials* (5th edn, London, Sweet & Maxwell, 2001) contains much more material on philosophies of punishment than most of its competitors.

extrapolated to the international context[36] (although the more sophisticated theories of retributive justice may not be as vulnerable to their criticisms as these authors sometimes seem to imply).[37] Peace and security might conceivably be better served in particular post-conflict situations by restorative justice processes, or even by non-judicial forms of accountability like truth and reconciliation commissions, rather than by trials and punishments on the traditional (ie Western) model.

To say that ICrimJ makes it impossible to ignore questions of fundamental values and objectives which are generally taken-for-granted at the domestic level, is not yet to say that ICrimJ scholarship is particularly distinguished by theoretical sophistication,[38] much less that international criminal tribunals have fully articulated and defended coherent penal philosophies.[39] The vital importance of re-examining fundamental objectives and underlying rationales is nonetheless a valuable lesson to take back to domestic Evidence scholarship and teaching. For such re-examination turns out to be essential not only for a proper appreciation of particular doctrinal rules and principles, but also in order to be able to conceptualise the discipline as a whole without unconsciously slipping into an arid conceptualism.

The argument for incorporating political morality within Evidence teaching and scholarship was briefly outlined in Chapter 1, partly by reference to ICrimJ (human rights) examples. In my view, it is impossible fully to grasp or confidently to apply rules of evidence without appreciating their underlying values and objectives. Whenever the content of the applicable rule stops short of determining the instant case, and equally whenever two or more legal rules contain conflicting directives, it is necessary to appeal to more general values and objectives—those encapsulated in intermediate principles, if not the system's ultimate rationales—in

---

[36] Eg MA Drumbl, 'Collective Violence and Individual Punishment: the Criminality of Mass Atrocity' (2005) 99 *Northwestern University Law Review* 539; JE Alvarez, 'Crimes of States/Crimes of Hate: Lessons from Rwanda' (1999) 24 *Yale Journal of International Law* 365.

[37] See further, P Roberts, 'Restoration and Retribution in International Criminal Justice: an Exploratory Analysis' in A von Hirsch *et al* (eds), *Restorative Justice and Criminal Justice* (Oxford, Hart Publishing, 2003).

[38] A plausible hypothesis: ICrimJ is likely to be strong in those fields of scholarship traditionally cultivated by most of its exponents, such as international law and international relations theory, and relatively weak in other areas, including doctrinal criminal law and penal philosophy.

[39] Indeed, it is possible to marshal considerable evidence for the contrary proposition; though academic commentary, at least, is lately becoming markedly more sophisticated. See eg, E Blumenson, 'The Challenge of a Global Standard of Justice: Peace, Pluralism, and Punishment at the International Criminal Court' (2006) 44 *Columbia Journal of Transnational Law* 801; B Wringe, 'Why Punish War Crimes? Victor's Justice and Expressive Justifications of Punishment' (2006) 25 *Law and Philosophy* 159; A Fichtelberg, 'Crimes Beyond Justice? Retributivism and War Crimes' (2005) 24(1) *Criminal Justice Ethics* 31.

order to fill the gap or resolve the conflict. Appreciating precisely why it is wrong to convict the innocent, for example, should inform the development and application of evidentiary rules on presumptions and burdens and standards of proof.[40] Understanding the moral and political objections to torturing the guilty into confessing should likewise inform exclusionary rules directed, in part, to preserving the moral integrity of criminal adjudication.[41] Of course, we all 'instinctively' know that suspects should not be tortured and that it is wrong to convict the innocent. However, whilst such commitments remain the unexamined reflexes of professional habit, they do not qualify as considered judgements which can be articulated and defended rationally; that is to say, by identifying *reasons* for holding particular beliefs, and for acting on them in appropriate circumstances. Where blind faith or habit have taken the place of reasoned, critical reflection, normative decision-making may appear to float free of any deeper theoretical moorings and come to seem essentially arbitrary, not only to those with competing interests and perspectives, but even (and in some ways, more to the point) to ourselves. A crisis of self-confidence in normative justification is threatened.[42] Is the criminal justice process in general, and the law of evidence and procedure in particular, nothing more than a collection of empty rituals or a confidence trick played by the ruling elite on the benighted masses? We had better hope not. If that were all there is to it, how could one continue in good faith to perpetuate such an abomination? There could hardly be more at stake on a personal and professional level. In terms of effective policy-making and advocacy, unexamined moral and political preferences are more vulnerable than fully rationalised commitments to being curtailed or even abandoned in pursuit of short-term instrumental political goals (security, crime control, populist rabble-rousing...).

At one extreme of the spectrum,[43] ICrimJ confronts us with the most profound questions of political morality. What is the appropriate punishment for genocide? When, if ever, is war legitimate? Who, if anybody, has the moral and political authority to punish international crimes? Or to forgive them? What kind of crime was the Holocaust? How can the

---

[40]   See further, Roberts and Zuckerman, above n 5, ch 8.

[41]   *Ibid* ch 4.

[42]   At least for those who believed in the first place that participating in the system, as a teacher, scholar or practitioner, had some legitimate point or genuine merit. This argument is not addressed to inveterate cynics.

[43]   It is a mistake to think that all international crimes must necessarily be very serious. In fact, some offending may be *relatively* trivial even by municipal standards, eg 'destroying or seizing the enemy's property' contrary to ICC Statute, Art 8(1)(b)(xiii). This is a codification of pre-existing IHL: 'Theft and robbery remain punishable crimes in peace and war. The solider in an enemy country must observe the same respect for civilian property as he would at home': UK Ministry of Defence, *The Manual of the Law of Armed Conflict* (Oxford, OUP, 2004) § 11.76.2.

international community strike an appropriate balance between judging the past and building a better future? Courts, including English criminal courts, occasionally have to grapple with questions exactly like these,[44] although of course the vast majority of domestic criminal litigation is mundane by comparison. Far from being disqualified from a more general discussion of criminal adjudication by its exoticism and extremity, however, it strikes me that ICrimJ holds up a mirror to domestic criminal proceedings which ought to induce a sobering sense of perspective. If a politician or general who ordered the murders of a thousand innocent civilians is subject, on conviction, to a maximum penalty of life imprisonment,[45] how does this compare to domestic sentencing tariffs? If restorative justice processes are appropriate for lower-level participants in genocide, why should their domestic application be limited to minor offending? I am not saying that questions such as these ipso facto expose the indefensibility of existing domestic practice, only that an international perspective both prompts searching questions about fundamental values and objectives in adjudication and rules out glib responses with nothing more than the deadweight of tradition to recommend them. Moreover, the political morality of international criminal justice is not limited to core debates in penal philosophy. It has distinctively procedural and evidentiary dimensions.

Consider, by way of illustration, the value choices underpinning relevant provisions of the ICC's Statute and Rules of Procedure and Evidence (RPE). These materials exhibit a strong commitment to truth-finding. By ICC Statute, Article 69(3), 'The Court shall have authority to request the submission of all evidence that it considers necessary for the determination of truth'. Rule 63(2) RPE adds that trial chambers 'shall have the authority ... to assess freely all evidence submitted in order to determine its relevance or admissibility in accordance with Article 69'. Even though evidence is normally presented by the adversarial parties, and facts can be agreed between the prosecution and defence as they are in England and Wales,[46] the ICC is not obliged to acquiesce in such agreements if 'the Chamber is of the opinion that a more complete presentation of the alleged facts is required in the interests of justice, in particular in the interests of

---

[44] See eg, *R v Sawoniuk* [2000] 2 Cr App R 220, CA, a prosecution for Second World War atrocities brought under the War Crimes Act 1991. Also see *David John Caldwell Irving v Penguin Books Ltd and Deborah E Lipstadt*, 2000 WL 362478, QBD, in which ascertaining the historical truth of the Holocaust was central to the court's determination of the claimant's libel action (notwithstanding the trial judge's protestations to the contrary).

[45] Being the maximum penalty that international criminal tribunals are empowered to impose: ICTY Statute, Art 24 and RPE Rule 101; ICTR Statute, Art 23 and RPE Rule 101; ICC Statute, Art 77.

[46] See eg, *R v Greenwood* [2005] 1 Cr App R 7, CA.

victims'.[47] Despite its evident priority, however, truth-finding is not the ICC's overriding concern, which is set out in Article 64(2): 'The Trial Chamber shall ensure that a trial is fair and expeditious and is conducted with full respect for the rights of the accused and due regard for the protection of victims and witnesses'. A further manifestation of the subordination of truth-finding to trial 'fairness' can be seen in the ICC's unique exclusionary rule for improperly obtained evidence:

> Evidence obtained by means of a violation of this Statute or internationally recognized human rights shall not be admissible if:
>
> (a) the violation casts substantial doubt on the reliability of the evidence; or
>
> (b) the admission of the evidence would be antithetical to and would seriously damage the integrity of the proceedings.[48]

Now, 'integrity'-based exclusionary rules are notoriously open-ended,[49] and it will be interesting to monitor how the ICC interprets this provision in practice and over time. It is nonetheless of considerable significance, if only as strong evidence of convergence in international attitudes, that 120 states with diverse legal traditions voted for an ICC Statute which not only prioritises rights and procedural propriety over truth-finding, but also contains something approximating a presumptive exclusionary rule for evidence obtained through serious breaches of human rights standards. For if the breach is regarded as sufficiently serious, admitting evidence obtained in consequence of the breach surely *would* be antithetical to the integrity of the proceedings: indeed the complementary normative standards of '(serious) human rights violation' and 'seriously damaging the integrity of the proceedings' appear to be mutually *constitutive* within the framework of the Rome Statute. Some commentators would like to see a similar approach adopted by courts in England and Wales under the

---

[47] RPE Rule 69.

[48] ICC Statute, Art 69(7). This provision has no exact precursor, but substantially derives from common Rule 95 of the ICTY and ICTR Rules of Procedure and Evidence: 'No evidence shall be admissible if obtained by methods which cast substantial doubt on its reliability or if its admission is antithetical to, and would seriously damage, the integrity of the proceedings'. In addition, Rule 89(D) of the ICTY's Rules of Procedure and Evidence states that: 'A Chamber may exclude evidence if its probative value is substantially outweighed by the need to ensure a fair trial'. This formulation was omitted from the ICTR's Rules of Procedure and Evidence.

[49] For discussion, see A Ashworth, 'Exploring the Integrity Principle in Evidence and Procedure' in P Mirfield and R Smith (eds), *Essays for Colin Tapper* (Oxford, OUP, 2003); P Mirfield, *Silence, Confessions and Improperly Obtained Evidence* (Oxford, OUP, 1997) 23–8.

Human Rights Act,[50] although the application of this decontextualised norm would presumably remain open to competing interpretations in practice.

A second notable feature of the ICC regime's hierarchy of values is the prominence afforded to victims' rights and interests. Article 68 of the ICC Statute, which is devoted entirely to 'Protection of the Victims and Witnesses and their Participation in the Proceedings', opens with the declaration that: 'The Court shall take appropriate measures to protect the safety, physical and psychological well-being, dignity and privacy of victims and witnesses'. Such measures extend to providing victims with their own legal counsel, empowered to make representations to the court on victims' behalf,[51] and to relaxing the normal expectation that witnesses will give live oral testimony at trial:

> As an exception to the principle of public hearings ... the Court may, to protect victims and witnesses or an accused, conduct any part of the proceedings *in camera* or allow the presentation of evidence by electronic or other special means. In particular, such measures shall be implemented in the case of a victim of sexual violence or a child who is a victim or a witness, unless otherwise ordered by the Court...[52]

> The Court may also permit the giving of *viva voca* (oral) or recorded testimony of a witness by means of video or audio technology, as well as the introduction of documents or written transcripts...[53]

There are evident parallels between these victim-orientated aspects of ICC trial procedure and recent developments in criminal adjudication in England and Wales, particularly in relation to the provision of 'special measures' for vulnerable or intimidated witnesses pursuant to the Youth Justice and Criminal Evidence Act 1999.[54] But three important differences are worth emphasising. First, the ICC Statute is scrupulous in insisting that 'These measures shall not be prejudicial to or inconsistent with the rights of the accused'.[55] This thrice-repeated affirmation strikes a rather different chord to the mood music of domestic British reforms, which are couched in terms of 'rebalancing' the criminal justice process with the implication that

---

[50] Choo and Nash, above n 9; D Ormerod, 'ECHR and the Exclusion of Evidence: Trial Remedies for Article 8 Breaches?' [2003] *Crim LR* 61: cf R Mahoney, 'Abolition of New Zealand's *Prima Facie* Exclusionary Rule' [2003] *Crim LR* 607.

[51] ICC Statute, Art 68(3); RPE Rules 89–93.

[52] ICC Statute, Art 68(2).

[53] ICC Statute Art 69(2).

[54] See Roberts and Zuckerman, above n 5, 280–6; P Roberts, D Cooper and S Judge, 'Coming Soon to a Court Near You! Special Measures for Vulnerable and Intimidated Witnesses I and II' (2005) 169 *Justice of the Peace* 748, 769; D Birch, 'A Better Deal for Vulnerable Witnesses?' [2000] *Crim LR* 223; D Birch and R Leng, *Blackstone's Guide to the Youth Justice and Criminal Evidence Act 1999* (London, Blackstone Press, 2000) chs 3–5.

[55] ICC Statute, Arts 68(1) and (3), 69(2).

suspects' and defendants' rights must be curtailed in order to achieve justice for victims and witnesses.[56] The ICC Statute does not play this 'zero-sum' game, and yet it still manages to give victims' rights considerable prominence. This merits emphasis as a second interesting contrast with criminal procedure and its reform in England and Wales. The provision of detailed defence rights, including an elaborated version of Article 14 ICCPR,[57] does not lead to a lopsided neglect of victims' interests. Instead, as we just saw, 'due regard for the protection of victims and witnesses' is placed alongside 'full respect for the rights of the accused' as an integral part of the Court's overriding Article 64 duty to 'ensure that a trial is fair and expeditious'. One must not underestimate the genuine practical difficulties of reconciling these potentially disparate values and interests in individual cases, or in relation to particular procedural policies. But at least at the level of general principle, the ICC Statute successfully affirms a fundamental duty of respect and compassionate treatment for victims and witnesses as part of a coherent, integrated conception of criminal justice.[58]

This balanced aspiration is closely connected to a third point. We have already noted that victims and witnesses before the ICC enjoy certain rights, such as access to legal representation, that are not available in England and Wales. Victims' procedural rights are buttressed by further innovative provisions which restrict the admissibility or use of certain kinds of information in sexual offence prosecutions,[59] require the Court to 'establish principles relating to reparations to, or in respect of, victims, including restitution, compensation and rehabilitation',[60] and mandate the creation of a state-maintained Trust Fund for paying compensation to victims and their families.[61] This package of provisions demonstrates that serious efforts can be made to accommodate the needs and interests of victims, not only in order to bolster the success of criminal prosecutions but also because it is intrinsically important to be attentive to their material comforts and personal wellbeing, without necessarily changing the basic structure of criminal trials. If this is an obvious point, it is apparently too easily overlooked or shouted down in the Punch and Judy Show politics of domestic criminal procedure reform.

---

[56] JD Jackson, 'Justice for All: Putting Victims at the Heart of Criminal Justice?' (2003) 30 *Journal of Law and Society* 309.

[57] ICC Statute, Arts 66–67.

[58] Cf Roberts and Zuckerman, above n 5, 20–1.

[59] RPE Rules 70 and 71, respectively, limit the circumstances in which consent can be inferred in cases of sexual violence, and render evidence of the complainant's previous or subsequent sexual conduct categorically inadmissible.

[60] ICC Statute, Art 75(1).

[61] ICC Statute Art 79.

PROCEDURAL AND INSTITUTIONAL DESIGN

The political morality of criminal adjudication extends beyond the specification of fundamental values—respect for human dignity, doing justice, safeguarding human rights, due process of law, etc—to inform the more concentrated jurisprudential tasks of designing institutions and procedures capable of serving those values and implementing penal objectives. Procedural innovation in international criminal adjudication has already been indicated, in the provision of legal counsel to victims in the ICC system. This is a significant departure from what English lawyers would regard as the procedural norm, and yet it would rarely raise an eyebrow in France or Germany where legal representation for the *partie civile* (complainant) is well-established.[62] This example encapsulates the broader potential of international criminal process as a case study in comparative institutional design. ICrimJ is the perfect antidote for blithe assumptions about the desirability, let alone the inevitability, of adopting the procedures and institutions of criminal justice which Anglophone common law jurisdictions, broadly speaking, share. Although English common law is represented on every continent,[63] Anglophone criminal procedure is very much a minority tradition in a world dominated, both geographically and in terms of population size, by the Napoleonic civilian Codes and their modern Western European, post-Soviet and colonial variations.[64]

This is not to suggest that choice of criminal procedure should be settled by global popularity contest. There should be no ex ante assumption that 'one size fits all' in criminal adjudication, or that a particular legal tradition's most celebrated or durable procedural practices could be successfully 'transplanted' into a different legal and cultural context. The point is to encourage critical reflection on our existing procedures, not to replace one set of unexamined assumptions supposing the inevitable superiority of common law adversarialism, with an equally uncritical preference for official inquisitions in the continental style. Indeed, the lesson of ICrimJ appears to be that it is possible to blend elements of both styles of adjudication into a sui generis procedure benefiting from the respective strengths of each municipal tradition. This has been the technique pioneered by the UN's ad hoc Tribunals, and subsequently followed by the ICC, whereby a recognisably inquisitorial pre-trial process, featuring strong prosecutorial direction and a supervisory Indictments Chamber, is combined with an essentially adversarial model of trial, complete with

---

[62] WT Pizzi and W Perron, 'Crime Victims in German Courtrooms: a Comparative Perspective on American Problems' (1996) 32 *Stanford Journal of International Law* 37.

[63] Antarctica excepted!

[64] For a valuable recent survey, see R Vogler, *A World View of Criminal Justice* (Aldershot, Ashgate, 2005). The classic theorisation is still MR Damaška, *The Faces of Justice and State Authority* (New Haven, Yale UP, 1986).

relatively active legal representation, guilty pleas, rules of admissibility, cross-examination of witnesses and discrete procedural phases for guilt determination and sentencing.[65]

At least since the creation of the Nuremberg International Military Tribunal (IMT), questions of basic institutional design in international criminal justice have been conceptualised in terms of perceived contrasts between 'adversarial' and 'inquisitorial' procedures. Notwithstanding the acknowledged limitations of this rather simplistic dichotomy,[66] it remains a useful starting-point for analysis. Reflecting on the stilted drafting process of the Nuremberg IMT's Charter, US Chief Prosecutor Robert H Jackson confided: 'From the very beginning it has been apparent that our greatest problem is how to reconcile two very different systems of procedure'.[67] There was considerable mistrust and misunderstanding infecting the relationship between the four principal victorious powers (Britain, France, Soviet Russia and the United States) not only regarding the overriding penal objectives of the IMT, but also arising from their markedly divergent conceptions of a properly conducted criminal trial.[68] The depth of this cultural incomprehension was succinctly, if inadvertently, revealed by the Soviet representative, and later judge of the IMT, Nikitchenko, who waited until the very last drafting meeting to inquire: 'What is meant in the English by "cross-examine"?' In the event, the Russians and their French civilian *confrères* were willing to let adversarial preferences prevail in order to placate the Americans, and 'differences were resolved by compromises which were crude but proved workable'.[69]

---

[65] ICC Statute, Art 76 and RPE Rule 143 contemplate supplementary hearings on sentence following a guilty plea or conviction after trial. The ICTY has conducted many such sentencing hearings. However, by ICTY RPE Rule 86(C) '[t]he parties shall also address matters of sentencing in closing arguments' at the end of the trial. An American judge at the ICTY has described this procedure as 'very prejudicial to the defence who must say in effect, "My client is not guilty, but if he is, there are some reasons to go easy on him"': PM Wald, 'Rules of Evidence in the Yugoslav War Tribunal' (2003) 21 *Quinnipiac Law Review* 761, 767.

[66] Cf John Jackson, Chapter 11; Jackson, above n 5; JF Nijboer, 'Common Law Tradition in Evidence Scholarship Observed from a Continental Perspective' (1993) 41 *American Journal of Comparative Law* 299.

[67] Quoted in T Taylor, *The Anatomy of the Nuremberg Trials* (Boston, Little Brown & Co, 1992) 64.

[68] Stalin sought to score political points off Churchill by insisting that the Nazi war criminals should stand their trial, whilst the British and Americans initially favoured summary execution for high-ranking Nazis. However, it should be appreciated that Stalin's conception of a 'trial', exemplified by the infamous show trials to which his political opponents were subjected throughout the 1930s, had more in common with summary drumhead courts martial, than with modern conceptions of criminal due process—or, indeed, with the protracted trial proceedings subsequently conducted in Nuremberg between November 1945 and October 1946. See GJ Bass, *Stay the Hand of Vengeance: the Politics of War Crimes Tribunals* (Princeton NJ, Princeton UP, 2000) ch 5.

[69] Taylor, above n 67, 64.

In more recent history, the ICTY, ICTR and ICC have all combined characteristic features of adversarial and inquisitorial process in novel and imaginative ways.[70] The inquisitorial caste of pre-trial international criminal process is personified in the figure of the prosecutor. In the ICC system, the Prosecutor 'may initiate investigations *proprio motu* on the basis of information on crimes within the jurisdiction of the Court', and to this end 'may seek additional information from States, organs of the United Nations, intergovernmental or non-governmental organizations, or other reliable sources ... and may receive written or oral testimony at the seat of the Court'.[71] The ICC Prosecutor must, however, obtain the authorisation of the Court's Pre-Trial Chamber in order to proceed with an investigation and prosecution.[72] This institutional arrangement, modelled directly on continental criminal procedure codes,[73] is in marked contrast to the rigid separation between English police and prosecutors enshrined in the Prosecution of Offences Act 1985, which has dictated a somewhat estranged relationship between police investigators and the Crown Prosecution Service in England and Wales.[74] The contrasting tendency of international criminal *trials* to adopt a broadly adversarial format, with party-orchestrated presentation of evidence and oral examination of witnesses, is attributable to several factors, prominently including the impact of the global human rights movement. In extending its activities into the sponsorship of international criminal trials, the United Nations has naturally been at pains to preserve its longstanding commitment to human rights.[75] The ICTY, ICTR and ICC all consequently reproduce within their respective Statutes a full suite of rights for suspects and the accused, including faithful translations of Article 14 ICCPR's right to a fair trial.[76] Thus, every person

---

[70] Generally, see A Cassese, *International Criminal Law* (Oxford, OUP, 2003) ch 20.

[71] ICC Statute, Art 15(1)–(2).

[72] ICC Statute, Art 15(3).

[73] Judicial supervision of criminal investigations and prosecutions is exemplified by the French juge d'instruction, albeit that the empirical realities of judicial supervision may belie professional ideologies and the strict letter of the law: cf J Hodgson, 'The Police, the Prosecutor and the *Juge D'Instruction*: Judicial Supervision in France, Theory and Practice' (2001) 41 *British Journal of Criminology* 342; EA Tomlinson, 'The Saga of Wiretapping in France: What it Tells Us about the French Criminal Justice System' (1993) 53 *Louisiana Law Review* 1091.

[74] Recent developments, culminating in a transfer of the initial power to charge suspects form police to prosecutors under the Criminal Justice Act 2003, are in the process of reducing this institutional distance: see ID Brownlee, 'The Statutory Charging Scheme in England and Wales: Towards a Unified Prosecution System?' [2004] *Crim LR* 896. Whether closer contact will facilitate effective prosecution, or damage Crown prosecutors' vaunted 'independence', remains to be seen. Cf A Sanders, 'An Independent Crown Prosecution Service?' [1986] *Crim LR* 16.

[75] The Preamble to the UN Charter reaffirms 'faith in fundamental human rights, in the dignity and worth of the human person, in the equal rights of men and women and of nations large and small'.

[76] ICTY Statute, Art 21; ICTR Statute, Art 20; ICC Statute, Arts 66 and 67.

facing criminal charges must be allowed to conduct their own defence, with the assistance of counsel if they prefer, and their entitlements shall include the right 'to examine, or have examined, the witnesses against him and to obtain the attendance and examination of witnesses on his behalf under the same conditions as witnesses against him'.[77]

In view of the fact that the ICC and its international precursors are sui generis institutions of criminal adjudication, it must be acknowledged that bespoke procedures designed for international tribunals like the ICC may not be appropriate for domestic criminal proceedings. But it is still well worth considering why, precisely, the institutions and procedures of the ICC have taken their current form. Those aspects of the process which appear to have been dictated by a moral conception of justice, or by human rights norms, are quite likely to have applications or analogues in domestic criminal proceedings that would repay further exploration and elucidation by Evidence scholars. This is merely to extrapolate the preceding section's argument, advocating closer attention to the normative values and objectives underpinning criminal adjudication, into the detailed specification of procedural and evidentiary norms. The methodology adopted might be conceptualised as a distinctively ICrimJ variation on comparative legal studies.[78]

Other aspects of ICC procedure have been heavily influenced by pragmatic institutional constraints. For example, the absence of a common world language effectively rules out the use of lay juries in trials before the ICC. This is only a genuine problem for ICrimJ, however, if trial by lay jury is a prerequisite of justice in international criminal proceedings. Some jurists have argued that it is,[79] but I am unable to discern anything more substantial than a culturally-conditioned projection of national constitutional arrangements behind such expressions of pro-jury sentiment. Most continental commentators (as far as I can gather) appear to view trial by jury as a curious, if not barbarous, Anglophone anachronism[80] that they would never have accepted for the ICC even in the absence of conclusive pragmatic objections. The bemusement of the rest of the world need not in-and-of-itself precipitate a loss of faith in English juries. However, we

---

[77] Article 14(3)(e) ICCPR.

[78] See further, Roberts, above n 3.

[79] Eg AJ Walker, 'When a Good Idea is Poorly Implemented: How the International Criminal Court Fails to be Insulated from International Politics and to Protect Basic Due Process Guarantees' (2004) 106 *West Virginia Law Review* 245.

[80] Cf T Hörnle, 'Democratic Criminal Process', in proceedings of a workshop on 'Democratic Criminal Justice', hosted by the Law Faculty of the University of Warsaw, 14–15 October 2006, 128–9: '[P]ublic support and perceived importance of lay participation is not uniform throughout Europe. In the German literature, scepticism about the necessity of lay participation prevails ... Lay participation is a symbolic token of scepticism towards the state ... From the normative point of view, however, there is no objection to abolishing lay participation'.

might want to reflect more carefully than we generally do on the implications of discovering—if this be the case—that the centrality of the jury in English criminal proceedings[81] is an essentially conventional and rather idiosyncratic artefact of British culture and heritage, rather than a conceptual imperative of justice, or even one of its more superficially plausible and internationally appreciated procedural extrapolations. This is particularly significant for the present discussion because jury trial is often said to be an important influence on the number, style and content of Anglo-American rules of evidence.

Neither an imperative of justice nor a consequence of pragmatic institutional constraints, a third dimension of the ICC's procedural regime comprises features which are quite transparently the outcome of diplomatic wrangling and geopolitical power-plays. There is no direct analogue to this style of politics at the level of domestic criminal proceedings (unless a pale reflection might be found in the relationship between central government and individual states in federal jurisdictions). Nonetheless, identifying the areas where the ideals of ICrimJ have been forced to defer to diplomatic pressures, at least for the time being, might throw into sharper relief the impact of (party-)political agendas on criminal procedure much closer to home.

The powers and independence of the prosecutor present one potentially fruitful source of such comparisons.[82] Prosecutorial independence was a hotly contested topic at the ICC Rome Conference.[83] Most states accepted the principle that the ICC Prosecutor must be independent of direct political influence in order to be a credible agent of international justice, both in reality and for the sake of appearances. However some states, notably including the USA, were concerned that a truly independent prosecutor would be free to launch 'politically-motivated' prosecutions against Western politicians or military personnel on active service overseas, and consequently sought to make the ICC Prosecutor answerable to the UN Security Council. But this proposal in turn was entirely unacceptable to many states, in view of the fact that the Security Council is an undemocratic institution rooted in historical inequalities (a critique that

---

[81] Recalling that this mooted 'centrality' is as much ideological as practical, and that jury trials are in fact limited to some 11,000 contested Crown Court trials, involving around 20,000 accused, annually in England and Wales: see Roberts and Zuckerman, above n 5, 40–2.

[82] ICC Statute, Arts 53–54.

[83] For general overviews, situating concern about the powers of the Prosecutor within broader critiques of the ICC Statute, see DE Edlin, 'The Anxiety of Sovereignty: Britain, the United States and the International Criminal Court' (2006) 29 *Boston College International and Comparative Law Review* 1; Walker, above n 79; R Wedgwood, 'The Irresolution of Rome' (2001) 64 *Law and Contemporary Problems* 193.

economically powerful states excluded from the Permanent Five, veto-holding, members are inclined to find persuasive). The final text of the Rome Statute incorporates a fudged compromise which satisfied neither side of the argument,[84] but did at least allow the Conference to conclude successfully with a Statute which, in its entirety, was acceptable to an overwhelming majority of states.

The historical evolution of the domestic prosecutorial system in England and Wales could hardly present a stronger contrast. Although the Crown Prosecution Service, with the Director of Public Prosecutions at its helm,[85] was created by statute as recently as 1985, the office of DPP is over a century old and the system whereby the DPP reports to the Attorney General, the government's principal law officer (and like the DPP himself, an executive appointee) rests on long-established constitutional convention.[86] Allegations of untoward political influence on decisions to prosecute, or to decline to prosecute, particular individuals surface in the media from time to time.[87] Whatever the truth of such allegations on their merits, the informal, conventional basis of the DPP's independence almost inevitably fans the flames of suspicion. Perhaps Evidence scholars and teachers should pay more attention to the possibility of conscious political influence on the types of cases that do, and do not, get to court. But I doubt whether isolated *cause celebres*—because that is, at most, what would emerge in the British context—could really shed much light on general features of English procedural law and practice.

More promising in this regard are the general rules and principles developed by prosecutorial authorities to regulate case-building and progression in routine criminal proceedings. In England and Wales, the Code for Crown Prosecutors[88] establishes some baseline principles, but these are augmented substantially by a complex framework of operational policies and practices targeting particular types of offence, identifying the special needs of designated groups of victims and witnesses, specifying criteria for diversion from formal process, and so on.[89] Operational selectivity in

---

[84] Thus, India and the United States both refused to sign the Statute partly owing to their dissatisfaction with the powers of the ICC Prosecutor, but for diametrically opposed reasons: see DF Orentlicher, 'Politics by Other Means: the Law of the International Criminal Court' (1999) 32 *Cornell International Law Journal* 489.

[85] Prosecution of Offences Act 1985, s 1.

[86] See eg, C Turpin, *British Government and the Constitution: Text, Cases and Materials* (5th edn, Cambridge, CUP, 2005) 208–9.

[87] Most recently in relation to the decision of the Serious Fraud Office to abandon efforts to prosecute alleged bribery by British arms exporters, in which the Prime Minister himself apparently intervened on several occasions: see D Leigh and R Evans, 'Scale of Pressure to Drop BAE Inquiry Revealed by Ministers', *The Guardian*, 23 January 2007; C Timmis, 'In the Line of Fire', 104/10 *Law Society Gazette*, 8 March 2007, 20.

[88] Available at www.cps.gov.uk/victims_witnesses/code.html.

[89] See CPS *Legal Guidance*, available at www.cps.gov.uk/legal/index.html. This detailed policy guidance is augmented by numerous ad hoc publications.

prosecutions is also a matter of intense policy concern and concerted activity at the ICC, reflecting the Rome Statute's foundational 'principle of complementarity'.[90] The ICC is intended to assert jurisdiction 'over the most serious crimes of concern to the international community as a whole' in a manner which is 'complementary to national criminal jurisdictions'.[91] In practice, this means that the ICC will normally allow national criminal processes to take their course, unless the ICC Prosecutor judges that the relevant state 'is unwilling or unable genuinely to carry out the ... prosecution'.[92] In accordance with the principle of complementarity, therefore, domestic criminal courts are envisaged as the primary agents of international criminal justice, with the ICC operating as supervisor and ultimate failsafe. In the words of the ICC's Office of the Prosecutor (OTP):

> The principle of complementarity represents the express will of States Parties to create an institution that is global in scope while recognising the primary responsibility of States themselves to exercise criminal jurisdiction. The principle is also based on considerations of efficiency and effectiveness since States will generally have the best access to evidence and witnesses. Moreover, there are limits on the number of prosecutions the ICC can bring ... The Court is an institution with limited resources. The Office will function with a two-tiered approach to combat impunity. On the one hand it will initiate prosecutions of the leaders who bear most responsibility for the crimes. On the other hand it will encourage national prosecutions, where possible, for the lower-ranking perpetrators, or work with the international community to ensure that the offenders are brought to justice by some other means.[93]

Devising robustly principled criteria for determining which cases to prosecute, and which referrals to reject, has accordingly become one of the ICC's most pressing operational priorities. It would be interesting to undertake a systematic comparison between the ICC's rapidly evolving criteria for implementing the principle of complementarity, within the framework of the Rome Statute, and policies structuring prosecutorial discretion at the domestic level. Such comparative studies would help to clarify the implications of prosecutorial decision-making for the types of cases, and forms of evidence, subsequently adduced in criminal trials. This is a relatively neglected dimension of the structure of proof in criminal adjudication. Questions of institutional and procedural 'design' are not exhausted by overt acts of primary legislation; they must also be traced into the subsidiary, 'soft' law-making and informal occupational routines

---

[90] See JT Holmes, 'Complementarity: National Courts *versus* the ICC' in A Cassese, P Gaeta and JRWD Jones (eds), *The Rome Statute of the International Criminal Court: a Commentary* (Oxford, OUP, 2002).

[91] ICC Statute, Preamble.

[92] ICC Statute, Art 17.

[93] ICC-OTP, *Paper on Some Policy Issues before the Office of the Prosecutor* (2003), available at www.icc-cpi.int/library/organs/otp/030905_Policy_Paper.pdf.

which structure professional legal practice, and which are devised and implemented in (amongst other places) prosecutors' offices.

CULTURAL INFLUENCES ON EVIDENCE, PROOF AND FACT-FINDING

Several Evidence scholars have recently drawn attention to the cultural determinants of forensic inference and fact-finding, partly in order to register their concern that 'common-sense' factual conclusions may conceal elements of prejudice or discrimination, especially within the context of pluralistic, ethnically and religiously diverse, multicultural societies.[94] If the meaning of conduct (including speech) is partly conditioned by an observer's cultural milieu and personal biography, witnesses or jurors with very different experiences of life may draw sharply divergent 'common-sense' inferences from the same event or testimony.

Comparativists continually encounter this phenomenon. A nice illustration, which attracted major press interest at the time,[95] involved 12 British and two Dutch plane-spotters participating in an organised tour around Greece (advertised on the tour-guide's website as 'a week-long excursion to one of the most interesting NATO countries in Europe'). Having themselves been spotted taking down details of aircraft on Greek military airbases, they were arrested and prosecuted for espionage. To the Greek magistrates presiding at trial, the defence claim that the accused had been filming Greek military aircraft in pursuit of their innocuous (if fatuous) hobby was, it would appear, virtually incomprehensible.[96] These foreigners

---

[94] See in particular, Christine Boyle, Chapter 3; CL Boyle and J Nyman, 'Finding Facts Fairly in Roberts and Zuckerman's *Criminal Evidence*' (2005) 2(2) *ICE* Article 3; M MacCrimmon, 'What is "Common" about Common Sense?: Cautionary Tales for Travelers Crossing Disciplinary Boundaries' (2001) 22 *Cardozo Law Review* 1433; RJ Allen, 'Common Sense, Rationality, and the Legal Process' (2001) 22 *Cardozo Law Review* 1417; AE Taslitz, 'An African-American Sense of Fact: the OJ Trial and Black Judges on Justice' (1998) 7 *Boston University Public Interest Law Journal* 219.

[95] O Bowcott, 'Spy Case Brings Spotters Down to Earth', *The Guardian*, 20 November 2001; N Smith and O Bowcott, 'Plane Spotters Face More Charges', *The Guardian*, 21 November 2001; H Smith and O Bowcott, 'Greeks Admit Concern at Air Spotters' Prison Plight', *The Guardian*, 23 November 2001; H Smith, 'Confusion at Trial of Planespotters', *The Guardian*, 26 April 2002. Also see BS Godfrey, C Emsley and G Dunstall, 'Introduction: Do You have Plane-spotters in New Zealand? Issues in Comparative Crime History at the Turn of Modernity' in BS Godfrey, C Emsley and G Dunstall (eds), *Comparative Histories of Crime* (Cullompton, Devon, Willan, 2003).

[96] I recall a not-too-dissimilar personal experience from many years ago, trying to explain to a Hungarian woman, with whom I happened to share an old-fashioned train compartment, why people wearing anoraks were stood at the end of the platform scribbling in notebooks and pointing videocameras at our train as it pulled into Birmingham New Street Station. Once you have said that these people are 'train-spotters', that train-spotting is their hobby, and that they do it for fun, it is actually quite difficult to think of anything else more constructive to say to somebody clearly eager to learn about British culture, but who still looks utterly bemused.

taking pictures and recording details of Greek military hardware just had to be spies; there was no other credible explanation for their behaviour from the magistrates' perspective.[97] Plane-spotting was apparently completely beyond the magistrates' experience, and it seems not to have occurred to them that the very eccentricity of this explanation, coupled with the elaborate arrangements that had been put in place to conduct an organised tour, vouched for its veracity. The accused were duly convicted and sentenced to terms of imprisonment extending up to three years' duration (although they were all freed pending an appeal, having previously spent 37 days in gaol on remand).[98] Six months later, these 'most unlikely spies in the history of international espionage' were acquitted on all counts by the Greek appeal court.[99]

Wittgenstein memorably declared that 'if a lion could talk, we could not understand him'.[100] This was a striking way of expressing the point that communication is rooted in a shared 'life-world' of meaning, not in the sounds we utter in speech or the abstract symbols which we use to commit our experience to writing. Criminal trials of animals are, literally speaking, a thing of the past.[101] However, if international criminal adjudication figuratively exemplifies Wittgenstein's conundrum of communicating with 'lions', its study might also reasonably be expected to illuminate the dynamics of domestic trials, in which the beguiling familiarity of a common language may serve to conceal the divisions of cultural experience. In this way, ICrimJ helps to make explicit what is often relatively opaque at the domestic level. The cultural conditioning of experience can hardly be ignored when trial participants do not even speak the same language (a situation hardly common, though not unknown,[102] in English criminal trials). In extreme cases, international criminal proceedings involve participants, as accused, victims and witnesses, whose cultural

[97] At least that is what they were told by Flight-Lieutenant Nectarios Samaras, who testified that he 'had no idea this hobby existed. But the handwritten notes these people made, the sort of details they recorded, were too expert to be made by amateurs' (quoted by Smith, above n 95). Earlier, a Greek London Embassy official remarked: 'It's unusual; we don't have plane spotters in our country' (quoted by Bowcott, above n 95). Also see K Myers, 'The Greeks don't have a Word for Plane-crazy', *Sunday Telegraph*, 28 April 2002 ('[T]he very notion of a "hobby", like anorak, belongs almost uniquely to males from a sodden island in the North Sea; trying to describe it to a woman judge in a Mediterranean culture is rather like explaining interplanetary travel to an oyster'); C Odone, 'A Nation of Anoraks: Why do the British Indulge in Such Strange Pastimes?', *The Observer*, 10 November 2002.

[98] H Smith and J Wilson, 'Dogs Barking, Lawyers Shouting and an Air of Disbelief as the Spotters are Guilty of Spying', *The Guardian*, 27 April 2002.

[99] S O'Neill, 'Joy after Plane-Spotters' Year of Hell', *Daily Telegraph*, 7 November 2002.

[100] L Wittgenstein, *Philosophical Investigations* (3rd edn, Oxford, Blackwell, 1967 [1953]) 223: for elucidation, see M McGinn, *Wittgenstein and the Philosophical Investigations* (London, Routledge, 1997) 51–60.

[101] Cf W Ewald, 'Comparative Jurisprudence (I): What was it Like to Try a Rat?' (1995) 143 *University of Pennsylvania Law Review* 1889, Pt I.

[102] Cf RG Parry, 'The Language of Evidence' [2004] *Crim LR* 1015.

experience and world-view are so divergent that their nations, tribes, parties or factions have recently resorted to genocidal violence in an attempt to obliterate each other from the face of the earth. In these desperate circumstances, the capacity of any model of criminal procedure to deliver justice founded on secure inferences of fact is truly tested to the limit.

The single richest source of primary documents and ancillary information about contemporary international criminal trials can be found on the respective websites of the UN's two ad hoc Tribunals.[103] These unique, and still rapidly accumulating, archives contain not merely appellate decisions, but full transcripts of first-instance proceedings, rulings and judgments of the ICTY and ICTR, materials of a type which cannot be obtained easily, if at all, for domestic criminal trials. Running to hundreds of thousands of pages,[104] keyword searchable transcripts of (to-date) some 80-odd trials offer a fascinating window into the world of international criminal adjudication. It is a vantage point which Evidence scholars and teachers might readily exploit, not least as a partial corrective to the disproportionate influence of appellate judgments on the pedagogic emphasis and popular conceptions of our subject. Even if transcripts of English criminal trials could be obtained more easily, they would not necessarily provide much indication of how the jury arrived at its peremptory general verdict of 'guilty' or 'not guilty'. Case analysis, for us, largely equates to dissecting what appellate courts have said about evidentiary norms or aspects of trial procedure, rather than having the opportunity to scrutinise fact-finding processes. The proceedings and reasoned judgments of the ICTY and ICTR therefore contribute a source of valuable insights which are generally absent from English criminal jurisprudence; and, it might be added, from the judgments of the ECtHR, which tend to adopt formulaic language and rarely explain how any factual conclusion has been proven or inferred.

Examining trials conducted by the ad hoc Tribunals brings into sharper focus the extent to which justice depends on a shared cultural background of norms, assumptions and expectations. A common natural language is only the starting-point. For as Rob Cryer explains more fully in Chapter 14 when considering the role of translators in international adjudication, meaning is embedded within language and sometimes resists literal translation. Moreover, language, culture and testimony are interrelated in complex ways. A single example must here suffice to illuminate the rich potential of international criminal trial records for more extended evidentiary analysis.

---

[103] See www.un.org/icty/cases-e/index-e.htm; www.ictr.org/.
[104] The ultimately abortive four-year trial of former Yugoslav president Slobodan Milosevic alone filled almost 50,000 pages of transcript: *Prosecutor v Slobodan Milosevic* (IT-02–54).

Tadic was the first decision handed down by the ICTY.[105] Dusko Tadic was a mid-ranking commander of a Serb paramilitary unit accused of various war crimes and crimes against humanity, including torture and murder of civilians, forced expulsions of non-Serb populations from the Prijedor region of Bosnia ('ethnic cleansing') and appalling mistreatment of prisoners of war. Amongst this grisly catalogue of indicted offences featured the cold-blooded murder of two Bosnian Muslim police officers, Edin Besic and Osman Didovic, who were allegedly pulled out of a line-up of surrendered prisoners standing with their hands behind their heads and stabbed to death by the accused. Although this was far from being the worst of Tadic's behaviour in these dark days of civil war and sectarian occupation, these particular murders were significant because the prosecution could produce an apparently impressive eyewitness claiming to have seen the victims die at Tadic's own hand, rather than as part of a common enterprise (potentially diluting criminal responsibility amongst several co-accused) or unwitnessed murders of the 'disappeared'. Nihad Seferovic had been at school with Dusko Tadic. Indeed, their families lived within 10 houses of each other on the same street where Tadic and Seferovic both grew up in a town called Kozarac in the Prijedor region of the former Yugoslavia. However, Seferovic was a Muslim, not a Serb like Tadic, and when the order came for Bosnian Muslims to report to Serb army collection points Seferovic fled to the hills, periodically thereafter venturing back down into the town on various errands. It was on one of these sorties that, whilst hiding in tall grass and concealed by overhanging plum trees, Seferovic caught sight of Tadic standing in a group of 15 or so Serb paramilitaries in front of the Serb Orthodox Church. The Serbs were apparently harassing a line of Muslim prisoners. Hiding less than 30 metres away, Seferovic was adamant that he recognised Tadic and saw him murder the two defenceless policemen. Basing itself on Seferovic's testimony, the ICTY Trial Chamber found 'beyond reasonable doubt that the accused ... killed two policemen, Osman [Didovic] and Edin Besic, in front of the Serbian Orthodox church in Kozarac'.[106] Tadic was accordingly convicted of murdering Besic and Didovic, amongst other atrocities.

On appeal, the defence took exception to Seferovic's evidence on several grounds, including the possibility that Seferovic was a Bosnian government 'plant' who had lied to the ICTY in order to exact revenge on Serbs.[107]

---

[105] *Prosecutor v Tadic* (IT-94–1, 'Prijedor'), Trial Chamber Judgment, 7 May 1997.
[106] *Ibid* para. 397.
[107] This is not, alas, a completely fanciful accusation. Another witness who testified against Tadic was exposed as a perjurer seeking revenge on Serbs: see *Decision on Prosecution Motion to Withdraw Protective Measures for Witness L*, 5 December 1996, where the Trial Chamber observed that '[W]itness L had admitted ... that he had lied about the death of his father while under oath. Witness L asserted that he had done this at the behest of the Bosnian government authorities who had allegedly "trained" him to give

Another argument, of particular interest to Evidence scholars, was that Seferovic's account was inherently implausible, for the reason later summarised by the ICTY Appeals Chamber:

> The Defence argues that the Trial Chamber erred in relying on the evidence of Mr Seferovic because it is implausible. Mr Seferovic, a Muslim who lived in an area under bombardment by Serbian paramilitary forces, fled to the mountains for safety. He testified at trial that he was so concerned about the welfare of his pet pigeons that he returned to town to feed them while the Serbian paramilitaries were still there. On his return to town, he saw Mr Tadic kill two policemen. Defence counsel contended at trial that the witness was never in town at the time of the killings…[108]

Indeed, this contention was advanced with some force in defence counsel's submissions to the ICTY Appeals Chamber. Appellate counsel called into question the Trial Chamber's willingness to conclude, beyond reasonable doubt, that Tadic had murdered Besic and Didovic solely in reliance on one eyewitness' testimony:

> That decision depended solely on the evidence of one witness, Nihad Seferovic. In our submission, the evidence of that witness was implausible when analysed … The background to his evidence is that he was a Muslim living in the area that had been under attack by Serb paramilitary forces. There had been a bombardment of the town where he lived, and he had fled to some nearby hills or mountains for safety. The cornerstone of his evidence was that before the bombardment, he had kept tame pigeons, and he was so concerned about their welfare that when the Serb paramilitaries were still in the town, he decided to return to the town in order to feed his pet birds. As a rational decision, that is, on any view, curious, because he was placing himself in the gravest of jeopardy in order to do no more than feed some pet birds who would have been most unlikely to have survived the bombardment of the town in any event; but that was the only explanation for him being in the town at the moment that these two men were killed, the evidence that he gave being that he approached the killing in an orchard to the distance of some 30 metres and, at that distance, was able to identify the defendant as the man who took two men out of a line of five and killed them in the area immediately in front of the Orthodox church. The evidence was identified in the judgment of the Trial Chamber at paragraph 393, and it merely recounts there the evidence that the witness gave … It was not, with respect to the Trial Chamber, the most critical analysis of the evidence of the witness Seferovic; it was, in truth, no more than a recitation of the effect of what he said … And the unlikelihood is obviously a reflection of the inherent improbability of anybody with any regard to their own safety willingly entering a town currently occupied by Serb paramilitaries when they were in the process

evidence against the accused, Dusko Tadic … Consequently, the Prosecution advised the Trial Chamber that it could no longer support Witness L as a witness of truth and invited the Trial Chamber to disregard his evidence entirely'.

[108] *Prosecutor v Tadic* (IT–94–1-A) (Appeals Chamber), 15 July 1999, para 58.

of actively deporting the Muslims to concentration camps in order to feed a pet bird. It is, we would submit, such an unlikely and improbable story that any Tribunal would want to reflect on whether it could possibly be true.[109]

Expressed in such stark terms, the proposition that a person would risk enemy bombardment and possible capture and internment in a concentration camp 'in order to feed a pet bird' does seem rather unlikely. Yet the ICTY Appeals Chamber remained unimpressed:

> The Appeals Chamber does not accept as inherently implausible the witness' claim that the reason why he returned to the town where the Serbian paramilitary forces had been attacking, and from which he had escaped, was to feed his pet pigeons. It is conceivable that a person may do such a thing, even though one might think such action to be an irrational risk. The Trial Chamber, after seeing the witness, hearing his testimony, and observing him under cross-examination, chose to accept his testimony as reliable evidence. There is no basis for the Appeals Chamber to consider that the Trial Chamber acted unreasonably in relying on that evidence for its finding that the Appellant killed the two men.[110]

The tale of Mr Seferovic's pigeons is worthy of extended commentary and analysis, but for present purposes I will confine myself to two brief observations. First, it is notable how the facts discussed on appeal are at variance with the testimony actually given by witness Seferovic at trial. For although Seferovic was asked several questions about feeding his pigeons under cross-examination, bird-feeding did not feature in his testimony-in-chief as Seferovic's overriding motivation for venturing back into Kozarac during the bombardment. His desire to find food and additional clothes and to locate his brother are mentioned as significant—and on their face, much more plausible—reasons for forsaking the comparative safety of his hillside bolthole for the perils of a town under hostile occupation. Not only does the witness' evidence-in-chief deflate defence counsel's ridicule of the notion that Seferovic would have risked death or capture 'to feed a pet bird' (a tendentious, if forensically unremarkable, adversarial distortion); it also significantly qualifies the Appeals Chamber's bald assertion that '*the* reason why he returned to the town where the Serbian paramilitary forces had been attacking, and from which he had escaped, was to feed his pet pigeons'.[111] The welfare of his pigeons was, at most, only one factor amongst several prompting Seferovic to steal back through the streets of Kozarac, where he would become witness to a double murder. Having taken advantage of this unusual opportunity to compare trial transcripts

---

[109]   *Prosecutor v Tadic*, IT-94-1-A (Appeals Chamber), Transcript of Proceedings, 385–389 (20 April 1999).
[110]   *Prosecutor v Tadic*, IT-94-1-A (Appeals Chamber), 15 July 1999, para. 66.
[111]   Emphasis supplied.

against the facts recited on appeal, and uncovering such material discrepancies between them, inevitably prompts the uncomfortable speculation that similar factual distortions might be creeping into English criminal appeals, and with very little prospect of detection after the event.

My second observation concerns the nature of the prosecution's response to the defence challenge mounted to Seferovic's evidence on appeal. Ms Brenda Hollis, appearing for the prosecution, adopted what might be termed a generic 'confession and avoidance' strategy. She conceded that Seferovic's actions might not appear very rational by normal standards, but insisted that people often do irrational things, especially where pet animals are concerned:

> The appellant seemed to argue that because this witness, Nihad Seferovic, would say that he would go into a town where the Serbs were taking it over to feed his birds, that his testimony is inherently incredible. Now, is this a decision many people would think is rational? Of course, it is not. But how many times have we heard stories of people going into burning buildings to rescue pets, of doing other things that subject them to a very real and immediate threat of death to save a pet? Are these rational acts? No, they're not. Are these acts that people do engage in? Yes, they are.[112]

There is nothing inherently wrong with the prosecution's strategy of locking horns with the defence on the issue of contextual rationality and its implications for witness credibility. It is difficult to argue with the general proposition that people sometimes behave irrationally, or that one person's rational errand is another person's folly. A more culturally sensitive analysis might nonetheless have provided greater assistance to the Court. On the one hand, Western perceptions of animals are notoriously sentimental. In a culture where every deer-calf is Bambi and even ants and fish can become CGI-conjured stars of Hollywood, small wonder that people anthropomorphise their pets! The story of Mr Seferovic's pigeons is almost inevitably viewed through these popular cultural filters by Western English-speakers, but I wonder just how much of this urban sentimentality can legitimately be projected onto the still predominantly agrarian Balkans of the early 1990s. Is it possible, in other words, that the prosecutor's burning-building analogy sounds more plausible to *us* than it would do to the average Bosnian as a rationalisation of Mr Seferovic's return to Kozarac at such a dangerous—and, as it turned out, evidentially vital—moment in time?

Then again, it does not take much imagination to appreciate that attitudes towards animals are highly culturally divergent. Vivid examples immediately spring to mind, in the reverence for cattle displayed by Hindus

---

and the Jewish disdain for pork, to say nothing of some Buddhists' aversion to crushing insects underfoot. As a Yorkshireman, I know from personal observation that pigeon-fanciers derive long hours of enjoyment and entirely unsentimentalised peer-group status and prestige from breeding champion racing birds. 'My pigeons are my life', or similar extravagant sentiments, would not astonish hardcore members of the pigeon-fancying fraternity. Do any of these cultural analogies resonate with Mr Seferovic's situation, and by extension help to illuminate the issue of his credibility as a witness? Since nobody took it upon themselves during the course of these lengthy proceedings to explore the cultural context of Seferovic's war-time pigeon-feeding, I suppose we will never really know.

CONCLUDING WITH A QUESTION

The programmatic discussion developed in this chapter does not lend itself to drawing 'conclusions' of the conventional kind, but it may be helpful to review and restate the argument's central contentions. I have tried to indicate, with reasonably detailed illustrations, why and how Evidence scholars might profit from greater familiarity with ICrimJ questions, sources, methods and materials. The only outstanding question of any immediate significance left dangling at the chapter's end, which by definition is not for me to answer, is whether I have done enough to encourage fellow Evidence teachers to 'get with the programme'.

The contention that 'Evidence' scholars and teachers should take greater interest in 'International Criminal Justice' is not even intelligible without some reasonably determinate notion of the distinctive questions, topics, materials and methods to which these disciplinary labels are supposed to refer. Questions of definition and disciplinary taxonomy are anyway worth exploring in their own right,[113] since this is the conceptual territory *par excellence* of unexamined and possibly unwarranted assumptions. On a sufficiently broad conception of ICrimJ, Evidence scholarship is already fully immersed in its cosmopolitan international jurisprudence, and necessarily so. Partly in recognition of legal globalisation, I personally favour broad conceptions of both 'Evidence' and 'ICrimJ'; and it might be retorted that if the connection between them is already so intimate and unavoidable, the argument developed in this chapter is a long-winded detour to a foregone conclusion. I would stress two points in reply. First, it does not necessarily follow from the fact that an argument is incontestably

---

[113] Also see Paul Roberts, Chapter 1; P Roberts, 'Penal Offence in Question: Some Reference Points for Interdisciplinary Conversation' in A Simester and A von Hirsch (eds), *Incivilities: Regulating Offensive Behaviour* (Oxford, Hart Publishing, 2006).

well-founded that its salience and implications are widely or fully appreciated. At this point in time, it seems to me that explaining how and why Evidence and ICrimJ overlap and interpenetrate, and exploring the opportunities for teaching and scholarship afforded by their interdisciplinary study, involves considerably more than merely stating the obvious. Secondly, even on the narrowest conceptions of ICrimJ, this fledgling discipline harbours untapped potential for Evidence scholars. Its possibilities can be glimpsed, for example, in the political morality of the ICC's Rome Statute, and in the cultural context of fact-finding before the ICTY, both of which have been explored in the preceding pages.

Much of the potential value for Evidence scholars and teachers of studying ICrimJ can be conceptualised as deriving from a distinctive brand of comparativism. Examining the work of international tribunals, staffed predominantly by civilian jurists, should help to dispel the myths surrounding inquisitorial criminal procedure. It is no longer a common conceit of English lawyers that 'in France you are presumed guilty until proven innocent'.[114] However, I wonder how many common lawyers would be surprised to learn that there is vigorous defence advocacy in France,[115] that the German legal system utilises exclusionary rules of evidence,[116] or that lay juries on the Anglophone model (*not* mixed panels) can now be found in Belgium, Denmark, Russia and Spain?[117] The judgments of the ICTY and ECtHR are highly educational in this regard, and should not be neglected as an important and readily accessible source of information for English lawyers striving to get to grips with the march of cosmopolitanism and 'convergence' in the global bazaar of criminal procedures. ICrimJ affords countless vivid and more-or-less unique illustrations of institutional

---

[114] According to a parody of French criminal justice circulating in the mid-nineteenth century and recently reproduced by C Allen, *The Law of Evidence in Victorian England* (Cambridge, CUP, 1997) 187–9, French law starts from the premiss: 'Prisoner, I am afraid you are an awful scoundrel. Why don't you confess, and make reparation to society? *Prisoner*. Because I am innocent. *The Law*. You say that with a certain impudence which proves you hardened in crime. How came you to rob your master? *Prisoner*. I never did. *The Law*. This reiteration of a plea which is clearly false is disrespectful to the Court, and will aggravate your punishment'. And so on.

[115] S Field and A West, 'Dialogue and the Inquisitorial Tradition: French Defence Lawyers in the Pre-trial Criminal Process' (2003) 14 *Criminal Law Forum* 261; cf J Hodgson, 'Constructing the Pre-trial Role of the Defence in French Criminal Procedure: an Adversarial Outsider in an Inquisitorial Process?' (2002) 6 *E & P* 1.

[116] CM Bradley, 'The Exclusionary Rule in Germany' (1983) 96 *Harvard Law Review* 1032.

[117] SC Thaman, 'Europe's New Jury Systems: the Cases of Spain and Russia' and N Vidmar, 'The Jury Elsewhere in the World', both in N Vidmar (ed), *World Jury Systems* (Oxford, OUP, 2000); R Vogler, *A World View of Criminal Justice* (Aldershot, Ashgate, 2005) ch 12.

design, operational cultures and the politics of criminal justice policy-making and practice which Evidence Scholarship and teaching might profitably exploit.

This exploratory chapter does not even aspire, let alone pretend, to contain all the answers to the questions that it has posed or will occur to readers. Certain avenues for further exploration are doubtless more enticing, and potentially more rewarding for Evidence scholars and teachers, than some of the suggested alternatives. Initially alluring vantage points can occasionally turn out to be dead-ends on closer inspection. Consistent results cannot be guaranteed. On my reckoning, however, the risks of expending wasted effort pale in comparison to the potential rewards of cultivating broader horizons; and to this end, I hope to have articulated questions and utilised methods and source materials of sufficient interest to inspire the imagination of fellow Evidence teachers, and to supply some useful signposts for the inquisitive to follow.

14

A Message from Elsewhere: Witnesses before International Criminal Tribunals

ROBERT CRYER*

INTRODUCTION

THIS CHAPTER ATTEMPTS to show that Evidence scholars and teachers, including those who regard themselves as exclusively interested in domestic law, might have something to learn from the (notably lengthy)[1] judgments of international criminal courts, in particular the International Criminal Tribunal for former Yugoslavia (ICTY) and the International Criminal Tribunal for Rwanda (ICTR).[2]

The main reason why Evidence specialists might benefit from paying more attention to the pronouncements of international criminal tribunals is very simple. Perhaps owing to their hybrid processes and input from civil law systems, the ICTY and ICTR spend considerable time openly evaluating evidence and discussing principles of fact-finding. In the common law world, the jury system (reinforced in the United Kingdom by the strictures of the Contempt of Court Act 1981)[3] makes detailed information about the processes of fact-finding difficult, if not impossible, to uncover. In addition, owing to the absence of rigid exclusionary rules that typically

---

* This chapter builds upon an earlier article 'Witness Evidence Before International Criminal Tribunals' published in (2003) 3 *Law and Practice of International Tribunals* 411–39.
[1] Judgments of the ICTY and ICTR are rarely shorter than 100 pages. The longest ICTY judgment to-date is *Prosecutor v Hadžihasanović* (IT-01–47), Judgment, 16 March 2006, which runs to 803 pp. The record, however, goes to the Tokyo International Military Tribunal's (Tokyo IMT's) judgment, which is in excess of 1,200 pages and was accompanied by separate and dissenting opinions that more than double its overall length.
[2] All of which are available on the websites of the ICTY and ICTR, www.un.org/icty and www.ictr.org respectively.
[3] Contempt of Court Act 1981, s 8 makes it a contempt of court, punishable by imprisonment, for any juror to reveal information about a jury's deliberations and verdict after the close of proceedings.

accompany jury trials, more time is spent on explaining the quality of evidence presented to international tribunals than in determining its admissibility. Such discussions provide exceptionally rich and extensive raw material which might fruitfully be studied by Evidence lawyers. Yet, for the most part,[4] this source has been overlooked.

There is far too much material to review within the compass of a single chapter.[5] The following discussion will therefore concentrate, by way of illustration, on just two aspects of the international tribunals' engagement with witness evidence. The first illustration explores issues of language, culture and interpretation; the second focuses on the relationship between trauma and memory. Both these dimensions of witness testimony are also pertinent to domestic legal proceedings, civil or criminal. Whilst the International Criminal Court (ICC) may prove in time to be the pre-eminent forum for international criminal adjudication, the ICC's trial phase only commenced in 2006 and it has yet to issue any decisions relating to evidence. This chapter consequently foregrounds decisions of the ICTY and ICTR. However, pertinent national cases are also mentioned where particularly illuminating.

INTERPRETATION, CULTURE AND WITNESS EVIDENCE

Commenting on a witness' apparently idiosyncratic turn of phrase in the English prosecution of Anthony Sawoniuk for Nazi atrocities committed during the Second World War,[6] Ian Bryan and Peter Rowe observe that 'it is a common feature of war crimes trials that witnesses' testimony has to be translated'.[7] Multilingual translation has been a recurrent theme of war crimes trials. Referring to the trial of Adolf Eichmann which took place in Jerusalem in 1961, Hannah Arendt commented that the interpretation was

---

[4] An honourable exception was the late Sir Richard May, whose final judicial appointment was to the ICTY.

[5] For more detailed review of the legal framework surrounding witness evidence before the tribunals, see R May and M Wierda, *International Criminal Evidence* (New York, Transnational, 2003); R May and M Wierda, 'Trends in International Criminal Evidence: Nuremberg, Tokyo, The Hague and Arusha' (1999) 37 *Columbia Journal of Transnational Law* 725; R Cryer 'Witness Evidence Before International Criminal Tribunals' (2003) 3 *Law and Practice of International Tribunals* 411, 412–17; H Brady, 'The System of Evidence in the Statute of the International Criminal Court' in W Schabas and F Lattanzi, *Essays on the Rome Statute of the International Criminal Court* (Ripa Fagano Alto, Sirente, 2001) 279; R May and M Wierda, 'Evidence Before the ICTY' in R May et al, *Essays on ICTY Procedure and Evidence in Honour of Gabrielle Kirk McDonald* (The Hague, Kluwer, 2001) 249.

[6] A prosecution witness said that he remembered the murder of three Jews in 1942 'beautifully': I Bryan and P Rowe, 'The Role of Evidence in War Crimes Trials: the *Sawoniuk* Case' (1999) 2 *Yearbook of International Humanitarian Law* 307, 312–13.

[7] *Ibid* 313.

'excellent in French, bearable in English, and ... frequently incomprehensible in German'.[8] This did not cause problems for the judges, who all spoke German and therefore did not need simultaneous translation into Hebrew.[9] Eichmann and his lawyer, Robert Servatius, only spoke German, however, and were thus placed at a disadvantage.[10] To ensure fairness to the defendant, the presiding judge, Moshe Landau, and his judicial colleagues spoke German to Eichmann during their discussions with him and intervened to 'correct and improve' translations.[11] The fact that the judges were obliged to double-up as *impromptu* interpreters in these domestic proceedings strongly hints at the seriousness and complexity of problems of language and communication likely to be encountered in international criminal trials.

The practice of international tribunals bears out this bald prediction. A translator working for an international criminal tribunal not only faces the usual technical challenges and difficulties attending simultaneous translation;[12] courtroom translation must, in addition, be accurate to a forensic standard. Although speech is in general more idiomatic than writing, and can often be translated without too many problems, spoken language cannot always be rendered literally or even by close approximation.[13] Indeed, translating witness evidence for an international criminal tribunal might be regarded as the acme of the professional translator's art.

Visible problems relating to interpretation and translatability go back at least to the Tokyo International Military Tribunal for the Far East (IMTFE) which sat from 1946 to 1948. The judgment itself recognised the extraordinary difficulties involved:

> [T]he need to have every word spoken in Court translated from English into Japanese, or vice versa, has at least doubled the length of the proceedings. Translations cannot be made from the one language into the other with the speed and certainty which can be attained in translating one Western speech into another. Literal translation from Japanese into English or the reverse is often impossible. To a large extent nothing but a paraphrase can be achieved, and experts in both languages still often differ as to the correct paraphrase. In the result the interpreters in Court often had difficulty as to the rendering they

---

[8] H Arendt, *Eichmann in Jerusalem: a Report on the Banality of Evil* (Harmondsworth, Penguin, 1994; revd edn 1964) 3.

[9] *Ibid* 4. See M Marrus, 'Eichmann in Jerusalem: Justice and History' in SE Aschheim, *Hannah Arendt in Jerusalem* (Berkeley, University of California Press, 2001) 205, 208.

[10] Arendt, above n 8, 3.

[11] *Ibid* 4.

[12] On which see B Hatin and I Mason, *The Translator as Communicator* (London, Routledge, 1997) ch 4.

[13] See KA Appiah, 'Thick Translation' in L Venuti, *The Translation Studies Reader* (London, Routledge, 2001) 417, 421.

should announce, and the Tribunal was compelled to set up a Language Arbitration Board to settle matters of disputed interpretation.[14]

The New Zealand Judge at the trial, Erima Harvey Northcroft, pithily summarised the problems of translated evidence in a written Memorandum: 'Translation from Japanese to English is not absolute. At best, it is only opinion. The translation received by the Court, however, becomes evidence'.[15] Justice Röling attempted to get the majority in that case to re-open proceedings in order to correct a document that he believed had been tendered in the form of a corrupted translation. The request was refused. According to Röling this alleged mistranslation might have influenced Koki Hirota's sentence,[16] although most of the other judges (with the notable exception of Judge Delfin Jaranilla) thought that Röling was confusing two separate documents.[17] Wherever the truth might lie on this particular occasion, the anecdote serves to demonstrate the great difficulties to which translated evidence may give rise, difficulties which can only multiply when simultaneous translations of witness testimony rather than translated documents are being presented to the court.

In more recent times, the ICTY has developed rules relating to interpretation. In particular, it has issued a Code of Ethics for translators and interpreters, containing a number of requirements relating to witness evidence. One prominent principle is that '[i]nterpreters, when working in the courtrooms, shall inform the Judges of any doubt arising from a possible lexical lacuna in the source or target language'.[18] The most detailed Code provision dealing with witness testimony is Article 10, which provides:

[14] Judgment of the IMTFE, Transcript, 48, 429–30.
[15] Memorandum from Northcroft J to the President and Members of the IMTFE re Exhibits 977 and 979, Australian War Memorial, Archives, 3DRL/2481, Papers of William Flood Webb, Box 4, wallet 19.
[16] Memorandum to the President and Members of the IMTFE, from the Member from Holland re Language Corrections by Language Board, 3 August 1948, Australian War Memorial, 3DRL/2481, Papers of William Flood Webb, Box 2, wallet 1. See BVA Röling and A Cassese, *The Tokyo Trial and Beyond: Reflections of a Peacemonger* (Cambridge, Polity, 1992) 53.
[17] Northcroft Memorandum, above n 15; Memorandum from Member from the United States to the President and Members of the IMTFE, 4 August 1948 re Language Corrections Received by Member for Holland, Australian War Memorial, Archives, 3DRL/2481, Papers of William Flood Webb, Box 1, wallet 9. The situation of Jaranilla is interesting, as he would have re-opened the proceedings 'for the reason that we are after the true meaning of the original document for the purpose of the best administration of justice': Memorandum, 3 August 1948, from the Member from the Philippines o the President and Members of the IMTFE, 4 August 1948 re Language Corrections Received by Member for Holland, Australian War Memorial, Archives, 3DRL/2481, Papers of William Flood Webb, Box 4, wallet 4. Jaranilla is often seen as biased against the defence. It would appear from these papers that the picture is more complex.
[18] The Code of Ethics for Interpreters and Translators Employed by the International Criminal Tribunal for the Former Yugoslavia (IT/144), Art 6(2).

10.1. Truth and Completeness

(a) Interpreters and translators shall convey with the greatest fidelity and accuracy, and with complete neutrality, the wording used by the persons they interpret or translate.

(b) Interpreters shall convey the whole message, including vulgar or derogatory remarks, insults and any non-verbal clue, such as the tone of voice and emotions of the speaker, which might facilitate the understanding of their listeners.

(c) Interpreters and translators shall not embellish, omit or edit anything from their assigned work.

(d) If patent mistakes or untruths are spoken or written, interpreters and translators shall convey these accurately as presented.

10.2. Uncertainties in Transmission and Comprehension

(a) Interpreters and translators shall acknowledge and rectify promptly any mistake in their interpretation or translation.

(b) If anything is unclear, interpreters and translators shall ask for repetition, rephrasing or explanation.

On their face, all these requirements and injunctions appear quite reasonable. However, a fundamental obstacle to faithfully and accurately conveying the wording of the speaker, as required by Article 10(1)(a), is that 'whilst translation is always possible, it may for various reasons not have the same impact as the original'.[19] To achieve the equivalent effect as the original for the benefit of an audience listening in a different language may require an effort of creative reinterpretation by the translator. This creative dimension of translation effectively interposes the translator between the witness and the court. Here problems may abound. The interpreter is caught in a difficult situation. If the testimony is rendered exactly literally, then it may not reflect the importance or vernacular sense of what was said. However, creative reinterpretation demands a form of editorial interpolation by the translator which appears to be prohibited by Article 10(1)(c).

A second source of difficulty is that the Code of Ethics does not require witnesses to have all their testimony translated by the same interpreter. This is unfortunate to the extent that interpretation is influenced by personal style. Evidence given by the same witness but translated by two different interpreters may appear less consistent than it really is, since different interpreters will translate the same words and phrases slightly differently.[20] Yet the consistency of testimony is regarded, by lawyers and

---

[19] P Newmark, *A Textbook of Translation* (London, Prentice Hall, 1988) 6.
[20] This point was suggested to me by Silvia de Bertodano at the conference at which this paper was first presented.

laypeople alike, as an important aspect of a witness' credibility. Interpretation by different translators consequently runs the risk of unfairly undermining the credibility of an honest and reliable witness.

Problems of interpretation have been considered at greatest length by the ICTR. The issue was confronted directly in *Akayesu*, where the Trial Chamber commented:

> The majority of the witnesses in this trial testified in Kinyarwanda. The Chamber notes that the interpretation of oral testimony of witnesses from Kinyarwanda into one of the official languages of the Tribunal has been a particularly great challenge due to the fact that the syntax and everyday modes of expression in the Kinyarwanda language are complex and difficult to translate into French or English. These difficulties affected the pre-trial interviews carried out by investigators in the field, as well as the interpretation of examination and cross-examination during proceedings in Court. Most of the testimony of witnesses at trial was given in the language, Kinyarwanda, first interpreted into French, and then from French into English. This process entailed obvious risks of misunderstandings in the English version of words spoken in the source language by the witness in Kinyarwanda. For this reason, in cases where the transcripts differ in English and French, the Chamber has relied on the French transcript for accuracy. In some cases, where the words spoken are central to the factual and legal findings of the Chamber, the words have been reproduced in this judgment in the original Kinyarwanda.[21]

It is notable that this case involved double translation: first from Kinyarwanda into French, then subsequently into English. The two European languages are not easily comparable to Kinyarwanda; and the difficulty of producing a reliable translation is exacerbated when the pace of a trial demands speed as well as accuracy. These problems were further alluded to by the Trial Chamber in *Musema*, where 'significant syntactical and grammatical differences between the three languages' were noted.[22] The Trial Chamber was satisfied, however, that '[t]hese difficulties have been taken into consideration by the Chamber in its assessment of all evidence presented to it'.[23] While the Chamber's candid recognition of the difficulties surrounding multiple translation is welcome, the simple assertion that such difficulties had been 'taken into consideration' might be regarded as complacent.

Similar reflections may be prompted by the Trial Chamber's remarks in *Rutaganda*:

> [T]he Chamber ... notes that many of the witnesses testified in Kinyarwanda and as such their testimonies were simultaneously translated into French and English. As a result, the essence of the witnesses' testimonies was at times lost. Counsel

---

[21] *Prosecutor v Akayesu* (ICTR-94–6-T), judgment, 2 September 1998, para 145.
[22] *Prosecutor v Musema* (ICTR-96–13-T), judgment, 27 January 2000, para 102.
[23] *Ibid.*

questioned witnesses in either English or French, and these questions were simultaneously translated to the witnesses in Kinyarwanda. In some instances it was evident, after translation, that the witnesses had not understood the questions.[24]

It should hardly be necessary to point out to lawyers that nuances of language are very important. The Trial Chamber in *Rutaganda* clearly appreciated that the 'essence' of a witness' testimony was sometimes being lost in translation, and these difficulties could to some extent be ameliorated by asking counsel to rephrase their questions or witnesses to rephrase their answers. But a more intractable obstacle to successful translation lurks in the Trial Chamber's remark that '[i]n some instances it was clear' that witnesses had not understood counsel's questions. The implication appears to be that in other instances the witness might have (only) failed to appreciate the more subtle nuances of the question, and that such misapprehensions remained hidden from the court.

The significance of subtle differences can be amplified with the help of some hypothetical illustrations. Imagine that a witness is asked the question 'Did you see a car?', but this is translated as 'Did you see the car?'. Or consider the likely implications of the question 'How fast were the cars going when they hit each other?' appearing in translation as 'How fast were the cars going when they smashed into each other?'. Neither of these mistranslations would necessarily become evident to the court from the witness' answers. Yet, as Elizabeth Loftus has shown, use of the definite article ('the' rather than 'a' car, in the first hypothetical) will tend to evoke more positive answers, all else being equal, than the use of the indefinite article. Likewise, the more dramatic 'smashed into' in the second hypothetical is likely to produce an increased estimate of speed compared with the more prosaic 'hit' to indicate a collision.[25] To be fair, the ICTR has attempted to deal with such semi-concealed pitfalls, and where errors in interpretation have occurred, it has tried to rectify them.[26] The enduring concern, however, is that some mistakes may simply fall 'under the bar' and pass unnoticed.

Translation problems before international tribunals have been exacerbated by the fact that most international crimes occur in conflict situations. During armed hostilities language is rapidly politicised, and it also mutates and becomes beguilingly euphemistic.[27] In Bosnia, for example, members of the Bosnian army were colloquially known as 'lilies' in a reference to symbols used on the Bosnian coat of arms.[28] The ICTR has struggled to

---

[24] *Prosecutor v Rutaganda* (ICTR–96–3–T), judgment, 6 December 1999, para 23.
[25] E Loftus, *Eyewitness Testimony* (Cambridge, Harvard UP, 1979) 78, 94–5.
[26] See the comments cited from *Akayesu*, above n 21, and *Rutaganda*, above n 24.
[27] See J Levinger, 'Language War–War Language' (1994) 16 *Language Sciences* 229.
[28] *Ibid* 223.

determine the precise meaning of various words relating to the 1994 genocide. In *Akayesu*, the Trial Chamber noted that certain words in Kinyarwanda could only be understood in their geographical and temporal context.[29] These included *Inkotanyi*,[30] *Inyenzi*,[31] *Icyitso*[32] and *Interahamwe*.[33] In the *Bagilishema* case, there was considerable discussion about who the *Abakiga* were.[34]

Technical words and expressions may assume specific meanings in certain contexts. During the Yugoslav conflict, the word 'genocide' was often misunderstood and misappropriated by participants in the conflict, or it was 'used so often that its meaning ... changed ... to something very dirty, ugly, but not otherwise defined'.[35] Knowledge and understanding of the specific idioms of a military or paramilitary force may be elusive to those (including international judges) who stand outside the conflict or are not members of the groups themselves. Furthermore, in conflict situations it may be difficult to obtain an interpreter with the relevant knowledge who is also willing and competent to translate for an international criminal court.[36] Where the language in question is not widely spoken, the prospect of finding suitable translators recedes even further.

The ICTY's Code of Ethics seeks to minimise these difficulties by requiring that interpreters and translators 'increase their knowledge of ... technical vocabulary that might be encountered during the performance of their duties'. Interpreters and translators must also 'provide their colleagues, whenever possible, with any specialised knowledge they acquire which may be useful to the exercise of their duties'.[37] These efforts to inculcate a level of institutional competence in the ICTY are laudable. However, it might not be possible to extend similar protocols to the ICC, which is likely to have to deal with fewer trials, arising from disparate

---

[29]   *Akayesu*, above n 21, para 147.

[30]   Rwandan Patriotic Front member or sympathiser.

[31]   The literal meaning of which is 'cockroach', but in the genocide referred to Tutsis.

[32]   Which meant collaborator, or moderate Hutu.

[33]   *Akayesu*, above n 21, para 151: 'Therefore Interahamwe could mean to attack or to work together, and, depending on the context, to kill together. The Interahamwe were the youth movement of the MRND. During the war, the term also covered anyone who had anti-Tutsi tendencies, irrespective of their political background, and who collaborated with the MRND youth'.

[34]   *Prosecutor v Bagilishema*, (ICTR-95-1A-T), judgment, 7 July 2001, paras 200–6. It appears that *abakiga* means either people from the North or, more generally, strangers.

[35]   Levinger, above n 27, 235.

[36]   The possibility that a translator is acting in bad faith cannot always be ignored: see R McGrath, 'Problems of Investigations into War Crimes and Crimes Against Humanity During and After Ethnic Conflicts' in MC Bassiouni (ed), *Post Conflict Justice* (New York, Transnational, 2002) 893, 904.

[37]   Article 11.

regions and conflicts (in contrast to the conflict-specific jurisdictions of the ICTY and ICTR) and interpreters may only be employed on a short-term basis.

It is not only conflict-specific neologisms and linguistic idiosyncracies that may prove problematic. In *Akayesu*, the Trial Chamber noted that a number of different Kinyarwandan words were being translated into English as 'rape' by the translators. Special care consequently had to be taken to ensure that words meaning sexual intercourse in general were not immediately equated with rape.[38] The court in *Akayesu* adopted a sensible course, by electing to hear expert evidence on the language and culture of the *locus delicti*. It is not easy to think of alternative solutions. Linguistic and cultural briefings by experts will be particularly important for the ICC, which, in accordance with the principle of complementarity,[39] may be confronted with cases from a large variety of linguistically and culturally diverse countries. However, translation issues do not appear to have been dealt with in a systematic way in the ICC Statute or in the supplementary Rules of Procedure and Evidence. Reference to expertise in translation is confined to Rule 18, which suggests that the Victims and Witnesses Unit may include experts in translation and interpretation on its staff.

When foreign language evidence is presented in domestic criminal proceedings, it is unlikely that a judge or other fact-finder will be fully conversant in both (or several) of the languages used in a trial.[40] In the South African case of *State v Mpopo*, the trial judge's attempt to second-guess an official translation proved to be 'undesirable and potentially dangerous'.[41] The trial judge mistakenly believed that the defendant was speaking in Xhosa, and formed his (negative) opinion of the defendant's testimony on the basis that he 'sufficiently understood the language to follow the evidence and form some impression of his demeanour'. In fact the defendant was speaking Sotho. As the appellate court observed, 'a Xhosa linguist would not necessarily understand fully evidence given in Sotho or be able to judge the demeanour of a witness testifying in the latter

---

[38] *Akayesu*, above n 21, paras 152–54. The Appeals Chamber commended the Trial Chamber's approach as 'well informed and vigilant about the problems of translation': *Prosecutor v Akayesu* (IT-94-6-A), judgment, 1 June 2001, paras 208–12.

[39] ICC Statute, Arts 17–19. See JT Holmes, 'Complementarity: National Courts *versus* the ICC' in A Cassese, P Gaeta and JRWD Jones (eds), *The Rome Statute of the International Criminal Court: a Commentary* (Oxford, OUP, 2002) 667.

[40] For discussion of translation problems in the Australian prosecution of Ivan Poly-ukhovich, see D Bevan, *A Case to Answer* (Kent Town, Wakefield, 1994) 124–6, 127–8, 185–7.

[41] *State v Mpopo* (2) *South African Law Reports* (1978) 424, 426. This appeal from a domestic murder conviction was heard by the South African Appellate Division on appeal from the Supreme Court of Transkei. Transkei was an illegal entity created by South Africa, in pursuit of its *apartheid* policies, which was never an independent state: see J Crawford, *The Creation of States in International Law* (2nd edn, Oxford, OUP, 2006) 338–48.

language'.[42] This case stands as a cautionary tale for many reasons, the most relevant here being the dangers of over-confidence in dealing with the cultural and linguistic dimensions of witness evidence.

CULTURE AND MISUNDERSTANDING

Mpopo also exemplifies the possibility of cultural misunderstanding.[43] Judges with different cultural backgrounds to witnesses or the accused may have problems accurately appraising their testimony and conduct. It would be all too easy for judges to apply socially and culturally relative standards to interpret the demeanour of witnesses who do not share the same behavioural norms and expectations. This blinkered approach is not merely insensitive and patronising,[44] it also threatens the integrity of the court's assessment of evidence, and the soundness of any inferential conclusions drawn from it, including the court's final verdict.

Issues of cultural difference, extending beyond simple problems of translation, plagued the Tokyo IMT.[45] The witnesses and at least the majority of the judges were failing to communicate in more than one sense. The majority judgment betrayed little sympathy for cultural difference and appeared oblivious to the possibility of intercultural misunderstanding. For example, the judges deprecated the 'tendency for counsel and witnesses to be prolix and irrelevant':

> This last tendency at first was controlled only with difficulty as on many occasions the over-elaborate or irrelevant question or answer was in Japanese and the mischief done, the needless time taken, before the Tribunal was given the translation in English and objection could be taken to it. At length it became necessary to impose special rules to prevent this waste of time.[46]

As far as the majority was concerned, much testimony from Japanese defendants and witnesses had simply been wasting the court's time, to no apparent purpose:

> A large part of the evidence which was presented had been a source of disappointment to the Tribunal. An explanation of events is unconvincing unless the witness will squarely meet his difficulties and persuade the Court that the

---

[42]   *Mpopo*, above n 41, 427.

[43]   See generally, S Marks and A Clapham, *International Human Rights Lexicon* (Oxford, OUP, 2005) 33ff.; J Almqvist, 'The Impact of Cultural Diversity on International Criminal Proceedings' (2006) 4 *Journal of International Criminal Justice* 745.

[44]   See eg, K Knop, *Diversity and Self-Determination in International Law* (Cambridge, CUP, 2002) 9–10.

[45]   For discussion of other cases in the Pacific Sphere along these lines, see A-M Prévost, 'Race and War Crimes: the 1945 War Crimes Trial of General Tomoyuki Yamashita' (1992) 14 *Human Rights Quarterly* 303.

[46]   Tokyo IMT judgment, 48, 430.

inference, which would normally arise from the undoubted occurrence of these events, should on this occasion be rejected. In the experience of this Tribunal most of the witnesses for the Defence have not attempted to face up to their difficulties. They have met them with prolix equivocations and evasions, which only arouse distrust.[47]

Such crude appraisals of witness testimony rooted in cultural norms and patterns foreign to tribunals have fortunately been less conspicuous in more recent international criminal proceedings. The ICTR has led the way in this regard, demonstrating sensitivity to the challenges of intercultural appreciation of evidence, and seeking the assistance of expert advice in an attempt to bridge the cultural divide. In its first full decision in *Akayesu*, the ICTR demonstrated how far international criminal proceedings have progressed since the Tokyo IMT castigated what they saw as Japanese time-wasting:

According to the testimony of Dr Ruzindana, it is a particular feature of the Rwandan culture that people are not always direct in answering questions, especially if the question is delicate. In such cases, the answers given will very often have to be 'decoded' in order to be understood correctly. This interpretation will rely on the context, the particular speech community, the identity of and the relation between the orator and the listener, and the subject matter of the question. The Chamber noted this in the proceedings. For example, many witnesses when asked the ordinary meaning of the term *Inyenzi* were reluctant or unwilling to state that the word meant cockroach, although it became clear to the Chamber during the course of the proceedings that any Rwandan would know the ordinary meaning of the word. Similar cultural constraints were evident in their difficulty to be specific as to dates, times, distances and locations. The Chamber also noted the inexperience of witnesses with maps, film and graphic representations of localities, in the light of this understanding, the Chamber did not draw any adverse conclusions regarding the credibility of witnesses based only on their reticence and their sometimes circuitous responses to questions.[48]

What might appear as evasiveness to a Western observer, and would harm credibility in certain cultures, is simply a cultural fact of life in Rwanda. This was explicitly acknowledged in the *Musema* case, in which the Trial Chamber noted the problems witnesses had in giving evidence outside their familiar cultural context.[49] José Alvarez has criticised the *Akayesu* judgment as 'present[ing] troubling, if predictable, issues of cultural misunderstanding or linguistic difficulties ... [which are] difficult to avoid when foreign judges need to have recourse to translators and cultural experts in order to determine, for example, whether a witness understands the

---

[47]   *Ibid*, 48, 431–2.
[48]   *Akayesu*, above n 21, para 156.
[49]   *Musema*, above n 22, paras 103–5.

difference between reporting something as an eyewitness and presenting a second-hand account'.[50] Alvarez identifies important issues, but his critique partly misses the mark. The reason such matters are clear to see in *Akayesu* is precisely because the Chamber was candid about the difficulties it faced in understanding and assessing witness evidence and consciously attempted to overcome them.

The ICTY, on the other hand, has been slower to take such considerations on board. The ICTY's celebrated first judgment in *Tadić* has been criticised for having 'dismissed the relevance of witnesses' ethnic or religious affiliations when stating its reasons for determining credibility'.[51] Such matters were first discussed in detail in *Limaj* in 2005, where the Trial Chamber observed that 'notions of honour and other group values have a particular relevance to the cultural background of witnesses with Albanian roots in Kosovo', and proceeded to quote from an expert report prepared by Stephanie Schwandner-Sievers:[52]

> [The] Albanian concept of honour governs all relations that extend beyond blood kinship ... Solidarity with those individuals that share the same 'blood' is taken for granted, but faithfulness to a group or cause that reaches beyond the family needs to be ritually invoked. Honour can also be explained in terms of an ideal-type of model of conduct, and a man's perceived potential of protecting the integrity of the family or any wider reference group (such as the clan or a political party) against outside attacks ... [The pledge of allegiance or *besa*] requests absolute loyalty, and it requires the individual's compliance with family and group values in general. At the same time it justifies the killing of those within the group who break this code ... However ... the members of a group can cho[o]se to avoid violence. The reaction to conflict, insult, treason, or other transgressions to group norms, depends on the members' interpretations of the facts and these may vary greatly.

To which the Chamber added:

> Some of these factors were also applicable, in the Chamber's assessment, to aspects of the evidence of some former KLA members who were called in the course of the Defence case. These are matters which the Chamber has taken into consideration in assessing the personal credibility of particular witnesses in this case, an assessment which in many cases has been most material to the Chamber's acceptance or rejection of the evidence of a witness, whether in whole or in part ... At times, the Chamber has been unable to make such determinations and has had to leave the evidence aside altogether.

---

[50] JE Alvarez, 'Lessons of the *Akayesu* Judgment' (1998–99) 5 *International Law Students' Association Journal of International and Comparative Law* 367, 368.

[51] JE Alvarez, 'Rush to Closure: Lessons of the *Tadić* Judgment' (1998) 96 *Michigan Law Review* 2031, 2066–7. Also see *ibid* 2048.

[52] *Prosecutor v Limaj, Bala and Musliu* (IT-03–66-T), judgment, 30 November 2005, paras 13–14.

The experiences of the ICTR and ICTY underline the importance of anthropological expert evidence and pertinent research findings in the fields of psychology and anthropology. In some cultures exaggeration is encouraged, whilst in others understatement is preferred. The significance of eye-contact and facial expression also varies widely across cultures,[53] and judicial fact-finders regard these factors as highly relevant in determining the credibility of a witness. It is well-known that 'some cultures consider looking one in the eye to be rude behaviour, while many Westerners would regard someone staring at the floor or the wall while talking as a sign of duplicity'.[54] Such anthropological evidence needs to be made available to international courts and should inform their deliberations.

The Tribunals' experience also raises other, more complex issues about culture and evidence. The use of expert evidence, in particular, requires us to 'scrutinise critically the processes of authenticating culture . . . [W]ho has authority to speak for culture? What is the relation between processes of cultural authentication and systems of social hierarchy?'[55] These considerations patently apply to self-appointed experts who speak from outside the relevant culture. Would it be advisable, for example, to accept Kipling as an expert on India?[56] Even outsiders who are basically sympathetic, bona fides, and have considerable ties to the relevant cultural group may be questionable expert witnesses. Albert Camus, notwithstanding his anti-colonial instincts, was hardly an impartial objective observer of Algerian society. His views were inevitably filtered through his French colonial heritage.[57]

Edward Said's *Orientalism* contains the following classic statement on the limits of intercultural understanding:

> No one has ever devised a method for detaching the scholar from the circumstances of life, from the fact of his involvement (conscious or unconscious) with a class, a set of beliefs, a social position, or from the mere activity of being a member of a society.[58]

As Said implies, questions of cultural authority, authenticity and conflict are not confined to the outsider looking in from elsewhere. Contested cultural hegemony may be an indigenous achievement, at least in part:

---

[53] See JC Yuille, D Marzsen and B Cooper, 'Training Investigative Interviewers: Adherence to the Spirit, as Well as the Letter' (1999) 22 *International Journal of Law and Psychiatry* 323, 330–1.

[54] McGrath, above n 36, 904.

[55] Marks and Clapham, above n 43, 41.

[56] E Said, *Orientalism*, (London, Penguin, 2003) 226–8.

[57] E Said, *Culture and Imperialism* (London; Vintage 1994) 224ff.

[58] Said, above n 56, 10. The same can be said for those speaking of an undifferentiated 'West' from elsewhere, see *ibid* 27–8; I Buruma and A Margalit, *Occidentalism* (London, Penguin, 2005).

Culture, of course, is to be found operating within civil society, where the influence of ideas, of institutions, and of other persons works not through domination, but by what Gramsci calls consent. In any society not totalitarian, then, certain cultural forms predominate over others, just as certain ideas are more influential than others; the form of this cultural form is what Gramsci has identified as *hegemony*.[59]

Further difficulties arise in determining the precise ambit of the relevant culture. Who is qualified to speak of and for Nigerian culture, for example? Someone from the Christian South, or a denizen of the Islamic North? Who can speak for Sudan, the largest state in Africa? Or for India, a multicultural and multifaith subcontinent of over one billion people? As the Chinese proverb has it (and the people who hail from this vast and most populous of states may know better than most), in many places 'the mountains are high and the Emperor is far away'. At the other end of the spectrum, in small and localised communities, it may be difficult to find anyone with the expertise or linguistic competence who has not become involved in some way in the events which are under scrutiny.[60] Moreover, the array of problems arising from potential witnesses' personal involvement in the subject matter of the trial is not confined to small societies, as the ICTY noted in the *Limaj* case:

> The Chamber heard evidence about witnesses requesting to be interviewed by investigators at night to avoid the fact of an interview becoming known, or in a third language rather than through Albanian interpreters, as they feared they would be compromised.[61]

Expert anthropological evidence can, of necessity, deal only in cultural generalities. But cultures are neither unchangeable monoliths, nor uniformly prescriptive. Many individuals buck the cultural stereotype. British reserve notwithstanding, there are individual Britons who are entirely comfortable discussing the details of their income with relative strangers. Whilst many English people might concede, with a characteristically wry smile, the perspicuity of some of the observations in the popular anthropological bestseller *Watching the English*, it is doubtful that any reader would identify unreservedly with the picture of Englishness it portrays.[62] To extend these general reflections on the nature of culture to the forensic

---

[59]   Said, above n 56, 7.

[60]   This has been a problem in East Timor where the relevant communities are very small, thus everyone with knowledge of the local language and culture is likely to know the victim and/or the perpetrator. This point was originally suggested to me by Sylvia de Bertodano.

[61]   *Limaj*, above n 52, para 15.

[62]   K Fox, *Watching the English: the Hidden Rules of English Behaviour* (London, Hodder & Stoughton, 2004). For example, it is difficult to agree, as a general proposition, that 'the only rule one can identify with any certainty in all this confusion over introductions and greetings is that, to be impeccably English, one must perform these rituals badly. One must appear self-conscious, ill-at-ease, stiff, awkward and, above all, embarrassed. Smoothness,

context, fact-finders dealing with evidence arising from different countries or cultures are likely to face considerable challenges of cultural translation and interpretation. In Foucauldian terms, testimony is 'disciplined'[63] by its filtration through expert knowledge on the culture. Just as Pierre Rivière[64] was caught between the bifocal lenses of law and medicine, witness evidence is subjected to two expert narratives (and perhaps the further narrative of the law) prior to its judicial reception, those of translation and cultural interpretation.

Alternative methods of attempting to overcome problems of understanding witnesses in context have been tried in national courts. In *Sawoniuk*, as well as in *Polyukhovic* in Australia[65] and the Belgian case of *Niyontenze v Public Prosecutor*,[66] fact-finders went to visit the localities from which the witnesses came and where the atrocities in question were alleged to have been perpetrated. The objective of the exercise was to better understand the topography of the *locus delicti* and the cultural context of witness testimony. Such methods are useful, but also underline the difficulties involved. This is not to deny the possibility of ever employing witness evidence,[67] but simply to argue for its sympathetic reception and critical evaluation.

TRAUMA AND MEMORY

Problems of culture and interpretation are exacerbated by the fact that victim-witnesses and others are often traumatised by the horrific events they have seen or suffered. High levels of adrenaline in the bloodstream at the time of events can damage recall.[68] The ICTY and ICTR have had to deal with the question of traumatised witnesses in a number of cases, beginning with *Furundžija*.[69] In this case witness A appeared before the Trial Chamber to testify about sexual offences, including rape, to which

---

glibness and confidence are inappropriate as un-English': *ibid* 41. As Fox also notes, *ibid* 80–1 and 162–7, many of the rules she identifies are class-related.

[63] See eg, M Foucault, *Discipline and Punish* (London, Penguin, 1977); D Garland, *Punishment and Modern Society* (Oxford, OUP, 1990) ch 6. Said, above n 56, 3, openly acknowledges his debt to Foucault.

[64] M Foulcault (ed), *I Pierre Rivière, a Case of Parricide in the 19th Century* (London, Penguin, 1978) esp P Moulin, 'Extenuating Circumstances', 212.

[65] *Polyukhovic v Commonwealth* (1992) 91 International Law Reports 1. See Bevan, above n 40, 223. The court also took expert evidence on culture: see *ibid* 185–7. However, it still might be argued that such evidence was not sufficiently taken into account.

[66] See L Reydams, 'Niyontenze v Public Prosecutor' (2002) 96 *American Journal of International Law* 231, 236.

[67] The difference between telling the truth and lying is (to my knowledge) appreciated in all cultures and societies, for example.

[68] *Prosecutor v Furundžija* (IT–95–17–T), judgment, 10 December 1998, para 102.

[69] *Ibid*.

she had been subjected during the Yugoslav conflict. It emerged after the trial proceedings closed that witness A had undergone some preliminary psychiatric counselling and had been diagnosed as having Post-Traumatic Stress Disorder (PTSD). As a result, proceedings were reopened to discuss the matter of trauma and memory. The Chamber heard expert evidence on witnesses and trauma, inter alia, from Professor Loftus.

After deliberating on the matter, the Trial Chamber decided, correctly, that 'even when a person is suffering from PTSD, this does not mean that he or she is necessarily inaccurate in the evidence given. There is no reason why a person with PTSD cannot be a perfectly reliable witness'.[70] Equally, the Trial Chamber noted that 'survivors of such traumatic experiences cannot be expected to recall the precise minutiae of events ... [or] every single element of a complicated and traumatic sequence of events'.[71] Thus, the Trial Chamber accepted that memory can be affected by trauma, but did not consider that corroboration[72] was necessary where traumatised witnesses gave evidence. The Appeals Chamber subsequently upheld the Trial Chamber's findings, noting that 'in the reopened proceedings, numerous experts gave evidence on the potential effects of PTSD on memory. The Trial Chamber was best placed to assess this evidence and to draw its own conclusions'.[73]

Later cases such as *Čelebići* have adopted a similar position to the Trial Chamber in *Furundžija*.[74] An ICTR Trial Chamber in *Kayishema and Ruzindana* took a rather robust line in relation to evidence relating to the reliability of victims. In response to evidence led by the Prosecutor to the effect that traumatic events may be recalled in an especially detailed and vivid way, the judges commented, rather sharply, that '[w]hat is apparent to the Trial Chamber is that different witnesses, like different academics, think differently'.[75] But the possibility of memory impairment is notably not denied in this statement.

These cases underline the necessity of continuing to bear in mind that many, if not most, victims and other witnesses to events amounting to

---

[70]   *Ibid* para 109.

[71]   *Ibid* para 113.

[72]   The Trial Chamber appears to have used the term 'corroboration' in the general, rather than the common-law technical, sense. That usage is followed here.

[73]   *Prosecutor v Furundžija* (IT-95-17-A), judgment, 21 March 2000, para 123.

[74]   See *Prosecutor v Delalić, Mucić, Delić and Landžo (Čelebići)* (IT-96-21-T), judgment, 16 November 1998, para 595 and IT-96-21-A, judgment, 20 February 2001, para 497; *Musema*, above n 22, paras 100-1; *Rutaganda*, above n 24, para 22; *Akayesu*, above n 21, paras 142-3; and *Prosecutor v Kunarac, Kovać and Vuković* (IT-96-32-T and IT-96-23/1-T), judgment, 22 February 2001, para 564.

[75]   *Prosecutor v Kayishema and Ruzindana* (ICTR-1995-1-T), judgment, 20 May 2001, para 74. See also *Limaj*, above n 52, para 15; *Prosecutor v Ntagerura* (ICTR-99-46-T), judgment, 25 February 2004, para 26; *Prosecutor v Kajelijeli* (ICTR-98-44-T), judgment, 1 December 2003, para 37; *Prosecutor v Kamuhanda* (ICTR-95-54A-T), judgment, 24 January 2004, para 31.

international crimes may have been traumatised by those events, and that these experiences may have important effects on witnesses' memories. Fortunately, the ICTY and ICTR have been mindful of these issues and have adopted a sensitive middle position relating to the reliability of evidence from trauma victims. As the Appeals Chamber in *Kunarac, Kovač and Vuković* succinctly summarised:

> [I]n principle, there could be cases in which the trauma experienced by a witness may make her unreliable as a witness and ... a Trial Chamber must be especially rigorous in assessing identification evidence. However, there is no recognised rule of evidence that traumatic circumstances necessarily render a witness's evidence unreliable. It must be demonstrated *in concreto* why the 'traumatic context' renders a given witness unreliable.[76]

Psychological Therapy and Memory

The possibility of trauma raises a further problem: the risk of witness evidence being contaminated during trauma counselling or in psychiatric treatment. Domestic legal controversies surrounding repressed or recovered memories of child abuse demonstrate the need for caution in relation to the use of evidence procured through therapy.[77] The possibility of evidence contamination through counselling was raised, but rejected, in *Furundžija*.[78] However, this ruling was premised on the narrow ground that witness A had received only preliminary treatment, and not relating to any facts in issue.[79] The possibility that further therapy might have contaminated her evidence seems implicit.

Certain forms of therapy, such as dream therapy or hypnosis, have led to evidence of questionable validity forming the basis for charges and allegations at the domestic level.[80] This is not to say that victims should be denied therapy; far from it. However, the issue raises difficult questions about the appropriate balance between the rights of defendants and victims. The psychological condition of a person is an intensely private

---

[76] *Prosecutor v Kunarac, Kovać and Vuković*, (IT–96–32–A and IT–96–23/1–A), judgment, 12 June 2002, para 324. See further, S Porter, AR Birt, JC Yuille and HF Hervé, 'Memory for Murder: a Psychological Perspective on Dissociative Amnesia in Legal Contexts' (2001) 24 *International Journal of Law and Psychiatry* 23, 32–3.

[77] See P Lewis and A Mullis, 'Delayed Criminal Prosecutions for Childhood Sexual Abuse: Ensuring a Fair Trial' (1999) 115 *LQR* 265; M Redmayne, 'A Corroboration Approach to Recovered Memories of Sexual Abuse: a Note of Caution' (2000) 116 *LQR* 147; P Lewis and A Mullis, 'Supporting Evidence and Illusory Double-Counting: Recovered Memory and Beyond' (2001) 5 *E & P* 111; M Redmayne, 'Another Note of Caution' (2001) 5 *E & P* 129.

[78] *Furindžija*, above n 68, paras 103–4.

[79] *Ibid* para 108.

[80] See GF Wagstaff, 'Hypnotically Induced Testimony' in A Heaton-Armstrong, E Shepherd and D Wolchover (eds), *Analysing Witness Testimony: a Guide for Legal Practitioners and Other Professionals* (London, Blackstone Press, 1999) 162.

matter. To make this a subject of public discussion in a courtroom is likely to be a humiliating experience for any victim-witness. The release of witness A's therapy records was controversial and has been criticised as a violation of her right to privacy.[81]

The right of the defence to full disclosure and the rights of victims to privacy appear to be in direct conflict. This is a serious matter, as '[d]isclosure of evidence goes to the heart of an accused's right to a fair trial'.[82] The drafters of the Rome Statute and the Rules of Procedure and Evidence for the ICC noted the problem of privacy and disclosure without settling it conclusively. Article 67(2) of the Rome Statute requires the Prosecutor to disclose all material which the Prosecutor believes may affect the credibility of evidence to be adduced before the court. On the face of it, this would include evidence relating to any therapy that a witness had undergone, and a failure to disclose such evidence was the basis for re-opening proceedings in *Furundžija*.[83] This approach might be regarded as excessively intrusive from a witness' point of view. On the other hand, if witnesses were afforded a blanket privilege to withhold intimate informa-tion about their psychological condition or experiences of treatment to overcome trauma the court might be forced, as the Trial Chamber was in *Akayesu*, simply to guess at which witnesses were suffering from PTSD or any other psychological condition or illness, which in turn imperils the court's evaluation of evidence and the soundness of its ultimate verdict.[84]

Talking About It

Risks of evidence contamination are not restricted to professional therapy and its effects on a witness' recall. Simply discussing or talking over events with family, friends or other acquaintances can have a significant impact on a witness' ability to recall those events accurately.[85] In *Kupreškić*,[86] for example, witness H, who was 18 years of age, and had been 13 at the material time, clearly impressed the Trial Chamber, not only by her bravery in coming forward to give evidence before the tribunal but also by her

---

[81]   KD Askin, 'Sexual Violence in Decisions and Indictments of the Yugoslav and Rwandan Tribunals: Current Status' (1999) 93 *American Journal of International Law* 97, 111–13.

[82]   H Brady, 'Disclosure of Evidence' in RS Lee (ed), *The International Criminal Court: Elements of Crimes and Rules of Procedure and Evidence* (New York, Transnational, 2001) 403.

[83]   *Furundžija*, above n 68, para 107.

[84]   *Akayesu*, above n 21, para 143.

[85]   Loftus, above n 25, 54–66.

[86]   *Prosecutor v Kupreškić, Kupreškić, Jospiović, Papić and Santić* (IT–95–16–A), judg-ment, 23 October 2001. See DM Amann, 'Prosecutor v Kupreškić' (2002) 96 *American Journal of International Law* 439, esp 442–4.

confident manner whilst testifying.[87] However, despite noting that the Trial Chamber had had the advantage of observing witness H in person and was thus better placed to determine her honesty, the Appeals Chamber overturned certain convictions based upon her evidence. The Appeals Chamber did not doubt witness H's honesty, which had not been questioned by the defence.[88] Nonetheless, the Appeals Chamber felt that the Trial Chamber had been overly impressed with witness H's confidence, which the appellate judges regarded merely as a character trait rather than a reliable indicium of accuracy.[89]

The Appeals Chamber also accepted that discussing with other family members the crimes she had witnessed could have altered witness H's recollection of events.[90] Although witness H honestly believed what she had told the Trial Chamber, the Appeals Chamber perceived that her memory of the event had 'developed' over time, and that discussions about her ordeal with her family might conceivably have been the source of distortions.[91] As the Trial Chamber said in the *Vasiljević* case, '[t]he fact that a witness gives their testimony honestly is insufficient to establish the reliability of that evidence. The issue is not merely whether the ... witness is honest, it is also whether the evidence is objectively reliable'.[92]

CONCLUSION

The use of witness evidence is beset by difficulties. But this should not be read as a counsel of despair or a compelling objection to the use of witnesses. Witness evidence is an extremely important and useful form of evidence and often the only evidence there is of extremely serious offences fully deserving punishment. Excessive scepticism of a witness' accurate recall has been a pernicious tactic frequently employed in denying international crimes, as was seen in the failed libel proceedings brought by the Holocaust denier David Irving.[93] Similar scepticism can also be seen, albeit in muted form, in the judgment of Pal J at the Tokyo IMT.[94] There is no

---

[87] *Kupreškić*, above n 86, paras 129–30, 136.

[88] *Ibid* para 193.

[89] *Ibid* paras 136–54.

[90] *Ibid* para 191.

[91] *Ibid* paras 191–201. The Chamber noted that another witness' evidence had similarly 'developed'.

[92] *Prosecutor v Vasiljević* (IT–98–32–T), judgment, 29 November 2002, para 16.

[93] *DJC Irving v Penguin Books Ltd and DE Lipstadt* (1996–I–1113) judgment, 11 April 2000, paras 7.110–7.111, 8.9, 8.17(vi), (viii), (xiii), (xiv), 9.5(v), (vii), (ix), (x), (xxvi), 9.12, 9.15, 13.74, 13.77, 13.83, 13.95, 13.150–13.151.

[94] See KD Askin, *War Crimes Against Women: Prosecution in International Tribunals* (The Hague, Kluwer, 1997) 181–5.

justification for using the natural frailties of memory to deny the reality and cogency of much witness testimony, as the *Sawoniuk* trial in England showed.[95]

This chapter has identified various potential difficulties attending reliance on witness evidence, but none of them is in principle insoluble. With sensitivity and care most of these challenges can be overcome, and without unreasonable expense. Nonetheless, as we have seen, the work of the ICTY and ICTR has thrown up a number of illuminating practical difficulties and imaginative solutions, building on the efforts of previous international criminal prosecutions and laying firmer foundations for a successful ICC. Particularly in the light of international judges' apparent willingness to discuss problems of evidence and fact-finding quite openly, all Evidence scholars, and not only those with a developed interest in international criminal law, might readily be encouraged to learn from and contribute towards studies of the practice and procedures of the international criminal tribunals. By doing so, a body of knowledge and understanding of how to gather, prepare and treat witness evidence in international criminal adjudication might be generated. The judgments in such cases may be long, but they are also, intentionally or otherwise, an extraordinary repository of reasoned decisions on evidence, the relevance of which ought not to be confined to the backwater of Evidence scholarship in which the work of international criminal tribunals currently flounders.

[95]   *R v Anthony Sawoniuk* [2000] 2 Cr App R 220, CA (Westlaw Transcript 2000 WL 473).

Index